Financial Services Firms

Governance, Regulations, Valuations, Mergers, and Acquisitions

Third Edition

ZABIHOLLAH REZAEE

WILEY

John Wiley & Sons, Inc.

Published by John Wiley & Sons, Inc., Hoboken, New Jersey.
Published simultaneously in Canada.

For general information on our other products and services or for technical support, please contact our Customer Care Department within the United States at (800) 762-2974, outside the United States at (317) 572-3993 or fax (317) 572-4002.

Wiley also publishes its books in a variety of electronic formats. Some content that appears in print may not be available in electronic books. For more information about Wiley products, visit our web site at www.wiley.com.

Library of Congress Cataloging-in-Publication Data:

Rezaee, Zabihollah, 1953-
  Financial services firms: governance, regulations, valuations, mergers, and acquisitions/ Zabihollah Rezaee.—3rd ed.
      p. cm.
    Rev. ed. of: Financial institutions, valuations, mergers, and acquisitions. 2nd ed. New York: J. Wiley, c2001.
    Includes index.
    ISBN 978-0-470-60447-2 (hardback); 978-1-118-09851-6 (ebk); 978-1-118-09852-3 (ebk); 978-1-118-09853-0 (ebk)
   1.   Banks and banking–Valuation–United States. 2.   Bank mergers–United States. 3.   Sale of banks–United States. 4.   Financial institutions–Valuation–United States. 5.   Financial institutions–Mergers–United States. 6.   Financial institutions–Purchasing–United States. 7.   Consolidation and merger of corporations–Law and legislation–United States.   I. Rezaee, Zabihollah, 1953- Financial institutions, valuations, mergers, and acquisitions.   II. Title.
    HG1707.7.R49 2011
    332.1'6–dc22

                                                                                2011012029

Printed in the United States of America

10 9 8 7 6 5 4 3 2 1

To the loving memory of my mother,
Fatemeh Rezaee.

Contents

Preface

T RADITIONALLY, CUSTOMERS HAVE HAD their checking and savings accounts at a bank, their mortgage at the savings and loan association, their insurance services with insurance companies, and their investment activities with investing companies, mutual funds, and brokerage firms. This conventional model of providing and receiving financial services has disappeared in the years after the Gramm-Leach-Bliley Financial Services Modernization Act of 1999. The recent wave of consolidations in the financial services industry has resulted in fewer but bigger financial institutions, and they are often perceived as "too big to fail" (TBTF). The distinctions among financial services and products of banks, insurance companies, mutual funds, and brokerage firms are now becoming less noticeable. The principal focus of this book is on banks, but many issues discussed throughout all chapters are relevant for all firms in the financial services industry, such as mutual and hedge funds and investment and insurance companies. Although it is not the purpose or this book to evaluate the relative importance of factors that contributed to the 2007–2009 financial crisis, their consequences and regulatory responses are discussed. As this book was going through production, the Financial Crisis Inquiry Commission issued a report that suggests the 2007–2009 financial crisis could have been avoided and was caused by inadequate and ineffective regulations to ensure the safety and soundness of the financial system. Other factors which contributed to the crisis range from lax oversight of derivatives to insufficient supervision by federal banking and securities regulators as well as greed, excessive risk taking, and mismanagement of executives of financial services firms.

A new regulatory framework has been established for the financial services industry, including the Dodd-Frank Act of 2010 and its related regulations, Group of 20 summits, and Basel committee requirements. This new regulatory framework defines boundaries, guidance, and requirements within which banks and other financial services firms can effectively operate in generating sustainable performance. It normally is supplemented by best practices of vigilant boards of directors, risk assessment, and effective corporate governance. In an open market economy and the free enterprise system, the achievement of sustainable performance depends on cost-effective and efficient regulations as well as effective corporate governance, best practices, and competent and ethical culture. There should be a right balance between rules and regulations governing banks' operations and oversight functions of the board to engage in business strategy and overseeing managerial decisions.

In summary, the new regulatory framework requires:

- Strengthening the quality and quantity of overall bank capital adequacy
- Assessing the market risk capital requirements
- Identifying systemically important financial institutions and measuring their sustainability, risks, and externalities to reduce the moral hazard of TBTF and risk to the global financial stability
- Stricter oversight of credit rating agencies
- Rationalizing the executive compensation program, which is linked to long-term performance and avoids incentives for undue risk taking
- Regulating over-the-counter derivatives and credit default swaps
- Enhancing the supervisory program for financial services firms
- Improving the corporate governance structure by increasing independence of directors and risk management functions
- Clearing banks' balance sheets of toxic assets by applying fair value in measuring, recognizing, and reporting assets
- Using the expected loss model instead of the current practice of incurred loss model for measuring credit losses
- Separating investment banks from commercial banks
- Developing more stringent prudential standards of enhanced capital and liquidity requirements
- Providing transparency and accountability for government bailout plans and stimulus programs
- Implementing close supervision and monitory of banks' debt, liabilities, and capital adequacy
- Maintaining ongoing and systematic assessment of banks' systemic risks

This book presents these and other regulatory and corporate governance measures for the financial services industry.

The past two decades have witnessed significant changes in the structure, characteristics, and types of products and services offered by financial services firms. The most significant changes were in four areas: consolidation, convergence, regulation, and competition. The modern financial services being offered by banks, insurance companies, and mutual funds, coupled with a new trend toward combinations between banks and financial services firms, make the subject matter of valuations and mergers and acquisitions (M&A) timely and relevant. It is expected that the steady global economic recovery and improved financial and credit market conditions in the post-financial crisis period will lead to increased M&A across all industrial sectors particularly the financial services industry. The 2011 KPMG survey indicates that: (1) 2010 M&A activity increased significantly by 23 percent, and it is expected to continue to grow in 2011 as a result of a rebound in both the debt and equity markets; (2) two-thirds of respondents reported that they were currently more optimistic about the M&A deal environment than a year ago; (3) factors that contributed to the recent growth in M&A activities according to the survey are: a more stable economic environment (66 percent), an improvement in buyer confidence (52 percent), improved debt and equity markets (41 percent), the return of the private equity buyer (27 percent), and certainty surrounding tax legislation (27 percent); and (4) the three industries that will be more actively involved in M&A are banking, financial services, and health care. Strategic M&A transactions will be the key driver of business combinations in industries such as financial services, natural resources, pharmaceuticals, health care, and technology. M&A activities of the emerging markets, such as China, India, and Brazil, are expected to continue to increase significantly. Every day a significant number of business executives, business owners, accountants, attorneys, investment bankers, tax and regulatory authorities, and judges are involved in various stages of business valuation and the M&A process. Knowledgeable and experienced valuation specialists can play a vital role in this exciting, dynamic, and rewarding process.

This book is intended to assist valuation and M&A practitioners in applying their knowledge and expertise in providing their services. No prior knowledge of financial institutions, valuations, or M&A is assumed in the third edition. The text presents current developments in the areas of valuations and M&A, which have progressed significantly since the first edition of the book in 1995 and the second edition in 2000. This third edition is designed primarily for business executives, banks, financial services organizations, attorneys, accountants, and appraisers interested in the valuation and M&A areas of the financial services industry. Throughout the book, every effort is made to integrate online, fair value valuation techniques into the due diligence process and practices for internal and external assessment purposes as well as M&A deals. The goals in preparing this edition are to: (1) refine the style and clarity of presentations to maximize the effectiveness of the book as an authoritative guide and learning resource for users; (2) refine the content and organization of the book to enhance its relevance and flexibility in accommodating new online valuation techniques for the financial services industry; (3) provide comprehensive and integrated coverage of the latest developments in the environment, accounting standards, laws, regulations, and methodologies pertaining to the valuation process, as well as the due diligence practices for M&A deals; and (4) present the emerging regulatory framework governing operations of financial services firms.

The third edition is designed to provide a useful reference for anyone wishing to obtain understanding and knowledge of financial services firms and their regulation, governance, and valuation as well as the wave of M&A in the financial services industry. This edition presents a new regulatory framework for financial institutions in this postfinancial crisis era. It will provide valuable guidance to bank professionals, their advisors, and business appraisers to assess risks, measure performance, and conduct valuation processes to create shareholder value while simultaneously protecting interests of other stakeholders (e.g., customers, regulators, government, and society). This edition is a superior reference for all business professionals who need an up-to-date understanding of financial services firms, their challenges, and their opportunities in the Dodd-Frank Act era. The substantial changes in the third edition reflect the intent of the book.

HIGHLIGHTS OF CHANGES FROM THE SECOND EDITION

These changes have been made in the third edition:

- Each chapter includes a conclusion.
- Emerging regulations for the industry financial services are discussed throughout the book.
- Bank valuation cases in the post–Sarbanes-Oxley (SOX) period are discussed.
- All chapters have been updated to address emerging initiatives affecting financial reporting and corporate governance and auditing functions (implementation rules of SOX and the Securities and Exchange Commission, auditing standards issued by the Public Company Accounting Oversight Board, technological advances, Dodd-Frank Act, Basel Committee, and globalization).
- Recent financial accounting standards, under U.S. generally accepted accounting principles and International Financial Reporting Standards on business combinations and fair value are incorporated throughout the book.
- Emerging initiatives on and models for the allowance for loan losses is incorporated into the related chapters.
- Risk management and assessment for bank loans and other major transactions is integrated into all chapters.
- Lending practices and overall health of financial institutions are addressed.
- Government efforts to influence bank rescues through the Trouble Asset Relief Program (TARP) are discussed.
- Bank credit markets, demands for commercial paper, and credit problems are examined.
- The misperception of too-big-to-fail banks is addressed.
- Derivatives risk and its regulatory oversight are examined.
- The emerging financial reporting and auditing initiatives, including the movement toward International Financial Reporting Standards as well as the use of Extensible Business Reporting Language (XBRL) reporting platform, are discussed.
- Government bailout of troubled financial institutions is covered.
- Capital allocation and performance measurement of the banking industry are discussed.
- Description of managing and assessing the value of financial institutions is presented.
- Corporate governance and executive compensation standards for the banking industry are discussed.
- Bank financial statement analysis and valuation assessments are covered.
- Financial and nonfinancial key performance indicators (KPIs) in the banking industry that affect the value of the bank are presented.
- Market performance, initial public offerings, and M&A transactions that affect the value of the bank are described.
- The Dodd-Frank Act of 2010 and recent Basel Committee requirements are presented.
- Integrated audit of both financial statements and internal control over financial reporting is incorporated into all related chapters.

- Bank sustainability performance and accountability reporting are examined.
- The role of new federal agencies to oversee Dodd-Frank regulations (Financial Stability Oversight Council, FSOC; Consumer Financial Protection Bureau, CFPB) is discussed.
- Risk management and assessment for bank major credit activities, loans, and other transactions is presented.

 ## ORGANIZATION OF THE BOOK

The organization of the third edition continues to provide maximum flexibility in choosing the amount and order of materials on regulation, corporate governance, valuations, and M&A for financial services firms. The entire valuation process is examined from an M&A perspective. Thus, in addition to valuation theory, concepts, methodology, and techniques, the M&A process, target bank analysis, applicable laws and regulations, and related accounting standards are thoroughly examined.

The third edition is organized into five parts.

Part	Subject	Chapters
I	Financial Services Industry: Its Markets, Regulations, and Governance	1–3
II	The Foundation: Financial Institutions, Valuations, Mergers, Acquisitions, and Regulatory and Accounting Environment	4–6
III	Fundamentals of Valuations: Concepts, Standards, and Techniques	7–10
IV	Assessment of Financial Institutions	11–13
V	Valuation of Mergers and Acquisitions	14–19

The first part contains three chapters that constitute the foundation of the book. Chapters 1 and 2 discuss the major topics of the book, including the nature, role, operation, and the regulatory framework of financial services firms. Chapter 3 describes corporate governance measures of the financial services industry. Part II consists of Chapters 4 to 6. Chapter 4 discusses M&A in general and convergence in the financial services industry in particular. Chapters 5 and 6 present an overview of M&A and examine the regulatory environment and the financial reporting process of financial institutions.

Part III, containing Chapters 7 through 10, addresses the fundamental issues related to valuation, including different types of value, approaches to measuring value, and the differences between tangible and intangible assets. The four chapters in Part III provide a thorough background on the basic principles needed to understand the calculation of the value of a bank.

Part IV, comprising Chapters 11, 12, and 13, addresses the various types of research that likely will be undertaken as part of a proper valuation. A major portion of the discussion relates to the financial analysis of the banking company, but there is ample discussion of nonfinancial aspects of bank operations and organizations as well as the external market environment in which the bank operates. Taken together, the discussions in Parts III and IV provide a solid foundation for applying the principles of valuation to the calculation of a banking company's value.

Part V contains Chapters 14 through 19, which focus on specific issues related to calculation of value for purposes of M&A. A description of the bank M&A process is provided as a background to put into context the role that valuation can play at various points in that process. Also covered are topics that are unique to banking, such as core deposits, branch acquisitions, unknown loan losses, derivatives, and accounting standards on M&A.

The analyses in this book are described in order to be useful to both buyers and sellers. As a buyer, a banker must be able to assess the value of a target bank and gauge the underlying business that has "created" that value. As a seller, a banker should understand how the value of the institution will be assessed, whether a buy offer is fair, and possible strategies to enhance value. Where possible, examples are given from both the buyer's and seller's perspective. However, whether the reader is a buyer or seller (or a professional assisting either), the concepts, principles, and techniques described can assist in making the M&A process more successful.

In one book, it is not possible to address the valuation of every type of subsidiary business a bank holding company may operate. Consequently, the focus is on what is commonly thought of as a commercial bank, often referring to the bank holding company legal structure that is common in U.S. banking. While the discussions that unfold generally focus on commercial banks and on those bank holding companies where the principal subsidiaries are commercial banks, the same valuation principles and techniques apply to nonbanking entities. Although the title of the book is *Financial Services Firms: Governance, Regulations, Valuations, Mergers, and Acquisitions,* and therefore the focus is on financial services firms, the issues of corporate governance, regulations, valuations, and M&A are relevant to all organizations in all industries. The first part of the book examines these issues in generic terms as they relate to all organizations. The other parts of the book discuss these issues as they pertain to financial services firms. Technical distinctions exist between mergers and acquisitions. Mergers often occur when two separate entities combine and both parties to the merger wind up with common stock in a single combined entity. In contrast, in an acquisition deal, the acquirer (bidding entity) buys the common stock or assets of the seller (target entity). However, in this book the terms "mergers" and "acquisitions" are used interchangeably to describe the method in which separate institutions are combined under the control of one entity. The vast majority of all business combinations are acquisitions rather than mergers.

Acknowledgments

THIS BOOK HAS BENEFITED from the assistance of numerous professionals and colleagues. I would like to thank specifically Tim Bell and Ram Menon for their invaluable review of earlier chapters of the book. I also thank the publishing team at John Wiley & Sons for their help, particularly John DeRemigis, Stacey Rivera, Natasha Andrews-Noel and Dexter Gasque in Hoboken, NJ. The assistance of my graduate students, Yue Zhang, Kyle Griffiths, Sudeshna Gunna, Mansi Gadi, and Amir Alimardani is greatly appreciated.

The encouragement and support of my family and colleagues are also acknowledged. I am thankful for the love, patience, and support of my wife, Soheila, my son, Nick, and my daughter, Rose, in making it easier for me to focus on completing the third revision of this book.

PART ONE

Financial Services Industry: Its Markets, Regulations, and Governance

CHAPTER ONE

Fundamentals of the Financial Markets and Institutions

 INTRODUCTION

More than half of all households (over 115 million) in the United States are now investing in the securities markets through private investments in company shares, mutual funds, and pension funds. Furthermore, due to the recent financial crisis, bank failures, the risks regarding Social Security, and the high-profile failure of some large pension funds, Americans are being forced to take responsibility for their financial future and retirement funds. The sustainability and financial health of public companies in general and financial services firms in particular is vital to keeping investor confidence high, and this sustainability requires public trust in the reliability of financial reports. Reliability of public financial information contributes to the efficiency, liquidity, and soundness of financial markets that may drive economic development and prosperity for the nation. This introductory chapter discusses the importance of our financial markets to the nation's economic prosperity, the promotion of the free enterprise system, the vital role of financial services firms in our society, and the importance of financial information as the lifeblood of financial markets.

 FINANCIAL MARKETS

The efficiency, liquidity, and safety of the financial markets, both debt and capital markets, have been threatened by the recent financial crisis and resulting global economic meltdown. These threats have significantly increased the uncertainty and volatility in the markets, which adversely affected investor confidence worldwide. These crises prevent investors from receiving meaningful financial information to make savvy investment decisions. U.S. capital markets traditionally have been regarded as the deepest, safest, and most liquid in the world. For many decades, they have employed stringent regulatory measures to protect investors, which has also raised the profile and status of listed companies. However, the recent global financial crisis and the competitiveness of capital markets abroad have provided global companies with a variety of choices of where to list, possibly subject to less vigorous regulatory measures. As these markets abroad become better regulated, more liquid, and deeper, they enable companies worldwide to raise their capital needs under different jurisdictions. Investors now have a wide range of options to invest globally to secure their desired return on investment.

To a significant extent, the global competitiveness of U.S. capital markets depends on the reliability of financial information in assisting investors to make sound investment decisions, cost-effective regulations that protect investors, and efficiency in attracting global investors and companies. The U.S. free enterprise system has transformed from a system in which public companies, including banks and other financial institutions, traditionally were owned and controlled by small groups of investors to a system in which businesses are owned by global investors. The United States has achieved this widespread participation by adopting sound regulations and by maintaining high-quality disclosure standards and enforcement procedures that protect the interests of global investors.[1]

Recent financial regulatory reforms—both the Sarbanes-Oxley Act of 2002 (SOX) and the Dodd-Frank Wall Street Reform and Consumer Protection Act of 2010 (Dodd-Frank)—are intended to protect investors and consumers.[2]

 ## FINANCIAL INFORMATION AND CAPITAL MARKETS

Reliability, transparency, and quality of financial information are the lifeblood of the capital markets. The efficiency of the markets depends on the reliability of that information which enables the markets to act as signaling mechanisms for proper capital allocation. Investor confidence in "the same level playing field" of all market participants has encouraged investors to own stock, and billions of shares trade hands to provide capital to businesses. Society, particularly the investing community, relies on the quality of corporate financial reports in making investment decisions. William McDonough, the former chairman of the Public Company Accounting Oversight Board (PCAOB), stated, "Confidence in the accuracy of accounting statements is the bedrock of investors being willing to invest, in lenders to lend, and for employees knowing that their firm's obligations to them can be trusted."[3] As investor confidence in financial information drives the willingness to invest, America's economic future is tied to how successfully companies respond to this call for greater transparency and reliability in financial information as well as cost efficiency and effectiveness of regulatory reforms of financial services firms.

A greater number of people are now investing through retirement funds or are actively managing their portfolios and therefore are affected by financial information disseminated to the market. Reliable and transparent financial information contributes to the efficient functioning of the capital markets and the economy. In recent years, investment banks and major brokerage firms have grown rapidly and generated record revenue. Recently five major financial institutions have failed: Goldman Sachs Group, Bear Stearns Co., Morgan Stanley, Lehman Brothers Holdings, and Merrill Lynch & Co. The subsequent government bailout of some of these firms raises serious concerns about the value-adding activities of financial services firms, their ethics and governance, as well as the professional accountability of their board of directors, senior management, internal and external auditors, and other corporate governance participants. The lack of public trust and investor confidence in corporate America, Wall Street, and its financial dealings and reports has continued to adversely affect the vibrancy of the capital market. Bailed-out banks and their continuous excessive executive compensation schemes have left us with a legacy of mistrust. Policy makers and regulators have been challenged to establish and enforce more effective and efficient regulatory reforms; business leaders have been challenged to change their culture, behavior, and attitudes to restore confidence and trust in Wall Street.

FINANCIAL CRISIS AND FINANCIAL REGULATORY REFORMS

A historical perspective of the financial crisis in the United States indicates that real estate markets started to collapse in the second half of 2007, and investors began shorting real estate markets. Where shorting or short selling is defined as; borrowing an asset from a third party and selling it with a promise to buy back at a future point in time at a predetermined price. Collateralized debt obligations (CDOs) and mortgage-backed securities were written down, and financial panic continued into 2008, which caused major financial institutions to go bankrupt. The persistence of the financial panic in 2009 and lack of public trust and investor confidence in the financial system have caused the disappearance or reorganization of once-prominent Wall Street firms, some of which have changed their corporate structures and become bank holding companies. The U.S. financial crisis eventually affected global financial markets. Financial institutions worldwide have lost more than $1.5 trillion on mortgage-related losses. The failed financial institutions Bear Stearns, Lehman Brothers, AIG, and Merrill Lynch played important roles in the recent financial crisis by engaging in risky mortgage lending practices, credit derivatives, hedge funds, and corporate loans. The Federal Reserve responded by reducing interest rates and flooding the market with money, and the Treasury Department asked for a $700 billion package dubbed the Troubled Asset Relief Program (TARP) to buy toxic mortgages and other assets. The U.S. government responses to mitigate the financial panic were the TARP stimulus packages, temporary increases in deposit insurance coverage of $250,000 per person by the Federal Deposit Insurance Corporation (FDIC), and the Dodd-Frank Act of 2010.

Recent financial reforms (Dodd-Frank), and corporate governance reforms, including SOX, convergence in regulatory reforms (from the Group of 20 [G-20]) worldwide, and TARP have shifted the power balance among shareholders, directors, and management of all entities, particularly banks. Shareholders including the U.S.

government have been more proactive in monitoring and scrutinizing corporations. Directors are held more accountable in fulfilling their fiduciary duties by overseeing management's strategic plans, decisions, risk assessment, and performance. Management is expected to achieve sustainable shareholder value creation and enhancement and to enhance the reliability of financial reports through executive certifications of internal controls and financial statements. Some provisions of SOX that were not previously practiced by public companies and that are intended to benefit all companies include:[4]

- Creating the PCAOB to oversee audits of public companies and to improve the ineffective self-regulatory environment of the auditing profession.
- Improving corporate governance through more independent and vigilant boards of directors and responsible executives.
- Enhancing the quality, reliability, transparency, and timeliness of financial disclosures through executive certifications of both financial statements and internal controls.
- Prohibiting nine types of nonaudit services considered to adversely affect auditor independence and objectivity.
- Regulating the conduct of auditors, legal counsel, and analysts and their potential conflicts of interest.
- Increasing civil and criminal penalties for violations of security laws.

Six provisions of SOX address the quality, reliability, transparency, and timeliness of public companies' financial reports:

1. The board of directors should adopt a more active role in the oversight of financial reports.
2. The audit committee is responsible for overseeing financial reports and related audits.
3. Management (chief executive officer [CEO], chief financial officer [CFO]) must certify the completeness and accuracy of financial reports in conformity with generally accepted accounting principles (GAAP).
4. Pro forma financial information must be presented in a manner that is not misleading and that is reconciled with GAAP items.
5. All material correcting adjustments identified by the independent auditor must be discussed with the audit committee and reflected in any reports that contain financial statements.
6. Management must assess the effectiveness of internal controls, audit of internal control over financial reporting (ICFR), communication of significant deficiencies to the audit committee, and public disclosure of material weaknesses in ICFR.

The first summit of the 20 largest advanced and emerging countries, better known as the G-20, was held in Toronto in June 2010 to ensure international economic cooperation by addressing the global economic crisis, reforming and strengthening global financial systems, and promoting a full return to growth with quality jobs.[5]

The 2010 G-20 agreed to:

1. Reduce budget deficits by cutting the global deficit in half by 2013.
2. Promote growth through global economic stimulus and more government spending.
3. Full return to growth with quality jobs.
4. Reform and strengthen financial systems.
5. Create strong sustainable and balanced global growth.
6. Reduce government debt–to–gross domestic product (GDP) ratios by 2016.

The important provisions of the 2010 G-20 are discussed next.

- The Framework for Strong, Sustainable, and Balanced Growth assesses global policy actions and strengthens policy frameworks.
- Financial service reform establishes a more resilient financial system, improving risk assessment, promoting transparency, and reinforcing international cooperation.
- International financial institutions (IFIs) should develop as a global response to the financial and economic crisis and a platform for global cooperation including $750 billion by the International Monetary Fund (IMF) and $235 billion by the multilateral development banks (MDBs).
- Fighting Protectionism and Promoting Trade and Investment by refraining from raising barriers or imposing new barriers to investment or trade in goods and services at least until the end of 2013.
- Moving toward convergence in accounting standards by adopting a single set of high-quality globally accepted accounting standards.

The most important declaration of the 2010 G-20 summit is the development of financial sector reform that encourages a systemic risk assessment, supports strong and stable global economic growth, requires prudential oversight, and promotes transparency and reinforces international cooperation. The G-20 financial sector reform consists of four pillars. The first pillar is a strong financial regulatory framework built on the progress of the Basel Committee on Banking Supervision. This regulatory framework would establish a new regime for bank capital and liquidity that will eventually raise levels of resilience for the global banking systems and enable banks to withstand the pressure of the recent financial crisis. This first pillar will come to fruition by the end of 2012 and is intended to strengthen financial market infrastructure by implementing effective measures to improve transparency and regulatory oversight of the over-the-counter (OTC) derivatives, credit rating agencies, and hedge funds.

The second pillar is effective oversight and supervision of global financial institutions. The Financial Stability Board (FSB) in consultation with the International Monetary Fund (IMF) issued its report, in February 2011, entitled "Progress in the Implementation of the G 20 Recommendations for Strengthening Financial Stability" which makes recommendations to finance ministers and central bank governors to strengthen oversight and supervision while providing adequate resources and defining roles and responsibility of supervisors.[6]

The third pillar is the development of a system that systematically restructures and resolves all types of financial institutions in crisis with no burden on taxpayers. This system would consist of policy framework, implication procedures, resolution tools, supervisory provisions, and core financial market infrastructures.

The fourth pillar is robust and transparent international assessment and peer review of global financial institutions. This pillar demonstrates G-20's commitment to the IMF/World Bank Financial Sector Assessment Program to support transparent peer review through the FSB. The review process would address noncooperative jurisdictions based on effective assessment regarding the fight against money laundering, tax havens, and terrorist financing.

The Basel Committee is intended to strengthen global capital and liquidity regulations to promote a more resilient banking sector with proper ability to absorb shocks arising from financial and economic stress and to improve risk management, governance, transparency, and disclosures. The Basel Committee addresses the market failures caused by the recent financial crisis and establishes measures to strengthen bank-level and micro-prudential regulation.

On September 12, 2010, global bank regulators agreed to require banks to significantly increase their amount of top-quality capital in an attempt to prevent further international crisis.[7] Basel III will require banks to maintain top-quality capital totaling 7 percent of their risk-bearing assets compared to the currently required 2 percent. Effective compliance with Basel III rules would require banks to raise substantial new capital over the next several years as the Tier 1 rule (4.5%) will take effect from January 2015 and the requirement for the capital conversation buffer (up to 10.5%) will be phased in between January 2016 and January 2019. The primary objective of Basel III rules is to strengthen global capital standards to ensure sustainable financial stability and growth for banks worldwide. The rules are intended to encourage banks to engage in appropriate risk business strategies to ensure their financial health and their ability to withstand financial shocks without government bailout supports. The increased capital requirement, however, could reduce the amount of funds available to lend out to customers.

Specifically, Basel III will require banks to: (1) maintain top-quality capital (tier 1 capital, consisting or equity and retained earnings) up to 4.5 percent of their assets; (2) hold a new separate "capital conservation buffer" of common equity worth at least 2.5 percent of their assets; and (3) build a separate "countercyclical buffer" of up to 2.5 percent when their credit markets are booming. The tier 1 rule will take effect from January 2015 and the requirement for the capital conservation buffer will be phased in between January 2016 and January 2019.

Other rules of Basel III include: (1) provisions for reducing risk-taking by banks, (2) requirements for liquid banks' assets, (3) promotion of financial stability, and (4) improvements in risk management, governance, banks' transparency and disclosures.

Eleven important provisions of Basel III are listed next.

1. Basel III rules are more robust than those of Basel II in the sense that they require higher capital standards (more than triple that required by Basel II) to withstand future financial crisis.

2. The effective implementation or Basel III is undermined by several potential pitfalls during the eight-transition period.
3. The new capital conservation buffer (2.5 percent) will not be effective until January 2019.
4. The total capital requirement of 7 percent is expected to become a norm or standard floor for banks in order to avoid curbs on their payouts such as dividends, bonuses, or share buybacks.
5. Basel III rules along with global liquidity standards that will become effective January 2015 will make banks build up reserves of cashlike assets and more capital than Basel II rules.
6. Financial institutions may reconsider financial market trading in light of the new tougher capital requirements.
7. Big financial institutions may build up more capital than Basel III rules to mitigate the negative effects of the perception of "too big to fail" (TBTF).
8. Regulators may require excess countercyclical buffer.
9. Banks may attempt to adopt Basel III capital requirements prior to the dates specified in Basel rules to demonstrate their commitment to a sound banking system and proper risk assessment. Investors will perceive early adoption of Basel III rules as positive steps toward a more sustainable, liquid, and sound banking sector.
10. It is also expected that large banks will adopt Basel III rules earlier than the required timetable because they have more resources and incentives to do so to rule out the perception of TBTF.
11. A relatively long transition period may put banks that delay adoption at a competitive advantage over early adopters.

On July 21, 2010, President Barack Obama signed into law the Dodd-Frank Wall Street Reform and Consumer Protection Act of 2010, which is called the most sweeping financial reform since the Great Depression. Dodd-Frank is named after Senate Banking Committee chairman Christopher Dodd (D-CT) and House Financial Services Committee chairman Barney Frank (D-MA). Its provisions pertain to banks, hedge funds, credit rating agencies, and the derivatives market. Dodd-Frank authorizes the establishment of an oversight council to monitor systemic risk of financial institutions and the creation of a consumer protection bureau within the Federal Reserve. Dodd-Frank requires the development of over 240 new rules by the Securities and Exchange Commission (SEC), the Government Accountability Office (GAO), and the Federal Reserve to implement its provisions over a five-year period.

Many provisions of Dodd-Frank are considered to be positive and useful in protecting consumers and investors, including the establishment of a consumer protection bureau and a systemic risk regulator and provisions requiring derivatives to be put on clearinghouses/exchanges. The new Consumer Financial Products Commission will make rules for most retail products offered by banks, such as certificates of deposit and consumer loans. Dodd-Frank requires managers of hedge funds (but not the funds themselves) with more than $150 million in assets to register with the SEC.

Some provisions are subject to study and further regulatory actions by regulators, including the so-called Volcker rule. Dodd-Frank fails to address the misconception of

TBTF financial institutions, the main cause of the financial crisis, inefficiencies in Fannie Mae, Freddie Mac, and the housing agencies and the excessive use of market-based short-term funding by financial services firms.

Provisions of the Dodd-Frank Act of 2010 are summarized next.

1. Broadening the supervisory and oversight role of the Federal Reserve to include all entities that own an insured depository institution and other large and nonbank financial services firms that could threaten the nation's financial system.
2. Establishing a new Financial Services Oversight Council to identify and address existing and emerging systemic risks threatening the health of financial services firms.
3. Developing new processes to liquidate failed financial services firms.
4. Establishing an independent Consumer Financial Protection Bureau to oversee consumer and investor financial regulations and their enforcement.
5. Creating rules to regulate OTC derivatives.
6. Coordinating and harmonizing the supervision, setting, and regulatory authorities of the SEC and the Commodities Futures Trading Commission.
7. Mandating registration of advisors of private funds and disclosures of certain information of those funds.
8. Empowering shareholders with a say on pay of nonbonding votes by shareholders approving executive compensation.
9. Increasing accountability and transparency for credit rating agencies.
10. Creating a Federal Insurance Office within the Treasury Department.
11. Restricting and limiting some activities of financial firms, including limiting bank proprietary investing and trading in hedge funds and private equity funds as well as limiting bank swaps activities.
12. Providing cooperation and consistency with international financial and banking standards.
13. Making permanent the exemption from its Section 404(b) requirement for non-accelerated filers (those with less than $75 million in market capitalization).
14. Requiring auditors of all broker-dealers to register with the PCAOB and giving the PCAOB rulemaking power to require a program of inspection for those auditors.
15. Empowering the Financial Stability Oversight Council to monitor domestic and international financial regulatory proposals and developments in order to strengthen the integrity, efficiency, competitiveness, and stability of the U.S. financial markets.
16. Making it easier for the SEC to prosecute aiders and abettors of those who commit securities fraud under the Securities Act of 1933, the Securities Exchange Act of 1934, and the Investment Advisers Act of 1940 by lowering the legal standard from "knowing" to "knowing or reckless."
17. Directing the SEC to issue rules requiring companies to disclose in the proxy statement why they have separated, or combined, the positions of chairman and CEO.

The effective implementation provision of Dodd-Frank requires more than 60 studies to be conducted and more than 200 rules and regulations to be established within the next several years (2010–2015). Dodd-Frank is organized in 16 title provisions of the Act, as shown in Exhibit 1.1.

EXHIBIT 1.1 Summary of Provisions of the Dodd-Frank Act of 2010

Title	Heading	Description
I	Financial Stability	Creating a Financial Stability Oversight Council to identify users and respond to existing and emerging systemic risk of bank holding companies and large nonbank financial companies.
		The Council is composed of ten voting members chaired by the head of the Treasury Department.
II	Orderly Liquidation Authority	Provides recommendations for receivership that may be made by the secretary of the Treasury or Federal Reserve and Federal Deposit Insurance Corporation (FDIC) or Securities and Exchange Commission (SEC) for the financial companies in default.
		Secretary will petition U.S. district court for an order to appoint the FDIC as receiver if a failing financial company does not consent to it.
		The liquidation process requires that: unsecured creditors bear losses; shareholders do not receive payment until all claims are fully paid; management and directors responsible for the failure are removed; any funds the FDIC borrows from Treasury to facilitate a liquidation be repaid through asset sales and risk-based assessments; no taxpayer funds to be used to prevent or pay for a liquidation.
III	Transfer of Powers to the OCC, FDIC, and the Federal Reserve	Abolishes the Office of Thrift Supervision; preserves the thrift charter.
		Allocates supervisory and rule-making authority for all thrift holding companies and their nondepositary institution subsidiaries to the Federal Reserve.
		All rule-making authorities for thrifts will be transferred to the Office of the Comptroller of the Currency (OCC). The OCC will be redefined as a bureau within the Department of Treasury.
		Imposes a number of deposit insurance reforms to: redefine the assessment base to reflect assets; requires the reserve ratio to reach 1.35% of estimated insured deposits; permanently increases deposit insurance coverage to $250,000; fully covers non-interest bearing transaction accounts through 2012.
IV	Regulation of Advisers to Hedge Funds	Eliminates the private advisor exemption and requires the investment advisor to maintain certain records and reports.
		Provides exemptions from the registration requirements for: advisors solely to venture capital funds; foreign private advisors with fewer than 15 U.S clients and less than $25 million in assets under management; family offices as defined by SEC.
		Requires the General Accountability Office (GAO) to study and report on appropriate criteria for determining the financial thresholds.
V	Insurance	Monitors the insurance industry and identifies issues contributing to system risk.
		Determines if the state insurance measures are preempted by certain international insurance agreements.
		Requires modernization and improvements of the U.S system of insurance regulation.
		Submits a report to Congress on the global reinsurance market.

(Continued)

EXHIBIT 1.1 (*Continued*)

Title	Heading	Description
VI	Improvements to Regulation of Bank and Savings Association Holding Companies and Depository Institutions	GAO conducts a study of elimination of exceptions as amended, for thrifts, loan companies and credit banks, etc.
		Modifies regulations related to transactions with affiliates, charter conversions, and SEC's elective investment bank that holds company framework and also requires the Federal Reserve to examine nondepositary institution subsidiaries engaged in activities as banks.
		Provides rules such as: banking entities to be prohibited from engaging in trading or investing funds; insured depositary institution not including an institution that functions solely in a trust or fiduciary capacity.
		Banking entities must bring their activities and investments into compliance within two years after the rules become effective.
		Includes activities such as transactions in U.S government obligations or in connection with activities related to market making to meet demand of clients/customers or risk mitigating hedging activities.
		Transactions will be prohibited if they have conflict of interest between clients or customers; or if they are prone to high-risk assets or trading strategies or even if they pose a threat to the safety of bank.
VII	Wall Street Transparency and Accountability	SEC and Commodity Futures Trading Commission (CFTC) will share authority for regulation of OTC's swaps that actually are required to be submitted for clearing must also be traded on or through exchange or swap execution facility. (The dealers and participants must register with SEC/CFTC.)
		An exemption is provided for end users who use derivatives to hedge against risks such as fuel prices and interest rates.
VIII	Clearing and Settlement Supervision	Council to design financial market utilities and payment; the Federal Reserve to prescribe uniform risk management standards for the payment and settlement activities.
		Requires conducting examinations to evaluate compliance with risk management and conduct standards besides the market utilities getting access to Federal Reserve's discount window under few restrictions.
		Requires that financial institutions not include swap data repositories, security exchanges, and the financial market utility not include the above not a broker, dealer or agent as well.
IX	Investors Protections and Improvements to Regulation of Securities	As per the Investors Protections, SEC is granted authority to promulgate rules to establish fiduciary duty. SEC must study and give suggestions within six months of enactment of care for brokers-dealers or persons associated while advising customers; study enhancing investment advisor examinations, mutual fund advertising, etc.
		Credit rating agencies to be established within SEC to administer the commission's rules with respect to nationally recognized statistical rating organizations (NRSROs) that in turn will be examined annually by SEC as its employees (of NRSRO) are covered by the whistleblower protections.

(*Continued*)

EXHIBIT 1.1 *(Continued)*

		Asset-backed securities would be required to retain economic interest and risk retention requirements for commercial mortgages to be determined by federal banking agencies and the SEC.
		Executive compensation to be provided as prerequisite for listing shares on an exchange.
		Create municipal securities; its dealers and advisors are to register with the SEC.
X	Bureau of Consumer Financial Protection	Establish a bureau that comprises of the consumer protection functions (Federal Reserve, OCC, OTC, FDIC and NCUA) to be resident within the Federal Reserve and to be funded by Federal Reserve system.
		Grants authority to the bureau to regulate any person engaged in offering or providing a consumer financial product or service.
		Banks and credit unions with total assets of $10 billion or less would be subject to examination and enforcement of their compliance with federal consumer laws.
		Exclusions to be provided for some persons including SEC/CFTC regulated entities; real estate brokers; home retailers; accountants, tax preparers; auto dealers.
		Bureau to take action against covered persons and service providers to stop unfair, deceptive, and abusive acts and practices.
		Additional offices to be established under the bureau including the Office of Fair Lending, Financial Literacy, Service Member Affairs, and Financial Protection for Older Americans.
		Interchange fees for electronic debit transactions to be required to be reasonable and proportional.
XI	Federal Reserve System Provisions	Federal Reserve to establish policies and procedures to ensure that a program is used to provide liquidity to the financial system.
		GAO to audit Federal Reserve loans and other financial assistance and to audit Federal Reserve Bank governance, including consideration of the selection and appointment of directors and conflicts of interest.
XII	Improving Access to Mainstream Financial Institutions	Establish grants to promote initiatives that enable low- and moderate-income individuals access to financial products that meet their needs.
		Establish multiyear programs to provide low-cost alternatives to small-dollar loans.
XIII	Pay It Back Act	Reduce authorization of the Troubled Asset Relief Program and requiring to proceed from the sale of Fannie Mae, Freddie Mac debt purchased under Treasury's emergency authority.
XIV	Mortgage Reform and Anti-Predatory Lending Act	To create laws/rules requiring mortgage originators to be qualified, registered, and licensed; to set a minimum standard that mortgage originators make a reasonable and good-faith determination while prohibiting steering where no mortgage originator may receive compensation, directly or indirectly based on terms of loans; to limit prepayment penalties.

(Continued)

EXHIBIT 1.1 (*Continued*)

Title	Heading	Description
		To increase protection for consumers by redefining high-cost mortgages with smaller spreads over the prime offer rate than currently used and by adding requirements regarding escrow accounts and appraisal standards.
XV	Miscellaneous Provisions	Requires the GAO to report to Congress in a year on relative independence, effectiveness, and expertise of appointed inspectors general and designated federal entities.
		Requires the FDIC to evaluate the definitions of core deposits and brokered deposits and their impact on the economy.
XI	Section 1256 Contracts	Adds a new provision to the Internal Revenue Code providing an exception for any securities future contact and any interest rate swap, currency swap, basis swap, interest rate cap, commodity swap, equity swap, or similar agreement.

Technological advances and global competition and regulatory reforms have enabled companies and their investors to "largely meet in the jurisdiction of their choosing . . . [they] have choices about where to invest, where to raise capital and where secondary trading is to occur."[8] Thus, companies can choose the regulatory regime they desire to operate under, and investors have a choice of safeguards and protections provided under different regulatory reforms. An effective regulatory reform creates an environment under which companies can operate in achieving their performance targets, being held accountable for their activities, and providing protections for their investors. Regulatory reforms in terms of their effectiveness and context can be classified into three concepts: (1) a race to the bottom; (2) a race to optimality; (3) a race to the top. The race to the bottom concept suggests that global securities regulators, in an effort to attract issuers, deregulate to the points that provide issuers with maximum flexibility for their operations at the expense of not providing adequate protections for investors. The race to the top concept suggests that global securities regulators provide maximum protection for investors through rigid regulations and highly scrutinized enforcements at the expense of putting companies in the global competition at a disadvantage with non-cost-justified regulations. The race to optimality concept is a hybrid of the first two concepts, in which both issuers (companies) and investors prefer a regulatory regime and jurisdiction that provides cost-justified investor protection. In a real-world global competition, a combination of these three concepts may work best, as many provisions of SOX have been globally adopted.

Many provisions of SOX, particularly those pertaining to strengthening auditor independence, assessment of internal control over financial reporting, the creation of an independent board to oversee the accounting profession, and the strengthening of audit committee requirements, have been effectively adopted in other countries. Dodd-Frank is one of the most comprehensive financial regulatory reforms intended to strengthen regulation and oversight of the U.S. financial system in order to reduce the likelihood of future financial crises. Dodd-Frank consists of 16 distinct titles addressing all aspects of financial institutions from financial stability to mortgage reforms. It requires more than 500 rules to be established, 60 studies to be conducted, and 90 reports to be prepared to ensure proper and effective implementation of its provisions over the next four years. Effective implementation of provisions of Dodd-Frank is expected to have significant impacts not only on financial services firms but also on credit rating agencies, banks and bank holding companies, insurance companies, hedge funds, private equity, broker-dealers, and large asset managers among others.

 ## TYPES AND ROLES OF FINANCIAL MARKETS

A vital financial system and reliable financial information is essential for economic development worldwide. The persistence of differences in global financial systems necessitates a move toward convergence in corporate governance measures and regulatory reforms. Emerging global corporate governance reforms are shaping capital market structure worldwide, their competitiveness and protection measures they provide to their investors in ensuring the desired return on investment (ROI). The financial markets typically are classified into debt and capital markets. In particular, financial markets can be classified into capital, bond, mortgage, equity, derivative, and international financial markets.

Capital Markets

Capital markets are intermediaries facilitating the exchange of securities where business enterprises, including companies and governments, can raise funds and money for long-term investments. Securities are comprised of both debt and equity. Hence, the capital market includes the stock and the bond markets, which are further regulated by the Securities Exchange Commission (SEC). The capital markets are further segregated into two types—primary and secondary markets. A new security—bond/stock—is issued for the first time through the process of underwriting in the primary market. The existing securities are traded to other investors in the secondary market on the organized securities exchanges or OTC.

Bond Markets

Bond markets, also known as debt markets, are a type of financial market where participants purchase and sell debt securities. According to statistical data from the Bank of International Settlements (BIS), the world bond market exceeds the security market almost by 100 percent. The total size of the U.S. bond market is estimated to be $34.2 trillion. Debt securities have different risk/return characteristics ranging from short-term government bonds to corporate bonds. The types of debt securities and their subsequent weights in a total current debt outstanding amount are illustrated in Exhibit 1.2.

The advantages of the debt market are that debt securities are highly liquid and are not subjected to the same form of credit risk, where principal and coupon rates are received in accordance with the contract. Traditionally when the volatility of the equity market is high, investors turn to safe havens (e.g., bond markets), which pay a "guaranteed" interest rate. Money market funds are considered to be the safest security currently, yielding on average 0.02 percent. The biggest disadvantage of money market

EXHIBIT 1.2 U.S. Bond Market Debt Outstanding

$6,927.80	U.S. Treasury (marketable securities out of a total debt of $12 trillion, $7.5 of which is public)
2,972.4	Agencies of the United States
2,726.8	State and municipal
6,778.4	Corporate
3,430.3	Money market
8,948.7	Mortgage backed
2,533.6	Asset backed
$34,318.0	Total

Source: Securities Industry and Financial Markets Association, www.sifma.org/.

funds[9] is their sensitivity to interest rate hikes. If the bonds are bought for the speculative purposes and are not intended to be kept to maturity, then they become subject to the volatility of interest rates. The largest segment in the debt market is the mortgage-backed bond market, which accounts for at least 35 percent of the total debt market. Failure of financial instruments, coupled with loose risk assessment standards for the collateral portfolio of loans, caused one of the worst subprime mortgage crises in history.

Mortgage Markets

The mortgage markets, so-called secondary mortgage markets, offer a diverse number of products. The secondary mortgage market is the market for the sale of securities or bonds collateralized by the value of mortgage loans. The mortgage lender, commercial banks, or specialized firms often group together many loans and sell loan portfolios as securities called collateralized mortgage obligations (CMOs) in an attempt to reduce the risk of the individual loans. The CMOs sometimes are further grouped in other collateralized debt obligations. The most popular mortgage-backed securities are mortgage-backed bonds, mortgage pass-through securities, mortgage pay-through securities, and CMOs.

The mechanism of the mortgage-backed bonds is similar to any other bond; the only difference is the pool of mortgages issued by the specialized lending institutions or banks acts as collateral. Mortgage-backed bonds have a higher yield than other types of bonds and are considered to have lower risk rate. The prepayment risk is the major risk that can affect the profitability of the security instrument. All the income generated by the pool of mortgages (part of interest and principal) is directly distributed to the mortgage pass-through securities investors (excluding the fee that intermediary collects). The mortgage pool can contain either residential property mortgages or commercial property mortgages.

Mortgage pay-through securities are similar to the pass-through securities except pay-through securities act like an amortized fixed-income instruments rather than equity instrument. The amortized payments are made from the cash flow generated by the mortgage pool, and prepayment risk comes into play.

CMOs are a type of pay-through security; the main difference is that CMOs separate the payments of the interest and principal on the pool into different revenue streams and as a result can offer different rates. CMOs combine features of both mortgage-backed bonds and pass-through securities. Unlike with pass-through securities, with CMOs, the investor assumes the prepayment risk. CMOs are very complex financial instruments that are designed specifically to meet an investor's financial criteria as they do not necessarily synchronize with the original pool payments. The payment schedule can be accelerated or decelerated depending on the investor's choice. Mortgage delinquencies, defaults, and decreased real estate values can make these collateralized debt obligations difficult to evaluate. The recent wave of foreclosures resulted in the highest rate of foreclosures and payment delinquencies in U.S. history. According to the Mortgage Bankers Association, more than 4.6 percent of homeowners were in foreclosure as of May 19, 2010, which a record high for the mortgage market.

The Community Reinvestment Act of 1977[10] encourages commercial banks and savings association to facilitate the lending process for low- to middle- income borrowers. A study conducted by Harvard University Joint Center[11] for housing studies suggest that secondary market mortgage investors have little knowledge of the complexity of the mortgage products they are investing in. As a result, the efficiency of the secondary mortgage market is questionable. The study also stated that the existing regulatory framework, which is intended to protect investors, is far from perfect.

Equity Markets

Equity or stock markets are public forums for the trading of public company stock and derivatives at an agreed price determined by demand and supply for these financial instruments. Equity markets comprise securities listed on a stock exchange as well as those only traded privately. Stocks are listed and traded on stock exchanges such as the New York Stock Exchange (NYSE) and Nasdaq in the United States, Euronext (European Union), MICEX (Russia), and Shanghai Stock Exchange (China). According to statistical data from the World Federation of the Exchanges, the total size of the U.S. equity $14,281trillion.[12] NYSE and Nasdaq are both the first and third largest exchanges in the world. Exhibit 1.3 shows capitalization of the exchanges in 2008 and 2009.

Derivative Markets

Derivatives are financial contracts that are designed to create market price exposure to changes in an underlying commodity, asset, or event. In general, derivatives do not

EXHIBIT 1.3 Change in Capitalization of U.S. Exchanges in 2009

Stock Exchange	Capitalization 2009	Capitalization 2008	Change 2009/ 2008
Nasdaq OMX	3,239,492.4	2,248,976.5	44.0%
New York Stock Exchange Euronext (U.S.)	11,837,793.3	9,208,934.1	28.5%

*Millions of Dollars

Source: Annual statistics. Equity markets, domestic capitalization. World Federation of Exchanges 2009. Available at: www.world-exchanges.org/statistics/annual/2009/equity-markets/domestic-market-capitalization.

involve the exchange or transfer of principal or title and are typically classified into futures, forwards, options and swaps, or some kind of hybrid of those described earlier.[13] Derivatives can be traded on organized stock exchanges or OTC exchanges. The most famous organized stock exchanges where futures and options are traded are Chicago Mercantile Exchange and NYSE Euronext. The size of the market, according to BIS statistics, was getting close to $86 trillion at the beginning of 2008. OTC derivative markets are much larger and poorly regulated. OTC derivatives include: commodities forwards, options swaps, equity-linked forwards, options, swaps, foreign exchange forwards, swaps, currency swaps, currency options, interest rate swaps, forward rate agreements and swaps, gold contracts, and many others. The total notional amount of the outstanding positions was around $615 trillion as of May 11, 2010.[14]

The recent financial crisis has underscored the lack of regulations for non-securities based derivatives contracts such as credit default swaps (CDS), which are primarily traded in the OTC markets. Unlike other derivative contracts (insurance, securities, commodities, futures), CDS are not regulated. Thus they are perceived as a form of legalized gambling. Proper regulations require transparent information on OTC transactions to restore investor confidence on speculative derivatives transactions (credit derivatives). Global regulators particularly in the United States and Europe have considered regulating CDS and other OTC derivatives by establishing clearinghouses to serve as a central counterparty for those derivatives.

Prior to 2000, almost all derivatives were traded on regulated central exchanges overseen by the Commodity Futures Trading Commission. After 2002, the derivative markets became unregulated and exempt from all regulations, including state gambling laws. With no regulation scrutiny on derivative trades, the determination of the true value of those exotic instruments became subjective, manipulative, and complex. The Commodities Futures Modernization Act of 2000 was passed by U.S. Congress and allowed the deregulation of financial derivatives. This deregulation enabled insurance giant AIG to engage in CDS. When AIG as a major player in CDS collapsed, other banks, insurance companies, and investment funds suffered tremendous losses. Deregulation of the CDS derivatives promoted speculative activities at the expense of derivative hedging activities, which substantially increased the systemic risks of CDS. Regulation of OTC derivatives has gained considerable attention since the Lehman Brothers collapsed and the AIG debacle. Lack of transparency in OTC markets, the excessive use of CDS, along with improper market discipline and mechanisms and the perceived complexity and speculation encouraged global legislators to issue legislative proposals to regulate OTC derivatives and transfer them from bilateral to multilateral trading.

Derivatives are important tools used by management for mitigating risks. The ever-increasing growth of derivatives suggests that market participants including management find derivatives useful tools for risk management. Credit derivatives can be useful to commercial banks to manage loan portfolio risks, to investment banks to manage risks of underwriting securities, and to asset managers or hedge funds to achieve the desired credit risk portfolio. Nonetheless, credit derivatives can create conflict of interest when a bank performs all three commercial, investment, and insurance activities. Credit derivatives enable banks to take additional risks or transfer risks of loans to another party.

Derivative markets should be better regulated and scrutinized to prevent further financial crises. Inadequate, ineffective, and unenforced regulations, particularly regarding OTC financial derivatives, have enabled and contributed to excessive speculative behavior of the use of credit derivatives.[15]

Global Financial Markets

Investor confidence in the global capital markets is the key driver of global economic growth, prosperity, and financial stability. Global capital markets are classified into those with either an inside system or an outside system. In an inside system, in such countries as France, Germany, and Italy, there is a high level of ownership concentration, illiquid capital markets, and liberal regulation of capital markets. Conversely, in an outside system, in such countries as the United Kingdom and the United States, ownership is widely dispersed, capital markets are liquid, markets are active for corporate control, and capital markets are highly regulated. There are more than 50 stock exchanges worldwide that assist companies to conduct their initial public offerings (IPOs). Stock exchanges in India, Italy, and South Korea recently have attracted many domestic IPOs; and many state-owned enterprises in China and France have done their fundraising domestically and have listed their IPOs on their home exchanges. Companies have traditionally listed on their domestic stock exchanges, and only about 10 percent of companies have chosen to list abroad.[16]

U.S. capital markets have traditionally been regarded as the deepest, safest, and most liquid in the world. For many decades they have required stringent regulatory measures in protecting investors, measures that also have raised the profile and status of their listed companies.[17] The U.S. financial markets are important sector of the nation's economy.[18]

1. The U.S. financial services industry's GDP in 2009 exceeded $800 billion, accounting for 6 percent of the U.S. GDP.
2. The securities industry accounted for more than $175 billion, about 17 percent of the total for financial markets.
3. The financial services sector employed about 6 million workers in the United States in 2008, accounting for 6 percent of the total private sector employment.

However, recent competitiveness of capital markets abroad has provided global companies with a variety of choices of where to list and possibly subject to less vigorous regulatory measures. As these markets abroad become better regulated, more liquid, and deeper, they provide companies worldwide opportunities to raise their capital needs under different jurisdictions. High compliance costs of SOX have prompted companies to think about whether their capital financing should come from U.S. capital markets or from capital markets abroad, which may be less strictness and have looser disclosure requirements. Globalization and technological advances have promoted tight competition among the world's leading capital markets (e.g., NYSE, London Stock Exchange [LSE], Hong Kong, Shanghai, Dubai), and thus regulations governing these markets can have a considerable impact on the balance of capital worldwide.

Stock exchanges in the United Kingdom and the United States are the most liquid in the world. In the United Kingdom, the LSE is primarily for established companies and the Alternative Investment Market (AIM) for smaller companies. In the United States, the NYSE comprises the large-cap company market while Nasdaq is typically the home for high-tech and growing companies. The American Stock Exchange usually lists smaller companies. The other active stock exchanges worldwide are the Tokyo Stock Exchange, NYSE Euronext, and Deutsche Börse. While listing standards in the United States and the United Kingdom are similar in terms of share ownership, market requirements, information disclosures, and board models, there are some differences with respect to shareholders' and directors' roles and responsibilities. Technological advances and globalization including cross-border share ownership necessitate that many global companies observe a variety of corporate governance reforms and guidelines—at least the listing standards of the country in which they are incorporated and the country in which they are listed. These listing standards and corporate governance guidelines are often in conflict, reflecting differences in regulatory, legal, and cultural traditions.

Stock exchanges in both the United States and the United Kingdom have attracted a number of international companies. Foreign companies choose these two main exchanges for raising their capital needs, and investors invest in these companies because of the higher protections provided by these exchanges. Some companies are listed on more than one stock exchange and often face difficult, duplicitous, and confusing listing standards that increase compliance costs. The pervasiveness of global financial scandals has encouraged policy members and regulators to respond by adopting laws and regulations to mitigate problems. The costs and benefits of these laws and regulations are often not assessed in considering their appropriateness on regulatory measures and the international impact of such measures. SOX's impact on foreign registrants is an example of the global reach of regulations and challenges associated with establishing national regulatory reforms. In response to the global reach and extraterritorial effects of national regulations, the Organization for Economic Co-operation and Development (OECD) published the OECD Principles of Corporate Governance in 1999, subsequently revised in 2004, and has already adopted by the International Corporate Governance Network. These principles provide a framework and a platform for all countries in developing their own corporate governance structure. Foreign private issues, while required to comply with listing standards in the United States, are not subject to the listing rules that govern U.K. companies.

U.S. capital markets provide four benefits for global companies' listings:

1. U.S. capital markets are the deepest and most liquid in the world.
2. Cross-listing securities in the United States promotes visibility for foreign listings.
3. Listing on U.S. exchanges subjects companies to increased disclosure requirements, which can lead to more investor confidence and thus lower risk premium.
4. Foreign investors are allowed to benefit from the high level of investor protection experienced by U.S. investors.

LSE is perceived as having less restrictive listing requirements and lower compliance costs. These advantages have resulted in the majority of IPOs being listed on the London AIM in the post-SOX period (870 IPOs listed on the AIM compared with 526 being listed on Nasdaq). Ten factors contributing to the switch include:

1. Higher U.S. underwriting fees than their foreign counterparts.
2. Because foreign exchanges are maturing, they attract and facilitate home IPOs.
3. The decrease of global dependence on the United States to raise capital.
4. The emergence of private equity within the U.S. financial markets.
5. Geographical convenience, as London is closer in proximity to many regional issuing companies.
6. Time zones are a factor, as the U.S. exchanges are in time zones that often conflict with business hours of many international companies.
7. Increased investor confidence in domestic markets resulting from more effective corporate governance reforms in other countries in the post-SOX period.
8. Substantial growth in Islamic financial markets providing many opportunities to foreign exchanges in London and Dubai.
9. Privatization of governmental institutions in countries such as China, India, and their preference for their local market listings.
10. The emergence of government-backed investment entities such as mutual funds and hedge funds outside the United States.[19]

 ## FINANCIAL SERVICES FIRMS

Financial services firms include commercial and investment banks and savings institutions, mortgage institutions, investment companies, credit unions, insurance companies, finance companies, real estate investment trusts, and securities brokers and dealers. The more common types of financial are described in this section.

Commercial Banks

Commercial banks normally provide a link between those that have capital and those that need capital. Commercial banks are privately owned financial institutions that accept demand and time deposits, make loans to individuals and organizations, and provide services such as documentary collections, international banking, trade financing cash management and other fiduciary services. The Federal Reserve Banks keeps the statistics about the assets and liabilities of the commercial banks. As of the week ending March 16, 2011, Large domestically chartered commercial banks had $993.8 billion and small domestically chartered commercial banks had $442.6 billion in residual assets (assets less liabilities).[20] The bank assets include but are not limited to: bank credit, securities in bank credit, treasury and agency securities, commercial and industrial loans, revolving home-equity loans, closed-end residential loans, commercial real estate loans, consumer loans, and credit cards and revolving plans, among others.

Bank liabilities include deposits, large time deposits, borrowing, and trading liabilities, among others.[21]

Investment Banks

Investment banks deal with the financing requirements of corporations, governments, and institutions and are usually organized as corporations or partnerships. Investment banks are financial institutions that assist corporations and governments in raising capital by underwriting and acting as the agent in the issuance of securities. Investment banks also assist companies involved in mergers and acquisitions, derivatives, and other financial instruments. Investment banks as opposed to the commercial banks typically act as short-term principals. However, recently the distinction has become less and less evident. Other countries historically never separated investment banking function from commercial banking function. The leading global investment banks are Goldman Sachs, Citigroup, JPMorgan Chase, Bank of America/Merrill Lynch, CitiGroup, UBS, Credit Suisse, Deutsche Bank, Barclay's Capital, and others. Investment banking fees collected in 2009 amounted to $59.8 billion, or 13 percent above 2008 fees, but significantly down from 2007 fees of $86.9 billion.[22]

Insurance Companies

The primary purpose of insurance is to manage risks, hedge against uncertainties, and spread unforeseen risks. The two major types of insurance companies are life insurance companies, which provide financial assistance at the time of death, and property and casualty insurance companies, which provide policies to individuals (personal lines including homeowners' and individual automobile policies) and to business enterprises (commercial lines including general liability and workers' compensation). Banks, mutual funds, and health maintenance organizations are aggressively trying to expand into products traditionally sold by insurance companies. The financial crisis had an increasing impact on the insurance industry through the companies' investment portfolios. However, the solvency of the insurance sector as a whole does not seem to be threatened. A majority of companies in the insurance sector have been adversely affected by the financial crisis, which revealed the exposure to credit and market risks in U.S. mortgage and financial guarantee insurance companies and other insurance-dominated financial groups.

Insurance companies have proved to be a stabilizing factor during the financial crisis. These insurance organizations are primarily large investors with a longer horizon of investments compared to the financial institutions such as banks. For this reason, insurance organizations can withstand and sustain short-term shocks. However, the insurance companies that were involved in activities traditionally associated with investment banks, valuation, and rating pressures have been deeply impacted by the recent financial crisis. The subsequent downgrading of business enterprises in the financial guarantee insurance sector led to downward pressures on market valuations of the securities. These activities had already led to imbalance in the market before the credit and financial crisis hit the market.

Some provisions of Dodd-Frank are relevant to insurance companies and their business transactions. The newly established Federal Insurance Office (FIO) will play an important role in overseeing and coordinating insurance activities between the international insurance market and the U.S. insurance market. Dodd-Frank directed the SEC to establish rules and standards for broker-dealers and investment advisors that would have a substantial impact on insurance companies. The FIO will oversee all aspects of the insurance industry, including systemic risk, capital standards, consumer protection, and international coordination of insurance regulation.

Pension Plans and Mutual Funds

A retirement plan is a financial vehicle that pays an individual, at a contractually agreed on time, a payment throughout retirement and is usually in the form of an annuity. Pension plans are a type of retirement plan, where an employer makes contributions toward a pool of funds set aside for an employee's future benefit. The pool of funds is then invested on the employee's behalf, allowing the employee to receive benefits upon retirement. Depending on the arrangements, retirement plans can be set up by government agencies, employers, trade unions, and other institutions and organizations. There are two distinct pension plans under the Employee Retirement Income Security Act of 1974: defined benefit plans and defined contribution plans. A defined benefit plan is designed to give employers an opportunity to contribute toward employee retirement. Employee contributions are voluntary and not required. Significantly, employers can contribute more under defined benefit plans than under any other plan and consequently can claim more as a tax deduction. Also, employees are promised the certain amount upon retirement and are eligible for the early retirement withdrawals. On the downside, defined benefit plans are expensive to manage, and if an overfunded plan is terminated the employer has to pay excise tax. According to the Pension Benefit Guaranty Corporation, there were about 38,000 insured defined benefit plans in 2010 compared to a high of about 114,000 in 1985. The Internal Revenue Service believes that the reason for the decrease in popularity is the complex nature of the plans.[23]

Defined contribution plans are gaining popularity. Under these plans, employers contribute a specific amount annually, and those contributions are later invested on the employees' behalf. Examples of defined contribution plans include 401(k) plans, 403(b) plans, employee stock ownership plans, and profit-sharing plans.[24] The total U.S. retirement market as of September 30, 2009, was getting close to $15.5 trillion and accounts for 35 percent of all household financial assets in the country. Mutual fund managers hold around 13 percent of the total retirement market and 51 percent of the total defined contribution plans.

Mutual funds are investment vehicles that are made up of a pool of funds collected from many investors for the purpose of investing in securities such as stocks, bonds, money market instruments, and similar assets. Mutual funds are operated by money managers, who invest the fund's capital and attempt to produce capital gains and income for the fund's investors. A mutual fund's portfolio is structured and maintained to match the investment objectives stated in its prospectus. Mutual funds are classified as open-end funds by the Investment Company Act of 1940 and the SEC.

Mutual funds also typically are organized in the form of equity funds. Depending on the investment strategy, mutual funds carefully choose the investment tools they are planning to manage within the portfolio, which include: bond funds, money market funds, funds on funds, growth funds, value funds, index funds, and other integrated funds, and often are invested based on the Russell Indexes. Individual or institutional investors can use the indexes to benchmark the mutual fund performance.

Sovereign Wealth Funds

Sovereign wealth funds (SWFs) are pools of money derived from a country's reserves, intended for investment purposes to generate revenue to benefit the country's economy and citizens. The funding for a SWF comes from central bank reserves that accumulate as a result of budget and trade surpluses and even from revenue generated from the exports of natural resources. The types of acceptable investments included in each SWF vary from country to country; countries with liquidity concerns limit investments to only very liquid public debt instruments. About 75 percent of the total global SWF pool comes from Middle East and Asia and 60 percent of the total global SWF pool comes from oil- and gas-related income. Abu Dhabi's Abu Dhabi Investment Authority is the biggest SWF with total holdings of $627 billion, according to statistics from the Sovereign Wealth Funds Institution.[25] The second and third largest SWFs in the world are the Norwegian Government Pension Fund- Global and Saudi Arabia's SAMA Foreign Holdings with $443 billion and $432 billion in holdings respectively. SWFs play a more important role in the capital markets as they become active buyers of the U.S. equity. To illustrate, Roland Beck and Michael Fidora estimated that the world's largest SWFs purchased more than $60 billion of newly issued equity from developed world's banks during the midst of the recent global economic meltdown.[26]

Despite the openness of U.S. markets, the U.S. government imposes some restriction on SWF investments. For example, foreign investments in such sectors as energy, communication, and transportations are restricted. Investments in other sectors must comply with the strict regulations as well. According to the GAO report, the legal restrictions on foreign investment exist on the state level for businesses like real estate, agricultural land, banks and financial institutions, insurance companies, and so on. The agencies that are responsible for the international investment law enforcement are the Federal Reserve Board, Federal Communications Commission, Nuclear Regulatory Commission, and the Departments of Transportation, Agriculture, and Interior. Examples of the laws that regulate or prohibit foreign investment are the Agricultural Foreign Investment Disclosure Act of 1978, Magnuson-Stevens Fishery Conservation and Management Act, Communications Act of 1934, Atomic Energy Act of 1954, General Mining Law of 1872, and others.[27]

 ### CONCLUSION

The financial services industry traditionally has been regarded as vital to the nation's economic growth, development, and prosperity. Nonetheless, recent financial difficulties in the industry prompted large government bailouts of TBTF financial institutions and has resulted in a series of mergers and acquisitions that consolidated the financial service industry further. If these TBTF financial firms assume that the government's reluctance to hold them accountable for their business failures signals aversion to tough regulatory reforms and actions, moral hazards can arise. To minimize this perceived moral hazard, the Dodd-Frank Act of 2010 establishes stricter regulations for the financial service industry to prevent significant adverse impact of large financial firm failures. Any financial regulations that do not address the real causes of the financial crisis and end TBTF will not be sustainable. Dodd-Frank indirectly addresses the TBTF phenomenon by requiring the newly established Financial Stability Oversight Council to identify and more effectively regulate "systemically important" financial institutions, including bank and nonbank financial companies.

 NOTES

1. C. D. Niemeier, "American Competitiveness in International Capital Markets: Background Paper for the Atlantic's Ideas Tour Commemorating the Magazine's 150th Anniversary," Washington, D.C., U.S. Public Company Accounting Oversight Board, 2006.
2. Dodd-Frank Wall Street Reform and Consumer Protection Act, H.R. 4173., Pub. L. 111-203 (2010).
3. D. Solomon and C. Bryan-Low, "Tough Cop for Accounting Beat," *Wall Street Journal*, April 16, 2003.
4. Sarbanes-Oxley Act of 2002, The Public Company Accounting Reform and Investor Protection Act (H.R. 3763). Available at: www.whitehouse.gov.
5. The G-20 Toronto Summit: Declaration, June 26–27, 2010. Available at: www.g20.org.
6. Financial Stability Board (FSB). "Progress in the Implementation of the G 20 Recommendations for Strengthening Financial Stability," February 15, 2011. Available at: www.financialstabilityboard.org/publications/r_11o219.pdf.
7. Basel III Accord: The New Basel III Framework. Available at: www.basel-iii-accord .com/.
8. T. Ethiopis, "Statement by SEC Statement by SEC Staff: A Rule to the Top." International Regulatory Reforms Post-Sarbanes Oxley, September 15, 2006. Available at: www.sec.gov.
9. Jason Kephart, "A New Star in the Bond Market," Smart Money, *Wall Street Journal*, March 22, 2010. Available at: www.smartmoney.com/investing/bonds/a-new-star-in-the-bond-market/.
10. Community Reinvestment Act. Available at: www.ffiec.gov/cra/default.htm.
11. Harvard Research, Joint Center for Housing Studies 2010, "Mortgage Market Complexity Foils Consumers and Undermines Fair Lending," September 2010. Available at: www.jchs.harvard.edu/media/understanding_mortgage_markets_04-26-07.html.
12. Annual statistics. Equity markets, domestic capitalization. World Federation of Exchanges 2009. Available at: www.world-exchanges.org/statistics/annual/2009/equity-markets/domestic-market-capitalization
13. Randall Dodd, "Derivative Markets, Sources of Vulnerability of the U.S. Financial Markets," May 10, 2004. Available at: www.financialpolicy.org/fpfspr8.pdf.

14. Bank of International Settlements Statistics, "OTC Derivatives Market Activity in the Second Half of 2009," May 11, 2010. Available at: www.bis.org/press/p100511.htm.

15. P. Krugman, "A Catastrophe Foretold," *New York Times,* October 26, 2007. Available at: www.nytimes.com/2007/10/26/opinion/26krugman.html.

16. Ernst & Young, Global Capital Market Trends, January 2007. Available at: www.ey .com.

17. Committee on Capital Markets Regulation, "Interim Report of the Committee on Capital Markets Regulation," November 302006. Available at: www.capmktsreg.org/research .html.

18. Securities Industry and Financial Markets association. "US Financial Services Industry Contributing to a More Competitive US Economy," July 2010. Available at: www.ita .doc.gov/td/finance/publications/U.S.%20Financial%20Services%20Industry.pdf

19. Z. Rezaee, *Corporate Governance Post-Sarbanes-Oxley* (Hoboken, NJ: John Wiley & Sons, 2007).

20. Board of governors of the Federal Reserve System. "Economic Research and Data: Assets and Liabilities of Commercial Banks in the United States," March 25th, 2011, Available at: www.federalreserve.gov/releases/h8/current/

21. Ibid.

22. Yalman Onaran, "Recovery and Anxiety," Bloomberg Markets, April 2010. Available at: www.bloomberg.com/news/marketsmag/mm_0410_story3.html.

23. Internal Revenue Service, "Choosing a Retirement Plan: Defined Benefit Plan," September 5, 2009. Available at: www.irs.gov/retirement/article/0,,id=108950,00.html.

24. U.S. Department of Labor, "Retirement Plans, Benefits & Savings." Available at: www .dol.gov/dol/topic/retirement/typesofplans.htm.

25. Roland Beck and Michael Fidora, "The Impact of Sovereign Wealth Funds on Global Financial Markets," European Central Bank, Occasional Paper 91, July 2, 2008.

26. Ibid.

27. United States Government Accountability Office, "Sovereign Wealth Funds Laws Limiting Foreign Investment Affect Certain U.S. Assets and Agencies Have Various Enforcement Processes," May 2009. Available at: www.swfinstitute.org/research/ GAOReport.pdf.

CHAPTER TWO

Introduction to Financial Institutions

INTRODUCTION

The past decade has witnessed significant changes in the structure, characteristics, and types of products and services provided by the financial services industry. The most significant changes were in four areas: consolidation, convergence, competition, and regulations. These changes, which are expected to continue to occur at a higher speed in the future, have been motivated and caused by a number of factors and forces, including the global financial crisis, globalization of business, geographic expansion, highly valued stock prices, product line expansion, technological advances, relatively low interest rates, and the worldwide economic downturn. Consolidation, convergence, competition, and regulations have transformed the financial services industry from traditional organizations such as banks, brokers, insurance companies, mutual funds, and securities providers to asset management companies such as bank holding companies (BHCs) and financial holding companies (FHCs).

LANDSCAPE OF THE FINANCIAL SERVICES INDUSTRY

The structure and characteristics of banks and banking organizations are changing from traditional brick-and-mortar branches to universal banking, personal computer banking, and Internet banking. Customers can now do one-stop shopping for all of their financial services. The range of options is not limited by geographic restrictions and/or product limitations. The majority of households and businesses can use local banks within 20 miles for their financial service needs because of availability, convenience, and personalized banking relationships. Financial institutions are also facing numerous challenges caused by rapid changes occurring in information technology, trends toward business combinations, statutory laws, marketplace, global competition, regulatory reforms, and accounting standards. Traditionally, financial services provided by banks, insurance companies, and mutual funds and their roles have been somewhat separate. Today, the differences between functions of these financial services provided by different entities in the industry are becoming less noticeable.

Today, financial holding companies provide the opportunity for one-stop shopping for all financial services and products, including checking and saving accounts, loans, asset management, insurance, and investment services as well as unlimited efficiency in finding the best financial services at the lowest cost nationwide or even across international borders. For example, customers now can easily find information about loans or mortgages online by visiting eloan.com, loanweb.com, lendingtree.com, mortgageloan.com, or national bank sites. This information efficiency offered to customers through e-commerce and Internet banking, coupled with the creation of financial holding companies, will accelerate the financial services movement toward commoditization. The new information technology (IT) not only empowers customers to shop for their financial services easily and effectively but also provides opportunities for competitors to identify, match, and duplicate any innovative financial services.

Many of the traditional barriers, including both geographic (e.g., interstate banking) and products (e.g., a variety of financial services), that once separated banks from insurance companies, mutual firms, or investment funds are now diminishing in the financial services industry. Thus, the ever-changing nature, structure, and competition of the financial services industry have received great attention primarily because of the recent elimination of geographic barriers and product barriers, especially those that related to cross-industry mergers and affiliations. The passage of the Gramm-Leach-Bliley (GLB) Act of 1999[1] has significantly increased the number and size of mergers within the financial services industry. During the past decade, the financial services industry has gone through significant changes influenced by technological advances, globalization, financial crisis, and the worldwide economic meltdown and related regulation.

STRUCTURAL CHANGES IN THE FINANCIAL SERVICES INDUSTRY

The financial services industry is undergoing unprecedented changes driven by consolidation, convergence, competition, and regulations. Traditionally, financial service organizations (e.g., banks, insurance companies, mutual funds, brokerage firms) in the industry were structurally and functionally distinct. Consolidation, convergence, and competition have brought these organizations together. The distinctions among banks, insurance companies, securities, and brokerage firms have diminished as the financial services industry transforms into a more consolidated, converged, competitive industry.

Consolidation

"Consolidation," in this book, refers to the integration and consolidation of financial institutions' resources into larger and fewer institutions by means of mergers and acquisitions (M&A). The driving forces behind substantial consolidation in 1990s and the early 2000s, especially among financial institutions, were (1) deregulation of geographical and product restrictions; (2) technological advances; (3) global competition; (4) healthy financial positions and profitable financial conditions; and (5) growing stock prices. These factors are not listed in any order of importance, and they are discussed thoroughly in this chapter and Chapter 4. The elimination of geographic restrictions under the Riegle-Neal Interstate Banking and Branching Efficiency Act of 1994, which allowed virtually nationwide branching as of June 1, 1997, was the biggest impetus for the consolidation of banks and banking organizations. Recent changes in technology, global competition, interest rates, and merger trends have profoundly affected the financial services industry. Internet banking has changed the low-touch customized financial services provided to local customers.

The use of derivative financial instruments is becoming more common as a means of managing risk. Foreign banks are now competing more freely and frequently in the United States and the global market. The wave of megamergers has substantially reduced the number of financial institutions as the industry consolidated. The Glass-Steagall Act (also called the Banking Act of 1933): (1) separates commercial banking (e.g., receiving deposits and making loans) from investment banking (e.g., underwriting, market maker of securities); (2) prohibits banks from paying interest on checking accounts; (3) restricts the types of assets banks can own; and (4) prohibits bank distribution of mutual funds.

The economic growth of the mid-1990s coupled with the low interest rates and diversity in operations of financial institutions gave large banks higher valuation and the currency of higher stock prices with which to pursue future M&A deals. Small banks, however, became more profitable, which made them a good target for acquisition at prices attractive to their shareholders. Traditionally, banks have expanded by adding more branches staffed by many salaried employees to provide retail transactions and costly commercial services to customers. Banks have faced regulatory restrictions that kept them from moving out of the commercial business into investments and insurance services. The recent wave of mergers in the financial services industry is driven by the emerging technologies to make the industry more competitive and efficient. There is no compelling evidence that the new mergers are motivated by a desire to monopolize markets and increase fees for financial services. Indeed, the financial services industry, especially the banking industry, remains far less concentrated than many other competitive industries, such as automobiles and communication. However, it is vital that the Federal Reserve continues to exercise its oversight responsibility to ensure that M&A deals and resulting changes in the structure of financial institutions are consistent with and in compliance with applicable laws and regulations and in the best interest of the public.

Banks are, by law, protected by a so-called federal financial safety net (e.g., deposit insurance, access to the Fed's discount window, and payment services) designed to protect bank customers and to serve the public. This provision of the banking industry,

EXHIBIT 2.1 Top 10 European and American Banks

American Banks	Market Value ($m)	European Banks	Market Value ($m)
JPMorgan Chase	143336.6	HSBC	114727.4
Wells Fargo	113953.0	Banco Santander	81474.4
Bank of America	106401.6	BNP Paribas	52974.1
U.S. Bancorp	38084.5	Banco Bilbao Vizcaya Argentaria	40028.3
PNC Financial	15608.4	Barclays	38204.3
Citigroup	14846.3	UniCredit	33613.7
BB&T	13844.3	Intesa Sanpaolo	31165.5
Northern Trust	13006.3	Standard Chartered	30238.8
Hudson City Bank	7259.2	Deutsche Bank	29571.5
M&T Bank	6963.5	RBS	27815.6

Based on the market capitalization of each bank in dollars. Data as of July 27, 2009.

Source: Thomson Reuters Datastream.

when it is not properly monitored, may create adverse incentives of "moral hazard" in the sense that depositors may think that their deposits are always safeguarded regardless of a bank's severe financial difficulties. Banks, however, may be motivated to take more than prudent business risk by undertaking risky loans and investments, expecting that higher returns will ease their financial difficulties. In the absence of proper balance between the risk and return assessment of banks and in the light of financial difficulties, the insurance fund and ultimately taxpayers are left to absorb the losses (e.g., the savings and loan debacle of the 1980s). The existence of moral hazard can be very detrimental to the success of megamergers in the financial services industry because the failure of a large combined financial institution could be very costly to resolve. Thus, the current merger wave may necessitate a reform in the financial services industry at least in the areas of safety net and deposit insurance coverage.

There have been many actions in the past two decades regarding consolidation in the financial industry. The governments in the United States, the United Kingdom, and Europe encouraged and supported consolidation and augmentation of the financial institutions. Mergers and acquisitions of banks all across the world complicated the global banking and financial industry and produced 17 large complex financial institutions (LCFIs). These institutions further determined the securities underwriting, syndicated lending, asset-backed securities, over-the-counter (OTC) derivatives, and collateralized debt obligations (CDOs). Exhibit 2.1 presents the top 10 American and top 10 European banks.

Convergence

Webster's *Third New International Dictionary* (1986) defines "convergence" as the "tendency or movement toward union or uniformity." Convergence in the financial services industry is defined in this book as the integration of banking organizations and other financial services providers (e.g., insurance companies, mutual funds, and securities firms) through the combination and expansion of the scope or breadth of their financial products and services. Convergence may occur through (1) M&A between financial institutions and other financial services organizations permitted under the GLB Act of 1999; (2) the creation of BHCs under the Bank Holding Company Act of 1956; and (3) the establishment of FHCs under the GLB Act of 1999.

Traditionally, the functional services of banks, insurance companies, mutual funds, and brokerage firms were distinguishable, and their roles were separate. Banks were engaged in offering traditional services, such as deposits, loans, and transaction activities. Insurance companies provided auto, property, and life insurance products. However, the financial services industry has experienced the evolutionary disappearance of the distinctions in their offered financial services. Today, the differences between functions of these financial services providers are becoming less noticeable. The logic of a universal financial service (e.g., one-stop shopping for all financial services and products) offering a variety of financial products and services is compelling. Furthermore, technological advances facilitate one-stop shopping for all financial products and services. Indeed, universal banking has been practiced in Germany, Canada, and other countries, yet it was not permitted in the United States until the year 2000. The trend toward convergence in financial services organizations can be viewed as desirable and socially beneficial in the sense that it leads to offerings of more financial products and services at a single location and more competition for customer dollars.

The GLB Act of 1999 (better known as the Financial Modernization Act), which officially went into effect in March 2000, repealed the Glass-Steagall Act of 1933, which prohibits the line-of-business expansion for banks. The GLB Act permits banks, securities firms, insurance companies, mutual funds, brokerage firms, and asset managers to freely enter each others' business or consolidate. It also allows creation of financial holding companies that may conduct a broad range of financial services, including insurance and securities underwriting, commercial banking, investment banking, asset management and distribution, and real estate development and investment, typically under separate subsidiaries. The passage of the GLB Act has raised some concerns that its implementation might have: (1) created concentration of economic power in the financial services industry; (2) caused lack of ability of regulators and government to properly oversee the industry's activities and to manage risk; (3) created too-big-to-fail (TBTF) financial institutions; and (4) been the overriding factor contributing to the recent financial crisis in the United States. Proponents of the GLB Act believe that its implementation has: (1) provided long-sought financial services supermarkets and one-stop shopping for all financial services; and (2) improved the ability of U.S. financial services providers to compete effectively in the global financial services market.

Provisions of the Gramm-Leach-Bliley Act

Provisions of the GLB Act can be summarized in nine categories:

1. Creation of the new types of regulated entities—namely, FHCs—that are authorized to offer a broad range of financial products and services. An FHC is a BHC

whose depository institutions are well capitalized, well managed, and rated by the Community Reinvestment Act (CRA) as "satisfactory" or better. A financial subsidiary, which can offer most of the newly authorized activities, is a direct subsidiary of a bank that satisfies the same conditions as the financial holding company.

2. Authorization of a wide variety of the newly permissible financial activities for financial holding companies, including securities, insurance, merchant, banking/ equity investment, financial in nature, and complementary activities. Provisions of the GLB Act permit banking organizations to engage in virtually every type of activity currently recognized as financial as well as new activities that will be authorized by the Federal Reserve and Treasury Department as "incidental" or "complementary" to a financial activity. The "merchant banking" provisions of the GLB Act permit a financial holding company to make a controlling investment virtually in any kind of company, financial or commercial.

3. Restrictions for commercial companies to acquire thrifts through unitary thrift holding companies. However, the existing commercial unitary thrift holding companies are grandfathered as of May 4, 1994, but such companies may not sell their thrifts to any other commercial company.

4. Substantial changes to laws governing the Federal Home Loan Bank System. The GLB Act created a new type of Federal Home Loan Bank member called a community financial institution (CFI), which is a community bank or thrift with less than $500 million in assets. A CFI may pledge small business and agricultural advances.

5. Requirements for protecting the privacy of customers' information. The GLB Act established four privacy requirements pertaining to the sharing of customer information with others, which apply equally to all financial institutions. The GLB Act requires each financial institution to: (1) establish and annually disclose a privacy policy; (2) provide customers the right to opt out of having their information shared with nonaffiliated third parties; (3) not share customer account numbers with nonaffiliated third parties; and (4) abide by regulatory standards to protect the security and integrity of customer information.

6. Community Reinvestment Act provisions. The GLB Act addressed the three controversial CRA provisions that nearly prevented the legislation from passing. These provisions are related to requirements for:
   a. Establishing "satisfactory" CRA ratings as a condition for engaging in the Act's new activities.
   b. Disclosing of CRA agreements between financial institutions and third parties.
   c. Establishing a lengthened CRA exam cycle for community banks and thrifts.

7. Other regulatory provisions. Other important regulatory provisions of the GLB Act affecting banks and financial institutions are:
   a. The Federal Reserve's "umbrella" supervisory authority over financial holding companies.
   b. Those affecting foreign banks.
   c. Limitations on the state's ability to establish regulations that discriminate against banking organizations.

  d. Revisions to federal antitrust authority affecting financial holding companies.
  e. Automated teller machine (ATM) disclosure provisions
  f. Elimination of the "special reserve" of the Savings Association Insurance Fund.
8. CRA ratings. The GLB Act states that BHCs cannot become financial holding companies or engage in the newly authorized financial activities unless all of their subsidiaries and affiliates have CRA ratings of satisfactory or better.
9. Effective dates of key provisions of the Act. These include the 120-day delayed effective date for the financial holding company and financial subsidiary sections of the Act (e.g., through mid-March 2000).

Implementation of the Gramm-Leach-Bliley Act

The proper implementation of the landmark GLB Act has created both opportunities and challenges for the financial services industry, including these:

- The Act has increased certain trends already under way in the financial services industry by enabling and promoting further consolidation of the industry.
- New authorized financial activities can be conducted only by a subset of bank holding companies (BHCs) to be called financial holding companies (FHCs). To be an FHC, each subsidiary bank must be well capitalized, well managed, and have a CRA rating of satisfactory or better.
- The "sunshine" language of the Act has required public disclosure of all written agreements made in fulfillment of the CRA involving payments by banking organizations in excess of $10,000 or loans in excess of $50,000.
- Financial services organizations affected by the Act established disclosure requirements and consumer "opt-out" procedures that protect consumer privacy without significantly burdening financial institutions or consumers. The purpose of the privacy provision of the Act is to restrict the ability of financial institutions to disclose to unrelated third parties nonpublic personal information pertaining to individuals who obtain financial products and/or services from the financial institution.
- Prior to the passage of the Act, a BHC could own no more than 5 percent of the voting equity and 25 percent of total equity of a company. The Act allows "merchant banking," which means that any FHC with a securities affiliate may engage in merchant banking by obtaining ownership of securities of a company.
- FHCs have been authorized to engage in a broad range of financial activities, including insurance underwriting and sales, securities underwriting and dealing, merchant banking, lending, investment advisory, financial data processing services, travel agency, and certain management consulting services.
- There has been a new challenge for bank supervisors to implement the new blend of umbrella and functional supervision established in the Act. The extent of the challenge depends on the degree of integration of financial activities within FHCs and the relative size of the bank and nonbank activities within such organizations.
- The Act requires communication, cooperation, and coordination among multiple banking regulators to share information among the umbrella, financial, and bank

supervisors in a manner that is satisfactory to all regulatory agencies. However, the Act states that the first-level supervisory authority lies with the functional regulators (e.g., the state, and the Securities and Exchange Commission [SEC].)

■ The Act limits extensions of the safety net by eliminating the need to impose banklike regulation on nonbank subsidiaries and affiliates of organizations that contain a bank.

■ The privacy provisions of the Act prohibit financial institutions from disclosing information to third parties unless customers first are given the opportunity to opt out of information sharing. Furthermore, all financial institutions, including banks, brokerage firms, and insurance companies, must establish a privacy policy, which should be presented to all current and future customers. The privacy policy must: (1) list all types of personal information the institution collects (e.g., accounting activity, credit reports); (2) inform customers of precisely where this information will be shared; and (3) disclose the security measures undertaken to safeguard the confidentiality of the information.

The 1994 Riegle-Neal Act, which went into effect in 1997, practically removed all geographic barriers to M&A activities within the banking industry. The 1999 GLB Financial Modernization Act, which went into effect in March 2000, removed the remaining products and services restrictions for convergence within the financial services industry. These two acts substantially deregulated the financial services industry by removing geographic and product barriers and set the stage for unprecedented consolidation and convergence in the financial services industry. The 1997 removal of all geographic barriers to M&A made it theoretically possible, subject to antitrust policy restrictions, for the top 50 U.S. banks to merge into just six megabanks and the next 50 banks to combine into seven banks of almost equal size.[2] The 2000 removal of products and services barriers allowed the potential six megabanks to become full-line financial service providers under the universal banking system.

The passage of the GLB Act of 1999 brought the financial services industry one step closer to the effective convergence of financial services and utilization of universal banking common in other countries. However, the full convergence necessitates resolution of obstacles and issuance of standard and universally applicable regulatory and supervisory laws and rules in the financial services industry. For example, the global banking community, with the issuance of the Basel Accord I (2001), has established standards and globally acceptable risk-based capital requirements for banks. The National Association of Insurance Commissioners has also established risk-based capital guidelines for insurance companies to prevent insurance company failures. Although there are some similarities in these two sets of requirements, they are not currently applicable to both banks and insurance companies.

There is a debate as to whether the GLB Act contributed to the recent financial crisis.[3] One school of thought says that it enabled financial diversification and thus paved the way for a number of mergers. During the financial crisis, the diversification has created more good than harm. A couple of examples are Citigroup, Shearson, and Primerica. The GLB Act also facilitated JP Morgan to buy out Bear Stearns and Bank of

America to buy Merrill Lynch. However, the high-profile consolidation and convergence cases in the financial services industry made possible by the implementation of provisions of GLB could have created the TBTF institutions. The GLB Act played a vital role in the organized resolution of distressed investment banks by offering their assets and liabilities to be absorbed into a BHC. This was complemented with full regulation, strong capital requirements, and on-site examination. Wall Street's financially distressed companies would have faced a worse situation without the GLB Act; there is a high probability that they would have failed.

The GBL Act's elimination of the artificial separations between financial firms allowed financial firms to diversify their activities. It created conflicts of interest by allowing financial institutions to combine their investment and commercial activities and to offer customers a full range of banking and brokerage services. Nonetheless, it makes no sense to attribute the financial crisis and particularly problems with subprime mortgages, mortgage underwriting practice, and inefficiency in Fannie Mae and Freddie Mac to the GLB Act.

Competition

Consolidation and convergence resulting from deregulation, technological advances, and favorable economic and business prospects have to be profitable, productive, and cost effective to survive. Productive and profitable consolidation and convergence cause cost efficiency, which in turn creates higher competitive intensity and tighter pricing. In the 1990s and the early 2000s, it was expected that consolidation and convergence in the financial services industry would have createed more competitive prices for financial products and services. Future pricing of financial services was expected to follow examples of other consolidated, deregulated industries, such as long-distance telecommunications companies, electricity providers, and airlines. In these industries, prices declined about 20 percent in the first five years following deregulation-consolidation and then another 20 percent in the subsequent five years.[4] Higher competitive intensity resulting from consolidation and convergence was expected to resuls in low cost. High-price providers were either acquired and restructured or driven out of the industry entirely.

Increased competition nationally and worldwide in the financial services industry is viewed as an important factor shaping the industry. Global competition in providing financial services can be achieved by striving to be the low-cost provider of financial products and services or by developing a niche product of different offered financial services and products. Being low-cost providers requires banks to be large enough to generate economies of scale. Differentiation is difficult to achieve in the banking industry because financial services and products (e.g., checking, saving, loans) are relatively homogenous, which is why many financial services organizations are currently engaged in a variety of activities, such as asset management, insurance, and mutual funds. Furthermore, differentiation often requires substantial investment in technology, an investment that is not readily available to small banks. Thus, for banks to become low-cost providers or to offer niche financial products and services, they ought to grow through M&A.

The profound effects of consolidation and convergence include increases in local market concentration, the move toward universal banking, and the commoditization of financial services and products. Banks and banking organizations have moved toward offering retail banking, insurance, and asset management services. The financial services markets have become relatively homogenous. Global competition and easy accessibility of financial services through the Internet have forced financial institutions to provide a variety of financial services and products at relatively competitive and similar rates through extensive branch networks. Today financial products and services are viewed mostly as commodities available to everyone through the Internet.

Commoditization of financial products and services for small business includes checking, savings, lines of credit, mortgages, transactions, cash management, and credit-related services. Transaction services consist of the processing of credit card receipts, wire transfers, the provision of currency and coin, and the collection of night deposits. Cash management services include lockbox services, zero-balance accounts, and the provision of sweep accounts. Credit-related services consist of letters of credit, factoring, and bankers' acceptances. The 1995 Survey of Consumer Finances revealed that 98 percent of households use a local depository institution, while the 1993 National Survey of Small Business Finances indicated that 92 percent of small businesses use a local depository institution.[5] According to the Survey of Consumer Finances 2007, the mean and median of families' holdings of financial assets increased overall from 2004 to 2007. But the financial assets as a percentage of total assets declined. This resembled an earlier trend. The homeownership rate had increased considerably from 2001 to 2004 but later declined slightly. Debts and assets rose in equal proportions from 2004 to 2007. Overall indebtness as a proportion of assets did not change much. A decrease was seen in home-secured debt as a proportion of total family debt, but it still remained the largest component of family debt.[6]

To compete successfully in the highly competitive global market, many banks have adopted a new management philosophy of being driven more by markets than by regulations. In the highly competitive global market of the 1990s and 2000s, banks that were strong and well capitalized acquired other banks and got stronger, and weak banks got weaker. The strong banks and banking organizations with effective and efficient performance and high capital ratios often are viewed and treated favorably by both financial markets and regulators. Banks also found that competitive edge and market value are the ultimate performance measures.

Consolidation, convergence, and competition may increase systemic risk and expand the safety net of financial institutions by changing the risk profiles of individual institutions. Especially as financial institutions are becoming larger through M&A, their activities and systemic risk would affect many other financial services organizations. This universal impact may give a wrong impression of TBTF and discourage the market and policy makers, including bank regulators, from responding to bank problems in a timely manner. One may argue that larger banks are in a better position to manage risk through diversification rather than by incurring additional risks. However, combined financial institutions are more interested in maximizing shareholders' return by reallocating their portfolios to higher-risk, higher-return investments. Current forces and trends in the financial services industry that have encouraged consolidation, convergence, and competition in the industry are:

- Changes in regulations
- Information technology
- Global marketplace
- Capital standards
- Supervisory activities
- Continuous quality improvement
- Valuation process

Recently, the governments of the United States, United Kingdom, and Europe have promoted and encouraged consolidation in the financial services sector. Regional banks have now become global. A few of the major M&A in the U.S. banking sector are listed next.

- Chase Manhattan Corporation with J.P. Morgan & Company
- Firstar Corporation with U.S. Bancorp
- First Union Corporation with Wachovia Corporation
- Fifth Third Bancorp with Old Kent Financial Corporation
- Summit Bancorp with FleetBoston Financial Corporation
- Golden State Bancorp, Inc. with Citigroup Inc.
- Dime Bancorp, Inc. with Washington Mutual
- FleetBoston Financial Corporation with Bank of America Corporation
- SunTrust with National Commerce Financial Hibernia National Bank with Capital One Financial Corporation
- Bank One with JPMorgan Chase and Company[7]

Information Technology

The rapid progress in IT has had a profound effect on the economy in general and the financial services industry in particular. IT has a great impact on the financial services and banking sector. With the help of IT, people can transfer funds between different accounts at the tip of their fingers. With the help of mobile and online banking, everything is easy. There has been some innovative mobile banking applications in the industry. Several banks offer a huge set of capabilities with their mobile applications. For example, leading banks such as Citi, Wells Fargo, State Farm's Bank, and J.P. Morgan Chase offer remote deposits, the ability to initiate or approve wire transfers and outgoing payments for corporate customers, and the ability to view transaction details, manage exception items, and monitor intraday activity.[8]

Technological advances have increased economies of scale and scope in the financial services industry. These advances have encouraged more consolidation, convergence, and competition in the industry and have shifted the traditional delivery of retail financial services toward electronic delivery modes that do not rely on a branch network. Indeed, many banks have replaced their full-service branches with supermarket branches that offer a variety of financial services, including ATMs and Internet banking.

The new technology, including e-commerce, business to business (B2B), and Internet banking, provides both financial services organizations and their customers with a greater degree of information efficiency. This information efficiency can significantly speed up the movement of the financial services and products offered by financial institutions toward commoditization. Global access to the Internet and especially Internet banking make customization of financial products and services less possible because they can be easily replicated by competitors. As customers gain access to more information and more readily available information, they can shop more competitively for financial products and services and can easily change providers. This suggests that future markets for financial services and products will be very competitive, and only those large institutions with opportunities for economics of scale and scope that offer the best-quality financial services and products at the lowest cost will survive. Technological advances may have increased economies of scale and scope in producing financial services by creating opportunities to improve efficiency and increase value through consolidation.

"Electronic banking" is a generic term that covers a broad range of financial services provided by banks. These services include: (1) the traditional electronic services, such as telephone banking, credit cards, ATMs, and direct deposits; (2) maturing electronic services, such as debit cards and electronic bill payment (e.g., Financial Electronic Data Interchange); and (3) developing electronic services, such as stored-value cards, Internet banking, and online investing. One of the current challenges in the financial services industry, especially banking, is the proper development of electronic commerce including the issues of customer identification and account verification for online purchases. The Internet is also changing the way financial institutions operate because customers now have unlimited choices of both financial services and pricing online, and often it is cheaper to complete transactions electronically than to use paper or the telephone. For example, banks now can conduct the majority of their financing and cash management services to automobile dealers across the nation over the Internet. The use of the Web in the financial services industry can achieve the three goals of marketing: information, delivering financial services, and improving customer relationships.

Electronic banking is growing rapidly as a result of continued development and advances in processing, analyzing, and transmitting vast quantities of data electronically. The key factors that are encouraging and facilitating the rapid growth of the use of electronic commerce and banking are convenience, confidence, and complexity.[9] "Convenience" reflects the availability of both human and physical resources required to optimize the use of electronic commerce in conducting and processing business transactions. "Confidence" refers to the assurance provided by electronic commerce in security, privacy, and the authentication of transactions and parties as well as safeguarding resources and data and reducing the risk. "Complexity" refers to the extent that the key features of electronic transactions can be easily standardized, automated, understood, and used by the parties to the transactions.

Electronic banking has created a convenient and an efficient financial services environment within which banks and their customers are able to transact a variety of financial services at virtually any time. Financial institutions' recent statistics reveal that: (1) approximately 40 percent of U.S. banks now have Web sites through which they communicate with their customers; (2) about 15 percent provide Web sites that can be used to conduct financial services transactions; and (3) over 50 percent of large banks (over $500 million in assets) provide Web sites for their customers' convenience to conduct banking transactions. [10] Through the use of Internet and Web sites, banks are now able to standardize and automate many of their financial services, such as loan services. In the past several years, B2B has evolved from being a facilitator of traditional business to a transformer of business in its entirety. Although B2B has revolutionized the global marketplace, it has not been fully utilized in the financial services industry. Online and electronic baking services have been much easier with the introduction of mobile banking. Mobile banking offers corporate customers the ability to deposit physical checks into bank accounts by simply taking pictures of the front and back of checks with their smart phones. New technology, such as near field communications technology, allows secure, two-way payment communications between mobile phones.[11]

Businesses of all sizes can benefit from Internet banking. Small businesses where cash flow is king benefit from Internet banking just as much as large corporations where continuous improvement in efficiency and effectiveness is the main goal of top executives. Internet banking can provide an online, real-time cash management tool by:

- Offering up-to-the-minute cash balances on checking and money market accounts
- Making free domestic wire transfers
- Viewing checks that have cleared
- Transferring funds
- Authorizing automatic payments
- Downloading data to computer applications

Internet banking also can be beneficial to large corporations in: (1) promoting B2B transaction processing; (2) establishing direct deposits for employee paychecks; and (3) authorizing payment of funds electronically that are immediately deposited into a vendor's account. Internet banking has not yet been universally accepted and used by businesses; breaking away from the traditional brick-and-mortar banks and moving into online banking takes time. Internet banking is now considered a handy (but still optional) way of doing banking transactions, but soon it will evolve into a high-priority requirement for conducting effective financial services activities.

Technological innovations have made financial products and services more standardized and commoditized, and these products and services are offered through electronic media (phone, e-mail, Internet, PC), which is much cheaper than offering them through traditional brick-and-mortar buildings.

In summary, technological advances, including the Internet and mobile banking applications on smart phones, are significantly changing the ways in which banks offer financial products and services. The Internet and the mobile banking applications provide banks with new opportunities and challenges of reevaluating their existing delivery channels and business activities, developing new online financial products and services, taking advantage of cost efficiencies, satisfying existing customers' demands, reaching new customers, and securing customers' privacy. Bank regulators, including the Office of the Comptroller of the Currency (OCC), have revised their regulations to reflect the use of new technologies by banks. For example, in 1996, the OCC revised its data-processing regulation to reflect the use of electronic activities by banks (61 FR 4849, February 9, 1996). The OCC issued "Technology Regulations and Publications for Financial Institutions" in April 2010. It addresses the regulations and publications including the Federal Deposit Insurance Corporation (FDIC) financial institution letters, OCC advisory letters, alerts, and bulletins, the Federal Reserve Board Supervision and Regulation Letters, and the OTS Chief Executive Officer Memoranda and Regulatory Bulletins.[12] This Internet Banking Handbook and other OCC-related technology handbook series are available on the OCC Web site (www.occ.treas.gov).

Global Marketplace

The globalization of capital markets and the demand for investor protection in response to financial scandals worldwide (e.g., Enron, WorldCom, Parmalat, Ahold) also requires consistency and uniformity in regulatory reforms and corporate governance practices. Before 1960, only a handful of banks had operations based outside the United States. Macroeconomic factors, such as the cost of capital, stage of the business cycle, and federal monetary policy, have influenced the inclination to grow overseas and become global. From the 1960s to the 1980s, U.S. banks started making their presence felt abroad.[13]

Competition among global capital markets can be healthy in producing adequate levels of protection for investors through right-balanced regulatory reforms. Since governments have eliminated barriers for the free flow of capital, international finance has changed a lot over the last two decades. Countries have opened up their domestic economies to foreign financial institutions and there has been a global integration of financial institutions. International regulation over this foreign integration of the financial industry is required, a fact that has been noted by lawmakers and policy makers.[14]

Global financial considerations are important issues that should be thoroughly examined to determine whether the financial sector is functioning effectively toward its goal of facilitating capital accumulation and enhancing real economic growth. The social cost of the global financial crises can be significant due to high unemployment rates following the crises. A sound macroeconomic policy of anticipating potential crises in the financial services industry and taking proactive actions to prevent them can be an effective way of dealing with national financial crises. However, even good macroeconomic policies would not be effective in dealing with global financial crises. More reliance on global market forces can be the most effective and efficient way of preventing global financial crises.

Market-driven forces are the result of: (1) the global competition in the financial services industry through the use of Internet banking and (2) demand by global customers for more convenient and broader financial services provided by technology. Recently there have been profound and fundamental changes in the way customers handle their financial services, mostly driven by the Internet. In the near future, providing financial services through national branching may be less relevant in conducting banking business. Local banking and even national branching may become obsolete under the new electronic delivery of financial services. Thus, the requirement for reform, particularly in the area of electronic delivery of financial services, is critical in order to keep up with all the changes that are affecting the industry.

To compete successfully in the global marketplace, financial institutions are adopting a new management philosophy of becoming more aggressive, leaner, more adaptable, more performance-oriented, and more responsive to market value. Banks are also realizing that to compete successfully in a global market, they have to move away from traditional commercial services into investment and asset-management businesses. Global capital markets are classified into those with an inside system (IS) or an outside system (OS). In an IS, in such countries as France, Germany, and Italy, there is a high level of ownership concentration, illiquid capital markets, and liberal regulation of capital markets. Conversely, in an OS, in such countries as the United Kingdom and the United States, there is a widely dispersed ownership, liquid capital markets, an active market for corporate control, and strict regulation of capital markets.

Too Big To Fail Misperception

The recent wave of consolidations in the financial services industry has resulted in fewer but bigger financial institutions. Often they are perceived as too big to fail (TBTF) Financial services and products of banks, insurance companies, mutual funds, and brokerage firms that once were distinguishable and had separate roles are now integrated. Large American companies, particularly huge banks, may believe that they are TBTF. Moral hazards can be raised if these TBTF firms assume that the government's reluctance to hold them accountable for business failures signals aversion to tough regulatory reforms and actions. To minimize this perceived moral hazard, the government plans to establish stricter regulations for the financial service industry to prevent significant adverse impact of failures of large companies. Recent debates suggest that different sizes of financial services organizations may receive different regulatory scrutiny and treatment. The elite of large public companies and banks may receive protection and benefits from the perception by policy makers, regulators, and capital market that they are TBTF. The common definition of TBTF firms is that these firms are so large that their failure will threaten the overall financial stability of the nation and thus government bailout is the only way to rescue them. Investors are concerned about the failure of these institutions, and markets tend not to discipline them adequately and regulators have not developed the proper tools to monitor them.

The TBTF perception may be detrimental if these financial companies do not receive adequate scrutiny from regulators and enjoy favorable treatment from regulators and market, particularly during the recent financial crisis and government's Troubled Asset Relief Program (TARP) program. Anecdotal evidence suggests that an important detrimental effect of TBTF protections is the subsidy of the TBTF banks at the expense of regional and smaller banks.[15] That is, the cost of capital of these TBTF banks can approach zero when the government implicitly and continuously guarantees their existence and rescues them from failure due to the lack of sustainable performance. TBTF protections concern investors, taxpayers, and policy makers, because about half of the reported profits of TBTF are basically subsidized by taxpayers. Congress passed the TARP in the aftermath of the Lehman Brothers failure in order to bail out and rescue TBTF institutions in a period of financial turbulence. The TARP has been perceived as government commitment to the TBTF policy for major banks and corporations. An implied result of the TBTF policy is the gap formed between the interest rates that smaller banks owe to derive the deposits and otherwise borrow funds. The rates for the TBTF banks would increase, since they are now able to borrow all their funds, including the big and the small deposits, with the federal government standing at their backs.[16]

Financial institutions have gone through significant changes with advances in technology, financial engineering, financial innovation, and deregulation. Consolidation, convergence, and competition have caused profound changes in the role of financial institutions. Traditionally, financial institutions have issued claims to back their holdings of primarily private illiquid assets. Today, financial institutions assist their customers in holding and managing highly diversified portfolios of marketable securities (e.g., pension funds, mutual funds) at low cost. Financial institutions are different from most other businesses. To demonstrate and better understand these differences, it is helpful to discuss the historical perspective of American banking.

HISTORICAL PERSPECTIVE OF AMERICAN BANKING

During the early life of the banking industry in the United States, banks operated locally with strict branch restrictions and negative perceptions regarding large and centralized financial institutions. This is evident by the opposition and refusal of renewal of charters of the First and Second Banks of the United States in the early nineteenth century.[17] There was a deep-seated distrust that large federal financial institutions would seek financial power and attempt to maximize their owners' profit at the expense of the broader public. Branching was not common or possible, primarily because of lack of sufficient technology to support inexpensive long-distance communication. Another impediment to branching by national banks was the general belief that the National Banking Act, passed during the Civil War, prohibited it. To promote more banking activities, an act was passed in 1900 that lowered the minimum capital requirements to establish a new national bank in a small town. As a result, during the early years of the twentieth century, there were over 13,000 banks in the United States with only 119 branches. The significant number of bank failures, especially of small banks during the 1920s and in the early years of the Great Depression, proves that large banks with branches were more resistant to failure. Thus, policy makers began to consider liberalization of the banking system by allowing branching as a means of diversifying individual bank portfolios and failure risk and by strengthening the banking system.

High interest rates and inflation in the late 1970s and early 1990s, coupled with inadequate and inappropriate policy and regulatory response, forced deposits out of banks and thrifts into money market funds and open-market instruments. This move was the major cause of the savings and loan crises of the 1980s and bank problems of the late 1980s and early 1990s. However, this crisis underscores the importance of market discipline and market-oriented forces over regulatory requirements, which in turn encourage deregulation in the financial services industry.

The passage of national deposit insurance in 1933, which guaranteed the stability of the banking system, encouraged many states to liberalize their branching laws. During the past three decades, three factors have encouraged substantial increases in the number of M&A in the banking industry:

1. In the early 1990s, more than 36 states authorized statewide branching.
2. States passed laws allowing BHCs from other states to buy banks within their borders with the restriction of operating these interstate acquisitions as separate banks.
3. The passage of the Riegle-Neal Interstate Banking Act of 1994 eliminated interstate banking restrictions. Banks now had the opportunity to have branches nationwide, which set the stage for the significant acceleration for M&A of financial institutions.

In the late 1990s and 2000s, banks faced the challenges of the subprime mortgage crisis affected by the burst in the housing market and substantial home foreclosures. In order to stabilize the financial system during the financial crises due to subprime mortgage in late 2007 and 2008, several bailouts were implemented by the governments in the United States, the United Kingdom, and some western European countries.

The next section on the recent trends in the financial industry elaborates on the subprime mortgage crises and the collapse of securitization market.

 ## CURRENT TRENDS IN THE FINANCIAL SERVICES BANKING INDUSTRY

Today's ever-changing business environment has created substantial challenges for all businesses, especially those in the financial services industry. These changes require management to establish a proper business strategy to compete effectively in the global market. Management should focus on value-added activities that contribute to improvements of the cash flow–based value of the business and its potential market value by identifying the key drivers of value. In the late 1990s, the banking industry showed record profits, improvement, and diversity in operations, which were reflected in their valuations. In addition, reasonable stable interest rates and favorable regulatory changes helped banks to improve their values.

The banking problems of the early 1990s encouraged the issuance of the 1991 FDIC Act amendments, which sharply raised bank deposit insurance premiums. The reduction of short-term interest rates by the Federal Reserve in the early 1990s encouraged banks to borrow short and lend long, which helped banks to get back to better financial health and generate excess capital for new acquisitions. In 1994, Congress passed the Riegle-Neal Interstate Banking Act, which allowed consolidation across state lines. This Act made interstate banking much easier by capping the amount of domestic deposits that a bank could hold at 10 percent of the national aggregate.

The financial services industry has undergone significant changes in recent years. The financial crisis caused a significant economic downturn in the United States comparable to the Great Recession in the 1930s where the real gross domestic product was lowered below 6 percent annual rate and monthly job losses averaged about 750,000.

Recent Crises in the Financial Industry

In 2008, the National Bureau of Economic Research declared that the United States had been in a recession since December 2007. In March 2009, the Dow Jones Industrial Average had fallen in value 54 percent from its peak in 2007, a greater amount than the decline of 1937–1938, when it fell 49 percent. Home foreclosures in the United States reached record highs in late 2008 and continued to increase into 2010. By mid-2010, 15 percent of mortgage borrowers nationwide were at least one payment past due. The U.S. unemployment rate reached over 10 percent in mid-2010. Commercial banking giant Citigroup required a massive government guarantee against losses and an injection of cash to prevent failure. All but two major financial services firms (Goldman Sachs and Morgan Stanley) have failed or been acquired and these two firms converted to commercial BHCs. AIG, one of the largest insurance companies, was bailed out by the U.S. government. The financial crisis hit the financial services industry hard. By August 2009, the FDIC reported that the list of troubled banks had climbed to over 400 banks, the highest level in 15 years.

Banks, insurers, and the financial industry worldwide have reported approximately $1.1 trillion in losses since the subprime mortgage crises from 2007. The majority of the losses are owed to the 17 globalized banks, better known as LCFIs. Out of those 17 banks, nine banks failed, were nationalized, or were funded by the government. In order to prevent the collapse of the global financial industry, the U.S., U.K., and European governments pumped money into the financial system. This money not only saved the banks from a disastrous collapse but also offered liquidity. The subprime crises also caused a credit crunch in the global economy.

The LCFIs formulated an origin to distribute strategy (OTD). The strategy included not only the originating consumer and corporate loans but also packaging the loans together creating CDOs, whose value is based on loans, and eventually delivering the securities to investors and clients. The OTD strategy not only maximized the fee income for LCFIs but also reduced capital charges with securitized loans. This strategy further helped LCFIs to transfer the risks associated with loans backed by securities to investors and clients. Through the securitization process, LCFIs managed to sell home mortgages and credit card loans to everyone, including subprime borrowers. Eventually, by 2006, the whole system had become a vicious circle. The borrowers were taking new loans to pay off the old ones. Once the real estate prices hit a peak and started falling, the nonprime borrowers could not refinance and loan defaults eventually led to the subprime mortgage crises.

The LCFIs and the globalized banks desined highly aggressive terms, which included interest-only provisions and high loan-to-value ratios for commercial mortgages, corporate sector, and homeowner mortgages. These terms reflected the highly imprudent nature of the policies and practices being followed by LCFIs. The market had become so aggressive that the basic rules to offer mortgages and loans were compromised and ignored completely. LCFIs did not screen borrowers before offering the loan; nor did they monitor the borrower postloan behavior. At the same time, LCFIs were still exposed to risks contained in contractual commitments made on the paper. By mid-2007, all the global banks and LCFIs faced with huge losses as the securitization markets collapsed. The existing control mechanisms, such as the regulatory policies and the internal risk mechanism for the LCFIs in the financial industry, were not sufficient to control the disruptive conflicts of interest and high risk-taking attitute. LCFIs have already been called TBTF.[18]

Troubled Assets Recovery Program

The decision to let Lehman Brothers and Bear Stearns collapse destroyed the assumption of government backing up the debts of major banks faced with bankruptcy. After the Lehman Brothers collapse, the government started TARP to provide hundreds of billions of dollars to support the financial industry.[19] TARP was created to strengthen the financial sector of U.S. financial institutions. It is one of the biggest and most vital measures taken by the government to rescue financially distressed companies from the subprime mortgage crises in 2008. The intention behind the creation of TARP is to bring liquidity for troubled assets, which could include CDOs. CDOs were sold in the booming economy until foreclosures started significantly impacting the underlying mortgages/loans. As per TARP, the U.S. Department of the Treasury can purchase up to $700 billion in troubled assets, defined as:

A. Either residential or commercial mortgages and any securities, obligations, or other instruments that are based on or related to such mortgages, that in each case was originated or issued on or before March 14, 2008, the purchase of which the Secretary determines promotes financial market stability.

B. Any other such financial instrument that the Secretary, after consultation with the Chairman of the Board of Governors of the Federal Reserve System, determines the purchase of which is necessary to promote financial market stability, but only upon transmittal of such determination, in writing, to the appropriate committees of Congress.[20]

The Treasury can then purchase the hard-to-value illiquid assets from banks and financial institutions. TARP has a restriction stating the banks and financial institutions cannot use the money to regain their losses already incurred with the troubled assets. The program has been created with the intention that these troubled assets can be traded once again and their prices will stabilize, and ultimately both parties—the Treasury and the banks—can gain from the trading. Another important objective of TARP is to encourage banks to start lending again to other banks as well as to consumers and businesses. TARP is seen as "revolving purchase facility." The Treasury's initial cap on TARP spending is $250 billion. After purchasing the assets with this money, the Treasury can either sell them or hold them to collect coupons. The money proceeds from the sale will be reinvested to facilitate more purchases of assets. However, the $250 billion cap can be increased to $350 billion, depending on the president's certification to Congress that such an increase is required. The balance of TARP funds will be released once the Treasury submits the detailed plan to Congress of how the money will be spent.

Government Bailout

In the United States, after the government-brokered sale of investment banks Bear Stearns and Lehman Brothers, Treasury secretary Henry M. Paulson and Federal Reserve chairman Ben Bernanke proposed a $700 billion bailout for the stabilization of the financial institutions in September 2008. The proposal, called the Troubled Asset Relief Program, had full support of former president George W. Bush. Although it was fully supported by the Democrats in Congress, most Republicans opposed it. It faced a lot of resistance before the money was released in a series of loans to financial institutions in order to stave off a global depression. In the course of next three months, Paulson pumped $350 billion into banks. This did not comply with the original plan of buying toxic assets, which essentially consisted of mortgage-backed securities (MBSs). In order to offer some liquidity in the economic system, the Federal Reserve cut interest rates to zero and bought back billions of dollars of MBSs. It also offered other extraordinary measures to provide liquidity. In 2009, the federal government decided to use the remaining TARP funds in partnership with private investors to buy as much as $2.5 trillion in toxic assets. Banks that were on the verge of recovering from the crises stayed away from this part of the program.

On June 9, 2009, the Treasury decided to ask ten banks to repay the Federal government and exit the TARP program. As a result, in December, Bank of America announced a plan to repay $45 million to the government. Citigroup is in the process of obtaining the permission to repay the balance amount of $20 billion to the government by selling its stock. Treasury officials estimate that the government would earn $19 billion in profit as a result of the bank loans.[21]

 ## REGULATORY REFORMS

Financial regulation has a number of objectives, including safety and soundness, fair disclosure, avoidance of abuses, competitiveness, resource allocation, and fair treatment. These objectives are not mutually exclusive and are independent and often conflict. For example, the requirements of the CRA may conflict with permission to branch and combine within the financial services industry. Another example is the capital adequacy requirement and the permission to expand by consolidation and convergence. Consolidation and convergence resulting from deregulation and techno-logical advances require proper attention to safety and soundness in the financial services industry. Vigilant, prudential supervision is essential to prevent excessive risk-taking by financial institutions under the newly established financial structure. Consolidation and convergence create large financial services organizations that present special challenges for regulatory authorities and supervisors because the failure of a large financial organization can have a severe effect on the financial system. Thus, bank supervisors in many countries have a TBTF policy that protects all depositors at a big bank (whether insured or uninsured) if the bank fails. The problem with this policy is that it may increase moral hazard incentives of big banks to take on excessive risk and therefore reduce market discipline.

Banks are regulated organizations operating under specific regulations issued by states and national agencies. One of these regulations is the requirement of the safety net by lowering the cost of banking, which (1) gives banks a competitive advantages over other financial institutions; (2) reduces substantially the concern about banks' financial risk, going concern, and creditworthiness; (3) encourages bank management to take more risk, which may impair the realistic balance between risk and reward (moral hazard) and create risk incentive distortions, allowing banks to obtain funds more cheaply by protecting customers who deal with banks through governmental subsidy; and (4) requires that taxpayers, who eventually bear the cost bailing out banks, protect themselves through the supervision and regulations of bank activities.

The U.S. government has responded to the financial crisis through both fiscal and monetary policies. Policies were intended to mitigate the impacts of the financial crisis and have been extensively and inconclusively debated, primarily because our economy is still weak, unemployment is high, home foreclosures are growing, and more government support is needed to ensure economic growth and reduce the likelihood of another recession and economic meltdown. The positive effects of these policies can be attributed to the fiscal stimulus and financial market, reforms, initiatives and mechanisms including TARP, the Fed's quantitative easing of and prime rate reduction, the Dodd-Frank Act of 2010,[22] and bank stress tests.

The effectiveness of these monetary and fiscal policies has been highly debated, with no consensus regarding the effects of each policy initiative. Nevertheless, many policy makers and the U.S. government, in justifying their policy responses to the financial crisis, argue that had they not reacted aggressively and timely, the economy might still be shrinking; unemployment might be much higher with no potential growth and high costs to tax payers.

The Federal Reserve undertook several initiatives to mitigate the negative impacts of the financial crisis:

- Extending credit facilities to financial institutions and thus improving market liquidity.
- Lowering interest rates to eventually a zero-interest-rate policy by the end of 2008.
- Taking several quantitative measures to reduce long-term interest rates and purchase Treasury bonds and Fannie Mae and Freddie Mac MBSs.
- Increasing deposit insurance limits and guaranteeing bank debt.
- Ordering the 19 largest BHCs to conduct compensation stress tests to ensure that they have sufficient capital to withstand financial difficulties and be able to raise needed capital.

Congress also passed the American Restoration and Recovery Act (ARRA) in early 2009. Both TARP and ARRA have been criticized for their ineffectiveness in bringing timely stability to the financial system, cost inefficiency, using taxpayer's money to bail out financial institutions that triggered the financial crisis, and low speed in lowering the unemployment rate. The perceived benefits of both these monetary and fiscal policies are their impacts on preventing further financial crisis and possible double-dip recession.

Dodd-Frank Act of 2010

On July 21, 2010, President Barack Obama signed into law the Dodd-Frank Wall Street Reform and Consumer Protection Act of 2010, which is cited as the most sweeping financial reform since the Great Depression. The Act is named for Senate Banking Committee chairman Christopher Dodd (D-CT) and House Financial Services Committee chairman Barney Frank (D-MA), and its provisions pertain to banks, hedge funds, credit rating agencies, and the derivatives market. Dodd-Frank is about 2,300 pages, and more than 200 regulations that will arise from it have not yet been written. Dodd-Frank authorizes the establishment of an oversight council to monitor systemic risk of financial institutions and the creation of a consumer protection bureau within the Federal Reserve. Dodd-Frank requires the development of over 240 new rules by the SEC, the Government Accountability Office (GAO), and the Federal Reserve to implement its provisions over a five-year period.

Many provisions of Dodd-Frank are considered positive and useful in protecting consumers and investors, including the establishment of a consumer protection bureau and a systemic risk regulator and provisions requiring derivatives to be put on clearing-houses/exchanges. The new Consumer Financial Products Commission will make rules for most retail products offered by banks, such as certificates of deposit and consumer loans. The Act requires managers of hedge funds (but not the funds themselves) with more than $150 million in assets to register with the SEC. Some provisions are subject to study and further regulatory actions by regulators, including the so-called Volcker rule, before they are implemented. Dodd-Frank fails to address the TBTF misconception, the inefficiencit practices at Fannie Mae, Freddie Mac, and the housing agencies and the excessive use of market-based short-term funding by financial services firms.

Dodd-Frank is intended to minimize the probability of future financial crises and systemic distress by empowering regulators to require higher capital requirements and establish a new regulatory regime for large financial firms, by developing regulatory and market structures for financial derivatives, and by creating systemic risk assessment and monitoring. Dodd-Frank created a Financial Services Oversight Council (FSOC) that identifies and monitors systemic risk in the financial system. The FSOC recommends appropriate leverage, liquidity, capital, and risk management rules to the Federal Reserve. The FSOC can practically take control of and liquidate troubled financial services firms if their failure would pose significant threat to the nation's financial stability. Complete implementation and effective enfocement of provisions of Dodd-Frank are expected to promote and strengthen safer and robust financial service firms, more stable and liquid financial market, more improved investor confidence, better protection for investors, more efficient capital markets, and sustainable economic growth and prosperity.

Former Federal Reserve chairman Volcker has made these suggestions for structural changes and improvements in markets and market regulation:[23]

1. Macroprudential regulation.
2. Separation of investment banking from commercial banking and other banking activities that can be better managed by the existing supervisory system.
3. Refinement of the financial system, particularly the mortgage market, which currently is broken.
4. Redesigning the business school curriculum to focus on risk assessment and market externalities as well as training the most competent and ethical future business leaders.
5. Better balanced supervisory authorities and responsibilities between central banks and the Federal Reserve.
6. Eliminating the basic disequilibrium in the real economy in order to move out of the recession.
7. "Potentially cumbersome" council of regulations.
8. Pure reliance on judgment of regulators and individual institutions can be challenging.
9. Procyclicality of being proactive rather than reactive.
10. Proper risk management.
11. Excessive derivatives that have exceeded the need for hedging.
12. Controlling and supervising money market funds.
13. The importance of the Dodd-Frank Act of 2010.

An effective regulatory reform creates an environment under which companies can operate in achieving sustainable performance, being held accountable for their activities, and providing protections for their investors. The regulatory environment of the banking industry is further discussed in Chapter 3.

Corporate Governance

The Dodd-Frank Act is intended to improve corporate governance effectiveness and disclosures in many areas, including shareholders' nonbinding or advisory votes on "say on pay" and "say on golden" parachutes that give payments to executives associated with M&A and major asset transactions. Companies also are required to disclose: (1) the relationship between senior executive compensation and the company's financial performance in terms of graphs and charts; (2) the ratio of chief executive compensation and the median total to employee compensation excluding the chief executive's compensation; and (3) whether employees or directors are allowed to hedge against a decrease in value of options included in their compensation scheme.

Other corporate governance provisions of the Dodd-Frank Act are:

■ Rules pertaining to compensation committee independence and standards on avoidance or conflicts of interest associated with retaining compensation consultants

- Corporate "claw-back" policies for reclaiming incentive-based compensation from formal and current executive officers when the company subsequently restates its financial statements due to material misstatement
- Revision of rules pertaining to the ability of brokers to vote proxies without instruction from beneficial holders, thus prohibiting brokers from voting on compensation matters
- Rules on shareholders' ability to nominate director candidates

For the purpose of discussing the key issues in the global economy, a group of 20 finance ministers and central bank governors was formed in 1999. During their meetings, a great deal of emphasis was placed on corporate governance. Good corporate governance is critical for sustaining the financial institutions. The G-20 meetings emphasized entrenching the good corporate governance culture.[24] The corporate governance structure, including its principles, mechanisms, and functions, is discussed in depth in Chapter 3.

Capital Standards

The 2007–2009 financial crisis and resulting global economic meltdown signify unhealthy financial environments and lack of capital adequacy in the financial services industry, especially banks. Frequent bank failures resulting from inadequate capital or fraudulent activities can cause substantial losses to the insurance fund. Capital standards determine how much of banks' operations should be funded by equity as opposed to debt. The general perception is that equity is expensive and that increasing capital requirements will raise the cost of capital and thus weaken banks' lending potential. Furthermore, banks prefer debt financing over equity because debts lower the amount of taxes. Banks and banking organizations have established internal risk management processes in evaluating risks for capital adequacy. These processes consist of four elements: (1) identifying and measuring all material risks; (2) relating capital to the level of risk; (3) stating explicit capital adequacy goals with respect to risk; and (4) assessing conformity to the institution's stated objectives. In 1988, the Basel Accord established the Basel Committee on Banking Supervision in an attempt to (1) create a level playing field for international banks to compete effectively in the global market, (2) provide a common international definition of bank capital, and (3) establish risk-based capital standards for banking organizations worldwide.

The Basel Committee assesses capital adequacy based on a set of three so-called pillars: minimum capital standards, supervisory oversight, and market discipline.[25] Pillar 1 requires sound minimum capital standards that effectively and accurately distinguish degrees of credit risk based on a standardized approach that ties capital requirements to external credit assessments (e.g., credit ratings), and banks' own internal ratings according to their estimates of default probabilities and unique risk profiles.

Pillar 2 of the Basel Committee requires vigilant supervisory oversight and review of capital adequacy by focusing on these principles. Supervisors:

- Have the authority to require banks to operate above the minimum regulatory capital ratios.

- Should require banks to assess and maintain overall capital adequacy in relation to underlying risks.
- Should review and evaluate the internal capital adequacy assessments and strategies of banks as well as their compliance with regulatory capital ratios.
- Should intervene at an early stage to prevent capital from falling below prudent levels and should require remedial action quickly if capital becomes inadequate.

Pillar 3 of the Basel capital framework relates to market discipline, which gives banks more incentive to manage their risks and maintain adequate capital. The effectiveness of market discipline and supervision depends on whether banks disclose timely, accurate, and reliable information regarding their capital structure and risk exposures. Based on the relevant and objective information disseminated to the market, market participants can assess and decide about their own risks in dealing with such institutions. The effectiveness of market discipline in controlling the risk-taking of banks depends on the adequacy of disclosure provided to the market and the reliability and quality of disclosure practices in banks.

The aim of the Basel Committee is to strengthen global capital and liquidity regulations to promote a more resilient banking sector with proper ability to absorb shocks arising from financial and economic stress and to improve risk management, governance, transparency, and disclosures. The Basel Committee addresses the market failures caused by the recent financial crisis and establishes measures to strengthen bank-level and microprudential regulation by issuing the new Basel III banking rules. These rules require banks to hold top-quality capital to 8 percent of their total assets and to modify their stress testing, capital management strategies, and counterparty risk. To comply with rules, banks can increase their capital by issuing new equity or through retained earnings, reduce their risk-weighted assets, or sell off assets and riskier business.

Dodd-Frank establishes stricter requirements and restricts risk-taking. It encourages banks to redesign their business lines and services. To comply with the Act, banks can sell their private equity funds to a third party with the right to manage and run those funds and to get the percentage of increase in value. This practice will produce the same results as holding the funds. Particularly, Dodd-Frank affects regulatory and corporate govern-ance measures of the financial services industry. The Act provides more funding and more information, and provides U.S. regulators with discretionary authority establish, interpret, and enforce new laws. The Volcker rule would prohibit much proprietary trading of banks and their affiliates by establishing strong restrictions on bank investment and hedging activities. It restricts the amount banks can invest in hedge funds or private equity funds to 3 percent of Tier 1 capital. Taken together, Dodd-Frank and Basel III requirements establish more restrictive capital definitions, tougher capital standards, additional capital buffers, higher risk-weighted assets, and higher standards for minimum capital ratios. Capital standards for banks are described further in Chapter 4.

Supervisory Activities

Consolidation, convergence, and competition in the financial services industry have created new challenges for policy makers, regulatory authorities, and supervisors in:

(1) defining geographic and product markets for antitrust policy implications; (2) establishing more vigilant methods based on new market parameters to preserve the safety and soundness of the financial systems; and (3) establishing a more relevant disclosure system to provide information on the current values of assets and liabilities. The new technological innovations should be used to create secure and reliable disclosure systems based on a real-time, online basis. Since the financial services industry is experiencing an unprecedented merger movement, which is changing the structure of the industry, the role of the Federal Reserve in effective implementation of its merger policy of encouraging competition in the industry is becoming vital.

Financial reporting of financial institutions should properly disclose the distribution of their internal ratings, asset quality, risk measurement, and management practices. Large banks should also attempt to strengthen their supervisory information systems. The supervisor's role in identifying and assessing weakness in financial institutions in the midst of strong economic conditions is crucial, primarily because bank supervisors are assuming an important public trust with a great responsibility of: (1) minimizing fraud incidents and excesses in the banking system, (2) reducing losses to insurance funds, and (3) maintaining a stable and productive banking system. The Dodd-Frank Act broadens the supervisory and oversight role of the Federal Reserve Board to include all entities that own an insured depository institution and other large and nonbank financial services firms that could threaten the nation's financial system. The Basel Committee supervisory guidance highlights the application of the Basel Core Principles for Effective Banking Supervision to microfinance activities in order to improve practices on regulating and supervising such activities. The guidance is intended to assist global banking organizations to develop a coherent and comprehensive approach to microfinance supervision. Supervision provisions of both the Dodd-Frank Act and the Basel Committee are discussed further in subsequent chapters.

Continuous Quality Improvement

An important asset of financial services organizations is their reputation and customer satisfaction and confidence, which are not measurable and are unrecognized in their financial statements. Financial institutions whose reputation is sound can compete more effectively in the global market. An institution whose reputation is impaired has a harder time regaining the confidence of customers, employees, creditors, shareholders, and regulators.

Recent trends of increased complexity of doing business, globalization of the economy, worldwide competition, deregulation, consolidation, and convergence have encouraged financial institutions to apply strategies of continuous improvement in the quality of their services. To remain competitive, financial institutions have begun to place a high premium on improving the quality of their services, meeting customers' expectations, and ensuring financial integrity. Financial institutions can achieve continuous improvements in the quality of their financial products and services by:

- *Identifying the nature of their financial products and services, categories of customers, markets, competitors, regulatory environment, and key quality attributes.* For example, direct competitors would be other banks, credit unions, savings and loan associations, and finance companies. Indirect competitors would include brokerage firms, insurance companies, and other financial service providers. However, the direct competition among banks, insurance companies, and securities and brokerage firm's increases as financial services providers continue to take advantage of convergence opportunities provided by the GLB Act of 1999.

- *Stating their quality mission and goals, as they are perceived by customers, and establishing appropriate methods of execution to attain these goals.* Doing this typically involves establishment of the mission of attaining high levels of customer satisfaction with a goal of attracting and retaining customers. The method of execution entails eliminating a customer's "expectation gap" by understanding customers' expectations and meeting them. To eliminate the expectation gap, banks should consider the quality expectations of different segments of customers served, including individual depositors, small businesses, commercial customers, institutional customers, and services provided to other financial institutions.

- *Obtaining top-level management commitment to continuous quality improvements.* Top-level executives should set a tone at top that customer satisfaction is the important mission of their financial institution; lack of leadership can cause any quality initiative to fail. The role of senior management should include communication of an understandable mission statement of quality to all employees. Top executives must assume an active role in dealing with customers' complaints, quality problems, and customer service.

- *Empowering employees to use their judgment in dealing with customers.* Internet banking, global competition, consolidation, and convergence caused by technological advances and deregulation create a need for better-trained, highly motivated, more productive, and more empowered employees. Development of quality programs for employees consists of monthly quality meetings, assignment of senior executives to quality programs, discussion of quality issues in general management meetings, quality recognition programs, and quality videos.

- *Gathering and analyzing relevant information related to customers' needs, products, and services as well as internal operations, suppliers, and competitors.* The information gathered should be analyzed to develop actionable responses in both short- and long-run planning. These actionable responses include criteria for targeting problem areas, proving appropriate information, and implementing responses. Surveys of customers chosen at random or as members of special groups (e.g., closing out accounts, opening new accounts, special services) can provide valuable quality information. These surveys can evaluate adherence to appropriate procedures and determine why customers are leaving or opening new accounts.

- *Ensuring compliance with four privacy requirements of the GLB Act as well as other privacy legislation to protect and safeguard the privacy of customers' personal information.* The GLB Act requires each financial institution to (1) establish and annually disclose a privacy policy; (2) provide customers the right to opt out of having their personal identifiable information shared with nonaffiliated third parties; (3) not share customer account numbers with nonaffiliated third parties; and (4) abide by regulatory standards to protect the security and integrity of customer information.

The passage of the GLB Act and the public outcry over privacy issues has encouraged almost all states to introduce privacy bills primarily directed toward financial institutions to give consumers choice and control over the information collected about them.

■ *Providing training for all personnel, including executives, managers, and employees, to get involved in quality-related activities to make continuous improvement in quality and productivity.* This training process must constantly communicate the message of total quality to the various levels of employees and empower them to make appropriate decisions to support this goal. Training programs should teach employees what quality means to customers and how this quality can be provided through each employee's function. Continuous employee training in focusing on customer retention, personal interaction, and customer feedback is necessary to ensure day-to-day quality.

■ *Recognizing and awarding employees for their commitment to quality.* Satisfied and rewarded employees would be more dedicated to improve the quality of their performance. Periodic surveys of employees and information on percentages and causes of turnover can provide valuable input regarding employee satisfaction. As the economy is transforming into a knowledge-based economy, it depends more on human capital than ever before. With the advent of technological developments and financial services over the past 30 years, an increasing number of businesses have become dependent on human resources. Organizations are now paying more attention to their business sustainability and corporate social responsibility, including employee satisfaction.

■ *Complying with corporate governance measures of the Dodd-Frank Act of 2010 and the 2010 Basel Committee.* This material is thoroughly addressed in Chapter 3.

Risk Assessment

One of the overriding causes of the recent financial crisis was the lack of proper risk assessment of subprime mortgage loans. Banks are now paying more attention to risk assessment and taking prudent risks when giving out loans.

The Dodd-Frank Act and the Basel III have higher capital requirements for banks. New ideas, such as that of capital floor, are being proposed for banks. New capital requirements will further act as a supplementary non-risk-based measure to provide bank leverage. The Financial Stability Forum and successor the Financial Stability Board (FSB) are established to promote international financial stability and often acted as a clearinghouse for fresh ideas of global regulation intended to strengthen financial stability through improving risk assessment. The G-20 occasionally has encouraged the Financial Stability Board's recommendations and has supported its efforts to become a global coordinator of banking policy. However, the topic of raising the capital requirements for banks has been debated because, in the current credit crunch, it is hard for banks to raise capital.

The board of directors of banks, particularly its compensation committee, should review executive compensation to ensure that management is not taking too many risks. The compensation committee should meet with the bank's chief risk officers at least annually to check the link between risk management and executive pay. Compensation for bank executives is another area addressed by the Financial Stability Board report because it has now become global issue. It is now considered important to align compensation standards.[26]

Financial and Nonfinancial Key Performance Indicators

Conventional financial statements provide historical financial information relevant to an entity's financial condition and results of operations. Investors demand forward-looking financial and nonfinancial information on key performance indicators (KPIs) relevant to the entity's governance, economic, ethical, social, and environmental activities. In today's business environment, global businesses are under close scrutiny and profound pressure from lawmakers, regulators, the investment community, and their diverse stakeholders to focus on sustainability and accept accountability and responsibility for their multiple bottom lines of economic, governance, social, ethical, and environmental performance. Organizations worldwide including banks recognize the importance of sustainability performance (SP) and accountability reporting (AR). However, proper determination of SP and AR concepts, guidelines, implementations, and best practices is evolving and remains a major challenge for organizations of all types and sizes.

Traditionally, banks have reported their performance on economic affairs in reports that have become overwhelmingly complicated and irrelevant. Although the primary focus of corporate reporting will continue to be an economic issue to create sustainable long-term shareholder value, the issues of social, ethical, and environmental perform-ance will gain momentum as we look ahead. The sustainability and financial health of banks are the keys to keeping investor confidence high. This sustainability requires public trust in the suitability, reliability, and timeliness of bank's reports in disclosing relevant information on financial and nonfinancial KPIs. The global competitiveness of U.S. capital markets depends significantly on the reliability of KPI information in assisting investors in making sound investment decisions. Financial markets should continue promoting and enforcing sustainability performance and demanding account-ability reporting to ensure transparent flows of reliable, accurate, and relevant financial and nonfinancial KPI information to the markets. Doing this requires policy makers, standard setters, regulators, investors, businesses, and educators to collaborate in promoting SP and AR in order to rebuild public trust and investor confidence in corporate America, including financial services firms, and thus to ensure effective functioning of our free enterprise system.

 VALUATION PROCESS

The current changes in the financial services industry raise two fundamental questions: (1) How much are these financial services firms actually worth? and (2) How should their value be measured? The primary goal of this book is to assist readers in understanding current changes in the industry and their possible impact on the valuation of financial services firms, specifically financial institutions. During the 1990s and the early 2000s, bank earnings grew and many stock prices continuously increased, thereby encouraging more consolidation and convergence in the financial services industry. This continuous rapid pace of business combination in the financial services industry has been criticized on the grounds that consolidation and convergence are happening at high costs and acquirer banks are paying too much for the target banks. The valuation computation process requires answers to these questions: What is being valued? Are we determining the value of the equity of the target? Do we calculate the value of the target company on a long-term basis or a short-term basis? Most M&A are aimed at acquiring the equity of the target company. The three primary issues addressed in this book are: (1) how much banks actually are worth, (2) how to value a target bank, and (3) how much premium over the book value of the target bank the acquirer should pay.

Traditionally, financial institutions have been defined by geographical markets. Thus, when Bank A sought to buy Bank B, it knew what it was buying (e.g., a number of branches, deposits, loans, market share). Today, financial institutions may enter and exit distant markets more freely, they may provide a variety of financial services (e.g., loans, insurance, credit cards, investment, financing), and their customers may buy financial services from a dozen institutions. It is becoming more difficult to value properly an institution because branch networks and bricks and mortar do not count for as much as they used to. Thus, four factors should be considered in the valuation of financial institutions:

1. Reasonably well-run institutions and management operating style
2. Simple earnings streams with stable, straightforward, basic earnings components not too sensitive to macro events such as interest rate changes and regulatory changes
3. Sustainable performance
4. The lowest price-to-earnings ratios

 ## CONCLUSION

In this chapter we examined current changes, such as consolidation, convergence, globalization, competition and regulatory reforms, that have significantly affected the structure and characteristics of financial services firms. The potential impact of these changes on the value of financial institutions will be discussed throughout this book. However, the traditional valuation methods of focusing on branches, deposits, and market share may not be appropriate for the valuation of currently formed financial holding companies. Core deposits, branch networks, and bricks and mortar are worth less than they once were. Technology and deregulation are two major factors driving the wave of consolidation and convergence in the financial services industry. Technological advances such as image processing, networking, and Internet banking enable larger banks to achieve additional cost savings and synergies, which might have resulted in the booming consolidation and convergence activities in the industry.

Deregulation (e.g., Riegle-Neal Act of 1994; GLB Act of 1999) virtually eliminated both geographic and product barriers in the U.S. financial services industry, which has been through significant structural changes in the past decade. Product and geographic deregulation, especially in the banking industry, coupled with increased global competition and technological innovations, has produced potential and likely acceleration of consolidation and convergence. Financial services organizations have responded to these changes by attempting to strategically position themselves for future challenges and opportunities. Invariably, the consideration of consolidation, convergence, and competition is a significant part of management strategic planning to succeed in this ever-changing economic and business environment. Thus, the valuation and financing aspects of M&A activities in the financial services industry will continue to be of significant interest to the business community in general and financial institutions in particular.

The GLB Act publicly and officially permits cross-industry financial conglomerates in the United States, although the cross-industry consolidation has been practiced often in the United States and abroad. FHCs can provide a broad range of financial services, including investment and commercial banking, asset management and distribution services, insurance and securities underwriting services, and even real estate development and investment services. These future FHCs, by consolidating their human and physical resources, will be able to gain economies of scale and scope. This perceived benefit of economies of scale and scope will increase M&A in the financial services industry. The recent financial crisis has created new challenges for financial firms. The Dodd-Frank Act of 2010 and the Basel Committee are addressing these challenges to ensure business sustainability of financial services firms.

The convergence in the financial services industry has raised many concerns including potential excessive market concentration and monopoly power in the industry and the creation of too much systemic risk in the economy resulting from fewer but larger financial services firms that are perceived as TBTF. Furthermore, the bull market in stocks has caused high-valuation multiples paid by the acquirer to buy the target, especially when the target is a public rather than a private company. The study of M&A activities requires consideration and assessment of numerous issues, including strategic planning, valuation, legal and regulatory, accounting, tax, negotiating, and integration strategies. These issues are discussed throughout this book, with the primary focus on their relevance issues for financial services firms.

 NOTES

1. The Gramm-Leach-Bliley (GLB) Act of 1999 (the Financial Modernization Act), Pub. L. 106-102, 113 Stat. 1338, enacted November 12, 1999.
2. Lenny Mendonca and Greg Wilson, "Financial Services Consolidation and Convergence: Advancing to the Endgame," *Business Economics* (October1998): 7–13.
3. "Gramm-Leach-Bliley Did Not Cause the Financial Crisis," American Bankers Association, January 2010. Available at: http://www.aba.com/NR/rdonlyres/9B9CA352-

C8CD-4BB1-BDB7-DEA69C625E36/64869/GrammLeachHelpedtoResolvenotCause theCreditCrisisJa.pdf.

4. Robert Crandal and Jerry Ellig, "Economic Deregulation and Customer Choice: Lessons for the Electric Industry," Center for Market Processes, 1997.

5. Myron L. Kwast, "Bank Mergers: What Should Policymakers Do?" *Journal of Banking and Finance* 23 (1999): 629–636.

6. Brian K. Bucks, Arthur B. Kennickell, Traci L. Mach, and Kevin B. Moore, "Changes in U.S. Family Finances from 2004 to 2007: Evidence from the Survey of Consumer Finances," March 2009. Available at: www.federalreserve.gov/pubs/bulletin/2009/pdf/scf09.pdf.

7. "Mergers and Acquisitions in Banking Sector," *Economy Watch.* Available at: www.economywatch.com/mergers-acquisitions/international/banking-sector.html.

8. Shane Kite, "The Five Best Mobile Banking Apps Now," *Bank Technology News* (October 2010). Available at: www.americanbanker.com/btn_issues/23_10/the-five-best-mobile-apps-now-1026278-1.html.

9. Federal Reserve Board, Remarks by Vice Chairman Roger W. Ferguson, Jr., at the 36th Annual Conference on Bank Structure and Competition, Chicago, IL, May 4, 2000.

10. Ibid.

11. Kite, "The Five Best Mobile Banking Apps Now."

12. Federal Deposit Insurance Corporation, "Technology Regulations and Publications for Financial Institutions," April 2010. Available at: www.fdic.gov/regulations/information/ebanking/index.html.

13. Mark S. Mizruchi and Gerald F. Davis, "The Globalization of American Banking, 1962–1981," *The Sociology of the Economy*, New York: Russell Sage Foundation, May 2003.

14. Thomas Oatley, "The Dilemmas of International Financial Regulation," *Regulation Magazine* 23, No. 4 (Spring 2001): 36–39.

15. Tyler Durden, "Qualifying for Too Big to Fail," government subsidy, October 2009. Available at www.zerohedge.com/article/quantifying-too-big-fail-governmental-subsidy.

16. Dean Barker and Travis McArthur, "The Value of the Too Big to Fail Big Bank Subsidy," Center for Economic and Policy Research, September 2009. Available at www.zerohedge.com/article/quantifying-too-big-fail-governmental-subsidy.

17. J. Alfred Broaddus, Jr., "The Bank Merger Wave: Causes and Consequences," *Economic Quarterly* 85, No. 3 (Summer 1998): 1.

18. Arthur E. Wilmarth, Jr., "The Dark Side of Universal Banking: Financial Conglomerates and the Origins of the Subprime Financial Crisis," *Connecticut Law Review* 41, No. 4 1-89 (May 2009).

19. Barker and McArthur, "The Value of the Too Big to Fail Big Bank Subsidy."

20. "A CBO Report: The Troubled Asset Relief Program: Report on Transactions Through December 31, 2008," January 2009. Available at: www.cbo.gov/ftpdocs/99xx/doc 9961/01-16-TARP.pdf.

21. "Credit Crisis—Bailout Plan," *New York Times*, December, 7 2009. Available at http://topics.nytimes.com/top/reference/timestopics/subjects/c/credit_crisis/bailout_plan/index.html.

22. Dodd-Frank Wall Street Reform and Consumer Protection Act of 2010, Pub. L. 111-203. Available at: www.gpo.gov/fdsys/pkg/PLAW-111publ203/pdf/PLAW-111 publ203.pdf.

23. Damian Paletta, "Volcker Spares No One in Broad Critique," *Wall Street Journal*, September 23, 2010. Available at: http://blogs.wsj.com/economics/2010/09/23/volcker-spares-no-one-in%20-broad-critique/.

24. Bassey Udo, "Step Up Financial Reforms, Transparency International Tells G20," April 2009 .Available at: http://234next.com/csp/cms/sites/Next/Money/Business/5558191 147/story.csp.

25. Federal Reserve Board. Remarks by Vice-Chairman Roger W. Ferguson, Jr., Institute of International Bankers, Washington, DC, March 6, 2000.

26. Damain Paletta, "Regulators Agree to Create Stricter Capital Requirements for Banks," *Wall Street Journal*, April, 2 2009 Available at http://online.wsj.com/article/SB123868295604882511.html.

CHAPTER THREE

Corporate Governance

 INTRODUCTION

Some of the overriding reasons for the 2007–2009 financial crisis include ineffective regulation, greed, and the ineffectiveness of executives at troubled financial institutions. Effective corporate governance plays an important role in addressing these crises. Indeed, the phrase "corporate governance" appeared for the first time in many legislative reforms. Section 111 of the Emergency Economic Stabilization Act of 2008, better known as the Government Bailout of Troubled Financial Institutions, requires establishing executive compensation and corporate governance standards for those financial institutions. Corporate governance has transformed from a compliance process to a business strategic imperative in the twenty-first century. The demand for ever-improving corporate governance and accountability for business organizations appears to be a global trend in recent years. The recent wave of financial scandals and resulting global financial crises has reinvigorated interest in corporate governance. Effective corporate governance plays an important role in addressing these crises. This chapter presents the ethical and professional responsibilities of all participants in the financial reporting process, including the board of directors, the audit committee, executives, internal auditors, external auditors, financial analysts, legal counsel, regulators, and standard setters.[1] Furthermore, this chapter examines corporate governance measures of the financial services industry.

CORPORATE GOVERNANCE EFFECTIVENESS

The collapse of major financial institutions such as Bear Stearns, Lehman Brothers, and Countrywide as well as the restructuring of others including AIG, Citigroup, and Bank of America brought corporate governance to the attention of policy makers, regulators, and the business community. A vital financial system and reliable financial information is essential for economic development worldwide. The persistence of differences in global financial systems necessitates a move toward convergence in corporate governance measures and regulatory reforms. The emerging global corporate governance reforms are shaping the structure of capital markets worldwide, their competitiveness and measures taken to protect investor interests. Corporate governance measures are defined as state and federal statutes, judicial deliberations, listing standards, and best practices. For example, the Sarbanes-Oxley Act of 2002 (SOX) has influenced regulatory reforms in the United States. In Canada, Bill 198 (often referred to as Canadian Sarbanes-Oxley, or C. SOX) was enacted in 2002 to ensure that investors are receiving reliable financial information. The U.K. corporate governance reforms are specified in the 2003 Combined Code on Corporate Governance.

The globalization of capital markets and the demand for investor protection in response to financial scandals worldwide (e.g., Enron, WorldCom, Parmalat, Ahold, subprime loans) also require consistency and uniformity in regulatory reforms and corporate governance practices.

> As good corporate governance is an essential prerequisite for the integrity and the credibility of financial institutions, stock exchanges, individual companies, and indeed the whole market economy. . . . In today's integrated markets, failure to deal with the regulatory issues associated with corporate governance can have strong repercussions on global financial markets and jeopardize financial stability.[2]

One argument is that there is no need for corporate governance reforms, policy interventions, or regulations, because product market competition provides incentives for public companies to adopt the most efficient and effective corporate governance structure. Companies that do not adopt effective corporate governance are presumably less efficient in the long term and ultimately are replaced. Nonetheless, the rash of financial scandals in the late 1990s and the early 2000s proves that market-based mechanisms alone could not solve corporate governance problems. The capital markets hit rock bottom in the early 2000s and again in 2007 and 2008 primarily because market correction mechanisms, lax regulations, inadequate risk assessment, unreliable financial reports, and poorly developed disclosure standards failed to protect investors and thus diminished public trust and investor confidence in the capital markets.

Furthermore, market correction mechanisms often are initiated and enforced after the occurrences of substantial management abuse and after shareholders sell their shares and depress prices. The sales of shares incur transaction costs and do not directly remove assets from management control; they simply pass shares to other investors who ultimately suffer from the same management malfeasance. Market correction mechanisms may affect corporate governance after significant wealth is destroyed due to management misconduct and corporate malfeasance and after considerable transaction costs for other stakeholders, including employees in the form of layoffs, lost wages, and pension funds and society in the form of lost taxes. Market mechanisms failed to prevent the corporate debacles of Enron, WorldCom, Global Crossing, Bear Stearns, and Lehman Brothers, among others, that were devastating to shareholders, employees, retirees, and society as almost all corporate wealth was destroyed. Thus, corporate governance reforms are expected to create an environment that promotes strong marketplace integrity and efficiency as well as investor confidence and public trust in the quality, reliability, and transparency of financial disclosures.

Corporate Governance Definition

Corporate governance can be defined in several ways. For example, it may be defined as a process of aligning management interests with those of investors in the context of the "agency theory." Corporate governance can also be defined from a legal perspective as a system that ensures compliance with all applicable laws, rules, regulations, and standards. This chapter adopts the most comprehensive definition of corporate governance:

> Corporate governance is an ongoing process of managing and running an entity with the primary goal of creating shareholder value while protecting interests of other stakeholders (including creditors, employees, suppliers, customers, government, competitors, and society) by clearly defining roles and responsibilities of all corporate governance participants (e.g., the board of directors, executives, legal counsel, internal auditors, external auditors, financial advisors, investment banks, credit agencies, regulators, policy makers, standard setters, investors, and other gatekeepers) as well as holding them accountable in fulfilling their responsibilities.

Corporate governance attributes addressed in this chapter include sources and functions of corporate governance, convergence in corporate governance, and corporate governance of financial services firms.

Sources of Corporate Governance

The primary sources of corporate governance in the United States are corporate law, securities law, listing standards, and best practices.[3]

1. *Corporate laws.* State corporate law establishes standards of conduct for corporations and defines fiduciary duties, authorities and responsibilities of shareholders, directors, and officers. The primary intent of state laws is to protect shareholder rights by empowering them to:
   a. Elect directors in the corporate annual meetings.
   b. Inspect the company's ledgers, books, records, and financial reports.
   c. Approve major business transactions such as mergers and acquisitions.
   d. Receive proxy materials and disclosures for related-party transactions.

While no uniform body of corporate law exists in the United States, the state of Delaware has been prominent in influencing corporate law.

2. *Federal securities laws.* Federal securities laws are passed by Congress and are intended to protect investors and improve investor confidence in the integrity and efficiency of the capital markets. The two fundamental federal securities laws pertaining to public companies are the Securities Act of 1933 and Securities Exchange Act of 1934. These acts are primary disclosure-based statutes that require public companies to file a periodic report with the Securities and Exchange Commission (SEC) and disclose certain information to their shareholders to make investment and voting decisions. U.S. Congress established the SEC to enforce provisions of the Securities Acts in protecting investors of public companies from receiving misleading financial information by enforcing compliance with federal securities laws, detecting problems in the markets, and preventing and deterring violations of the laws. The rash of financial scandals during the late 1990s and the early 2000s and the resulting loss of investor confidence encouraged Congress to pass SOX. SOX expanded the role of federal statutes in corporate governance by providing measures to improve corporate governance, financial reports, and audit activities. Eight years after the passage of SOX to combat the rash of corporate and accounting scandals, businesses have taken appropriate measures to improve their professional accountability and corporate governance. The subprime mortgage crisis and the resulting government bailout of major financial institutions and subsequent economic meltdown compelled Congress to pass the Dodd-Frank Wall Street Reform and Consumer Protection Act of 2010.[4] Dodd-Frank is intended to minimize the probability of future financial crises and systemic distress by empowering regulators to require higher capital requirements, develop regulatory and market structures for financial derivatives, and establish mechanisms for systemic risk assessment and monitoring. Dodd-Frank created a Financial Services Oversight Council (FSOC) that identify and monitor systemic risk in the financial system. The FSOC recommend appropriate leverage, liquidity, and capital and risk management rules to the Federal Reserve. The FSOC can practically take control of and liquidate troubled financial services firms if their failure would pose significant threat to the nation's financial stability.

3. *Listing standards.* Listing standards adopted by national stock exchanges (New York Stock Exchange, Nasdaq, American Stock Exchange) establish corporate governance standards for listing companies to promote high standards of shareholder democracy, corporate responsibility, and accountability to shareholders, and to monitor the operation of securities markets. Corporate governance listing standards address a variety of governance issues of listing companies from uniform voting rights to mandatory audit committee formation, shareholder approvals of broad-based option plans, and requiring internal audit function and risk assessment.

4. *Best practices.* Corporate governance best practices suggested by professional organizations (e.g., Conference Board, Business Roundtable) and investor activists (Council of Institutional Investors) are nonbinding guidelines intended to improve corporate governance policies and practices of public companies above and beyond state and federal statutes and listing standards. The best practice of "say on pay,"

which requires nonbinding votes by shareholders in determining executive compensation, is an obvious example of these best practices.

Corporate Governance Sources Relevant to Financial Services Firms

Financial Reforms

The U.S. financial reform legislation signed into law in July 2010 titled the Dodd-Frank Wall Street Reform and Consumer Protection Act establishes U.S. federal agencies, including the Consumer Financial Protection Bureau for implementation purposes (usual and customary activities), and will create new regulations for companies that extend credit to customers. Dodd-Frank addresses many corporate governance aspects of financial services firms to enhance their accountability and shift governing power from their directors and officers to shareholders. Dodd-Frank is expected to have significant impact on governance of financial services firms. The overriding governance provisions of Dodd-Frank are changes in the way executive compensation arrangements are determined, disclosed, and approved; more effective whistleblower incentives and protections to report securities laws violations; shareholder use of the proxy materials to nominate directors; shareholder say on pay; independence of compensation committees and their advisors; restrictions on the voting of shareholders by brokers; and registration of advisors to private funds.

Dodd-Frank consists of 16 separate titles and requires more than 500 rules, 60 studies, and 90 reports over the next four years to implement its provisions effectively. The Dodd-Frank Act requires many changes to corporate governance, disclosure, and compensation practices of all public companies including those in the financial services industry. Many of the provisions of Dodd-Frank require further SEC rulemaking and interpretation, including those related to proxy access, executive compensation, and whistleblower protections. The provisions reflect the lawmakers' focus on strengthening corporate governance, disclosure, and accountability, and are expected to shift significant governing power from boardrooms to shareholders. These provisions and related implementation rules will have a profound impact on the design and disclosure of compensation arrangements and shareholder monitoring of the terms of executive compensation programs. Whistleblower policies, programs, practices, and protections will be improved. Dodd-Frank directs the SEC to adopt changes to the federal proxy rules to facilitate the exercise of shareholders' traditional state law rights to nominate and elect directors to company boards. Companies will be required to include a provision in certain proxy statements for an advisory shareholder vote on the compensation of executives at least once every three years. Shareholders also will have a separate vote at least every six years on whether they want that say on pay vote to occur annually, biennially, or triennially. The board compensation committee should be authorized to retain and oversee compensation consultants and other advisors in fulfilling its duties independence of any consultants retained.

Dodd-Frank mandates national securities exchanges to prohibit member brokers from voting customer shares without first receiving voting instructions from the beneficial owner with respect to director elections. Dodd-Frank directs the SEC to require listed company to implement and disclose a "clawback" policy mandating that if a company is made to restate its financial statements due to material noncompliance with relevant reporting requirements, the company must recover from current and former executive officers any excess incentive compensation paid based on the erroneous financial information during the three-year period preceding the date of the restatement. The SEC must issue rules requiring companies to disclose in annual proxy statements the link between paid executive compensation and the company's financial performance. Public companies are required to disclose in their Form 10-K: (1) the median of the annual total compensation of all the company's employees except the chief executive officer (CEO); (2) the annual total compensation of the CEO; and (3) the ratio of the median of total compensation to the median of CEO compensation. These and other provisions of the Dodd-Frank Act will be thoroughly discussed later in this chapter.

Basel Committee

The Basel Committee finalized its "Principles for Enhancing Corporate Governance" in October 2010 to address deficiencies in bank corporate governance and to promote adoption of sound and effective corporate governance practices for banks worldwide. These corporate governance principles highlight the importance of supervisory oversight of banks' corporate governance policies and practices in these six areas:

1. The oversight role of the board of directors
2. The qualifications, independence, and composition of the board
3. The importance of the position of the chief risk officer in risk management function
4. The board's oversight of the executive compensation arrangements in discouraging excessive risk-taking activities
5. Directors' and officers' understanding of the bank's operational structure and ongoing risk assessment
6. Disclosure and transparency of principles of good corporate governance[5]

The Basel Committee is expected to have an immediate effect on stemming the financial crisis, to have a long-term structural impact on global banks' corporate governance, to strengthen the global financial and monetary structure, and to commit to fundamentally reforming the governance of the international financial institutions. To achieve these objectives, the Basel Committee will address a wide area of: financial regulation, scope of regulation, oversight of credit rating agencies, private pools of capital, liquidity, infrastructure, accounting standards, compensation schemes and risk management, transparency, enforcement, and technical assistance and capacity building in emerging market economies.

GLOBAL REGULATORY REFORMS

Regulations vary significantly throughout the world in response to each country's economic, cultural, and legal circumstances. One emerging trend is toward a demand for the protection of global investors. Effective regulations can align the interests of directors, management, and shareholders in achieving sustainable performance, which promotes market efficiency and economic prosperity. However, as stated by the U.S. Treasury Secretary Henry Paulson, "Excessive regulation slows innovation, imposes needless costs on investors, and stifles competitiveness and job creation."[6] In a perfect global market, a company can be incorporated in one jurisdiction (Country A), listed in a foreign market (Country B), operate in another country (Country C), be subject to the regulatory and financial services of another country (Country D), and be taxed in several countries. Technological advances, globalization, and cross-country investments demand that regulators worldwide cooperate in reducing regulator conflict and excessive regulatory reforms. The global overreach of SOX underscores the need for convergence in corporate governance reforms. More emphasis on national regulations is not relevant to emerging global investment, capital markets, or the economy. The issues that need to be resolved are: (1) what measures are considered good corporate governance practices; (2) how such practices can be converged while maintaining domestic market confidence in both national and global regulations affected by differences in legal, political, and cultural environments; and (3) to what extent effective global regulatory cooperation can facilitate the emergence of global corporate governance.

Each country has its own corporate governance reforms that are shaped by its economic, cultural, and legal circumstances. The effectiveness of corporate governance is influenced by many factors and typically is measured in terms of creating shareholder value and protecting interests of other stakeholders. The worldwide responses to corporate scandals promote convergence in corporate governance across borders. Convergence is particularly vital in the areas of investor rights and protections, board responsibilities, and financial disclosures. Although total convergence in corporate governance reform may not be feasible, global corporate governance practices should be promoted to improve efficiency and liquidity in the global capital markets. Corporate scandals worldwide caused regulators to respond through regulations to reinforce business integrity and restore market confidence. In the United States, SOX was enacted in response to the financial scandals of Enron and WorldCom, among others. The United Kingdom responded to several high-profile scandals, such as Parmalat and Ahold, by strengthening the Combined Code on Corporate Governance.

The U.K. approach to corporate governance reforms is more principles-based that the U.S. approach; it requires companies to "comply or explain why not." This flexible approach to corporate governance coupled with the fact that U.K. shareholders are in much stronger position than U.S. shareholders to nominate directors and forward their resolutions have recently made the U.K. capital market more attractive to global initial public offerings (IPOs). Different types of corporate governance structure are exposed to different financial misconduct and scandals. For example, the dispersed ownership system of governance in the United States is prone to earnings management schemes (e.g., Enron, WorldCom) whereas concentrated ownership systems are more vulnerable to the appropriation of private benefits of control (e.g., Parmalat).[7]

There are no globally accepted corporate governance reforms and best practices. Differences are driven mainly by a country's statutes, corporate structures, and culture. Country statutes could pose challenges for regulators in adopting corporate governance reforms and financial reporting disclosures for home companies as well as multinational corporations. The United States and United Kingdom, for example, operate under common law, which tends to give more antidirector privileges to minority shareholders compared to countries under code law (e.g., Germany) in the sense that regulators allow too many or too few rights to minority shareholders. Another example is that regulations in the United States typically are regulator-led—established by the SEC to protect investors—whereas reforms in the United Kingdom are normally shareholder-led indicating that investors are responsible to safeguard their own interests.

Corporate and capital structure can also influence corporate governance and financial disclosure requirements. One of the key differences in corporate structure is ownership of the company. In the United States, ownership of shares is dispersed as more than 110 million Americans own company shares through direct investment and retirement plans. Comparative stock ownerships in Europe are more concentrated, and thus controlling shareholders are in better position to influence corporate governance and business operations. Corporate governance in a dispersed share ownership system is designed to align interests of management with those shareholders as management may have incentives to engage in earnings management and focus on short-term considerations at the expense of sustainable shareholder value creation and long-term performance. Conversely, with concentrated ownership, corporate governance creates a right balance between interests of minority and majority shareholders. The primary purpose of corporate governance in the United States is to enhance shareholder value creation while protecting interests of other stakeholders (creditors, employees, suppliers, customers, and government); in Germany, in contrast, the focus is more on protecting creditors as banks play an important role in financing companies.

The board system can also influence corporate governance. In the one-tier boards in the United States, directors are elected to oversee management in running the company; in the two-tier board system in Germany, the supervisory board advises, appoints, and supervises the management board in managing company operations. Japan's companies operate through a complex system of committees, and these committees oversee and run the company. Cultural and political differences can also influence corporate governance as some cultures are more collective and risk averse than others (e.g., Germany compared to the United States).

An appropriate question is whether these differences in corporate governance can be reconciled and whether convergence in corporate governance is possible. A move toward corporate governance integration was attempted in 1999 by the Organization for Economic Co-operation and Development (OECD). The OECD has established a set of corporate governance principles designed to protect all stakeholders, particularly shareholders; later these principles were adopted by the International Corporate Governance Network. Each country legislates its regulatory reforms relevant to its political, cultural, economical, and investment preferences. Furthermore, each capital market in each country establishes listing standards to list and maintain public companies in its exchange. Global companies have a choice of whether to list in exchanges home or abroad by evaluating advantages and disadvantages in terms of cost of capital and of regulatory compliance. When a company is listed in a selected exchange, payoffs to investors and companies are determined in part by the extent and nature of regulatory reforms and listing standards. Securities markets worldwide operate under the premise of fair transparent disclosure of information and protection of shareholder rights. Regulations are designed to achieve this premise, and stringent regulations are considered to provide higher investor protection at higher compliance costs. In Anglo-Saxon countries, securities regulations are intended to promote market efficiency and investor confidence where all market participants have equal access to information, financial information is reliable, and there is a level playing field. Regulations are not designed to ensure that all investors make a desired return on investment. In countries with efficient capital markets based on reliable financial information, there is less need for stronger regulations to protect investors. Thus, the safety, strength, and efficiency of capital markets determine the severity of the securities regulations, and differences in regulations across countries can be linked to differences in investor protections against unfair trading.[8]

Factors that differentiate corporate governance in the United States from other countries are corporate ownership and control, capital markets, culture, and legal systems.[9]

1. *Corporate ownership and control.* Corporate ownership in countries other than the United States is much more highly concentrated through large banking institutions of family ownership. The concentration of corporate ownership and control and government ownership of corporate shares can significantly influence corporate governance in those countries. Ownership structure is an important aspect of corporate governance; it determines the nature and extent of both internal (e.g., composition of the board) and external (e.g., rules and regulations) mechanisms needed to protect investors and minimize the agency costs (e.g., information asymmetries and self-dealing by management). The ownership structure can be either *highly dispersed* with significant ownership by institutional investors (e.g., pension funds, mutual funds, insurance companies), as is the case in the United States and the United Kingdom, where ownership usually is open to cross-border portfolio holdings; or *concentrated* primarily in hands of families, as in Europe and Japan, where there is an agency cost of potential conflict between controlling owners and minority shareholders.

2. *Capital markets.* Public companies in the United States raise capital through public equity and debt markets. In other countries (e.g., Europe and Asia), banks are the primary source of capital for companies. Public companies' lending arrangements with banks and ownership of large blocks of shares by banks empower them to monitor and control the company's affairs and influence its corporate governance structure (e.g., board independence). Capital markets are the means of alleviating scarce financial resources, facilitating access to global investments, and providing the forum for global exchanges to list public companies. Capital markets facilitate the investment process through more efficient allocation of capital by scrutinizing management and mitigating financial constraints.

3. *Culture.* Under the U.S. market-based corporate governance structure, shareholder value creation and enhancement is the primary objective of public companies. In many other countries, corporations are responsible for protecting interests of a variety of stakeholders, including shareholders, employees, customers, suppliers,

government, and the public. Thus, the corporate governance structure in other countries is driven by the need to balance the interests of *all* stakeholders. The corporate decision-making process also is affected by the close family culture compared with the U.S. open and social culture.

4. *Legal system.* A country's legal system is the key driver of corporate governance in determining corporate responsibility, authority, and structure and fiduciary duties of its directors and officers. Literature in accounting and finance examines the relationship between legal protection of investors and the development of financial markets and corporate governance. It concludes that the legal system is an integral component of corporate governance, and, thus, better legal systems contribute to market liquidity.[10] Corporate governance listing standards do not normally exist outside the United States. The legal system determines the nature and the degree of investor protection across countries due to differences in legal regimes. Two traditional legal regimes influencing corporate governance are civil law and common law.[11] Civil law has its origin in Roman law and is practiced in Austria, Denmark, Finland, France, Germany, Greece, Italy, Japan, Norway, Spain, Switzerland, and Sweden. Common law of English origin is dominant in Australia, Canada, the United Kingdom, and the United States. The effectiveness of the legal system in protecting investors depends on the type of law where common law is perceived to be more efficient in protecting investors and the level of enforcement.

SARBANES-OXLEY ACT OF 2002

On July 30, 2002, President George W. Bush signed into law the Public Company Accounting Reform and Investor Protection Act of 2002, better known as the Sarbanes-Oxley Act of 2002 (SOX).[12] SOX is one of the most far-reaching laws addressing the conduct of corporate boards, executives, auditors, lawyers, financial analysts, investment banks, and others involved in corporate governance and the financial reporting process. The main purpose of SOX is to restore integrity to financial markets and confidence in corporate conducts, financial reports, and related audit functions. SOX establishes an independent regulatory structure for accountants who audit public companies; creates increased disclosure and reporting requirements to improve transparency of financial reports; changes accountants' relationships with their clients and audit committees; increases criminal penalties for violations of securities and related laws; requires senior executives (CEOs and chief financial officers [CFO]) to certify both financial statements and internal controls; and imposes substantial and unprecedented requirements on public companies, their directors, officers, and accountants, to improve corporate governance. SOX was enacted to respond to the wave of financial scandals, a series of high-profile alleged financial statement frauds, an erosion in investor confidence, and extreme market volatility. SOX is intended to improve the quality and transparency of financial reports through: (1) higher standards for corporate governance, (2) executive certification of financial reports and internal controls, (3) creating an independent regulatory body for the auditing profession, and (4) establishing new civil and criminal remedies for violations of federal securities laws. SOX and the SEC-related rules provide guidelines and opportunities for companies to engage in self-examination of their corporate governance, internal controls, financial reporting process, audit functions, and what it takes to be a good corporate citizen.

SOX should be regarded as a process that: (1) can prevent and control conflicts of interest (e.g., independence of directors, internal control reporting, prohibiting nonaudit services, regulation of the auditing profession, rules for security analyst(s) that provide opportunities and temptation to mislead investors); and (2) establishes incentives and penalties (e.g., CEO/CFO certification of financial reports and internal controls; auditors' report to the audit committee; loans to directors or executive officers; audit committees' responsibility for hiring, firing, compensating and overseeing auditors; penalties for violations of securities laws and securities fraud) to encourage directors, executives, auditors, security analysts, lawyers, and others involved with published financial reports to fulfill their professional responsibilities. It is also believed that the implementation of SOX has created a more conservative financial reporting and auditing environment.

There are primarily two types of certification requirements. The first type, certifications of periodic financial reports filed with the SEC after August 29, 2002, requires each officer (principal executive and financial) to affirm that the filed report is accurate and complete and that, accordingly, the financial statements and other financial information are, in all material respects, fairly presented. The second certification pertains to the company's "disclosure controls and procedures," which goes beyond the existing requirements of internal control. In every periodic report filed with the SEC for periods ending after August 29, 2002, CEOs, CFOs, and/or other certifying officers affirm that they:

1. Are responsible for establishing and maintaining disclosure controls and procedures.
2. Established the disclosure controls and procedures to ensure that material information is known to them.
3. Evaluated the effectiveness of the disclosure controls and procedures within 90 days prior to the filing date and presented in the field report their assessments on the effectiveness of these controls and procedures.
4. Informed the audit committee and auditors of all significant deficiencies in the design and/or operation of internal controls and any fraud by those who have a significant role in internal controls.
5. Indicated in the report whether there were any significant changes in the effectiveness of internal controls subsequent to the date of their most recent evaluation.

Like the Securities Acts of 1933 and 1934 as well as the Private Securities Litigation Reform Act of 1995, SOX was enacted to address corporate misconduct and the related business and accounting scandals that eroded investors' confidence in the capital markets. Unlike the previous acts, SOX contains sweeping measures dealing with corporate governance, financial reporting, conflicts of interest, corporate ethics, disclosure controls and procedures, new civil and criminal penalties, and the new regulatory structure for oversight of the accounting profession. In addition, unlike other related regulations, certain provisions of SOX were effective immediately; other provisions require the SEC to issue implementation rules to carry out the purposes of the Act. On June 27, 2002, the SEC issued an order that practically requires CEOs and CFOs of large public companies to certify, individually and personally, under oath, the accuracy and completeness of their company's most recent SEC filings (e.g., 10-K, 10-Q, and 8-K). Section 302 of the Act: (1) requires that the principal executive officers and the principal financial officers, or persons performing similar functions, to certify annual and quarterly reports to the SEC and (2) directs the SEC to publish rules pertaining to certification requirements within 30 days of enactment. On August 27, 2002, the SEC issued new rules pertaining to certification requirements of SOX. These rules apply to CEOs and CFOs of all publicly traded companies under the SEC jurisdiction who must personally certify that their filings with the SEC (quarterly, annual, and 8-K) are accurate and complete.

Implementation of the provisions of SOX should have positive effects for essentially everyone directly or indirectly associated with financial reports or participating in capital markets. Corporations can benefit from the implementation of SOX by improving corporate governance, quality and transparency of financial reports, and effectiveness of related audit functions, thus restoring public confidence in corporate America. Management can benefit by utilizing cheaper capital to improve profitability and thus offer higher bonuses, stock options, and other compensation plans. Investors, including shareholders and creditors, will benefit by being better able to assess the risk and return associated with their investment through more accurate and complete financial information. More reliable financial information disseminated to the capital markets can make the security markets more efficient and in turn can result in more effective allocation of the nation's resources and result in economic growth and prosperity.

In the wake of recent corporate and accounting scandals, public companies and their auditors have been under close scrutiny by legislators and regulators. SOX was intended to fundamentally change the relations between public corporations and their auditors by restricting the scope of nonaudit services that auditors can provide to their clients and establishing an independent board to oversee the auditing profession. These regulations are expected to foster a more independent and adversarial role for auditors of public companies. Although the ultimate responsibility for quality, reliability, and integrity of financial statements lies with management, auditors in many cases have failed in their role as financial watchdogs.

It has been argued that provisions of SOX have encouraged auditors to be more conservative. SOX was enacted in response to the revelations of business and accounting scandals and perceived audit ineffectiveness. One way that auditors can improve their effectiveness in compliance with the provisions of SOX is to lower their threshold for issuing modified audit reports, an action that encourages them to be more conservative primarily because they will be under more scrutiny by regulators and the newly established Public Company Accounting Oversight Board (PCAOB). A conservative auditor approach reduces the likelihood of failing to issue a modified report where appropriate.

The passage of SOX affects corporate governance and financial reporting for organizations of all sizes and types, particularly financial services firms for at least three reasons. First, SOX applies equally to and is intended to benefit investors of all public companies. Multinational and private companies and even not-for-profit organizations have benefited from some best practices of SOX in areas such as the majority of independent directors, mandatory audit committee, internal control reporting, whistleblowing programs, code of business conduct, and ethics. Some of the provisions of SOX that were not previously practiced by public companies and that are intended to benefit all companies are:

- Creating the PCAOB to oversee the audit of public companies and to improve the perceived ineffective self-regulatory environment of the auditing profession
- Improving corporate governance through more independent and vigilant boards of directors and responsible executives
- Enhancing the quality, reliability, transparency, and timeliness of financial disclosures through executive certifications of both financial statements and internal controls
- Prohibiting nine types of nonaudit services
- Regulating the conduct of auditors, legal counsel, and analysts and their potential conflicts of interest
- Increasing civil and criminal penalties for violations of security laws[13]

If SOX improves corporate governance, financial reporting, and audit functions, and increases criminal penalties for willful misrepresentation of financial information (which was previously unachievable through market mechanisms), it will improve investor confidence, decrease the cost of capital, increase firm value, and enhance benefits to all public companies, the investing public, and the capital markets.[14]

Second, the mandatory level of compliance with the provisions of SOX regarding corporate governance, accounting, and auditing practices is much higher than that of the pre-SOX era. The achievement of this mandatory level of governance is ensured by SEC-related implementation rules. Investor protection laws, including SOX, have provided corporations in the United States with the lowest cost of equity capital in the world.

Third, SOX imposes significant new compliance costs on public companies. The compliance costs vary depending on the firm's level of compliance with SOX provisions prior to its passage. The pre-SOX financial environment is characterized as an era of ample incentives and opportunities for engaging in conflicts of interest that caused financial manipulation. Nonetheless, the compliance cost of SOX should be weighed against its possible benefits of positive impacts on investor confidence, improved reliability of financial reports, and improved effectiveness of internal controls in preventing, detecting, and correcting financial statement fraud.

The debate over the possible impacts of new corporate governance reforms and their compliance costs on U.S. capital market global competitiveness centers around two key issues. The first issue is that SOX and its implementation costs have: (1) increased compliance costs of regulation and the potential for liability; (2) contributed significantly to the loss of global competitiveness of U.S. capital markets as the majority of recent IPOs have been listed on capital markets abroad; (3) encouraged U.S. companies to go private in order to reduce their regulatory compliance costs; and (4) reduced the corporate risk taking that produces economic growth. The other view is that SOX and its implementation rules have significantly improved the accountability of corporate America, the quality and reliability of its financial reporting, and the integrity and efficiency of its capital markets, and some of its best practices have been adopted globally. It is expected that companies that were actually closer to complying with SOX provisions and that have good compliance infrastructures experience higher net benefits than companies that were farther away from compliance due to the substantial costs in bringing their governance practices and financial reporting process to the level required by SOX. If SOX has aided in improving investor confidence in cost-effective compliance, we expect SOX to have positive effects on shareholder wealth. The extent of positive effects depends on the induced net benefit, which is the difference between the realized benefit of providing investor protection and the imposed compliance costs.

 ## DODD-FRANK ACT

Seven provisions of the Dodd-Frank Act of 2010 address corporate governance and executive compensation practices of financial services firms:

1. *Say on pay and say on golden parachutes.* Shareholders are empowered with a nonbinding vote on executive compensation at a minimum of every three years with the right to vote on the frequency of say on pay every one, two, or three years. Financial services firms should also disclose their executive compensation policies and practices in their proxy compensation discussion and analysis (CD&A) and related tables. Investment managers are required to disclose how they voted on executive compensation. Shareholders are now able to have a separate, nonbinding vote on all executive change-in-control arrangements (mergers and acquisitions). Best practices suggest an annual say on pay nonbinding vote by shareholders.

2. *Institutional investment managers votes.* Institutional investment managers are required to disclose at least annually how they voted on say on pay and its frequency and say on golden parachute votes.

3. *Mandatory clawback policies.* The Dodd-Frank Act requires that all U.S. public companies incorporate so-called clawback provisions into incentive compensation arrangements for executive officers. It expanded the provisions of SOX on clawback practices by requiring companies to implement and report on their policies and practices for recouping payments to current and former executives when published financial statements subsequently are restated (restatements of financial statements) caused by material noncompliance with financial reporting standards. The recouped pay is the exact amount paid based on misstated financial statements and is recoverable for the three-year preceding the restatement date. Dodd-Frank requires national securities exchanges and associations to revise their listing

standards to prohibit listings for any company that does not implement a clawback policy as required by the Act.

4. *Corporate governance disclosures.* The Dodd-Frank Act requires extended corporate governance disclosures pertaining to: (a) the link between pay and performance; (b) the rationale for choosing a combined or separate role of CEO and the chair of the board of directors (CEO duality); (c) policies and practices on the hedging of company securities; and (d) internal equity ratios (the ratio of the annual total compensation of the CEO and the median annual total compensation of all employees excluding the CEO). Companies should adopt the governance disclosures, particularly the relation between compensation and financial performance.

5. *Compensation committee and its advisors.* Members of the compensation committee must be independent. The committee must assess the independence of its advisors in the context of their fees and any other director affiliations with the company and other factors to be determined by the SEC.

6. *Executive compensation at financial services firms.* Financial firms must disclose their incentive-based arrangements designed to discourage inappropriate risk taken by management. Financial firms must not provide excessive compensation, fees, or benefits that encourage inappropriate risks.

7. *Elimination of broker discretionary vote.* Brokers may not vote without customer instruction on some governance issues, such as say on pay and say on golden parachute and board elections.

In summary, the Dodd-Frank Act influences corporate governance measures of public companies as well as certain private financial services firms. Some provisions of the Act regarding say on pay will be required at all public companies in their upcoming proxy season (2011), and other provisions need to be considered by the SEC in its future rules. Corporate governance provisions of the Act that will require immediate actions are the proxy access rules that became effective on November 15, 2010, and will apply to large companies for their 2011 proxy season, disclosure of whether directors or employees are allowed to hedge company stock, whistleblowing policies and procedures of offering cash incentives to reward and encourage whistleblowers who come forward to the SEC, and assessment of current and potential derivatives transactions by the board of directors. Provisions that require the SEC to adopt long-term implementation rules are compensation practices and disclosures and brokers' discretionary voting and advance voting instructions.

 ## CORPORATE GOVERNANCE FUNCTIONS

The seven essential corporate governance functions are oversight, managerial, compliance, internal audit, advisory, external audit, and monitoring.[15] Corporate governance participants fulfill their responsibility when their role in corporate governance is viewed as a value-added function and they are held accountable in discharging their responsibilities effectively. Three of these functions, however, are crucial to the protection of investor interests and the achievement of sustainable corporate performance. These functions are the oversight function assumed by the board of directors, the managerial function delegated to management, and the monitory function exercised by shareholders.

1. *Oversight function.* This function is granted to the board of directors with the fiduciary duty of overseeing the managerial function in the best interests of the company and its shareholders. The effectiveness of the oversight function depends on directors' independence, due process, authority, resources, composition, qualifications, and accountability. The board of directors should provide consultation and advice to management and oversee managerial performance while avoiding micromanaging. Corporate directors are elected by shareholders. As such, they are representatives of shareholders and guardians of their interests. The board of directors ultimately is responsible for the entity's business affairs, achievement of its objectives, and enforcement of its governance. The board may delegate its decision-making authority to the company's executives, but it is still responsible for running the company and accountable to shareholders. Prior to the corporate governance reforms, the board of directors was characterized as having personal and financial ties to management, as lacking independence and proper authority, resources and accountability, and as being ineffective in overseeing of managerial functions. After the corporate governance reforms, the board of directors still faces the challenges of striking a right balance among its independence, diversity, accountability, and effective oversight functions.

2. *Managerial function.* This function is given to management in order to run the company and manage its resources and operations. The effectiveness of the managerial function depends on the alignment of management's interests with those of shareholders. Management's primary responsibilities are to achieve operational efficiency, present high-quality financial reports, and ensure compliance with applicable laws, regulations, rules, and standards. The management team led by CEO and supported by CFO, controller, treasurer, and other senior executives is in the driver's seat of effectively managing the company for the benefit of its stakeholders. Prior to the governance reforms, management of some companies and particularly major financial institutions had been criticized for being greedy, incompetent, and focusing on short-term performance and self-dealing while receiving outrageous compensation. After the governance reforms, management is striving to meet the challenges of proper certification of both financial statements and internal controls, creating sustainable performance, effective assessment of risk, and compliance with all applicable laws, rules, regulations, standards, and norms.

3. *Compliance function.* This function is composed of a set of laws, regulations, rules, standards, and best practices developed by state and federal legislators, regulators, standard-setting bodies, and professional organizations to create a compliance framework for public companies in which to operate and achieve their goals. Policy makers, regulators, and standard setters are being criticized for being reactive rather than proactive in establishing and enforcing cost-effective, efficient, and scalable rules, regulations, and standards to prevent and detect financial scandals

and crises as well as to create an environment and culture of honesty, integrity, and accountability for corporations to earn sustainable performance. Regulators should develop effective and enforceable corporate governance rules and guidelines to hold companies accountable to their shareholders and other stakeholders.

4. *Internal audit function.* Internal auditors provide both assurance and consulting services to the company in the areas of operational efficiency, risk management, internal controls, financial reporting, and governance processes. Internal auditors are now assisting management in complying with Section 302 and 404 requirements of SOX by reviewing management's certifications on internal controls and financial statements and providing some type of assurance on the accuracy of those certifications. Internal auditors recently have been asked to provide audit opinions on their organization's governance measures, risk management process, and internal control systems for internal as well as regulatory purposes.

5. *Legal and financial advisory function.* Legal counsel provides legal advice and assists the company and its directors, officers, and employees with complying with applicable laws, regulations, rules, and other legal obligations and fiduciary duties. Financial advisors provide financial advice and planning to the company and its directors, officers, and employees. Legal and financial advisors assist companies in evaluating legal and financial consequences of business transactions. Financial analysts and investment bankers, by providing financial advice to corporations, their directors, officers, and other key personnel, and by following companies and making stock recommendations, can influence corporate governance.

6. *External audit function.* This function is performed by external auditors in expressing an opinion that financial statements truly and fairly represent, in all material respects, the company's financial position and the results of operations in conformity with generally accepted accounting principles. External auditors lend credibility to the company's financial reports and, thus, add value to its corporate governance through their integrated audits of both internal control over financial reporting (ICRF) and of financial statements. Auditors are also required to express an opinion on the effectiveness of the design and operation of ICRF in compliance with Section 404 of SOX. The external audit function is intended to lend credibility to financial reports and reduce the risk that financial reports are biased, misleading, inaccurate, and incomplete.

7. *Monitoring function.* This function is exercised by shareholders, particularly institutional shareholders, who are empowered to elect and, if warranted, remove directors. Shareholders can influence corporate governance through their proposals and nominations to the board of directors. Other stakeholders, such as creditors, employees, financial analysts, and investor activists, can also affect corporate policies and practices. Shareholders elect directors and directors appoint officers (CEO, CFO) to manage the company. By being attentive and engaged, shareholders and other stakeholders can play an important role in corporate governance. An effective monitoring function of corporate governance can be achieved by investors monitoring business and financial affairs of corporations or through direct participation by intermediaries, such as securities analysts, institutional investors, and investment bankers.

BOARD OF DIRECTORS AND ITS COMMITTEES

The board of directors, as a representative of the investors, is responsible for overseeing the company's financial reporting and internal control reporting to safeguard the company's assets and shareholders' investments. The board of directors and its audit committee should conduct at least an annual review of the reliability and quality of audited financial statements and the effectiveness of internal control over financial reporting (ICFR). In particular, the audit committee should report annually to shareholders its review of audited financial statements and ICFR.

Corporate boards, through vigilant oversight of the company's governance, financial reporting, and audit activities, can strengthen quality of financial reports. The board should oversee financial reports and ICFR to ensure that management has effectively carried out its financial and internal control reporting. This oversight function by the audit committee is particularly essential because controls are designed and performed by management, subject to management override, and often cannot be monitored objectively by management. The board should also oversee the entire financial reporting process to evaluate the fair and true presentation of financial statements and obtain an understanding of how management has met its ICRF responsibilities. Thus, the board of directors should have reasonable assurance that management and external auditors are meeting their financial reporting responsibilities.

PricewaterhouseCoopers (PwC) in its 2007 publication *Global Best Practices: Building Blocks of Effective Corporate Boards* discusses eight bonus attributes that assist directors in creating an appropriate balance between their role as compliance watchdogs and that of participating in managerial strategic planning, thus effectively overseeing the financial reporting process:[16]

1. *Establish an open and engaging boardroom culture.* Effective boards are those whose directors work well in teams, possess good listening and problem-solving skills, have the diverse experience to address relevant business and industry issues, and are independent-minded. Directors should advise management in strategic planning without micromanaging and oversee management operational, compliance, and reporting functions, including IFCR.
2. *Define clearly roles and responsibilities of the board to maximize its efforts in adding value.* To be effective, directors should focus their efforts on the most relevant and important issues that contribute to the achievement of sustainable performance in creating shareholder value.
3. *Provide the board with relevant and timely information.* The company's board should receive the right information in the right format and at the right time to fulfill its oversight function effectively. In particular, the audit committee of the board should receive adequate information about the company's internal control and financial reports, risk assessment, and compliance reports.
4. *Pay careful attention to strategic issues.* The board of directors should be proactively engaged with management in establishing strategic planning, setting strategic priorities, and executing these priorities in a timely manner.
5. *Design and implement a performance-based, transparent, and accountable executive pay scheme.* Executive compensation should be linked to the company's long-term

sustainable performance and aligned with benchmarks of the market and peer groups. It should also pass the commonsense test in the public eye and be fully transparent.

6. *Be proactive regarding the CEO succession process.* The board of directors should plan and be committed to the CEO succession process for replacement of a CEO in case of crisis and establish CEO selection criteria for a successor under normal circumstances.

7. *Monitor the strength of management talent.* The management team led by the CEO is crucial in ensuring the effectiveness of corporate governance and long-term sustainable shareholder value creation. The board of directors should ensure that the company has committed adequate resources to attract, train, and retain a competent and ethical management team.

8. *Oversee the assessment of the company's enterprise risk management system.* The board of directors should oversee the adequacy and effectiveness of the company's risk management system. Some companies have established a position of chief risk officer (CRO) to coordinate risk management activities among the board of directors, management, and key personnel. The CRO under the direct oversight of the board of directors and close cooperation with senior executives (CEO, CFO) should establish the strategy for the company's risk management, provide guidance for the proper implementation of the strategy, and review the implementation of the guidance.

The three mandatory board committees that listed companies are obliged to form are the audit, compensation, and nominating/governance committees. The audit committee is responsible for protecting investors by overseeing internal controls, financial statement risk assessment, and external and internal auditor activities. The compensation committee has the responsibility of evaluating executive and director performance and establishing top management compensation and benefit programs. The nominating/governance committee usually is responsible for identifying, evaluating, and nominating new directors for the board, renominating existing directors, and facilitating the election of new directors by shareholders. These three mandatory board committees should be composed of at least three independent directors. The audit committee roles and responsibilities are examined in the next section.

The primary functions of the *compensation* and *nominating* committees are to: (1) review and recommend to the board compensation and equity plans, policies, and programs; approve executive officer compensation; and prepare the annual report on executive compensation and the CD&A required to be included in the company's proxy statement; (2) assess the appropriate levels of risk within the corporation's compensation policies and practices; and (3) review and recommend to the board the nominees for election as directors of the company and to review related board development issues, including succession planning and evaluation.

The purposes of the *compensation committee* are to: (1) determine and approve the compensation of the company's CEO and other executive officers; (2) approve, or recommend to the board that it approve, the company's incentive compensation and equity-based plans; (3) assist the board in its oversight of the development, implementation, and effectiveness of the company's policies and strategies relating to its human capital management function, including but not limited to those policies and strategies regarding recruiting, retention, career development and progression, management succession, diversity, and employment practices; and (4) prepare any report on executive compensation required by the rules and regulations of the SEC.

The role of the *nominating committee* is to recommend nominees to the board to fill current and anticipated vacancies of any board position. The nominating committee shall be comprised solely of three independent directors. The purposes of the nominating committee are to: (1) identify qualified individuals to become members of the board of directors; (2) recommend the director nominees to the board to be presented for election at each annual meeting of stockholders; (3) develop, review, evaluate, and recommend for approval to the board corporate governance practices and principles; and (4) provide oversight of the corporate governance affairs of the board.

AUDIT COMMITTEE ROLES AND RESPONSIBILITIES

A survey of audit committee members reveals that the primary responsibilities of audit committees are to understand the implications of significant transactions regarding financial reporting and internal controls.[17] Thus, review of the effectiveness of IFCR is an essential part of the audit committee roles and responsibilities. The audit committee should review the adequacy and effectiveness of overall internal control relevant to operation, financial, and compliance controls, not just ICFR, and report publicly that it has undertaken the review. The audit committee should review: (1) management's assessment of the effectiveness of ICFR; (2) the independent auditor's report on the effectiveness of ICFR; and (3) the independent auditor's report on fair presentation of financial statements.

Internal Controls

The audit committee should oversee the adequacy and effectiveness of the company's internal control structure to ensure: (1) the efficiency and effectiveness of operations; (2) the reliability of financial reporting; and (3) compliance with applicable laws and regulations. The committee's oversight of Section 404 on internal control is becoming more important as public companies are required to certify their ICFR. The audit committee should:

1. Know the senior executive who is directly responsible and ultimately accountable for Section 404 compliance.
2. Understand the process of establishing and maintaining adequate and effective internal control.
3. Understand procedures for assessing the effectiveness of both the design and the operation of ICFR.
4. Understand the proper documentation of compliance with Section 404.
5. Review management's report on the effectiveness of ICFR.

6. Review auditor reports expressing an opinion on management's assessment of the effectiveness of ICFR.
7. Evaluate the identified significant deficiencies and material weaknesses in internal control.
8. Be satisfied with management and auditor efforts and reports on ICFR.
9. Ensure that management has properly addressed the identified material weaknesses.

In February 2005, the American Institute of Certified Public Accountants (AICPA) issued a report titled "Management Override of Internal Controls: The Achilles' Heel of Fraud Prevention."[18] This report is part of an ongoing effort of the AICPA to provide guidance to audit committees to effectively oversee their company's internal controls and address the risk of management override of ICFR. The guidelines provided in the report were intended to assist audit committees to prevent, deter, and detect fraudulent financial reporting. Management is primarily responsible for the design and operation of adequate and effective ICFR. Thus, there is always the risk that management may override internal controls, which makes the otherwise effective internal controls inoperative. The audit committee should be aware of such a risk and address the likelihood of its occurrence in overseeing the company's financial reporting.

The AICPA report indicates that management may override internal control and engage in financial statement fraud by: (1) recording fictitious business transactions and events or altering the timing of recognition of legitimate transactions; (2) recording and reversing biased reserves through unjustifiable estimates and judgments; and (3) changing the records and terms of significant or unusual transactions.[19] The report offers several recommendations and actions that can be taken by audit committees to address the risk of management override of ICFR.

The suggested actions for addressing and assessing financial statements fraud risk caused by management override of internal controls are:

1. Exercising an appropriate level of skepticism.
2. Strengthening the audit committee's understanding and knowledge of the company's business and industry to identify and assess business and financial risks that increase the likelihood of financial statement fraud.
3. Brainstorming and open discussion among members of the audit committee about the potential for fraud, including identification of events and transactions that are most likely to be susceptible to fraud, management motivations to engage in fraud, opportunities provided to management to override internal control or perpetuate fraud, and corporate culture and environment that enable management to rationalize the commission of fraud.
4. Establishing and implementing the business code of conduct including an appropriate tone at the top of promoting ethical behavior and legal conduct throughout the company.
5. Cultivating a vigorous whistleblower program including a telephone hotline to receive tips regarding fraud and concerns pertaining to accounting and internal controls from employees, suppliers, customers, and others.

6. Establishing a broad information and feedback network that extends beyond senior management and requires the audit committee to communicate with the internal auditor, independent auditors, compensation committee, and key employees regarding the likelihood of occurrence of fraud and how to prevent and detect fraud.[20]

The audit committee is responsible for addressing internal control activities and issues and asking these questions:

1. What are the internal control priorities?
2. Are there adequate internal control investments?
3. Are internal control resources properly allocated?
4. Is the company getting the right return for its investment in internal control?
5. Are entity-level controls adequate and effective?
6. Are process-level controls adequate and effective?
7. Have management and the independent auditor coordinated their plans to implement the requirements of the SEC's Interpretive Guidance and PCAOB Auditing Standard No. 5?
8. Are the design and operation of ICFR effective?
9. Are the design and operation of internal control over operational performance effective?
10. Are the design and operation of internal control over compliance functions effective?
11. Is the management report on ICFR appropriate?
12. Is the independent auditor's report on ICFR appropriate?
13. What are the causes and effects of reported material weaknesses in ICFR?
14. What, if any, remediating actions have been taken or are planned by management to correct reported material weaknesses?
15. Has the independent auditor issued a report on management corrections of the reported material weaknesses?
16. What are the effects of internal control significant deficiencies and material weaknesses on potential misstatements in financial statements?

Financial Reporting

The audit committee should oversee the financial reporting process by reviewing annual and quarterly financial statements, including: (1) management discussion and analysis; (2) accounting principles, practices, estimates, and reserves; and (3) independent auditors' suggestions, comments, and adjusting and clarification entries. The committee is responsible for overseeing the integrity, reliability, quality, and transparency of the company's financial disclosures. In the post-SOX period, the audit committee should prepare and submit a formal annual report to the shareholders stating that:

1. Financial standards prepared in accordance with generally accepted accounting principles are included in the annual report on Form 10-K or Form 10-KSB.

2. The committee has adopted a charter and has satisfied its oversight responsibilities as specified in the proxy statement.
3. The committee has reviewed the audited financial statements with management.
4. The committee discussed with the independent auditor those matters required to be communicated to the committee in accordance with generally accepted auditing standards.
5. The committee received the independent disclosures from the independent auditor and discussed the matters relevant to auditor independence.
6. The committee discussed with management and the independent auditor their reports on ICFR.

Audit Activities

The audit committee is responsible for overseeing both internal and external audit activities. The committee has the direct responsibility for hiring, compensating, and firing the company's independent auditor and chief audit executive (CAE, the head of the internal audit department). Sections 201 and 202 of SOX require the company's audit committee to preapprove all audit and permissible nonaudit services. The preapproval of permissible nonaudit services may be delegated to a member of the audit committee who must present preapproved nonaudit services to the full committee in its regular meeting. Thus, the audit committee must establish preapproval policies and procedures to: (1) increase the committee's knowledge and understanding of all permissible nonaudit services; (2) evaluate the qualifications of providers of preapproved nonaudit services; and (3) select the best provider considering reinforcement of auditor independence from management. Although SOX and SEC-related implementation rules permit certain tax services to be performed by the company's independent auditor contemporaneously with audit services, the PCAOB in its *Ethics and Independence Rule 3523* limits the performance of a number of tax services, such as tax shelters. Both the independent auditor and the CAE ultimately should be held accountable to the audit committee.

The audit committee should receive and review reports of the independent auditors on financial statements and ICFR. The committee should also receive and review significant internal audit reports. On July 24, 2007, the PCAOB proposed its new *Ethics and Independence Rule 3526* concerning communications with audit committees and an amendment to its existing tax services rule along with an implementation schedule for the tax services rule.[21]

The PCAOB has approved a new rule prohibiting audit firms from allowing lower-level employees to conduct final reviews of clients' financials before releasing opinions. Under the new Auditing Standard No. 7, such reviews—which the PCAOB officially calls "engagement quality reviews" but often are referred to as concurring reviews—are expected to be done by a partner or other high-level auditor who has not worked on the audit under review. PCAOB inspectors have found some reviews to be ineffective because reviewers lacked expertise and experience or because they were conducted at an improper time during the audit process. The new rule allows smaller firms to use partners from other firms for the evaluations.

The PCAOB has adopted an amendment to the inspection frequency requirements of Rule 4003 that will give the PCAOB the ability to postpone, for up to three years, the first inspection of any foreign-registered public accounting firms that the PCAOB is otherwise required to be conducted before the end of 2009 and that was in a jurisdiction where the PCAOB had not conducted an inspection before 2009.[22] The PCAOB also announced that it will implement certain transparency measures related to its international inspections program. The amendment to Rule 4003 will take effect upon approval by the SEC.

The proposed Rule 3526 would require independent auditors to communicate to the company's audit committee any relationships between the audit firms and the company that may reasonably be thought to bear on auditor independence. This communication would be required both before the auditor accepts a new engagement and annually for continuing engagements.

 ## EXECUTIVE COMPENSATION

Executive compensation decisions have received considerable attention after the Enron and other financial scandals. Reported financial scandals and crises have raised serious concerns regarding the reasonableness of executive compensation. The question of how executives should be compensated, particularly after reported financial scandals and congressional responses, has also received great attention. There are commonly two ways to determine executive compensation. The first method is performance-based compensation, suggesting that companies use cash compensation (salary and bonus) to reward executives for past performance. The second method is pay-for-performance compensation, where companies attempt to promote future performance by offering stock options (noncash compensation) to optimize executives' equity incentives. The use of stock-based executive compensation has increased substantially during the past two decades, to align executive incentives with the shareholders' goal of increasing firm value.

Several provisions of SOX directly or indirectly affect executive compensation packages. These provisions are: (1) prohibition of personal loans to directors and executives (Section 404); (2) reporting insider trading (Section 403); (3) insider trading during pension fund blackout periods; and (4) forfeiture of certain bonuses and profits. SOX is also intended to make directors and executives more vigilant and due diligent, which may increase executives' liability (e.g., executive certification of financial statements and internal controls). Any increase in executives' liabilities should affect their compensation as well. Executive compensation is defined as the total compensation including salary, bonus, value of stock options, restricted stock, long-term incentive pay, and other compensation paid to CEOs and other top executives.

The Dodd-Frank Act requires more transparency and disclosures of executive compensation in many ways, including shareholders' nonbinding or advisory votes on say on pay and say on golden parachutes that give payments to executives associated with mergers and acquisitions and major asset transactions. Companies also are required to disclose: (1) the relationship between senior executives' compensation and the company's financial performance in terms of graphs and charts; (2) the ratio of CEO compensation to the median total for employee compensation excluding the CEO compensation; and (3) whether employees or directors are allowed to hedge against a decrease in value of options included in their compensation scheme.

The Dodd-Frank Act requires that all U.S. public companies incorporate clawback provisions into incentive compensation arrangements for executive officers. It expanded the provisions of SOX on clawback practices by requiring companies to implement and report on their policies and practices for recouping payments to current and former executives when published financial statements subsequently are restated (restatements of financial statements) caused by material noncompliance with financial reporting standards. The recouped pay is the extra amount paid based on misstated financial statements and is recoverable for the three-year period preceding the restatement date. Dodd-Frank requires national securities exchanges and associations to revise their listing standards to prohibit listings for any company that does not implement a clawback policy as required by the Act.

The federal securities laws require clear, concise and understandable disclosure about compensation paid to CEOs, CFOs, and certainly other high-ranking executive officers of public companies. Several types of documents that a company files with the SEC include information about the company's executive compensation policies and practices. Large financial institutions should ensure that their compensation frameworks are consistent with their long-term goals and with prudent risk taking. Boards of directors of financial institutions should set clear lines of responsibility and accountability throughout their organizations to ensure that the design and operation of their remuneration system supports the firms' goals, including their overall risk tolerance. Shareholders may have a role in this process. Boards should also ensure that there are appropriate mechanisms for monitoring remuneration schemes. Compensation practices at financial institutions are regarded as one factor among many that contributed to the financial crisis. For instance, bonus payments that may be tied to short-term profits without adequate regard to the longer-term risks they impose on their firms and this misalignment of incentives amplify the risk taking that may severely threaten the global financial system. Financial institutions should have clear internal incentives to promote stability, and action needs to be taken, through voluntary effort or regulatory action, to avoid compensation schemes that reward excessive short-term returns or risk taking.

In December 2009, the SEC amended Items 401, 402, and 407 of Regulation S-K to elicit enhanced disclosures regarding risk, compensation, and corporate governance matters. In particular, the new rules require disclosure about:

1. The relationship of a company's compensation policies and practices to risk management
2. The background and qualifications of directors and director nominees
3. How the board (or its nominating committee) considers diversity when identifying director candidates
4. Board leadership structure (e.g., one person serving as both the chair of the board and the CEO versus split roles)
5. The board's role in risk oversight

6. Revised reporting of stock and option awards to company executives and directors in the summary compensation table
7. Potential conflicts of interests of compensation consultants

In summary, one of the important contributing factors to the financial crisis was excessive risk taking by executives of financial services firms. Dodd-Frank addresses excessive risk taking that drives from executive incentives. The two overriding sources of excessive risk-taking incentives are executives' keen focus on achieving short-term targets and their main efforts and concern to enhance shareholder value at the expense of other contributors of capital, including bank customers and lenders. Some of the important aspects of executive compensation that are not adequately addressed in Dodd-Frank are: (1) selection of peer group companies for determining executive pay benchmarks by the compensation committee; (2) continuous assessment of such benchmarks and their link to long-term performance; and (3) requirements for setting a minimum restricted stock ownership level and holding periods.

 CONCLUSION

The demand for and interest in corporate governance has increased significantly in the post-SOX era. Corporate governance has transformed from a compliance process to a business strategic imperative. The global overreach of SOX underscores the need for convergence in corporate governance reforms. More emphasis on national regulations is not relevant to emerging global investment, capital markets, or the economy. The Dodd-Frank Act is intended to improve corporate governance effectiveness and disclosures of financial services firms in many areas, including shareholders' nonbinding or advisory vote on say on pay and say on golden parachutes that give payments to executives associated with mergers and acquisitions and major asset transactions. Effective corporate governance should address and influence both corporate culture and control structure. Corporate culture should create an environment that sets an appropriate tone at the top that promotes ethical behavior and demands doing the right thing always. Corporate culture provides incentives for everyone in the company, from directors to officers and employees, to act competently and ethically. An effective control structure should eliminate opportunities for individuals to engage in questionable, unethical, and fraudulent activities.

 NOTES

1. Much of this chapter is extracted from the introductory chapter of Zabihollah Rezaee, *Corporate Governance and Ethics* (Hoboken, NJ: John Wiley & Sons, 2008).
2. Keynote address by Alexander Schaub, director-general of DG Internal Markets and Services, European Commission, at Transatlantic Corporate Governance Dialogue event organized by the European Corporate Governance Institute and the American Law Institute, September 27, 2005. Available at: www.tcgd.org/2005/13_schaub_keynote.php.

3. Zabihollah Rezaee, *Corporate Governance Post Sarbanes-Oxley: Regulations, Requirements, and Integrated Processes* (Hoboken, NJ: John Wiley & Sons, 2007).

4. Dodd-Frank Wall Street Reform and Consumer Protection Act of 2010, Pub. L. 111-203.

5. Basel Committee on Banking Supervision, "Principles for Enhancing Corporate Governance," June, 2010, Bank for International Settlements. Available at: www.bis.org/publ/bcbs168.pdf.

6. H. Paulson, Remarks on the Competitiveness of U.S. Capital Markets, Economic Club of New York, November 20, 2006. Available at: www.ustreas.gov/press/releases/hp174.htm.

7. J. C. Coffee, Jr., "A Theory of Corporate Scandals: Why the USA and Europe Differ," *Oxford Review of Economic Policy* 21, No. 2 (2005.): 198–211.

8. R. LaPorta, F. Lopez-de-Silanes, A. Shleifer, and R. Vishny, "Legal Determinants of External Finance," *Journal of Finance* 52 (1997): 1131–1150.

9. Ibid.

10. Ibid.

11. Rezaee, *Corporate Governance Post Sarbanes-Oxley*.

12. Sarbanes-Oxley Act of 2002, Public Company Accounting Reform and Investor Protection Act. Available at: www.whitehouse.gov/infocus/corporateresponsibility.

13. P. K. Jain, and Z. Rezaee, "The Sarbanes-Oxley Act of 2002 and Capital Market Behavior: Early Evidence," *Contemporary Accounting Research* 23, No. 3 (2006): 629–654.

14. Ibid.

15. Rezaee, *Corporate Governance Post Sarbanes-Oxley*.

16. PricewaterhouseCoopers, *Global Best Practices: Building Blocks of Effective Corporate Boards*, September 2007. Available at: www.globalbestpractices.com.

17. Ernst & Young, "Audit Committee Survey and Industry Insights—Executive Summary," Audit Committee Perspectives, 2006.

18. American Institute of Certified Public Accountants, "Management Override of Internal Controls: The Achilles' Heel of Fraud Prevention," February 2005. Available at: www.aicpa.org/ForThePublic/AuditCommitteeEffectiveness/AuditCommitteeBrief/DownloadableDocuments/management%20override%20achilles_heel.pdf.

19. Ibid.

20. Ibid.

21. Public Company Accounting Oversight Board, "Board Proposes New Ethics and Independence Rule Concerning Communications with Audit Committees and an Amendment to Its Existing Tax Services Rule and Adjusts Implementation Schedule for Tax Services Rule," July 24, 2007. Available at: www.iasplus.com/usa/pcaob/0707ethicsrulepr.pdf.

22. http://pcaobus.org/Rules/PCAOBRules/Pages/Section_4.aspx

The Foundation: Financial Institutions, Valuations, Mergers, Acquisitions, and Regulatory and Accounting Environment

CHAPTER FOUR

Overview of the Valuation Process

 INTRODUCTION

Business valuation is a specialized field with a variety of valuation standards, statutory guidelines, case laws, and techniques offering valuation services for a variety of purposes. Traditionally, a business value (e.g., selling price) is determined based on the bargaining power of negotiation between the buyer and the seller. Today's business climate is made up of the boards of directors, executives, investors, suppliers, customers, government, and employees who are looking for customized valuation services. Businesses have built infrastructures that not only deliver timely, relevant, reliable, and useful information but also consist of networks of specialists who can provide critical assistance and advice to constantly changing situations. The appraisers can play an important role and be a key member of this team.

The business valuation market has grown at a steady pace and will continue to grow as long as the demand for business valuation services increases, due to factors such as: (1) increasing merger and acquisition (M&A) activities in all industries, especially financial services; (2) high-volume creation of executive and employee stock ownership plans; (3) enhanced financing opportunities for individuals and businesses; and (4) litigation involving shareholder disputes, small businesses, taxation issues, business damages, and divorces. A number of professionals and individuals, including academics, accountants, attorneys, bankers, business brokers, economists, financial analysts, and real estate appraisers, can perform a variety of valuation services for their clients. An appraiser is defined in this book as a person or firm that has expertise in providing valuation services based on relevant and reliable information, standards, methodology, knowledge, integrity, and objectivity.

Appraisers provide value-added advice, assistance, or services to their clients. Appraisers are those experts with adequate training, experience, proficiency, and knowledge about valuation concepts, standards, and techniques as well as reporting and documentation requirements. Appraisers should have both didactic and technical understanding and knowledge of tax, accounting, financial, theory, and valuation methods. Appraisers should possess both appraisal and industry qualifications to provide a credible valuation opinion. Appraisers are typically members of one or more valuation professional organizations, such as the American Society of Appraisers (ASA), Institute of Business Appraisers (IBA), American Institute of Certified Public Accountants (AICPA), National Association of Certified Valuation Analysts (NACVA), or other appraisal organizations that are required to observe and comply with the Business Valuation Standards, the Principles of Appraisal Practice, and Code of Ethics of the American Society of Appraisers.

Appraisers often possess professional valuation certification and designation and prepare their valuation reports in accordance with the requirements of their professional affiliations, such as the Uniform Standards of Professional Appraisal Practice issued by the Appraisal Foundation. The current demand for and interest in business valuation services have encouraged professional organizations to offer a vast line of business valuation tools and methodologies to their members. Valuation profession organizations offer certification, conferences, publications, continuing professional education self-study, and software programs to their members in order to provide a framework, foundation, and continuing education in business valuation.

VALUATION SERVICES

Valuation services are becoming an interesting, profitable, and exciting market niche for appraisers. The types of valuation services, their purposes, and related valuation standards are summarized in Exhibit 4.1. The four basic standards of value commonly used in the valuation process are fair market value, fair value, investment value, and intrinsic value. These and other valuation standards are described thoroughly in Chapter 7. Fair market value is the most commonly used standard of value, especially for estate, gift, or marital disputes valuation purposes. "Fair market value" is defined in Revenue Ruling 59-60 as what a willing buyer would pay a willing seller at a specific date based on the best-educated judgment using all the knowledge available on that date. Fair value is defined statutorily, applies to certain specific transactions, such as shareholders' disputes, and is an estimate of the price that would have been realized by selling an asset under normal business conditions.

More specifically, "fair value" is the amount at which an asset could be bought or sold or a liability could be incurred or settled in the normal course of business between willing parties. "Investment value" is the strategic value to the specific group of investors and is the specific value assigned to goods or services by this group of investors based on investment requirements. "Intrinsic value" is the fundamental or theoretical value, often determined based on the discounted value of future operating cash flows.

EXHIBIT 4.1 Valuation Services, Purposes, and Standards

Valuation Services	Purposes	Standards
Ad valorem taxes	To establish the value of property used in a trade or business for tax purposes	Fair market value
Allocation of purchase price	To support uniform allocation of the total purchase price to the component parts for tax purposes based on an appraisal of the underlying assets	Fair market value
Buy-sell agreements	To determine a value for a transaction between the partners or shareholders in the event of withdraws, death, disability, or retirement	Investment value (agreed-on value)
Charitable contributions	To establish the value of the gift that exceeds $10,000 to charity	Fair market value
Employee stock ownership plans (ESOPs)	To determine the price per share to support ESOP transactions with participants, plan contributions, and allocations within the ESOP	Intrinsic value (public price quotations if available)
Damages litigation	To estimate the amount of damage resulting from the disputed issues, such as breach of contract, lost business opportunities, and discrimination	Fair value
Eminent domain actions	To establish the value of the property seized by government	Fair value
Estate and gift taxes	To determine the value of a business interest for the purpose of the unified estate and gift tax credit	Fair market value
Financing	To establish the value for the business to obtain additional funds	Fair value
Incentive stock option considerations (ISOC)	To determine the price of the exercised stock option mostly for income tax purposes	Fair market value
Initial public offerings (IPOs)	To establish the price of the stock for the initial public offering purposes	Intrinsic value (pro forma estimate of earnings, market price of comparable stock)
Liquidation or reorganization of a business	To determine the value of distributed assets in the case of split-up or spin-off for financial reporting or tax purposes	Fair value
Marital dissolution	To establish value for asset and liability interests of a couple involved in a divorce case	Fair value
Mergers and acquisitions	To determine the value of both the target and acquirer entities involved in the business combination	Investment value/ Intrinsic value
Stockholder disputes	To establish the value for shares of dissenting shareholders	Fair value
Legal structure conversions of S-to-C corporation	To determine the value of business interest in the case of S-to-C corporation conversions	Fair value/Investment value

(Continued)

EXHIBIT 4.1 *(Continued)*

Valuation Services	Purposes	Standards
Casualty loss	To estimate the value of assets lost due to casualty	Fair value
Allocation of lump-sum assets	To allocate the cost of assets in a bulk purchase between depreciable and nondepreciable assets such as land and goodwill	Fair value

Valuation services as they pertain to financial institutions (banks) are typically performed for these reasons:

- At any time during the life of a business to determine the value of the institution
- M&A transactions or takeover deals
- Changes in ownership
- Selling part or the entire stock
- Giving all or a portion of the institution's stock as gifts
- Exercising stock option or warrant
- Establishing employee stock ownership plans
- Initial public offerings
- Damages litigation
- Valuation of assets donated to charitable organizations
- Valuation of assets lost due to casualty
- Allocation of the cost of assets in a bulk purchase between depreciable and nondepreciable assets, such as land and goodwill
- Financing

A number of factors, valuation standards, and valuation methodologies can be utilized in valuing a financial institution. Financial institutions may be valued differently for different purposes. Practically, the appraisal value depends on the purpose for which the institution is being assessed, not what the institution is worth in an appraisal. For example, in M&A deals, the value depends on what a potential acquirer is willing and able to pay for the target institution. This willing and able price is known in accounting, finance, and business literature as fair market value or simply fair value. The general public may confuse fair market value with fairness. Fair market value is not about fairness; rather, it is determined as of a specific date based on the price that a willing buyer would pay a willing seller, using all available relevant knowledge. In addition, the net income of the target institution and the price to earnings ratio of the potential acquirer's stock can play an important role in the valuation process.

 VALUATION PROFESSION

In contrast to the centuries-old preeminence of medicine, law, and engineering as professions, valuation services gained prominence as a profession only during the twentieth century. The evolution of the valuation profession is summarized by Trugman:[1]

- Prior to the 1920s, a business's selling prices were primarily a matter of negotiation between the buyer and the seller based on their horse-trading sense.
- During the 1920s, business valuation began changing when breweries and distilleries incurred substantial losses in the intangible value of their business. Thus, the Internal Revenue Service (IRS) issued Appeals and Review Memorandum (ARM) 34 suggesting consideration of the value of intangibles and goodwill for estate and gift tax purposes. Business specialists then started applying ARM 34 by adding the value of intangibles, including goodwill, to the tangible assets in establishing the total value of a business.
- In 1959, the IRS issued Revenue Ruling 59-60, which established basic guidelines for business appraisers by identifying eight factors to be considered in the valuation of closely held businesses for estate and gift tax purposes. Exhibit 4.2 discusses these eight factors, their description, and related court cases. The application of these factors for appraisers will be discussed later in this chapter. Revenue Ruling 65-192 extended the applicability of Revenue Ruling 59-60 to other business valuations.
- The IRS issued Revenue Ruling 68-609 in 1968, suggesting the use of a formula in determining the fair market value of intangible assets.
- During the 1970s and 1980s, the demand for business valuation expanded greatly due to a downward slide in the real estate market and economic losses suffered by banks and thrifts. This period was considered the period of the emergence and growth of professional appraisal organizations, such as the American Society of Appraisers, the Institute of Business Appraisers, and the Appraisal Foundation.
- In 1984, the Financial Institutions Reform, Recovery, and Enforcement Act (FIRREA) was enacted, which mandates the licensing and certification of real estate appraisers. Although the FIRREA was intended to affect only real estate appraisers, several states have expanded its applicability to cover other business valuations. Business valuation as a profession has evolved from simple valuation of intangible assets for estate and gift tax purposes under ARM 34 in 1920 to a complex and sophisticated valuation of megamergers of the 1990s and 2000s that promulgated standards and certifications (e.g., 2010 Developments in Privete Equity Transactions). Exhibit 4.3 shows organizations that have influenced the development of business valuation as a profession with prospect and prosperity.
- Congress as the source of appraisal standards and appraiser qualifications author-izes the Appraisal Foundation (AF). The AF has formed the Appraisal Standard Board (ASB), which has promulgated a set of Uniform Standards of Professional Appraisal Practice (USPAP). All real estate appraisers must comply with USPAP in accordance with FIRREA. Other organizations and agencies, such as state appraiser certification and licensing boards, appraisal services, appraisal trade associations, and federal, state, and local agencies, require compliance with USPAP. The ASB has issued a set of: (1) USPAP, which provide guidelines for real property, mass, business, and personal property appraisal and consulting; (2) statements that clarify, interpret, explain, and elaborate on appraisal standards; (3) advisory

opinions that offer advice and resolutions for appraisal issues; and (4) Uniform Commercial/Industrial Summary Appraisal Report (UCISAR) manuals, which guide appraisers in appraising existing income-producing and small, un-complicated income-producing properties. Exhibit 4.4 summarizes the content of the 2008–2009 USPAP. That USPAP, which is 370 pages long and is available at the Appraiser Foundation Web site, is discussed in depth throughout the book.

EXHIBIT 4.2   Revenue Ruling 59-60, Its Description, and Related Court Cases

Factor	Description	Court Cases
Nature of the business and history of the entity	Nature and history of an entity reveals its condition and past performance (e.g., stability, growth, diversification), which is very important in determining the degree of risk involved in the business.	*Estate of Victor P. Clarke* (35 TCM. 1482, 1976). Characteristics of the company, its products, markets, management, position in industry, book value, dividend-paying capacity, and earnings considered to be important in determining value.
Economic outlook in general and specific outlook for industry	Analysis of economic conditions and industry specifications and considerations (e.g., economic growth, interest rates, government regulations, market share) are very important in the valuation.	*Tallichet v. Commissioner* (33 TCM. 1133, 1974). Nature of competition considered as a factor in determining value.
Book value of stock and financial condition of the entity	Financial statements analysis (comparative analysis of balance sheets, ratio analysis) can be helpful in assessing book value and financial condition.	*McIntosh* (26 TCM 1164, 1967); *Turner* (23 TCM 952, 1964). Book value by itself is not relevant in determining fair market value of the stock. Book value, however, should serve as a basis if the result is to be anything more than a dignified guess.
Earnings capacity	Earnings capacity is a major factor in many valuations of closely held stock. Historical earnings records are often the most useful and reliable sources of assessing future earnings. Recurring earnings components should be given special attention in the valuation. The capitalization rate for earnings and dividends is key in determining the value.	*Knowles* (24 TEM 129, 1965); *Harrison* (17 TCM 776, 1958); *Huntsman* (66 TC 861, 1976); *Tebb* (27 TC 671); *Clarke* (35 TCM 1482, 1976). Significant considerations were given to recurring earnings capacity and prospects for future profits.
Dividend-paying capacity	Revenue ruling states that primary consideration should be given to dividend-paying capacity, not actual dividends paid in the valuation of closely held corporations. In a close corporation, dividends often are authorized based on the needs of	*C. D. Baker* (172 F. Supp. 833, 1959). Dividend-paying capacity was given considerable weight in determining value. The three factors considered important in determining value were earnings (50 percent weight), book value

(Continued)

EXHIBIT 4.2 *(Continued)*

	executives and/or shareholders (e.g., avoiding double taxation, executive compensation), which may not be a good measure of dividend capacity.	(25 percent weight), and dividend-paying capacity (25 percent weight).
Goodwill and other intangibles	Goodwill (excess of appraised value of assets over book value of assets) and other intangibles (patents, trademarks, and copyrights) should be considered in the business valuation.	*Richard M. Boe and Marglois Boe v. C.T.R.* (307 F.2d 339, 1962). Goodwill is an unidentifiable intangible asset that affects the earning entity.
Previous sales and size of block of stock to be valued	Previous sales of stock in a closely held corporation should be considered carefully to ensure that the sales were made at arm's length, not distress sales, which may not reflect fair market value. The size of the block of stock is also relevant because isolated sales in small amounts may not provide an accurate measure of value.	*White* (35 TCM 1726, 1976), *Levenson* (18 TCM 535, 1959); *DuPont* (19 TC 281, 1960); *Brown* (25 TCM 498, 1966); and *Thalheimer* (36 TCM 101, 1977). Prior sales that were based on "arm's length" were given much weight in these cases.
Market price of stocks or corporations engaged in a similar line of business	Value of unlisted stocks and securities is to be determined partly by market price of stocks of corporations engaged in a similar line of business. For example, a business in an expanding market should not be compared with one in a declining market.	*Tallichet v. Commissioner* (33 TCM 1133, 1974). Factors such as capital structure, credit status, depth of management, personnel experience, nature of competition, and maturity of the business were used in determining comparability.

 ## VALUATION OF THE BUSINESS

Valuing a business is a complex process that involves not only valuing tangible assets, such as furniture, fixture and equipment, and future cash flows, but also intangible assets, such as intellectual property, goodwill, and human capital. The accurate valuation requires extensive knowledge of the up-to-date standards as well as specific knowledge of the industry. Results of the business valuation may vary depending on the assumptions made and the choice of the standard. Several methods can be used for business valuation purposes: discounted cash flow, gross revenue multiplier, adjusted book value, capitalized adjusted earnings, and analysis of the comparables. Usually business valuation methods are classified into three categories: income approach, asset-based approach, and market approach. The use of the models is very case specific, thus they have to be supported by the adequate assumptions. The market approach is the most common for the business valuation process. For example, for the discounted cash flow model, the appropriate discount rate has to be chosen. A discount rate is calculated based on three categories: cost of equity, cost of debt, and cost of capital. To estimate the cost of capital, an appraiser needs an appropriate beta, which is a measure of volatility.

EXHIBIT 4.3 Organizations Influencing Business Valuation

Organization	Purpose	Certification, Publication, Standards
American Institute of Certified Public Accountants (AICPA) 1211 Avenue of the Americas New York, NY 10036-8775 Phone: (212) 596-6200 Fax: (212) 596-6213 Web: www.aicpa.org/members/div/mcs/abv.htm	The Management Consulting Services (MCS) Division of the AICPA issues Management Consulting Standards, which typically are applicable to all consulting engagements including business valuations. The AICPA Consulting Services Team also assists CPAs to develop specific consulting nontechnical core competencies to create specializations and certificates in educational achievement (CEA) programs including business valuation programs. In December 1999, the Accounting and Review Services Committee of the AICPA issued an exposure draft that would exempt financial statements included in written business valuations from the applicability of Statement on Standards for Accounting and Review Services (SSARS).	AICPA MCS Division's Business Valuation and Appraisal Subcommittee has been working on standards relevant to business valuations. In 1997, the AICPA developed the Accredited in Business Valuation (ABV) accreditation program. To earn the ABV designation a candidate must: Be a member in good standing of the AICPA and hold an unrevoked CPA certificate or license. Provide evidence of ten business valuation engagements. Take and pass a written examination. Meet CPE requirements of 60 hours and involvement in five business valuation engagements every three-year period.
American Society of Appraisers (ASA) 555 Herndon Parkway, Suite 125 Herndon, VA 20170 Phone: (703) 478-2228 Fax: (703) 742-8471 Web: www.appraisers.org	The ASA offers education and professional accreditation in many appraisal disciplines, including business valuation, real property, machinery and equipment, and personal property. The ASA through its Business Valuation Committee issued a set of business valuation standards. These standards provide guidance for implementation of business valuation approaches and methods and must be observed by members of ASA.	The ASA sponsors Accredited Senior Appraiser (ASA) and Accredited Member (AM) professional designations. To obtain the ASA or AM designation, candidates must: Have work experience in the discipline in which the designation is granted (two–five years of full-time equivalent experience). Pass the relevant examinations (both technical and ethics exams). Submit two appraisal reports that meet the examining committee's standards. These two levels of accreditation are granted based on the experience of the applicant. The ASA publishes a multidisciplinary appraisal Journal of Valuation and the Business Valuation Committee of the ASA publishes the quarterly Journal of Business Valuation Review.

(Continued)

EXHIBIT 4.3 *(Continued)*

The Appraisal Foundation (AF)
1029 Vermont Avenue, NW
Suite 900
Washington, DC 20005-3517
Phone: (202) 347-7722
Fax: (202) 347-7727
Web: www.appraisalfoundation.org

1. The AF consists of nine appraisal organizations and was established in 1987. The board of trustees of the AF consists of representatives of the sponsoring organizations plus 14 trustees-at-large.
2. The board of trustees appoints two independent boards of the Appraisal Standards Board (ASB) and the Appraisal Qualifications Board (AQB).

1. The Appraisal Standards Board has promulgated the Uniform Standards of Professional Appraisal Practice (USPAP). The content of the USPAP is summarized in Exhibit 4.4.
2. The USPAP Standards and the Statements of Appraisal Standards are mandatory for members of professional appraisal organizations that have adopted USPAP. Advisory opinions are, however, illustrative and offer advice, and therefore, are not mandatory.
3. The Appraisal Qualifications Board issues appraiser qualifications for different disciplines such as real estate, personal property, and business appraisers.

Association for Investment
Management and Research (AIMR)
560 Ray C. Hunt Drive, PO Box 3668
Charlottesville, VA 22903-0668
Phone: (804) 951-5499, (800) 247-8132
Fax: (804) 951-5262
Web: www.aimr.org
E-mail: info@aimr.org

1. The AIMR is not an appraisal organization; however, it does provide educational materials, conducts seminars, and publishes monographs on valuation services.

1. The AIMR sponsors a professional designation and Chartered Financial Analyst (CFA). The AIMR requires a minimum three-year program for passing examinations given annually for three consecutive years.
2. CFAs are well qualified to conduct the analysis of publicly traded securities, the management of investment portfolios, and valuation of companies in the case of mergers, acquisitions, and spin-offs.

Institute of Business
Appraisers (IBA)
PO Box 17410
Plantation, FL 33318
Phone: (954) 584-1144
Fax: (954) 584-1184
Web: www.instbusapp.org
E-mail: ibohg@instbusapp.org

1. The IBA offers seminars on business appraisal topics. It publishes a code of ethics and issues a set of business appraisal standards.
2. IBA standards are very comprehensive and fully embrace Uniform Standards of Professional Appraisal Practice (USPAR) and provide in-depth guidance for business appraisals.

1. The IBA grants the professional designation of Certified Business Appraiser (CBA). The CBA designation requires an examination and the approval of reports but no requirement for experience.

(Continued)

99

EXHIBIT 4.3 *(Continued)*

Organization	Purpose	Certification, Publication, Standards
National Association of Certified Valuation Analysts (NACVA) 1245 E. Brickyard Road, Suite 110 Salt Lake City, UT 84106 Phone: (801) 486-0600 Fax: (801) 486-7500 Web: www.nacva.com E-mail: nacva@nacva.com	1. The NACVA is a professional association providing business valuation and litigation consulting education and training support programs. 2. The NACVA offers a range of support services, including marketing tools, software, reference materials, and customized databases. 3. The NACVA assists its members to seize the opportunities providing valuation, litigation, and consulting services to the business community. 4. NACVA has issued a set of valuation standards.	1. NACVA currently offers three designations in the field of business valuation: Certified Valuation Analyst (CVA), Government Valuation Analyst (GVA), and Accredited Valuation Analyst (AVA). 2. To obtain a CVA designation, the practitioner should be a licensed CPA. To become a GVA, the candidate must be employed by a government agency and have a college degree. The AVA designation requires a business degree. All three designations require successful completion of a comprehensive exam
Canadian Institute of Chartered Business Valuation (CICBV) 277 Wellington Street, W., 5th Floor Toronto Ontario, Canada M5V3H2 Phone: (416) 204-3396 Fax: (416) 977-8585 Web: www.businessvaluators.com E-mail: admin@cicbv.ca	1. The CICBV was founded in 1971 and provides educational meetings and publishes a code of ethics and practice standards.	1. The CICBV sponsors the professional designation of Chartered Business Valuator (CBV). 2. The CBV designation requires candidates to successfully complete an examination and have either three years of full-time experience, five years of part-time experience, or two years of experience and a required course of study.
Employee Stock Ownership Plans (ESOP) Association 1726 M Street, NW, Suite 501 Washington, DC 20036 Phone: (202) 293-2971 Fax: (202) 293-7568 Web: www.the-esop-employer.org	1. The ESOP Association is an organization of companies that have ESOPs and those that provide professional advisory services to ESOP companies. The association has created the Valuation Advisory Committee composed of 25 members who meet twice a year to discuss issues concerning the valuation of ESOP shares.	1. The ESOP Association does not sponsor any certification or designation nor does it endorse business appraisers or any other specialists. It has not yet issued any valuation standards. 2. The ESOP Association has published a book titled *Valuing ESOP Shares* providing guidance for the valuation of ESOP shares of most closely held companies.

(Continued)

EXHIBIT 4.3 (Continued)

E-mail: esop@esopassociation.org
Internal Revenue Service (IRS)
1111 Constitution Avenue, NW
Washington, DC 20224
Phone: (202) 566-5000
Web: www.irs.gov

1. The IRS has issued a number of regulations and pronouncements (e.g., revenue rulings, revenue procedures, letter rulings, technical advice memorandums, and general counsel memorandums) on various tax matters, including the valuation of businesses, business interests, and related intangible assets. Although the IRS regulations and pronouncements are intended to provide valuation guidance for tax purposes, they often contain general valuation guidance that can be used for a variety of valuation purposes.

1. The most important IRS rulings pertaining to valuations discussed throughout this book are:

59-60: Provides guidance on minimum factors to consider for valuation of estate and gift taxes.

61-193: Modified Revenue Ruling 59–60 regarding separation of tangible and intangible assets.

66-49: Provides guidance for making appraisals of donated property for federal income tax purposes.

68-609: Suggests "formula approach" or excess earnings methods of appraisals for determining fair market value of intangible assets.

77-12: Suggests methods for allocating a lump-sum purchase price to inventories.

77-287: Covers marketability discounts related to restricted stock.

81-253: Describes allowance of minority discounts.

83-120: Discusses factors that should be considered in valuing common and preferred stock.

85-75: Describes the basis for determining depreciation deductions or income taxes on capital gains from a subsequent asset sale.

93-12: Allows appropriate minority discounts to be applied when minority interests of family members in a closely held corporation are valued.

EXHIBIT 4.4 Uniform Standards of Professional Appraisal Practice, 2008–2009 Edition

	Contents	Introduction
Standards and Standards Rules	Standard 1: Real Property Appraisal, Development	Preamble
	Standard 2: Real Property Appraisal, Reporting	Ethics Rule
	Standard 3: Appraisal Review, Development and Reporting	Competency Rule
	Standard 4: Real Property Appraisal, Consulting, Development	Departure Rule
	Standard 5: Real Property Appraisal, Consulting, Reporting	Jurisdictional Exception Rule
	Standard 6: Mass Appraisal, Development and Reporting	Supplemental Standard Rule
	Standard 7: Personal Property Appraisal, Development	
	Standard 8: Personal Property Appraisal, Reporting	
	Standard 9: Business Appraisal, Development	
	Standard 10: Business Appraisal, Reporting	
Statements on Appraisal Standards	SMT-1: Standard Rule 3-1(g) has been retired	Preamble
	First three elements apply to all the practices SMT-2: Discounted Cash Flow Analysis	Ethics Rule
	SMT-3: Retrospective Value Opinions	Competency Rule
	SMT-4: Prospective Value Opinions	Departure Rule
	SMT-5: Confidentiality Section of the Ethics Rule statement retired	Jurisdictional Exception Rule
	SMT-6: Reasonable Exposure Time in Real Property and Personal Property Market Value Opinions	Supplemental Standard Rule
	SMT-7: Permitted Departure from Specific Requirements for Real Property and Personal Property Appraisal Assignments—retired	
	SMT-8: Electronic Transmission of Reports—retired	
	SMT-9: Identification of the Client's Intended Use in Developing and Reporting Appraisal, Appraisal Review, or Consulting Assignment Opinions and Conclusions	
Advisory Opinions	AO-1: Sales History	Preamble
	Al four elements apply to Standards 1 through 10 AO-2: Inspection of Subject Property Real State	Ethics Rule
	AO-3: Update of Prior Appraisal	Competency Rule
	AO-4: Standards Rule 1-5(b)	Departure Rule
	AO-5: Assistance in the Preparation of an Appraisal retired; instead AO-31 assignments involving more than one appraiser	Jurisdictional Exception Rule
	AO-6: The Appraisal Review Function retired, substituted to Appraisal Review Assignment that includes the reviewer's own opinion of value	Supplemental Standard Rule

(Continued)

EXHIBIT 4.4 (*Continued*)

AO-7: Marketing Time Opinions

AO-8: Market Value vs. Fair Value in Real Property
Appraisals— retired

AO-9: The Appraisal of Real Property That May Be
Impacted by Environmental Contamination

AO-10: The Appraiser-Client Relationship—retired;
adequate information can be found at AO-25,
Clarification of the Client in a Federally Related
Transaction; AO-26, Readdressing (Transferring) a
Report to Another Party; and AO-27, Appraising the
Same Property for a New Client

AO-11: Content of the Appraisal Report Options of
Standards Rules 2-2 and 8-2

AO-12: Use of Appraisal Report Options of
Standards Rules 2-2 and 8-2

AO-13: Performing Evaluations of Real Property
Collateral to Conform with USPAP

AO-14: Appraisals for Subsidized Housing

AO-15: Using the Departure Rule in Developing a
Limited Appraisal—retired

AO-16: Fair Housing Laws and Appraisal Report
Content

AO-17: Appraisal of Real Estate Property with
Proposed Improvements

AO-18: Use of an Automated Valuation Model (AVM)

AO-19: Unacceptable Assignment Conditions in Real
Property Appraisal Assignments

Source: Uniform Standards of Professional Appraisal Practice, 2008–2009 Edition. USPAP is available
from the Appraisal Foundation Web site and online at: www.vanderwerffandassociates.com/Links%
20Page/2010-11_USPAP.pdf

Betas could be estimated based on comparable firm betas or on the same risk/return
category, but if the firm is not publicly traded and has unique features, a unique growth
pattern, or unique risk management applications, comparables might not be applicable.
The asset-based method, also known as the adjusted book value approach, is a more
straightforward business valuation method. The book value of assets must be adjusted to
fair value whenever applicable. But the value of the goodwill and other intangible assets
is hard to estimate sometimes, which is why the asset-based approach is not the best
choice for the going-concern business. It is used mostly when business is liquidated or as
a commonsense check to estimate the accuracy of the other methods findings. Market-
based estimation of the value of the business is based on the assumption that a firm
operates under the economic rationale of the competition. The guideline public
company method compares the business to the established public company. The
main metrics used are: stock price and earnings; earnings before interest and taxes;

or earnings before interest, taxes, depreciation, and amortization; operating cash flow; free cash flow; and economic value added.The public company chosen has to be very similar to the comparison subject in terms of product/services offered, growth prospects, earnings, and, most important, risks.

The valuation computation is determined by providing answers to three questions:

1. What is being valued?
2. Is the value assigned to the equity of the target company?
3. Is the target company being valued on a long-term basis or a short-term basis?

Business valuation is a challenges process which requires proper determination of the purpose and circumstances surrounding the business valuation and valuation strategies and methods. The most commonly used approaches for valuation are:

▪ Income
▪ Asset
▪ Market
▪ Discounted cash flow (DCF)

The income-based approach derives the fair market value of the business by multiplying the income generating stream with the target company times a discount or capitalization rate. There are three common methods under the income-based approach: discount or capitalization rates, capital asset pricing model (CAPM), and weighted average cost of capital.

The CAPM method includes the risk premium, risk-free rate, discount rate, and the beta. The beta measures the price risk volatility of an industry or an asset.

$$E(R_i) = R_f + \beta_i(E(R_m) - R_f)$$

where
$$R_f = \text{Risk-free rate}$$
$$R_m = \text{Expected market rate of return}$$
$$\beta = \text{Beta}$$
$$E(R_i) = \text{Expected return on stock i}$$
$$B_i = \text{Systemic risk of stock i}$$

However, the CAPM method does not cover every aspect of the market. According to the critics, beta is calculated from the volatility of prices of publicly traded companies, which will vary for private organizations because of the diversification of products, markets, access to credit markets, size, and so on.

The DCF often is used in the valuation process, primarily because it captures all of the elements important to valuation and assumes that investments add value when returns exceed the cost of capital. The DCF model: (1) discounts the future expected cash flows over a forecast period; (2) adds a terminal value to cover the period beyond the forecast period; (3) includes present values of excess cash, investment income, and other nonoperating assets; and (4) subtracts the fair market value of debt to determine the value of equity. These and other valuation approaches will be discussed thoroughly in the next chapters.

The bank valuation approach differs due to the specifics of the business. Deposit activities are the core of the banking business, and the government heavily regulates banking lending activities. Financial service firm value depends a lot on intangible assets, such as goodwill, brand, and human capital. Banks typically do not have high capital expenditures; thus they carry low depreciation values on their books. The definition of debt is also different for financial institutions. That is why appraisers believe that equity multipliers are much better ratios to measure the value of the bank. In banking valuation, it is common to use dividend payments as a measure of the free cash flow; thus the dividend discount model is an appropriate method for banking valuation.

 ## ATTRACTING VALUATION CLIENTS

Appraisers are constantly seeking new valuation clients or looking for ways to expand valuation services to existing clients. Today's competitive valuation environment dictates that every appraiser consider how best to market their valuation services. Appraisers can market their valuation services through target advertising, surveys of client needs, and identification of targeted industries and companies for unsolicited preliminary proposals. New clients can be obtained by these means:

- *Referrals from existing clients.* Referrals and recommendations from existing clients are not only the best source of obtaining new clients but also attest to the quality of valuation services.
- *References from other professionals, especially accountants, lawyers, bankers, and analysts.* This is the best method of establishing a network of professional contacts. Appraisers often work closely with accountants, certified public accountants (CPAs), lawyers, bankers, and analysts in providing comprehensive services to mutual clients. This coordination and cooperation can lead to valuable future references.
- *Online advertising.* In today's era of information technology, using the Internet or Web is the most effective and efficient method of marketing valuation services and obtaining new clients. Exhibit 4.5 shows a list of valuation services specialists found by using a keyword search for "valuation services" on the Internet.
- *Professional and social contacts with key business executives.* Becoming acquainted with key executives in the business community is a sure way of obtaining new clients. Business relationships fostered in community activities, at golf clubs, in voluntary organizations, or membership at the Chamber of Commerce often expand an appraiser's potential client base.
- *Mergers and acquisitions.* The potential for M&A often leads to the expansion of valuation services for most appraisers. Appraisers can establish M&A valuation and consulting services to assist their clients in the M&A process.

EXHIBIT 4.5 Valuation Services Organizations

Organization	Specialization	Address, Telephone, Web Site
American Valuation Group	Provides business valuation, economic analysis, and expert witness services for taxation, litigation, mergers and acquisitions, and condemnation	21860 Burbank Boulevard, Suite 110 Woodland Hills, CA 91367 Tel: 818-992-4917 Fax: 818-992-4925 www.ameri-val.com/
Baker-Meekins Company, Inc.	Business valuation analysts, consultants, and advisors	1404 Front Avenue Lutherville, MD 21093 Tel: 410-823-2600 Fax: 410-823-8455 www.bakermeekins.com/
Banister Financial, Inc.	Valuations of closely held companies, professional practices and family limited partnerships	1914 Brunswick Avenue, Suite 1-B Charlotte, NC 28207 Tel: 704-334-4932 Fax: 704-334-5770 www.businessvalue.com
Bear, Inc.	Provides a snapshot valuation of companies or small businesses by submitting a web form	865 Laurel Street San Carlos, CA 94070 Tel: 650-592-6041 Fax: 650-508-4410 www.bearval.com
Business Valuation Services	Provides a coordinated approach to business damages, valuation and litigation issues for privately held corporations	529 North Ferncreek Avenue, Suite A Orlando, FL 32803 Tel: 407-898-7099 Fax: 407-898-7095 www.valuationanalysis.com
CBIZ Valuation Group LLC	Provides business and business asset valuations for merger and acquisition, taxation, litigation, and management consulting purposes	3030 LBJ Freeway, Suite 1650 Dallas, TX 75234 Tel: 972-620-0400 Fax: 972-620-8650 www.bvs-inc.com
Columbia Financial Advisors	One of the top business valuation firms in the U.S. Also offering investment banking and research consulting services	650 Morgan Building 720 SW Washington Street Portland, Oregon 97205 Tel: 503-222-0562 Fax: 503-222-1380 www.cfai.com
Corporate Appraisal, Inc	Specializing in the valuation of closely-held businesses, partnerships, and proprietorships	10452 Fawns Way Eden Prairie, MN 55347 Tel: 612-829-5406 Fax: 612-829-7464 www.corpappraisal.com
Edward G. Detwiler & Associates	Valuations of high technology businesses in medical and scientific fields	1515 East Woodfield Road, Suite 730 Schaumburg, IL 60173 Tel: 847-995-9885 Fax: 847-995-9887 www.egdetwiler.com/
Equipment Appraisal Group, Inc.	Provides machinery and equipment appraisals following USPAP guidelines	PO Box 90255 San Antonio, TX 78209 Tel: 210-822-7473 Fax: 210-822-7144 www.eagi.com

(Continued)

EXHIBIT 4.5 *(Continued)*

Fowler Valuation Services, LC	Offers services for merger and acquisition, taxation, shareholder transactions, and provides litigation support	211 W. 7th Street, Suite 920 Austin, TX 78701 Tel: 512-476-8866 Fax: 512-476-4625 www.fowlervalue.com
Gordon Associates	Business valuation, damage analysis, and corporate financial consulting	One State Street, Suite 750 Boston, MA 02109 Tel: 617-227-2707 Fax: 617-227-7625 www.gordonassociates.com
Halas & Associates	Uses the HBVS appraisal system to determine the reasonable market value for any present or planned U.S. or offshore business	425 Rose Lawn Place Charlotte, NC 28211 Tel: 704-364-4440 Fax: 704-364-1494 www.halas.com
D. L. Heisey & Co, Inc.	Business valuation for purchases and sales, estates and gifts, litigation support, lost profits damages, and intellectual property matters	D.L. Heisey & Co, Inc. Parker, CO 80134 Tel: 303-840-2875 Fax: 303-840-2875 www.dlheisey.com
Institute of Business Appraisers (IBA)	IBA is a professional society devoted to the appraisal of closely-held businesses, and a pioneer in business appraisal education and accreditation	PO Box 17410 Plantation, FL 33318 Tel: 954-584-1144 Fax: 954-584-1184 www.instbusapp.org
Mentor Group, Inc.	Investment banking firm specializing in valuations and appraisals	777 E. Tahquitz Canyon Way, Suite 200 Palm Springs, CA 92262 Tel: 760-325-6411 Fax: 760-325-7260 www.mentorgroup.com
Mercer Capital	Provides independent business valuation services for ESOPs, litigation support, estate and gift tax, mergers and acquisitions, fairness opinions, corporate transactions, and research services	5860 Ridgeway Center Parkway, Suite 410 Memphis, TN 38120 Tel: 901-685-2120 Fax: 901-685-2199 www.bizval.com
Wharton Valuation Associates, Inc.	Provides valuation studies for manufacturing, distribution, financial, and service industries	PO Box 2042 Livingston, NJ 07039 Tel: 973-992-4979 Fax: 973-992-1128 www.whartonvaluation.com

■ *Advertising.* Advertising is one way of creating images for your quality and commitment to valuation services. Appraisers can highlight their areas of valuation expertise, qualifications, certification, and associations. Advertising not only brings new clients to the business but also creates a positive image of, and positive recognition for, appraisers.

- *Requests for proposals.* In this demanding environment for business valuation services, many organizations are shopping for valuation services or reassessing their current level of valuation services and fees. In a competitive environment, clients often shop for valuation services by testing the market to determine whether significant cost savings can be achieved by changing appraisers. Appraisers often are asked to submit proposals for potential new clients. An appraiser must be able to write an effective proposal that thoroughly explains the valuation services that can be provided and properly demonstrates understanding and knowledge of the client's business, industry, and potential problems. This written proposal typically should include an overview of the valuation services, particular areas of expertise, a description of the qualifications, designations of appraisers, types of valuation services, service fee structure, and billing requirements for the engagement. Exhibit 4.6 shows a more detailed description of the contents of a proposed package.

EXHIBIT 4.6   Proposal Package for a New Client

Overview of the Appraiser Team

This section provides an overview of the appraiser team, its members' expertise, qualifications, designations, achievements, and affiliations.

Valuation Service Capabilities

This section normally emphasizes the appraiser team's ability to provide a variety of valuation services, including mergers and acquisitions, estate and gift taxes, allocation of purchase price, and employee stock ownership plans. Included are descriptions of unique valuation capabilities of the team suitable for this particular client.

Valuation Approach

This section describes the appraiser team's overall valuation approach and standard of value that will be used. (Standards of value are defined and discussed in the next section.) The team should also use this opportunity to extol its computerized online valuation capabilities.

Timing and Fees

This section contains a detailed description of the valuation service fees and the method of determining the fee. The basis of billing is generally outlined and fees are allocated among various valuation services. The section also includes the preliminary valuation service schedule, including any plans and a target date for completion of the agreed-on valuation services.

Qualifications and Resumes of the Valuation Engagement Team

This section contains a description of the qualifications of the members of the valuation engagement team, their education, experience, designations, certifications, and unique expertise in relation to valuation of the client's industry. This narrative description should be followed by a formal resume of all members of the valuation engagement team.

Client List and References

This section includes a list of all local office clients and selected individual references from the client list. Any industry references on a regional or national basis are also included to emphasize the firm's overall qualification for valuation services in that industry.

(Continued)

EXHIBIT 4.6 *(Continued)*

Publications and Periodicals

Any publications or periodicals, including manuals and membership rosters, published by the appraiser organization, either online or in hard copy, should be described here.

Web Site

The Web site of the appraiser team or organization is a focal point and the most effective means of introducing, marketing, and advertising the appraiser valuation capabilities, services, expertise, knowledge, and qualifications.

- *Direct proposals to a targeted industry or company.* Many valuation appraisers or organizations establish strategies to target a specific industry or a company. For example, an appraiser wishing to become known as an M&A specialist might target all potential business combination companies as clients. This targeted approach includes building key contacts with the important decision makers in the organization, developing an understanding of the business and industry, and promoting a positive image.
- *Referrals by other valuation appraisers or organizations.* As surprising as this may sound, referrals by other valuation appraisers or organizations are the most effective method of obtaining new clients. For example, when an appraiser is providing valuation services to a growing client with business throughout the nation, client needs may exceed the appraiser's service ability. The appraiser might refer the client's local valuation services to a local valuation appraiser. Thus, it is important to cooperate and develop relationships with peers throughout the nation and even internationally.
- *Other professional contacts.* Contact through other professional organizations, such as CPA firms, banks, attorneys, and valuation and appraiser associations, can be an effective way of getting referrals. Thus, membership in these professional organizations and associations would be very helpful in attracting more clients.

 ## ACCEPTING A CLIENT

Within the valuation profession, there is considerable competition among appraisers. Although selling valuation services is important, appraisers do not want to accept all potential clients. Association with the wrong valuation client can be detrimental to an appraiser's financial situation as well as reputation. Clients with financial difficulties or lack of management integrity may not be able to pay the valuation fee or may create additional risk for the appraiser. An appraiser is not obligated to perform valuation services for every client that requests it. Before accepting a new client, an appraiser should investigate the client to determine its acceptability. To the extent possible, the prospective client's standing in the business community, financial stability, and relations with its previous appraiser should be evaluated. Thus, a decision to accept new valuation clients or continue services to existing clients should not be taken lightly.

In summary, the appraiser should make a preliminary assessment of these factors and consider them when deciding to accept a new client or continuing with an existing client:

- The client's standing in the community
- Client management's integrity and reputation
- Any legal proceedings involving the client's organization
- The overall financial position of the client's organization
- The client's working relationships with the predecessor appraiser
- Client credit ratings and business risk assessment

These factors are, to some extent, interrelated. Several sources of information regarding management integrity, honesty, and trustworthiness are available to the appraiser, including correspondence with other professionals and predecessor appraisers' information in regulatory findings, news media, and interviews with management. The appraiser should be prepared to pursue many of the sources of information shown in Exhibit 4.7 if there are any indications that there may be problems with management integrity.

EXHIBIT 4.7 Sources of Information Regarding Management Integrity

Preliminary Interviews with Management

Such interviews can be very helpful in better understanding your client's valuation needs as well as management operating style and frankness in dealing with important issues affecting the valuation.

Communication with Predecessor Appraiser(s)

Information obtained directly through inquiries of predecessor appraisers regarding integrity and operating style of client's management and any disputes with the client over valuation fee or method of determining the fee can be very helpful to the successor appraiser in making acceptance decisions.

Communication with Other Professionals in the Business Community

Inquiries of lawyers, CPAs, and bankers known to the appraiser with whom the client has working relationships is a good way of obtaining knowledge about the client and its management.

News Media

Information about the client's organization and its management may be available online, or in financial journals or magazines or industry trade magazines.

Public Databases

Public databases on the Internet (e.g., Yahoo, and Google) can be searched to obtain sufficient information and knowledge about the client, its business, industry, and management. In addition, online databases, such as National Automated Accounting Research System (NAARS) and LEXIS/ NEXIS, can be searched to obtain sufficient information about the financial situation and other information, such as the existence of legal proceedings against the client's organization or key members of management.

Inquiries of Government Regulatory Agencies

Inquiries should be done when the potential client indicates any reason regarding pending actions against the client's organization or its management.

Hiring Private Investigation Firms

While the use of this method of obtaining information about the potential client may be rare, it can be very helpful when there are serious issues regarding the creditworthiness or the integrity of management.

Many appraisers have developed a checklist to assist them in determining whether to accept or continue with a valuation client. The checklist should include these factors:

- *Competency and capability to do the job.* Almost all appraisal organizations and associations (e.g., USPAP, AICPA, and ASA) have competency standards for members who perform valuation services.
- *Nature of the relationship between the appraiser and the client.* Validity and reliability of the appraiser's opinion, to a great extent, determines the degree of independence from the client. Thus, the appraiser or the appraisal firm should assess the impact of any previous or existing business or personal relationships with the client and consider the ability to express valuation opinions independently and without bias. The existence of such relationships, however, should be disclosed in the valuation report to enable potential readers or users of the report to make their own judgment about appraiser independence and possible impact on reliability and objectivity of opinions. In accordance with ethical standards of most appraisal professional organizations, the relationship between the appraiser and the client is confidential in nature. This confidential relationship requires that the appraiser disclose information about an appraisal assignment only to the client or to other parties with the client's permission unless demanded by court of law.
- *Purposes of the valuation.* The appraiser must understand the purpose of the valuation assignment in order to determine the standard of valuation being used, the valuation approach employed, the type of appraisal opinions furnished, and the intended use of the valuation report.
- *Form and extent of the valuation report.* The form and extent of the anticipated appraisal report plays an important role in the determination of the fees to be charged and the amount of time required to complete the assignment. Furthermore, the nature and amount of paperwork and documentation necessary to support the appraisal report helps the appraiser to assign personnel, budget staff time, and meet the time budget. The appraiser should ensure that the assignment meets the minimum documentation standards for appraisal reports set forth in USPAP and the Business Appraisal Standards.

 ## PRICING VALUATION SERVICES

Valuation appraisers should price their valuation services to support their continuous growth and to attract and retain competent personnel as well as to attract and retain valuation clients. There should be a link between the price of valuation services and sustainable valuation service performance. Competition within the valuation profession demands that valuation services be reasonably priced. Appraisers' professional qualifications and certifications can also influence their valuation prices. The two prevailing valuation certifications are Certified Valuation Analyst (CVA) and Accredited in Business Valuations (ABV). The CVA is sponsored by the National Association of Certified Valuation Analysts (www.nacva.com) and the ABV is sponsored by the

AICPA (www.aicpa.org). An appraiser can, on occasion, cut valuation prices to obtain a key client in an important industry, but services cannot routinely be priced at unprofitable levels.

 ## IMPORTANCE OF THE ENGAGEMENT LETTER

A clear understanding of the terms of the valuation engagement should exist between the client and the appraiser. It is good professional practice to confirm the terms of each engagement in an engagement letter, as illustrated in Exhibit 4.8. The form and

---

EXHIBIT 4.8 Sample Engagement Letter

Smith & Jones Associates
123 Courtside
Any City, NY 10011

Mr. John Clark
500 West Main Street
Any City, NY 10011

Dear Mr. Clark:

Thank you for meeting with us to discuss the requirements and terms of our forthcoming engagement. This will confirm our understanding of the arrangements for appraisal of the fair market value of a 100 percent, nonmarketable, controlling interest in the outstanding common stock of XYZ Company, Inc., a New York Corporation, held by Mr. John Clark, as of May 30, 2010, for gift tax purposes. Fair market value standard used in this engagement is defined as "value at which a willing seller and willing buyer, both being informed of the relevant facts about the business, could reasonably conduct a transaction, neither party acting under any compulsion to do so."

Client warrants that this appraisal report will be relied on for the use and the date indicated in this engagement. The appraisal will be subject to, at least, the following contingent and limiting conditions.

1. The appraiser needs prompt and free access to all related documents, materials, records, facilities, and/or client's personnel to effectively and efficiently perform the agreed-upon valuation services in a timely and professional manner. Lack of proper cooperation in this regard may result in withdrawal from the assignment and/or a delay of the completion date of the assignment.
2. Information, estimates, opinions, and evidence contained in this report are gathered from reliable sources. However, no independent verification of such evidence is performed by the appraiser.
3. Client warrants that the information and evidence provided to the appraiser is reliable and accurate to the best of the client's knowledge.
4. Contingent and limiting conditions may be required, and the client agrees that all conditions disclosed by the appraiser will be accepted and incorporated into the appraiser's report.

Our engagement will also include providing expert witness testimony as it may require. Client agrees that payment of all fees and expenses related to this service be paid prior to the performance of expert witness testimony. Client agrees to indemnify and hold the appraiser harmless against any and all liability, claim loss, cost, and expenses that the appraiser may incur as a result of providing expert witness testimony.

It is our intention to complete this assignment by the agreed-upon date (e.g., 120 days from the receipt of signed agreement and all requested documents). Our billings for the services set forth in

(Continued)

EXHIBIT 4.8 *(Continued)*

this engagement will be based upon our per diem rates for this type of work plus out-of-pocket expenses; billings will be rendered at the beginning of each month on an estimated basis and are payable upon receipt. This engagement includes only those valuation services specifically described in this letter, and appearance before judicial proceedings or government organizations such as the Internal Revenue Service, or other regulatory bodies, arising out of this engagement will be billed to you separately.

We look forward to providing the valuation services described in this letter as well as other valuation services agreed upon. The appraiser reserves the right to withdraw from this engagement at any time for reasonable cause. In the unlikely event that any differences concerning our services or fees should arise that are not resolved by mutual agreement, we reserve the right not to make a court appearance in this matter.

If you are in agreement with the terms of this letter, please sign one copy and return it for our files. We appreciate the opportunity to (continue to) work with you.

Sincerely,
Smith & Jones Associates
Robert E. Smith
Engagement Partner

The foregoing letter fully describes our understanding and is accepted by us.

May 30, 2011	Signature of John Clark
Date	John Clark

content of engagement letters may vary for different clients, but they generally should include:

- Clear identification of the client and their appraiser
- Precise specification of the valuation subject including the business interests or the legal interest being valued
- The objective or purpose of the valuation
- Reference to the standard of value that will be used or any applicable valuation professional standards
- An explanation of the nature and scope of the valuation and the appraiser's responsibility
- Date(s) of the valuation
- Form and type of the valuation report (e.g., written, oral)
- A statement regarding the intended use of the valuation report, including any assumptions and limitations of it
- The responsibilities of the client to provide valid and timely records and documentation necessary to complete the appraisal report
- The valuation fee or the method of determining the fee and any billing arrangement
- Method of dispute resolution
- A request for the client to confirm the terms and conditions of the engagement by signing and returning a copy of the letter to the appraiser
- The date of the engagement letter

PLANNING AN APPRAISAL ENGAGEMENT

The preliminary planning of an appraisal engagement consists of arranging a conference with client personnel, gaining knowledge of the client's business including legal structure and policies, and understanding the client's industry and economic conditions.

Conference with Client Personnel

Soon after acceptance of a valuation assignment, the appraiser should have conferences with key client personnel. The appraiser should meet with principal administrative, financial, operating officers, and executives to discuss matters expected to have a significant effect on the conduct of the valuation assignment and the appraiser's opinion.

Assistance of client personnel often is needed to obtain documents, records, evidence, and explanations of various matters. Thus, effective early conferences can establish a foundation for a good working relationship with all client personnel. Effective communication with top management is particularly important.

Knowledge of the Business

The appraiser's knowledge of the client's business and industry is very important in understanding the events, transactions, and practices that affect business valuation. The evidence-gathering part of the valuation assignment typically requires the appraiser to obtain knowledge of the client's business and the factors affecting its value. The knowledge of the client's business that the appraiser should obtain includes:

- *Organization structure.* In any business, the structure of the organization is important in specifying the tasks and responsibilities of its various components. The organization structure and operating style are influenced by roles, responsibilities and abilities of management, tax and legal issues, regulatory considerations, product diversification, and geographical location. In a large complex business, the organization structure takes the form of organization charts, charts of accounts, rules, office memos, manuals, contracts, and internal control structure, including control environment, communication, monitoring, and control activities and risk assessment.
- *Operations.* The appraiser should obtain an understanding of the client's operating characteristics, its legal structure, applicable laws, rules, and regulations as well as managerial policies and procedures. Operating characteristics consist of types of products and services, locations, and methods of production, distribution, and compensation. The appraiser should list brief operating characteristics of the client and other significant factors that have a bearing on valuation. To interpret the evidence gathered throughout the valuation properly, the appraiser must understand the client's business and the many factors that will have an influence on the client's operations. A review of legal documents is important for rational interpretation of the evidence gathered throughout the valuation assignment. The appraiser should review the corporate charter and bylaws or partnership

agreements, the corporate minute book, tax returns, regulatory requirements, and filing systems, and consider their implications for the valuation process. For example, the corporate charter includes information on the corporate structure, the authorized capital, and the power and rights granted to as well as responsibilities and restrictions placed on the corporation by state law. A partnership agreement includes similar information about the organization and operating requirements of a business organized as a partnership.

Legal Structure

The legal status of the business (e.g., partnership, corporation) plays an important role in the valuation engagement and can have a significant impact on valuation opinions. In the case of limited partnership or when earnings allocation among partners is different from allocation in the liquidation process, the value assigned to different groups or partners may not be the same. Thus, the appraiser should read the partnership agreement first to understand the partners' legal rights and privileges and then consider their implications for the valuation assignment.

Policies

Minutes of meetings of the corporate board of directors contain an official record of important information, economic events, transactions, and agreements that can have a significant impact on the valuation conclusions. The declaration of dividends, capital expenditures, and authorization of stock-based compensation plans are examples of the important information contained in corporate minutes. Contracts and correspondence with customers, suppliers, employees, labor unions, and various government agencies contain information that will enable the appraiser to understand the business practices and problems of the clients as well as provide information for valuation reports.

Industry and Economic Conditions

The appraiser must understand the broad economic environment in which the client operates, including the effects of national economic polices (e.g., various government regulations), the geographic location and its economy (northeastern states versus southwestern states), and developments in taxation and regulatory requirements. The appraiser should have a basic understanding of the global market and economy, national economic conditions, government regulations, changes in technology, and competitive conditions that affect the value of the client's business or business interest. Information about the industry in which the client operates may be obtained by searching for data from online sites, trade journals, and books of industry statistics and publications. To obtain knowledge about the client's business and business interest, the appraiser may:

- Review the articles of incorporation and bylaws or partnership agreements.
- Read the minutes of the board of directors' and shareholders' meetings to gather information about dividend declarations, employee stock-based compensation plans, and approval of mergers and acquisitions.

- Review and analyze recent (e.g., past five years) annual financial statements, tax returns, and reports to regulatory agencies.
- Review government laws and regulations that apply to the client.
- Read important continuing contracts, such as labor contracts, loan agreements, and bond indentures.
- Read trade and industry publications regarding current business and industry developments. Exhibit 4.9 shows some sources of business and industry information.
- Obtain nonfinancial information, such as the form of organization and ownership of the client's business, products, and services, through inquiries of client's management, key personnel, or a document request.

EXHIBIT 4.9 Sources of Economic, Industry, and Business Information

General Economic Information
1. *Federal Reserve Bulletin*
2. Survey of Current Business (U.S. Department of Commerce)
3. Statistical Abstract of the United States (U.S. Department of Commerce)
4. Economic Report of the President (U.S. Council of Economic Advisers)
5. Economic and Business Outlook (Bank of America)
6. Economic Trends (Federal Reserve Bank of Cleveland)
7. U.S. Financial Data (Federal Reserve Bank of St. Louis)
8. Monthly Labor Review (U.S. Bureau of Labor Statistics)
9. Congressional Information Service
10. Regional Economics and Markets
11. The Complete Economic and Demographic Data Source
12. Office of the Comptroller of the Currency

Industry Information
1. Federal Deposit Insurance Corporation
2. U.S. Industrial Outlook
3. Standard & Poor's Industry Surveys
4. Moody's Investor's Industry Review
5. National Trade and Professional Association of the United States
6. *Statistical Abstracts of the United States*
7. *Encyclopedia of Associations*
8. Moody's Manuals (various industries)

Business Information
1. Dun & Bradstreet Principal International Business
2. Standard & Poor's Register of Corporations, Directors, and Executives
3. Value Line Investment Survey
4. Standard & Poor's Corporation Records
5. Dun & Bradstreet, Key Business Ratios
6. Business press (e.g., *The Wall Street Journal, Forbes, Fortune,* and *Barron's*)
7. National Mortgage News
8. United States Banker
9. Federal Reserve Banks
10. SNL Securities
11. Online data sources (e.g., Google, Yahoo, Lycos, America OnLine, and LEXIS/NEXIS)

- Search available Web sites to gather general economic, industry, and business information. The online information search provides powerful flexibility, easy and fast accessibility, and relatively cheap availability and control for the appraiser. Exhibit 4.10 provides a list of Web sites that can be very helpful to the appraiser in gathering sufficient and competent information.

EXHIBIT 4.10 Online Sites for Economic, Industry, and Business Information

Site	Feature
www.bls.gov/eag/eag.us.htm	Provides a section on Economy at a Glance, which gives a statistical breakdown of the labor market in hours, earnings, and productivity.
www2.fdic.gov/hsob/	Posts daily, weekly, monthly, quarterly, and annual statistics releases and historical data of commercial banks.
www.bloomberg.com	Provides information about earnings, investments, and trades.
www.edgar-online.com http://documentresearch.morningstar.com/ www.sec.gov www.freedgar.com http://learn.westlawbusiness.com/	All these sites provide information on publicly traded companies often needed in performing valuations on estate and gift taxes, ESOPs, and M&A. The SEC's EDGAR database provides information on more than 15,000 publicly traded companies.
www.hoovers.com	Provides extensive information on more than 12,000 publicly traded companies in easy-to-use format.
www.ebscohost.com	Offers comprehensive research on publicly traded companies' stock information, earnings estimates, comparison ratios, and brokerage reports.
www.esopassociation.org/media/ media_statistics.asp	Provides ESOP statistics on the number of ESOPs, their magnitude, and types of ESOP.
www.nceo.org/main/article.php/id/11/	Nonprofit membership organization that provides broad information on employee-owned companies.
www.stockpickr.com/	Stock idea network.
http://valuewalk.com/	Provides global value investing with stock valuation including detailed information about value investing, the process of stock screening, selection, and pricing.
www.investopedia.com/	Provides free encyclopedia information using the collaborative software wiki.
	Provides the definition and meaning for investment and financial terms
www.NACVA.com	National Association of Certified Valuation Analysts provides a variety of business valuation, M&A, and forensic accounting services.
www.aicpa.org/InterestAreas/ ForensicAndValuation/Pages/FVS.aspx	The AICPA's Forensic and Valuation Services provides forensic accounting and business valuation resources.

GENERAL PLANNING

The valuation process and appraisal plan consist of three interrelated and sequential aspects: (1) the decisions the appraiser needs to make; (2) the knowledge to be obtained and the evidence to be gathered in making these decisions; and (3) the valuation procedures that typically are applied to obtain that evidence and knowledge. To distinguish these aspects clearly, consider the next separate listings of valuation decisions, knowledge, and evidence as well as procedures. These aspects of the valuation process for financial institutions are discussed in depth in Chapters 5 through 18 of this book.

General Planning Decisions to Be Made

It is vital that general planning decisions be made before conducting a valuation service. In general, these decisions need to be made:

- The agreed-on purpose(s) of the valuation
- Detailed description of the valuation subject (e.g., business or business interest)
- The applicable standard of value that will be used (e.g., fair market value, fair value, investment value, intrinsic value)
- The type, nature, form, and extent of the report to be issued
- Overall timing of the valuation assignment
- Staffing requirements and the expected assistance from client personnel in valuation evidence gathering and data preparation
- Any assumptions and limiting conditions that will be part of the valuation report
- Other services, such as providing expert witness or litigation testimony

Evidence and Knowledge Obtained to Prepare Preliminary Appraisal Plan

The effectiveness of valuation services depends to a great extent on the understanding and knowledge of the client's business and industry obtained by the appraiser during the preliminary appraisal planning phase. Appraisers must have knowledge in these areas:

- *Business.* Description of the business and its operations, types of products and services, capital structure, location, and methods of production, marketing, and distribution. The purpose is to obtain knowledge of how effectively and efficiently the client is carrying out its operations.
- *Industry.* Specification of the industry in which the client operates, including economic conditions, government regulations, changes in technology, and competitive conditions can assist the appraiser in learning more about the client's business and industry. This knowledge can have a significant impact on valuation conclusions.
- *Interviews.* Interviews with the client's key personnel can provide information regarding management integrity, operating style, and business operations to develop a realistic process of establishing an appropriate valuation conclusion.

- *Audited financial statements.* Audited financial statements (statement of financial position, income statement, statement of cash flows, and statement of owner's equity) can provide reliable and useful financial information regarding the client's financial position, results of operations, and cash flows as well as equity situations. Although audited financial statements prepared in conformity with generally accepted accounting principles (GAAP) are based on historical cost, not the fair market value, they provide financial information that is relevant to the appraisal.
- *Normalized financial statements.* Appraisers often use audited historical financial statements to develop and present their appraisal report of a business's value. The primary purpose of using financial statements is to assist in developing and presenting the value of an entity. These financial statements, which are utilized in the preparation of the valuation report and often included in the written business valuations, frequently contain departures from GAAP or other comprehensive basis of accounting. The accounting and review services committee of the AICPA issued an exposure draft (ED) in December 1999 titled *Financial Statements Included in Written Business Valuations*. The ED defines "normalized financial statements" as "financial statements that contain necessary and appropriate adjustments in order to make an entity's financial information more meaningful when presenting and comparing on a consistent basis the financial results of that entity to those of a comparable entity as part of a business valuation engagement." The ED exempts such financial statements from the provisions of Statements on Standards for Accounting and Review Services (SSARS) No. 1, *Compilation and Review of Financial Statements*, which requires compliance. The ED exempts from SSARS No. 1 historical financial statements and normalized financial statements included in a written business valuation.
- The accounting and review services committee of the AICPA issued an ED published August 1, 2008 titled *Applying AICPA Business Valuation Standards in Tax Practice*. The AICPA issued a statement on Standards for Valuation Services (SSVS) No. 1, *Valuation of a Business, Business Ownership Interest, Security, or Intangible Asset*, effective for all engagements accepted on or after January 1, 2008. The new standards apply to an AICPA member and to a nonmember CPA who has adopted SSVS No. 1 and who is engaged to estimate the value of a business, business ownership interest, security, or intangible asset. The AICPA has also established a new practice called a practice aid: AICPA Statement on Standards for Valuation Services (SSVS) No. 1, *Nonauthoritative Implementation Guidance Toolkit*, and Implementation Guide No. 1, *Application of SSVS No. 1 to Various Illustrative Client Engagement Situations*. The implementation Guide provides further guidance on best practices of valuation and interpretation of SSVS No.[2]
- *Other financial data.* Financial information other than financial statements, such as federal income tax returns, reports with regulatory agencies, management forecasts and projects, internal and managerial reports, and capital and operating budgets, can provide relevant data for the valuation assignment.
- *Operating information.* A history of the client's organization, its business, mission, and a brief chronology of major changes in the form and ownership of organization, background of key personnel, brochures, catalogs, price lists, organization charts,

major customers and suppliers as well as information regarding long-term and continuous agreements and obligations (e.g., leases, loans, bonds) can assist the appraiser in completing the valuation assignment effectively and successfully.

▪ *Key performance indicators.* Clients' key performance indicators (KPIs)—both financial, such as earnings and other financial information, and nonfinancial, such as composition of the board of directors, executives' tenure and compensation, social responsibility, and environmental issues—should be considered.

Procedures in Preparing the Preliminary Appraisal Plan

Every appraisal engagement requires the choice of certain valuation procedures. Valuation procedures performed as part of the preliminary appraisal plan are an important component of the valuation process. These procedures include:

▪ Reviewing and analyzing economic data to (a) determine its impact on the future performance of the client's organization and (b) assess the economic risk that the client organization is exposed to.

▪ Reviewing various sources of industry information, such as industry or trade publications and annual reports of companies in the industry.

▪ Reviewing and analyzing financial information, including trend analysis, comparative analysis, ratio analysis, and common-size financial analysis, assists the appraiser in assessing the client's future trends, performance, risk, and unusual items (abnormalities) that may have an impact on valuation conclusions.

▪ Considering the applicable valuation standards and methods issued by professional appraisal organizations (e.g., ASA, IBA, NACVA, AICPA).

▪ Inquiring of management about current business developments.

▪ Reading the current year's interim financial statements.

▪ Discussing the type, scope, and timing of the valuation assignment with the client.

▪ Touring the client's physical facilities, plants, and offices.

▪ Reading the corporate charter, bylaws, major contracts, and minutes of directors' and shareholders' meetings.

▪ Completing a generalized questionnaire, checklist, or narrative memorandum that organizes and summarizes the information needed to complete the valuation assignment.

The appraiser should choose valuation techniques that best combine reliable values with relevant information about the economic characteristics of the business or business interest under consideration. The usual approach to valuation is to determine the present value of the future cash flows. In other words, the projected cash flows are discounted at an appropriate discount rate and then the sum of the discounted cash flows is an indication of the value. Appraisers often try to be realistic by providing a clear caveat in their report stating: "The value developed in this report is calculated based on the premises that the firm will be able to continue its existence according to its business plan. If the plan is fulfilled in terms of projected revenues, expenses, and cash flows, then the value determined in this report can be relied on."

The second approach is the comparable method. The appraiser looks at revenue trends, earnings potential, and the firm's competitive position relative to other comparable firms in the same industry. The most commonly used valuation approaches are presented and described in depth in Chapter 8 of this book. The appraiser should consider these questions in selecting the appropriate valuation approach(es):

- What future economic, industry, and business factors should be included in or excluded from the valuation process?
- To what extent should joint inputs, interaction, and grouping affect the valuation?
- How and to what extent should the assessed risk be factored into the valuation estimates?
- What valuation standard(s) should be used?
- What discount rate should be used?
- How should changes in value be reported?

 APPRAISER'S TRAITS

According to Elizabeth Danziger, CPAs who have been successful in offering business valuation services share these traits.[3]

- *Able to function well under intense pressure.* Business valuation clients often have a specified goal (e.g., marital dissolution, M&A, stockholder disputes, estate and gift taxes), and they also know whether a high or low valuation will benefit them most. In performing valuation services, appraisers should maintain their objectivity and independence by refusing to be pressured by a client to reach a particular value. Appraisers should also be able to handle the pressures of meeting deadlines and being cross-examined by attorneys when serving as expert witnesses or litigation consultants.
- *Communicate well both orally and in writing.* Successful appraisers typically are effective communicators who can convey their findings (valuation opinions) succinctly to interested parties (e.g., client, judge, jury, tax authorities, and bank regulators). Good public relations with the business community, appraisal professionals, and other professionals (banks, accountants, and attorneys) can assist in establishing appraisal services and secure future growth. Effective writing skills in preparing the appraisal report are essential in conveying valuation findings to interested parties.
- *Utilize both qualitative and quantitative data.* Successful appraisers should have the training and experience of meshing the data by using both quantitative information (e.g., historical financial statements, market value, discount rate, and cash flows) and qualitative information (e.g., economic conditions, market trends, judgment, goodwill, management reputations, and skills) in reaching valuation conclusions. Appraisers should have adequate skills of gathering, analyzing, synthesizing, and interpreting data by employing appropriate valuation methodologies to generate reliable and relevant valuation information.

EXHIBIT 4.11 Appraisal Certifications and Their Attributes

Certifications/Attributes	Sponsoring Organization	Year Established	Education
1. Accredited in Business Valuation (ABV)	American Institute of Certified Public Accountants (AICPA)	1997	Education requirements for CPA designation
2. Accredited Senior Appraiser (ASA)	American Society of Appraisers (ASA)	1952	College degree or equivalent
3. Accredited Senior Member (ASM)	ASA	1952	College degree or equivalent
4. Chartered Financial Analysts	Association for Investment Management and Research (AIMR)	1963	College degree
5. Certified Business Appraiser (CBA)	Institute of Business Appraisers (IBA)	1978	College degree or equivalent
6. Business Valuator Accredited for Litigation	IBA	1998	None
7. Accredited by IBA (AIBA)	IBA	1991	None
8. Certified Valuation Analyst (CVA)	National Association of Certified Valuation Analysts (NACVA)	1991	Education requirements of CPAs
9. Government Valuation Analyst (GVA)	NACVA	1996	College degree
10. Accredited Valuation Analyst (AVA)	NACVA	1999	Business degree
11. Chartered Business Valuator (CBV)	Canadian Institute of Chartered Business Valuation (CICBV)	1971	Business degree

EXHIBIT 4.11 (*Continued*)

Experience	Examination	Continuing Education	Others
Ten business valuation agreements	Written examination	60 hours and involvement in five business valuation engagements every three-year period	CPA in good standing
a. Five years of full-time equivalent experience b. Two appraisal reports	a. Technical and ethics examination b. Four courses and related technical exams	40 hours every five years	Two appraisal reports No continuing experience
None	Eight hours of technical exam and one hour of ethics exam before sitting for the exam	40 hours every five years	Public company orientation
Significant professional experience	Minimum three-year program for passing examination; three extensive annual examinations	Professional continuing education	Investment management
None	Four-hour written examination	None	Two full valuation reports
None	Four-hour written examination	None	None
None	Four-hour exam	None	None
Licensed CPAs	a. Two-day AICPA course with open-book take-home exam; or b. Five-day other related course and take-home exam	Continuing education requirements of CPAs; 24 hours first two years; 36 hours every three years thereafter	Periodic report writing course and quality enhancement
Governmental employee	Five-day course with open-book take- home exam	24 hours first year and 36 hours every three years thereafter	Quality enhancement
Holding ASA or CFE designation	Five-day course with open-book take- home exam	24 hours first year and 36 hours every three years thereafter	Quality enhancement
Three years of full-time experience; or five years of part time; or two years of experience and a required course	Written exam	40 hours every five years	

- *Be unfazed by ambiguity and uncertainty.* In performing valuation services, appraisers often use their judgment and experience in estimating appraisal data (e.g., future cash flows, discounted rate, and growth rate). Thus, appraisers should support their findings by applying several valuation methods, test these methods to determine their sensitivity to ambiguities and uncertainties, and be able to justify estimations used in forming valuation opinions.
- *Continuously improve valuation expertise and skills through ongoing professional education.* Being a successful appraiser requires proper training, education, work experience, and proficiency. To achieve these credentials and skills in the professional valuation community, appraisers must first earn a business valuation designation offered by a number of organizations (e.g., ASA, IBA, NACVA, Association for Investment Management and Research, AICPA). Exhibit 4.11 presents appraisal certifications and their attributes. Understanding business valuation theory, concepts, and methods is a prerequisite for getting into the business valuation profession but is not sufficient. After achieving the knowledge base and initial designation, the appraiser should obtain proper experience and continuous training and education to be successful.
- *Continuously market.* Obtaining valuation clients requires an effective marketing and contacting strategy. Appraiser can obtain clients in several ways:
  - Targeting your marketing efforts and expertise to a particular profession or industry (e.g., valuing employee stock ownership plans, estate and gift taxes, mergers and acquisitions).
  - Contacting other professionals and assisting them with valuation services (e.g., attorneys, accountants, bankers, security brokers).
  - Personal direct contact with local businesses.
  - Advertising in local and national business and appraisal journals.
  - Getting referrals from fellow appraisers.
  - Attending conventions, conferences, and other meetings of professional associations (e.g., appraisal organizations, accountant's societies, attorneys, chamber of commerce, banks).
  - Creating a Web site to get local, national, and even global exposure.

 ## APPRAISER'S DUE DILIGENCE PROCESS

Conducting effective business valuation services requires appraisers to develop proper valuation strategies and perform the due diligence valuation process of using different valuation methods, concepts, a number of sources of financial and strategic information, various state and federal valuation regulations, and professional valuation standards. Frank C. Evans suggested these tips for appraisers in performing a business valuation due diligence:[4]

- Understand the valuation assignment.
- Comply with competency and independence standards.
- Watch the market.
- Know the difference between fair market and investment value.

- Know when to use the invested capital versus equity model.
- Do not let rates of return distort value.
- Beware of earnings measures—cash is king.
- Verify all rates of return.
- Always challenge long-term growth rates.
- Challenge premiums or discounts.
- Take pride in your report.

The *Journal of Accountancy* has laid down steps for smaller firms to keep in mind when entering business valuation. A few of those steps are:

- Start and utilize the existing customer base.
- Invest more time on the first few valuations.
- Capitalize on offering valuation services to existing firms that do not have the capability to do valuations for their customer base.
- Ensure that the procedures are in compliance with the applicable guidelines.
- Get your first few reports reviewed by an expert.
- Obtain a valuation credentials offered by the ASA and the NACVA.[5]

 ## RISK ASSESSMENT

Lack of adequate and effective risk assessment is often cited as a contributing factor to the recent financial crisis and resulting economic meltdown. Risk assessment is an integral component of a risk management process of determining both quantitative and qualitative value of risk associated with certain events, transitions, or threats. Successful risk assessments require full support of senior management and must be conducted by teams that include functional managers and information technology administrators. The risk assessment tool can be used to identify assets as well as the risks to those assets, to estimate the likelihood of security failures, and to identify appropriate controls for protecting assets and resources. An effective risk assessment enables financial services firms to safeguard against potential downturns in the business environment and the economy. The Dodd-Frank Act and the 2010 Base Committee III underscore the importance of proper risk assessment and detrimental of excessive risk taking by executives of financial services firms.

According to a PricewaterhouseCoopers (PwC) report, the cumulative loss of $50 trillion in wealth during the recent financial crisis can be attributed to the poor risk management practices and excessive risk undertaken by financial companies. As policy makers assess the causes of the recent financial crisis, it is becoming more clear that improvements will need to be made both in the way that senior executives approach risk management activities within their organization and the role of their boards of directors in risk oversight. The 12th annual survey of the CEO conducted by PwC confirmed that even though 92 percent of the executives believe that assessing and managing the risk is crucial to the success of the organization, only 23 percent believe that they have all the tools in place to manage the risk at their organization. Companies that have used the practice of risk management to the full extent have higher chances to be valued with higher book-to-value multipliers.[6] A risk assessment matrix typically is used to evaluate that risk. That valuable business tool allows companies to organize information in a way that enables them to see the breakdown between the function and the areas of risk that need to be addressed and, as a result, link the risk to performance later during the execution process.

 ## CONCLUSION

This chapter provides background information regarding the market and demand for valuation services, valuation service providers (appraisers), the various appraisal organizations, and their standards and certifications. This chapter also discusses the appraisal process, including information about engagement letters, the initial document request, and internal and external sources of information gathered by the appraiser. Gathering and analyzing the required information will provide a framework for the appraiser to conduct a variety of valuation service assignments, including those pertaining to financial institutions (e.g., M&A, initial public offerings, and employee stock ownership plans). An understanding of background materials presented in this chapter is crucial to the further development and application of valuation methodologies and techniques to financial institutions presented in Parts II, III, and IV of this book.

 ## NOTES

1. Gary R. Trugman, "Conducting a Valuation of a Closely Held Business," Management Consulting Services Division of ASCPA, 1993, p. 13/100–1.
2. F. Gordon Spoor, "Applying AICPA Business Valuation Standards in Tax Practice," AICPA (August 2008). Available at: www.aicpa.org/Publications/TaxAdviser/2008/aug/Pages/ApplyingAICPABusinessValuationStandardsinTaxPractice.aspx.
3. Elizabeth Danziger, "Is Business Appraising for You?" *Journal of Accountancy* (March 2000): 28–33.
4. Frank C. Evans, "Tips for the Valuator," *Journal of Accountancy* (March 2000): 35–41.
5. Parker Eddy, "Breaking into Business Valuation," *Journal of Accountancy* (March 2010). Available at: www.journalofaccountancy.com/Issues/2010/Mar/20092383.htm.
6. Ibid.

CHAPTER FIVE

Overview of Mergers and Acquisitions

 INTRODUCTION

Mergers and acquisitions (M&A) are occurring at a record pace in almost every industry, especially in the financial services industry. Falling regulatory and geographic barriers (e.g., interstate and even global banking, the passage of the Financial Services Modernization Act of 1999 [Gramm-Leach-Bliley (GLB) Act]) along with banks' unprecedented performance and levels of private equity, are contributing to this increased M&A activity at the turn of the twenty-first century. It is expected that the recent economic recovery and resulting improvements in the financial and credit markets in the post 2007–2009 financial crisis led to increased M&A transactions across all industries—particularly healthcare, energy, natural resources and financial services industries. The objective of this chapter is to present a basic understanding of the M&A process from the standpoints of both the target and the acquirer. This chapter provides a generic discussion of M&A transactions that can be used by all entities wishing to grow through business combinations. More in-depth discussion of M&A transactions for financial institutions is presented in Chapters 14 and 15. M&A deals typically are viewed by both the acquirer and the target as an important means of achieving economies of scale, especially in a multiple-product market such as the financial services industry. The wave of M&A activities and the determinants of their behavior in the financial services industry have begun to gain importance and have surfaced as a core issue in the financial community. In a merger deal, two separate entities combine, and both parties to the deal wind up with common stock in a single, combined entity. In contrast, in an acquisition transaction, the acquirer (bidding entity) buys the common stock or assets of the seller (target entity). The vast majority of all business combinations are acquisitions, not mergers. M&A activities within the financial services industry have continued with varying levels of intensity since the end of World War II. Recent waves of M&A in financial institutions have been motivated by a favorable regulatory environment (e.g., elimination of intrastate and interstate branching restrictions), continuous increase in bank earnings and stock prices, opportunities for market expansions, favorable stock prices and a strong stock market, substantial advances in communication and data processing technologies (e.g., e-commerce, Internet banking), greater efficiency following acquisition, and economies of scale. As M&A deals continue to grow, as shareholders lean toward liquidity, and as acquirers offer higher premiums for their targets, the use of the appropriate valuation process in considering the pros and cons of these deals and estimating their values become more apparent. Hence, M&A form an important part of companies' strategies. The possible motives may include: search for efficiency gains through new combinations of material and immaterial assets; a drive to increase market shares and market power; a desire to safeguard access to important inputs; a search for access to new technologies and know-how; a drive to gain access to new customer groups or new geographic markets; and a desire for diversification.

 ## HISTORICAL PERSPECTIVE OF MERGERS AND ACQUISITIONS

Prior to World War II, the primary motivations for M&A in corporate America were centered on the effectiveness and efficiency in operations expected to be generated from the incorporation of economies of scale. Prior to the 1980s, geographic restrictions, especially the prohibition against interstate banks and even intrastate branching, limited where and how banks could compete. The formation of bank holding companies (BHCs) allowed banks to acquire banks and other nonbanking companies in different geographic locations or markets, lower their inherent tax burden, and issue commercial paper. During the 1980s, banks began to acquire other financial services companies, such as mutual funds, investment, and finance companies. Many banks focused on acquiring other banks and thrifts or commercial banks to have immediate access to the federal funds market.[1] Hence, in the post 2007–2009 financial crisis era banks are set to see a wave of M&A as the market seems to be heading toward greater consolidation in an uncertain financial environment. The sooner this happens, the better, given the prospect of the shrinking economy and an increase in bad loans. On the contrary, the aim of M&A during the 1980s was primarily to remove troubled banks and thrifts; M&A in the late 1990s focused on additional growth, increase in efficiency and effectiveness in operations, and diversification of financial services. The situation remained the same during the early 2000s. Exhibit 5.1 shows large bank mergers in the United States during the early 2000s for target banks with assets of acquirer over $1 billion.

According to the American Bankers Association, the largest bank merger occurred in 2004, when JPMorgan Chase & Company acquired Bank One Corporation for $59 billion. Exhibit 5.2 presents the top 10 bank mergers from 2004 to 2009.

EXHIBIT 5.1 Large Bank Mergers in 2000s

Year	Target Bank	Acquiring Bank	Total Assets of Target ($billions)
2000	Bank United Corp.	Washington Mutual	1.5
2000	Morgan Keegan	Regions Financial Corp	7.89
2000	First Security Corp.	Wells Fargo & Co.	23
2001	Wachovia Corp.	First Union Corp.	N/A
2002	Golden State Bancorp	Citigroup Inc.	N/A
2002	Dime Bancorp, Inc.	Washington Mutual	N/A
2003	First Virginia Banks, Inc.	BB&T Corp.	N/A
2004	FleetBoston Financial Corp.	Bank of America Corp.	47
2004	Bank One	JPMorgan Chase	
2004	Union Planters	Regions Financial Corp.	5.9
2004	National Commerce Financial	SunTrust	6.98
2004	SouthTrust	Wachovia	14.3
2005	Riggs Bank	PNC Bank	0.78
2005	Hibernia National Bank	Capital One Financial Corporation	4.9
2005	MBNA Corporation	Bank of America Corporation	35
2006	Westcorp. Inc	Wachovia	3.91
2006	North Fork Bank	Capital One Financial Corporation	13.2
2006	Golden West Financial	Wachovia	25
2006	AmSouth Bancorp	Regions Financial Corp.	10
2007	Republic Bancorp	Citizen Banking Corporation	1.048
2007	Compass Bancshares	Banco Bilbao Vizcaya Argentaria USA	9.8
2007	Lasalle Bank	Bank of America Corporation	21
2007	Investors Financial Services Corporation	State Street Corporation	4.2
2007	Mellon Financial Corporation	Bank of New York	18.3
2007	Worlds Savings bank	Wachovia	25
2008	Commerce Bancorp	TD Banknorth	8.5
2008	Bear Stearns	JPMorgan Chase	1.1
2008	Merrill Lynch	Bank of America	50
2008	Washington Mutual	JPMorgan Chase	1.9
2008	Wachovia	Wells Fargo	15.1
2008	National City Corp.	PNC Financial Services	5.08
2008	Fremont Investment and Loan	Capital Source Bank	7.66
2008	National City Corp	PNC Financial Services	5.08

Source: Extracted from FDIC Merger Decisions Annual Report 2008, Lists of the Bank Mergers in the United States, www.fdic.gov/bank/individual/merger/2008/merger2008.pdf.

EXHIBIT 5.2 Top 10 Bank Mergers by Deal Price (2004–2009)

Buyer Name	Target Name	Completion Date	Transaction Value $ in Millions	Deal Price $ in Millions
JPMorgan Chase & Company	Bank One Corporation	6/30/2004		59,240
Bank of America Corporation	FleetBoston Financial Corporation	4/1/2004	47,000	49,604
Bank of America Corporation	Merrill Lynch & Co	1/1/2009		47,182
Bank of America Corporation	MBNA Amro North America HC NY	1/1/2006	35,000	35,810
Mellon Financial Corporation	Bank of New York Company Inc	7/1/2007	18,300	29,055
Wachovia Corporation	Golden West Financial Corp.	10/2/2006	25,000	25,501
Bank of America Corporation	ABN Amro North America HC NY	10/1/2007		16,000
Capital One Financial Corp.	North Fork Bancorporation	11/30/2006	13,200	15,133
Wells Fargo & Company	Wachovia Corporation	12/31/2008	15,100	15,117
Wachovia Corporation	SouthTrust Corporation	11/1/2004	14,267	14,267

Source: Highline Financial as of June 6, 2009.

RECENT TRENDS IN MERGERS AND ACQUISITIONS

The anticipated steady global economic recovery and potential improvements in financial and credit market conditions are expected to promote M&A activities across all industry sectors in 2010 and 2011. Industries that are anticipated to experience an increasing level of M&A activity are technology and pharmaceuticals/health care, financial services, and energy/natural resources.

All Industries

The most remarkable deal that occurred in 2005 was the acquisition of Gillette by Procter & Gamble (P&G) for $54.91 billion. It was the largest acquisition in P&G history and resulted in the creation of the largest consumer product company in the world. The year 2006 was the biggest year for global M&A market, totaling $3.3 trillion of total announced deal value. The deal that received the most publicity was the buyout of Clear Channel Communications by private equity groups. Clear Channel Communications' original intent was to go private by partitioning its businesses and selling them off. Various lines of businesses were sold to the different business groups—for example, all Clear Channel's television stations were sold to Newport Television, while more than

100 radio stations were sold to Aloha Station Trust, LLC. But the $19 billion deal did not go through smoothly. Lenders (Deutsche Bank, Credit Suisse, Citigroup, Royal Bank of Scotland, and Wachovia) declined to provide financing to fund Clear Channel Communications' buyout, so the company filed a lawsuit against banks that walked away from the deal. A Texas district court judge ruled that lenders cannot just walk away from deals and have to proceed with the fulfillment of commitments they made earlier.

The year 2007 was probably one of the biggest years for M&A since 2000 in terms of the number of deals. The AT&T acquisition of Bell South for $85.6 billion contributed to the statistics. One of the most notable acquisitions of the year was the combination of Wachovia and Golden West Financials. The deal between ConocoPhillips and Burlington Resources was also one of the largest deals in the energy sector in a few years. The $35.6 billion deal made ConocoPhillips one of the nation's biggest producers of natural gas.

The volume of the M&A in 2009 was down significantly (approximately 40 percent from 2010) due to the crisis in the credit markets, the inability of companies to get financing, and overall uncertainty about the future. Cross-border acquisitions were not as popular as they had been few years earlier, and most M&A occurred within similar industries. The largest deal took place in the health care industry with Pfizer Inc., acquiring Wyeth for $68 billion in both cash and stock. According to the official version, the main reason for the merger was the synergy that can be achieved and the creation of the diversified portfolio of brands.

The merger of Burlington Northern Santa Fe Corporation into Berkshire Hathaway Inc. is another notable merger that was closed in 2010. The deal received a lot of publicity, not only because of its size (Berkshire will pay a total of $35 billion both in cash and stock) but also because of the strategic importance of the deal. According to the *Logistics Management Journal*, Burlington Northern Santa Fe Corporation is one the largest U.S. Class I railroads company; it is heavily involved as a provider of intermodal services and transports the most grain of all U.S. Class I railroads as well as high levels of coal. Consequently, the strategic benefit to the Berkshire Hathaway Inc. portfolio is obvious. To illustrate, privately held Mars, Inc. acquired William Wrigley Jr. Co. in partnership with Warren Buffett for $23 billion (including the premium of $5.7 billion over Wrigley's market value), creating a confectionary giant that potentially could force other industry leaders to consolidate in order to compete with the newly merged company. On April 14, 2008, Northwest Airlines, Inc. and Delta Air Lines, Inc. merged, creating a colossal airline with services to all major travel destinations; the deal cost Delta $10.3 billion. Another major deal was the merger between United Airlines and Continental Airlines forming the largest airline based on revenue generated from passenger miles and second largest in fleet size. One of the most important mergers in recent history also took place in 2008. Belgian Inbev purchased Anheuser-Busch Companies Inc. for about $52 billion, creating the world's biggest beer market leader with sales of more than $36 billion a year. Another important combination happened between Hewlett-Packard and Electronic Data Systems Corporation. The $16.9 billion deal created a strong force in a global information technology marketplace. Other notable electronic industry M&A activity includes: Cisco buying Linkedin, Google acquiring Ruku, and Netflix purchasing Flixster.

Bank of America's acquisition of Merrill Lynch can be considered as one of the biggest deals in the recent banking M&A history as well as one of the most controversial. The $50 billion all-stock transaction has created an unparalleled financial institution in terms of size and breadth of operations. Merrill Lynch was not in good condition when Bank of America made an offer during the 2007–2009 financial crisis. Merrill Lynch's business was going down due to huge losses from subprime mortgages and other risky derivative trading.

Merrill Lynch was in the midst of panic when the deal was announced (just an hour before Lehman Brothers officially went bankrupt). The company was priced at 1.8 times its stated book value. The deal resulted in a combination of wealth management, capital markets, and advisory business. As a result of the deal, Bank of America now has the largest advisory network in the world and has the largest amount of assets under management (including the 50 percent ownership of Blackrock, Inc.). Bank of America also became the largest underwriter of global high-yield bonds, M&A advice, and global equity.

Bank of America was advised by J.C. Flowers & Co. LLC, Fox-Pitt Kelton Cochran Caronia Waller and Bank of America 7. It was represented by Wachtell, Lipton, Rosen & Katz. Merrill Lynch was represented by Shearman & Sterling.[2]

The deal was considered to be controversial. According to the *Wall Street Journal*, Federal Reserve chairman Ben Bernanke and then-Treasury Department chief Henry Paulson were afraid that the U.S. financial system could collapse and pressured the chief executive of Bank of America, Ken Lewis, not to discuss Bank of America's plan to buy troubled Merrill Lynch. If Merrill Lynch had disclosed its fourth-quarter loss of $15.48 billion to the company's shareholders, they could have stopped the deal. Ken Lewis's testimony suggest that he was not verbally pressured to remain silent but rather was advised to do so.

The 2010 merger between Ohio-based First Energy Corp and Pennsylvania-based Allegheny Energy for $8.5 billion, created the largest electric utility with more than six million customers in seven Northeast and Midwest states in the United States. Other notable M&A activity included BP selling off assets to cover the increasing cost of the oil spill in the Gulf of Mexico and ConocoPhillips eliminating noncore assets streamlining their operations. The combined sales from these two companies made up 14.1% of M&A activity in the energy industry totaling $29.8 billion. In America Exxon Mobile bought XTO for $41 billion in 2009 spurring activity into 2010.[3]

Financial Services Industries

There are two types of business combinations in the financial services industry: consolidation and convergence. Consolidation entails a combination of resources of similar financial institutions (e.g., banks) through M&A of, for example, banks and bank holding companies. It is done to increase the size of financial institutions and reduce the number of small, independently owned banks and financial service providers. With convergence, the scope or breadth of financial institutions expand into a variety of financial services through M&A between banks and other financial services firms (e.g., insurance companies, securities underwriting, and mutual funds). It brings together the firms from different industries to create conglomerate firms offering multiple services.

Clearly, these two trends are related. In their effort to compete with each other, banks and their closest competitors have acquired other firms in their industry as well as across industries to provide multiple financial services in multiple markets. Consolidation is very common in the financial services industry; convergence of banks with other financial service providers has been rare. The consolidation of banks may not significantly affect the functioning of various segments of the financial markets. In a liberalized environment, the mere size of a bank may not be an enabling condition for distorting pricing mechanisms. M&A, consolidations, and convergence are all valid positioning tactics intended to assist combined companies to compete more effectively in the global marketplace by shoring up existing lines of business, extending into new lines of business, and eliminating former competitors.

The evolution of M&A in the financial services industry starts with consolidation of local banks to improve their efficiency and effectiveness and moves to mergers across the nation to expand geographical services and create synergies, and finally results in convergence to consolidate all financial services. The ultimate liberalization in the financial services industry would be achieved by globalization of the industry through cross-border integration. The torrid role of M&A in the financial services industry is expected to continue in the twenty-first century. Future M&A deals will be motivated by a loosening in regulations, technological advancements, a desire by large financial institutions to offer a variety of financial services (e.g., insurance, loans, and investments), and the lure of new markets.

The total number of bank mergers has decreased significantly from 598 deals in 1997 to 260 in 2008, according to Federal Deposit Insurance Corporation (FDIC) historical statistics. The number of transactions not only followed the same pattern but decreased even at a faster pace. In 2009, the M&A value in banking and finance was just $29 billion, as opposed to over $100 billion in 2007. M&A in the banking industry have undergone significant changes because of the 2007–2009 financial crisis. The recent financial crisis caused most banks, regardless of their size and asset holdings, to report over $1 trillion in losses and write-downs of their mortgage holdings. The situation did not change significantly in 2009, a year in which there were a record number of bank failures; bank failures increased 500 percent from 2008 and compromised about 70 percent of the total failures during the last decade. But the situation also provided a once-in-a-lifetime opportunity for healthy banks to grow quickly in assets, locations, and market share with the government assuming part of the risk through the FDIC loss-sharing agreements. Half of the deals that were approved were government-backed transactions. The FDIC provided merger assistance by taking part of the credit losses incurred by buyers. (The government agency generally pays for 80 percent of losses up to a certain threshold and 95 percent above it.) There are pros and cons to acquiring failed banks using the loss-sharing agreement with the government. The acquirer has to do a lot of work in terms of cleaning money-losing losses under the strict supervision of regulators. That kind of work may require the acquirer to free up substantial resources while qualifying for FDIC-assisted deal. Under the FDIC risk-based premium system, banks must have a total risk-based capital ratio of at least 10 percent (total capital to estimated risk-weighted assets), a Tier 1 risk-based capital ratio of at least 6 percent, and a Tier 1 leverage capital ratio 4 percent or greater.[4] In other words, banks that want to receive government assistance in purchasing failed banks must fall into well-capitalized capital group category. Banks must also have a CAMELS rating (the composite rating based on capital, asset quality, management, earnings, liquidity, and sensitivity to market risk) of 1 or 2, satisfactory anti–money laundering records, a bank holding company composite risk, financial condition, impact (RFI) rating of 1 or 2, and at least a satisfactory Community Reinvestment Act rating.

The CAMELS rating is an international rating system given by bank supervisory authorities. It rates banks based on the six listed criteria. Capital adequacy examines the financial statement performance, growth prospects, earnings potential and quality, and others. The asset quality component scrutinizes all the assets of the holding bank, including off balance sheet transactions. The management component is considered by some experts the most important element of the rating system. The earnings component has to include all sources of current and potential earnings, including nonrecurring and extraordinary items. Liquidity measures the ability of the bank or financial institution to generate cash quickly to cover short-term liabilities. Sensitivity concerns the exposure of the financial institution to market risks.[5]

The RFI composite is a rating adopted in 2005 that consists of three major components: (1) risk management measures the ability of the top executives and board of directors to control risks; (2) financial condition components measure the total amount of consolidated capital, asset quality, earning, and liquidity; and (3) impact is a more indirect component that measures risks that come from nondepository institutions.

Those ratings mean that banks should exhibit the strongest performance and adequate risk-management practices relative to their size, complexity, and risk profile should be in place. Banks with a rating 2 and higher should not have any material concerns and must comply with all existing laws and regulations. The disclosed high RFI rating leads to a possible assumption that the largest banks are in a more favorable position to consolidate with failed institutions. Meeting qualification requirements is just one step toward acquiring banks with government assistance. According to the Grand Thornton's 17th Bank Executive Survey, even considering the fact that 62 percent of bank executives are interested in acquiring a failed bank, only 2 percent have completed an acquisition of a failed bank and 7 percent have been unsuccessful bidders.[6] The FDIC applies the least-cost test in selecting winning bidder, which suggests that the highest bid is not always deemed to be less costly; safety and soundness appear to play a key role in the FDIC decision-making process.

The survey also indicated that more smaller banks (with assets less than $500 million) are interested in bidding than large banks, but small banks may not have adequate resources to handle the transaction. It is of crucial importance for banks to be able to manage loss-sharing agreements as well as adequately value assets, service them, and use proper accounting methods to record transactions. Hence the general trends that companies are now paying attention to are:

1. Very few distressed deals. That is, the deals will be smaller and the timing of the sales and the competitiveness and structure of the bidding processes will be driven more by pricing considerations than by an immediate need for capital.
2. More unsolicited bids.

3. More leveraged deals.
4. More postclosing purchase price protections.
5. Timing and currency issues, such as credit crisis and stock market volatility impacts.
6. Reducing private equity activity and working on hedge funds.
7. Updating greater strategic defenses.

Since the pooling of assets through M&A can lead to efficiency gains, there are benefits to consumers if the gains are passed on in the form of lower prices, higher quality, or new products and services. However, if M&A are not controlled by an effective competition policy, they may lead to excessive market concentration and anticompetitive behavior so that consumers must pay higher prices or acquire poorer-quality goods and services.

According to the Federal Reserve Bank of Philadelphia study, as presented in Exhibit 5.3, a price-to-book ratio at which banks were valued continued to decline sharply from 2007. The study also suggests that larger banks receive a lower valuation ratio. Banks with assets exceeding $1 billion received an average price-to-book ratio of 0.88 while banks with less than $1 billion in assets received an average of 1.02 price-to-book premium.[7] Strong connection between CAMELS and RFI ratings, core deposits, and price-to-book valuations were found.

Target banks with a high percentage of core deposits received a higher price-to-book premium. This continues to be the case, as banks with core deposits over 20 percent received a 2.33 price-to-book premium while banks with lower core deposits of 5 percent or less received only a 0.78 average price-to-book value. The highest price-to-book premium paid in the nation from July 1, 2008, to June 30, 2009, was Hillister Enterprises II Inc.'s purchase of Crosby Bancshares in the Atlanta District for 3.37

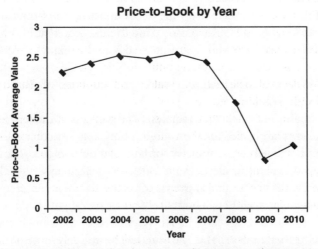

EXHIBIT 5.3 Recent Trends in Bank Valuations and Mergers and Acquisitions

Source: Author's calculations based on data from http://www.philadelphiafed.org/bank-resources/publications/src-insights/2010/third-quarter/pace-of-bank-mergers.cfm.

times book value. The lowest price-to-book premium in 2008 was Wells Fargo & Co.'s purchase of Wachovia for 0.23 times book value. It is interesting to note that the Wachovia Corp. deal was also the highest amount, at $15 billion.[8]

 ## REGULATIONS OF BANK MERGERS

It is important to examine M&A laws and regulations in order to understand the continuous trend toward M&A deals in the financial services industry. A number of laws and regulations are applicable to M&A proposals in the financial services industry, and they influence M&A approvals. M&A proposals are being reviewed by both the financial institutions' regulatory agencies and the DOJ for compliance with applicable laws and regulations. All M&A must follow the regulatory framework when they are planning to engage in a combination. Regulatory considerations can be general (or applicable to any industry) or industry specific. The two conventional federal regulations pertaining to bank mergers are the Bank Merger Act (BM Act) of 1960 and the Bank Holding Company Act (BHC Act) of 1956 and its 1970 amendment.

The BM Act requires that applications for M&A by banks be processed through bank regulators. The federal regulator responsible for bank M&A typically has regulatory authority over the final form of the bank emerging from the M&A deal regardless of the agency that regulated the bank prior to the merger.

The BHC Act requires approval by the Board of Governors of the Federal Reserve System of any M&A action making a bank part of a BHC affiliation. Chapter 3(c) of the BHC Act specifies the required forms that disclose this information:

- The financial history and condition of the company or companies and the banks concerned
- Prospects after the merger, if the merger is permitted
- The charter of management
- Effects of the proposed merger on the needs and welfare of the communities
- Whether the proposed M&A would expand the size or extent of the bank involved beyond limits consistent with adequate and sound banking

The New Merger Guidelines that were released on April 20, 2010, emphasize the different approach to the merger analyses. The main focus of regulators shifted from more generic analysis of the M&A to analysis of the effects of the particular M&A. For example, regulators are going to be examining how the particular merger of two big financial institutions will result in increased financial services fees. The Department of Justice (DOJ) and Federal Trade Commission (FTC) will likely revise the Herfindahl-Hirschman Index (HHI) thresholds from 1000 to 1500. Combinations of firms that result in an HHI index of 1500 will most likely not be investigated. Merger of firms with an HHI index of 1500 or below are classified as unconcentrated markets and normally will require no further analysis. The FTC and the DOJ will rely more on the diagnosis of the unilateral price effects. Adverse unilateral price effects can arise when the merger gives the merged entity an incentive to raise the price of a product previously sold by one merging firm and thereby divert sales to products previously sold by the other merging firm, boosting the profits on the latter products.[9]

It is emphasized by the FTC in *Horizontal Mergers Guidelines* that agencies will rely more on the unilateral price effects analysis rather than on HHI levels. Other tools will be used to analyze the possibility of a merger resulting in a diminished level of competition. Three new sections were added to the Merger Guidelines: powerful buyers, merger of competing buyers, and partial acquisitions. The FTC and the Department of Justice (agencies) will evaluate those choices that powerful buyers have and how those choices will change if the merger does not take place. Partial acquisitions are treated the same as mergers, in case the acquisition results in effective control of the target firm or involves substantially all of the relevant assets of the target firm. These three principal effects are of major importance to the agencies: (1) whether the proposed acquisition will result in one firm having a significant voting interest in another; (2) whether the proposed acquisition will result in a reduced incentive of the target firm to compete; and (3) whether the proposed acquisition will influence the buyer's ability to obtain information about the target's activities that is not meant for public use—in other words, insider information. Mergers of competing buyers is another serious issue of big concern to government agencies. Agencies will apply the same procedure to the mergers of competing buyers and determine whether the merger will result in enhanced market power of buyers and thus impair seller chances to compete.

Antitrust Regulations

The Antitrust Department of the DOJ has advisory responsibility over bank merger activities primarily because the Sherman Act and the Clayton Act often apply to M&A deals in the banking industry. The antitrust policy, as related to M&A, is designed to prevent business combinations that would lead to a substantial increase in market power. Market power is not easily determinable and can be driven by a variety of forces (e.g., profitability, efficiency) unrelated to business combinations. Thus, regulators and antitrust authorities examine the structural characteristics of the affected markets measured by market concentration to determine the likely market power and competitive impact of a proposed business combination.

The antitrust regulation seeks to fulfill several objectives for bank customers and the general public, mainly to prevent monopoly prices (excess profits) in banking industry and also to maintain public access to bank products and services, an issue that can be especially problematic in small markets. These laws seek to avoid static markets and to allow efficiency increasing, service-enhancing mergers. The two regulatory authorities assessing M&A transactions among commercial banks in the United States, the Federal Reserve Board and the DOJ, traditionally have employed different approaches in enforcing antitrust policies. The Office of the Comptroller of the Currency (OCC) and FDIC also have regulatory jurisdiction for antitrust enforcement in the banking industry. The OCC and the FDIC have followed more lenient antitrust policies than the Federal Reserve Board and DOJ in recent years. This is evidenced by the fact that neither the OCC nor the FDIC has denied a proposed M&A deal on competitive grounds in the past 10 years while the Federal Reserve Board and DOJ have challenged and caused modification of many proposed M&A transactions.

Section 5 of the Federal Trade Commission Act (FTC Act) also relates to the banking M&A in a way that it prohibits "unfair or deceptive acts or practices in or affecting commerce." Along with that, the board of directors at the financial institution is entitled under Section 8 of Federal Deposit Insurance Act to take appropriate actions when unfair or deceptive acts are discovered. The FTC and Antitrust Division of the DOJ are expected to continue vigorous antitrust merger enforcement.

The four important antitrust issues relevant to all M&A in the banking industry are:

1. Geographic market definition
2. Product market definition
3. Structural guidelines
4. Mitigating factors

Geographic Market Definition

The first step in antitrust assessment is to determine the proper market definition, which can be defined as a product (or group of products) and a geographic area in which the product is sold.[10] Geographic markets are often defined locally, such as a metropolitan statistical area (MSA) or a non-MSA county. Since financial institutions provide a wide variety of financial services to a wide variety of customers throughout the nation and now, with the use of Internet banking, worldwide, it is difficult to define geographic banking markets. Global competition opportunities and technological advances have reduced barriers to entry and expanded the size of markets. Markets are becoming more open, which in turn makes it more difficult for antitrust policy makers to define precisely the relevant geographic and product market.

Product Market Definition

The Federal Reserve Board and DOJ traditionally have defined the relevant banking product market for antitrust assessment and purposes as the cluster of financial services offered by commercial banks. Financial institutions provide a cluster of financial services to their clients, including deposits, loans, transaction activities, and other asset management services. However, regulators commonly have used total deposits as measures of concentration. These agencies traditionally have used total deposits as a proxy for the ability of commercial banks to provide this cluster of financial services to both businesses and individuals in a given local geographic banking market. However, the use of Internet banking has expanded the geographic boundaries of banking markets and made it possible and easier for bank customers to split their various financial services among a number of providers. This may result in a substantial weakening of the clustering of bank services, which makes the antitrust policies in banking less predictable. Furthermore, the recent wave of consolidation and convergence makes the use of total deposits less relevant as a proxy for the measure of concentration and market power.

Structural Guidelines

The impact of proposed M&A deals on market structure is the next step in assessing the deal for antitrust policy purposes after clearly defining geographic and product markets. The primary purpose of U.S. antitrust policy is to prevent M&A activities that could lead to a substantial increase in market power, which may discourage healthy competition in the market. Determination of direct market power is not easy because of the lack of specific, reliable, and relevant information for measuring market power. Thus, antitrust authorities generally investigate the structural characteristics of the affected market to determine the likely competitive effect of a proposed M&A deal. The competitive impact is measured in terms of the potential effect of the proposed M&A deal on market concentration.

The Justice Department and banking authorities use the HHI as a first-cut assessment of the likely impact of a proposed M&A on competition. The HHI is calculated as the sum of the squares of the deposit market shares of all entities (e.g., banking organizations) in the market. The HHI is a static measure that determines market concentration at a single point in time. Mathematically, it can be depicted as:[11]

$$HHI = \sum_{i=1}^{n} (MS_i)^2$$

where
MS = market share of bank i
n = number of banks in the market

Market structure (e.g., number, size, distribution, market shares) affects the degree of competition in the banking industry, which is often measured by the HHI. The HHI is calculated by adding up the squares of the deposit shares of participants in a banking market and multiplying by 10,000. For example, if there are four banks in a given market and their deposit shares are 25 percent each, the HHI would be calculated as $[(.25)^2 + (.25)^2 + (.25)^2 + (.25)^2] \times 10,000 = 2500$. The HHI index of 10,000 is set for a monopoly market and decreases as the number of banks entering the market increases. Here is another example: If the number of banks increases to 5, each having 20 percent of the market, the HHI would be $[(5)(.20)^2 (10,000)] = 2000$. This shows that an M&A deal may cause increases in the HHI because the number of banks in a given market decreases. Thus, antitrust regulators often use the HHI to screen bank M&A applications for potential monopoly or anticompetition. According to the 1982 DOJ guidelines, an HHI level of less than 1,000 is presumed to be unconcentrated and therefore not anticompetitive. An HHI level of 1,000 is considered moderately concentrated, and an HHI level of greater than 1,800 is viewed as highly concentrated and therefore anticompetitive.

The DOJ has issued merger guidelines based on the HHI for all industries, including the banking industry. The HHI is relevant in assessing the proposed bank M&A by considering every competitor in a market and by measuring the structural effect of the proposed merger in a particular market. The antitrust enforcement agencies have developed a numerical standard using the HHI to determine the degree of concentration resulting from a proposed M&A. If a proposed M&A would result in an HHI less than 1,800 (equivalent to having five or six equal-size firms) or would increase the HHI by fewer than 200 points (market share of 10 percent), then the proposal would be very unlikely to raise antitrust concerns. These numerical standards are not deciding rules; rather they are guidelines to assess the changes and level of concentration that may be caused by the M&A proposal. The Federal Reserve Board has also employed the acquiring firm's market share as an additional merger screen. For example, if an acquirer's pro forma market share would exceed 35 percent, the acquisition proposal would be subject to a more stringent antitrust assessment.

Mitigating Factors

The primary purpose of antitrust analysis is to determine whether a merger is likely to result in the exercise of market power. The Federal Reserve Board or the DOJ assesses the effects of each merger or market concentration and the ability of the combined institution to influence the pricing of financial services to both individuals and businesses. Thus, in addition to other considerations, the mitigating factors in M&A transactions are important in assessing M&A proposals. The Federal Reserve Board, in 1997, performed a major review of its antitrust policies and procedures. This review confirmed existing policies in two areas: (1) use of the cluster of banking services as the standard product line for this assessment of the effects of M&A activities on competition, and (2) use of local geographic markets as the standard for defining a market or changes in market concentration. The Federal Reserve Board cited several mitigating factors grouped into categories consisting of strong remaining competition, misleading HHI, potential competition, convenience and need considerations, and pro-competitive effects on the market. The rest may include thrift competition, nonbank and out-of-market competition, numerous remaining competitors, partial divestiture, deposit run-off, passive investment, total deposits incorrect, limited competition, financial health of the target firm, benefits to the acquiring bank, and applicants' small size in the market.[12] In assessing the effectiveness of current antitrust policies and procedures, Myron Kwast wrote "while antitrust constraints will occasionally affect the terms and conditions for consummation of a bank merger, the antitrust laws do not significantly constrain the vast majority of bank mergers and acquisitions."[13]

When a proposed M&A would violate the benchmark 1800/200/35 percent initial merger screen, the Federal Reserve Board examines various factors that might mitigate any anticompetitive effects that might arise from the change in structure. Examples of mitigating factors considered in assessing a proposed banking M&A are: (1) the competitive effect of potential entrants into local banking markets; (2) long-term market decline, acquisition of a failing banking organization; and (3) improved efficiency and effectiveness of the combined institution.[14]

Noncompliance with the established antitrust policies should prevent M&A deals. Nevertheless, the number of proposed M&A denials for financial institutions has been very low during the past several years. Indeed, the Federal Reserve Board has denied only two merger applications in the past several years, and both denials were of acquisitions of thrift institutions in rural banking markets.[15] However, simulations have indicated that the number of banking organizations in the United States could drop from its level of 7.300 to 6 without ever violating the Federal Reserve Board HHI M&A guidelines.[16]

The DOJ and bank authorities apply the HHI to all mergers in the banking industry to assess the effects of a proposed bank merger on competition and to determine possible violations of antitrust laws. The DOJ has issued M&A guidelines based on the HHI for banking and other industries. The guidelines suggest that if a banking merger shows an increase in the HHI of over 200 points in a given market (50 points in other industries) to a level greater than 1,800, the bank should be further assessed for antitrust enforcement. It is obvious that the more lenient standard, as measured by the changes in the HHI, applies to the banking industry as compared to other industries. This more lenient standard is designed to account roughly for competition from nonbank financial services providers (e.g., credit unions and finance companies). Furthermore, the Federal Reserve Board takes into consideration the 50 percent of the deposits held by nonbank thrift institutions in a market in calculating the HHI. This HHI typically is used as a first-cut indicator of the effects of a proposed merger on competition. Merging banks that violate these standards are often approved upon the presence of some mitigating factors demonstrating potential competition. Even disapproved mergers eventually may get approved conditional on the merging bank selling some of its branches to other banks to reduce the noncompetitive structural impact of the merger.

Traditionally, banks were restricted by law to operate locally. Restrictions on interstate and intrastate banking made them unable to expand their geographic markets. These restrictions were somehow relaxed in the 1980s and especially with the passage of the Riegle-Neal Interstate Banking and Branching Efficiency Act of 1994. This Act allows interstate branching into almost all states that promote M&A in the banking industry. The deregulation of geographic restraints on bank competition has improved bank performance in increasing shareholder value by becoming more efficient or otherwise being acquired by more profitable banks. However, the Riegle-Neal Act, by restricting the total amount of deposits of the merged banks to 30 percent in a single state and 10 percent nationally, did not significantly liberalize consolidation and integration in the banking industry. The Glass-Steagall Act and related legislation significantly restricted convergence in the financial services industry by limiting banks' ability to underwrite securities. Liberalization of these restrictions began in the late 1980s with the Federal Reserve allowing bank holding companies to underwrite corporate debt and equity through "Section 20" affiliates and revenue from underwriting corporate debt and equity to be as much as 25 percent of the affiliate's total revenue. This liberalization has been a powerful force behind several large M&A between bank holding companies and securities firms. Finally, the passage of the GLB Act of 1999 significantly liberalized M&A in the financial services industry by allowing business combinations among banks, insurance companies, investment firms, and mutual funds. The removal of many legal restrictions on statewise branching and out-of-state acquisitions decreased the anticompetitive effects of mergers in many markets by substantially increasing the likelihood of new entry.

PLAYERS IN MERGERS AND ACQUISITIONS

M&A is a transaction, and every transaction has a buyer and a seller. Knowing "market" terms is an important part of any negotiation, but sometimes the most basic challenge for small business buyers and sellers involves agreeing on a company's valuation. Buyers and sellers need to carefully consider the issues and options prior to sitting at the negotiation table.

Buyers

Buyers in an M&A process are those entities that desire to improve their company's performance through acquiring another business entity. Private equity, investment banks, hedge funds, and strategic companies also can represent the buy side of the M&A process. Trade buyers who come back in force compete head on with private equity, and, with the continued emergence of hedge funds, the range of participants in M&A make the market a crowded place. Hedge funds that are prominently involved in the debt capital structure of buyouts take the subordinated debt that sits between bank debt and equity. As transaction sizes increase, an increasing number of consortium deals may occur where private equity houses come together. Buyers need a successful implementation strategy so that the deal will be executed and the sought-after goals will be achieved (economies of scale, economies of scope, taxation benefits, synergy effect). The acquirer initially has to identify the key acquisition targets that would allow it to achieve the set goals. That is usually done by performing the initial due diligence process and solicitation of the prospective target. During the due diligence process, all possible material issues that can influence the M&A transaction must be assessed and resolved. Valuation and modeling are other major parts of the M&A process, although one of the hardest parts of M&A process is obtaining financing. Cash financing is used primarily in the acquisition process because shareholders of the target company have to be eliminated.

Sellers

Just like a buyer, a seller has a direct interest in the process. The only difference is that the buyer wants to buy as low as possible, and seller wants to sell as high as possible. Only in strategic merger are both sides willing to compromise and try to create a long-lasting partnership. Sale of the business can be both result of the overall development strategy (exit strategy) or an unfortunate part of a friendly/hostile takeover. For a seller, selling a business might be a turning point. There is tremendous pressure on the seller to be able to maximize the return to the company's shareholders. The seller has to be careful in preparing all the documents that might be needed for the due diligence process. If the seller is the one who initiates the M&A process, then it would have to be able to pitch the business to a few buyers simultaneously. The seller has to invest significant resources in understanding what market compensation it can expect from selling the business. (Valuation has to include not only the physical assets but also goodwill or going-concern value.) The business market price can fluctuate tremendously over time, so whenever possible, the seller would be better off forecasting the timing of exit to make sure that the transaction outcome is favorable to it. The seller also takes an active role in deal structuring and has to account carefully for the tax implications that might result after the deal is finalized.

Stakeholders Including Shareholders

When planning the M&A initiatives it is of critical importance to understand what parties (both on the individual and the organizational level) will be affected and how the deal can best accommodate their interests. Most common stakeholders that are directly or indirectly involved in the deal are bank employees, customers, existing vendors, business partners, governmental organizations, local communities, media, and shareholders. To be successful, deal makers must have a simple, transparent, and disciplined approach to measuring shareholder value creation. Cumulative abnormal shareholder returns due to the announcement of a merger reflect a revision of the expected value resulting from future synergies or wealth redistribution among stakeholders. A majority vote of shareholders generally is required to approve a merger.[17]

There is no question that stakeholders' interests must be prioritized based on their influence and interest in the transaction. For example, shareholders and employees must be given greatest focus because they have a direct interest in the forming entities. The best way to identify how stakeholders' interest can be served is to communicate with them. To reiterate, communication is key, simply because people and organizations directly involved in the process (employees, business partners, clientele, and shareholders) have a right to know what is going to happen with the entity in the future as soon as that information becomes available. As history suggests, the most successful M&A have been the most structured with the most organized and direct communication program.

Regulators

The United States and more than 60 other countries have adopted a so-called merger control regime that aims to prevent the development of monopoly. A variety of structures are used in securing control over the assets of a company, and these structures have different tax and regulatory implications. At a time when banks are strapped for capital and acquirers capable of taking over troubled banks seem in short supply, regulators may propose to let buyers count some goodwill toward capital. M&A are governed by both state and federal laws. State law sets the procedures for the approval of mergers and establishes judicial oversight for the terms of mergers to ensure that shareholders of the target company receive fair value. Mergers also are regulated by the Merger Guidelines, which are a set of internal rules adopted by Antitrust Division of the DOJ in conjunction with the FTC. The latest version of the Merger Guidelines became available for the public review on April 20, 2010. The main regulatory authority in the process of banking M&A is the FDIC. According to Section 18(c) of the Federal Deposit Insurance Act, also known as the Bank Merger Act, a written approval has to be granted to the bank by the FDIC before any bank can proceed with merging or consolidating deal. An application must be filed with the FDIC that weighs carefully all the potential deal consequences. Approved decisions appear on the annual FDIC Mergers Decisions Report.[18]

Advisors

M&A advisors usually assist the transaction flow between the banks. Acting as consultants, they prepare the business for sale and depending, on which side they represent (buyer or seller), assess or improve business valuation. Ideally, M&A advisors are there to add considerable value to the deal by forecasting the after-sale consequences and effects on the financial statements.

Advisors can represent both buy and sell sides, but typically more buy-side companies prefer to engage M&A professionals than sell-side companies.

Financial advisors or legal advisors can perform numerous advising roles in the M&A process. However, their main role can be defined as processing and mobilizing information to ensure that the intended deal is in compliance with all regulations currently in place and benefits both parties.

Typically there are three types of the financial advisors in the market: business brokers, midmarket M&A advisors, and investment and commercial bankers. The type of advisor is usually chosen based on the size of the acquirer and the transaction type. Investment bankers primarily deal with companies with revenues over $50 million and above and specialize in the stock placement or other securities underwriting. Business brokers are authorized to do only asset sales and apply the general valuation multiplier to price businesses. Midmarket M&A advisors are authorized to do both asset and stock sales and use sophisticated techniques to value businesses. Typically both midmarket M&A advisors and investment bankers have enough expertise to apply sophisticated valuation methods, such as discounted cash flow or strategic value.

Allen, et al.[19] argue that commercial banks themselves have great expertise to offer advising services because they have been able to establish long-term relationships with clients and can obtain information about the company's cash flows and sources of financing that would be relevant for the prospective merger. From a legal standpoint, information obtained through commercial banking relationships can be transferred, whereas information obtained for the investment banking purposes has to remain secret under Securities and Exchange Commission (SEC) regulations and U.S. Bankruptcy Code.

Others

M&A success entirely depends on the people who drive the business and their ability to execute, create, and innovate. It is of utmost importance to involve human resources (HR) professionals in M&A discussions as M&A has an impact on key participants (personnel) issues. Plenty of attention is paid to the legal, financial, and operational elements of M&A. But executives who are involved in the merger process recognize that management of the human side of change is the real key to maximizing the value of a deal.

Participant issues occur at several stages, but at the integration phase of M&A issues include: (1) retention of key talent; (2) communications; (3) retention of key managers; and (4) integration of corporate cultures. Often the role of HR is lost in the intense data crunching and financial negotiations that take place before the M&A; hence 70 percent of M&A fail due to HR issues. The HR issues can be broken down into three categories:

1. *Precombination.* Identifying reasons for the intended M&A, forming M&A team/ leader, searching for potential partners, selecting a partner, planning for managing the process of the intended merger and/or acquisition, planning to learn from the process.
2. *Combination and integration of the partners.* Selecting the integration manager, designing/implementing teams, creating the new structure/strategies/leadership, retaining key employees, motivating the employees, managing the change process, communicating to and involving stakeholders, deciding on the HR policies and practices.
3. *Solidification and advancement.* Solidifying leadership and staffing, assessing the new strategies and structures, assessing the new culture, assessing the new HR policies and practices, assessing the concerns of stakeholders, revising as needed learning from the process.

Therefore, the role of the HR department includes:

- Developing key strategies for a company's M&A activities
- Managing the soft due diligence activity
- Providing input into managing the process of change
- Advising top management on the merged company's new organizational structure
- Overseeing communications
- Managing the learning processes
- Recasting the HR department itself
- Identifying and embracing new roles for the HR leader
- Identifying and developing new competencies

The strategic contribution of HR consists of the "five Ps": philosophy, policies, programs, practices, and processes. As M&A activity continues to step up globally, companies involved in these transactions have the opportunity to adopt a different approach, including the increased involvement of HR professionals. By doing so they will achieve a much better outcome and increase the chance that the overall deal is a total success.

Culture (norms, common practices, values, attributes) can be ranked as the most challenging people issue in M&A. Culture is followed by effective leadership from the top; a well-executed employee communication program; integrating benefits, pay, and other rewards program on a global basis; and, most important, the correct selection of the top management team.

A highly productive business invariably has a high-performing organizational culture that aligns well both internally and externally to support the overall objectives of the business. This organizational culture shapes the employee experience, which in turn impacts customer experience, business partner relationships, and, ultimately, shareholder value. During a merger, two or more distinct organizational cultures must be integrated and fused. As M&A transactions increasingly become globalized, their complexity increases, and differences in national cultures and legal systems need to be considered. The criteria for employee recruitment, promotion, retirement, and exit;

formal and informal ways of socialization; recurrent systems and procedures; organizational design and structure; design of physical spaces, stories, and myths about key people and events; and formal statements, charters, creeds, and codes of ethics: all these count toward an organization's corporate culture.

 ## MOTIVES FOR BUSINESS COMBINATIONS

The primary goal and motive behind almost all M&A deals in the financial services industry is congruent with the main purpose for the existence of business entities—maximizing shareholder value. The most general motive is simply that the purchasing firm considers the acquisition to be a profitable investment. The increase in shareholder wealth of the acquiring entity could be a result of value created by the M&A deal or could result from a wealth transfer from bondholders to shareholders with no change in the total market value of the combined entity. This can be achieved by:

1. Improving the efficiency and effectiveness of the combined institutions through economies of scale and cost saving
2. Increasing their market power in selling prices and service fees (market power)
3. Increasing their access to the safety net
4. Financial and tax benefits
5. Management greed and self-aggrandizement
6. Obtaining a good buy
7. Stockholder expropriation

When two entities combine, the merged entity is expected to make more money. Other factors that may be important in an M&A deal are operational or financial synergies, economies of scale and scope, market presence, culture, cost cutting, revenue improvement or market share, cross-selling, taxation, geographic diversification, vertical integration, resource transfer, and expanding operations and territory. Although we can consider a number of different motives for acquisition, a coherent acquisition strategy has to be based on factors such as acquiring undervalued firms, diversification to reduce risks, improving efficiency and effectiveness, increasing market share or market presence, achieving tax shields and benefits, lowering financing costs, using of excess cash, achieving economies of scale and scope and improving performance.

Several hypotheses have been advanced to explain the motives for business combinations, especially the current M&A wave. These hypotheses, their justifications and rationales, and empirical evidence substantiating the hypotheses are presented in Exhibit 5.4. These hypotheses attempt to explain the capital market reaction to target and acquirer firms. Some of these hypotheses assume a non–wealth-creating behavior on the part of acquirers (e.g., hubris hypothesis) and predict that the share price of target firms will rise and that of the acquirers will drop with no net aggregate wealth creation. Other hypotheses assume a wealth-creating behavior predicting that the share prices of target firms will rise with no impact on share prices of acquirers.

EXHIBIT 5.4 Motivational Hypotheses for Mergers and Acquisitions

Motivational Hypothesis	Justifications and Reasonings	Empirical Evidence
Economies of scale	Combination of two or more entities yields an increase in effectiveness and efficiency of the combined business (e.g., increases in productivity and outputs; decreases in long-term costs). Unit cost decreases as size increases.	Jensen and Ruback (1983) found evidence of economies of scale resulting from M&A deals.
Inefficient management	The acquirer tends to buy out inefficient management of target firms and make it efficient.	Hannan and Rhoades (1987) rejected the hypothesis that poorly managed firms are more likely acquisition targets than other firms.
Reengineering	Cost savings resulting from divestiture and internal restructuring decisions made prior to or subsequent to the business combination.	Cheng, Gup, and Wall (1989) found evidence in support of reengineering as a motivational factor for bank acquisition.
Power	Optimizing size by eliminating duplication and lowering unit costs of financial services. Increases in size of business resulting from M&A and relationship between size and proposed management compensation and self-interest.	Phillips and Pavel (1986) found acquiring firms use mergers as a vehicle to increase market share and profits.
Geographic and product diversification	Enhanced profitability and risk moderation through geographic and product diversification.	Piper and Weiss (1971) argued that M&A occurs to overcome geographical limits on bank expansion.
Revenue enhancement	Impact of business combination on wealth of shareholders of combined entity (e.g., shareholder wealth maximization).	Hunter and Wall (1989) found that profitability measured by return on equity and core-deposit growth of acquired banks had consistently important effects on a merger premium.
Tax	Merger will create wealth to shareholders whenever tax liability of combination is smaller than sum of tax liability of the two individual firms.	Rose (1988) concluded that expected (1) increases in profitability, market share, growth rate, market power, and stock price and (2) decrease in tax liabilities were considered the important motives to pursue merger activities.
New business opportunities	Creation of new business opportunities and market expansion through M&A.	Cheng, Gup, and Wall (1989) and Palia (1993) concluded that new business opportunities play an important role in bank's takeover.
Decrease risk	Reduction in inherent business risk resulting from diversification.	Asquith and Kim (1982) did not find evidence in support of the diversification hypothesis.

(Continued)

EXHIBIT 5.4 *(Continued)*

Hubris	There is no gain to be realized from corporate takeovers primarily because financial markets, product markets, and labor markets are assumed to be totally efficient.	Roll (1986) concluded that any perceived monetary gains of mergers are offset by true economic value of combined firm.
Synergy	There is potential reduction in production and/or administrative costs when two or more entities combine.	Mueller (1980) found that nonmerging firms outperformed merging firms, indicating that mergers lead to reduction in profitability with no synergic effect.
Information	Shares of some firms are incorrectly valued by the market because relevant information about the firms are not available to public.	Firth (1980) found a permanent rise in price of target firms even in the case of unsuccessful tender offers.

Bank consolidations unquestionably affect the competitive environment due to changes of size and scope of the banking operations provided by banks. On one hand, advocates of the efficiency hypothesis believe that bank consolidations allow banks to achieve needed economies of scale, thus benefiting all the involved stakeholders. On the other hand, opponents support the structure-conduct performance hypothesis, which states that when banks grow in size and become too big, they start dictating their interest rates and, consequently, that results in the failure of the efficient market hypothesis. Academic research on bank mergers and the dynamics of deposit interest rates suggests, bank mergers have a positive short- and midterm effect on the deposit interest rates and may increase the value of deposit insurance.[20]

DETERMINANTS OF MERGERS AND ACQUISITIONS

The late 1980s to late 1990s were very fruitful times for the financial services industry in terms of megamergers. That wave was a part of a convergence trend in the financial services industry that began in the early 1980s. M&A activity is significantly larger in countries with better accounting standards and stronger shareholder protection. The premier reason behind the mergers was the aim to share risk and save costs. This is evident by a substantial decrease in the number of financial institutions in the past two decades. Exhibit 5.5 shows the trend in the number of banks and saving associations from 1980 to 2010. For example, between 1981 and 1997, the number of banks and savings and loan associations decreased about 40 percent (from more than 18,000 to less than 11,000). That trend continued all throughout 2010. To illustrate, the number of commercial banks decreased from 8,315 in 2000 to 6,839 in 2009 and the number of savings institutions dropped from 1,589 in 2000 to 1,173 in 2009.

Another significant wave of mergers occurred in the late 2000s as a result of government regulations. In 2006, the Federal Deposit Insurance Act of 2005 became effective. According to legislation, the FDIC guarantees depositors up to $250,000 in

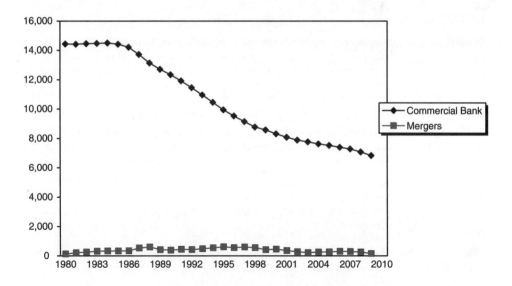

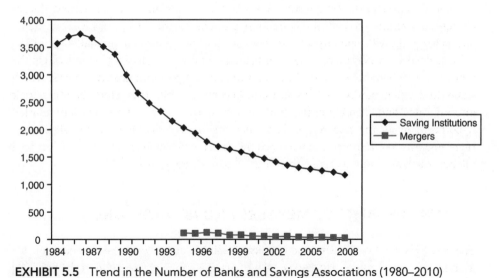

EXHIBIT 5.5 Trend in the Number of Banks and Savings Associations (1980–2010)

Source: Author's calculations based on data from the FDIC. Available at www2.fdic.gov/hsob/index.asp.

case a bank goes bankrupt. It is important to note that only deposit and deposit-related accounts are insured. Stocks, bonds, mutual funds, money market accounts, and any other accounts are not insured by the FDIC. In compliance with regulations, banks that are unable to cover their deposits and are in danger of bankruptcy can be taken over by FDIC administrators temporarily to prepare for sale or forced merger. To receive insurance and FDIC backing, banks must meet the rigid requirements of capitalization and liquidity requirements. Based on those criteria, banks are classified into five groups that represent that subsequent risk levels. Despite the strict regulations and liquidity requirements during the 2007–2009 financial crisis, 25 banks became insolvent and were taken over by the FDIC. In 2009, that number increased almost five times, with more than 140 banks becoming insolvent. To address the situation, the FDIC initiated the Legacy Loans Program that is aimed at helping troubled banks clean toxic assets from their books so they can obtain financing.

Even though M&A deals have become a common practice in the financial services industry, related challenges should be addressed to ensure success of these deals. Based on the general conclusion that M&A are failed strategies, analysis of the causes of failure often has been shallow and the measures of success weak. The determinants of the merger success include strategic vision and fit, deal structure, due diligence, premerger planning, postmerger integration, and external factors. Failure of any one of these can impede the achievements of the merger goal.

The challenges to execute an M&A deal include both the opportunities to achieve a profitable M&A deal (e.g., financial benefits to shareholders of both the acquirer and the target institution) and obstacles during the combination process where both human and physical resources eventually are forced to join. Thus, both financial opportunities and the related obstacles (e.g., different corporate cultures) should be examined and assessed when contemplating an M&A deal.

Although it is impossible to identify all causes and effects of the past merger waves in the financial services industry, we can explain and understand the most recent mergers. The current rapid pace of M&A can be attributed to several factors. Exhibit 5.6

EXHIBIT 5.6 Determinants of Mergers and Acquisitions

Factors	Description
Strategic vision and fit	1. Clear focus on scale to increase efficiency and cost cutting. 2. Clarity of the strategic vision is critical and hence real growth should be the only expectation. 3. Leadership from both companies must carefully analyze the strategic vision, how each company fits into that vision, and their compatibility in terms of culture, systems, and processes.
Deal structure	1. Attention paid to price premium and financial type. 2. Decision of whether to finance with cash, stock, or a combination depends on a number of factors, including accounting and tax implications. 3. Check whether a company's stock is overvalued or undervalued at the time of the deal.
Due diligence	1. Ensures that there are no disruptive surprises in the integration process. 2. The team should comprise members from both companies' functional areas (managerial, oversight) as well as accountants, lawyers, technical specialist, and so on. 3. Includes the formal financial review of assets, liabilities, revenues, and expenses and substantiation of the financial records along with numerous nonfinancial elements, including investigation and evaluation of organizational fit, ability to merge cultures, and technological and human resources capabilities and fit.

(Continued)

EXHIBIT 5.6 (*Continued*)

Premerger planning	1. Key decisions are made in the areas of leadership, structure, and timeline for the process. 2. Establishes clarity in roles and responsibilities for those involved in the integration process versus those involved in operating the businesses. 3. Source of final authority, direction, and responsibility should be made clear. 4. Early dates should be set for making key decisions and establishing metrics and targets.
Postmerger planning	1. Begins with proper premerger planning and a new well-defined organizational structure as part the strategy. 2. Processes including management of human resources, technical operations, and customer relationships must be carefully blended, and important decisions should made. 3. This process should generate a culture where employees see the merger as enabling them to develop the business rather than inhibiting them from progress.
External factors	1. Drastic/unexpected changes during the integration due to the success, failure, or actions of peer firms or economic conditions may affect fortunes of a single client or partner. 2. Distinguish between external factors that actually damage the value of the merger and those external factors that only damage perception of the merger.
Regulations	1. Lowering the restrictions on branching. 2. The passage of the Riegle-Neal Interstate Banking Act of 1994 eliminating interstate banking restrictions. 3. The passage of the Financial Modernization Act of 1999 (GLB) allowing consolidation in the financial services industry. 4. FDIC insures accounts up to $250,000 for accounts as of August 22, 2008.
Reporting and accounting standards	1. Generally accepted accounting principles (GAAP) versus regulatory accounting principles (RAP). 2. Fair value standards. 3. Exposure draft on eliminating pooling-of-interest methods.
Technological advancements	1. Advances in communication and data processing technology. 2. Internet banking. 3. Use of Web sites.
Business practices	1. Increases in the nationwide level of concentration in financial institutions. 2. Increases in earning power and earning quality. 3. Expanding financial services provided. 4. Steady increases in bank stock prices. 5. Increases in number of banks. 6. Reduction in bank failures.
Economic factors	1. Economic growth. 2. Low interest rates. 3. Abundance of money available for investment. 4. Excess financial capital.

summarizes possible determinants of current M&A in financial institutions. Four points are clear:

(1) The ever-increasing number of M&A would have been impossible without the elimination of traditional interstate and branching restrictions.
(2) The level of concentration gives more market power and purchasing power to acquire other banks. Although banking in the United States is relatively fragmented nationally compared to other industries (e.g., automobile, soft drinks), the two largest banks recently have doubled their market share. Unlike other industries (automobile, manufacturing), banks traditionally have provided financial services to local customers, which discourages excessive concentration at the national level. Thus, most mergers occur across local markets rather than within them to create synergy, which in turn makes measures of concentration virtually constant at the local level.
(3) The substantial advances in information technology, communications, and data processing play an important role in facilitating and making M&A possible in the banking industry. The use of automated teller machines (ATMs), electronic data interchange (EDI), financial EDI, and Internet banking enables banks to manage information databases more effectively and efficiently. The benefits of the techno-logical advances in offering financial services via the Internet and computer networks and reducing the data processing costs can be realized more effectively by bigger banks. Thus, technology is considered as the fundamental force driving the merger wave.
(4) The extraordinary abundance of financial capital (money) and stock prices result-ing from high earnings available for investment has encouraged the ever-increasing merger wave. The excess capital has gone into stocks, which has pushed their values to a high level in the past decade and encouraged shareholders of both acquirers and targets to take advantages of M&A deals. The globally abundant financial capital resulted from the globalization of economies and businesses, lower trade barriers, technological advances, and privatization, which are considered other important forces driving M&A transactions.

PERCEIVED SHORTCOMINGS OF MERGERS AND ACQUISITIONS

Merger critics have argued several perceived shortcomings of an M&A deal: the effect of Sarbanes-Oxley, higher financial service fees, diminished services, decreased credit availability, and undesirable impacts on competition.

Sarbanes-Oxley and M&A

Introduction of the Sarbanes-Oxley Act of 2002 (SOX) changed the way that businesses manage M&A transactions. As stated earlier in chapter 3, SOX (especially Section 404) has increased the costs of compliance significantly. Recently, financial executives have been flooded with information on the internal control requirements of Section 404 intended to improve the effectiveness of internal controls and reliability of financial reports . . . Critics argue that high compliance costs of SOX have disadvantage U.S. firms competing with foreign firms subject to less rigid regulatory regimes. According to the Foley and Lardner's 2005 National Directors Institute Study, SOX had three significant effects on the M&A process, even though the legislation does not explicitly regulate it. First, SOX complicates the laborious due diligence process. Both target and acquirer have to be Section 404 compliant. If the target is not compliant, the acquirer has to make sure that it has a plan to exercise to impose adequate internal control over financial reporting procedures in a timely manner. Second, SOX affects legal matters of the acquisition, as special SOX-specific warranties and representations must be included in the legal draft. For example, under Section 402 of SOX, it is prohibited to lend to executives and other officers through the companies' funds. Third, SOX changes the time frame of the deal process. It also significantly affected the timing of the deal, even though SOX Section 404 allows for the grace period of up to one year when the acquired entity can be excluded from the financial statements. There is no grace period for Sections 302 or 906 (executive certifications). That is why companies need to craft the deal timing to allow the acquirer more time to prepare for the compliance reporting.[21] A public company can face real challenges when it acquires a target of significant size that was privately held and therefore historically not subject to SOX. Public company acquirers should address these and related concerns by conducting more comprehensive due diligence of a target's SOX compliance and financial disclosure and systems before effecting a transaction. Hence, the issues that public company management should examine in conducting a SOX "audit" of an M&A target are controls and procedures and financial statement certifications (ensures accurate SEC reporting, and the chief executive and chief financial officers must certify as to the accuracy of their company's periodic reports).

Diminished Services

People are naturally resistant to change. Especially when a bank is taken over, they find it easy to complain about the quality of financial services they receive. The perception of diminished services can be explained by three main reasons: (1) The consolidation and convergence may cause changes in the mix and pricing of financial services, which may not be viewed favorably by customers who prefer the traditional financial services mix; (2) the economies of scale that make the merger more cost effective may dictate the standardization of financial services offered by the combined financial institution, which can inconvenience customers who are accustomed to tailored services; and (3) as banks merge into larger institutions, the combined institution may lose its focus on providing high-touch financial services tailored to satisfy customer demands. The possibility of lower-touch banking may adversely affect the well-established banking relationships with many customers.

High Financial Services Fees

No empirical evidence indicates that merged financial institutions charge higher fees for similar services after the combination. However, service fees on deposits as a percentage of deposits have risen by 42 percent for all banks and by 67 percent for large banks during the past decade.[22] This steady increase in service charges, especially by bigger banks, may increase customers' perception that merged banks charge higher fees than smaller local community banks. Larger national banks often do charge higher fees for services such as checking accounts, overdrafts, and the use of ATMs than small local commercial banks.[23]

Credit Availability

In most cases, small community banks, by virtue of having high-touch banking relationships with local customers, can tailor their financial services to customer needs. These specialized, customized financial services can positively affect the availability of credit to small businesses. The larger, megamerged banks may not be able to maintain close lines of communication between their lending officers and customers. However, large banks can overcome this perceived negative effect by offering loan convenience, such as loan applications being made over the phone or the Web.

Undesirable Impacts on Competition

Changing the ownership structure will affect firm behavior and the resulting price and quantity decisions. The change in firm behavior and strategic decisions takes into account new incentives for the merged entity but also competitors' reactions to the merger. The tendency of merged firms to set higher prices would be the basic ingredient for business combinations. From the viewpoint of competitors, the merged firm acts less competitively since it sets higher prices. A merger reduces the competitive pressure faced by nonmerging firms. Given that the merged entity raises prices of its products, the demand for competitors' products is higher in the postmerger situation. Moreover, as the discipline imposed by the prices set by the merged firm diminishes and its products become less attractive to consumers, competitors will face a lower risk of losing their clientele by substitution toward these products. Typically, competitors will raise their own prices in reaction to the merger.

The wave of mergers in the financial services industry that occurred in the mid-2000s has raised concern about their impact on competition. This concern has gotten the attention of policy makers and bank authorities to assess the social and private benefits of M&A and to ensure that consolidations in financial institutions are not detrimental to potentially vulnerable bank customers. Straham and Weston[24] found that smaller banks tend to invest a greater proportion of their assets in smaller loans than do larger banks. Two works by Berger and associates[25] concluded that consolidations resulting from loosening of geographic restrictions led to a decline in the supply and quality of small business loans. Prager and Hannan[26] found evidence that merging banks tend to significantly decrease deposit interest rates compared to nonmerging banks during the 12 months prior to and subsequent to a merger, which suggests that merging banks are not passing on efficiency gains to their customers.

There is a gap between what managers and investors expect from an M&A deal and what employees and customers desire from such a deal. Generally speaking, shareholders and managers are expecting a more efficient and effective combined institution resulting from an M&A deal. Employees and customers, however, may view business combinations as reductions in jobs and services. One reason for these expectations is too much emphasis on management and financial issues and inadequate attention to other factors, such as corporate culture, team-spirit chemistries, technological advances, banking systems, human resources, general negative attitudes toward M&A deals, and hostile feelings associated with convergence.

Employees typically view M&A deals as threats to their positions by jeopardizing their job security through cost reduction, downsizing and resulting layoffs, or competition between staff. Nonmanagerial employees might view an M&A deal as a threat and react with apathy due to lack of participation and involvement during the initial planning stages. Managerial employees may view the M&A deal as an opportunity to seize power and to advance, especially if they were involved during the transition phase of the M&A deal. Thus, proper communication with affected employees and encouragement of their participation during the various stages of M&A can prevent many problems during the due diligence, execution, and implementation of the business combination.

Continuous communication with all affected management, employees, shareholders, and major customers of both the acquiring and target institution is an effective means of reducing and controlling rumors and wild predictions during the M&A process. Since there can be a long period of time between the announcement of a merger and the consummation of the M&A deal, negotiation teams should continuously communicate steps of the process to the affected employees by means of conferences, speeches, newsletters, direct mail, lobby displays, and videotapes. This allows people to feel that they are participating in the process and gives them an opportunity to understand the changes that will be taking place and the reasons for them. This communication should focus on the advantages of the consolidation and convergence, the growth potential and opportunities to improve services, the role of employees in the combined institution, and how the business combination can contribute to the achievement of employees' personal and professional goals.

 ## STUDIES ON MERGERS AND ACQUISITIONS

Early empirical studies on M&A (e.g., Smith)[27] found that the profitability of acquired firms was not significantly greater than that of nonmerging firms. Empirical results on capital market reactions to M&A announcements are controversial and inconsistent. For example, Piper and Weiss[28] found that acquisitions by bank holding companies between 1947 and 1967 yielded no increase in earnings per share. James and Wier[29] concluded that gains to acquirer firms are positively related to the number of alternative target firms and negatively associated with the number of other potential bidders in the market. More recent studies[30] have found that merger premiums were associated with the regulatory environments for both acquirer and target banks and their characteristics (e.g., inefficient management, synergy, and new business opportunities). Exhibit 5.7 summarizes the findings of a number of studies on M&A.

Rose[31] surveyed 591 national and state-chartered banking institutions to gather information on their motives for M&A deals. The survey results indicate that expected

EXHIBIT 5.7 Empirical Studies of Mergers and Acquisitions

Studies	Findings
Smith 1971	Found that the profitability of acquired banks was not significantly greater than that of nonmerging banks.
Lev and Mandelker 1972	Focusing on areas of risk, growth rate, and financial structure, they found that monetary returns to shareholders of acquiring firm were higher but not statistically different from those of shareholders of nonmerging firms.
Dodd 1980	Shareholders of target firms earned large positive abnormal returns from announcement of merger proposals.
Piper and Weiss 1971	Acquisitions by bank holding companies between 1947 and 1967 yielded no increase in earnings per share.
Hannan and Wolken 1989	Found evidence that target firms show positive returns on average of 11.2 percent the day before merger announcement while acquiring firms accrue negative returns of 4 percent on two days before merger announcements.
Asquith and Kim 1982	Using a paired comparison of bond returns, found no evidence in support of the diversification hypothesis.
James and Weir 1987	Found that gains to acquirer firms are positively related to number of alternative target firms and negatively associated with number of other potential bidders in the market.
DeAngelo, DeAngelo, and Rice 1984	Offers (bids) are made in cash when bidding firm perceives its stock to be undervalued. Bid offers are typically made with stock when bidding firm perceives its stock to be overvalued.
Varaiya 1986	Found that any premium paid over market price in an M&A deal is result of positive error in estimate of value by buyer management.
James and Weir 1987	Found evidence in support of positive target shareholders returns and negative bidding shareholder returns.
Cheng, Gup, and Wall 1989	Concluded that target bank profitability, capital adequacy, management efficiency, size, diversification, and leverage are collectively significant in explaining premium paid by acquirer bank.
Servacs 1991	Found that takeover gains were larger if target company is performing poorly and buying company is performing well.
Healy, Palepu, and Ruback 1992	Found significant improvements in operating cash flows from increased asset productivity resulting from business combinations.
Cornett and Tehranian 1992	Found improved returns and cash flow for a sample of bank acquisitions resulting from attracting more loans and more deposits, improving productivity, and increasing assets.
Palia 1993	Concluded that merger premiums were associated with regulatory environments for both acquirer and target banks as well as characteristics of both acquirer and target banks (inefficient management, synergy, and new business opportunities).
Gart and Al-jafari 1993	Found that banks' core deposits, leverage, return on assets, state deposit cap restrictions, and nonperforming assets as well as the method of accounting (pooling versus purchase) are statistically significant in explaining premium paid by acquirer bank to target bank.

(Continued)

EXHIBIT 5.7 (*Continued*)

Hadlock, Houston, and Ryngaert 1999	Found that banks with higher levels of management ownership are less likely to be acquired, especially when target managers depart from their jobs following the acquisition.
Brewer, Jackson, Juliani, and Nguyen 2000	Provided evidence that indicates that passage of the Riegle-Neal Interstate Act has increased demand for target banks as the number of potential bidders increases, resulting in higher M&A prices.
Ismail and Magdy 2010	Synthesized prior literature on M&A and acquisitions transactions and their effects on financial performance; found that there are inconclusive results: Corporate performance is improved in some cases but not in others.

increases in profitability, market share, growth rate, market power, and stock price were considered the important motives needed to pursue their merger activities.

Curry[32] examined a large sample (1,156 banks) to determine the preacquisition characteristics of the banks acquired by multibank holding companies (MBHCs) during the period of 1969 to 1972. Curry found significant associations between dependent variables, such as risk, pricing behavior, operating efficiency, and profitability, and independent variables of market growth, bank growth, the state branching code, and the size of banks. Curry concluded that MBHCs tend to acquire "typical" commercial banks instead of acquiring banks with unique operating attributes.

Hannan and Rhoades[33] analyzed 201 Texas banking organizations acquired between 1971 and 1982 according to the locations of their acquiring banks (e.g., outside or inside the markets of the target banking organizations). They found that: (1) a poorly managed bank measured by several different ratios (e.g., return on equity, return on assets) did not have significant influence on the probability of being acquired; (2) the bank capitalization ratio (e.g., capital assets) showed a significant negative relationship with the probability of being acquired; and (3) a higher market share of a target bank increased the probability of being acquired, especially when its acquirer comes from the outside market.

Beatty et al.[34] examined a number of factors that may determine a bank merger premium and found that higher merger premiums (purchase price–to–book ratio) were paid to target banks that had a higher proportion of risky assets in the asset portfolio, were well managed and profitable, and were located in a noncompetitive banking environment.

Rose[35] analyzed data for all U.S. commercial banks that completed mergers between 1970 and 1980 and concluded that: (1) acquiring banks had a larger market share of deposits and loans as well as faster growth and less efficiency in comparison with nonmerging banks; and (2) target banks showed larger market shares, faster growth in deposits and loans, and more efficiency than nonmerging banks.

Fraser and Kolari[36] found a positive relationship between merger premiums defined as the market-to-book ratio and financial ratios of target banks measured as net income/total assets, demand deposits/time deposits, and leverage. Hunter and Wall[37] concluded that profitability measured by return on equity and core-deposit growth of acquired banks had consistently important effects on a merger premium. Cheng et al.[38] found a significant positive relationship between a target bank's profitability, core-deposit growth, loan quality, and a merger premium and a negative association between the total asset growth of the acquiring bank, the relative ratio of the asset sizes (e.g., the total assets of the acquired/the total assets of the acquiring bank), and a merger premium.

O'Keefe[39] analyzed merger-related data for U.S. commercial and savings banks between 1984 and 1995 and found that acquired banks, in general, had lower earnings and higher liquid asset portfolios than nonmerging banks and that the probability of becoming a target increases when the regulator rate on earnings is poor measured by capital adequacy, asset quality, management quality, earnings, and liquidity.

Several studies examined the effect of certain variables, such as interest rates, interest rate exposures, management incentives, corporate governance, and perform-ance, on the level of M&A activities. Esty et al.[40] concluded that the level of M&A activity is more positively associated with equity indices and more negatively correlated with interest rates for banks than nonbanks and that merger pricing is a function of the interest rate environment in the sense that acquirers are paying higher prices and earning lower returns when rates are low. Hadlock et al.[41] found that: (1) banks with higher levels of management ownership are less likely to be acquired, especially in a situation where target managers depart from their jobs following the acquisition; (2) high rates of management turnover follow bank acquisition; and (3) corporate governance or performance variables are not systematically related to the probability that a bank will be acquired.

Brewer et al.[42] investigated whether prices offered to target banks have been increased over time, increased prices encourage bank owners to sell, and prices are correlated with the financial characteristics of target banks and their market structure. They concluded that, prior to the Riegle-Neal Interstate Banking and Branching Efficiency Act of 1994, the number of potential bidders for a given target bank was limited by laws governing intrastate and interstate M&A activities. The passage of the Riegle-Neal Act has increased the demand for target banks as the number of potential bidders increases, resulting in higher M&A prices. Brewer et al. found:

1. Higher performance targets, as measured by both return on assets and return on equity, receive higher bids.
2. The lower the capital-to-deposit ratio, the larger the bid the acquiring bank is willing to offer.
3. Larger target loan-to-assets ratios are associated with larger bid premiums.
4. Bank size is positively correlated with bid premiums.
5. Market concentration is not related to bid premiums.
6. Changes in state and federal banking regulations have a significant impact on both bank merger activity and prices.
7. There are higher bid premiums in Southeast states relative to other parts of the country.
8. When target banks are large, but not megamergers of equals, there is a greater stock market reaction to the merger announcement than for other target banks, which indicates that large banks are using their increased freedom to merge in a way intended to increase the value of their deposit insurance.

LEVERAGED BUYOUT

A leveraged buyout (LBO) is an acquisition process by which one company purchases another company using borrowed money (leverage), and usually assets of both the acquired and acquiring companies are used as collateral for the loans. The debt is paid with funds generated by the acquired company's operations or sale of its assets. In fact, the transaction variations are endless, and the only part of the press definition that seems to apply in all leveraged buyouts is "leveraged." The main goal of the LBO is to generate the desired return on equity through a successful liquidity event. The leveraged buyout investment firms are better known as private equity firms (PE-LBO). It is a new type of institution, reflecting a type of finance capitalism that emerged in the late 1970s and early 1980s, rapidly grew until 1990—when it caused and experienced a financial and liquidity crisis—and then contracted before again growing even more rapidly and much larger through 2007, when it became involved in another liquidity crisis. The leveraged purchases historically are able to outperform the market indexes; thus they provide a larger return for private equity firms. Another great advantage of LBO is a tax shield it creates. Investors' interest payments are tax free, so the cash flow generated is much higher if it would be with pure equity purchase. The higher the risk, the higher return investors should expect. For this reason, LBO firms typically are looking at internal rates of return that are higher than 20 percent. The debt structure contains a combination of loans: bank loans, loans from different financial institutions (e.g., insurance companies, credit companies), and bonds or other public markets financial instruments. Since LBO transactions are risky, the underwritten bonds are typically low grade and high yield. Typically an LBO involves outside investors, and it is especially attractive to private equity firms because of the deal requires very little equity commitment.

The first LBO transaction occurred in 1955, when McLean Industries Inc. purchased Pan-Atlantic Steamship Company and Waterman Steamship Corporation. McLean borrowed the total amount of $49 million, and when the deal went through, $20 million of Waterman Steamship Corporation assets and cash reserves were used to retire debt, and a few months later the other $25 million was paid to McLean the form of dividend.

LBOs became increasing popular in early 1980s when the debt market was gaining popularity. However, after realizing the riskiness of these transaction methods, lenders started to require more and more equity to contribute. Based on Standard & Poor's portfolio data, in 2000, the average equity contribution to LBOs was almost 38 percent, and for the first three quarters of 2001 the average equity contributions were above 40 percent.

The years 2005 to 2006 were peak years for LBOs conducted by private equity groups. In 2006 alone, private equity firms purchased 645 U.S. companies for the total of $375 billion. The debt multiples available for borrowers hit the astonishing 10 times earnings before interest depreciation taxes and amortization during those years, and bankers demanded less equity. But as the economy started deteriorating, the number of LBOs went down and banks were very reluctant to finance deals. Lending standards have tightened so much that any deal with less than 40 percent equity did not have a chance to obtain financing in 2007.[43]

Not any company can become a target of an LBO; the acquisition target has to meet certain criteria to be qualified for the transaction. The main criteria are: very strong balance sheet, strong sustainable growth, no major future capital expenditures, diversifiable assets, room for the cost-cutting initiatives, limited working capital needs, and strong growing market share.[44]

A growing proportion of corporate restructuring is in the form of leveraged management buyouts, but this activity is controversial as it involves ethical problems and redistribution issues. Principal issues concerning LBO accounting include the question of whether LBOs are to be regarded as a purchase business combination by new investors, a step acquisition by existing owners, or a purchase of treasury stock by the old company. Other issues that may need attention to attain a complete understanding of LBOs are the different levels of research and development (R&D) spending and R&D investments long-term performance, which would depend on how well they do under the conditions of economic downturn or prolonged recession.

After an LBO, there should be significant improvements in profitability and operating efficiency. Managers have a large personal stake in the success of the business, and the pressure of debt along with the monitoring by debtholders provide strong pressures to increase efficiency while not sacrificing long-term profitability. Restructuring may force managers to concentrate on bottom-line results at the expense of long-term investments in R&D. The number of LBO M&A is expected to continue to increase because of the potential stability in valuations and increased availability of leveraged financing. Implementation of provisions of Dodd-Frank will have several effects on private equity M&A transactions through the Advisers Act applicable to private equity fund advisors. These advisors should register with the SEC rather than the states, and they are required to provide more transparent reports. Furthermore, private equity fund and hedge fund activities are limited by the "permitted activity" conditions of the Volcker rule of Dodd-Frank.

 POST MERGERS AND ACQUISITIONS PERFORMANCE

Post M&A performance is extremely important because it is one thing to announce the synergy effects and cost-cutting and other benefits while still in process and another thing to successfully implement the integration strategy so that they have a positive effect on the company's sustainable performance. Business combinations (M&A) can be motivated by improving the competitiveness of companies through gaining greater market share and broadening the portfolio to reduce some business risks. Customer and HR retention, alignment of organizational responsibilities, and merging two opposing corporate environments are just a few challenges that can arise during the integration. Solving those problems takes a considerable amount of energy, time, and resources.

The research conducted by Boston Consulting Group on real-world M&A and their success in postmerger integration process identified these lessons that need to be learned:

- The leader's role in guiding postmerger process is unarguably important. Tone has to be set at the top.
- A communication strategy that supports the M&A process throughout has to be tailored specifically according to the situation.

- The planning process is crucial to the success of the integration, so companies have to start planning well in advance.
- It is also critical to dedicate a special team responsible for continuously monitoring and supporting the postmerger integration process and making sure that the amount of possible added value is maximized.
- Ensure the customers are an integral part of the integration process.
- Postmerger provides an excellent opportunity to upgrade the leadership executive talent and create a knowledge curve that can be applied to the next merger.[45]

Merged bank holding companies (BHCs) typically experience postmerger profitability below the industry average. The market reaction to the merger announcements is significantly negative. The most important causes of the poor postmerger performance are credit quality and inadequate generation of fee income. Asset mix and capitalization also play a major part. Proper assessment of the postmerger effects presents significant challenges for management and ultimately determines the success of a material merger.

■ SHAREHOLDER WEALTH AND EFFECT OF MERGERS AND ACQUISITIONS

Most M&A experts argue that combinations typically adversely affect shareholder wealth. They state that there could be a multiple of reasons, but inability to retain top talent is one of the arguments. Lately companies have started to realize that they need to retain top talent and improve their statistics on shareholder wealth creation. A Bain & Co. study suggests that the percentage of deals that fail to increase shareholder value has declined in recent years, from 65 percent to 50 percent. Reasons include the fact that companies are getting better at the deal execution process, acquire the targets that are more closely related to their core business, and use more cash deals rather than stock deals, which results in more transparent due diligence and fair value pricing.[46]

Sometimes shareholders do not support the proposed M&A; gaining shareholder support is critical to the deal outcome. These next deals had to overcome a tremendous amount of shareholder resistance: Genesis Healthcare acquisition by Formation Capital, Lone Star Steakhouse acquisition by a private equity group, Inter-Tel acquisition by Mitel, and Reckson Associates acquisition by SL Green Realty. In these cases shareholders did not agree to the price offered by buyers, so buyers had to raise the price to meet shareholders' demands.

According to a Latham and Watkins report on M&A deals, here are a few reasons that could explain increased shareholder attention to the deals[47]:

- Since more and more hedge funds became shareholders of big companies over time, they started demanding that a certain return on investment be achieved.
- Following the hedge fund trends, traditional mutual fund investors also took a more defined position in the M&A process and expressed their opinion if they felt the price was insufficient.
- Media and other sources recommended that shareholders oppose deals if they are not satisfied with the price.

Two-step M&A and shareholders analysis are two of the most common ways to address shareholder pushback.[48]

Stock prices set in a rational, efficient market contain information that is useful in diagnosing anticompetitive mergers. Arguments arose that the purpose of the GM-Toyota joint venture was to prepare the firms for a predatory price to drive Chrysler and Ford out of business. That case would generate significant economic efficiencies, helping the antitrust agencies to decide on whether to opposing the business combination. The impact of U.S. antitrust enforcement suggests that the market power hypothesis rests on an extremely weak empirical foundation in the context of mergers. Thus, as long as the enforcement agencies continue to insist on rigid structural standards for evaluating the competitive effects of mergers, it is reasonable to suspect that special interest groups, including those representing relatively inefficient producers and/or a rigid workforce, will continue to attempt to take advantage of the regulatory process. It is possible that the threat of a challenge also deters a sufficient number of collusive mergers from even reaching the state of a merger proposal.

 ## JOINT VENTURES AND STRATEGIC ALLIANCES

As economies become more globalized, more and more firms are participating in foreign markets. The most popular participation strategies include exporting, licensing, strategic alliances, joint ventures, and direct foreign investment. Moreover, each of these strategies involves different levels of risk, capital, and returns. Strategic alliances and joint ventures are rapidly becoming popular with a growing number of multinational firms, and they play an increasingly important role in interorganizational relationships, allowing firms to capture benefits from new markets more quickly and at lower risk than through horizontal or vertical integration strategies. The rapid rate of change in competitive markets means that companies may not have the time to develop necessary resources and capabilities internally. Forming joint ventures and strategic alliances is one of the few available ways to strategically grow the company (along with organic growth or growth through M&A).[49] Joint ventures and strategic alliances force companies to share revenues and profits, but they also share less risk of loss and failure than M&A, besides allowing the companies to achieve similar synergy effects. Thus, the popularity of cooperative strategies increases as projected risk increases, because joint ventures allow firms to take on projects that are otherwise too risky or too costly. Economies of scale can be achieved when two or more firms pool their resources, maximizing efficiency based on the project's needs. In the cases where firms do not have the same strengths, creating alliances can allow them to share technology that can help firms produce more efficiently or at a higher quality. Firms must learn to recognize which other companies can offer complementary skills or technology.

Alliances empower two or more parties to engage in a contractual agreement for the purpose of executing a particular business undertaking. All parties agree to share in the profits and losses of the enterprise. Strategic alliance is an arrangement between two companies that have decided to share resources in a specific project and includes less involvement than a joint venture. Signing the confidentiality agreement is usually the very first step in a strategic alliance. Alliances may or may not be legally binding combinations, but that is always recommended for security purposes. Strategic alliances are based on trust and ideally have to facilitate the continuous learning process. There are typically three types of strategic alliances: cooperative agreements, outsourced arrangements, and licensed arrangements. All are applicable in different business situations and demand significant commitment from both sides. The strategic alliance life cycle approach recommends that organizations consider more than simply those factors leading to alliance formation. Examining the issues and factors affecting all stages of a strategic alliance's life will enhance the understanding of the alliance process and improve the likelihood of increasing both the longevity and the value of alliances to organizations.

Joint ventures are more sophisticated alliances that call for creation of the separate business entity and exist for a strictly defined time period. A limited liability company (LLC) is the most common legal structure for a joint venture. Since the LLC has limited liabilities and is not required to pay taxes at a corporate level, the legal structure allows partners to test the viability of the alliance without forming the corporation. Tax and financial/accounting considerations have to be discussed prior to entering into a joint venture.

ETHICS IN MERGERS AND ACQUISITIONS

M&A may sound like an exciting way to grow the business, but in reality it is a very tedious process that may affect many people's lives for a long time. Minority stakeholders and employees tend to suffer the most from that turbulent process. To illustrate, minority shareholders do not have much power over the decision-making process, and they cannot take an aggressive stance on the M&A issues. Moreover, the M&A decision sometimes is announced after the process has begun. All those factors may affect the performance of minority investors' portfolios and potentially result in adverse consequences.

Multiple layoffs are another serious aftermath of the M&A. The synergy effect is achieved by applying cost-cutting techniques on a larger scale, and companies can get rid of variable costs relatively pain-free. In October 2009 Pfizer bought Wyeth creating Pfizer-Wyeth. The combination could eventually result in as much as 20,000 layoffs across both companies.[50]

As a rule, companies focus more on the internal communications program than the internal one. The continuously deteriorating global environment and business scandals have rekindled interest in business ethics since an extreme case of unethical practice can literally destroy a company and incur an immense corporate loss. Typically department managers and HR are the ones who have to deal with complex ethical issues on a daily basis after the deal is officially announced. Since M&A is an efficient way for corporations to expand their operational domain in search for external growth, unethical practice is most likely to occur during the M&A phase.

Best practices suggest that the best way to confront ethical dilemmas is to communicate clearly; the company has to make sure that people know where they stand. Companies have to remember that human capital is an asset as well and that retaining and structuring human capital may be a critical input to the successful outcome of the deal. Failure to handle M&A ethical issues properly can result in employee cynicism, reduced employee morale, and increased employee turnover. Clark argues that employees whose organizations are going through the M&A process feel ethics-related pressure almost twice as much as employees at other organizations.[51]

Business ethics includes an array of issues, including macro environmental issues, human rights principle, industry-specific practices, organizational philosophy, and individual conducts. Business ethics has been widely studied in the areas of marketing, information management, labor relations, and human resource management. Yet, its influence is less explored by M&A scholars as M&A success lies not only in the completion of the financial transaction but also in the post-acquisition human resources integration and the realization of the synergy effects of the parties involved. M&A ethics is represented by employee perceived employment security, justice, and caring practices in this research.

GOVERNANCE IN MERGERS AND ACQUISITIONS

The success and the amount of wealth generated by M&A transactions largely depend on the effectiveness of corporate governance including internal and external control mechanisms such as independent directors, executive share ownership, and independent stockholders.

Board of Directors

According to the 2007 National Directors Institute study conducted by Foley and Lardner LLP, the role of the board of directors in the M&A process is crucial. Fiduciary duty and responsibility to the shareholders is the major duty for any board member. The board is responsible for obtaining all available information about the transaction and informing shareholders in a timely and accurate manner. The board can also play a role in the creation and revision of the investment strategy. Both companies' boards should approve the merger scheme and authorize the directors to make an application to the higher court under Section 391 of the 1956 Companies Act. Success of the deal sometimes is directly correlated with board involvement in the scrutiny process, a clearly defined M&A strategy, and implementation policies and procedures. The board plays a significant role not only during the initial stages of the process but later down the road. Once the positive decision has been made, the board's role becomes more interactive and requires board members to take subsequent actions on the information they obtained. Foley and Lardner LLP state that the board's focus at this point should be looking at the red flags. Continuous revision of the deal's status is necessary. Ideally, board members should come up with their own ideas on deal valuation. The board of the acquiring company also has to play an active role in the integration process. Board members have to review the integration plan in advance and give constructive feedback throughout the execution process. Directors should use their critical thinking abilities and business acumen and act as a "reality check" as they monitor the deal.[52]

Shareholder Voting

Voting on M&A is arguably one of the most important corporate decisions shareholders have to make. Whether this shareholder decision is influenced by the opinions of financial advisors has important consequences for shareholder wealth and the effectiveness of regulatory oversight. Further, studies show that shareholders on average experience significant losses when a firm undertakes an acquisition while the merger advisors stand to gain substantial fees when a deal is closed. The apparent conflict of interest between the merger advisors and the shareholders prompts the board of directors to examine the relation between acquirer shareholder voting and financial advisor opinions. It is possible that shareholders listen to financial advisors' opinions regardless of the potential bias and are more likely to support a deal when the merger opinion is more favorable. Alternatively, shareholders may choose to ignore financial advisors' opinions, and no relation exists between shareholder voting and financial advisor opinions. Finally, it is plausible that the acquirers' shareholders are able to recognize the more severe conflict of interest of their own advisors and are more willing to follow the less biased opinions of target advisors. Typically after the deal is officially announced, the proxy statement with information regarding the deal is sent to the target's shareholders. Then the special meeting is organized where the target's shareholders can express their opinion regarding the M&A. Under state and federal regulations, the shareholders of the takeover target have all legal rights to vote down the proposal. Although we cannot observe how institutions share the votes, we can observe the association between institutional trading around record dates and shareholder voting in aggregate.

Interesting enough from a legal standpoint, shareholders of the acquirer do not have to be notified until the newly issued shares used to finance the acquisition equal to or exceeding 20 percent of common shares outstanding before the issuance. For example, in the Pfizer-Wyeth merger contract, the voting provisions for Wyeth shareholders were included, but Pfizer shareholders were not required to approve the merger or the stock issuance as a part of the merger considerations.[53]

Shareholder voting clauses typically are incorporated in the M&A agreement. There are three types of provisions: voting provisions, "force-to-vote" provisions, and inter-shareholders' voting provisions agreements. The force-to-vote provision typically means that shareholders still must vote on the bids. There are two distinct rights that shareholders have in a voting process: contractual right, or the right to vote in favor of the combination, and statutory right, often the right to demand their shares to be appraised at a fair market value. There is also an option to vote the merger down, if the majority of shareholders vote the merger down during the special shareholders meeting. In short, all those issues need to be taken into consideration during the initial process to make sure there are no surprises.[54]

 MERGERS AND ACQUISITIONS PROCESS

Exhibit 5.8 summarizes the eleven phases of a typical M&A process. Although every M&A transaction is unique, this eleven-step process provides an overview of most M&A

EXHIBIT 5.8 Mergers and Acquisitions Process

Phase	Description
1. Strategy development	Establish M&A strategy consistent with organization's overall mission, goals, and needs to grow through business combinations.
2. Growth, synergy, and diversification	Identify strategies for growth, synergy, and diversification to reduce risks, and costs, while maintaining growth objectives.
3. Target identification and selection	Identify, screen, and select potential targets based on criteria designed to achieve M&A strategy and to minimize M&A risk.
4. Key issues identification	Identify key relevant issues and trends and incorporate them into due diligence team.
5. Transaction structure	Schedule initial meeting between two parties (potential target and acquirer). Key issues to discuss in this meeting include negotiating strategies, financing options, deal structure, and price. Structure M&A transaction in such a way that is good for both buyer and seller.
6. Due diligence process	Identify and evaluate potential deal breakers and gather information that can be used to determine purchase price and transaction structure reflected in nonbinding letter of intent. Ensure that functional specialists (e.g., accountants, appraisers, arbitragers, attorneys, risk management consultants) all get involved in this due diligence process. Analyze target's historical operations, products, profitability, capital spending, and working capital sensitivity.
7. Risk assessment	Identify all related M&A risks including: (1) operating risk that combined business does not perform as expected at time the M&A was approved; (2) overpayment risk of paying too much premium to target entity; and (3) financial risk of not having adequate financial resources to meet debt service requirements of combined entity. These risks should be assessed and then minimized in order for an M&A transaction to be successful.
8. Negotiation	Negotiate final M&A transaction by addressing issues such as purchase price, structure, and other key important issues and considerations, including accounting, tax, and employee benefits.
9. Financial structure	Financial structure depends on size of transaction and nature and quality of both target and acquirer organization. Incorporate these factors in financial structure: estimated purchase price; maximum amount of equity needed; projected amount of cash flow needed; and method of financing required cash flow (e.g., debt, equity).
10. Closing	Consummate M&A transaction by completing due diligence, reviewing all closing documents, exchanging financial consideration, and distributing all necessary documents to proper authorities.
11. Integration	Design and implement changes necessary to integrate new acquisition into existing business. Consider relevant actions such as downsizing, eliminating duplicate overhead, developing new cash management/treasury systems, consolidating accounting and management information systems, and transitioning new employee benefits plans.

transactions and describes many of the aspects of a carefully planned M&A deal. Chapter 14 describes the M&A process in more depth from the banks' point of view. The chronology of M&A activities in financial institutions consists of:

1. Developing M&A strategy.
2. Growth, Synergy, and Diversification
3. Identifying and selecting the potential M&A target(s).
4. Identifying key issues.
5. Structuring the transaction.
6. Starting the due diligence process of dialogue with the target.
7. Assessing all relevant M&A risks.
8. Negotiating the transaction.
9. Discussing financial issues including pricing the transaction.
10. Closing the transaction.
11. Designing and implementing integration.

Strategy Development

Companies need to determine their strategic objectives very early, as they form the foundation for all that follows. The first consideration in developing M&A strategy is to decide whether an acquisition or even a merger is an appropriate strategy for growth. For buyers, M&A is almost strategic and should be consistent with an acquirer's overall mission, objectives, and goals to grow through business combinations. The M&A strategy should clearly define financial objectives, acquisition criteria, and acquisition budget. Financial objectives, including purchase price, will vary depending on the unique characteristics of a target entity and its industry. The acquisition criteria should specify the objective(s) of acquisition as: (1) diversification of products, services, and related business risk; (2) expansion of market share by acquiring competitors; and (3) vertical integration by acquiring suppliers and distributors. The acquisition budget should specify qualifications, talents, and plans of management for postacquisition integration, risk profile of management (e.g., high-risk target with a greater potential for high returns versus low-risk probability of lower returns), and the required cash flow including the method of financing the purchase price (e.g., debt, equity, or a combination of both). The M&A strategy should also specify the types of financial advisor(s) and intermediaries needed for M&A consultations. Advisors and intermediaries include accountants, attorneys, business brokers, investment bankers, lending sources (e.g., commercial bankers), and M&A specialized consultants. Exhibit 5.9 provides a list of financial advisors, ranked by number of deals and total deal value in by the first quarter of 2010.

Growth, Synergy, and Diversification

Some scholars are convinced that the ultimate goal of the consolidation is the realization of synergies. However, companies may become involved in M&A for various reasons. Some companies look at a merger possibility as a way to save taxes; some want to expand into new markets and regions or diversify their portfolio of brands.

EXHIBIT 5.9 Top U.S. Financial Advisors Ranked by Deal Value[a] (U.S. and U.S. Cross-Border Transactions)

Financial Advisor	Total Deals Announced[b]	Disclosed Deal Value[c] ($mil)
Goldman Sachs Group, Inc.	21	$99,398.0
Morgan Stanley	22	$78,360.4
Credit Suisse Group	26	$76,531.1
Lazard Ltd.	9	$62,516.6
Citigroup, Inc.	16	$61,983.8
Deutsche Bank AG	16	$61,853.3
Blackstone Group LP	6	$50,399.1
Bank of America Corp.	15	$30,315.6
JPMorgan Chase & Co., Inc.	14	$23,212.2
UBS AG	10	$22,751.1
Barclays Plc	12	$20,732.8
Allen Holding, Inc.	3	$13,328.9
Greenhill & Co., Inc.	4	$13,195.5
HSBC Holdings PLC	6	$11,988.2
Rothschilds Continuation Holdings AG	7	$ 8,362.8
Centerview Partners LLC	3	$ 7,742.2
Guggenheim Capital LLC	1	$ 6,928.2
Perella Weinberg Partners LP	1	$ 6,928.2
ORIX Corp.	11	$ 4,606.4
Stifel Financial Corp.	4	$ 4,536.7
Peter J. Solomon Co.	3	$ 4,250.2
Royal Bank of Canada	6	$ 3,280.7
PricewaterhouseCoopers International Ltd.	2	$ 3,175.2
Government of United Kingdom	3	$ 2,522.4
Evercore Partners, Inc.	4	$ 2,393.2
Deloitte & Touche Tohmatsu	6	$ 2,061.1
Nomura Holdings, Inc.	1	$ 1,546.2
SunTrust Banks, Inc.	1	$ 1,273.1
Waller Capital Corp.	1	$ 1,273.1
Jefferies Group, Inc.	13	$ 1,224.9
Groupe Rothschild	4	$ 1,125.0
Close Brothers Group PLC	4	$ 924.3
Tegris LLC	1	$ 887.1
Violy Byorum & Partners	1	$ 887.1
William Blair & Co. LLC	9	$ 842.6
Wells Fargo & Co.	2	$ 600.3
Baird Holding Co.	7	$ 512.5
Cooperatieve Centrale Raiffeisen-Boerenleenbank BA	2	$ 510.0

(Continued)

EXHIBIT 5.9 *(Continued)*

Hodges Ward Elliot, Inc.	2	$ 459.7
P&M Corporate Finance LLC	1	$ 443.8
FBR Capital Markets Corp.	3	$ 437.4
Macquarie Group Ltd.	2	$ 429.3
KPMG Australia	1	$ 416.8
Lonergan Edwards & Associates Ltd.	1	$ 416.8
Raymond James Financial, Inc.	2	$ 411.9
Genesis Capital Corp.	1	$ 364.7
Canadian Imperial Bank of Commerce	3	$ 338.2
Broadpoint Gleacher Securities Group, Inc.	1	$ 329.4
WH Ireland Group PLC	1	$ 291.4
Piper Jaffray Cos.	1	$ 253.4
Stone Key Partners LLC	1	$ 225.6
Canaccord Financial, Inc.	2	$ 213.3
KBW, Inc.	15	$ 176.1
KeyCorp	2	$ 160.1
Bridge Street Advisory Services	1	$ 151.8
Danske Bank A/S	1	$ 145.5
Erik Penser Bankaktiebolag	1	$ 145.5
SNS Reaal Groep NV	1	$ 145.5
Needham & Co., Inc.	3	$ 123.0
Greene Holcomb & Fisher LLC	3	$ 111.6
Haywood Securities, Inc.	1	$ 100.5
Oppenheimer Holdings, Inc.	1	$ 100.0
BB&T Corp.	2	$ 99.1
JMP Group, Inc.	1	$ 89.0
Enam Securities Pvt Ltd.	1	$ 84.8
China eCapital Corp.	1	$ 80.0
Esae Capital Partners LLC	1	$ 77.7
PGP Capital Advisors LLC	1	$ 77.7
GMP Capital, Inc.	1	$ 73.5
The Stephens Group LLC	1	$ 60.0
The Jordan Edmiston Group, Inc.	4	$ 56.0
Arbuthnot Banking Group Plc	1	$ 55.4
Milestone Merchant Partners LLC	1	$ 52.9
Paradigm Capital, Inc.	1	$ 51.1
Marks Baughan Securities LLC	1	$ 50.0

[a]Value is the base equity price offered.
[b]Includes deals that have disclosed a price and deals that have not disclosed a price.
[c]Enterprise value.

Includes public and private transactions. Statistics as of year to date March 17, 2010.

Source: Factset Mergerstat LLC, available at www.factset.com/data/data/factsetmergers.

Growth and expansion is the most common motive behind initiation of M&A activities. Studies prove that typically the growth rate achieved through M&A is faster than organic growth.

Achieving synergy effect is the second most cited motive for mergers. Two types of synergies theoretically can be achieved: revenue enhancement and cost cutting. Synergies from cost cutting are obtained through spreading fixed and overhead costs and eliminating the redundant payroll, thus resulting in a lower per-unit cost.

The realization of the benefits of the diversification is an important element of the M&A strategy. Diversification allows companies to mitigate risks. The diversification effect is harder to achieve, because to capitalize on that risk management technique, the company's product/services should be very closely related. Banking M&A have higher chances to capitalize on M&A simply because they have similar clientele and vendors. Deng and Elyasiani identified that in the U.S. banking industry, geographic diversification leads to lower bond-yield spread and lowers the cost of capital.[55]

Target Identification and Selection

Identification and selection of acquisition target(s) should be done according to established acquisition criteria. The first step in searching for target(s) is to select the industry or industries that the acquirer wishes to consider. The industry candidate(s) can be the industry in which the acquirer has business experience with the intention of acquiring potential competitors, suppliers, or customers. The other approach is to consider other industries that have growth potential. The acquirer's acquisition criteria, strengths, and experience should be matched with the particular characteristics of the industry under consideration. The second consideration in target selection is the size and price of the target. The acquisition strategy should specify the minimum and maximum price the acquirer is willing and able to pay for the target. Searching for the potential target(s) can be handled in several ways, including through: intermediaries; personal contacts; professional referral sources such as lawyers, bankers, accountants, and appraisers; industry contacts; and business or M&A publications. The screening process should be based on sound screening criteria that incorporate marketing, production, financing, management, and administrative issues.

The screening criteria should be consistent and unbiased to reduce the broad universe of potential acquisition candidates to a handful of manageable, likely candidates. The reduced pool of candidates then should be prioritized according to the established screening criteria. The acquirer should obtain adequate relevant information regarding the pool of candidates for acquisition. Exhibit 5.10 provides a sample list of M&A information sources, which should be of great interest to acquirers.

Identifying Key Issues and Contacting Targets

Once a group of potential candidates has been carefully selected, they should be contacted and presented with a range of prices in order to create price competition and to maximize shareholder value. The potential candidates are selected by identifying and considering a number of key issues and factors unique to the acquirer, such as industry, location, marketing, products, management, size, earnings potential, and

EXHIBIT 5.10 Sample List of Mergers and Acquisitions Information Sources

Source	Information
Google Finance, Yahoo Finance	Financial information on public companies including stock prices
Bureau of Labor Statistics	Economic data
Dow Jones Financial	Newsletters, newswires, databases, and events for venture capital and private equity arenas, including coverage of portfolio company M&A
Daily Deal	Daily publication
Red Herring	M&A deal coverage in technology sector
Financial Trader	Magazine covers many recent trends on Wall Street and lists recent security issues
SEC Edgar Database	SEC filings and annual reports
Lexis/Nexis	M&A database
D & B Credit Reports	Financial information on more than 700,000 U.S. businesses.
Mergers & Acquisitions	M&A database
Mergerstat	Public company information
SNL Securities	M&A database including banks and thrifts
Moody's	Corporate profiles
Standard & Poor's	Public company information
Wall Street Journal Interactive Edition	Public company information
Corporate Growth Report	Weekly publication provides coverage of mergers and acquisitions, takeover speculations, and divestitures
M&A Journal	M&A history, deal coverage, takeover defense cases, rankings, legal, and regulatory cases

operating results. The acquirer should ensure that these candidates are genuinely interested in engaging in merger or sale discussion. The price range presented to potential candidates typically is driven by the acquirer's ability to reduce the operating expenses of candidates through downsizing, which may pose significant risk to candidates' employees and management. This process should assist the acquirer in selecting the appropriate and suitable target that meets the established acquisition criteria and ensures that its initial valuation fits the previously defined criteria.

Structuring the Acquisition Transaction

Structuring the acquisition transaction starts with scheduling the initial meeting between the acquirer and the target. Key issues discussed are negotiating strategy, valuation of the acquisition transaction, and financing options. Determining the value of the target is probably one of the most difficult aspects of the M&A transaction, primarily because every business is unique, and it is difficult to set the worth of the target at a single figure. The best way of structuring and specifying terms of a transaction is to reach an agreement that is suitable and acceptable to both the target and the acquirer. These issues should be addressed when structuring the transaction:

- The needs expressed by the target
- The requirements of the acquirer
- Considerations exchanged between the target and the buyer (e.g., cash, capital, combination of cash and equity)
- Income or estate tax situation of both parties
- Accounting method used for the transaction
- The role of the target and its management in the operations after the transaction is completed
- Compensation and employment issues for the target and key members of its management
- Financial structure of the purchase price
- The valuation methods used in establishing purchase price
- Postclosing issues (e.g., responsibility and obligation of the target, ownership of real estate or other fixed assets)

Due Diligence Process

Due diligence is the process of examining thoroughly the information provided by the target to determine the accuracy and reliability of the information, the acquirer's final decision to buy the target, the purchase price, and how to finance the M&A transaction. The primary objectives of this process are to: (1) examine all relevant information; (2) evaluate the key issues and potential areas of the business including financial, operational, legal, and contractual activities; (3) assess the potential risks of the M&A transaction; and (4) decide the purchase price and the methods of financing the transaction. The due diligence process consists of financial, operational, and legal due diligence. The due diligence process is a very important and time-consuming process requiring participation of key members of the management team as well as other professionals, such as attorneys, accountants, insurance experts, investment bankers, business brokers, operational and marketing consultants, and environmental specialists. This due diligence team should gather relevant and reliable information about the target by:

- Interviewing all key management personnel to determine the target's strengths and weaknesses of each functional area and the target's future prospects.
- Identifying and resolving deal breakers, which could delay or preclude pursuing the transaction any further.
- Determining the integrity and competence of all key personnel of the target organization especially those who are going to stay after the transaction is completed.
- Obtaining a thorough knowledge and understanding of the target's business and industry by reviewing the target's industry specifications as well as corporate records (e.g., articles of incorporation, bylaws, minutes, stock records), material

and continuous contracts, loan agreements, pending and potential litigation, employment contracts, stockholder agreements, royalty agreements, environmental liability, labor agreements, and any other important legal documents.

■ Examining the financial information and representations received from the target to: (a) evaluate the target's financial strengths and weaknesses including historical earnings, cash flows, financial position, and earnings potential; (b) corroborate assertions made through interviews and other sources; and (c) provide a basis for determining financial projections and forecasts.

■ Selecting valuation method(s) in determining the purchase price.

■ Considering all possible financial methods to finance the transaction.

The due diligence process should be completed before finalizing the financial terms of the M&A deal. Due diligence, consisting of an extensive due diligence checklist, should be prepared by the acquirer and can be scheduled at different stages of the acquisition process. It is usually in the best interest of both the target and the acquirer to schedule due diligence before final price negotiation and before any letter of intent or definitive agreements are signed. This gives the acquirer plenty of time to review the information and representation received from the target and allows the acquirer to put forth its best and highest offer price and reduce the risks of subsequent acquisition price changes. The target should sign a mutual confidentiality agreement before exchanging information with any potential acquirers.

Risk Assessment

A number of benefits can be derived from M&A deals, including:

1. The potential reduction in costs resulting from the adoption of more economical and efficient technology (synergy).
2. Expanding territory by creating better market for products or services.
3. Combining managerial positions and removing inefficient management.
4. Economies of scale.
5. Strengthening financial position.
6. Stabilizing a cyclical or seasonal business.

However, growing through business combinations is a decision fraught with risk that may cause failure of M&A transactions. The highest priority must be to mitigate risks where due diligence is expected. The acquisition team should identify, assess, and minimize all relevant M&A risks to a prudent, rational, and intelligent business risk. For starters, the team has to review the target's financial performance, asset, quality, market share, and risk management practices. This risk assessment consists of identifying all relevant M&A risk, quantifying the risk, determining the probability of risk occurrence, and minimizing the M&A risk to the acceptable prudent business risk. Relevant M&A risks, in addition to the typical business uncertainties of competition, demand and supply changes, pricing volatility, and technological changes, are operating, legal, overpayment, and financial risks.

Business and Legal Due Diligence

Proper assessment and planning for the possible business or legal complications that may arise later during the due diligence process add tremendous challenges for the M&A process to be successful.

Operating or business risk is the failure of the business combination to perform as intended and expected when the M&A transaction was completed. Factors that may cause occurrence of excessive operating risk are insufficient understanding and knowledge of the target business and industry, lack of a sound postacquisition integration plan, inexperienced management team in conducting a postintegration plan, mistakes in proper execution of the integration plan, and unrealistic expectations of the target's prospects.

Overpayment risk is the risk of paying too much premium to the target. Many factors can contribute to the overpayment risk, including:

- Undefined objectives for the valuation.
- Use of inappropriate valuation methods.
- Overestimating the market potential of the target's products.
- Inadequate and ineffective analysis of financial position and results of operations of the target.
- Mistakes in forecasting prospects of the target.
- Underestimating the impact of competition.
- Overestimating the potential benefits of the integration (e.g., synergies, cost saving, economies of scale).

Operational due diligence intends to ensure that the business operation will be run smoothly and that the planed operational improvements are achieved. Operational due diligence typically looks at vendors' effectiveness and managerial effectiveness and identifies ways to make them more controllable and structured.

Financial risk is the risk of not having adequate financial resources to meet debt service requirements of the combined entity. Factors that increase the financial risk are:

- Underestimation of the purchase price.
- Inability to raise the projected amount of equity.
- Mistakes in calculating the target's assets and cash flow in determining the financing gap to be filled by additional debt or equity.
- Ignoring the effect of changes in key variables (e.g., competition, economy, marketing, products, interest rates, revenue, and operating margin) on the proposed financial structure.
- Inability to generate sufficient cash flow to fund not only operations subsequent to integration but also the incurred significant debt service.

Financial due diligence involves a number of different estimations. The goal is to identify high-risk areas that would impact the decision to proceed with the transaction. The teams would look into cash flow projections, revenue validation and growth assumptions, testing, and so on. Cash flow analysis aims to identify the real sources of cash, specifically free cash flows, and confirms the value of the target company. Overall, financial due diligence has to provide a clear picture on the feasibility of the proposed combination and verify the possibility to achieve financial goals as well as verify the costs of the process.

Legal risk is the probability that the legal due diligence fails to:

1. Provide adequate and relevant information on legal issues and contingencies of the target.
2. Investigate the affairs of the target.
3. Uncover potential liabilities.
4. Ensure compliance with applicable laws and regulations.
5. Ensure the legality of the transaction.
6. Determine properly the target's capability to convey agreed-on assets, liabilities, and other attributes of the business.

Legal due diligence is an essential part of the M&A process. It determines predeal and postdeal transaction structuring and helps companies to navigate through complex legal issues. Legal due diligence helps the company to assess the contracts, intellectual property issues, assets, and corporate status of the acquisition target.

Business Judgment Rule

The business judgment rule is a legal doctrine that provides directors with broad discretion to make good faith business decisions. In fulfilling their oversight functions, directors are entitled to rely on available information, reports, financial statements, advice, and legal opinion provided to them by the company's management, independent auditors, legal counsel, and other advisors. Consequently, the business judgment rule implies that directors when making their decisions are reasonably informed and rational when using the information available for decision-making purposes. Directors may be held liable under the federal securities laws for engaging and distribution of materially false, fraudulent, or misleading information to investors that then influence the company's stock prices. SOX prohibits directors from fraudulently misleading investors or from trading during the pension blackout periods. Directors may be regarded as unfit to serve on boards when the company they serve is in violation of the securities laws, display unethical conduct, undergo a major bankruptcy, have financial restatements, have ineffective corporate governance, or fail to protect investor's long-term interests.[56]

Throughout the M&A process, a business judgment rule applies specifically to shareholders' protection issues: lock-up period and controlling shareholders' transactions. Consequently, in the M&A process, the business judgment rule intends to provide a fair and equal protection to all shareholders regardless of their proportionate ownership of the company. Other factors that may affect business judgment are duty of care and loyal issues, disinterestedness and independence issues, compensation, stock option backdating, appraisal and defensive measures, shareholder derivative litigation and the prelitigation demand requirement, and so on.

Negotiation

Negotiations play a crucial role throughout the M&A process primarily because the buyer and seller have different objectives, mind-sets, and incentives. For example, the seller desires to complete the M&A transaction quickly, collect the money without any strings attached, market the business to many potential buyers, and lock in the most desirable buyer. The buyer, however, wants to have the opportunity to conduct due diligence in making sound decisions, be able to get out of the M&A deal if certain conditions are not met, and have a concrete exclusivity period to complete the M&A transaction without competition from others. Continuous effective negotiations addressing these conflicting objectives, mind-sets, and incentives as well as other key issues should be conducted at every step of the process, especially when new information becomes available. The acquisition team should get all key personnel in both the target and the acquirer organization involved in developing a negotiating strategy. Outside experts should also be consulted when establishing an effective negotiating strategy. The negotiating strategy should be flexible enough to consider the needs, objectives, strengths, and weaknesses of both the target and the acquirer.

The negotiation of M&A transactions consists of two phases: preparing the letter of intent and finalizing the acquisition agreement. The purpose of the letter of intent is to confirm in writing the interests of the two parties (target and acquirer) and to document the basic terms and conditions of the M&A transaction that have been agreed on in the initial phase of negotiation. Legal counsel should be advised in preparing the letter of intent to ensure the nonbinding aspects of the letter. Although the letter of intent is not legally binding, it brings the parties closer to agreement by spelling out the interests of the two parties and reducing the possibility that other buyers will make an offer.

The definitive purchase agreement should be drafted by the acquirer's attorney to address the new issues that may arise during the due diligence process and to confirm terms and conditions of the acquisition. The content of a definitive purchase agreement depends on the structure of the M&A transaction. Exhibit 5.11 presents a typical

EXHIBIT 5.11   Sample of Definitive Purchase Agreement

1.   Description of the M&A transaction structure.
2.   Types of consideration used in the M&A transaction.
3.   Warranties by both the potential acquirer and the target.
4.   Purchase price and what is being purchased.
5.   Descriptions of any specific conditions that should be met at or before closing the M&A deal.
6.   Provisions regarding the operation of the target between the date of the agreement and closing of the M&A deal.
7.   Applicable law of specifying which state laws will govern the agreements.
8.   Descriptions of other terms of agreement such as general information relating to closing procedures, expenses, indemnification, and termination of the deal.
9.   Provisions for lock-up agreements, limiting the target's ability to negotiate with other acquirers.
10. Statement pertaining to truthfulness and accuracy of the target's information, representations, and warranties.
11. Any agreed breakup fee.
12. Provision for signature.

definitive purchase agreement. After the agreements are signed and publicized, the acquirer and the target should work together to satisfy the provisions and terms of the agreement. Specifically, the acquirer should closely monitor the operations of the target to ensure that the representations and warranties from the definitive agreement are true and accurate and that there are no material adverse changes in the operations or policies of the target.

Financial Structure

The financial structure depends on the size of the transaction, purchase price, and nature and quality of both the target and the acquirer. The first step in the financial structure is to determine the purchase price. The valuation methods constitute a starting point for establishing purchase price. Valuation methods typically being used for M&A transactions are industry rules of thumb, comparable company methods, comparable acquisition methods, asset-based methods, capitalization methods, discounted cash flow analysis, and leveraged buyout methods. These valuation methods are discussed thoroughly in Chapter 7. After the long process of finding a good target company, performing due diligence, negotiating a fair purchase price, and structuring the transaction, the acquirer should find a means of financing the deal.

The amount of financing is determined based on this formula:

Established Purchase Price	XXXX
Add: Transaction Expenses	XX
Total Funds Needed	XXXX
Less: Equity that can be raised	(XX)
Assets that can be converted to cash	(XX)
Financing needed through additional debt or equity	XXX

Sensitivity analysis should be performed to determine the possible impact of changes in key variables (revenue, operating margins, interest rates, economy, and competition) on the amount of financing. The transaction can be financed using equity, debt, or a combination of equity and debt. A variety of funding resources may consider equity investments (e.g., common or preferred stocks). Examples are business corporations, banks, investment companies, individual investors, institutional investors, insurance companies, and domestic and multinational corporations. Unlike debt, there are no scheduled payments for equity funding; however, equity investors have residual interests in the company and may exercise their controlling rights. Sources of debt financing are: (1) asset-based borrowings against the assets of the acquired company; (2) cash flow leveraged buyouts, which are financed in part by a lender who is willing to lend based on future cash flows; (3) long-term debt (bonds); and (4) sale/leaseback transactions.

M&A transactions should be executed according to applicable tax laws and rules. This requires examination of both the target's and the acquirer's financial reports and tax returns. Tax returns of the past eight to ten years should be reviewed to provide information on potential tax attributes, business relationships, tax-sharing agreements, accounting for loan fees, income taxes, M&A expenses, and projected liabilities. M&A transactions can be in the form of stock or assets, and depending on their specifications, they can be taxable or nontaxable. If the target bank will be taxed upon receipt of stock or cash, it will ask for higher premiums for the M&A deal. However, under the existing Internal Revenue Service guidelines, the merger may be considered tax-free when target shareholders receive stock equal to 50 percent of what they have given up.

Closing the Deal

The letter of intent and the purchase agreements usually specify a timetable to ensure that both parties move expeditiously and prudently to close the deal after a long process of finding the target, conducting due diligence, structuring the transaction, negotiating the purchase price, and securing financing. Several procedures should be performed to close the transaction professionally and legally. Among these procedures are:

- Completing the due diligence process, particularly the legal due diligence of reviewing all important legal documents and complying with the terms of the purchase agreement and other applicable laws and regulations.
- Obtaining a tax ruling if necessary.
- Receiving financing commitments.
- Completing the purchase agreement.
- Receiving audited financial statements.
- Complying with applicable laws and regulations.
- Securing key employment agreements.
- Resolving tax accounting issues of the transaction. (Tax and accounting issues of M&A transactions are discussed in depth in Chapter 9.)
- Maintaining minimum net worth requirements.
- Obtaining of third-party consents on the transfer of material agreements, licenses, or rights.
- Consummating the deal of distributing all necessary documents to the proper parties.
- Preparing for integration.

Integration

Subsequent to successful closing of the transaction, the acquirer should design and implement the changes necessary to integrate a new acquisition into an existing business. An effective integration plan, which specifies all appropriate postclosing decisions and actions, plays an important role in making the M&A deal a success. The integration plan typically is prepared by the acquirer's management; however, participation of the target's key personnel in finalizing the plan can improve tremendously its success and the speed of postmerger integration, an area that is usually neglected. The benefits and detriments of speed of integration may depend on the magnitude of internal and external relatedness between the merging firms prior to the merger or acquisition. Thus, the integration plan should clearly define the organizational structure of the newly merged entity including appropriate functional responsibilities (e.g., manufacturing, marketing, and accounting), their proper authority and responsibility, and their required human and capital resources.

Merger integration is a long-term process that includes a number of planned activities, such as downsizing, eliminating duplicate overhead, developing new cash management/treasury systems, consolidating accounting and management information systems, and transitioning new employee benefit plans. The HR aspect of postmerger integration is crucial to the success of the combined entity. Merger announcements typically cause anxiety on the part of employees who wonder about the future of the merged entity and their role, if any, in that future.

It is inevitable that not all employees, both in managerial and nonmanagerial positions in both the acquirer and the target, will be offered positions with the combined entity. In this case, it is advantageous to the combined entity to be generous with compensation and severance packages in order to improve new management's reputation, morale of the retained employees, and future alliances as well as to create goodwill among customers and employees. Employee compensation plans to compensate or protect the target's employees should be properly designed in advance, even before the preparation of the letter of intent, primarily due to these reasons:

- Any stock option, severance, or other similar arrangements with employees should be negotiated with employees; discussed with legal, accounting, tax, and professional advisors; and finally approved by the board of directors.
- Employees' compensation packets are often priced in the M&A transaction, especially any payments in excess of normal compensation.
- The acquirer typically considers any excess compensation in calculating the purchase price, which in turn may reduce the amount received by the target's shareholders.

The integration plan should consider all important issues and processes of the combined entity's HR, capital resources, organization structure, and business processes, such as sales, manufacturing, supply chain, and distribution. The integration plan should also have provisions for an annual postmerger audit for the primary purpose of determining whether the merged entity has achieved its intended goals and is continuously working toward achievement of objectives of broadening product lines, increasing market share, strengthening financial position, and increasing shareholder value. After the integration, the acquirer and the target (the combined entity) should work together to achieve their organization's goals.

Achieving Integration and Synergy

The main incentive for M&A is the added value creation for both parties of M&A as a result of synergies. However, postacquisition integration and resource reconfiguration may be necessary to exploit potential synergies between the acquired and acquiring firms. Moreover, effective integration of the target firm entails a substantial commitment of managerial resources of the buying company. It is said by practitioners that integration processes during the postmerger integration period are critical to synergistic effects and performance of the merged companies over time, although the relation among the postmerger integration process, synergy potential exploitation, and its influence on M&A deal success, especially in the case of international M&A, is not clear. The majority of researchers in the realm of M&A utilize a fairly conventional postacquisition integration perspective and thus rely heavily on quantitative methodological and analytical tools.

The quality of the postacquisition decisions will determine the long-term viability of the newly created entity. Board of directors and executive managers have to be exceptionally careful in making their decisions, as some may have negative impact on the combined organization. Harbir Singh and Maurizio Zollo proved that replacement of leadership has a negative effect on M&A process due to the continuous and lengthy interruptions in the process and routines as well as damaged professional motivation of those managers who survived the turmoil. Similarly, the study demonstrates that integration, in contrast, affects the performance of the newly created entity in an constructive way. The positive effects of integration of the two cultures offset the costs associated with integration process.[57]

Successful integration should be incorporated in firm's overall strategy, which has to be strictly followed. Adopting a convergence strategy, which implies a low degree of replacement and a high level of integration, could be a good alternative to a more standard consolidation strategy for the company that has not been able to establish an M&A learning curve yet but is planning to continue growing business through acquisitions in the future. A convergence strategy is more suitable for firms that are looking to improve their bottom line in the longer term; a consolidation strategy provides quick payoff but is also more risky for the organization.

Documenting in Mergers and Acquisitions Deals

In an M&A process, responsible management will require a comprehensive assessment of the possible legal risks related to the corporate status, assets, contracts, securities, and intellectual property of the target company concerned. The implementation of the ideal transaction structure, whether predeal or postdeal, often requires complex corporate legal documentation. In most cases the negotiation of the transaction will require a legal expert, as numerous legal pitfalls need to be tackled early on. The drafting of the transaction contracts and related documents cannot be done without special attention from a business-minded lawyer.

"Documentation" here refers to the legal documentation of the transaction that includes all associated agreements with the closing. Generally, creating the documentation begins during the due diligence once it seems likely there are no issues. The reason the buyer waits is to avoid large legal bills resulting from the documentation. These documents serve three key aims: lend structure to the process for shaping the deal, signal ideas and intentions from one side to the other, and manage risks in important ways. Sometimes deals may fall apart during the documentation phase. Effective documentation includes a copy of the purchase agreement that clearly highlights all aspects of the M&A transaction, any agreements with senior management and key employees of the acquired company, and agreed compensation schemes for senior executives and key personnel including stock option plan and other major agreements (escrow, equity option award, buyouts).

Legal Compliance Review

M&A best practices suggest effective compliance with all applicable laws, regulations, rules, and standards relevant to M&A transactions. As mentioned, the M&A process involves several critical steps. The legal compliance review is important for the entire process by both the buyer and the seller. The compliance review studies M&A strategies, mission, plan design, provisions, objectives, financial arrangements, investments, administration, communication, education, commitments, risk assessment, contribution amounts, and other costs for the seller, purchaser, or merging companies. The legal compliance review should be conducted for all stages, particularly in the early stage in the process, to understand the process of any liability before signing the final deal. Parties involved in M&A transactions should address various issues related to the Investment Advisor's Act of 1940 and state and federal regulations at the time of external transition process. Regulatory compliance is crucial and a key challenge for financial services industry, with the ever-increasing regulatory reforms (SOX, Dodd-Frank) and standards (Basel Committee) governing nearly all aspects of M&A transactions.

CONCLUSION

M&A within the financial services industry have continued with varying levels of intensity since the end of World War II. Prior to the Riegle-Neal Act, the number of M&A was limited by state law governing interstate and intrastate acquisitions. During the late 1970s and the early 1980s, some states formed regional banking pacts to permit banks to combine with or acquire target banks in pact states. The 1980s, 1990s, and early 2000s have witnessed substantial increases in M&A deals in the banking industry. Ever-increasing bank consolidation has been motivated by a favorable regulatory environment, opportunities for market expansion, greater efficiency following M&A, a strong stock market, favorable stock prices, economies of scale, and technological advancements. But the late 2000s proved that M&A happen in waves.

The wave of bank consolidations during the 1990s significantly changed the characteristics and structure of the banking industry in the United States. The number of banks has decreased substantially with far fewer local and small banks and more large and regional or national banks. The market shares of large banks have also increased as a result of megamergers. This rapid pace of bank M&A is likely to continue into the future and possibly accelerate in the financial services industry as a result of the passage of the Gramm-Leach-Bliley Act of 1999.

Regulators typically consider three fundamental factors—motives, value to society, and optimal response—when assessing an M&A deal. Motives refer to the reasons for consideration and the expectations of the acquirer from the M&A deal, such as achieving economies of scale, gaining larger market share, spreading best-management and practice techniques, and decreasing competition. Value to society is a trade-off between potential social benefits of increases in effectiveness, efficiency, and diversification and possible social costs of concentration, influence, and monopoly power. Optimal response refers to M&A activities undertaken to minimize undesirable effects of the deal, such as employee compensation, branch divestitures, and increasing quality and quantity of products.

Empirical studies of M&A transactions discussed in this chapter found evidence in support of the hypothesis that:

- Target shareholders incur positive abnormal returns while acquirer (bidding) shareholders experience negative abnormal returns.
- Banks that make larger acquisitions perform better than banks making small acquisitions.
- Cash tenders are more significant than stock transactions in determining premiums paid to targets (e.g., price to book value).
- Bank takeover valuations (price-to-book) have increased.
- The number of banks has declined.
- The size of M&A deals has increased.
- The number of M&A deals has substantially increased.

The decision to expand through consolidation or even sell a company that is a strong acquisition candidate is one that should be made by management and owners of the company. However, a professional, competent, and experienced appraiser or valuation firm can provide valuable valuation services in determining the appropriate asking price based on market forces. Consulting and using an experienced appraiser or valuation firm can make the tedious M&A process easier and the M&A deal more profitable to shareholders of the target company. Acquirers, especially public consolidators, often pay for their acquisitions with their own publicly traded shares, which are typically restricted. Restricted shares obtained through the M&A deal cannot be sold to third parties for some period of time, often one to two years or more. Thus, owners of the acquired company should have reasonable assurance and confidence that the acquiring company will be as strong as it is now in one or two years; otherwise, their restricted stock may be worth much less. A professional, competent, and experienced appraiser can assist the target company in determining the market value of restricted stocks and provide reasonable assurance that the stock is appropriately discounted from its currently stated market value.

Typical problems with most M&A deals are overpayment, lack of proper assessment of M&A risks presented in this chapter, and improper implementation and integration. Successful M&A deals, however, involve consolidation of closely related entities, small premiums, and participation and retention of acquired management. M&A decisions involve proper analysis and assessment of strategic, financial, and integration factors discussed in this chapter. The strategic review determines whether growth, especially through M&A, is a desirable choice. Financial institutions should perform financial analysis to determine whether the M&A deal increases shareholder value creation and reduces the risk of overpayment. Finally, the integration review determines the ability of the acquirer to successfully integrate the acquired financial institution into its own organization. Empirical studies show that ultimate success of M&A deals is measured in terms of the creation of shareholder value. To be considered a successful M&A deal, the merger should be effective operationally, and it should also create value for acquiring shareholders. The anticipated steady global economic recovery along with potential improvements in the financial and credit market conditions are expected to promote M&A activities across all industry sectors in 2010 and 2011. Industries that are anticipated to experience an increasing level of M&A activities are technology and pharmaceuticals/health care, financial services, and energy/natural resources.

NOTES

1. J. Spiegel and A. Gart, "What Lies Behind the Bank Merger and Acquisition Frenzy?" *Business Economics* (April 1996): 47–52.
2. Liz Rappaport, "Bank of America Chief Says Bernanke, Paulson Barred Disclosure of Merrill Woes Because of Fears for Financial System," *Wall Street Journal*, April 23, 2009. Available at: http://online.wsj.com/article/SB124045610029046349.html.
3. Richard Mason, "Global Oil and Gas Upstream M&A 2010 Review," *2010 PR Newswire*. Available at: http://conocophillips.einnews.com/pr-news/298293-global-oil-and-gas-upstream-m-a-2010-review
4. FDIC, Risk-Based Assessment System, Capital and Supervisory Groups, July, 2007 Available at: www.fdic.gov/deposit/insurance/risk/rrps_ovr.html.
5. United States Agency for International Development,-Funded Economic, CAMELS Ratings, October 2006. Available at: http://pdf.usaid.gov/pdf_docs/PNADQ079.pdf.
6. Grant Thornton, "Troubled Bank Opportunities: What You Need to Know about FDIC-Assisted Transactions," March 2010. Available at: www.gt.com/staticfiles/GTCom/Financial%20services/LSA%20white%20paper%20-%20FINAL%20linked_to%20post.pdf.
7. William Lenney and Paul Matteo, "Bank Mergers and Acquisitions Continue at Slow Pace," Federal Reserve Bank of Philadelphia (2009). Available at: www.phil.frb.org/bank-resources/publications/src-insights/2009/third-quarter/q3si5_09.cfm.
8. William Lenney and Lauren Jones, "Factors Affecting Bank Acquisition Valuations." Federal Reserve Bank of Philadelphia" (2008). Available at: www.phil.frb.org/bank-resources/publications/src-insights/2008/first-quarter/q1si4_08.cfm.
9. Federal Trade Commission, Horizontal Mergers Guidelines for Public Comment, April 20, 2010. Available at: http://www.ftc.gov/os/2010/04/100420hmg.pdf.
10. U.S. Department of Justice, "Merger Guidelines," June 14, 1984, p. 4.
11. Stephen A. Rhoades, "Competition and Bank Mergers: Directions for Analysis from Available Evidence," *Antitrust Bulletin* 41, No. 2 (Summer1996): 339–364.
12. Federal Reserve Board of Atlanta, "The Use of Mitigating Factors in Bank Mergers and Acquisitions: A Decade of Antitrust at the FED," April 1993. Available at: www.frbatlanta.org/filelegacydocs/holder_marapr93.pdf.
13. Myron L. Kwast, "Bank Mergers: What Should Policymakers Do?" *Journal of Banking and Finance* 23 (1999): 629–636.
14. David B. Humphrey, "Why Do Estimates of Bank Scale Economies Differ?" *Economic Review* (Federal Reserve Bank of Richmond) 76, No. 5 (September/October 1990): 38–50.

15. See "Order Denying Acquisition of First State Bancshares of Blakely, Inc.," *Federal Reserve Bulletin* 82, No. 10 (October 1996): 953–958; and "Order Denying Acquisition of BancSecurity Corporation, Marshalltown, Iowa," *Federal Reserve Bulletin* 83, No. 2 (February 1997): 122–126.

16. Stephen A Rhoades, "The Herfindahl-Hirshman Index," *Federal Reserve Bulletin* 79 (March 1993): 188–189.

17. www.articlesbase.com/management-articles/role-of-human-resources-in-mergers-and-acquisitions-957835.html.

18. FDIC Statement of Policy on Bank Merger Transactions, July 7, 1998. Available at: www.fdic.gov/regulations/laws/rules/5000-1200.html.

19. L. Allen, J. Jagtiani, S. Peristiani, and A. Saunders, "The Role of Commercial Bank Advisors in Mergers and Acquisitions," *Journal of Money, Credit and Banking* 36 (2004): 197–215.

20. Ben R. Craig and Valeriya Dinger, "Bank Mergers and the Dynamics of Deposit Interest Rates," Deutsche Bundesbank Euro System Working Paper, 2008. Available at: www.iiw.uni-bonn.de/people/dinger/papers/paper_wp08-06.pdf.

21. Foley and Lardner's 2005 National Directors Institute Study, "SOX Impact on M&A/Financial Transactions." Available at: www.diversitymbamagazine.com/wp-content/uploads/2009/09/NDI_SOXMandA_final.pdf.

22. J. Alfred Broaddus, Jr., "The Bank Merger Wave: Causes and Consequences," *Economic Quarterly* 84, No. 3 (Summer 1998): 1.

23. Eric Dash, "Bank Fees Rise as Lenders Try to Offset Losses," *New York Times*, July 1, 2009. Available at: www.nytimes.com/2009/07/02/business/02fees.html.

24. Phillip F. Strahan and J. P. Weston, "Small Business Lending and Bank Consolidation: Is There Cause for Concern?" *Current Issues in Economics and Finance* (Federal Reserve Bank of New York) 2 (1996): 1–6.

25. Allen N. Berger, Joseph M. Scalise, and Anil K. Kushyup, "The Transformation of the U.S. Banking Industry: What a Long, Strange Trip It's Been," *Brookings Papers on Economic Activity* 2 (1995): 55–218. Allen N. Berger, Anthony Saunders, Joseph M. Scalise, and Gregory F. Udell, "The Effects of Bank Mergers and Acquisitions on Small Business Lending," *Journal of Financial Economics* 50 (1998): 187–229.

26. Robin A. Prager and Timothy H. Hannan, "Do Substantial Horizontal Mergers Generate Significant Price Effects? Evidence from the Banking Industry," *Journal of Industrial Economics* 46 (1998): 433–452.

27. D. Smith, "The Performance of Merging Banks," *Journal of Business* 44 (April 1971): 184–192.

28. T. R. Piper and S. J. Weiss, "The Profitability of Multibank Holding Company Acquis-itions," *Journal of Finance* 29 (1971): 163–174.

29. C. James and P. Weir, "Returns to Acquirers and Competition in the Acquisition Market: The Case of Banking," *Journal of Political Economy* 95, No. 2 (1987): 355–357.

30. D. Palia, "The Managerial, Regulatory and Financial Determinants of Bank Merger Premiums," *Journal of Industrial Economics* 41, No. 1 (1993): 91–102. A. Gart and M. K. Al-Jafari, "Revisiting the Determinants of Large Bank Merger and Acquisition Premi-ums." *Journal of Applied Management and Entrepreneurship* 4, No. 2 (1998): 76–86.

31. Peter S. Rose, *Bank Mergers in a Deregulated Environment*. Rolling Meadows: Bank Administration Institute, 1988. Chicago, IL.

32. Timothy J. Curry, "The Pre-Acquisition Characteristics of Banks Acquired by Multibank Holding Companies," *Journal of Bank Research* (Summer 1981): 82–89.

33. T. H. Hannan and S. A. Rhoades, "Acquisition Targets and Motives: The Case of the Banking Industry," *Review of Economics and Statistics* (February 1987): 67–74.

34. Randolph P. Beatty, Anthony M. Santomera, and Michael L. Smirlock, *Bank Merger Premiums: Analysis and Evidence*, Monograph Series in Finance and Economics, New York University, 1987.

35. Peter S. Rose, "Characteristics of Merging Banks in the United States: Theory, Empirical Results, and Implications for Public Policy," *Review of Business and Economic Research* 24 (Fall 1988): 1–19.

36. Donald R. Fraser and James W. Kolari, "Pricing Small Bank Acquisitions," *Journal of Retail Banking* 10 (Winter 1988): 23–28.

37. William C. Hunter and Larry O. Wall, "Bank Merger Motivations: A Review of the Evidence and an Examination of Key Target Bank Characteristics," *Economic Review* 74 (September/October 1989): 2–19.

38. S. Cheng, L. Gup, and R. Wall, "Financial Determinants of Bank Takeovers," *Journal of Money, Credit and Banking* 21, No. 4 (1989): 524–536.

39. John P. O'Keefe, "Banking Industry Consolidation: Financial Attributes of Merging Banks," *FDIC Banking Review* 9 (December 1996): 18–37.

40. B. C. Esty, S. Harris, and K. Krueger, 1999, An overview of the project finance market, Harvard Business 31School case study 9-200-028.

41. Charles Hadlock, Joel Houston, and Michael Ryngaert, "The Role of Managerial Incentives in Bank Acquisitions," *Journal of Banking and Finance* 23 (1999): 255–285.

42. Elijah Brewer III, William E. Jackson III, Julapa A. Jagtiani, and Thong Nguyen, "The Price of Bank Mergers in the 1990s," *Economic Perspectives* (Federal Reserve Bank of Chicago) (first quarter 2000): 2–23.

43. Robert L. Samuelson, "The Private Equity Boom," *Washington Post*, March 15, 2007. Available at: www.washingtonpost.com/wp-dyn/content/article/2007/03/14/AR2007031402177.html.

44. Colin Blaydon and Fred Wainwright, "The Balance between Debt and Added Value," *Mastering Transaction/Leveraged Buyouts*, Tuck Business School. Available at: http://mba.tuck.dartmouth.edu/pecenter/research/Financial_Times.pdf.

45. Boston Consulting Group, "Trends in a Post-Merger Integration IV. Real World PMI, Learning from Company Experience." Available at: www.bcg.com/documents/file23276.pdf.

46. David Harding and Darrell Rigby, "Pursue Game-Changing M&A and Partnerships," *Harvard Business Digital*, February 11, 2009. Available at: www.bain.com/bainweb/publications/article_detail.asp?id=26897&menu_url=articles.asp.

47. Latham & Watkins, M&A Deal Commentary, December 2007. Available at: www.lw.com/upload/pubContent/_pdf/pub2065_1.pdf

48. Latham & Watkins, M&A Deal Commentary, December 2007. Available at: www.lw.com/upload/pubContent/_pdf/pub2065_1.pdf.

49. "Growth through Joint Ventures and Strategic Alliances," web.ebscohost.com.ezproxy.memphis.edu/ehost/pdfviewer/pdfviewer?vid=1&hid=104&sid=bcde8c90-b941-400f-911a-81d41b0d0fce%40sessionmgr113.

50. http://blogs.wsj.com/health/2009/10/15/pfizer-wyeth-deal-wraps-up-layoffs-to-follow/.

51. M. M. Clark, "Corporate Ethics Programs Make a Difference, but Not the Only Difference," *HR Magazine* 48, No. 7 (2003): 36.

52. 2007 National Directors Institute study, "The Board's Role in M&A Foley and Lardner LLP." Available at: www.foley.com/files/tbl_s31Publications/FileUpload137/3962/BoardsRoleMA.pdf.

53. Jim Hsieh and Qinghai Wang, "Acquirer-Shareholder Voting Rights in Mergers and Acquisitions," December 2006. Available at: http://69.175.2.130/~finman/Orlando/Papers/vote_121106.pdf.

54. "M&A Standards: Voting Rights and Wrongs," *Westlaw Business Currents*, April 21, 2009. Available at: http://m-currents.westlawbusiness.com/Article.aspx?id=ecb5366e-4904-40ac-af0b-3377556d78a5&cid=&src=&sp=

55. Saiying Deng, Connie X. Mao, and Elyas Elyasiani, "Diversification and the Cost of Debt of Bank Holding Companies," September 29, 2006. Available at http://papers.ssrn.com/sol3/papers.cfm?abstract_id=944728=.

56. Zabihollah Rezaee, *Corporate Governance Post Sarbanes-Oxley: Regulations, Requirements, and Integrated Processes* (Hoboken, NJ: John Wiley & Sons, 2007).

57. Harbir Singh and Maurizio Zollo, "Creating Value in Post-Acquisition Integration Process," Wharton Financial Institutions Center. Available at: http://fic.wharton.upenn.edu/fic/papers/98/9833.pdf.

CHAPTER SIX

Regulatory Environment and Financial Reporting Process of Financial Institutions

 INTRODUCTION

The safety, soundness, efficiency, and effectiveness of the U.S. banking system is best served by: (1) a stable monetary policy; (2) effective market discipline; (3) adoptive regulatory environment; (4) effective corporate governance; and (5) reliable financial reporting process. Given the significant changes that are taking place in financial institutions, the purpose of this chapter is to discuss the banking regulatory and financial reporting environment. This chapter examines the three most fundamental public policy issues facing the financial services industry: consolidation, regulatory reform, and financial reporting.

 CONSOLIDATION

The recent wave of consolidations in the banking industry, as discussed in Chapter 2, has resulted in fewer but bigger banking organizations. Consolidations have been viewed positively in the sense that they enhance the value of the combined institution to its owners by reducing the number of financial services organizations chasing marginal business and running up the cost of funds. Consolidations are also considered as effective vehicles for reducing overhead costs and creating economies of scale and scope, which in turn would benefit customers seeking desirable financial service. Consolidations can be very beneficial to the financial services organizations and their customers as the industry attempts to take advantage of economies of scale and scope and risk-reduction opportunities offered by geographic diversification. The financial services industry consolidation could be the result of natural global market forces driving the industry toward bigger organizations to achieve lower costs, higher profitability, and ability to compete effectively in the global market. Several factors have played important roles in promoting the current wave of consolidation in the financial services industry. Among these factors are technological innovations, geographic diversifications, and global competition.

Government regulations have traditionally affected consolidation in the financial services industry in two different ways. First, the McFadden Act of 1927, by vesting states with authority to limit branch banking and to prohibit interstate banking, placed limitations on geographic expansion of banks. Second, the Glass-Steagall Act of 1933 prohibited the line-of-business expansion for banks expanding into fields such as insurance and securities underwriting. Two important acts passed in the early 1980s have effectively nullified the McFadden Act. These are the Depository Institutions Deregulation and Monetary Control Act (DIDMCA) of 1980 and the Garn-St. Germain Depository Institutions Act (GSGDIA) of 1982. The passage of the DIDMC and GSGDI Acts and the corresponding changes in state banking laws encouraged a substantial consolidation and expansion in the banking industry during the 1980s. For example, in 1980, there were 12,679 banking organizations (including 14,737 banks). These numbers decreased to 9,688 organizations (including 12,526 banks) by 1990, indicating a 24 percent decline in organizations and a 15 percent decline in the number of banks.[1] The passage of the Riegle-Neal Interstate Banking and Branching Efficiency Act (RNIBBEA) of 1994 permits a bank holding company (BHC) to acquire target banks located in any other state. The RNIBBEA, by allowing national and state bank mergers across state lines, has lowered the previous interstate banking barriers and has had a significant impact in stimulating the ongoing merger and acquisition (M&A) activities in the banking industry. The Glass-Steagall Act was reversed in 1999 by the Gramm-Leach-Bliley Act (GLB Act), which permits line-of-business expansion combinations among banks, insurance companies, investment firms, and mutual funds.

Technological Innovations

Technology (e.g., Internet banking, visual and audio communication systems, and e-commerce) is crucial to providing financial services effectively and efficiently. Technological innovations have made it possible to reduce the cost and to increase the speed of providing financial services across distances, including national and cross-border boundaries. It is assumed that bigger financial services organizations have a higher potential to expand the scale and scope of technology in which they can invest and spread over a larger customer base. If enhanced technology lowers the cost of offering financial services, then the bigger financial services organizations may have economies of scale and scope advantage over small organizations. Thus, the cost and ability to afford investment in technological innovations can be viewed as a relevant factor in explaining consolidation in the financial industry.

The new technology has facilitated mergers in the financial services industry by enabling financial institutions to take advantage of economies of scale and related cost reduction. The use of technology has created opportunities for financial institutions to develop more sophisticated computerized financial instruments (e.g., derivatives) by unbundling risks and reallocating them to parties willing and able to take the risk. The new technology has also fostered full development of e-commerce and Internet banking. The new information technology (IT) has made universal banking possible, which enhances global competition in the financial services industry. Technological advances are viewed as an important impetus toward consolidation because they have made it more efficient for banks to grow larger and consolidate their operations.

Geographic and Activity Diversification

Prior to 1970, interstate banking was not practiced. In the late 1970s and 1980s, some states established regional banking pacts as other states allowed even nationwide banking systems with reciprocal arrangements.[2] Exhibit 6.1 presents interstate banking laws prior to RNIBBEA. The RNIBBEA allowed banks to expand across state lines and branch interstate by combining existing out-of-state bank subsidiaries and/or acquiring banks or individual branches through M&A. The Act also permitted BHCs to acquire banks in any states effective September 29, 1995, and merge with other banks located in different states beginning June 1, 1997.

EXHIBIT 6.1 Interstate Banking Laws Prior to Riegle-Neal Act

State	Area Covered and Reciprocity
Alabama	Reciprocal, 13 states (AR, FL, GA, KY, LA, MD, MS, NC, SC, TN, TX, VA, WV)
Alaska	National, no reciprocity
Arizona	National, no reciprocity
Arkansas	Reciprocal, 16 states (AL, FL, GA, KY, LA, MD, MO, MS, NC, NE, OK, SC, TN, TX, VA, WV)
California	National, reciprocal
Colorado	National, no reciprocity
Connecticut	National, reciprocal
Delaware	National, reciprocal
District of Columbia	Reciprocal, 11 states (AL, FL, GA, LA, MD, MS, NC, SC, TN, VA, WV)
Florida	Reciprocal, 11 states (AL, AR, GA, LA, MD, MS, NC, SC, TN, VA, WV) and DC
Georgia	Reciprocal, 11 states (AL, FL, KY, LA, MD, MS, NC, SC, TN, VA, WV) and DC
Idaho	National, no reciprocity
Illinois	National, reciprocal
Indiana	National, reciprocal
Iowa	Reciprocal, 6 states (IL, MN, MO, NE, SD, WI)
Kansas	Reciprocal, 6 states (AR, CO, IA, MO, NE, OK)
Kentucky	National, reciprocal
Louisiana	National, reciprocal
Maine	National, no reciprocity

(Continued)

EXHIBIT 6.1   *(Continued)*

State	Area Covered and Reciprocity
Maryland	Reciprocal, 14 states (AL, AR, DE, FL, GA, KY, LA, MS, NC, PA, SC, TN, VA, WV) and DC
Massachusetts	National, reciprocal
Michigan	National, reciprocal
Minnesota	Reciprocal, 16 states (CO, IA, ID, IL, IN, KS, MI, MO, MT, ND, NE, OH, SC, WA, WI, WY)
Mississippi	Reciprocal, 13 states (AL, AR, FL, GA, KY, LA, MO, NC, SC, TN, TX, VA, WV)
Missouri	Reciprocal, 8 states (AR, IA, IL, KS, KY, NE, OK, TN)
Montana	Reciprocal, 7 states (CO, ID, MN, ND, SD, WI, WY)
Nebraska	National, reciprocal
Nevada	National, no reciprocity
New Hampshire	National, no reciprocity
New Jersey	National, reciprocal
New Mexico	National, no reciprocity
New York	National, reciprocal
North Carolina	Reciprocal, 13 states (AL, AR, FL, GA, KY, LA, MD, MS, SC, TN, TX, VA, WV) and DC
North Dakota	National, reciprocal
Ohio	National, reciprocal
Oklahoma	National, no reciprocity for initial entry; after initial entry, bank holding company must be from state offering reciprocity or wait 4 years to expand
Oregon	National, no reciprocity
Pennsylvania	National, reciprocal
South Carolina	Reciprocal, 12 states (AL, AR, FL, GA, KY, LA, MD, MS, NC, TN, VA, WV) and DC
Rhode Island	National, reciprocal
South Dakota	National, reciprocal
Tennessee	National, reciprocal
Texas	National, no reciprocity
Utah	National, no reciprocity
Vermont	National, reciprocal
Virginia	Reciprocal, 12 states (AL, AR, FL, GA, KY, LA, MD, MS, NC, SC, TN, WV) and DC
Washington	National, reciprocal
West Virginia	National, reciprocal
Wisconsin	Reciprocal, 8 states (IA, IL, IN, KY, MI, MN, MO, OH)
Wyoming	National, no reciprocity

Source: Donald T. Savage, "Interstate Banking: A Status Report," *Federal Reserve Bulletin* 73 (December1993): 1075–1099.

Consolidation can provide financial services with the opportunity and potential to diversify across products (financial services) and geographic regions. For example, large banks can offer a greater variety of loans to a variety of customers in a variety of geographic areas through branching networks and specialized loan production officers. With the financial crises hitting the American economy, a term called "too big to fail" (TBTF) emerged.

The consolidation in the industry was one of the answers to TBTF companies. TBTF companies are those that are essential for survival of the economy. Their failure would lead to a disaster in the economy. This term became very prominent in public discourse from 2007 to 2010. The consequences of the collapse of Bear Stearns and Lehman Brothers were so disastrous that the federal government decided to back up other investment houses. The federal government also passed the Troubled Asset Relief Program program to protect the interests of investors and investment houses. However, many economists argue that TBTF is now virtually an official policy.

Moral hazards can be raised if these TBTF firms assume that the government's reluctance to hold them accountable for their business failures signals aversion to tough regulatory reforms and actions. To minimize this perceived moral hazard, the government plans to establish more severe regulations for the financial service industry to prevent significant adversarial impact of failures of large companies. Recent debates suggest that different sizes of financial services organizations may receive different regulatory scrutiny and treatment.

National and Global Competition

The current banking crisis is caused, in most part, by the excessive buildup of short-term debt. The excessive level of short-term debt systematically increases the risks of a financial crisis and causes a global economic meltdown. Thus, the stability of the international financial system is important. The financial crisis proved that the minimum Basel capital adequacy ratio of 8 percent was not sufficient to compensate the systemic risk that was taken by global banks and that there was no adequate and effective risk management system. Thus, the need for sound and consistent global banking policies and procedures became more important as the financial services industry and financial institutions are integrating worldwide. The widespread effect of the recent financial crisis demonstrated the growing integration of the global financial markets and the need for the global supervisory requirements, capital adequacy, and risk management assessments.

Economies of scale and scope as well as the potential cost reductions and geographic and activity diversification of consolidations should enable financial services to compete more effectively in national and global markets. Consolidation in the financial services industry may serve the public interest by creating social benefits if competition is maintained and consumer convenience of one-stop shopping is enhanced. U.S. laws governing bank acquisitions are neutral regarding the nationality of the acquirers. Indeed, banks and banking organizations in the United States have been open to foreign acquisitions in line with the U.S. government's commitment to the free flow of capital among nations.[3] The fourth meeting of the Group of Twenty Finance Ministers and Central Bank Governors (the G-20) Summit was held in June 2010 in Toronto, Canada. The summit was held to discuss the global financial system and the world economy. The theme of the meeting was "Recovery and New Beginnings." The summit included such current topics as evaluating the progress of financial reform, global bank tax, developing sustainable growth and stimulus measures, reducing global deficits, and promoting markets.

Global financial services firms should be keenly aware of and monitor and implement, whenever required, the regulations enacted under Dodd-Frank, the Basel III accords, and other initiatives endorsed by the G-20 to ensure compliance with the global regulatory requirements. The United States has been a major participant in efforts to develop global regulatory systems to identify and address issues and factors that contributed to the financial crisis. An important issue challenging to the global financial system is identification and proper monitoring of financial institutions that are deemed to be systemically important financial institutions (SIFIs). The G-20, meeting in Seoul, South Korea, on November 11, 2010, resulted in the development of a policy framework developed by the Financial Stability Board to monitor and mitigate potential risks and externalities associated with SIFIs worldwide. The suggested policy framework addresses the systemic and moral hazard risks associated with SIFIs and monitoring them through effective supervision. The Basel Committee will begin to implement the framework on January 1, 2013, with the phase-in process to be completed by January 1, 2019. The framework addresses five important aspects of SIFIs:

1. Establishment of proper measures to ensure that all troubled financial institutions can be resolved safely, quickly, and without destabilizing the global financial system and exposing taxpayers to the risk of loss
2. The requirement that SIFIs have higher loss-absorbency capacity to guard against the potential risks that these institutions pose to the global financial system
3. Development of more effective and intensive supervisory oversight for financial institutions that may pose global systemic risk
4. Establishment of robust core financial market infrastructures to reduce risk of losses from the failure of individual institutions
5. Development of other supplementary prudential and other requirements as deemed necessary by the national authorities to deal with SIFIs[4]

 ## REGULATORY ENVIRONMENT

There are several sources of bank supervision and regulation. Exhibit 6.2 reveals regulations pertaining to financial institutions. A bank, a savings and loan association (S&L), or a financial service firm may operate under a state or federal charter. National banks: (1) operate under federal charter; (2) are supervised by the Office of the Comptroller of the Currency (OCC); (3) are required to be members of the Federal Reserve Board System; and (4) are required to have their deposits insured by the Federal

EXHIBIT 6.2 Regulations Related to Financial Institutions

Year	Regulation	Provisions
1913	Federal Reserve Act	Created the Federal Reserve, the central bank of the United States.
1927	McFadden Act	Restricts geographic expansion of banks by limiting branch banking and prohibiting interstate banking.
1932	Federal Home Loan Bank Act	Created Federal Home Loan Banks (FHLB), which lent to savings and loan banks (S&Ls).
1933	The Banking Act	Created the Federal Deposit Insurance Corp. (FDIC).
		Separated commercial and investment banking (by the Glass-Steagall Act).
1933	The Glass-Steagall Act	Separates commercial banking from investment banking to ensure financial safety.
		Bars banks from paying interest on deposits.
		Restricts the types of assets banks could own.
		Prohibits bank distribution of mutual funds.
		Prohibits the line of business expansion for banks expanding into fields such as insurance and security underwriting.
1933	The SEC Act	Protects initial investors' rights.
		Requires full disclosure of all relevant information needed to make a decision about investing in corporate securities including banks' stock.
1934	The SEC Act	Protects the right of investors who trade securities.
		Requires full disclosure and audited annual financial statements of publicly traded corporations.
		Regulates all national securities' exchanges.
1934	National Housing Act	Created the Federal Savings and Loan Insurance Corp. Until its 1989 bankruptcy, FSLIC insured S&L deposits. Now the FDIC does.
1940	Investment Company Act	Separates fund management from other financial services.
		Establishes rules for selling practices, capital structure, and accounting.
1956	Bank Holding Company Act	Puts the Federal Reserve Board in charge of multibank holding companies.
		Grants the Federal Reserve Board to review the effects of consolidation in the banking industry.
1960	Bank Merger Act	Requires the Federal Reserve Board to review the impacts of merger in the banking industry by applying the competitive standards of the Sherman Act and Clayton Antitrust Acts on bank mergers.
1968	Federal National Mortgage Association	First Fannie Mae and then Freddie Mac were chartered as for-profit entities to encourage home buying by moderate income people.

(Continued)

EXHIBIT 6.2 (*Continued*)

Year	Regulation	Provisions
1970	Securities Investor Protection Act	Indemnifies brokerage customers against losses from a failed broker/dealer.
1977	Community Reinvestment Act	Pressed banks and S&Ls to provide credit to buyers from "red-lined" neighborhoods.
1980	Depository Institutions Deregulation and Monetary Control Act	Nullifies the McFadden Act. Permits branch banking and interstate banking.
1982	Garn-St. Germain Depository Institution Act	Encourages substantial consolidation and expansion in the banking industry. Permits branch banking and interstate banking.
1989	Financial Institutions Reform, Recovery, and Enforcement Act	FIRREA created the Resolution Trust Corp. (RTC) to solve the S&L crisis. It accelerated the move toward full-scale financial deregulation.
1994	Riegle-Neal Interstate Banking and Branching Efficiency Act	Permits a bank holding company (BHC) to acquire target banks located in any other state. Allows national and state bank consolidations across state lines.
1999	Gramm-Leach-Bliley Act or Financial Services Modernization Act (GLB)	Repeals Glass-Steagall Act. Permits banks, securities firms, insurance companies, mutual funds, brokerage firms, and asset managers to freely enter each others' business or merger. Creates financial holding companies that can conduct a broad number of financial services including insurance and securities underwriting, commercial banking, investment banking, merchant banking, asset management and distribution, and even real estate development and investment typically under separate subsidiaries.
2002	Public Company Accounting Reform Act (Sarbanes-Oxley)	Restore investor confidence in corporate America and its financial reporting. Regulate the auditing profession. Improve corporate governance.
2010	Dodd-Frank Financial Reform and Consumer Protection Act	Authorizes the establishment of an oversight council to monitor systemic risk of financial institutions and the creation of a consumer protection bureau within the Federal Reserve. Creates a new regulatory framework for financial services firms.

Deposit Insurance Corporation (FDIC). Federal S&Ls are chartered by the Office of Thrift Supervision and insured through the Savings Association Insurance Fund and the FDIC. Banks and federally insured mutual savings are insured by the Bank Insurance Fund of the FDIC. Dodd-Frank establishes several new supervisory agencies including the Financial Stability Oversight Council (FSOC) and the Consumer Financial Protection Bureau. Exhibit 6.3 outlines a typical national bank's supervisory and regulatory services.

EXHIBIT 6.3 Bank Supervisory and Regulatory Environment

Source	Date of Establishment	Mission	Applicability	Provisions
Offices of the Comptroller of the Currency (OCC)	1863 as part of national banking system	Comptroller of the Currency is: (a) Chief Regulatory Officer for national banks; and (b) responsible for governing operations of national banks. OCC has authority to charter national banks.	Examines all national banks to determine their financial condition, soundness of operations, quality of management, and compliance with federal regulations. Oversees regulation of federally licensed branches and agencies of foreign banks.	Operates as an independent unit within the Department of the Treasury.
Federal Reserve System	1913 by Federal Reserve Act	To perform as central bank of the United States. To assume responsibility for administering and making policy for nation's credit and monetary affairs. To act as fiscal agent, legal depository, and custodian of funds for the U.S. government. Oversee safety and soundness of state-chartered banks that choose to become members of Federal Reserve System.	State member insured banks (other than DC). Bank holding companies and their subsidiaries.	Holding legal reserves of banks and other depository institutions. Providing wire transfers of funds. Facilitating clearance and collection of checks. Examining and supervising state-chartered member banks and bank holding companies. Collecting and disseminating economic data.
Federal Home Loan Bank System	1932 by Federal Home Loan Bank Act	To provide a flexible credit reserve for member savings institutions engaged in home mortgage lending.	Savings associations, insured banks, and insured credit unions with at least 10 percent of their assets in residential mortgage loans.	Provides advances to members as a supplement to savings flows in meeting recurring variations in supply and demand for residential mortgage credit.

(Continued)

195

EXHIBIT 6.3 (Continued)

Source	Date of Establishment	Mission	Applicability	Provisions
Federal Deposit Insurance Corporation (FDIC)	1933 as part of the Federal Reserve Act and in 1950 under the Federal Deposit Insurance Act	To promote and preserve public confidence in financial institutions. To project the money supply through insurance coverage for deposits.	Insures deposits of up to $100,000 in: (1) national banks; (2) state banks that apply for federal deposit insurance; and (3) federally insured S&Ls.	Maintains separate insurance funds to insure financial institutions: (a) Bank Insurance Fund (BIF); and (b) Savings Association Insurance Fund (SAIF). Requires regular financial reporting on the part of insured banks.
Federal Financial Institutions Examination Council	1978 by Congress	To provide consistency and progress in federal examination and supervision of financial institutions.	Insured bank	Authority to establish principles, standards, reporting forms, and systems.
Office of Thrift Supervision (OTS)	1986 as part of FIRREA	Has responsibility for chartering and regulating federal savings associations and their holding companies. Supervising state-chartered savings associations.	Assures safety and soundness of federally chartered S&Ls and federal savings banks.	Operates as independent unit within Department of the Treasury.
Resolution Trust Corporation (RTC)	1989 by Financial Institutions Reform, Recovery & Enforcement Act	To manage and resolve financially troubled thrift institutions. Dispose of residual assets in a manner that: (a) maximizes returns and minimizes losses to FDIC Insurance fund; (b) minimizes impact on local real estate and financial markets; and (c) maximizes preservation of availability and affordability of	Acts as conservator or receiver for savings associations that are under direct control of government or that have failed.	Develops policies and programs for management and disposition of all real property assets under its jurisdiction. Funding comes from three sources: (1) Resolution Funding Corporation; (2) a line of credit from U.S. Treasury; and (3) unsecured obligations issued by the RTC.

(Continued)

EXHIBIT 6.3 *(Continued)*

		residential property for low- and moderate-income individuals.
State Banking Departments		Every state has an agency that supervises and monitors state-chartered banks.	Many state-chartered banks are also: (1) members of Federal Reserve System; (2) insured by FDIC; and (3) subject to regulation of those agencies.
Financial Stability Oversight Council (FSOC)	Dodd-Frank Act of 2010	To identify risks to U.S. financial stability.	To identify systemically important bank and nonbank financial companies.
Consumer Financial Protection Bureau (CFPB)	Dodd-Frank Act of 2010	To control certain mortgage industry practices that contributed to 2007–2009 financial crisis.	To issue rules designed to ensure U. S. consumers receive clear and accurate information to assess mortgages, credit cards, and other financial products offered by financial services firms.

BANK SUPERVISION

The Federal Reserve and other U.S. and foreign bank supervisory agencies through the Basel Committee have developed an approach for measuring and managing bank risk based on three so-called pillars: capital standards, supervision, and market discipline.[5] To supervise large, complex, and globally active banks effectively, U.S. regulators (e.g., the Federal Reserve) have developed a special supervisory program that focuses on continuous risk-assessment approach. Market discipline can provide oversight functions more closely to business practice by linking banks' funding costs of both debt and equity more closely to their risk taking and providing a supplementary reliable and objective source of information to the examination process.

The former chairman of the Federal Reserve Board, Alan Greenspan suggested a multitrack approach to bank supervision and prudential oversight by seeking to strengthen market discipline, supervision, and minimum capital regulation.[6] Dodd-Frank requires higher capital requirements and establishes a new regulatory regime for large financial services firms, by developing regulatory and market structures for financial derivatives, and by creating systemic risk assessment and monitoring. Dodd-Frank creates the FSOC to identify and monitor systemic risk in the financial system. The FSOC recommends appropriate leverage, liquidity, and capital and risk management rules to the Federal Reserve. The FSOC can practically take control of and liquidate troubled financial services firms if their failure would pose significant threat to the nation's financial stability.[7]

Market Discipline

Market discipline now plays an important role in banking behavior and supervision through disclosing adequate and relevant information to market participants. This market discipline is more important and evident when a large portion of bank assets is funded by non-insured liabilities. An effective market discipline requires (1) the enhancement in the amount and kind of public disclosure that uninsured claimants need about bank activities and on– and off–balance sheet assets and (2) the establishment of new disclosure standards to uniformize and improve banks' public disclosure and risk management practices.

Effective market discipline can be achieved when market participants, including investors, financial intermediaries, regulators, and policy makers, receive timely, reliable, and relevant information. This requires that financial reporting of financial institutions properly disclose the distribution of the institutions' internal ratings, asset quality, risk management, and management practices. Lack of existence of uniform international accounting standards based on fair value and ineffective enforcement of these accounting standards hamper the quality of information being received by global market participants. Improper financial disclosure can cause bad decision making and poor risk management assessment, which may result in ineffective market discipline.

One argument is that there is no need for corporate governance reforms, policy interventions, or regulations because product market competition provides incentives for public companies to adopt the most efficient and effective corporate governance structure. Companies that do not adopt effective corporate governance presumably are less efficient in the long term and ultimately are replaced. Nonetheless, the rash of financial scandals in the late 1990s and the early 2000s prove that market-based mechanisms alone could not solve corporate governance problems. The capital markets hit rock bottom in the early 2000s primarily because market correction mechanisms, lax regulations, and poorly developed disclosure standards failed to protect investors and thus diminished public trust and investor confidence in the capital markets.

Furthermore, market correction mechanisms often are initiated and enforced after the occurrences of substantial management abuse and after shareholders sell their shares and depress the price. Sale of shares has transaction costs and does not directly remove assets from management control as it involves simply passing shares to other investors who ultimately suffer the same management malfeasance. Market correction mechanisms may affect corporate governance after significant wealth is destroyed, resulting from management misconduct and corporate malfeasance and after considerable transaction costs for other stakeholders, including employees in the form of layoffs, lost wages and pension funds, and society at large in the form of lost taxes. Market mechanisms failed to prevent the corporate debacles of Enron, WorldCom, and Global Crossing, among others, that were devastating to shareholders, employees, retirees, and society, as almost all corporate wealth was destroyed. Thus, corporate governance reforms are expected to create an environment that promotes strong marketplace integrity and efficiency as well as investor confidence and public trust in the quality, reliability, and transparency of financial disclosures.

There should also be effective and comprehensive procedures for monitoring the performance of banks worldwide in meeting the established international banking standards (e.g., Basel Committee) as well as international accounting standards in reporting compliance with banking standards. Finally, failure to require fair value accounting (FVA) for financial reporting purposes of financial institutions worldwide can induce serious distortions in financial reports because there is always an incentive to realize gains on assets whose value has increased and retain assets whose value has declined.

Supervision

The most effective and efficient approach to bank supervision is to examine the safety and soundness of the overall structure and operation of banks' risk management systems. Proper emphasis and reliance on banks' internal risk management systems can also be used to enhance prudent assessment of a bank's capital adequacy. Indeed, the Federal Reserve, in June 1999, issued examination guidance encouraging banks to perform self-assessment of their capital adequacy in light of objective and quantifiable measurement of risk. This internal self-assessment will be evaluated during on-site examinations and will be considered in assigning supervisory ratings.

According to the provisions of the GLB Act, banking organizations can elect to become financial holding companies (FHCs) and perform a variety of financial services now allowed under the GLB Act. The Federal Reserve Board also applies capital and managerial standards to foreign banks wishing to establish financial holding companies comparable to those of U.S. banking organizations. The U.S. bank risk-based capital standards of 6 percent Tier 1 capital and 10 percent total capital are also applied to foreign banks becoming FHCs. In supervising FHCs, especially global FHCs, the Federal Reserve considers provisions of the GLB Act and relies on the Basel Committee to continue coordinating banking supervisory policies and practices worldwide. The global capital adequacy, determined based on the level of underlying systematic and economic risk, is an essential supervisory tool for fostering the safety and soundness of banks worldwide.

Reform of the supervisory role for the Federal Reserve and regulatory structure for financial institutions is needed to keep pace with the ever-changing characteristics and environment of the financial services industry. The passage of the Bank Holding Company Act Amendments of 1970 increased the role of the Federal Reserve in bank supervision and regulations. There has been debate in the financial community around the issues of whether there is a conflict of interest in this dual role of the Federal Reserve as related to monetary policy objectives on one hand and the supervision and regulation role on the other hand. Other countries (e.g., United Kingdom) have addressed the issue of reforming regulatory structures to better deal with the current changes in the financial services industry. Indeed, the Financial Services Authority (FSA) has been established in the United Kingdom to authorize, supervise, and regulate all forms of financial services including banks.[8] The primary reason for transferring bank supervision to the FSA was the current changes in "financial innovation and globalization." This important issue of separating central banking and bank regulation has received considerable attention in the United States and has been addressed by the Shadow Financial Regulatory Committee.[9] The committee made these observations and recommendations regarding the Federal Reserve perceived conflict-of-interest problems:

> There is at times a clear conflict of interest inherent in the Fed's carrying on roles as both a promoter of stability in the domestic and international financial markets and as a supervisor of banking organizations. . . . The authority to supervise national banks and their holding companies should rest with the Comptroller of the Currency, while similar responsibility for state chartered banks and their holding companies should be transferred to the Federal Deposit Insurance Corporation.[10]

According to Spillenkothen, effective bank supervision in the twenty-first century depends on the proper development and implementation of these strategies:

- Enhanced supervisory focus on the quality of internal systems and processes for identifying, measuring, monitoring, and controlling risks
- Active encouragement of banks to continually develop, reassess, and upgrade sound risk management policies and practices
- Substantial improvements in public disclosure by banks and greater reliance on financial markets to discipline and "regulate" bank risk taking[11]

The Basel Committee on Banking Supervision issued its guidance on "Microfinance Activities and the Core Principles for Effective Banking Supervision." in August 2010.[12] This supervisory guidance highlights the application of the Basel Core Principles for

Effective Banking Supervision to improve practices on regulating and supervising microfinance activities. The guidance is designed to help global banking organizations establish a coherent and comprehensive approach to microfinance supervision by focusing on these important elements:

- Proper and specialized knowledge of supervisors to identify, assess, and monitor risks that are specific to microfinance and microlending
- Efficient and effective allocation of supervisory resources to microfinance activities
- Development of regulatory and supervisory framework that is cost effective, efficient, and adequate

Minimum Capital Requirements

The regulatory capital requirements can be viewed as the third pillar of bank supervision and prudential oversight. The 1988 Basel Accord, in an attempt to create a level playing field for international banks, for the first time provided a common international definition of bank capital. The regulatory capital requirements should be linked to banks' internal risk ratings to ensure the adequacy of capital. During the past decade, banks and bank holding companies worldwide have been subject to a set of regulatory capital guidelines that define minimum amounts of capital to be held against various categories of on– and off– balance sheet position. The guidelines are established based on the 1988 Basel Accord adopted by the Basel Committee on Banking Supervision, comprised of bank supervisors from the G-10 countries.[13] Other countries have also adopted bank capital standards based on the Basel Accord that specify which debt and equity instruments on a bank's balance sheet qualify as regulatory capital. The U.S. risk-based capital standards conform to the guidelines of the Basel Accord.

The initial Basel Accord and U.S. risk-based capital guidelines focused primarily on a bank's credit risk exposure in suggesting minimum capital standards. The primary purposes of the risk-based capital measure according to the Basel Committee and as implemented by the Federal Reserve are to: (1) ensure that regulatory capital requirements are sensitive to differences in risk profiles among banking organizations; (2) achieve greater uniformity and consistency in the assessment of the capital adequacy of major banks worldwide; (3) factor off–balance sheet exposures (e.g., derivatives) into the measurement of capital adequacy; and (4) minimize disincentives to holding liquid, low-risk assets.

The risk-based capital measure is intended to evaluate the credit risk associated with the nature of banking organizations and provides a definition of capital and a framework for determining risk-weighted assets by relating assets and off–balance sheet items to broad categories of credit risk. A bank's risk-based capital ratio is then calculated by dividing its qualifying capital by its risk-weighted assets. This risk-based capital ratio establishes minimum supervisory capital standards that apply to all banking organizations on a consolidated basis. This ratio focuses primarily on credit risk and its impact on capital adequacy. Thus, for overall assessment purposes of capital adequacy, the other components of risk, including interest rate, liquidity, funding, and market risks, should be taken into consideration.

The two elements of the risk-based capital ratio are the qualifying capital and risk-weighted assets. Banking organizations' capital consists of two major components: core capital and supplementary capital. Core capital elements, also known as Tier 1 capital, consist of common equity (e.g., common stock and retained earnings), qualifying noncumulative perpetual preferred stock, and minority interest in the equity accounts of consolidated subsidiaries. Supplementary capital elements, also known as Tier 2 capital, include a limited amount of the allowance for loan and lease losses, perpetual preferred stock that does not qualify as Tier 2 (e.g., perpetual preferred stock of bank holding companies exceeding the 25 percent cap of Tier 1 capital), mandatory convertible securities and other hybrid capital instruments, long-term preferred stock, intermediate preferred stock, limited amounts of subordinated debt, and unrealized holding gains on qualifying equity securities. The qualifying capital for the purpose of calculating the risk-based capital ratio is the sum of Tier 1 and Tier 2 capital less any deductions.

The denominator of the risk-based capital ratio is the risk-weighted assets, which are calculated by assigning one of four broad risk categories (e.g., 0, 20, 50, and 100 percent) to each asset and off–balance sheet item. The four broad risk categories are determined based on the obligor, guarantor, or type of collateral. However, the standard risk category most often used for the majority of assets is 100 percent. The risk-weighted assets are calculated by multiplying the dollar value of the amount in each category by associated risk and then adding them together to determine the risk-weighted assets. Nevertheless, in 1996, both the U.S. risk-based capital guidelines and the Basel Accord were amended to incorporate minimum capital standards for a bank's exposure to market risk.[14] "Market risk" is broadly defined as the risk of loss from an adverse movement in the market value of an asset, liability, or off–balance sheet position. Market risk is determined by the volatility of underlying risk factors, such as interest rates, exchange rates, equity prices, or commodity prices, as well as the sensitivity of the bank's portfolio to movements in these risk factors.

Currently, capital standards focus on the market risk resulting from a bank's trading activities as well as its overall exposure to interest risk. The market risk capital standards require both a quantitative minimum capital charge based on the output of a bank's internal risk management model and a number of qualitative standards for the measurement and management of market risk. The qualitative standards incorporate some of the basic principles of sound risk management into the capital requirement and consist of:

- A risk measurement system that is conceptually sound and adequate and is implemented effectively with integrity.
- Periodic stress tests of its portfolio to assess the impact of extreme market conditions.
- An independent risk control unit that is separate from the business units that generate market risk exposure.
- An independent review of the bank's risk management and measurement process conducted by internal and/or external auditors.

The qualitative capital requirements consist of separate capital charges for general market risk and specific risk. "General market risk" is defined in the capital standards as the risk resulting from movements in the general level of underlying risk factors, such as interest rates, exchange rates, and equity prices and commodity prices. "Specific risk" is defined as the risk of an adverse movement in the price of an individual security due to factors related to the individual insurer, which is intended to cover even the credit risk.

The Federal Reserve amended its risk-based capital framework in August 1996 to incorporate a measure of market risk. Financial institutions with $1 billion or more trading activity or global trading activity greater than 10 percent of their total assets should assess their market risk using their internal value at risk (VaR). Financial institutions may calculate VaR using an internal model based on variance-covariance matrices, historical simulations, Monte Carlo simulations, or other statistical approaches.

The 1996 market-risk amendment requires that a supervisor request this quarterly market-risk related information:[15]

- Total trading gain or loss for the quarter
- Average risk-based capital charge for market risk during the quarter
- Market-risk capital charge for general risk during the quarter
- Average one-day VaR for the quarter
- Maximum one-day VaR for the quarter
- Larger one-day loss during the quarter and the VaR for the preceding day
- The number of times the loss exceeded the one-day VaR during the quarter and, for each occurrence, the amount of the loss and the prior day's VaR
- The cause of back-testing exceptions, either by portfolio or major risk factor
- The market-risk multiplier currently in use

An institution's VaR measures must also meet these quantitative requirements:

- The VaR methodology must be commensurate with the nature and size of the institution's trading activities and risk profile.
- VaR measures must be computed each business day based on a 99 percent (one-tailed) confidence level of estimated maximum loss.
- VaR measures must be based on a price shock equivalent to a 10-day movement in rates and prices.
- VaR measures must be based on a minimum historical observation period of one year for estimating future price and rate changes.
- VaR model data must be updated at least once every three months and more frequently if market conditions warrant.
- VaR measures may incorporate empirical correlations both within and across broad risk categories.
- VaR measures must be reviewed for aggregating VaR estimates across the entire portfolio.

The general market risk charge is based on the bank's internal VaR model, which determines an estimate of the maximum amount that the bank can lose on a particular portfolio over a given holding period with a given degree of statistical confidence level and precision. A number of empirical approaches have been used to calculate VaR-estimates based on the behavior and movements of underlying risk factors (e.g., interest rates, exchange rates).[16] For the purposes of the supervisory standard, these VaR estimates are calculated on a daily basis using a minimum historical observation period of one year, or the equivalent of one year if observations are weighted over time. The capital charge for general market risk is equal to the average VaR estimate over the previous 60 trading days (approximately one quarter) times a "multiplication factor," typically equal to three (3), and calibrated to a ten-day, 99th percentile standard. This common supervisory standard is required to ensure that the capital charge entails a consistent prudential level across banks. For example, if the ten-day, 99th percentile VaR is calculated to be $100, it means that the bank would expect to lose more than $100 on only 1 out of 100 ten-day periods. The purpose of this supervisory minimum capital standard is to ensure that banks hold adequate capital to withstand the impacts of prolonged and/or severe adverse movements in the market rates and prices that affect the value of their trading portfolios.

The specific risk capital charges are intended to cover the risks of adverse price movements related to factors pertaining to the issuer of an individual security and are applicable to long- and short-term debt and equity positions in the bank's trading portfolio. Under the initial risk-based capital guidelines, long-term debt and equity positions in the trading portfolio were subject to capital charges ranging from zero percent (for government securities) to 8 percent (for corporate debt and equity) of the book value of the positions.[17]

Basel III will require banks to: (1) maintain top-quality capital (Tier 1 capital, consisting of equity and retained earnings) up to 4.5 percent of their assets; (2) hold a new separate "capital conservation buffer" of common equity worth at least 2.5 percent of their assets; and (3) build a separate "countercyclical buffer" of up to 2.5 percent when their credit markets are booming. The Tier 1 rule will take effect from January 2015, and the requirement for the capital conversation buffer will be phased in between January 2016 and January 2019.[18] Basel III also introduces a new leverage ratio requirement. Items to be included in the leverage ratio are on–balance sheet items, such as repurchase agreements, securities financing transactions, and derivatives, as well as off–balance sheet items, such as commitments, direct credit substitutes unconditionally cancelable commitments, acceptances, trade letters of credit, standby letters of credit, failed transactions, and unsettled securities. Adjustments are contemplated to be made before full implementation. Basel III also would require banks to disclose their leverage ratios and their components beginning January 1, 2015.

Dodd-Frank also addresses capital requirements for financial services firms through its established FSOC. The FSOC is directed to identify and monitor systemic risk in the financial system. The FSOC is expected to recommend stricter capital, leverage, liquidity, and risk management rules to the Federal Reserve through its comprehensive authority to regulate the largest bank holding companies and systemically important financial institutions. The FSOC also has the authority to oversee nonbank financial companies that are systemically significant. The Supervisory Capital Assessment Program has increased capital levels for banks, in the United States, by (1) requiring banks to increase their capital levels (the current Tier 1 common median for many U.S. banks is at

9 percent); and (2) providing an adequate transition period of eight years to generate further capital buffers through earnings generation.

Safety and Soundness

Approximately once every 12 to 18 months, federal or state supervisors examine each U.S. commercial bank to assess its safety and soundness. This examination reveals the CAMELS rating measuring the bank's *c*apital adequacy, *a*sset quality, *m*anagement, *e*arnings, *l*iquidity, and *s*ensitivity to market risk determined by the supervisor. Each bank is rated from 1, the highest, to 5, the lowest, on each of the component categories and given a composite rating. Banks with a rating of 1 (sound in every respect) or 2 (fundamentally sound) are not likely to be constrained in any way by supervisory oversight. Banks with a CAMELS rating of 3 (flawed performance) are likely to have potential problems addressed by the examiners that are considered to be correctable. Banks with a 4 rating (potential of failure, impaired viability) are viewed to incur a significant risk of failure. Banks with a CAMELS rating of 5 (high probability of failure, severely deficient performance) are those banks with the most severe problems. These ratings are determined by the examination of a combination of publicly available information (e.g., financial statements, audit reports) and private information produced by bank examiners during their investigation (e.g., the quality of individual loans).

These CAMELS ratings on individual institutions are viewed as extremely confidential by each of the bank regulators. Until recently, the FDIC had a policy of not disclosing the CAMELS rating even to bank management. Recently, supervisors report these ratings only to top management of the bank, who may not reveal them to employees, customers, or financial market participants. Therefore, neither the public nor any financial market participants (e.g., financial analysts) have access to CAMELS rating data on individual banks. It is assumed that the public release of such data can be very detrimental to a bank, particularly if it became widely known that examiners determined a bank had a very high probability of failure. Even though the CAMELS ratings are not publicly available, banks prefer to have a good rating because it can affect the extent of their minimum capital requirements, the frequency and nature of future supervisory examinations, the types of activities undertaken, and the amount a bank pays for deposit insurance.

 ## FINANCIAL MODERNIZATION: THE GRAMM-LEACH-BLILEY ACT

Mergers and acquisitions among U.S. banks and thrifts, which trailed off in 1999 (total M&A deals of 349) compared to a booming 1998 (total M&A deals of 506) are expected to increase substantially for several reasons, including improvements in bank profitability, the expected elimination of pooling-of-interest accounting, the implication of the GLB Act, and increases in the number of prime acquisition targets. The 1990s experienced an unpredictable pace of bank mergers and acquisitions. The number of bank M&A deals grew from 170 in 1990 to 413 in 1998. As a result of M&A activities, the number of banks operating in the United States has declined over 30 percent since 1990.

On November 12, 1999, President Clinton signed the GLB Act (known as the Financial Services Modernization Act) allowing banks to merge with securities firms and insurance companies within financial holding companies. The Act makes banking regulations more consistent with marketplace realities and financial services more aligned with the needs of consumers. This Act has expanded the merger opportunities for banking organizations and may tend towards a new wave of convergence in the financial services industry. The Act:

- Permits commercial banks to affiliate with investment banks by repealing provisions of the Glass-Steagall Act of 1933.
- Allows companies that own commercial banks to offer any type of financial services by modifying the Bank Holding Company Act of 1956.
- Permits subsidiaries of banks to offer a broad range of financial services that are not allowed for banks themselves.
- Removes remaining statutory limitations on the financial activities allowable in banking organizations for qualified bank holding companies.
- Creates FHCs that may conduct a broad range of financial activities including insurance and securities underwriting, merchant banking, real estate development, and investment.
- Delays approval of cross-industry mergers until 120 days after enactment (mid-March 2000).
- Establishes restrictions on the locations of the new or expanded nonbank financial activities within the banking organization.
- Blends functional supervision of the component entities with umbrella supervision of consolidated financial holding companies by requiring that: (a) the Federal Reserve supervises the consolidated organization; (b) bank regulators regulate and supervise the banking subsidiaries; and (c) functional regulators supervise and regulate selected nonbank components.
- Improves privacy protections on disseminating information about customer accounts to third parties.
- Affects the implementation of the Community Reinvestment Act of 1977 (CRA) including the requirement that a BHC cannot become an FHC unless all the company's insured depository institutions have a CRA rating of at least satisfactory. The CRA requires banks that take deposits in a community to also make a certain level of loans available to that community, including low- and moderate-income areas. Banks are regularly examined for compliance with the CRA on their lending investments and community development activities in particular areas and can obtain one of four ratings: outstanding, satisfactory, needs to improve, and substantial noncompliance.

Proponents of the Act argue that it has benefited consumers by allowing "one-stop shopping" for all of their financial services and will enable U.S. financial services providers to compete more effectively in the global market. Critics argue that the Act's implementation will lead to unhealthy concentration of financial services, will weaken requirements that banks reinvest funds in local communities, and inadequately protect consumers' private financial information. The banking industry would benefit from the provisions of the Act in these ways:

- National banks, including community banks through their established subsidiaries, will be able to offer their financial services without geographic limitations.
- Community banks under $500 million in assets obtain much greater access to Federal Home Loan Bank advances, which expands their ability to obtain lendable funds and meet other liquidity needs.
- National and state banks remain protected from discriminatory state rules on the sale of insurance and other financial services.
- Banks of all sizes are able to offer a wide range of financial products and services without the costly restraints of outdated laws (e.g., the "town of 5000" provision).
- Banking organizations and other financial services companies (e.g., securities, insurance, financial technology) are able to combine much more readily.

The GLB Act of 1999 has affected the CRA in three ways: qualification process, examination process, and sunshine provisions.

1. *Qualification process.* Based on the provisions of the GLB Act, all subsidiaries and affiliates of banking organizations should have CRA ratings of at least satisfactory to qualify for establishing FHCs or converting the existing BHCs to FHCs. These provisions of the GLB Act further extend the review of CRA performance to transactions involving nonbanking financial activities.
2. *Examination process.* Prior to the Act, small insured depository institutions are examined on a three-year cycle for compliance with applicable laws and regulations including CRA, Equal Credit Opportunity, and Truth in Lending. The GLB Act changed this three-year cycle, for small institutions only, to a four-year interval or a five-year cycle if the institution's last CRA rating was "satisfactory" or "outstanding," respectively.
3. *Sunshine provisions.* Sunshine provisions of the GLB Act require financial institutions to provide new data on their lending agreements with community groups. If these lending agreements involve loans of $50,000 or above a year and payment of $10,000 or above per year, both the institution and the community groups must publicly disclose the agreements and make annual reports to the institution's regulator. Even though institutions' regulators do not influence these lending agreements with community groups, they enforce compliance with their reporting requirements under the GLB Act.

The GLB Act permits creation of new types of regulated institutions— FHCs—that are authorized to offer a broad range of financial products and services. An FHC is a BHC whose depository institutions are well capitalized and well managed. The GLB Act and the Federal Reserve Board have established rules that specify conditions that must be met for a BHC or a foreign bank to become an FHC authorized to engage in expanded activities. To become an FHC, a domestic BHC must file with the appropriate Reserve Board a written declaration that contains this information:

- A statement that the BHC elects to be an FHC
- The name and head office address of the company and of each depository institution controlled by the company
- A certification that all depository institutions controlled by the company are well capitalized
- The capital ratios for all relevant capital measures
- A certification that all depository institutions controlled by the company are well managed

The GLB Act authorizes an FHC to engage in these activities:

- Activities pertaining to banking under the Bank Holding Company Act (e.g., lending, leasing, investment advice).
- Normal activities in connection with the transaction of banking abroad (e.g., management consulting).
- Financial activities such as underwriting and dealing in securities, insurance underwriting, and merchant banking.
- Any other activities that are financial in nature, incidental to financial activities, or complementary to financial activities. (Prior Federal Reserve Board approval is required for the cases of being incidental to financial activities and complementary to financial activities.)

 ## FINANCIAL REPORTING PROCESS OF FINANCIAL INSTITUTIONS

Traditionally, Securities and Exchange Commission (SEC) registrants have been required to comply with certain industry-specific financial statement requirements, set forth in Article 9 for Bank Holding Companies of SEC Regulation S-X. Furthermore, they must comply with other nonfinancial disclosures required by Guide 3 for Bank Holding Companies of Regulation S-K. Current financial statements of banks are combinations of values derived from fair value, cost basis, depreciation, amortization, impairment, and other accounting standards. The 1980s and early 1990s witnessed the greatest number of financial institution failures in U.S. history. The savings and loan association crisis of the 1980s and banking organization financial problems of the early 1990s caused many to question the usefulness and relevance of historical cost financial reporting in reflecting the true economic net worth of troubled financial institutions. Many troubled financial institutions had negative economic net worth, even though based on historical cost accounting (HCA), they reported positive net worth in excess of regulatory requirements.

The highly publicized crisis in the S&L industry has been attributed to a number of causes, including economic downturn, deregulation, fraud, changes in tax laws, problems in real estate markets, and lax lending standards. Mandated accounting standards have also been criticized for their tendency to overstate financial institutions' earnings, net worth, and underlying asset values. No evidence indicates that the use of HCA caused financial institutions to fail; however, many argue that FVA would have provided warning signals of possible financial difficulties and led regulators, bank supervisors, and other financial statement users to address the institutions' financial difficulties earlier.

During the S&L crisis, many S&Ls had a negative spread between the asset yields and cost of funds that resulted in both a negative cash flow and a decrease in the value of the loans. These decreases in S&L net worth encouraged financial institutions to use regulatory accounting principles (RAP) as a means of meeting government-mandated minimum capital requirements. During the S&L crisis, the Federal Home Loan Bank Board permitted S&Ls to deviate from generally-accepted accounting principles (GAAP) in certain ways as part of a program of regulatory forbearance. There are several differences between RAP and GAAP used by business firms. For example, under RAP, financial institutions could defer losses of sales of assets with below-market yield. This practice allowed the write-off of loans over the life of the loan rather than when the loss occurred (as GAAP required). Another example of following RAP in violation of GAAP was that regulators permitted an increase to the capital account of S&Ls for the appraisal value of owned property, which helped boost the S&Ls' net worth above the minimum capital requirements. Brewer stated: "GAAP reveals that many of the currently insolvent S&Ls have been insolvent for quite some time. In contrast, RAP suggests that the problem is more recent."[19]

The S&L debacle has demonstrated the insufficiency and irrelevancy of historical costs in reflecting economic reality of business. The lack of FVA encouraged S&Ls to recognize transactions that were not in the best interest of the institutions. For example, S&Ls often recognized the increase in value of the bonds sold as income or net worth while any decline in the value of bonds was ignored or not written down. The seriousness of problems facing the S&L industry led to the passage of the Financial Institutions Reform, Recovery, and Enforcement Act (FIRREA) in August 1989. Furthermore, in 1991, the Federal Deposit Insurance Corporation Improvement Act (FDICIA) introduced mandatory procedures called prompt correction action, which requires regulators to promptly close depository institutions when their capital falls below predetermined quantitative standards. The FDICIA also required that RAP be no less conservative than GAAP in determining the regulatory capital requirements.

During the past two decades, there has been considerable interest in the reporting by financial institutions of the fair values of their financial instruments either as complements or substitutes for historical book values. Traditionally, the financial community, regulatory bodies, standard-setting authorities, and the accounting profession have continued to express conflicting views of the desirability and feasibility of using the FVA approach for financial reporting purposes. The terms "fair value," "market value based," "mark to market," and "market value accounting" are frequently used interchangeably as synonyms.

The adoption of FMV for financial reporting purposes has long been a subject of controversy, in both the financial community and the accounting professions. Proponents of FVA (e.g., Morris and Sellon; Mondschean)[20] assert that its use in financial reporting provides more useful and reliable financial information and reduces the alleged gain-trading problems of selling high-quality assets to recognize gains while retaining poor-quality assets to avoid realizing related losses. Advocates of FVA also believe that fair value provides more relevant and useful measures of assets, liability, and earnings than the use of historical cost. Opponents of FVA (e.g., Mergh; Sulton and Johnson)[21] take the position that it is not justifiable nor reasonable to report intermediate fluctuations in investment value until it is realized. In addition, the major arguments against FMV center on the possible volatility in reported earnings and owner's equity resulting from the use of FMV and the lack of reliability and objectivity in determining FMV of items that are not publicly traded. Nevertheless, disclosure of objectivity-measured and reliable fair values could improve the effectiveness of market and regulatory discipline. To the extent that the use of FVA improves the measurement of capital, it could lead to more timely supervision action of capital-impaired institutions.

The usefulness of historical cost-based financial statements is extensively debated in the literature. Historical balance sheet measurements are viewed as irrelevant, and more useful concepts such as fair value are suggested as measurement attributes. If the purpose of financial institutions is to increase shareholder value, the existing historical financial reporting fails to properly report changes in shareholder value. PricewaterhouseCoopers, one of the Big Five certified public accounting firms, has developed an approach called Value Reporting, which focuses on cash and nonfinancial measures driving shareholder value creation.[22] Value Reporting is a comprehensive set of financial and other non-financial performance benchmarks tailored to the company that provide both historical and predictive indicators of shareholder value creation. It focuses on value creation and the underlying activities that are crucial to a company's ability to generate sustainable shareholder value.

The main theme of Value Reporting is that management should compile and report relevant, reliable, and timely information regarding the company's value derivers and factors that increase shareholder value. Factors driving the change in corporate reporting are changes in the capital market and the internal characteristics of the company. Changes in the capital market consist of: (1) ever-increasing globalization of capital markets; (2) growing interest in the concept of shareholder value; (3) consolidation and convergence in most industries, especially the financial services industry; (4) greater use of technology and sophisticated valuation models; and (5) investors' investment strategies of holding stock on a long-term basis to create value. Changes in the internal characteristics of companies include: (1) shareholder value orientation (greater focus on cash flow); (2) increasing use of balanced scorecards linking performance to shareholder value creation; and (3) embedding of value-based management systems and procedures. Value Reporting can be used as supplementary reporting to the existing financial reports to provide additional relevant information to users of financial reports, especially investors. The Value Reporting approach provides fair value information for all financial items that can be useful as the global economy and business shift away from industrial and move toward a more service-based business and economy. For example, it is easier to determine the value of manufacturing inventory than the value of the user base of an Internet shopping site. Thus, as intangible assets grow, more value-relevant information on these assets should be disclosed on a timely basis.

Theoretically, there are three possible approaches to the implementation of FVA for financial reporting purposes: (1) adopt FVA for certain assets, with an objectively determinable fair market value (FMV; e.g., trade investments); (2) piecemeal adoption of FMV for selected assets and liabilities (e.g., match funds with liabilities of similar duration); and (3) adopt a comprehensive FVA system to determine and disclose fair value of all on– and off–balance sheet assets, liabilities, and owner's equity. The Financial Accounting Standards Board (FASB) has moved toward the possible requirements of a comprehensive FVA system for financial institutions over the past 20 years by issuing a number of Statements of Financial Accounting Standards (SFAS) pertaining to the fair value of financial instruments, including loans, equity securities, and derivatives. They are:

- SFAS No. 105, *Disclosure of Information about Financial Instruments with Off-Balance Sheet Risk and Financial Instruments with Concentration of Credit Risk* (March 1990)
- SFAS No. 107, *Disclosure about Fair Value of Financial Instruments* (December 1991)
- SFAS No. 114, *Accounting by Creditors for Impairment of a Loan* (May 1993)
- SFAS No. 115, *Accounting for Certain Investment in Debt and Equity Securities*, FASB, (May 1993)
- SFAS No. 118, *Accounting by Creditors for Impairment of a Loan—Income Recognition and Disclosure* (August 1994)
- SFAS No. 119, *Disclosure about Derivative Financial Instruments and Fair Value of Financial Instruments* (October 1994)
- SFAS No. 133, "Accounting for Derivative Instruments and Hedging Activities (June 1998)
- SFAS No. 140, *Accounting for Transfer and Servicing of Financial Assets and Extinguishments of Liabilities* (September 2000)
- SFAS No. 141, *Business Combinations*; FASB Statement No. 141 (Revised 2007), *Business Combinations*; Accounting Standards Codification (ASC) No. 805 (December 2007)
- SFAS No. 142, *Goodwill and Other Intangible Assets*, and ASC No. 350
- SFAS No. 144, *Accounting for the Impairment or Disposal of Long-Lived Assets*

These SFAS require additional disclosures of the fair value information on both assets and liabilities as well as the accounting treatment for loan impairment. A loan is impaired when it is probable that the creditor cannot collect all amounts due according to the loan agreements.

One major difficulty with these standards is that they permit a wide variety of approaches, which may impair comparability of financial statements. Another concern with these standards is that the valuation exercise often takes place at the end of the reporting period, and management has a variety of options in determining fair value. Since market information at year-end is the key criterion in most valuation methods, and a variety of methods can be used, year-end valuation estimations may not properly reflect the performance of the banks secured or unsecured loans during the fiscal year. Although SFAS Nos. 105, 107, and 118 were steps in the right direction, fair values suggested in these standards did not address the risk aspect of loan types or asset composition. The FASB has issued SFAS Nos. 115 and 133, which establish guidelines for the measurement, recognition, and reporting of fair values of investment in debt and equity securities as well as derivatives, respectively.

The financial crisis of 2007 to 2009 can be attributed to many factors, including the improper application of fair value estimates by the real estate appraising industry. The conflicting interests between real estate brokerage firms and real estate appraisal firms provided incentives for appraisers to provide fair value estimates above and beyond reasonable and realistic fair value to get financing to close deals. Banks had incentives to get the highest fair value estimates to provide subprime loans to customers and then sell the mortgages to mortgage buyers, such as Freddie Mac and Fannie Mae, quasi-government corporations established to buy up mortgages from banks. Inappropriate use of fair value measures has contributed to the crisis.

STATEMENT OF FINANCIAL ACCOUNTING STANDARDS NO. 115

The FASB issued SFAS No. 115, *Accounting for Certain Investment in Debt and Equity Securities*, in May 1993. SFAS No. 115 is one of the challenging accounting standards pertaining to financial institutions. It intended to: (1) provide better uniformity in the financial reporting process of financial institutions; (2) standardize portfolio accounting practices across industry lines; (3) establish guidelines for the fair value measurement, recognition, and reporting of investments in debt and equity securities; and (4) discourage financial institutions from selectively selling securities recorded at historical cost in an attempt to manage their reported earnings (gains trading). SFAS No. 115 has generated widespread interest and criticism by requiring the use of FVA for certain investments in debt and equity securities. SFAS No. 115 defined these terms:

- *Financial instruments.* SFAS No. 115 defines a financial instrument as a debt or equity security that evidences an ownership interest in an entity or a contract that: (1) contractually obligates an entity to transfer cash or another financial instrument to a second entity or exchange financial instruments on potentially unfavorable terms with the second entity; and (2) provides that second entity a contractual right to receive cash or other financial instruments from the first entity or exchange other financial instruments on potentially unfavorable terms with the first entity.
- *Security.* SFAS No. 115 defines a security as a share, participation, or other interest in property or in the issuer's enterprise that is represented by a financial instrument that can be divisible into classes of shares, participations, interests, or obligations. Securities include debt securities (also called credit instruments) and equity instruments, which represent ownership interests in a company.
- *Fair value.* SFAS No. 115 retains SFAS No. 107's definition of fair value as the amount at which buyers and sellers are willing, not forced as in a liquidation sale, to exchange financial instruments. Management should determine these values from the most active stock exchanges as possible using quoted market prices. For example, auction markets (e.g., the New York Stock Exchange) would be preferable to dealer markets that usually contain buy-sell "spreads" (e.g., the over-the-

counter [OTC] markets). Similarly, broker markets, where buyers and sellers often do not know each other's needs (e.g., private placements) are preferable to principal-to-principal markets, where buyers and sellers exchange securities for cash using services of intermediaries. Techniques now available to measure fair value include closing prices for auction markets, the average of closing bid and asked prices for dealer markets, using broker prices or quoted values of "similar" financial instruments to ascertain the value of certain not readily available fair values, and relying on "valid" mathematical models (e.g., capital pricing, binomial pricing, or Black-Scholes models) for certain types of financial instruments.

■ *Debt securities.* Debt securities include U.S. Treasury bonds, U.S. agency securities, municipal securities, convertible debt, corporate bonds, commercial paper, and secured debt instruments, such as collateralized mortgage obligations, but not unsecured trade accounts receivable and consumer loans payable.

■ *Equity securities.* Equity securities consist of an entity's ownership interest in another entity or right to acquire or dispose of such an interest at a fixed or determinable price, including common stock, stock rights and warrants, and put and call options. Financial instruments also include foreign currency forward contracts, loan agreements, financial options and guarantees, loan commitments and letters of credit, but not convertible debt or redeemable preferred stock.

SFAS No. 115 specifies that fair values of equity securities are readily determinable if they are traded on a securities exchange registered with the SEC or in the OTC market, provided that sales prices or bid-and-asked quotations are currently determinable (i.e., if they are published and based on current transactions). However, SFAS No. 115 does not apply to investments in equity securities that were accounted for under the equity method or financial statement consolidation.

SFAS No. 115 classifies securities into three categories: held to maturity, trading, and available for sale. It also establishes different financial reporting treatments for each category of securities.

1. *Held to maturity.* A financial institution should carry, at amortized cost, all debt securities that it has both the positive intent and ability to hold to maturity. Thus, management may not include securities in this category that it plans to hold for an indefinite amount of time or lacks a specific intent to sell or redeem by a specific date. Since the FMV of such securities will normally reverse in the long term, management should recognize no gains and losses on such debt instruments until the financial instruments mature.

2. *Trading.* Entities purchase trading debt and equity securities for resale purposes, primarily to make short-term profits rather than holding them for longer-term capital appreciation. Financial institutions should thus carry at market value and include in income all unrealized gains and losses of such securities that were bought and held for the purpose of selling them in the near term (e.g., within the entity's operating cycle). Trading securities also include mortgage-backed securities held for sale in conjunction with mortgage banking activities. Portfolio managers often continually trade financial instruments in this category.

EXHIBIT 6.4 Reporting Requirements of SFAS No. 115

Investment Type	Held to Maturity	Trading Securities	Available for Sale
Basis for measurement	Amortized cost	Fair value	Fair value
Recognition of unrealized gains and losses	No recognition Footnote disclosure only	Recognize in earnings	Recognize in stockholders' equity

3. *Available for sale.* Entities should classify all securities that are not classified in the held-to-maturity or trading categories as available for sale. This catchall category includes debt securities that do not meet the intent-to-hold criteria and equity securities that are not classified as trading securities. Financial institutions should carry these investments at market value and include unrealized gains and losses as a separate component of stockholders' equity without first going through the income statement, thereby minimizing earnings fluctuations on changes in the market values of such debt and equity securities. Management should defer recognizing in income unrealized gains and losses until realizing the revenues from these financial instruments. Exhibit 6.4 reveals reporting requirements of SFAS No. 115 for each securities categories.

AUDITING PROPER CLASSIFICATIONS OF MARKETABLE SECURITIES

SFAS No. 115 in establishing accounting for certain investment securities relies heavily on management's intent and the entity's ability to hold the investment, but auditors needed some guidance to help "verify" this "ability." Thus, Statement on Auditing Standards (SAS) No. 81, *Auditing Investments*, which became effective for periods ending on or after December 15, 1997, provides further guidance to auditors to evaluate such intent and ability. When evaluating management's intent, auditors should consider if actual investment activities are consistent with management's stated intent, which ordinarily requires examining records of investment strategies, records of investment activities, instructions to portfolio managers, and minutes of meetings of the board of directors or the investment committee. In evaluating an entity's ability to hold a debt security to maturity, auditors should consider factors such as the entity's financial position, working capital needs, operating results, debt agreements, and other relevant contractual obligations as well as laws and regulations.

SAS No. 81 also provides guidance regarding valuation of investments and evaluation of other-than-temporary impairment conditions. SAS No. 81 discusses various circumstances that may require differing auditing procedures, ranging from testing quoted market prices for marketable securities to the need to consider the use of a specialist when a fair value estimate is based on a complex valuation model. The SAS also gives examples of factors to consider when an other-than-temporary impairment condition exists.

When auditing an entity's investments, auditors should be familiar with applicable accounting guidance and with the rules that apply both to the particular type of entity and to the types of investments it holds. SAS No. 81 discusses the evidence needed to corroborate assertions related to debt and equity securities investments primarily since the FASB now requires greater use of management's intent and ability to hold financial instruments and the related measuring of FMV. Since valid approaches to determine fair value can vary with the type of investment, auditors should determine if the entity's fair value is consistent with the approach specific in SFAS No. 115. For example, the use of market value quotations as opposed to estimation techniques is required when measuring the fair value of equity securities accounted for under SFAS No. 115.

TAX CONSIDERATION OF FAIR VALUE

The Revenue Reconciliation Act of 1993 expressed the position of the U.S. Congress on FVA for the financial services industry. Section 13223 of the 1993 Act requires the use of FVA for securities dealers and added Section 475 to the Internal Revenue Code. Section 475 affects the tax treatment of banks and other financial institutions that qualify as "dealers in securities" and provides a new boost toward the ultimate adoption of FVA for financial reporting and tax purposes. Exhibit 6.5 compares the provisions of SFAS No. 115 and Section 475.[23] The major similarities between Section 475 and SFAS No. 115 are: (1) the requirement of the use of FVA for securities reported for 1994 and thereafter; (2) establishment of more uniformity for certain investments in debt and equity securities; and (3) changes in managerial and financial activities of affected entities. The major differences are in: (1) the application of FVA rules; (2) classification of securities; (3) definition and nature of affected entities (dealers in securities); and (4) timing and character of gain or loss recognition for financial reporting and tax purposes.

Under Section 475:

1. Securities dealers are required to use the mark-to-market method with respect to securities held in inventory.
2. A security may be any stock, bond, or other evidence of indebtedness; a beneficial interest in a widely held partnership or trust; various notional principal contracts; and any option, forward, contract, currency, short position, or other derivative financial interest in the listed securities.
3. The mark-to-market rules do not apply to:
   a. Any security held for investment.
   b. Any evidence of indebtedness that dealers acquire or originate in the normal course of their business provided they are not held for sale to customers.
   c. Any security that is issued as a hedge for another security that is not subject to the mark-to-market rules or as a hedge for a position, income right, or liability that is not a security in the taxpayer's hands.
4. A "dealer in securities" is defined as any taxpayer who:
   a. Regularly purchases securities from or sells securities to customers in the ordinary course of a trade or business or
   b. Regularly offers to enter into, assume, offset, assign, or otherwise terminate positions in securities with customers in the ordinary course of a trade or business.

EXHIBIT 6.5 Comparison of Provisions of SFAS No. 115 and IRC Section 475

Provisions	SFAS No. 115	IRC Section 475
Application	Any entities holding certain investments in debt and equity securities.	Any taxpayer that is a dealer in securities.
Purpose	Establish guidelines for recognition and measurement of investment in debt and equity securities by requiring piecemeal adoption of market value accounting (MVA) for certain securities.	Use mark-to-market accounting method for any securities held in inventory for U.S. tax purposes.
Reporting requirements	Market value adjustments of any realized or unrealized holding gains or losses of "trading securities" and realized gains and losses of "available-for-sales securities" should be included in determination of net income.	Any nonexempted market adjustment gains or losses on securities held in inventory should be included in taxable income. Any sales of securities during tax year are recognized as ordinary income or losses.
	Any market adjustments of unrealized holding gains or losses of "available-for-sales securities" should be reported as net amount in separate component of shareholders' equity until realized.	A security may be a stock, bond, or other evidence of indebtedness.
Security classifications	*Trading.* Any securities bought and sold to make short-term profits rather than to realize long-term gains from capital appreciation.	*Held for investment.* Any security that is not held by taxpayer primarily for sale to customers in ordinary course of taxpayer's trade or business.
	Held to maturity. Debt securities with positive intent and ability to hold to maturity.	*Held in inventory.* Any securities for sale.
	Available for sale. Any debt and equity securities not assigned to above categories, which may be sold prior to maturity.	
Possible impacts	Changes in asset/liability management strategies and funding decisions.	Recording of earnings and investment portfolio on more timely and realistic bases.
	Fluctuations in reported earnings and equity due to market adjustments for securities.	Taxpayers who make or sell loans may be considered dealers in securities.
	Reclassification of securities.	
Effective dates	Effective for fiscal years beginning after December 15, 1993.	Effective for tax years ending on or after December 31, 1993.
Implementation	Obtain complete knowledge and understanding of provisions of SFAS No. 115, including circumstances in which debt and equity are reported at amortized cost. Establish policies and procedures regarding securities classification into the three suggested categories.	Maintain proper records on an ongoing basis to determine which accountants (securities) are subject to or excepted from the mark-to-market requirements.

(Continued)

EXHIBIT 6.5 (Continued)

Evaluate how: (1) investment securities should be recorded, measured, and adjusted for market value; (2) securities should be transferred between categories; (3) earnings and capital volatility resulting from market adjustments can be minimized; and (4) to manage a securities portfolio to minimize negative impacts on cash flows. Establish an adequate and effective internal control system for investment securities to ensure compliance with provisions of SFAS No. 115.	*Planning.* Monitor new transactions and activities usin the identification procedures outlined in Reg. 1.1236-a(d). Identify exempted securities in records before close of day on which they were acquired, originated, and entered into. Evaluate tax planning opportunities to minimize possible negative impacts on income tax liability. Avoid IRS investigation or enforcement action by complying with all tax rules and regulations on MVA.

Source: Cecilia Leung and Zabihollah Rezaee, "Interactions between Financial and Tax Rules on Market Value Accounting," *Journal of Taxation of Investments* (Winter 1997): 132–151.

The mark-to-market tax rules complement SFAS No. 115 and force financial institutions to report their earnings and investment portfolios on a more timely and realistic basis. The adoption of Section 475 significantly affects asset/liability management strategies of many financial institutions that have not traditionally been considered as securities dealers. Under Section 475, a community bank, thrift, or any other taxpayer that makes and then sells loans may be a dealer in securities. The implementation of SFAS No. 115 and Section 475 can: (1) reduce gains trading (the practice of selling appreciated securities to recognize gains while retaining those that have fallen in value as long-term investments); (2) cause financial institutions to manage their investment portfolios more cautiously by requiring disclosure of fair value, which better reflects the true economic value of assets and liabilities; and (3) provide early warning signals of financial difficulties by reflecting the fair value of assets and liabilities.

 ## RECENT DEVELOPMENT OF FAIR VALUE ACCOUNTING

Many in the financial community believe that the existing financial reporting model, based on historical cost, is not keeping up with rapid changes in information technology, the global economy, and business. In the wake of the 2007–2009 financial crisis, the FASB proposed to make FVA mandatory for virtually the entire bank balance sheet. However, as of April 2011 the use of FVA is still in the preliminary stages. The release of preliminary views suggesting FVA has moved the FASB a step closer to adopting this controversial method of valuing assets and liabilities. FVA would present investors with relevant and useful information on the true current value of a loan, derivative, security, or deposit.

In December 1999, the FASB issued its Preliminary Views (PV) titled *Reporting Financial Instruments and Certain Related Assets and Liabilities at Fair Value.*[24] The objective of the PV is to solicit comments on FASB's views regarding issues pertaining to reporting financial instruments at fair value. The FASB has reached preliminary decisions about the definition of "fair value" and "financial instrument" and general guidance for determining fair value. The FASB, however, has not yet decided when, if ever, it will be appropriate and feasible to report fair values of all financial instruments in the basic financial statements.

The FASB in its Statement of Financial Accounting Standards No. 159, now Accounting Standards Codification (ASC) No. 825, allows banks to value many financial instruments of the acquired institution at fair value. The fair value measurement should be applied and customized to each and every financial instrument, with a few exceptions. The FASB states that a financial instrument is one of the following:[25] (1) cash; (2) an ownership interest in an entity; (3) a contractual obligation of one entity to deliver a financial instrument to a second entity and a corresponding contractor's right of the second entity to receive that financial instrument in exchange for no consideration other than release from the obligation; and (4) a contractual obligation of one entity to exchange financial instruments with a second entity and a contractual right of the second entity to require an exchange of financial instruments with the first entity. To further clarify this broad definition of a financial instrument, the FASB provided examples of the types of financial instruments as well as items that are considered as financial instruments and items that are not financial instruments. These items are summarized in Exhibit 6.6.

EXHIBIT 6.6 Contractual Rights and Obligations that Are/Are Not Financial Instruments

Contractual Rights and Obligations that Are Financial Instruments

Contractual obligations to deliver financial instruments and corresponding rights to require delivery of financial instruments.

- Obligations to pay and corresponding rights to require payment; e.g., accounts, notes, and loans payable and receivable, debt securities, demand and time deposits, insurance claims payable and receivable, and derivative settlements after settlement amount is fixed.
- Obligations to return borrowed securities, obligations to deliver financial instruments for which payment has been received, and corresponding rights to require return or delivery.
- Insurance policies and warranty contracts that will be settled in cash.
- Reinsurance contracts that will be settled in cash.
- Derivatives that require net settlement in cash or other financial instruments.
- Contracts excluded from Statement No. 133 in paragraph 10(e), i.e., "weather derivatives."
- Financial guarantees.

Contractual obligations to exchange financial instruments and corresponding rights to require exchange of financial instruments.

- Cardholder's options in credit card contracts.
- Loan commitments.
- Lines of credit.
- Securities options.
- Forward exchanges of securities.

Similar Contractual Rights and Obligations that Are Not Financial Instruments

Contractual obligations to deliver items other than financial instruments and corresponding rights to require deliveries of those items.

- Obligations to deliver goods or services that have been prepaid.
- Obligations to return a borrowed item other than a financial instrument.
- Warranty guarantees that provide for repair or replacement of warranted items.
- Insurance policies that provide for services or property replacement.

Contractual obligations to exchange financial instruments for items other than financial instruments and corresponding rights to require those exchanges.

- Forward exchanges or optional exchanges of services or goods other than financial instruments; e.g., purchase orders and sales orders, whether they are considered "normal purchases and normal sales" under paragraph 10(b) of Statement No. 133 or not; commodity contracts that are required to be settled by deliveries of commodities.

Other Similar Assets and Liabilities that Are Not Financial Instruments

- Taxes payable.
- Tax refunds receivable.
- Deferred taxes.
- Legal (other than contractual) requirements to issue or renew insurance policies.
- Certain accruals of revenues and expenses; e.g., obligations to repair environmental damage that is not yet a liability to a particular entity.

The FASB defines "fair value" in its SFAS No.157 as "an estimate of the price an entity would have realized if it had sold an asset or paid if it had been relieved of a liability on the reporting date in an arm's length exchange motivated by normal business considerations. That is, it is an estimate of an exit price determined by market interactions."[26] The FASB is in favor of exit prices as a proxy for fair value. The exit price for an asset or a liability is the price at which it could be sold or settled at present, which is determined by the market's estimate of the present value of its expected future cash flows. The exit price should reflect the amount, timing, and uncertainty of future cash flows of the entity that owns the asset or owes the liability. The estimated market exit price for a financial instrument can be determined based on:

■ The price of the identical instrument, if it is available and traded in the same active market.
■ Prices in observed transactions. If more than one active market exists for the particular instrument and if a similar instrument is traded more recently than the identical instrument, the price of the identical instrument should be adjusted for changes in market factors since the date of the last transaction.
■ Estimates of actual transactions if they are available. In some cases, transaction prices require adjustment especially when: (a) the observable transactions are not recent and there is compelling evidence that a current price would be different; (b) two parties to the transaction are affiliates (e.g., related parties transactions); and (c) one party to the transaction is subject to financial or regulatory difficulties.

When there is more than one market for certain instruments, the portfolio of items can be used in estimating the exit price. The exit price of the portfolio might be higher than the total of the exit prices of the individual instruments. In this case, the fair value should be based on the market with the most advantageous price, which is the optimum accessible market price. The most advantageous price would be a higher exit price for an asset and a lower exit price for a liability.

The market exit price is considered to be the best evidence of the fair value of an asset or liability when it is obtainable in a market to which the entity has reasonable access.

The market exit price on which to base fair value may not be obtainable when: (1) a current exchange is not possible or readily available; (2) the instrument is unique or highly unusual; and (3) market participants do not disclose prices or valuation models regarding similar instruments. Under these circumstances, the exit price must be determined based on a combination of general market information (e.g., interest rates, exchange rates) and internally developed estimates and assumptions based on the present value (PV) of future cash flows.

■ The PV calculations should be based on the projected cash flows for a financial instrument including contractual rights and obligations and cash expected to be delivered or exchanged under the contract.
■ The projected cash flows should be adjusted for:
   ■ The time value of money (e.g., discount rate).
   ■ Expectations and changes in future conditions about possible variations in the amount or timing of these cash flows.

- The risk premium (the price marketplace participants expect to receive for bearing the uncertainty inherent in the asset or liability).
- Other factors, such as market imperfections, anticipated profit margins, and illiquidity.

Under GAAP, the best evidence of fair value is quoted market price in an active market. However, in the absence of quoted market prices, the fair value should be estimated based on reasonable, justifiable, and relevant assumptions. For example, in valuing the interests retained from the sale of the higher-risk assets (e.g., subprime and high loan-to-value assets), the fair value of these expected future cash flows should be recorded on balance sheets as assets under retained interests. The fundamental assumptions in the valuation of these retained interests, among others, include default rates, loss severity factors, discount rates, and prepayment or payment rates.

The FASB's long-term goal is to have all financial items (assets and liabilities) recognized and reported at their fair values in financial statements. The major conceptual advantages of fair value over historical costs as a measurement attribute are that fair value: (1) does not depend on the date or cost at which an asset or liability was acquired or incurred; (2) is the same for all entities having access to the same markets in determining the market exit price of assets or liabilities; (3) does not depend on the intended disposition of an asset or liability; and (4) provides relevant information about assets and liabilities that is more useful than historical cost information. The changes in fair value should be reported in earnings when they occur, whether they are realized or not. Exhibit 6.7 summarizes the conceptual advantages of fair value information over historical cost information.

The FASB has been considering the issue of fair value as a measurement attribute for all financial items including assets, liabilities, and instruments for over a decade. Other alternatives, such as the requirement for improved disclosure of fair value of financial items or a separate supplementary set of fair value financial statements, are also being considered. The FASB issued the Statement of Financial Accounting Concept (SFAC) No. 7, titled *Using Cash Flow Information and Present Value in Accounting Measurements*, in February 2000. SFAC No. 7 emphasized PV accounting for assets and liabilities through a pure balance sheet approach. This SFAC establishes a framework for using future cash flows as the basis for accounting measurements at initial recognition or fresh-start measurements and for the interest method of amortization. It is based on the concept that a true PV of future cash flow is unknown, and the next closest measurement is current (market) value or fair value. "Fair value" is defined as the amount at which an asset could be bought or sold or a liability could be incurred or settled in a current transaction between willing parties in the normal course of business.

SFAS No. 140 defines the fair value of an asset or a liability as the amount at which that asset or liability could be bought or sold in a current transaction between willing parties, that is, other than in a forced or liquidation sale. Quoted market prices in active markets are the best evidence of fair value, and under SFAS No. 140, they shall be used as the basis for the measurement, if available. SFAS No. 157, *Fair Value Measurements*, sets the source of information used in fair value measurements into three levels: Level 1, where there are observable inputs from quoted prices in active markets; Level 2, where

EXHIBIT 6.7 Pertinent Features of Fair Value–Based and Historical Cost–Based Measures of Financial Assets and Liabilities

Fair Value	Historical Cost
Improves comparability by making like things look alike and unlike things look different.	Impairs comparability by making like things look different and different things look alike.
Provides information about benefits expected from assets and burdens imposed by liabilities under current economic conditions.	Provides information about benefits expected from assets and burdens imposed by liabilities under economic conditions when they were acquired or incurred.
Reflects effect on entity performance of management's decisions to continue to hold assets or owe liabilities as well as decisions to acquire or sell assets and to incur or settle liabilities.	Reflects effect on entity performance only of decisions to acquire or sell assets or to incur or settle liabilities. Ignores effects of decisions to continue to hold or to owe.
Reports gains and losses from price changes when they occur.	Reports gains and losses from price changes only when they are realized by sale or settlement, even though sale or settlement is not the event that caused gain or loss.
Requires current market prices to determine reported amounts, which may require estimation and can lead to reliability problems.	Reported amounts can be computed based on internally available information about prices in past transactions, without reference to outside market data.
Easily reflects effects of most risk management strategies.	Requires complex rules to attempt to reflect effect of most risk management strategies.

there are indirectly observable inputs from quoted prices of comparable items in active markets, identical items in inactive markets, or other market-related information; and Level 3, where there are unobservable, firm-generated inputs in determining fair value.

FINANCIAL REPORTING REQUIREMENTS OF FINANCIAL INSTITUTIONS

Financial institutions should maintain sound accounting and reporting procedures and systems to prepare regulatory reports in conformity with GAAP or U.S. RAP. Effective on March 31, 1997, the reporting standards set forth for the Consolidated Reports of Condition and Income (known as call reports) are based on GAAP for banks. Any deviation from GAAP is allowed only in those instances where statutory requirements or overriding supervisory concerns warrant a departure from GAAP. Certain differences between GAAP and RAP remain after the amendments to the March 1997 Call Report Instructions. Many of these differences remain because the agencies generally default to SEC reporting principles for registrants. The more significant remaining differences between call report instructions and GAAP are related to these areas: impaired collateral-dependent loans; pushdown accounting; credit losses on off–balance sheet commitments and contingencies; related party transactions; and the application of accounting changes.

Financial institutions should also maintain clear and concise records with special emphasis on documenting adjustments and reconciliation when converting foreign accounting principles to either GAAP or RAP. Domestic and foreign financial institutions are required to file timely and accurate regulatory reports with the Federal Reserve System. Financial information compiled in the regulatory reports can serve several purposes: (1) facilitating early identification and signaling of problem situations that can threaten the safety and soundness of reporting institutions; (2) ensuring timely implementation of the prompt-corrective-action provisions required by banking legislation; and (3) assessing the financial conditions and position of the reporting institution by the public, including investors, depositors, and creditors. The call reports are used to prepare the Uniform Bank Performance Report, which uses ratio analysis and analytical procedures to detect unusual or abnormal (red flag) changes in an institution's financial condition and position.

The FIRREA and the Federal Deposit Insurance Corporation Improvement Act of 1991 (FDICIA) have given authority to the Federal Reserve to assess civil money penalties against state member banks, BHCs, and foreign institutions that file late, false, and misleading regulatory reports. The civil money penalties can also be assessed against individuals including outside auditors who cause or participate in filing late, false, or misleading regulatory reports. These reports should be reviewed by the assigned examiner for verification of the accuracy of the reports and assurance that they meet statutory and regulatory requirements. National banks, state member banks, and insured state nonmember banks are required to file call reports as of the close of business on the last calendar day of each calendar quarter. Call reports should be received by the appropriate supervisory agencies (e.g., national banks and state nonmember banks submit the reports to the FDIC, state member banks submit the reports to the appropriate Federal Reserve Bank) no more than 30 calendar days after the report date. The nature and extent of financial reports and disclosures depend on the size and characteristics of the financial institution (e.g., total assets of less than $100 million, global operations). The call report plays an important role in ensuring the customization of the bank supervisory approach to the activities and risks undertaken by financial institutions. The regulatory requirements of the call report are in the process of revision and modernization to ensure the elimination of many financial items that are not relevant to today's banking environment and to reflect the kinds of activities that banks are undertaking today such as securitization and venture capital.

The Report of Condition provides consolidated and detailed information on: (1) assets, liabilities, capital, and off–balance sheet activity; and (2) certain aggregated information and figures on loans to executive officers, directors, principal shareholders, and their related interests.

The Report of Income provides information on: (1) consolidated earnings; (2) changes in capital accounts; (3) allowance for loan and lease losses; and (4) charge-offs and recoveries. Call reports typically contain financial reports and supplement disclosures of these major financial attributes and items:

- Statement of financial position (balance sheet)
- Statement of income

- Statement of changes in owner's equity
- Applicable income taxes by taxing authorities
- Charge-offs and recoveries and changes in allowance for loan and lease losses
- Loans and lease-financing receivables
- Deposit liabilities
- Cash and balances due from depository institutions
- Securities
- Quarterly average balances
- Past-due and nonaccrual loans and leases
- Risk-based capital
- Off–balance sheet items
- Supplemental disclosure on significant nonrecurring items or changes of accounting method

Call reports are filed with the appropriate agency and generally are made available to the public upon request by the federal bank supervisory agencies. State member banks are no longer required to publish their report of condition, according to Section 308 of the Riegle-Neal Act. However, they may still be required to publish their report of condition under state law. S&Ls are required to file less extensive call reports with the Office of Thrift Supervision.

Reports Required under Regulation H and the SEC Act of 1934

Financial institutions under the SEC jurisdiction (e.g., publicly traded banks) must file quarterly (Form 10-Q) and annual (Form 10-K) reports and proxies with the SEC. Section 208.16(a) of Regulation H requires that state member banks whose securities are subject to registration under the SEC Act of 1934 file special reports with the Federal Reserve Board and the SEC including:

- Form 8-A, which is the registration of certain classes of securities, pursuant to Section 12(b) or 12(g) of the 1934 act, especially those listings on national securities exchanges
- Form 8-B, which is the registration of securities of certain successor issuers pursuant to Section 1(b) or 12(g) of the 1934 Act
- Form 10, which is the general form for registration of securities pursuant to Section 12(b) or 12(g) of the 1934 Act for classes of securities of issuers for which no other form is prescribed
- Form 8-K, which must be filed within 15 days after the occurrence of the earliest of one or more specified events, such as changes in control of registrant or acquisition of disposition of significant assets
- Form 10-Q, which is for quarterly and transition reports and must be filed within 45 days after the end of each of the first three fiscal quarters
- Form 10-K, which is for annual and transition reports that must be filed within 90 calendar days after the end of the registrant's fiscal year
- Form 3, which is an initial statement of beneficial ownership of registered companies, including securities of the bank

- Form 4, which is a statement of charges of beneficial ownership of registered companies, including the securities of the bank
- The Financial and Operational Combined Uniform Single report, required by the SEC, which discloses the details of securities revenue and capitalization information of financial institutions

Reporting Requirement for International Activities

The next reports should be filed with the Federal Financial Institutions Examination Council (FFIEC) for banks that conduct or intend to conduct international activities through either foreign branches or agreement corporations. Exhibit 6.8 presents regulatory reports of banks including types, description, frequency, and content. The reports are:

- *FFIEC 009, Country Exposure Report.* This report should be filed quarterly by all U.S. banks and bank holding companies that meet certain ownership criteria and have total consolidated outstanding claims on foreign residents in excess of $30 million.
- *FFIEC 009, Country Exposure Information Report.* This quarterly supplement to the FFIEC 009 provides public disclosure of significant country exposures of U.S. banking institutions.
- *FFIEC 030, Foreign Branch Report of Condition.* This report should be filed by every insured commercial bank with one or more branch offices in a foreign country as of December 31 of each year. Significant branches with either total assets of at least $2 billion or commitments to purchase foreign currencies and U.S. dollar exchange of at least $5 billion should submit this report quarterly.
- *FFIEC 035, Monthly Consolidated Foreign Currency Report of Banks in the United States.* This report should be filed by U.S. financial institutions that have greater than $1 billion in commitments to purchase foreign currencies. This report consists of monthly data on institutions' gross assets, gross liabilities, and positions in foreign currencies, on a fully consolidated basis.
- *FR (Federal Reserve) 2058, Notification of Foreign Branch Status.* This report should be filed within 30 days of the opening, closing, or relocation of a foreign branch of that U.S. organization or of its foreign subsidiary(ies).
- *FR 2064, Report of Changes in Investment Made under Regulation K, Subparts A and C,* for the acquisition or disposition of reportable investment.
- *FR 2314, Annual Report of Condition for Foreign Subsidiaries of U.S. Banking Organizations.* This report should be filed as of December 31 of each year by foreign companies.
- *FR 25029, Quarterly Report of Assets and Liabilities of Large Foreign Offices of U.S. Branches.* This report represents large foreign branches of U.S. banking institutions and large foreign bank subsidiaries.
- *FR 2886b, Report of Condition and Income for Edge Act and Agreement Corporations.* This report represents the operations of the reporting corporation, including any international banking facilities of the reporter.
- *FR 2915, Report of Foreign Currency Deposits.* This report collects seven-day averages of the amounts outstanding of foreign currency.

EXHIBIT 6.8 Bank Regulatory Reports

Type	Description	Frequency	Content
FFIEC 031	Consolidated reports of condition and income for a bank with domestic and foreign offices	Quarterly	Contains Schedules RC-B and RC-D, which capture all types of securities, and Schedule RC-L, which shows off–balance sheet financial instruments.
FFIEC 030	Report of condition for foreign branch of U.S. bank	Annually for all overseas branch offices, quarterly for significant branches	Captures information on balance sheet data and selected off–balance sheet instruments.
FFIEC 035	Monthly consolidated foreign currency report of banks in the United States	Last business day of each month	Captures information on foreign exchange transactions.
FFIEC 002	Reports of assets and liabilities of U.S. branches and agencies of foreign banks	Quarterly	Shows information pertaining to balance sheet and off–balance sheet transactions reported by all branches and agencies.
FFIEC 069	Weekly report of assets and liabilities for large U.S. branches and agencies of foreign banks	As of close of business every Wednesday	Includes all on–balance sheet and off–balance sheet instruments.
FFIEC 019	Country exposure for U.S. branches and agencies of foreign banks	Quarterly	Presents country distribution of foreign claims held by branches and agencies.
FR 2314a	Report of condition for foreign subsidiaries of U.S. banking organizations	Annually	Should be filed annually by banks with total assets exceeding U.S. $100 million and quarterly for significant subsidiaries.
FR 2314b	Report of condition for foreign subsidiaries of U.S. banking organizations	Annually	Should be filed by banking organizations with total assets between U.S. $50 and 100 million as of report date.
FR 2314C	Report of condition for foreign subsidiaries of U.S. banking organizations	Annually	For banking organizations with total assets less than U.S. $50 million.
FR 2886b	Report of condition for Edge Act and agreement corporations	Quarterly	Reflects consolidation of all Edge and agreement operations, except for those majority-owned Edge or agreement subsidiaries.

Source: Trading and Capital Markets Activities Manual, 1998. Section 2130-5. www.federalreserve.gov.

BHCs, owning stock of one or more banks, established according to the Federal Regulation Y, can engage in a number of activities considered closely related to and a proper incident to banking (e.g., insurance, brokerage, discount stock brokerage, third-party fee appraisals, and third-party data processing). BHCs are chartered as corporations under the laws of their home states and, therefore, must file a registration statement and an annual report of operations with their district Federal Reserve Bank and the Board of Governors. Exhibit 6.9 presents regulatory reports of BHCs including types, description, frequency, and content. BHCs should file these reports:

- *Y-6 Annual Report.* This report contains the parent's consolidated financial statements and must be filed by all domestic BHCs.
- *Y-7 Annual Report of Foreign Banking Organizations.* This report must be filed by BHCs that are established under the laws of a foreign country.
- *Y-9 Financial Supplement.* This report must be filed by BHCs with consolidated assets of $50 million or more.

EXHIBIT 6.9 Regulatory Reports (Bank Holding Companies)

Type	Description	Frequency	Content
FR-Y-9C	Consolidated financial statements for (1) top-tier BHC with total consolidated assets of $150 million or more; (2) lower-tier BHC with total consolidated assets of $1 billion or more; and (3) other multibank BHC with debt outstanding to general public or that are engaged in certain nonbank activities.	Quarterly	Schedule HC-A securities including U.S. Treasuries, municipal mortgage-backed, foreign governments, corporations, IDC debt, equities. Schedule HC-F instruments including futures and forwards, forward rate agreements, interest rate swaps, foreign exchange, currency swaps, options commodities, hybrids, index-linked activities.
FR-Y-95R	Parent company–only financial statements for one BHC with total consolidated assets of less than $150 million	Semiannually	Includes only securities, no off–balance sheet items.
FR-Y-9LP	Parent company–only financial statements for each BHC that files the FR-Y-9C	Quarterly	Examiners review only securities transactions. No off–balance-sheet items are captured.
FR-Y-8	Report of BHC intercompany transactions and balances	Semiannually and on an interim basis	BHCs with consolidated assets of $300 million or more are required to file this report of large asset transfers.
FR-Y-8f	Report of intercompany transactions for foreign banking organizations and their U.S. bank subsidiaries	Semiannually and on an interim basis	Presents intercompany asset transfers (loans and securities) and foreign exchange transactions for foreign banking organizations.

(Continued)

EXHIBIT 6.9 *(Continued)*

Type	Description	Frequency	Content
FR-Y-20	Financial statement for a BHC subsidiary engaged in ineligible securities underwriting and dealing	Quarterly	Schedules SUD and SUD-A capture securities transactions and transactions involving equities, futures, forwards, and options.
FR-Y-11Q	Financial statements for each individual nonbank subsidiary of a BHC with total consolidated assets of $150 million or more	Quarterly	Captures both balance sheet securities and off–balance sheet instruments.
FR-Y-111	Financial statements for each individual nonbank subsidiary that is owned or controlled by a BHC subject-size consideration	Annually	Captures both balance sheet securities and off–balance sheet instruments.
FEIEC 035	Monthly consolidated foreign-currency report of banks in the United States	Last business day of each month	Shows information on foreign exchange transactions (spot, forwards, futures), cross-currency interest rate swamps, and options for a BCH that files an FR Y-9 and has foreign exchange commitments in excess of U.S. $100 million.
FFIEC 009	Country exposure information report	Quarterly	Filed by U.S. commercial banks and/or BHCs that meet certain ownership criteria.
FFIEC 009a	Country exposure information report supplements FFIEC 009	Quarterly	Provides public disclosure of significant country exposures of U.S. BHCs.
X-17A-5	Focus report	Quarterly	Captures data on securities and spot commodities owned by broker-dealers.

Source: Trading and Capital-Markets Activities Manual, 1998. Section 2130-2. www.federalreserve.gov.

The review of the required regulatory reports is aimed toward achievement of three goals of determining whether the: (1) required reports are being filed on time, (2) content of reports is accurate, and (3) corrective actions are being taken when official reporting, practices, policies, or procedures are deficient. Thus, the examiner's primary purpose when reviewing the regulatory-reporting function is to vouch for the timeliness, accuracy, and consistency of reporting requirements.

 ## CORPORATE GOVERNANCE OF FINANCIAL INSTITUTIONS

This past decade (2000s) has witnessed significant improvement in the financial reporting process and corporate governance activities of financial institutions. The final rule of the Federal Deposit Insurance Corporation (FDIC) implementing Section 112 of the FDIC

Improvement Act of 1991 (FDICIA) was approved in May 1993.[27] The final rule required state member banks and other insured depository institutions with $500 million or more in total assets, for their fiscal years beginning after December 31, 1992, to submit to their regulatory agencies, within 90 days after the end of their fiscal year, a copy of: (1) an annual report, (2) a management report, and (3) an auditor's attestation report. Furthermore, affected institutions are required to establish and maintain audit committees consisting of outside, nonexecutive, and independent directors. The final rule affects all aspects of financial institutions' financial reporting, internal control, and audit committees, ensuring corporate governance and accountability.

Financial Statements

Traditionally, financial institutions have prepared annual reports in response to the needs and wants of shareholders as well as in compliance with requirements of regulatory agencies. Recently, an institution's annual report has become more of a compliance document to satisfy regulatory requirements than a communication vehicle for providing relevant, reliable, and useful financial information to shareholders. The FDIC rule (Section 363.2) requires affected institutions to submit their annual reports to the Federal Reserve Bank, the FDIC, and their state regulatory agency within 90 days after the end of their fiscal year.

The submitted annual reports should contain: (1) comparative financial statements including balance sheets, income statements, statements of cash flows, and statements of changes in owners' equity and related footnote disclosures prepared in accordance with GAAP; (2) a report indicating management's responsibility for preparing the submitted annual financial statements; and (3) an independent auditor's report on the institution's annual financial statements audited in accordance with generally accepted auditing standards. The final rule does not mandate any additional reporting requirements for covered institutions. Management is primarily responsible for the fair presentation of an institution's financial statements in accordance with GAAP by establishing and maintaining a sound accounting information system and an adequate and effective internal control structure. The independent auditor lends credibility, objectivity, and reliability to an institution's financial statements by expressing an opinion regarding the fair presentation of the financial statements in conformity with GAAP.

Internal Control Structure

Recently, the challenges of globalization, rapid technological advancements, business failure, and fraudulent financial activities (e.g., savings and loan crisis) have sharpened the ever-increasing attention of internal controls. Internal control is a widely used concept, and its importance to the business community and banking industry has grown significantly. Yet until recently, there was no common view of what internal control encompasses and what it should achieve. Management and internal auditors typically view internal control very broadly to cover both internal administrative control, ensuring achievement of the organization's goals and compliance with applicable laws and regulations, and internal accounting control, ensuring reliability of financial statements and safeguarding economic resources. External auditors and regulators, however, consider internal control from a narrow perspective as being primarily internal accounting controls. While the final FDIC rule did not attempt to determine a common definition and standards for internal controls, it clearly sets forth additional responsibility for management as well as internal and external auditors. Section 404 of SOX provides further clarifications and requirements for internal control reporting for public companies including banks as explained later in this chapter.

Management Responsibility for Internal Control

The FDIC rule requires a statement of management's responsibility in the institution's annual report for: (1) establishing and maintaining adequate internal controls over financial reporting and for complying with applicable laws and regulations; and (2) management's assessment of the effectiveness of internal controls and the institution's compliance with the designated laws and regulations. Traditionally, management has been responsible for establishing and maintaining adequate and effective internal controls to ensure: (1) achievement of the organization's goals; (2) adherence to managerial policies and procedures; (3) safeguarding of economic resources; (4) enhancement of the reliability of financial statements; and (5) compliance with applicable laws and regulations. Thus, the rule for covered institutions reemphasizes the importance of an adequate internal control structure to ensure reliable financial reporting and responsible corporate governance.

The idea of a management report on the effectiveness of internal controls to external parties and an independent auditor's report on management's assertions regarding the effectiveness of internal controls over financial reporting has been debated in the accounting profession and authorization bodies (e.g., American Institute of Certified Public Accountants and SEC) since the passage of the Foreign Corrupt Practice Act (FCPA) of 1977.[28] Subsequently, the National Commission of Fraudulent Financial Reporting (Treadway Commission, 1987)[29] stated that accounting controls set forth by the FCPA are not sufficient to reduce the incidence of fraudulent financial reporting. Furthermore, the Treadway Commission recommended that the SEC be required to publicly report its responsibility for the establishment and maintenance of an adequate internal control system and its assessment of the effectiveness of such a system in achieving established internal control objectives. The Treadway Commission also recommended that its Committee of Sponsoring Organizations (COSO) work to integrate the various internal control concepts and definitions and to develop a common reference point.

The COSO issued its report titled "Internal Control: Integrated Framework" in September 1992.[30] The provisions of the COSO report help: (1) businesses and interested users understand the value and use of internal controls; (2) establish a common definition for internal control; and (3) provide a criterion against which all entities can assess their internal control systems. Since the FDIC regulations do not establish standards for internal controls and determine the criterion against which institutions can assess the effectiveness of their internal control systems, this is management's responsibility. However, the COSO report can be used as a source of guidelines by management of affected institutions to comply with the FDIC rule.

The COSO report consists of four volumes. The first volume is the executive summary, which is a high-level overview of the internal control framework. It gives a broad outline of the nature of internal control structures, defines internal control, and discusses what internal control can do. The second volume describes internal control components and provides criteria against which management, board of directors, internal auditors, and external auditors can assess the effectiveness of internal control systems. The third volume provides guidance for reporting publicly on the effectiveness of internal control. Finally, the fourth volume provides guidance and evaluation tools that management and auditors can use in evaluating the effectiveness of internal control systems.

To comply with the requirements of the FDIC rule, the banking industry is using the COSO framework to create or modify their internal control structure (e.g. JPMorgan Chase, Bank of America).[31] The COSO report defines internal control objectives for achieving effectiveness and efficiency in operations, reliability of financial reporting, and compliance with applicable laws and regulations. These internal control objectives are similar to those suggested in the FDIC rule. The COSO report defines the five components of an adequate internal control structure as control environment, risk assessment, control activities, information and communication, and monitoring. These five components can help an institution's management establish and maintain an adequate internal control structure and establish procedures for financial reporting and compliance with designated laws and regulations relating to the bank's safety and soundness as required by Section 363.2(b) of the FDIC rule.

The third and fourth volumes of the COSO report should help an institution's management evaluate the effectiveness of an internal control system and report on the effectiveness of such a system to external parties. While the COSO report takes no position on whether entities should issue a management report, currently about 25 percent of publicly traded companies and approximately 60 percent of Fortune 500 companies include in their annual reports a management report discussing some aspects of internal control.[32] The COSO report provides a framework for those companies that are required to report on internal control.

The FDIC regulations require an institution's management to make a public statement regarding its responsibilities for the effectiveness of internal controls over financial reporting, operating activities, and compliance requirements. This reporting requirement necessitates adequate documentation of understanding, determination, and assessment of deficiencies in internal controls on financial reporting as well as the degree of compliance with applicable laws and regulations. The COSO report should help management with such documentation. However, the report focuses only on those internal controls that relate to the effectiveness of internal controls assessment regarding the reliability of published financial statements.

Although the definition of internal control includes controls over financial reporting, operations, and compliance with applicable laws and regulations, the scope of external reporting on internal control, in Volume 3 of the COSO report is not extended to operations and compliance objectives. Therefore, the affected institutions should establish their own reporting format for management reporting on internal controls over compliance with applicable laws and regulations. The management-required report on the assessment of the effectiveness of the internal control structure over financial reporting should document deficiencies in internal control at the end of the fiscal year; documentation of the assessment of compliance with applicable laws and regulations is required for the entire fiscal year. The proper documentation assists independent auditors in ascertaining management's assertions on the internal control structure.

Management's report on internal controls should include:

1. An assessment of the effectiveness of internal controls over the reliability of the financial statements and compliance with applicable laws and regulations.
2. A statement regarding the existence of mechanisms for monitoring and reporting on identified financial control deficiencies and noncompliance with applicable laws and regulations.
3. A statement regarding the inherent limitations of internal control systems.
4. The criteria against which the internal control structure is evaluated.
5. A description of any material deficiencies or weaknesses that exist at year-end and all matters of noncompliance found throughout the year that come to the attention of management.
6. The date of the report and proper signatures.

Auditor's Involvement with Internal Controls

The FDIC regulations have a tremendous impact on the independent auditor's consideration of institutions' internal control structure. Traditionally, independent auditors have been concerned more with the adequacy and effectiveness of their clients' internal control system in safeguarding assets and enhancing the reliability of financial information. Thus, independent auditors have not concentrated much on the assessment of compliance with applicable laws and regulations. The FDIC regulations require that the independent auditor attest to and report separately on the assertions in the management report concerning the institution's internal control structure and procedures for financial reporting. The independent auditor should also perform agreed-on procedures to test compliance with the specified laws and regulations.

The FDIC regulations also encourage and promote the role of institutions' internal auditors from the traditional reactive role of just investigating internal control systems to the new proactive role of participating in all aspects of the institution's internal control structure. The proactive role of internal auditors is to assist and participate with management in:

1. Defining internal control and related objectives over the financial reporting process and compliance with certain laws and regulations.
2. Establishing and maintaining an adequate internal control structure and its components.
3. Determining appropriate evaluation tools in measuring the adequacy and effectiveness of established internal controls.
4. Monitoring internal control continuously and periodically to ensure its objectives are being achieved.

5. Preparing and reporting on the effectiveness of the internal control structure and procedures for financial reporting.
6. Assessing the institution's compliance with the specified safety and soundness laws and regulations.

Internal auditors may also provide direct assistance to the independent auditors in auditing financial statements and the internal control attestation. Internal auditors can provide a variety of accounting and nonaccounting services to the institution's audit committee in fulfilling its responsibilities as stated in the FDIC regulations.

Integrated Financial and Internal Control Reporting

Regulations vary significantly throughout the world with one emerging trend toward a demand by global investors for more transparent and reliable financial reports. The Sarbanes-Oxley Act of 2002 requires directors, particularly audit committees, executives, and auditors, be held more responsible for overseeing their companies' internal controls, financial reporting, risk management, and audit activities. Now public companies, including banks, are required providing integrated financial and internal control reports (IFICR) composed of both audited financial statements and audited internal control over financial reporting (ICFR).These integrated reports should be useful to investors because effective ICFR is vital in preventing and detecting financial misstatements including fraud.

The primary goal of IFICR is to provide persuasive information to investors, including shareholders and other stakeholders (e.g., customers, employees, suppliers, government, competitors, and society), about both financial statements and internal controls in order for them to make sound investment decisions. Persuasive information is information that is adequate, reliable, useful, transparent, timely, and relevant to the fair presentation of financial statements and the effectiveness of ICFR. Effective IFICR provides reasonable, but not necessarily absolute, assurance about the quality of financial information disseminated to investors. IFICR as defined in this section includes: (1) the management report and certification of financial statements; (2) the management report and certification of ICFR; (3) the independent auditor's opinion on fair and true presentation of financial statements; (4) the independent auditor's opinion on the effectiveness of ICFR; and (5) the audit committee's review of audited financial statements and both management and auditor reports on ICFR. The effectiveness of IFICR depends on a vigilant oversight function by the board of directors, particularly the audit committee, a responsible and accountable managerial function by senior executives, a credible external audit function by the independent auditor, and an objective internal audit function by internal auditors, as depicted in Exhibit 6.10.

IFICR adds value by lending credibility to both financial statements and internal controls, which promotes investor confidence and reinforces public trust in public financial information. IFICR reports are expected to reduce the information risks of financial information being misleading, biased, incomplete, inaccurate, or fraudulent. In this context, audits reduce financial information asymmetries between management and shareholders and thus help investors to make more informed decisions that in turn make the capital markets more efficient and add to the nation's economic prosperity.

EXHIBIT 6.10 Integrated Financial and Internal Control Reporting Process

Oversight Function	Managerial Function	External Audit Function	Internal Audit Function
1. Establishes clear roles and responsibilities of board of directors, particularly the audit committee, for integrated financial reporting process.	1. Performs quarterly review and assessment of financial statements and ICFR.	1. Ensures that audit committee is in charge of hiring, compensating, and overseeing work of independent auditor as related to integrated audit of financial statements and ICFR.	1. Assists board of directors, particularly audit committee, in effectively overseeing IFICR.
2. Ensures that audit committee reviews financial statements with independent auditor and recommends to board of directors that financial statements be released.	2. Performs quarterly assessment of ICFR to ensure effective ICFR is maintained throughout year.	2. Plans audit to gather sufficient and competent evidence to form an opinion on effectiveness of ICFR.	2. Assists management with certification of both financial statements and ICFR and preparation of financial statements and report on internal controls.
3. Ensures that audit committee reviews ICFR with independent auditor and recommends to board of directors that auditor report on ICFR be released.	3. Provides management assurance for Section 302 reporting.	3. Plans audit to gather sufficient and competent evidence to form opinion on fair presentation of financial statements in conformity with GAAP.	3. Cooperates with external auditor for audits of both financial statements and ICFR.
4. Ensures that audit committee reviews management's report on ICFR with management and recommends to board that report be released.	4. Assesses ICFR in compliance with Section 404 of SOX and the SEC's new interpretative guidance.	4. Prepares audit report on management's recommendation of previously identified material weaknesses in ICFR.	4. Prepares internal auditor report on adequacy and effectiveness of overall internal controls.
5. Ensures that audit committee reviews management certifications on financial statements and ICFR, particularly quarterly assessment in compliance with Section 302.	5. Identifies significant control deficiencies and takes remediation action.	5. Documents audit evidence relevant to integrated audit for at least seven years.	5. Assists management with enterprise risk management (ERM) assessment as pertains to internal controls.
	6. Builds SOX compliance into financial reporting process.		
	7. Develops standardized documentation methods, including narratives, control flowcharts, and control matrices, for both financial statements and ICFR.		
	8. Works with audit committee and independent auditors to explore ways to improve quality of financial statements and effectiveness of ICFR.		

To facilitate the move toward cost-effective IFICR, the SEC and the PCAOB have taken several initiatives. The SEC issued interpretive guidance for management's assessment of the effectiveness of ICFR. The PCAOB revised its auditing standards, particularly AS No. 5, for audits of ICFR. These initiatives are intended to make Section 404 of SOX on internal control compliance more cost effective, efficient, and scalable and to design a framework for effective implementation of IFICR. The effective implementation of IFICR requires a well-balanced functioning of all participants in the financial reporting process, as depicted in Exhibit 1.4. It is expected that both the SEC Interpretive Guidance and the PCAOB's Auditing Standard (AS) No. 5 will substantially improve IFICR by enabling management and auditors to fairly present their financial statements and to tailor their assessment of ICFR to the facts and circumstances of their company using a top-down, principles-based, and risk-based approach.

SEC Interpretive Guidance and AS No. 5 provide guidance for the effective implementation of Section 404 of SOX in six key areas:

1. Management must assess the effectiveness of the company's ICFR.
2. The independent auditor must opine only on the effectiveness of ICFR, not management's assessment.
3. The focus of the internal control audit should be on the most important matters that present the greatest risk that a company's internal controls will fail to detect, prevent, or correct material misstatements in its financial statements by using a top-down, risk-based approach of focusing on company-level controls and its control environment.
4. Unnecessary audit procedures should be eliminated to achieve the intended benefits of the audit by using the experience gained in previous years' audits and from the work of others (e.g., internal auditors, management) and focusing on the assessment of the opinion on the effectiveness of internal controls rather than adequacy of management's process to reach its conclusion.
5. The integrated audit should be scaled to fit the size and complexity of the company, in particular, making the auditing standards more scalable for smaller companies.
6. Auditing standards should be simplified by making them shorter, more transparent, and more clearly scalable to audits of companies of all sizes and complexity.

Electronic Financial Reporting

IT has changed the way financial information is prepared and disseminated. Pressure to standardize electronic financial reporting started in early 1993, when the SEC began to require electronic filings through its Electronic Data Gathering, Analysis, and Retrieval System (EDGAR). The EDGAR system is intended to make information readily available to investors and the financial community, ease the burden of regulatory filings, and enhance the speed and efficiency of SEC processing. Although EDGAR delivers the advantages of speed and efficiency of a centralized database, its usefulness is limited due to the methods available to retrieve stored information. In its current form, users must download reports and manually extract data of interest for use in other applications.

The future of financial reporting is in the electronic format, which can be based on different languages. The first attempt resulted in Hypertext Markup Language (HTML), which controls the way information is displayed (e.g., appearance, size, shape, color) without changing its content. The HTML format does not allow searching, analysis, and manipulation of information without downloading and transferring data to a spreadsheet or some software application with search and manipulation capabilities. Thus, the eXtensible Markup Language (XML) was designed to structure data for online use. XML is a set of rules for designing text formats that allows data to be structured and makes it easy for a computer to generate and read data. eXtensible Business Reporting Language (XBRL) was then developed to code financial information into a machine-readable format compatible with most technological platforms. XBRL is an XML-based platform for analysis, exchange, and reporting financial information with the purpose of integrating business reports and technology solutions. Under XBRL format, descriptions in the form of tags or labels attached to the business data in terms of agreed upon vocabulary known as taxonomy. Development of the appropriate taxonomy is the key to the application of XBRL in financial reporting. XBRL tags the data in the financial statements to assist users in extracting comparable and consistent information from electronic financial statements by providing a universal format for a system or tagging data. XBRL can provide these benefits to organizations:

- Reduce information collection, processing, and analysis costs
- Make information analysis and use more effective and efficient
- Enable organizations to better identify financial information risks and, through immediate feedback, manage the risks
- Enable organizations to adopt different taxonomies for financial reporting, tax purposes, and government filings
- Make the development of electronic financial information processes on an ongoing basis
- Enable organizations to comply with electronic processing requirements of regulators and tax authorities (The IRS will require corporations with $50 million or more in assets to file some of their tax return forms electronically; the SEC allows companies to submit financial information in XBRL in an exhibit to the regulatory filings.)
- Improve the transparency of financial information by allowing organizations to respond much more quickly on a timely basis to changes in business conditions, regulatory requirements, and economic developments[33]

XBRL components and documentation are the XBRL specifications, taxonomies, instance documents, reports, and assurance.[34] XBRL specification provides a technical explanation of XBRL and its operation, including the framework, taxonomies and instance documents. The XBRL specification is available for download from the XBRL Web site (www.xbrl.org). Taxonomies are XBRL's dictionary that describes the key data elements (numbers and text) included in XBRL instance documents designed for particular financial reporting purposes and in compliance with requirements of regulatory, financial reporting provisions, or tax authorities. Various taxonomies have been released based on U.S. GAAP International Financial Reporting Standards. XBRL instance documents are a collection of data elements and explanatory tags in a machine-readable format, designed based on the rules and concepts of particular taxonomies to ensure the data are reliably and consistently moved between systems. XBRL style sheets are used to convert instance documents that are in machine-readable format to human-readable reports. Style sheets can present XBRL data in the format of financial statements in HTML, PDF, word processing, or other specified presentation formats. Three control issues of XBRL need to be addressed. First, organizations using the XBRL format should ensure that they utilize an appropriate taxonomy suitable for their financial reporting, regulatory, and tax purposes. Second, organizations should establish policies, procedures, and controls to ensure that the tagging of data is accurate, complete, and meets the requirements of the selected taxonomies. Finally, control policies and procedures should be designed for the approval of the selected taxonomy, tagged data, and reporting of XBRL data applicable to financial reporting and other regulatory and tax purposes.

The SEC XBRL program, as of April 2011, is a voluntary program; public companies have the opportunity to participate in the program and stop participation as they wish. XBRL documents can be submitted simultaneously with the official filings with the SEC or subsequent to official filings. The XBRL-submitted documents are viewed as furnished in addition to the official filings with some flexibility in the tagged data being submitted. The SEC strongly encourages companies to participate in the voluntary filing program and assessment of XBRL and tagged data as well as submission of XBRL documents on EDGAR.

The first mandatory e-filing using XBRL format was implemented under the system of the call report modernization project for about 8,400 financial institutions in 2005.[35] The call report uses the Central Data Repository, a secure shared database of the quarterly schedules of nation's commercial banks. The Call Report Modernization Project is designed to simplify and increase the transparency of the call report process to supervise and evaluate financial conditions and results of operations of financial institutions. Call report filings are used to compile and verify financial reports of financial institutions used by the FDIC, the Federal Reserve Bank, the OCC, and the public. The FFIEC estimates that about 192,500 hours are spent compiling and filing call reports comprised of 2,000 fields of data including 400 pages of instructions and 1,500 formulas to support the data.

 CONCLUSION

This chapter examined three fundamental issues of consolidation, regulatory environment, and financial reporting pertaining to the financial services industry in general and banking organizations in particular. Technological advances coupled with the demand by customers for a broad range of financial services (e.g., banking, insurance, and securities) have encouraged financial institutions to expand their territory and assets to compete in the global market. By the late 1990s, banks realized that to compete successfully in a global market, they had to move away from traditional commercial services into investment and asset-management businesses. Thus, distinctions in financial services including banking, insurance, and securities in the financial industry are vanishing. Today, financial institutions may enter and exit distant markets more freely and may provide a variety of financial services (e.g., loans, mutual funds, insurance, investment, financing, and credit cards), and their customers may receive financial services from a dozen institutions. Thus, financial institutions' financial reporting should properly disclose the distribution of their internal ratings, asset quality, risk measurement, and management practices. Large banks should also strengthen their supervisory information systems. It is becoming more difficult to properly value an institution because branch networks and bricks and mortar do not count for as much as they used to.

The accounting profession has addressed FVA for financial reporting purposes during the past two decades. Regulatory agencies and bank examiners have also been considering the use of FVA for financial institutions since the savings and loan disaster of the 1980s to prevent similar crises in the industry. The issuance of SFAS Nos. 115 and 157 by the FASB was an important step in the evolutionary process toward the adoption of a comprehensive FVA system for financial institutions. IRS Section 475 has also provided a new boost toward the ultimate adoption of FVA for financial reporting and tax purposes. Although the regulations explicitly exclude institutions with less than $500 million in total assets, almost all depository institutions are implicitly required to: (1) report to the FDIC and other regulatory agencies on internal control and compliance with certain laws and regulations; (2) have an audit committee composed of independent outside directors; and (3) prepare and disseminate audited financial statements. This chapter examined financial reporting, internal controls, and corporate governance and accountability requirements of affected institutions under the new FDIC and SOX regulations as well as providing some guidance and implementation suggestions for covered institutions to better comply with the provisions of the FDIC and SOX regulations.

 NOTES

1. John LaWare, Member, Board of Governors of the Federal Reserve System, Statement before Committee on Banking, Finance, and Urban Affairs, U.S. House of Representatives, September 24, 1991, as reported in the *Federal Reserve Bulletin* (November 1991).
2. Donald T. Savage, "Interstate Banking: A Status Report," *Federal Reserve Bulletin* 73 (December 1993): 1075–1089.
3. Steven J. Weiss, "National Policies on Foreign Acquisitions of Banks," *Bankers Magazine* (March 1999): 25–29.
4. Financial Stability Board, "G20 Leaders Endorse Financial Stability Board Policy Framework for Addressing Systemically Important Financial Institutions (SIFIs)," No. 53/2010, November 12, 2010. Available at: www.financial stabilityboard.org.
5. Federal Reserve Board, Remarks by Vice Chairman Roger W. Ferguson, Jr., before the Bond Market Association, New York, New York, October 28, 1999.
6. Remarks by Chairman Alan Greenspan, "The Evolution of Bank Supervision," before the American Bankers Association, Phoenix, AZ, October 11, 1999.
7. Dodd-Frank Wall Street Reform and Consumer Protection Act of 2010, Pub. L. 111-203, 2010.
8. Carter H. Golembe, "Global Financial Crises: Implications for Banking and Regulation," Conference on Bank Structure and Competition, Federal Reserve Bank of Chicago, Chicago, IL, May 6–7, 1999.
9. Ibid., 8.

10. Shadow Committee, " Statement of the Shadow Financial Regulatory Committee on The Federal Reserve Board and Prudential Supervision," Statement No. 153, Chicago, IL December 7, 1998.

11. Federal Reserve Board, Remarks by Richard Spillenkothen, Director, Division of Supervision and Regulation, at the New York State Banking Department, New York, NY, October 25, 1999.

12. Basel Committee on Banking Supervision, "Microfinance Activities and the Core Principles for Effective Banking Supervision—Consultative Document," August 2010. Available at: www.bis.org/publ/bcbs175.htm

13. J. D. Wagster, "Impact of the 1988 Basel Accord on International Banks." *Journal of Finance* 51 (1996): 1321–1346.

14. Basel Committee on Banking Supervision, "Amendment to the Capital Accord to Incorporate Market Risks," January 1996.

15. Department of the Treasury (Office of the Comptroller of the Currency), Federal Reserve System and Federal Deposit Insurance Corporation, "Risk-Based Capital Standards: Market Risk," August 1996. Federal Reserve, "The Market-Risk Amendment," *Commercial Bank Examination Manual*. Regulation H (12CFR 208, Appendix E, and 12CFR 225, Appendix E), 1996.

16. Darryll Hendricks, "Evaluation of Value at Risk Models Using Historical Data," Federal Reserve Bank of New York, *Economic Policy Review* (April 1996): 36–69.

17. E. Dimson and P. Marsh, "Capital Requirements for Securities Firms," *Journal of Finance* 50 (1995): 821–851.

18. Basel III Accord, "The New Basel III Framework." Available at: www.basel-iii-accord.com/.

19. Elijah Brewer III, "Full-Blown Crisis, Half-Measure Cure," *Economic Perspectives*, Federal Reserve Bank of Chicago, (November/December1989): 2–17.

20. Charles S. Morris and Gordon H. Sellon, Jr., "Market Value Accounting for Bankers: Pros and Cons," *Economic Review*, Federal Reserve Bank of Kansas City (March/April 1991): 5–19. Thomas Mondschean, "Market Value Accounting May Cure Banking Net Worth Distortions," *Business Credit* (June 1992): 14.

21. David L. Mergh, "Market Value Accounting and the Bank Balance Sheet," *Contemporary Policy Issues* (April 1990): 82–94. Michael H. Sulton and James A. Johnson, "Current Value: Finding a Way Forward." *Financial Executives* (January/February1993): 39–43.

22. PricewaterhouseCoopers, *Audit Committee Update 2000: Current Financial Reporting Model and Meeting Users' Needs*, 37.

23. Cecilia Leung and Zabihollah Rezaee, "Interactions Between Financial and Tax Rules on Market Value Accounting," *Journal of Taxation of Investments* (Winter 1997): 132–151.

24. Financial Accounting Standard Board, *Preliminary Views: Report Financial Instruments and Certain Related Assets and Liabilities at Fair Value* (Norwalk, CT: Author, December 14, 1999).

25. Financial Accounting Standards Board, Statement of Financial Accounting Standards (SFAS) No. 159, *Financial Instruments* (Norwalk, CT: Author, 2006).

26. Financial Accounting Standards Board, Statement of Financial Accounting Standards (SFAS) No. 157, *Fair Value Measurements* (Norwalk, CT: Author, 2006).

27. Board of Directors of the FDIC, Supervisory Guidance on the Implementation of Section 112 of the Federal Deposit Insurance Corporation Improvement Act, 1991, May 11, 1993.

28. Foreign Corrupt Practice Act, pp. 95–213, Title 1; 91 Stat. 1494, December 19, 1977.

29. National Commission on Fraudulent Financial Reporting, "Report of the National Commission on Fraudulent Financial Reporting" October 1987.

30. Committee of Sponsoring Organizations of the Treadway Commission, "Internal Control—Integrated Framework," *Coopers and Lybrand* 1–4 (September 1992).

31. Mary Colby, "New Audit and Reporting Rule Generates Yet More Paperwork," *Bank Management* (August 1993): 47–49.

32. Committee of Sponsoring Organizations of the Treadway Commission, "Internal Control."

33. Organizations interested in the emerging developments of XBRL taxonomies, tools, and solutions should visit the XBRL Web site: www.xbrl.org.

34. Canadian Institute of Chartered Accountants, Information Technology Advisory Committee, *Audit & Control Implications of XBRL* (December 2005). Available at: www.cica .ca.itac.

35. Accounting Web, "A Closer Look at the First Mandatory E-Filing System Using XBRL," September 1, 2005. Available at: www.accountingweb.com/cgi-bin/item.cgi?id= 101260.

PART THREE

Fundamentals of Valuations: Concepts, Standards, and Techniques

CHAPTER SEVEN

Value and Valuation: A Conceptual Foundation

T HE CONCEPT OF VALUE is not as straightforward as many people believe. The value of any asset depends on several factors: the party for whom the valuation is made, the type of value being measured, the point in time at which the value is being estimated, and the purpose of the valuation. This chapter presents key concepts and definitions of value and valuation that are important to understand when applying the various valuation approaches described in Chapter 6.

 ## ASSET-LIABILITY MANAGEMENT

Asset-liability management (ALM) is a risk management technique that often is employed in banking or insurance business that monitor and try to prevent an asset/liability mismatch. ALM has evolved since the early 1980s, and the scope of its activities has widened. In financial firms, ALM is associated with assets and liabilities in those business lines that are accounted for on an accrual basis. This includes bank lending and deposit taking. It includes essentially all traditional insurance activities. The function of ALM is to measure and control three levels of financial risk: interest rate risk (the pricing difference between loans and deposits), credit risk (the probability of default), and liquidity risk (occurring when loans and deposits have different maturities). Today, ALM departments are addressing (nontrading) foreign exchange risks and other risks besides extending to nonfinancial firms. Corporations have adopted techniques of ALM to address interest rate exposures, liquidity risk, and foreign exchange risk. They are using related techniques to address commodities risks. For example, airlines' hedging of fuel prices or manufacturers' hedging of steel prices are often presented as ALM.

Asset-liability risk is leveraged by the fact that the values of assets and liabilities each tend to be greater than the value of capital. ALM practice manages risks that arise due to mismatch between assets and liabilities (debts and assets) that can cause very serious damages to the banking business. Typically banks want to make sure that the short- or long-term interest earning assets match interest expense liabilities. Banking assets come from various sources: building, furniture and fixtures, land and other real estate owned, cash in vault, loans and discounts, overdraft collectibles, debit on customers' letters of credit and acceptances outstanding, government bonds, bonds, stocks and other financial market securities, dues from other branches or from other financial institutions, reserve with Federal Reserve, interest earned but not collected, exchanges from clearinghouses, checks on other banks, due from Treasurer of the United States, items with the Federal Reserve in a process of collection, and stocks of the Federal Reserve. It is important to note that commercial banks that are members of Federal Deposit Insurance Corporation (FDIC) are required to hold a portion of their capital in Federal Reserve stock; they receive 6 percent annually on their holdings and are eligible to elect six of nine members of Federal Reserve Bank board of directors.[1] A primary objective in ALM is managing the net interest margin (i.e., the net difference between interest-earning assets [loans] and interest-paying liabilities [deposits]) to produce consistent growth in the loan portfolio and shareholder earnings, regardless of short-term movement in interest rates. The dollar difference between assets (loans) maturing or repricing and liabilities (deposits) is known as the rate sensitivity gap (or maturity gap). Banks attempt to manage this asset-liability gap by pricing some of their loans at variable interest rates. A more precise measure of interest rate risk is duration, which measures the impact of changes in interest rates on the expected maturities of both assets and liabilities. In essence, duration takes the gap report data and converts that information into present-value (PV) worth of deposits and loans, which is more meaningful in estimating maturities, and the probability that either assets or liabilities will reprice during the period under review. Besides financial institutions, nonfinancial companies also employ ALM, mainly through the use of derivative contracts to minimize their exposures on the liability side of the balance sheet.

Banking liabilities also differ from liabilities of other commercial organization. The most common types of liabilities come from: capital stock, surplus, undivided profits, unpaid dividends, discount collected but not earned, amount reserved for taxes, interest, or expenses accrued, circulating notes outstanding, amounts due to other banks, demand depostis, time deposits, government or state/municipal deposits, certified checks outstanding, cashier check outstanding, bonds borrowed, bills payable outstanding, letter of credit and acceptance outstanding.[2] The bank's conventional principle is to borrow short term and lend long term; that is why ALM is so critical to the banking operations. If assets are more than liabilities, the bank becomes "insolvent." The value of assets usually fluctuates more than the value of liabilities. In a banking business, the accounting equation (assets equals liabilities plus shareholders capital) has a different meaning. Capital in a banking business correspond to claims on the assets. It is important to remember that the banking business is heavily regulated by the government.[3] In addition to the requirement to submit financial information on a daily, weekly, quarterly, and annual basis, banks are required to comply with International

Financial Reporting Standards, and they are obligated to report the information on all nonperforming loans, financial assets and liabilities and their subsequent durations, and other details.

The Diamond-Dybvig model was developed in 1983 and is widely used as a risk management tool to prevent bank runs. The main assumption that lays the foundation for the model is that the bank's main purpose is to generate liquidity. ALM is an ongoing process that considers a wide range of risks that banks are exposed to, including interest rate risk, equity risk, liquidity risk, and currency risk. Value at risk (VaR) is an advanced risk management tool that measures the magnitude of expected loss (total risk) over a given time frame based on the probability distribution and a specified confidence level, and is usually not the maximum possible loss.[4] VaR can measure the absolute risk of a portfolio of assets and/or liabilities or the active risk of the difference between a portfolio and its benchmark. VaR can aggregate across multiple risk factors such as currency, interest rate risk, and equity. VaR can also be forward looking (ex ante) or backward looking (ex post) as it can be based on market and/or historical data (i.e., VaR can be parametric or historical).

INVESTMENT MANAGEMENT

Investment management, also known as portfolio management, is the management of various securities and assets with a purpose to achieve specific returns for the benefit of the investors. Its provision includes elements of financial statement analysis, asset selection, stock selection, plan implementation, and ongoing monitoring of investments. Every fund has it own philosophy, strategy, and investment objectives that are to be achieved. In 1997, the Gramm-Leach-Bliley Act gave banks the opportunity to expand into a securities services markets in addition to traditional banking. Before that, as mentioned in Chapter 2, the Glass-Steagall Act mandated a separation of commercial and investment banking activities. Asset management activities at banks, depending on the size and the scale of operations, may be organized in a separate division of the bank. A smaller bank may have a separate "trust" department that handles asset management activities and deals with third parties. Asset types also vary within banking industries. Banks may manage their own assets (asset management account) or invest on behalf of their clients, giving them broader alternatives of the investment options, which otherwise would not be available to the individual investor. Wealth management departments at banks usually deal with high-net-worth individuals and are aimed to help them increase their wealth as well as choose the most tax-favored solutions. Banks and other sizable financial institutions have resources and years of accumulated experience to perform estate planning, risk management, and legal compliance.

Active asset management exposes banks to a broad range of risk factors due to the nature of the off–balance sheet activities. That was especially evident during the recent financial crisis, when the total amount of global funds under management fell 17 percent, totaling around $90 trillion.[5] However, analysts predict that the crisis will continue to have long-term effects on the wealth management industry, as investors will be more cautious in selecting funds and their subsequent investment strategies. To illustrate, according to the Merrill Lynch report *World Wealth Report 2009*, wealth management strategies shifted from equities and diversified portfolios to cash, fixed income, and domestic investments. Cash-based holdings increased 21 percent by the year-end 2008 and investments in equity dropped 33 percent from 2007, which proves that high-net-worth individuals remain very conservative during turbulent times.[6] As a result, more than a quarter of high-net-worth individuals withdrew assets from wealth-management firms due to the loss of confidence in wealth managers as well as market performance.

 ## LENDING MANAGEMENT

The concept of lending management is closely related to credit risk management. Credit risk is the likelihood of failure of borrowers to repay a loan or otherwise meet a contractual obligation which may result in loss of principal and/or interests incurred. Credit risk arises whenever a borrower is expecting to use future cash flows to pay a current debt. Investors are compensated for assuming credit risk by way of interest payments from the borrower or issuer of a debt obligation. Credit risks are calculated based on the borrower's ability to repay, which is derived from a combination of factors: the size and quality of collateral, the ability to generate revenue, and borrower's liabilities.

Kashyap, Rajan, and Stein[7] argue that banks stand ready to provide liquidity on demand to depositors through checking accounts and to extend credit as well as liquidity to borrowers through lines of credit. The use of risk management techniques (hedging risk by both buying and selling loans) increases the bank returns and mitigates the risks. Banks that enhance their ability to manage credit risk will operate with greater leverage and will lend more of their assets to risky borrowers. Thus, the benefits of advances in risk management in banking will likely be greater credit availability rather than reduced risk in the banking system.[8] A number of techniques are used to facilitate effective lending management practices at financial institutions, and managing credit risk concentration is one example. Management of credit risk concentration is achieved through diversification. Financial history holds a number of examples when financial institutions fail to diversify their borrowers and geographic regions, which resulted in a loss of liquidity (Parmalat, Enron, hurricane damage to the U.S. Gulf Coast). Consequently, by spreading the institution's risk over many borrowers, industries, or regions, the lending institution can minimize the collective impact of economic events or trends on its earnings and capital. Other popular techniques that are used in lending management are setting exposure limits (collateral size and quality, lending to only certain industries, single borrowers), altering bank product mixes, asset management and alteration, hedging and securitization, and use of credit derivatives.

Setting bank exposure limits based on economic capital is a more common practice in the industry as best practices suggest that no more than 10 percent of the economic capital can be allocated to the single borrower. A large deal with a high level of risk would use a large percentage of the portfolio's available economic capital and therefore might exceed exposure limits. A smaller deal and/or a more favorable risk rating would "consume" less economic capital and would more likely fall within prescribed lending policy guidelines.

Setting lending limits alone is not sufficient. Basel II explicitly states that idea in its definition of credit concentration and approaches to lending management. Basel II requires banks to explicitly state the extent of credit concentration when estimating the capital adequacy. Regulators strongly support the idea that concentration levels have to be identified and matched with appropriate risk factors. Basel III will require banks to maintain top-quality capital totaling seven percent of their risk-bearing assets compared to currently required two percent. Effective compliance with Basel III rules will require banks to raise substantial new capital over the next several years when the rules become effective in January 2019. The key is to identify risk variables and understand how they correlate inside the loan portfolio.[9]

 ## LIQUIDITY MANAGEMENT

Investment and liquidity management are analyzed in a sector in which firms are exogenously cash constrained. Liquidity is managed through dividend policy and access to short-term bank finance, in which bank lines of credit smooth variation in available cash flow and accelerate investment. Cash and liquidity management is about forecasting the company's cash needs to run its businesses and then managing the group's wide cash flows, short-term borrowings, and cash in the most efficient manner to ensure that those cash needs can be met. With the help of information technology and communications systems, cash can be pooled internationally and used appropriately. Funding and liquidity needs are intimately connected by understanding and managing working capital and the payments and cash reporting systems accurately. The core purpose of liquidity management is being able to obtain funding when it is needed.

The Bank of International Settlements defines liquidity as the ability of a bank to fund increases in assets and meet obligations as they come due, without incurring unacceptable losses. The fundamental role of banks in the maturity transformation of short-term deposits into long-term loans makes banks inherently vulnerable to liquidity risk, of both an institution-specific nature and due to broad market influences. That is why liquidity management is so crucial for banks because all bank operations involve implications on the bank's liquidity position.

Effective liquidity risk management is vital to banks to ensure their ability to meet cash flow obligations. The Basel Committee has established guidance on managing liquidity risk. The guidance provides details on eight functions of managing liquidity risk:

- The importance of establishing a liquidity risk tolerance;
- The maintenance of an adequate level of liquidity, including through a cushion of liquid assets;
- The necessity of allocating liquidity costs, benefits and risks to all significant business activities;
- The identification and measurement of the full range of liquidity risks, including contingent liquidity risks;

- The design and use of severe stress test scenarios;
- The need for a robust and operational contingency funding plan;
- The management of intraday liquidity risk and collateral; and
- Public disclosure in promoting market discipline[10]

Maintaining adequate liquidity is not only a matter of regulatory compliance, but also a determinant of the long-term solvency of the bank or financial institution. The lack or shortage of liquidity creates a vicious circle and threatens the viability of the whole banking system. To illustrate, a massive withdrawal of deposits threatens a bank's cash position and imposes the risk of illiquidity. If the bank is short on cash, depositors will lose their confidence in the bank and start withdrawing their deposits, forcing the bank to sell its assets at a loss and jeopardizing its opportunity to earn future interest or noninterest income on those assets. The inability to manage liquidity risk was one of the main reasons the financial crisis occurred in 2007–2009.

To address the issue, the Basel Committee of Banking Supervision came up with an international framework for liquidity risk measurement, standards, and monitoring. The committee proposed to tighten banking supervision as well promote as active usage of the liquidity risk management tools: liquidity and limits scenario stress testing and comprehensive cash flow forecasting. The committee increasingly focuses on the convergence of the global liquidity risk management standards and recommends that banks preserve and continuously monitor substantial high-quality liquid assets to meet their liabilities. The liquidity coverage ratio was designed specifically to test whether banks have enough liquidity to endure a one-month severe stress scenario. The stress test involves these events: loss of deposits, increase in collateral calls, downgrading of the institutional credit rating, and loss of a major type of funding. For further accuracy, banks have to report their contingent (contractual and noncontractual) liabilities.

The next formula is used to assess a bank's liquidity coverage ratio:

$$\frac{\text{Stock of high quality liquid assets}}{\text{Net cash outflows over a 30-day time period}} \geq 100\%$$

The standard suggests that banks must hold a stock of unencumbered (free of obligations, not pledged as collateral for any other operation), high-quality liquid assets that is clearly sufficient to cover cumulative net cash outflows (as will be defined) over a 30-day period under the prescribed stress scenario.

The net stable funding ratio was designed to promote banks to fund their activities with a less risky capital, thus creating a good foundation for long-term solvency. Funds have to be widely available and remain stable over the year period. The next formula is used to calculate the net stable funding ratio:

$$\frac{\text{Available amount of stable funding}}{\text{Required amount of stable funding}} > 100\%$$

Available stable funding is defined as the total amount of an institution's: (1) capital; (2) preferred stock with maturity of equal to or greater than one year; (3) liabilities with effective maturities of one year or greater; and (4) that portion of "stable" nonmaturity deposits and/or term deposits with maturities of less than one year that would be expected to stay with the institution for an extended period in an idiosyncratic stress event. The required amount of stable funding is calculated as the sum of the value of the assets held and funded by the institution, multiplied by a specific required stable funding factor assigned to each particular asset type, added to the amount of off–balance sheet activity (or potential liquidity exposure) multiplied by its associated required stable funding factor.

The Basel Committee suggests that banks concentrate on intraday risk management issues and use appropriate risk liquidity tools.[11] To illustrate, the so-called concentration of funding metric allows bank supervisors to understand the extent of the bank's balance sheet exposure if one of the wholesale funding sources were to be withdrawn. The unavailable encumbered asset tool measures the bank's capacity to raise additional funds to fund its operations, keeping in mind different economic scenarios.

 NATURE OF VALUE

In the context of valuation for bank mergers and acquisitions, "value" means *economic value*. Such value is an amount, expressed in dollar terms, that would be paid in exchange for an asset or the right to receive future benefits from the use of that asset. Based on three measures of operating merger and acquisition (M&A) performance, no value creation can be realized in the M&A in terms of research productivity, return on investment, and profit margin. Economic value is, therefore, the monetary worth of an asset.[12]

Value is not a static or homogeneous concept. It can be defined as the amount of money received back from a product. The value of any asset depends on many factors, which can change over time, such as:

- Total economic environment
- Potential use of the asset
- Timing of the value estimate
- Location of the asset
- Relative scarcity and values of substitutes
- Extent of ownership involved
- Liquidity of and market for the asset
- Physical condition of the asset

The concept of value is different from *price* or *cost*. Price is the actual amount spent to acquire an asset. Cost typically means the dollar value of the factors of production (land, labor, capital, and management) required to create an asset. The expression "He overpaid for that house" indicates a difference between the price someone paid for the house and the value someone else placed on it. A similar difference exists between value and cost. The cost of developing a shopping center, for example, may not reflect its value if it is located in a community that loses its largest employer the day after the shopping center opens. In this case, the cost could far exceed the value.

Given the increasing number of cross-border M&A, along with their economic and social importance, a better understanding of post-M&A performance is called for. Besides some extensive research on M&A as an international market entry strategy, the nature of value creation in cross-border M&A has not received enough attention in international business research. Investment property in companies involved in M&A is measured at fair value. Gains or losses arising from changes in the fair value of such property are included in net profit or loss for the period in which they arise. In relation to owner-occupied property, it can encompass market value or its surrogate (in the absence of an identified market), depreciated replacement cost. Fair value is synonymous with the definition of market value given by the International Valuation Standards Committee. "Market value" is defined as the estimated amount for which an asset should exchange on the date of valuation between a willing buyer and a willing seller in an arm's-length transaction after proper marketing wherein the parties had each acted knowledgeably, prudently, and without compulsion. The best evidence of fair value is normally given by current prices on an active market for similar property in the same location and condition and subject to similar lease and other contracts. The acquiring and consolidating companies have to take fair value into consideration in their respective negotiation or bargaining positions.

Value, price, and cost are different concepts and seldom are of equal monetary amounts. The discussion in this and other chapters focuses on value. Where price and cost come into play, they are explicitly identified.

TWELVE CONCEPTS OF VALUE

A Chinese proverb states that "wisdom begins with calling things by their right names." This saying has direct applicability to valuation, where different concepts of value have very different definitions, uses, and interpretations. Often bankers and other professionals are surprised to learn that the meaning of "value" is more complex than "what something is worth." As discussed in the preceding section, value depends on the person assessing it, the purpose, the timing, and a host of other factors. In other words, there is no one *right* value. Consequently, it is important to define the various concepts of value that can be used to establish a bank's value for a merger or acquisition.

Fair Market Value

The most common type of value definition is the *fair market value method*, also known as market value or cash value. The generally accepted definition of fair market value (FMV) is:

> The amount, expressed in cash or equivalent, at which a property (or any other asset) would exchange between a willing buyer and willing seller, each having a reasonable knowledge of all pertinent facts, neither being under compulsion to buy or sell and with equity to both.

This definition of value applies to virtually all federal and state tax matters as well as to many other valuation situations. It is the price that a given property or asset would fetch in the marketplace, subject to certain conditions, such as: (1) The price that an interested but not desperate buyer would be willing to pay and an interested but not desperate seller would be willing to accept on the open market assuming a reasonable period of time for an agreement to arise; and (2) a reasonable time period is given for the transaction to be completed. It is important to remember that the willing buyer and willing seller described in the definition are not "particular" buyers and sellers. They are hypothetical parties in an arm's-length transaction. Consequently, if the price paid for an asset reflects factors that are atypical to the hypothetical willing buyer and willing seller, then that price reflects something other than FMV. For example, the developer of a parcel of real estate may have more interest than anyone else in an adjoining strip of land because it would round out a total development. This unique situation of one particular buyer should not be taken into account when establishing a FMV of that adjoining strip of land.

The concept of a hypothetical willing buyer and willing seller is sometimes difficult to grasp, because no one considers himself or herself hypothetical. An alternate way of viewing this concept is to consider the hypothetical willing buyer and willing seller as the "most likely" buyer or seller. Therefore, FMV could be considered the "most likely" transaction price. This value would reflect consensus of assumptions of typical or likely buyers of the asset.

FMV is determined as of a specific date based on the price that a willing buyer would pay a willing seller with all relevant knowledge. The general public may confuse FMV with fairness. FMV is not about fairness but rather what a willing buyer would pay a willing seller at a specific date based on the best educated guess and judgment using all of the knowledge available on that date.

FMV assumes a continuation in the general pattern of the property being valued. In other words, FMV is, more or less, an *as-is* value, without improvements that a particular buyer may be able to implement. The buyer, in the process of establishing a price to offer for a particular asset, often considers the potential impact of improvements to the property. The results of such "value creation" efforts are not (and should not be) reflected in FMV. In the real world of buying and selling assets, however, it is very common for a seller to benefit from at least some of the *value creation potential* in the form of a price higher than a theoretically "pure" FMV. In a competitive market, more than one buyer will be bidding for the property of the seller, and the ultimate price paid may reflect the FMV plus some portion of the value creation opportunity the buyer believes it can realize. The price ultimately paid by a particular buyer is usually attributable to *investment value*, an extremely important M&A value concept described in the next section.

Investment Value

The most familiar type of value to professionals involved in M&A is *investment value* (IV). This type of value is usually thought of as the value of the future benefits of ownership of an asset to a particular buyer. IV is often a more easily understood concept, because it is the value of a specific asset to a specific buyer. It can be computed from the estimate of the market price it would sell at if it were straight (did not have the conversion feature) or computed from the value of the underlying asset.

The investment value can differ significantly from one potential buyer to another for a variety of valid reasons. Some factors that can affect a particular buyer's estimate of IV in a business include:

- Perceived synergy and value creation opportunities
- Desire on the part of the buyer to enter a new market
- Perception of riskiness and/or volatility of the asset's earning power
- Tax status of buyer
- Optimism of buyer

All of these factors influence a particular buyer's estimate of the future earning power of the business and therefore that buyer's estimation of value.

FMV and IV are related but seldom equal. If all potential buyers had the same assumptions and situations, the two types of values would be equal. As this is an improbable situation, it will always be the case that some buyers are willing to pay more for an asset than others. The techniques and approaches used to estimate FMV and IV are essentially the same; it is the assumptions that differ.

Fair Value

The concept of *fair value* has recently received considerable attention from standard-setting bodies [e.g., Financial Accounting Standards Board (FASB)] and judicial process through case law. Fair value is the statutory standard of value that has evolved from case law and applies to certain specific transactions. It is the estimated value of all assets and liabilities of an acquired company used to consolidate the financial statements of both companies. In the futures market, fair value is the equilibrium price for a futures contract. This is equal to the spot price after taking into account compounded interest (and dividends lost because the investor owns the futures contract rather than the physical stocks) over a certain period of time.

The concept of fair value has been developed by case law, and, accordingly, states have different interpretations of fair value with almost no consensus about its definition and application. However, in most court cases, the concept of fair value is equated to FMV and applied primarily in dissenting or oppressed shareholder actions in mergers or sell-outs. In cases when the fair value concept should be used, the appraiser must obtain a definition of fair value by consulting local case law, statutes, and attorneys in the jurisdiction in which the case would be filed.

The FASB in its 2000 pronouncements defined fair value as "an estimate of the price an entity would have realized if it had sold an asset or paid if it had been relieved of a liability on the reporting date in an arm's length exchange motivated by normal business considerations. That is, it is an estimate of an exit price determined by market interactions."[13] In this definition, the FASB equates fair value with exit price (i.e., the price at which an asset or liability could be sold or settled). The exit price is determined by the market's estimate of the PV of the expected future cash flows of the entity that owns the asset or owes the liability. Thus, based on the preceding definition, the fair value is the amount at which (1) an asset could be bought or sold between willing parties in a normal course of business, or (2) a liability could be incurred or settled in a current transaction between willing parties.

In current accounting standards, the FASB defines fair value in terms of current market value as the price that would be received for an asset or paid to transfer a liability in a current transaction between marketplace participants. The suggested framework for measuring fair value defines a fair value hierarchy that ranges from quoted prices for identical assets or liabilities in an active market (highest level) to the fair value information derived from extrapolation or interpolation that is not corroborated by other observable market data (lowest level). New fair value disclosures would include both tabular quantitative disclosures for all report filing periods (quarterly, annual) for fair value remeasurements and qualitative disclosures about valuations techniques used for annual reporting.

On September 15, 2005, the FASB issued Statement of Financial Accounting Standards (SFAS) No. 157 titled *Fair Value Measurements*.[14] SFAS No. 157 provides enhanced guidance for using fair value to measure assets and liabilities and expanded transparent information concerning the definition of fair values, the extent to which companies measure fair value for their assets and liabilities, the information used to measure fair value, and the impact of fair value measurements on their earnings. The definition of fair value in SFAS No. 157 focuses on the price that "would be received to sell the asset or paid to transfer the liability at the measurement data (at exit price), not the price that would be paid to acquire the asset or received to assume the liability at the measurement date (an entry price)." The fair value hierarchy set forth in SFAS No. 157 ranges from Level 1 (e.g., items with quoted prices for identical assets or liabilities inactive markets) to Level 5 (e.g., items valued using substantial entity-derived inputs through extrapolation or interpolation data). SFAS No. 157 focuses on market-based measures as opposed to entity-specific measures for fair value by giving the highest priority to quoted prices in active markets. However, it permits the use of unobservable inputs for circumstances where there is no or little market activity for assets or liabilities being measured.

The key eight provisions of SFAS No. 157 are:

1. Enhanced guidance for using fair value to measure assets and liabilities.
2. Proposed transparent disclosures concerning fair-value measurements.
3. Disclosure of the effect of fair value measurements on earnings.
4. Clarification of the definition of fair value based on an exit price instead of an entry price on the measurement data.
5. Requirement that fair value is a market-based measurement, not an entity-specific measurement.
6. Market participant assumptions used in determining fair value should include the risk inherent in a particular valuation technique and the effect of a restriction on the sale or use of an asset.
7. Clarification that a fair value measurement for a liability reflects its nonperformance risk such as credit risk.

8. Disclosures concerning the use of fair value to measure assets and liabilities in interim and annual periods subsequent to initial recognition.

Arguments in favor of fair value are:

- Fair value could increase market discipline and lead managers to take the right value-maximizing decisions.
- Fair value accounting may help preventing systemic crises.
- Increased volatility in accounting numbers resulting from the use of fair value is not necessarily a problem if investors correctly interpret the information disclosed.
- The market value of an asset is more relevant than historical cost because it reflects the amount at which that asset could be bought or sold in a current transaction between willing parties.
- The market value of a liability is more relevant than historical cost because it reflects the amount at which that liability could be incurred or settled in a current transaction between willing parties.
- A measurement system that reflects the market values of assets and liabilities would therefore lead to better insights into the risk profile of firms currently in place so that investors could exercise better market discipline and thake corrective action on a firm's decisions.
- The historical cost regime relies on past prices, so accounting values are insensitive to price signals. This leads to one type of inefficiency arising from excessive conservatism.

Arguments against fair value are:

- Fair value accounting increases the volatility of bank's profits.
- Fair value accounting lacks accuracy as it relies on subjective proxies for the market value of nontradable financial products (such as loans).
- Book value accounting minimizes expected costs of bankruptcy industry.
- Fair value increases the volatility of income.
- The very definition of market value by the FASB and the International Accounting Standards Board assumes the existence of deep and liquid secondary markets for their assets and liabilities.
- Fair value accounting does not properly reflect the way in which banks and insurance companies manage their core businesses of granting long-term loans and underwriting insurance policies.
- Reliance on market values for assets and liabilities runs the risk that the information disclosed will embody excess volatility driven by short-term fluctuations in financial market valuations in addition to the fundamental volatility driven by fluctuations in the riskiness of the financial institution's long-term cash flows.

Marking to market overcomes this conservatism by relying on current market prices, but it also distorts this information.

The subprime scandals of 2008 can be attributed to many factors, including the improper application of fair value estimates by the real estate appraising industry. The conflicts of interest between real estate appraisal firms and real estate brokerage firms provided incentives and opportunities for appraisals to present fair value estimates above and beyond reasonable and realistic fair value to get financing needs to close deals. Banks had all the incentives and opportunities to get the highest fair value estimates to provide subprime loans to customers and then sell the mortgages to mortgage buyers, such as Freddie Mac and Fannie Mae, quasi-government corporations established to buy up mortgages from banks. The other factor is banks' securitization vehicles of variable interest entities or special-purpose entities. The appropriate tone set at the top by management regarding corporate culture within which financial reports are produced is vital to the integrity of the financial reporting process. When the tone set at the top is lax, fraudulent financial reporting is more likely to occur and not be prevented.

Intrinsic Value

Intrinsic value, also known as fundamental value, is the concept used frequently by financial analysts to estimate the value of stocks based on all of the facts and circumstances of the business or the investment. It is the actual value of a company or an asset based on an underlying perception of its true value including all aspects of the business, in terms of both tangible and intangible factors. This value may or may not be the same as the current market value. Value investors use a variety of analytical techniques in order to estimate the intrinsic value of securities in hopes of finding investments where the true value of the investment exceeds its current market value. For call options, intrinsic value is the difference between the underlying stock's price and the strike price. Intrinsic value of an investment (e.g., security) is determined based on both the earning power and earnings quality of the investment. Earning power is measured in terms of the entity's capability to increase profitability constantly and rate of return in light of plausible assumptions including both internal sources and external economic and benchmark data. Earnings quality is assessed by factors such as customer base, profitability, customer satisfaction, employee satisfaction, relative risk, competitiveness, and steadiness of earnings forecasts.

The intrinsic value is the PV of the future earnings stream discounted at the current market yield. Intrinsic value of an investment is a function of estimated discounted periodic earnings stream, market gains or losses, and time horizon of earnings stream. If the market value of a stock is above its calculated intrinsic value, the stock is a good "sell," and investors will be able to earn excess return. Conversely, if the market price of a stock is below its predicted intrinsic value, the stock is a good "buy." The term "intrinsic value" often is used incorrectly and interchangeably with the concept of investment value. Investment value commonly refers to the value perceived by a specific buyer in light of a specific set of circumstances at a specific point of time. Intrinsic value, however, typically is viewed as the value of a going concern to a particular owner, regardless of the marketability of a business or a business interest under consideration.

Value in Use/Value in Exchange

Value in use is not a type of value but a condition under which certain assumptions are made in valuing assets. It is associated with assets that are in productive use and can be described as the value of an asset, for a particular use or to a particular user, as part of an operating enterprise. There is no official definition of value in use by professional valuation societies or the Internal Revenue Service (IRS). It is, however, important to understand the concept since the value of acquired assets (especially furniture, fixtures, equipment, and premises) in most bank M&A is influenced significantly by their use as part of the bank. When specific assets used by any ongoing business are valued, it is usually assumed that those assets will remain in their most productive use.

    Value in exchange is essentially the opposite of value in use. The concept of value in exchange relates to the value of a property or asset as exchanged by itself separate from an operating entity. Typically, the value in exchange is less than the value in use of an asset in an ongoing business enterprise. For example, the teller counters in a bank branch have less value if sold separately than if sold as part of a total branch sale.

Goodwill Value

Goodwill is an amount that can be found in the assets portion of a company's balance sheet. Goodwill often can arise when one company is purchased by another company. In an acquisition, the amount paid for the company over book value usually accounts by the target firm as a goodwill. Goodwill is a specific type of intangible asset that arises when a business as a whole has value greater than the value of its tangible and specifically identified intangible assets. A 1960 court case defined goodwill as "the sum total of imponderable qualities which attract the customers to a business; in essence it is the expectancy of continued patronage for whatever reason."[15]

    From an M&A perspective, the value of goodwill is calculated as the difference between the price paid for an acquired business and the FMV of the assets acquired (both tangible and separately identified intangible) net of the liabilities. The concept of goodwill value has important applicability to banks for tax, financial reporting, and regulatory reasons.

Going-Concern Value

Going-concern value is the value of a company as an ongoing entity and its value differs from the value of a liquidated company's assets, because an ongoing operation has the ability to continue to earn profit while a liquidated company does not. Going-concern value is used for a company that has the resources needed in order to continue to operate indefinitely. If a company is not a going concern, it means the company has gone bankrupt. Going-concern value is somewhat of a misnomer since it is not a standard of value, as is FMV or investment value. In other words, it would be incorrect to state that "the going-concern value of XYZ Bank is $100 million." A proper statement would be "the fair market value of XYZ Bank *as a going concern* is $100 million." This distinction appears to be a minor semantic difference, but the subtle differences in terminology is one key to understanding valuation.

The concept of going-concern value typically is brought into play when a business (such as a bank) is being valued as a viable operating unit, with no immediate threat of discontinuance of operations. In tax situations, however, going-concern value carries a somewhat different connotation. The IRS has taken the position that going-concern value is a nonamortizable (for tax purposes) intangible asset acquired by a buyer of a business, a value that reflects the fact that the purchased entity has staff and management in place, a sales and marketing organization, established customer and supplier relationships, and so on. The IRS has used this concept when the existence of goodwill was difficult to demonstrate or was nonexistent. A number of court cases admitted that no specific guidelines exist to measure going-concern value in the absence of goodwill.[16] Nonetheless, the IRS has been able to argue successfully that even without the goodwill, some assets of a business that are acquired have intangible value because they are in place and part of a "going concern." The real controversy, however, is not whether going-concern value exists or not but whether it is amortizable for tax purposes. The IRS generally has been successful in having at least some part of the purchase price of a business allocated to nonamortizable going-concern value when goodwill is difficult or impossible to measure. (Chapter 10 specifically addresses intangible assets and the related valuation issues.)

Book Value

One of the most misleading uses of the term "value" is in conjunction with *book value*. It is an accounting and tax concept only, not a valuational or economic one. For a particular asset (such as a piece of equipment), book value is simply the historical cost of that asset less accumulated depreciation.[17] For a business enterprise, book value is the total book values of all individual assets less the book value of individual liabilities. In an accounting sense, this is also called *net worth* or *book equity*. It is the value of accumulated depreciation taken out from the cost of an asset (i.e., the net asset value of a company calculated by total assets minus intangible assets—patents, goodwill—and liabilities).

An extremely important concept to bear in mind when valuing M&A candidates is that book value may or may not have any relation to FMV value or investment value of a bank. Consequently valuing a bank using a multiple of book value is an unreliable technique. A real-life example illustrates the difference between book value and measures of economic value such as FMV.

The financial statistics in Exhibit 7.1 represent a bank that is being valued as a potential acquisition candidate. The adjustments from book value to FMV of all assets and liabilities would be based on in-depth analysis of the underlying loans, securities, premises, and deposits. The book value of equity was $6,271,000 whereas the FMV of the equity was $5,509,000: a 12.2 percent decline and over $750,000 difference. Using book value to gauge any type of valuation estimate would be, at best, misleading.

Despite the failings of book value, it is used extensively in bank acquisitions as a means to gauge the appropriateness of a price paid. It is important to keep in mind the weaknesses inherent in book value and the potentially misleading information it can generate.

EXHIBIT 7.1 Illustration of Equity Valuation—Book Value versus Fair Market Value ($000)

Assets	Book Value	Fair Market Value*
Cash and due forms	$ 11,694	$ 11,694
Investments	34,369	31,812
Total loans	56,718	52,892
(Loan loss reserves)	(780)	(780)
Net loans	55,938	52,112
Premises and fixed assets	3,517	4,703
Real estate owned	810	525
Other assets	2,860	2,487
Core deposit intangible	—	4,646
Total assets	$109,188	$107,979

Liabilities	Book Value	Fair Market Value*
Customer deposits	$ 99,261	$ 98,814
Fed funds purchased	2,125	2,125
Other liabilities	1,531	1,531
Total liabilities	$102,917	$102,470
Equity	$ 6,271	$ 5,509

*Fair market value is derived by valuing the financial, tangible, and identifiable intangible assets and liabilities individually.

Liquidation Value

Liquidation value is not, by itself, a separate type of value but a condition under which value is estimated. It is the net amount that can be realized if a business is terminated, its assets sold individually, and its liabilities satisfied. In a normally growing profitable industry, a company's liquidation value is usually much less than the current share price. As with going-concern value described earlier, it would be incorrect to state "the liquidation value of asset X is $100." The correct statement would be "the value of asset X in liquidation is $100." In practice, however, the term "liquidation value" is used for simplicity.

Liquidation can be *forced* or *orderly*, with the major difference being the time allowed to find a buyer. The generally accepted definitions are:

- *Forced liquidation.* This is an emergency price assuming that the enterprise must sell all its assets at or near the same time to one or more purchasers. The net amount that an asset will bring if exposed for immediate sale on the open market, both buyer and seller having knowledge of the uses and purposes to which it is adapted and for which it is capable of being used, the seller being compelled to sell and the buyer being willing, but not compelled, to buy.
- *Orderly liquidation.* The net amount that an asset will bring if exposed for sale on the open market with a *reasonable time* allowed to find a purchaser, both buyer and

seller having knowledge of the uses and purposes to which it is adapted and for which it is capable of being used. Orderly liquidation occurs when the seller is being compelled to sell and the buyer is willing, but not compelled, to buy. This assumes that the enterprise can afford to sell its assets to the highest bidder. It assumes an orderly sale process and that the seller can take a reasonable amount of time to sell each asset in its appropriate season and through channels of sale and distribution that fetch the highest price reasonably available.

The *net amount*, as used in these definitions, is the price less any commissions and administrative cost associated with the liquidation.

From the standpoint of the value of a business, the lowest value possible is its liquidation value.[18] In other words, the worst scenario from a value perspective is to terminate the business, liquidate its assets, and satisfy its liabilities with the remaining balance being distributed to stockholders.

The liquidation value concept is involved when the FDIC does not accept bids for failed banks. In such cases, the agency has determined that the failed bank's value is higher (or its losses are less) if the FDIC liquidates the bank, pays depositors, and collects loans as best as possible. In other words, the bank had less value as an ongoing business than the value of the individual assets (net of liabilities) of that bank.

Insurable Value

Insurable value is very straightforward; it is simply the dollar value of destructible portions of an asset that will be insured to indemnify the owner in the event of loss. This type of value has little relevance to bank M&A, except possibly in a postacquisition review of insurance coverage of premises and equipment. It is the replacement cost or actual cash value for which standard insurance policies provide indemnity cover. It is less than the property's appraised or market value.

Replacement Value

The *replacement value* of an asset is simply the cost of acquiring a new asset of equal utility. An estimate of replacement cost takes into account how an asset would be replaced with newer materials and current technology. It applies unless the limit of insurance or the cost actually spent to repair or replace the damaged property is less. Replacement value is not the same as reproduction value. The latter is the cost of a duplicate asset based on current prices. Replacement value and reproduction cost are used mostly in the valuation of tangible assets that do not produce income directly, such as furniture, equipment, and fixtures.

Salvage Value

Salvage value is the amount realizable upon sale or other disposition of an asset after it is no longer useful to the current owner and is to be taken out of service. This is different from the concept of scrap value, which assumes the asset is no longer useful to anyone for any purpose. The value is used in accounting to determine depreciation amounts and in the tax system to determine deductions; it may be zero or a positive amount. The value can be a best guess of the end value or can be determined by a regulatory body such as the IRS.

During a bank M&A, salvage value may be involved if the combined banks will have excess equipment (e.g., computers or proof machines). It may be useful to the buyer to know the salvage value of such equipment.

TYPES OF PROPERTY THAT CAN BE VALUED

Valuation is an economic concept closely aligned with the legal concept of *property*. When involved in valuation, the term "property" usually means the rights and benefits associated with ownership. The legal concepts of property and ownership are very complex, but a few points are beneficial in providing a better understanding of valuations for bank M&A.

The most obvious type of property is a *tangible asset,* such as buildings, equipment, and furniture. These are "hard" assets that have physical shape and substance. Ownership of tangible assets is secured through titles and deeds. In a bank, the bulk of the physical tangible assets is shown on the balance sheet under *premises and fixed assets* and *other real estate owned.*

In a bank, loans and investments are considered tangible financial assets. Although they do not have true physical substance, loans and investments represent a contractual claim on future income at a stated rate and for a specified period of time. The FMV of a loan or investment is the net present value (NPV) of the income stream based on the timing and riskiness of that income stream.

Property can also be *intangible.* Such property, in the context of an ongoing business, includes those assets that have no physical substance but are important contributors to the success of the business. The benefits of ownership of intangible assets usually are measured by the financial return from those assets. Typical intangible assets in a banking environment include:

- Core deposit base
- Loan servicing contracts
- Safe deposit box contracts
- Proprietary computer software
- Leasehold interests
- Assembled workforce
- Name recognition
- Goodwill

Each of these types of intangible assets can be valued.

The third type of property that can be valued is the business in total, a combination of the tangible and intangible property. To understand the concept of a business as a property to be valued, distinct from the value of the underlying tangible and intangible assets, it is useful to understand the legal concept of *unity of use.*

Any combination of tangible and intangible assets, integrated so that they function as a unit, are considered to have unity of use. When valuing a bank as an ongoing business, it is being valued as a combination of tangible and intangible assets functioning with unity of use.

 ## RELATIONSHIP AMONG DIFFERENT TYPES OF VALUE

Within the context of total business (or total enterprise) value, the relationship among the various types of value described earlier can be seen. Exhibit 7.2 illustrates how different levels of future income of a business affect the various types of value.

The lowest conceivable value of a business is the scrap value of the tangible assets, which is the same no matter what the income level is of the enterprise. For example, the scrap value of a piece of equipment is constant, at a given point in time, irrespective of the earnings of the business that owns it.

Forced liquidation value is the second lowest potential value, but from a practical perspective, this is probably the lowest value a business as a whole would bring. Like scrap value, the forced liquidation value is the same no matter what the income of the enterprise. Orderly liquidation value is conceptually identical to forced liquidation, except that a higher value usually is received because more time is allowed to find a buyer.

Value in use of the tangible assets typically increases with the income of the business (up to the point at which the value in use equals the replacement value of the asset). At zero income, the value in use and orderly liquidation value are theoretically equivalent, but as the business becomes more successful, the importance of the tangible assets becomes more significant; thus value in use exceeds orderly liquidation value.

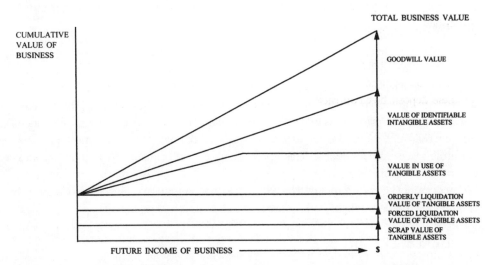

EXHIBIT 7.2 Illustration of Relationship among Various Types of Business Value and the Future Income of That Business

Value of identifiable intangible assets also tends to increase as the income of the business grows. As with tangible assets, the importance of the identifiable intangibles grows along with the income of the business.

Goodwill value will nearly always increase with the earnings of the business because goodwill is computed as the difference between the value of the total business and the value of the tangible and identified intangible assets. Consequently, as the earnings of the business grow, so does its total goodwill and enterprise value.

The cumulative result is the total business value. This is the value of the tangible and intangible assets, and it increases along with the future income prospects of the business. Most valuations of a business measure total business value.

The value of an asset is the benefit one receives from it. The PV rule is applicable to all types of value: The value of an asset in dollar amount today is more than the value in dollar amount tomorrow due to the inflation and opportunity costs.

 ## PRINCIPLES OF VALUATION THEORY

Basic economic principles—such as supply and demand—affect the value of a property or asset. There are, however, four specific economic principles that affect valuation in important ways. These principles are described next.

Principle of Alternatives

The *principle of alternatives* states that in any contemplated transfer of ownership, both the buyer and the seller have alternatives to consummation of the transaction. This principle does not mean that all alternatives are equally desirable. It simply means that a seller is not forced to sell to a given buyer, and a buyer is not forced to buy from a given seller. If this were not the case, the market mechanism would be distorted and an FMV could not be established. A normal valuation assumes that the principle of alternatives is satisfied.

Principle of Replacement

The *principle of replacement* states that a prudent buyer will pay no more for a property or asset than the cost necessary to reproduce it with one of equal utility. The simplest illustration of this principle is in the value of used machinery and equipment. A prudent buyer would not pay more for a used piece of equipment than for a new one that performs the same functions. The application of this principle to a total business enterprise is much more difficult, since the estimation of costs required to replace a business would be very complex. The *cost approach* to valuation (described in Chapter 8) is based on the principle of replacement.

Principle of Substitution

The *principle of substitution* is an extremely important concept of valuation. It states that the value of a property or asset tends to be determined by the cost that would be incurred to acquire an equally desirable substitute. An example, although somewhat improbable, illustrates this principle. Consider two banks of the same size, same staff, same earnings, same spreads, and so on. Common sense and valuation science would conclude that both banks are of equal or very nearly equal value because they are equally desirable substitutes (and in this case identical substitutes).

A more realistic example would be an investor group considering the acquisition of a bank. As prudent investors, they would examine not only the target bank itself but also the prices paid for comparable banks (i.e., for equally desirable substitutes). The principle of substitution is the theoretical basis for the *market approach* to valuation, which is described in Chapter 8.

Principle of Future Benefits

The *principle of future benefits*, which is particularly important in an M&A context, states that the value of a property or asset reflects anticipated future economic benefits from ownership or control of that property or asset. From this perspective, the value of a bank, or any business, is the NPV of all future economic benefits attained as a result of the ownership of that bank or business. In a theoretical sense, what a bank has accomplished in the past has no relevance to value. From a practical standpoint, however, past performance is usually one good indicator of future performance, unless unusual outside events have distorted past trends.

The application of the future benefits principle is very complex and requires numerous assumptions about the future of the business. Nonetheless, the NPV of future economic benefits is often the best indicator of value.[19] The principle of future benefits is the foundation for the *income approach* to value, described in Chapter 8.

Net present value is a financial concept and is defined as the difference between the PV of cash inflows and the PV of cash outflows. If NPV turns outs to be positive, the project is profitable and may be accepted. The basic NPV concept can also be used in the context of M&A with some minor modifications. In assessing M&A transactions, analysts typically perform the same basic calculations of estimating the incremental cash flows, selecting the appropriate discount rate, and computing the NPV. The key difference is the consideration of the synergy effect as combined companies are expected to produce more value and thus cash flows than two companies individually.

 PRICING VALUE VERSUS REPORTING VALUE

As mentioned previously, one factor affecting value estimates is the purpose for the valuation. Different valuation purposes influence the value assumptions and the type of value to be measured. Often different people assess the value of a property or business for different reasons and from different perspectives. In general, the points of view usually fall into two categories: pricing and reporting.

The pricing point of view is taken by an investor who is assessing a company for purposes of acquisition. From this perspective, measures of earnings, cash flow, tax benefits, discount rates, synergy potential, and value creation opportunities are important. These types of considerations are crucial to an assessment for pricing and economic return analysis.

The reporting point of view, however, is concerned with supporting an estimate of value for tax or accounting purposes. To provide the requisite support, it is necessary to use techniques that satisfy taxing and regulatory bodies. Such techniques may or may not coincide with those used for pricing.

The distinction between these two points of view is sometimes difficult to understand but provides one way of reconciling seemingly disparate approaches to, and estimates of, value. Consider the acquisition of a bank. To the buyer, the sole determinant of price may be the future dividend potential—the future economic benefits of ownership. The buyer may have little or no concern for the prices other similar banks have brought. For tax or accounting reporting purposes, however, that same buyer would have to follow certain guidelines that require consideration of prices paid for comparable banks as a basis of establishing value. The buyer is not being inconsistent but is simply reflecting different valuation needs at different points in time for different purposes.

 ## LIMITATIONS OF THE VALUATION PROCESS

Valuation is an inexact science. It requires judgment, assumptions, and opinion. Consequently, two equally qualified appraisers could easily derive two different, yet equally supportable, value estimates for the same asset or property. In financial terms, valuation is the process of estimating the potential market value of a financial asset or liability. The valuation approach is the general way that is followed to determine a value indication of a business, corporate ownership interest, security, or intangible asset.

 ## CONCLUSION

This chapter presented key concepts, definitions and techniques of value and valuation. Value is not a static or homogeneous concept. It can be defined as the amount of money received back from a product. The value of any asset depends on many factors discussed in this chapter including legal, regulatory and accounting standards and practices. It is important to remember that a value estimate is an opinion of value. If prepared by a competent valuation professional, it is an informed opinion based on accepted analyses and techniques. It is, however, still an opinion.

 ## NOTES

1. Federal Reserve Board, Frequently Asked Questions. Available at: www.federalreserve .gov/generalinfo/faq/faqfrbanks.htm.
2. H. Parker Willis, George W. Edwards Banking and Business, reproduction. April 6, 2010, Bibliolife.

3. Glen Tasky, "Introduction to the Banking Supervision." Prepared for the United States Agency of International Development, June 25, 2008. Available at: http://pdf.usaid .gov/pdf_docs/PNADM889.pdf.

4. Society of Actuaries, *2002–2003 Asset-Liability Management Specialty Guide.* Available at: www.soa.org/library/professional-actuarial-specialty-guides/professional-actuarial-specialty-guides/2003/september/spg0308alm.pdf.

5. International Financial Sevices London, *Fund Management 2009*, October 2009. Available at: www.ifsl.org.uk.

6. Merrill Lynch Wealth Management, *World Wealth Report* 2009. Capgemini. 2009. Available at: www.ml.com/media/113831.pdf.

7. Anil K. Kashyap, Raghuram Rajan, and Jeremy C. Stein, "Banks as Liquidity Providers: An Explanation for the Co-Existence of Lending and Deposit-Taking," *Journal of Finance* 57, No. 1 (2002). Available at: http://faculty.chicagobooth.edu/anil.kashyap/research/papers/liquidity.pdf.

8. A. Sinan Cebenoyan and Philip E. Strahan, *Risk Management, Capital Structure and Lending in Banks*, Wharton Financial Institutions Center. Available at: http://fic .wharton.upenn.edu/fic/papers/02/0209.pdf.

9. Automated Financial Systems, Inc, Risk Management Association," *The Fine Line Between Managing Concentrations in Credit Risk and Managing the Credit Risk in Concentrations"* 2 (February 2006). Available at: www.rmahq.org/NR/rdonlyres/FC2692A6-0161-46F8-A7FB-49CE397EB915/0/RASPerspective_feb2005.pdf.

10. Basel Committee on Bank Supervision, "Principles for Sound Liquidity Risk Management and Supervision," June 2008. Available at: www.bis.org/publ/bcbs138.htm.

11. Basel Committee on Banking Supervision, *International Framework for Liquidity Risk Measurement, Standards and Monitoring*, Consultative Document, April 16, 2010. Available at: www.bis.org/publ/bcbs165.pdf.

12. Throughout this book, the term "value" is synonymous with "economic value," and "asset" is used interchangeably with "property."

13. Financial Accounting Standards Board. *Preliminary Views on Reporting Financial Instruments and Certain Related Assets and Liabilities at Fair Value*, May 31, 2000, p. 47.

14. Financial Accounting Standards Board, Statement of Financial Accounting Standards No.157, *Fair Value Measurements* (Norwalk, CT: Author, 2006).

15. *Boe v. Comr.*, 35 T.C. 1038 (1960), *aff'd* 287 F.2d 1 (2nd Cir. 1961).

16. For example, *Concord Control, Inc. v. Comr.*, T.C. Memo 1976-301, *aff'd* and *rem'd*, 615-F.2d 1153 (6th Cir. 1980), and *Northern Natural Gas v. U.S.* 420 F.2d, 1107 (8th Cir. 1973).

17. Book value can be either accounting or tax book, but the basic principles are the same.

18. One scenario where liquidation value may not be the lowest value is a business that has assets that are of no use at all and would have only scrap value. This is, however, an unlikely possibility.

19. Situations often arise where the estimate of value by means of calculating the NPV of future income is much more or less than what the market seems to be paying for equally desirable substitutes. Such situations require judgment by the appraiser to reconcile the differences and determine which is the more reasonable approach, or if a combination of approaches is appropriate.

CHAPTER EIGHT

Approaches to Measuring Value

THIS CHAPTER ADDRESSES SPECIFIC approaches used to value property. Such property can be real estate, machinery, equipment, stock of a company, a privately held business, or an intangible asset. These techniques of valuation are conceptually the same irrespective of the particular type of property being appraised. Specific applications of these techniques to valuing a bank are described in Chapter 16.

There are three primary approaches to valuation:

1. Cost approach
2. Market approach
3. Income approach

Each approach is discussed in this chapter, along with special topics relating to valuation of intangible assets and businesses.

 OVERVIEW OF THE VALUATION PROCESS

Regardless of which particular approach to valuation is appropriate in a given circumstance, there is a basic process to any value estimation undertaking. A valuation professional normally uses five major steps in the process of conducting the assignment:

1. *Initial phase (defining the assignment).* The first step is to define what is to be valued, the date of the value, the purpose of the valuation, and the means by which the results will be communicated. It is important to all parties concerned that these

267

issues be addressed. The subsequent research, analysis, and approach will be determined by the answers.

2. *Selecting the appraiser.* The second step is to analyze carefully the property being appraised, whether it is a business, a parcel of real estate, equipment, or machinery. The types of analysis will differ significantly depending on the property being valued. Nonetheless, the asset must be analyzed thoroughly.

3. *Engagement phase.* The third major step is to gather data that will be input to the valuation of the subject property. To value a business, data on other companies would be gathered. For real estate, reproduction costs of similar properties and comparable sales would be gathered.

4. *Valuation phase.* The fourth step is to use the information generated in steps 2 and 3 and apply the appropriate valuation techniques in order to arrive at a value.

5. *Report phase.* The last step is the preparation of a written report of the valuation. All valuation estimates should be in writing. The form of the report may be brief and simple or long and complex, depending on the situation. In addition to the value estimate, the report should identify the purpose of the appraisal, the date of the value, assumptions underlying the value estimate, and limiting conditions.

The elapsed time to complete these steps can range from a few days for a simple property to months for a complex assignment with multiple properties and/or locations.

The discussions in this chapter focus on the application of valuation techniques once the valuation assignment has been defined and information on the subject asset and any other relevant data have been gathered. In other words, the focus of the balance of this chapter is step 4 of the valuation process.

 ## COST APPROACH TO VALUATION

The cost approach to valuation is based on a comparison of the property being appraised with the cost of replacing it. This approach makes intuitive sense because property should be worth the cost of another one of similar utility, with appropriate adjustments for any physical, functional, and economic obsolescence.

The cost approach to valuation is applied most frequently to the valuation of non-income-producing machinery, equipment, and real estate that are part of a business as this approach seeks to determine the value by aggregating the costs involved in the development of the property. It is one of the three main methods used to determine the value of intellectual property (the others are the market approach and the income approach). Typically, only when specific underlying assets of the business are being appraised is the cost approach applicable. The cost approach, using improved real estate as an example, determines the property's value by estimating the cost to reproduce the improvements (e.g., buildings, parking, landscaping) deducting for physical, functional, and/or economic obsolescence; then adding the market value of the land. (The land must be valued separately because the cost approach is not a valid valuation technique for land—every parcel of land is, by definition, unique because of location and cannot be "replaced" by one exactly like it.)

EXHIBIT 8.1 Illustration of Cost Approach to Valuation (Apartment Complex as Example)

Item	Reproduction Cost	Obsolescence	Market Value
Building			
(235,000 sq. ft. @ $42.00/sq.ft.)	$ 9,870,000	10%	$ 8,883,000
Appliances and interior fixtures	$ 770,000	20%	$ 616,000
(350 units @ $2,200/unit)			
Yard improvements			
Asphalt paving	$ 250,000	15%	$ 212,500
Concrete walks	275,000	10%	247,500
Maintenance shed	7,500	25%	5,625
Street lights	80,000	10%	72,000
Landscaping	110,000	15%	93,500
Swimming pool	80,000	20%	64,000
Other	10,000	10%	9,000
Total	$ 812,500		$ 704,125
Total reproduction costs	$11,452,500		$10,203,125
Value of land*	N/A	N/A	$ 897,000
	Total value (rounded)		$11,100,000

*Valued by the market approach. Land cannot be valued by the cost approach.

In order to estimate the cost to reproduce the improvements, a thorough analysis of those improvements must be undertaken. Then, using current local prices for each item, the cost to reproduce the improvements is calculated. Exhibit 8.1 illustrates the results of the cost approach to valuing an apartment complex after in-depth analysis of the property and current costs to reproduce each improvement are determined. Obsolescence is then calculated to derive market value.

The cost approach usually is useful in cases where there is no economic activity to review, such as early-stage technology; its main drawback is that it does not recognize the economic benefit provided to the owner of the property through its use. There is no mechanism to incorporate revenue or profit data, and therefore it ignores the standard of the value by which many assets are measured. A critical element in applying the cost approach is the obsolescence factor. Obsolescence measures the true decline in utility of an asset from one, two, or all three potential sources.

1. *Physical obsolescence.* This is the actual physical deterioration of a property through wear and tear. Under normal circumstances, this is the source of most obsolescence in physical assets.
2. *Functional obsolescence.* This source of obsolescence is a result of "defects" in design of the property. Such defects are not physical but functional in nature, such as obsolete materials or design. Functional obsolescence, which can be curable or incurable depending on the situation, is usually a result of either size (too large or

too small) or outdated design (requires modernization). An example of functional obsolescence in a banking situation is a "superadequate" branch—one that is too large or too opulent to be justified economically in today's environment. Because of automated teller machines and other electronic delivery systems, many older bank branches suffer from some functional obsolescence due to superadequacy.

3. *Economic obsolescence.* This type of obsolescence is a result of the diminished utility of a property due to external factors. For example, a piece of equipment that manufactures Beta videotapes has suffered economic obsolescence through the evolution of VHS as the standard. By definition, economic obsolescence is always incurable.

Estimates of the extent of the obsolescence are a major factor in determining the value of a property and often are very subjective.

In the context of valuations as part of bank mergers and acquisitions (M&A), it is likely that the cost approach will be used only to value individual tangible assets. When pricing an acquisition target or evaluating a purchase offer, the cost approach is seldom, if ever, used. The exception might be the case in which the bank has significantly undervalued fixed assets on its books that could be sold for a substantial profit after the transaction is complete. Chapter 10 discusses valuation of individual tangible assets of a bank in more detail.

 MARKET APPROACH TO VALUATION

The second major technique of valuation is the market approach that is established in the economic rationale of competition (i.e., in case of a free market, the demand and supply effects direct the value of business properties to a particular balance). In its simplest form, this approach states that a property's value is equal to the cost of acquiring an equally desirable substitute.[1] The process requires a comparison and correlation between the subject property and similar properties being exchanged in the current market with appropriate adjustments as necessary. The market approach entails using comparative valuation techniques according to specific guidelines in similar industries, for similar business interests, in similar publicly traded companies. This approach is most appropriate in determining the value of a marketable minority interest. The market approach of business valuation ascertains the value of a firm by performing a comparison between the firms concerned with organizations in the similar location, of equal volume or operating in the similar sector.

The market approach is relatively easy to understand but can be difficult to apply unless there is a reasonably active market for properties similar to the one being valued. For example, it is difficult to use the market approach to value a nuclear power plant, since there is, for all intents and purposes, no historical transaction data for these types of properties. Conversely, the market approach is valid when the comparable property types, such as office buildings in major cities or common stock of businesses, are actively traded.

The market approach is widely applied to bank M&A. Because of the reporting requirements of the industry, there is an abundance of information available on sales of banks as well as information on trades of widely held bank stock. This excellent base of information allows for the application of the market approach in most cases. However, there are problem in finding a comparable public company that discloses comparable information for comparison. In addition, in case of a private company, the liquidity of the equity is lower (in other words, its stocks are less easy to buy or sell) in comparison to a public company. The value is regarded as somewhat less in comparison to that a market-based valuation would render. Hence the guided public company method is the technique applied in the market approach that implies a relation between the companies that are publicly traded and the firm in question. The process of comparison is commonly carried out on the basis of printed information about the return and share prices of public companies, revenues, and sales. This is represented as a component or quotient called a multiple.

Even with an abundance of market transaction data, the use of the market approach requires thorough and thoughtful analysis. There are two key challenges in applying the market approach: (1) Comparable transactions must be identified; and (2) adjustments to those comparables must be made.

Each of these issues is discussed next.

Identifying Comparables

A company would be an appropriate comparable if it shares a similar risk and growth profile as the company being valued. The first issue is the identification of comparable properties. Such comparables (*comps* in valuation jargon) must meet two basic require-ments: (1) The comparables must be generally desirable substitutes for the property being appraised; and (2) the terms and conditions of the comparable transaction must reflect meaningful market conditions and "arm's-length" criteria.

These two requirements mean that the comparables should be as similar as possible to the criteria such as subject property, size, products, industry classification, growth rate, number of employees, technology, clientele, leverage, growth anf similar key financial and nonfinancial key performance indicators (KPIs). Within the general limitation of these requirements, there are four basic considerations used when identifying comparables.

(1) *Availability of data on actual transactions.* (Offers that were not consummated are not valid because they do not reflect market actions.) The information on the transac-tion must be reliable and reasonably complete. Fortunately, in the banking industry, information about change of control prices available through regulatory agencies and private sources usually meets both these criteria.

(2) *Number of comparable transactions* that can be identified. Information may be reliable and complete, but if statistics on only one or two transactions are available, use of the market approach is effectively eliminated. Normally, four or five truly comparable transactions are the minimum number necessary for a valid application of the market approach. In general, it is desirable to have as many comparable transactions as possible.

(3) *Degree of similarity between the subject property and the comparables.* Ideally, all comparables would be identical, not just similar, to the subject property. In the real

world, however, this will never happen. Nonetheless, the greater the degree of similarity between the subject property and the comparables, the more meaningful the information on the transaction. In the context of a bank valuation, this means the comparable transaction should involve a bank of roughly the same size, market type, and balance sheet composition.

(4) *Conditions and terms of the transaction.* The transaction must reflect arm's-length negotiations and sale, with no insider influence. Also, the form of payment must be known. Prices can vary significantly with different forms of payment—for example, all cash, cash and notes, or stock.

Once comparable transactions are identified and they meet these four considerations, it is necessary to adjust the comparables to match the subject property. The factors considered when making these adjustments are described next.

Adjusting for Lack of Comparability

It can be determined that there is no reasonable way to address the comparability issues for robust analyses of the available data or to use modelling or other statistical methods to adjust for lack of comparability in the original sources. Comparables are never identical to the subject property; therefore, adjustments are nearly always necessary. Such adjustments can be made either to the actual sales price of the comparable or to a meaningful financial ratio though the adjustments that are prompted by noncash features may be assumed as reasonably nonjudgemental. For example, using comparable bank sale data, the selling price could be adjusted up or down, depending on the situation, or adjustments could be made to ratios, such as price to earnings or price to book.[2] In either case, the adjustments are based on the informed opinion of the valuation professional.

With respect to a single tangible asset, the types of factors for which adjustments might be required include:

- Age of the asset
- Timing of sale
- Physical condition
- Functional obsolescence
- Possible amenities or extra features

When estimating the value of an entire business, the factors that usually lead to adjustments in sales transaction data include:

- Size of the business
- Form of ownership (e.g., closely held versus publicly held)
- Degree of liquidity and marketability
- Degree of profitability
- Liability and capital structure
- Market position and location
- Fixed assets
- Past growth rates

Whether adjustments to the comparables are made up or down will depend on the particular situation. Ideally, the comparables used should require a minimal amount of adjustment.

 ## INCOME APPROACH TO VALUATION

The income approach to valuation is based on the principle that the worth of a property is equal to the net present value (NPV) of future economic benefits—the income—it will bring to the owner. It is the core reason for running a business—making money, which is where the economic principle of expectation applies. This approach views a property in terms of its ability to generate income. Consequently, it is applicable only for income-producing assets (e.g., a business, rental property, etc.). Non-income-producing assets, such as special-use property, furniture, and fixtures, cannot be valued properly by the income approach. In the context of bank M&A, the income approach can be used effectively to value a bank as a total business. It also can be used to value selected individual assets of the bank, such as loans, investments, core deposit base, loan servicing rights, and safe deposit box contracts.

The income approach is most relevant when valuing a business as an acquisition target. This approach examines the particular business, its unique circumstances, and its ability to generate income in the future. As described in Chapter 7, "value" can be defined as the dollar amount that would be paid for a property or the right to receive future benefits from use of such property. The income approach bases value on these future economic benefits.

The income approach estimates the future income generated by a property, determines the appropriate relation between future income and value, then converts that future income to an estimate of value. As with the other approaches to valuation, the concept is fairly straightforward, but the application can be difficult.

Two variations of the income approach are typically used. They differ only in complexity, not in concept. The two variations are:

1. *Business valuation by direct capitalization (the stabilized income method).* Mathematically, the income approach is derived from the simple concept that the amount of income from an investment is equal to the invested amount (net operating income [NOI]) multiplied by the rate of return (capitalization rate [cap rate]). or in equation form:

$$\text{Annual income} = \text{Invested amount} \times \text{Annual rate of return or}$$
$$= \text{NOI} \times \text{Cap rate}$$

For example, if $12,500 is invested at 8 percent, the annual income is $1,000 ($12,500 × .08).

The equation can be rewritten as:

$$\text{Invested amount} = \text{Annual income}/\text{Annual rate of return}$$

If the annual income is again $1,000 and the annual rate of return is 8 percent, the amount invested would be $12,500, calculated as $1,000/.08. In terms of valuation, this formula can be interpreted as answering the question: "What is the value of a property generating $1,000 annually to an investor requiring an 8 percent annual return?" The value of that property to that investor would be $12,500. This process is known as *capitalization* and is simply the conversion of a stream of future income to a single value. In equation form, capitalization is:

> Value of a property(V) = Annual income from property (NOIO
> /Appropriate capitalization rate (Cap rate)
> or V = NOI/Cap rate

The mathematics of capitalization are simple. The difficulty of applying the approach lies in determining the future annual income and identifying the appropriate capitalization rate. To use the income approach properly, these two inputs must be determined carefully and only after thorough analysis.[3]

The selection of a capitalization rate can be especially difficult, as it must reflect the riskiness of the future income as well as the long-term growth of that income. Therefore, the capitalization rate and required rate of return are not necessarily equivalent, as the example shown implies. The differences are discussed later in this chapter along with techniques for selecting the capitalization rate.

2. *Valuation of a business by discounting its earnings growth (the discounted future income method).* At the initial phase, the business income stream over future period of time is projected, and then the discount rate which reflects the risk of getting this income on time is selected. The determination of what the business will be worth at the end of the projection period (called the residual or terminal business value) is also estimated. As a result, the discounting calculation would give the so-called PV of the business, or what it is worth today.

The capitalization rate equals the discount rate plus or minus a factor for anticipated growth.

$$CR = DR - K$$

where
   CR = capitalization rate
   DR = discount rate
   K = expected average growth rate in the income stream

Assuming that the discount rate is 40 percent and the projections show that the business profits are growing at a steady 10 percent per year. Then the capitalization rate is $40 - 10 = 30$ percent. Hence, the biggest difference between capitalization and discounting is the income input that is used. Capitalization uses a single income measure, such as the average of the earnings over several years. The discounting is done on a set of income values, one for each year in the projection period.

Business valuation using the discounted cash flow (DCF) model. The DCF model is appropriate for valuation because it: (1) captures all of the factors important to valuation (expected cash flow, discount rate, terminal value, time horizons); (2) assumes that investments add value when returns exceed the cost of capital; and (3) uses the time value of money concept.

The valuation computation using DCFincludes these four steps:

1. Discounting the future expected cash flows (both cash inflows and cash outflows) over a forecast period.
2. Adding a discounted terminal value to cover the period beyond the forecast period.
3. Adding investment income, excess cash, and other nonoperating assets at their PVs.
4. Subtracting out the fair market values (FMVs) of debt to arrive at the value of equity.

Stabilized Income Method

The *stabilized income* approach uses a single measure of annual income (i.e., the stabilized income) and a single capitalization rate to determine value. The example used previously—in which income was $1,000, rate was 8 percent, and value was $12,500—is an application of the stabilized income approach.

To use this approach, a level of stabilized income that is *representative* of the asset is estimated. The term "stabilized" does not mean that income is stagnant and will not increase in the future. The projected annual growth of the income is reflected in the capitalization rate, as discussed in the next section of this chapter.

One common method used to estimate the stabilized income level is to compute a *weighted average* of the last five years' income, with more recent years' income weighted most heavily. An example is shown in Exhibit 8.2. In this example, the stabilized level of income to be used in the valuation process would be $631.

The next requirement is the selection of the appropriate capitalization rate. This rate reflects the return a prudent investor would expect on an investment in the property, given its risk characteristics and the long-term income growth prospects of the property. For example, assume that the appropriate capitalization rate is 11 percent. The value would then be:

$$\text{Value} = \text{Stabilized income}/\text{Capitalization rate}$$

or

$$\$631/.11$$

$$= \$5,736$$

EXHIBIT 8.2 Calculation of Weighted Historical Income

Year	Historical Income	Weight	Weighted Income
2005	$500	1	$ 500
2006	580	2	1,160
2007	620	3	1,860
2008	620	4	2,440
2009	700	5	3,500
		Total 15	9,460
		Weighted Average:	$ 631
		(9,460/15)	

The process used to determine the stabilized level of income in this example is just one of a number of possibilities. Other ways to determine income and techniques used to select a capitalization rate are described in detail later in this chapter.

Discounted Future Income Method

The second variation of the income approach involves projecting income and converting the income to a PV through the process of *discounting.* This process is central to the application of the discounted future income approach. A simple example will illustrate the technique.

Assume an income-producing asset with a five-year life, at which time it will be worth zero (i.e., it will have no scrap or salvage value) with projected income as shown in Exhibit 8.3. The value of this asset can be computed as:

$$
\begin{aligned}
\text{Value of asset} = {} & \text{Year 1 income} \times \text{Year 1 discount factor} \\
& + \text{Year 2 income} \times \text{Year 2 discount factor} \\
& + \text{Year 3 income} \times \text{Year 3 discount factor} \\
& + \text{Year 4 income} \times \text{Year 4 discount factor} \\
& + \text{Year 5 income} \times \text{Year 5 discount factor}
\end{aligned}
$$

The computation of the discount factor is accomplished by this formula:

$$
\text{Discount factor for year } N = 1/(1 + \text{discount rate})^N
$$

The discount rate is a percentage that reflects the yield a prudent investor would require to purchase the asset, given that asset's risk characteristics. (As discussed later in this chapter, discount rate and capitalization rate are *not* the same.)

If the discount rate was assumed to be 13 percent, the discount factor for each year would be as shown in Exhibit 8.4. Under these assumptions, the value of the asset would be about $4,200, calculated as shown in Exhibit 8.5.

The preceding example has the unrealistic assumption that the income will be produced by the asset over a finite *and* predictable period of time and then will be worth nothing. Such conditions rarely exist. More typically, income is produced over a long period, the extent of which is not known exactly at the date of the valuation.

A business is a good example of this situation. The life of a business is unknown, and, with proper management, the business can exist, for all intents and purposes, into

EXHIBIT 8.3 Projected Income for Five-Year Asset

Year	Income
1	$ 900
2	1,050
3	1,200
4	1,450
5	1,600

EXHIBIT 8.4 Calculation of Discount Factor

Discount Formula	Factor
Year 1: $1/(1 + 1.3)^1$	.885
Year 2: $1/(1 + .13)^2$	.783
Year 3: $1/(1 + .13)^3$	.693
Year 4: $1/(1 + .13)^4$	.613
Year 5: $1/(1 + .13)^5$	.543

perpetuity. Valuation in this circumstance is accomplished using the discounted future income approach for a defined period of time (usually five to ten years), then using the stabilized income method to compute the *residual* value of the business at the end of the finite period.

Continuing with the preceding example, suppose that the stabilized level of future earnings after Year 5 is estimated to be $1,750 and a capitalization rate of 11 percent is determined to be appropriate. The value of the asset would then be about $11,850, calculated as shown in Exhibit 8.6.

Discounted Cash Earnings

A discounted cash earnings stream is a commonly used method of determining the value of financial institutions. This method assesses an institution's value as a function of two variables: (1) an estimate of continuous cash earning power, and (2) a discounted rate, usually the weighted average cost of capital to capitalize cash flow earnings. Assessment of cash flow earning power is the most essential and difficult component in the valuation process because it is a function of a number of internal and external factors. Internal factors that may influence the cash flow earning power are, among others, (1) the mix of assets and liabilities; (2) management's philosophy and operating style regarding composition, maturity, yield, and costs of debt and equity instruments; (3) the credit, business, and financing risks inherent in the loan portfolio; and (4) the institution's ability to generate fee income determined by the customer base as well as products and services offered. External factors are industry specifications, competitive

EXHIBIT 8.5 Calculation of Present Value of Future Income

Year	Income	Discount Factor	Present Value of Income
1	$ 900	.885	$ 796.5
2	1,050	.783	822.2
3	1,200	.693	831.6
4	1,450	.613	888.9
5	1,600	.543	868.8
			$4,208.0

EXHIBIT 8.6 Calculation of Present Value of Future Income with Residual

Year	Income	Discount Factor	Present Value of Income
1	$ 900	.885	$ 796.5
2	1,050	.783	822.2
3	1,200	.693	831.6
4	1,450	.613	888.9
5	1,600	.543	868.8
Residual	$1,750	.480	$ 7,636.4*
			Total $11,844.44

*Assumes residual income is capitalized at 11 percent, then discounted to present value.

environment, fluctuations in interest rates, regulatory laws and regulations, market conditions, and general economic conditions.

Financial Accounting Standards Board (FASB) issued the Statement of Financial Accounting Concepts (SFAC) No. 7, which provides a framework for using PV to estimate fair value of assets and liabilities.[4]

SFAC No. 7 establishes guidelines for using future cash flows as the basis for accounting measurements at initial recognition or fresh-start measurements and for the interest method of amortization. SFAC No. 7 provides a framework for using PV, especially when the amount of future cash flows, their timing, or both are uncertain. PV captures the economic difference between sets of estimated future cash flows by reflecting the uncertainties inherent in the estimated cash flows. If a price for an asset or liability or identical one can be determined in the marketplace, there is no need to use PV primarily because the marketplace assessment of PV is already embodied in such prices. However, in most cases, the PV of expected future cash flows can be used to estimate fair value. The PV formula,

$$PV = FV/(1+I)^n$$

where

PV = present value
FV = future value
I = interest rate
n = number of periods

is a tool used to incorporate the time value of money in a measurement to capture the PV of the amount that will be received in the future.

Financial assets and liabilities are regulated by the FASB No. 159, *The Fair Value Option for the Financial Assets and Financial Liabilities*. This standard, issued in February 2007, makes it easier to compare two companies that chose different approaches to value measurement but have similar assets/liabilities structure.[5]

Selecting the Type of Income to Use

In the preceding examples it was assumed, for purposes of illustrating the concept, that the type of income, income levels, and capitalization and discount rates all were known. These are the essential elements in using the income approach, and in real life they must be computed *before* applying the income approach.

In the context of a bank valuation analysis, the most appropriate type of income measure to use is *available cash flow*. This is the amount of cash that is available each year to the owner in the form of dividends. In the context of bank valuations, available cash flow usually means the cash that can be distributed to owners as dividends or proceeds of a sale. The accounting definition of cash flow is not as meaningful for valuation purposes. Calculation of available cash flow from dividends is discussed in detail in Chapter 16.

For purposes of presenting the concept and mechanics of the income approach to valuation, the term "income" is used.

Estimating the Stabilized Level of Income

Once the type of income is selected, it is necessary to determine the stabilized level of income and/or to project that income for a five- to ten-year period. Four basic characteristics of the income need to be considered in the projection process:

1. *Amount of income.* The first consideration examines the amount of past income, carefully assessing whether the amounts are realistic compared with the size of the property or business, the market environment, and competitive conditions. The major factor is whether abnormal circumstances have skewed historical income performance so that it is not indicative of the future.
2. *Regularity of income.* In this case, the pattern of income must be considered. The critical aspect is the volatility of past income trends. If a property, especially a business, exhibits excessive income variations, it is more difficult to forecast the income, unless those variations were a result of predictable market phenomena (e.g., it might be a seasonal business). Occasionally, the volatility of income is so great that the income approach to valuation is not appropriate, and other approaches are required.
3. *Duration of income.* Occasionally, the income will have a known and finite life. An office building leased at a fixed rate for a fixed term is an example of such a situation. In such a case, the stabilized income approach would not be the valid valuation technique. In cases of a business enterprise valuation, it is not necessary to assume that income goes on forever, but only that it will continue for a substantial number of years. This is a reasonable expectation with most healthy banking institutions.
4. *Certainty of income.* Future income is never certain, but some sources of income have greater certainty than others. In most cases, the greater the degree of certainty, the less risk involved (a factor that affects the discount and capitalization rates).

When determining a stabilized income level or when projecting future income levels, the process and results will be influenced by these four characteristics of the income. To assess these characteristics, the historical income of the subject property or

EXHIBIT 8.7 Stabilized Income Trend Example

Year	Income	Percent Change
2005	$1,000	—
2006	1,050	5%
2007	1,103	5%
2008	1,158	5%
2009	1,216	5%

business must be analyzed carefully. Depending on the situation, it may be necessary to adjust the actual reported income if it has extraneous or unusual elements. For example, a business may have had an unusual, one-time event that raised or lowered income (sale of property, legal costs, etc.) or excessive salaries may have been paid that would not continue into the future under prudent management. In certain cases, it may be necessary to adjust past earnings to gain a true picture of the past. In the examples used in this chapter, the income figures exclude any abnormal occurrences.

A stabilized income level to be capitalized into value can be determined by way of analysis of past income trends. There are typically three patterns that historical income trends can follow, each affecting the way that stabilized income level is estimated.

The *steady trend* pattern is the easiest method. In such a circumstance, income is increasing (or decreasing) at a more or less steady rate, in either dollar or percentage terms. The most straightforward way to deal with this situation is to use the latest year's income as being a representative, stabilized level of income. For example, if the income pattern shown in Exhibit 8.7 is being valued, the 2009 income could be considered a stabilized level of income.

The appropriate level of stabilized income to use in this example would be $1,216. (The 5 percent annual increase in earnings, which is expected to continue, will be reflected in the value estimate through the selected capitalization rate, as discussed in the next section of this chapter.)

The next type of income pattern is the *growing erratic trend*, which is typical of businesses in a cyclical but expanding market. In this case, the best way to determine the stabilized level of income is usually a simple average of historical income, as in Exhibit 8.8. In this example, a stabilized income level of $1,164 would be appropriate. (Again, the growth rate and instability of earnings will be reflected in the selected capitalization rate.)

The third type of income is the *erratic trend.* In this case, a careful assessment must be made of whether the income is too erratic to use. If so, it may not be possible to use the income approach. Otherwise, the simple average techniques used in the growing erratic case may be appropriate.

Projecting Future Income Levels

Projecting income for use in the discounted future income approach requires an in-depth analysis of past financial trends to identify the steadiness or instability of the income and the reasons for the pattern.[6] Income usually is projected for a five- to ten-year period and can be forecasted in one of three ways.

EXHIBIT 8.8 Erratic Income Trend Example

Year	Income	Percent Change
2005	$1,000	—
2006	1,200	20.0%
2007	1,080	(10.0%)
2008	1,290	19.0%
2009	1,250	(3.0%)
Average	$1,164	

The most straightforward method to forecast income is the development of a time series equation of past income and then assuming a continuation of the time series. Exhibit 8.9 illustrates a time series calculation and the resulting equation used to forecast income. The statistical technique *regression analysis* is used to compute the equation based on historical income data. That equation then is used to calculate the unknown variable, future income, based on the known variable, the year. The time series approach is appropriate when past income has exhibited a reasonably steady growth pattern.

A second method to forecast total income is to project the individual components of income, then aggregate to a total. This approach is appropriate when the subject property has more than one major source of income, such as a business with multiple product lines. Each such source may have different growth characteristics and future potential. If each income source is reasonably steady, the time series technique could be used on each individual source.

Exhibit 8.10 illustrates the forecasting of total income for a business that has three product lines. The approach is the same as forecasting total income, except that each component is analyzed separately. In the example, Product A is a small, slow-growth product and has more risk. Product B is a rapidly growing product and has more opportunity. Product C is the large, modestly growing cash cow that is more stable and predictable. The advantage of separating the components is in the identification of the different opportunity and risk characteristics associated with each source of income.

The third method is an indirect way to forecast income. Underlying drivers of income and expenses are first identified, then the quantitative relationships between income and those drivers are established, the income drivers are forecasted, and finally income based on the future levels of the drivers is estimated. In a bank, the principal drivers of net income include loans and investments (which create interest income), deposits (which create interest expense), loan loss provision, operating expenses, and noninterest income. It is usually more accurate to project loans, investments, and other income drivers (based, e.g., on market potential) than it is to project income directly. The relationship among loans, investments, deposits, and the associated income and expenses is then calculated to derive income for valuation purposes.

This indirect approach to forecasting income is probably the most difficult because it requires an in-depth analysis of income and expense drivers. In the application of

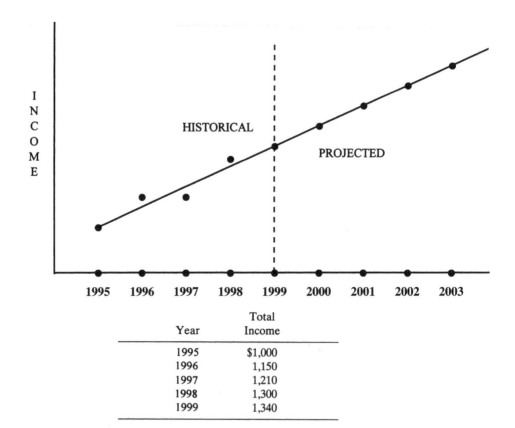

Year	Total Income
1995	$1,000
1996	1,150
1997	1,210
1998	1,300
1999	1,340

CALCULATED TIME SERIES
REGRESSION EQUATION:
Total income = (year × 83) − 163,638

Year	Projected Total Income
2000	$1,532
2001	1,615
2002	1,698
2003	1,781
2004	1,864

EXHIBIT 8.9 Using the Time Series Equation to Forecast Total Income of a Business

valuation techniques to bank M&A described in Chapter 16, this indirect approach is used as it is a more realistic basis of estimating future income levels.

Selecting the Capitalization and Discount Rates

The second crucial area of decision making in the income approach is the selection of capitalization and discount rates. It should be noted that these rates are related, *but they are not the same.*

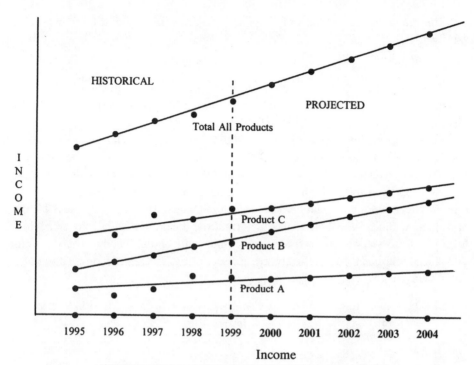

Year	Product A	Product B	Product C	Total
		Income		
1995	$500	$600	$1,000	$2,100
1996	500	780	950	2,230
1997	490	810	1,050	2,350
1998	520	900	1,040	2,460
1999	518	920	1,060	2,498

CALCULATED TIME SERIES EQUATION

Product A income = (year × 6.0) − 11,412
+ Product B income = (year × 76.0) − 150,134
+ Product C income = (year × 21.0) − 40,686
= Total income

Projected Income

Year	Product A	Product B	Product C	Total
2000	$528	$1,106	$1,104	$2,738
2001	534	1,182	1,125	2,744
2002	539	1,258	1,146	2,943
2003	545	1,334	1,167	3,046
2004	551	1,410	1,188	3,149

EXHIBIT 8.10 Using Time Series Equations to Forecast Components of Total Income of a Business

The mathematical relationship between the discount rate and the capitalization rate is:

Capitalization rate = Discount rate − Annual future growth of income

The capitalization rate converts a single estimate of annual income into a current capitalized value of that income, whereas the discount rate converts a flow of future income to PV.

Future income flows must be converted to PV because "a dollar tomorrow is worth less than a dollar today," and the farther into the future one projects, the less that dollar is worth in today's terms. This is the fundamental principle of the *time value of money*. If income is received today, it can be invested in an interest-bearing asset, resulting in interest plus the original balance. This basic financial concept has a significant impact on valuation. Since the valuation date is normally at the present and the income is in the future, it is necessary to compensate for the time value of that income. This compensation is accomplished through the process of discounting. The calculations of discounting are shown next:

PV of income to be received in year N = Income to be received in year N

$\times [1/(1 + \text{year } N \text{ discount rate})N]$

where

PV = present value

year N = future year corresponding to the receipt of the income

$1/(1 + \text{discount rate})^N$ = discount factor used previously in the illustration of the income approach.

For example, if $500 is to be received in three years, PV, discounted at 9 percent, is $386, calculated as:

$$\$500 \times [1/(1 + .09)3] = \$386$$

Income that is to be received in multiple years is discounted in exactly the same way. The income in each year is converted to PV, then the individual results are totaled. For example, if $400 is to be received in one year, $550 in two years, and $775 in three years, the PV of that stream of income discounted at 9 percent is $1,386, calculated as:

$$[\$400 \times 1/(1 + .09)1] + [\$500 \times 1/(1 + .09)2] + [\$775 \times 1/(1 + .09)3] = \$1,386$$

The discount rate can be thought of as the rate of return required to invest in the income flow, taking into account alternative investments and the riskiness and uncertainty of the income. The next two components constitute a discount rate:

- *Risk-free rate of return.* The return an investor could earn without risk. (All investments have risk, but a risk-free rate reflects the safest investment possible, usually a U.S. government security.)

■ *Risk premium.* The additional return an investor would require to invest in the particular property being valued.

The capitalization rate also reflects the risk-free rate and a risk premium. In addition, however, the capitalization rate reflects the long-term income growth prospects of the asset. The mathematical comparison between the discount rate and the capitalization rate is shown as:

$$\text{Discount rate} = \text{Risk-free return} + \text{Risk premium}$$

$$\text{Capitalization rate} = \text{Discount rate} - \text{Annual growth rate}$$

The annual growth rate of income is subtracted because faster growth, all other things being equal, has higher value (i.e., a lower capitalization rate). The only time the discount rate equals the capitalization rate is when the long-term growth of income is expected to be zero.

Theoretically, a potential problem can exist if the growth rate exceeds the risk-free rate plus the risk premium. In practice, however, this problem will not be encountered for two reasons: (1) It is unlikely that any business can be expected to sustain very rapid income growth into perpetuity; and (2) faster growth usually implies greater risk, thus requiring an increase in the risk premium.

An illustration of the discount rate and capitalization rate is shown next. Assume the risk-free return is 7 percent, the risk premium for the particular investment is 8 percent, and the long-term growth is 4 percent per year. The calculations would be:

$$\text{Discount rate} = .07 + .08 = .15$$

$$\text{Capitalization rate} = .15 - .04 = .11$$

If the stabilized income method is used, the single measure of income is capitalized at 11 percent. If estimates of future income—the discounted future income method—are used, those estimates are discounted at 15 percent.

The critical step is to select the proper discount rate, which can then be used as a basis to calculate the capitalization rate. Three principal approaches can be used to determine an appropriate discount rate:

1. Summation
2. Weighted cost of capital
3. Market comparison

The summation approach builds up the discount rate by component parts. The weighted cost of the capital approach creates a discount rate based on the costs of debt and equity, which is based on the capital structure associated with the subject property. The market comparison approach estimates the discount rate in total by comparing the subject property with other similar investments.

The *summation method* is based on the view that a discount rate can be thought of as comprising two parts, the risk-free rate of return and a risk premium. Each component can be dealt with separately, then they can be added together to arrive at the discount

EXHIBIT 8.11   Yields on Selected U.S. Government Securities

(As of May 28, 2010)	
3-month Treasury bill	0.16
6-month Treasury bill	0.22
1-year Treasury bill	0.34
Long-term Treasury securities	4.05

Source: Daily Treasury yield curve rates, May 28, 2010. U.S. Treasury. Available at www.ustreas.gov/offices/domestic-finance/debt-management/interest-rate/yield.shtml.

rate. A risk-free rate is the return an investor can be more or less certain to receive on an investment that has a ready market. U.S. government securities typically are used as a proxy for measuring a risk-free return. These rates are reported in a variety of business publications and are easily obtainable. Rates for U.S. government securities in May 2010 are shown in Exhibit 8.11. Short-term U.S. government securities (e.g., three-month Treasury bills) often are viewed as the most risk-free investment. However, for purposes of valuation, it normally is better to use the rate on government securities of longer maturities (one year or more) as a base rate. Long-term securities have greater risk of not selling at par, but because valuations usually involve value based on long-term income trends, the rate on longer-maturity securities is often a more comparable and relevant proxy for a risk-free rate.

The risk premium portion of the discount rate must reflect the risk associated with the particular property or business being appraised and the risk associated with the market. Some factors that should be considered in the risk premium are shown in Exhibit 8.12.

The actual determination of the risk premium, after due consideration of the above-mentioned factors, can be a difficult process and will differ among various potential buyers. To establish a starting point, it is useful to analyze the rates on various investments less the risk-free rate, the difference being the risk premium. A good starting point is the rate charged by a commercial bank for a loan on a similar asset. For example, if a bank will charge 13 percent to finance the purchase of a property similar to that being appraised and the risk-free rate is 8 percent, then a starting point for the risk premium would be 5 percent. Additional risk with a particular property may require additional risk premium.

Another technique that can be used to quantify the risk premium portion of the discount rate is the *capital asset pricing model* (CAPM). This model is an analytical approach that uses actual data on publicly traded equity instruments to describe the way prices of individual assets are determined in efficient markets. The CAPM theorizes that the expected rate of return on an asset is equal to the risk-free return *plus* an overall risk premium that reflects risk associated with the specific industry and the specific company. In equation form, the CAPM is applied to discount rate determination as:

$$\text{Discount rate} = \text{Risk-free rate} + (\text{Risk premium} \times \beta \text{ factor})$$

EXHIBIT 8.12 Factors Impacting Level of Risk Premium

Risks Associated with Subject Property*

- Type of product/service
- Size of business
- Financial condition
- Quality of management
- Quality and quantity of income
- Market position
- Liquidity of investment in business
- Location

*Using a business as an example.

Risk Associated with Market

- General outlook for industry
- Conditions of overall economy
- Availability/cost of credit
- Condition of local economy
- Outlook for customers of the business
- Legal or regulatory restrictions

where

Risk premium = systematic market risk for all businesses in the industry

β factor = risk associated with the specific business being valued relative to all other businesses

This model is most applicable to businesses that have widely traded stocks. A good history of stock sales usually is necessary to have a historical basis for estimation of the beta factor.

Essentially, use of the CAPM to determine a discount rate is a variation of the summation approach. An added enhancement of this approach is that it reflects the historical volatility of the specific business being valued. Practically speaking, however, this methodology is applicable only for fairly actively traded, publicly held businesses.

A second technique used to establish a discount rate is the *weighted cost of capital approach.* A weighted average of the cost of debt and required return on equity is computed as in the example shown in Exhibit 8.13. In this illustration, an investor requires 20 percent pretax return on equity, with debt costs at 11 percent for senior debt and 13 percent for subordinated debt, resulting in a discount rate of 13.84 percent. This figure is simply a weighted average based on the mix and cost of capital.

The third technique used to establish an appropriate discount rate is the *market comparison approach.* With this technique, discount rates are examined for situations similar to the subject asset in terms of type of sale, income levels, riskiness, and liquidity.

EXHIBIT 8.13 Calculation of Weighted Cost of Capital

Component of Capital	Percent of Capital	Pretax Cost	After-tax Cost
Senior debt	30%	11%	7.15%
Subordinated debt	20%	13%	8.45%
Equity	50%	20%*	20.00%
Weighted cost of capital			13.84%

*Often estimated using the capital asset pricing model described in text.

A rate is then selected, as opposed to the summation method, where the rate is built up from components.

For business valuations, data on publicly traded stocks provide a surrogate measure of a discount rate, assuming the publicly traded businesses are similar to the one being valued. The widely reported price-to-earnings (P/E) ratios provide a general idea of the yield the market requires. The deficiencies of the P/E ratio are, unfortunately, substantial: Price reflects investors' expectations for the future while earnings are historical; the P/E is for one particular company, which may or may not be comparable to the business being valued; and the quoted price used in the P/E is usually for a minority position.

Notwithstanding these deficiencies, the P/E ratio can be a useful way to begin the determination of a discount rate. The P/E ratio is based on reported earnings; therefore, it cannot be applied directly to cash flow measures. The best way to apply the P/E is to use an average P/E for a sample of comparable businesses. The calculations would be as shown next.

$$\text{Initial discount rate estimate} = (1 + \text{Control premium})/\text{Average P/E for companies}$$
$$+ \text{Projected income growth rate for companies}$$

The control premium factor must be applied to the inverse of the P/E ratio because the P/E reflects a minority position in the company. The expected growth of the sample companies must be added because the inverse of the P/E actually computes a capitalization rate and, as described earlier, the discount rate is the capitalization rate plus annual growth. An example of the P/E method is shown in the next equation. Assume that:

Average P/E for sample companies: 13
Control premium: 37 percent
Projected growth of sample companies: 4 percent annually

Initial discount rate estimate is:

$$(1 + .37)/13 + .04 = .105 + .04 = 14.5 \text{ percent}$$

The business being valued may have unusual risk characteristics, which would require an increase in the initial 14.5 percent rate estimate. This is a subjective factor based on a case-by-case analysis.

Public company P/Es should be used very cautiously in deriving an initial discount rate estimate. The control premium percentage is used to adjust the P/E to a majority position that is then used as a proxy for the required rate of return. Such a relationship implies that greater control allows greater influence over the systemic risks of the business. This is probably not true because systemic risks are, by definition, beyond the control of the owner. The control premium is more directly related to the ability of the majority owner to influence future cash flow and earnings.

One solution to this problem is to use acquisition P/Es rather than stock trade P/Es. This approach avoids the control premium adjustment problem. The formula to use is:

$$\text{Discount rate estimate} = \text{Earnings of sample companies/price paid for companies} + \text{Projected growth rate of companies}$$

An example of the calculations is shown in the next equation.

Average earnings of sample companies: $3,100,000
Average price paid for sample companies: $30,000,000
Projected annual growth of sample companies: 4.0 percent
Initial discount rate estimate is:

$$\$3,100,000/\$30,000,000 + .04 = .103 + .04 = 14.3 \text{ percent}$$

As before, the business being valued may have more or less risk associated with it, resulting in the need to adjust the 14.3 percent upward or downward.

Once the discount rate has been estimated, by one or more of the techniques described, it is possible to calculate the capitalization rate. To reiterate the formula:

$$\text{Capitalization rate} = \text{Discount rate} - \text{Growth rate of income}$$

The expected annual growth rate of the income stream of the property being valued is subtracted from the discount rate to arrive at the appropriate capitalization rate. Exhibit 8.14 illustrates how the discount, capitalization, and growth rates work together to value a projected income stream.

Dividend Capitalization Model

A variant of the income approach that can be used to value businesses is the dividend capitalization model. This approach can be used whether the business actually pays dividends to stockholders or not. The easiest case is valuation of a business that has a record of paying dividends. Instead of capitalizing total income, income per share is capitalized to derive a per-share value. This value is on a minority basis, with a majority position determined by adding a control premium. An example is shown in Exhibit 8.15. This approach can be used to value publicly held, widely traded stock.

The dividend capitalization model also can be used when the business does not pay dividends but has the financial capacity to do so. This is often the case with closely held businesses. The key is to evaluate comparable companies to determine the industry average for dividends (expressed as a percent of net income or as a return on book value

EXHIBIT 8.14 Valuation of an Income Stream to Illustrate Discount, Capitalization, and Growth Rates

	Year 1	Year 2	Year 3	Year 4	Year 5	Residual
Income (rounded)	$1,000	$ 1,050	$1,180	$1,300	$1,400	$ 1,500
Annual growth	—	5.0%	12.4%	10.2%	7.7%	5.0%
Discount rate	15%	15%	15%	15%	15%	15%
Discount factor	.870	.756	.657	.571	.497	.432
Capitalization rate	—	—	—	—	—	10%*
Capitalized value (rounded)	—	—	—	—	—	$15,000
Present value	$ 870	$ 794	$ 775	$ 742	$ 696	$ 6,480
Sum of present values	$10,357					

The income stream for years 1 through 5 is converted to present value by multiplying the income in a given year by the discount factor for that year (e.g., for Year 3, the income of $1,180 is multiplied by the discount factor of .657 to equal $775). The residual income level is capitalized at 10 percent (to equal $15,000), then converted to present value by multiplying by the discount factor of .432 (to equal $6,480). The individual present value figures are summed to arrive at a value estimate.

*15% discount rate less 5% expected growth of the $1,500 level of residual income.

of equity). The next step is to assess whether the business being appraised has the financial capacity to pay the industry average dividends. If so, the dividends can be imputed and value assessed as if the company actually had paid dividends.

The dividend-paying capacity concept plays an extremely important role in the valuation of a bank for acquisition purposes. The basis of the income approach described in Chapter 15 is that the available cash flow to the owner of a bank is equal to the bank's dividend paying capacity.

EXHIBIT 8.15 Valuation of a Business Using Dividend Capitalization Model

Dividends per share*	$ 2.50
Capitalization rate[†]	15%
Control premium	40%
Shares outstanding	100,000
Per-share value on minority basis (dividends per share/capitalization rate) ($2.50/.15)	$ 16.67
Aggregate minority value (per-share value on minority basis 3 shares outstanding) ($16.67, 3, 100,000 shares)	$1,667,000
Per-share value on control basis (per-share value on minority basis 3 control premium) ($16.67, 3, 1.4)	$ 23.34
Value of business on control basis	$2,334,000

*A "stabilized" level of dividends, analogous to stabilized income used earlier.
[†]Selected using techniques described earlier, with consideration of dividend yields on stocks of comparable risk.

Effects of Inflation

As every businessperson knows, inflation can have a devastating and uncontrollable effect on the value of a property. Consequently, it would seem logical to value an income-producing property using estimates of *real* future income, excluding any inflationary growth. If real income is used, however, the capitalization and discount rates would have to be reduced by an amount equal to the expected rate of inflation. This adjustment is needed because the various measures of return on investment already reflect the *market's consensus* on expected inflation. Therefore, if *real* income is to be used, *real* rates of return must be the basis for discounting. Valuations by the income approach usually are made with projected income (including whatever level of inflation is expected) and discounted by a rate that includes the market's assessment of inflation.

SPECIAL TOPICS—APPROCHES TO INTANGIBLE ASSET VALUATION

Intangible assets are those that have no physical substance but are positive contributors to the success of a business.[7] Such intangibles include, among others, customer lists, patents, proprietary computer software, assembled workforce, copyrights, brand names, and goodwill. Intangible assets often constitute a large portion of the total value of a business, which by definition is:

Total value of a business = Tangible asset value + Intangible asset value − Liabilities assumed

Intangible asset value, in turn, is made up of several components:

Intangible asset value = Amortizable identified asset value + Nonamortizable identified asset value + Goodwill

The segregation of the three components of intangible assets is important for tax reasons rather than for pricing, except if tax attributes will have a significant impact on cash flows. The term "amortizable" means that the intangible asset is allowed a deduction from taxable income, similar to the way tangible assets are depreciated. An identified intangible asset is one that can be valued separately. Goodwill and other intangibles are part of important tax issues and are discussed in Chapter 10. General approaches to intangible asset valuation are described next.

Cost of Replacement of an Intangible Asset

The cost of replacement approach to valuing an intangible asset is based on the current costs that would be incurred to replace the asset with one of comparable utility. An example of an intangible that can be valued by this technique is proprietary computer software. The person-hours required to create the software are multiplied by an hourly rate (salary, consultant's fees, etc.) to arrive at a replacement cost. This approach does not consider any income benefit to the business as a result of having the intangible asset.

EXHIBIT 8.16 Valuation of a Patent with Income

Year	Income	Discount Rate	Discount Factor	Present Value
1	$500,000	10%	.909	$454,500
2	540,000	10%	.826	446,040
3	583,200	10%	.751	437,983
4	629,856	10%	.683	430,192
5	680,244	10%	.621	422,432
6	734,664	10%	.564	414.351
7	793,437	10%	.513	407,033
				Value of patent = $3,012,531

Income from Intangible Asset

If an intangible asset generates income, the various income approaches described in the preceding section can be used. Copyrights and patents are examples of intangible assets that can be valued based on the income generated to the owner. For example, assume a business owns a special process patent that it has licensed to other companies, the income (fees, net of administrative expenses) from which is $500,000 annually and increasing at 8 percent per year. Also assume the patent has seven years remaining on its 17-year life. The value of that patent can be calculated as shown in Exhibit 8.16.

This approach is applicable if the intangible has a known and finite life. For intangibles without a definite life, or a life so long it is virtually indefinite (such as a copyright that runs for the author's life plus 50 years), the capitalization of income approach may be more appropriate. This technique estimates the stabilized income from the intangible asset and capitalizes it to a value (exactly as described earlier in the section "Income Approach to Valuation"). For example, assume that the income from a copyright is estimated at $750,000 annually and projected to increase at 5 percent per year. If the risk-free return and the risk premium total 14 percent (the discount rate), the capitalization rate is 9 percent (14 percent minus 5 percent). Therefore, the value of the copyright is $8,333,333 ($750,000/.09).

If ownership of an intangible asset results in tax benefits from amortization, the value should also reflect the net present value of those tax savings. The calculations become very complex because the value of the intangible is influenced by the tax savings, but the tax savings are influenced by the value. The value of the intangible including tax benefits of amortization can be estimated by this formula:

PV of Cash flow/[1 − (Tax rate × Annuity factor)/Remaining life]

The PV of cash flow factor excludes amortization. The tax rate is the marginal tax rate of the business owning the intangible. The annuity factor is based on an interest rate equal to the cost of capital and a term equal to the remaining life of the asset. This

EXHIBIT 8.17 Valuation of a Patent with Income and Cost Savings

Year	Income	Cost Savings	Discount Rate	Discount Factor	Present Value
1	$500,000	$55,000	10%	.909	$ 504,495
2	540,000	60,000	10%	.826	495,000
3	583,200	64,800	10%	.751	486,648
4	629,856	69,984	10%	.683	477,991
5	680,244	75,580	10%	.621	469,367
6	734,663	81,629	10%	.563	459,573
7	793,437	88,160	10%	.513	452,259
					Value of patent = $3,345,933

formula provides for the valuation of the intangible based on income and tax savings from amortization.

Cost Savings from Intangible Asset

Occasionally, a business is able to avoid costs because it owns an intangible asset. The cost savings approach can be illustrated using the patent process example again. If the company not only licenses the process but also uses it, the value of that patent would be the income received plus the savings to the company from not having to pay a license fee to someone else. If this were the case, the valuation would be as shown in Exhibit 8.17. The cost savings adds about 11 percent to the value of the patent compared to the valuation under an assumption of income only.

Excess Earnings Method

The excess earnings method is a technique that was originally used by the Internal Revenue Service (IRS) to estimate the value of the goodwill of a business. The technique has evolved, however, into one way to estimate the value of the total business by valuing net tangible assets and calculating the value of excess earnings attributable to intangibles.

The excess earnings method requires five steps:

1. Value net tangible assets of the business (i.e., the market value of tangible assets less market value of liabilities of the business).
2. Determine a stabilized total income level.
3. Select a rate of return on net tangible assets and compute income attributable to net tangible assets.
4. Subtract income attributable to tangible assets from stabilized total income, and capitalize the difference, which equals the value of excess earnings (the value of the intangible assets).
5. Add net tangible asset value to the value of "excess" earnings to estimate total value of the business.

An example of the excess earnings method is shown next.

Net tangible asset value	$1,000,000
Stabilized total income	$ 200,000
Rate of return on net tangible assets[8]	13%
Earnings attributable to net tangible assets (.13 × $1,000,000)	$ 130,000
Excess earnings ($200,000 – $130,000)	$ 70,000
Capitalization rate on excess earnings	20%
Value of excess earnings ($70,000/.20)	$ 350,000
Value of business ($1,000,000 + $350,000)	$1,350,000

The excess earnings method generally is not used in determining the value of intangible assets.

SPECIAL TOPICS—BUSINESS VALUATION

Most property types can be valued by using one, two, or all three of the approaches to valuation. Businesses, whether publicly or privately held, can also be valued using the three basic approaches. There are, however, some special aspects of business valuations that would not apply to other types of property. These special aspects are discussed in this section.

Market-to-Book Value Method

The ratio of market-to-book value method is another method that can be utilized to assess the value of financial institutions. The excess capital or equity should be taken into consideration when using the market-to-book value method. Typically, during favorable economic periods (e.g., 1999–2000, and 2003–2007), financial institutions may generate favorable returns, which if retained (e.g., no increase in dividends, no stock buy-backs, no expansion or acquisition) can result in higher than the industry norm or benchmark for equity-to-asset ratio. Investors typically do not capitalize excess equity, but they are willing to pay dollar for dollar for it.

Total Enterprise Value versus Value of Equity

From a technical standpoint, the phrase "value of a business" is somewhat ambiguous. What is usually meant is the "fair market value of the equity of the business as a going concern." Another term commonly used is "total enterprise value." This term often is erroneously used interchangeably with "value of a business and value of equity." The difference is that total enterprise value is based on a debt-free financial structure while value of equity is based on the income considering the debt structure. The relation between total enterprise value and value of equity is shown next.

$$\text{Value of equity} = \text{Total enterprise value} - \text{Long-term debt}$$

or conversely:

$$\text{Total enterprise value} = \text{Value of equity} + \text{Long-term debt}$$

Throughout this book, value of a *business* means the value of the *equity* of that business. The objective in most business valuations is to value the equity. This can be accomplished directly or indirectly.

The direct approach to valuing equity uses historical financial performance as it actually exists for a business, given whatever long-term debt structure was in place during the period under analysis. Determination of future income and selection of comparable transactions for use in the valuation are done directly. This approach is appropriate in two main instances: (1) when the company has little long-term debt relative to equity; or (2) when most comparable businesses have very similar long-term debt/equity structure.

The other method to valuing equity, the indirect approach, uses historical financial performance without the cost of long-term debt and projects future income without debt. This calculation provides the value of the business on a debt-free basis. Subtraction of any long-term debt produces the value of the equity. Exhibit 8.18 illustrates the calculation of the value of equity directly and indirectly. These examples illustrate that slightly different results will be obtained depending on which method is used.

A situation where the total enterprise value rather than the value of equity would be of more interest is when a business is being acquired but long-term debt is not to be assumed by the buyer. If that debt is not to be assumed and is a substantial part of the

EXHIBIT 8.18 Illustration of Direct and Indirect Approaches to Valuing Equity of a Business

	Direct Valuation of Equity					
	Year 1	Year 2	Year 3	Year 4	Year 5	Residual
Income (after debt service)*	$1,000	$1,075	$1,200	$1,350	$1,525	$ 1,650
Capitalization rate	—	—	—	—	—	.11%
Discount rate	15%	15%	15%	15%	15%	15%
Discount factor	.870	.756	.657	.571	.497	.432
Present value (rounded)	$ 870	$ 813	$ 788	$ 771	$ 758	$ 6,480
				Value of Equity by Direct Approach = $10,480		

	Indirect Valuation of Equity					
	Year 1	Year 2	Year 3	Year 4	Year 5	Residual
Debt-free income*	$1,045	$1,120	$1,245	$1,395	$1,570	$ 1,695
Capitalization rate	—	—	—	—	—	11%
Discount rate	15%	15%	15%	15%	15%	15%
Discount factor	.870	.756	.657	.571	.497	.432
Present value (rounded)	$ 909	$ 847	$ 818	$ 797	$ 780	$ 6,656
	Enterprise Value	$ 10,807				
	− 2 Long-term Debt					− 500
	= Value of Equity by Indirect Approach = $ 10.307					

*Assumes business had $ 500 in long-term debt at 9 percent annual interest cost.

capital structure, it is usually more appropriate to value the entity on a debt-free basis and then subtract the long-term debt to arrive at value of the equity.

Existence of Preferred Stock

When the equity of a company consists only of common stock, the value of the stock is synonymous with the value of the equity of a business. When preferred stock is involved, the value of the business consists of the value of both types of stock. The next equation illustrates the relationship:

Value of the equity of business = Value of common stock + Value of preferred stock

When the objective is to value the common stock only, it is necessary first to value the business in total and then to value the preferred stock, with the difference being the value of the common stock. Under most circumstances, ownership of preferred stock does not entail control. Therefore, when the value of preferred stock is subtracted from the total value of the business (by definition a majority position value), the result is the value of the common stock on a majority basis.

Preferred stock represents a portion of ownership of a company and therefore is similar to common stock. Preferred stock can also be like perpetual debt if it is not convertible to common stock. Basically, preferred stock is a security that generates income (i.e., a yield) to the holder. Consequently, it can be valued as an entity separate from the total business or the common stock. The income approach, specifically the capitalization of expected dividends, is normally used to value preferred stock. The formula for the value of a preferred issue with a fixed-rate dividend is:

Per-share value of preferred stock = (Dividend rate × Par value)/Capitalization rate

The equation becomes more complex with adjustable dividend rates but is conceptually the same.

The most significant factor in preferred stock valuation is the selection of the capitalization rate. The usual way to estimate this rate is to examine the current yields on similar types of preferred stock. These yields, which can be thought of as proxies of capitalization rates, reflect the dividends of the stock, the current market price, and investors' expectations of the issuing company's growth and performance. The key is to analyze preferred stock issues that are comparable to the issue being valued. Eight factors that indicate comparability of preferred stock issues are described next.

1. *Similarity of businesses.* If possible, the preferred stock should be issued by a company in the same line(s) of business as the company being valued. Preferred stock yields are driven by the creditworthiness of the issuing company as well as the overall risk associated with the industry. Therefore, companies in different industries of comparable risks could be used. Assessing such industry risk can be difficult. Consequently, selecting companies in the same industry can provide for a more certain selection of equal risk companies.
2. *Rating.* The assessment of risk provided by a rating agency such as Moody's or Standard & Poor's should be similar. If, however, the preferred issue being valued is

not rated, it is necessary to focus on leverage ratios, fixed charge coverage ratios, business risk levels, and other measures of creditworthiness to determine appropriate yields.

3. *Cumulative versus noncumulative.* If a preferred issue is cumulative, all dividends owed to date must be paid to preferred shareholders prior to any common stock dividends. The cumulative provision is a protective device that ensures preferred stockholders will be paid before any common stock dividends are declared. If the preferred stock is noncumulative and a dividend was omitted in a quarter (or year), the holder has no priority claim to that omitted dividend. Few, if any, preferred stock issues are noncumulative.

4. *Dividend policy.* A major comparison factor is whether the dividend is a fixed percentage of par or a variable based on some market index. All other things being equal, yields on variable rate preferred stock typically are less than fixed-rate issues.

5. *Convertibility.* If preferred stock can be exchanged for common stock at a preset formula, it is a convertible issue.

6. *Participation.* Participation refers to the right of preferred stockholders to participate in the profits of the company, usually based on a formula.

7. *Call provision.* The call provision is the right given to the company to require preferred stockholders to redeem their shares for par value plus a stated call premium.

8. *Voting rights.* Occasionally, preferred stockholders have limited voting rights, typically activated when preferred dividends have not been paid for a stated period of time. These voting rights usually have little impact on value on a minority basis.

Other types of comparisons could include the size of the issue (hence its marketability), redemption provisions, and whether it is listed on an exchange or traded over the counter. Once preferred stocks that are generally comparable to the stock being appraised have been identified, the yields can be analyzed to compute a capitalization rate for the subject preferred stock. Exhibit 8.19 illustrates the valuation of a preferred stock issue. In this example, the value of the preferred stock is $43,750,000. If the total value of the business was calculated to be $90,000,000, the value of the common stock would be $46,250,000 ($90,000,000 − $43,750,000).

Adjusted Book Value to Compute Market Value of Equity

Another way to value the equity of a business is to calculate its adjusted book value (sometimes called net asset value). This approach adjusts the tangible assets from book value to FMV, values the intangible assets, then subtracts liabilities. The result is the FMV of equity. This approach is useful for valuing a business that has had very erratic earnings or has had successive years of losses, both situations that could render the income approach inapplicable. It is also used when market comparables are unavailable.

To compute the adjusted book value, it is necessary to convert the value of each asset from its book value to its FMV. Technically, this process requires that each asset of the company be appraised individually, which is rarely done. More often, the substantial assets are valued individually, the market values of minor assets are estimated, the values of any intangible assets are established, and the liabilities are subtracted.

EXHIBIT 8.19   Illustration of Preferred Stock Valuation

Company	S&P Rating*	Yield
Comparable A	A+	5.3%
Comparable B	A+	6.2%
Comparable C	AA−	9.3%
Comparable D	BBB	9.0%
Comparable E	NR	6.5%
Comparable F	A+	7.1%
Comparable G	A−	7.5%
Comparable H	NR	5.9%
Comparable I	NR	8.2%
Comparable J	NR	7.1%
Average		7.2%
Par value of subject preferred stock		$100.00/share
Stated dividend rate		7%
Expected annual dividend		$7.00/share
Capitalization rate		8%[†]
Value per share ($7.00/0.8)		$87.50/share
Total value of preferred stock (500,000 shares)		$43,750,000

*The assessment of the capacity and willingness of an issuer to pay preferred stock dividends and any applicable sinking fund obligations as provided by Standard & Poor's Corporation. These ratings range from AAA 1 to BBB 2 for investment-grade preferred issues, BB 1 to CCC 2 for speculative-grade issues, and CC 1 to D 2 for issues in arrears or default.
[†]Used rate higher than the 7.2 percent average to illustrate situation where subject preferred stock is felt to be slightly riskier on average than comparables.
(All comparable preferred issues are cumulative, adjustable rate, nonconvertible, nonparticipating, perpetual, nonvoting.)

Exhibit 8.20 illustrates the adjustments to book value of each asset to compute FMV of the equity of a bank. The adjusted book value approach as applied to banks is discussed more fully in Chapter 14.

Liquidation of Business

Occasionally, a business is worth more as a collection of assets to be sold individually than as an ongoing entity. In this case, valuation of the business would require the liquidation approach.

Conceptually, the liquidation value, whether orderly or forced, is simple:

Liquidation value of a business = Liquidation value of tangible assets − Liabilities

This is virtually identical to the adjusted book value approach just described, except that adjustments are made from book value to liquidation value, not to market value. The liquidation value of the assets should reflect the costs associated with the

EXHIBIT 8.20 Illustration of Adjustments to Book Value of a Bank to Compute Market Value of Equity (Off–Balance Sheet Items Excluded for Simplicity, $000)

Assets	December 31, 2009 Book Value	December 31, 2009 Fair Market Value
Cash and due forms	$ 4,190	$ 4,190
Investments	6,000	6,000
Fed funds sold	9,250	9,250
Total loans	46,940	44,950
(Loan loss reserves)	(6,520)	(6,520)
Net loans	40,420	38,430
Premises and fixed assets	5,710	7,520
Real estate owned	10,490	9,210
Other assets	1,050	1,050
Core deposit base	—	3,040
Total assets	$77,110	$78,690
Deposits	$75,970	$75,970
Other liabilities	770	770
Total liabilities	$76,740	$76,740
Equity	$ 370	$ 1,950

liquidation, such as broker's fees and legal costs. Estimating liquidation value can be useful even when there is no immediate danger of actual liquidation. The liquidation value provides a lower limit of the company's value. With respect to a bank acquisition, the liquidation value approach may have relevance if a bank is considering a regulatory assisted takeover.

Free Cash Flow

Free cash flow (FCF) is an alternative approach in determining business valuation. FCF reflects future investments that must be made to sustain cash flow. The formula for determining FCF is:

$$FCF = \text{Earnings before interest and tax (EBIT)}(1 - t) + \text{Depreciation} - \text{Capital expenditures} + / - \text{Net working capital}$$

where

$(1 - t)$ = after-tax percent, used to convert EBIT to after taxes

Depreciation is added back because it is a non–cash flow item included in the calculation of EBIT

Capital expenditures = investments that must be made to replenish assets and generate future earnings and cash flows.

Net working capital = requirements associated with capital investments

Calculation of Free Cash Flow

EBIT	$600
Less cash taxes	(180)
Operating profits after taxes	420
Add back depreciation	100
Gross cash flow	520
Change in working capital	62
Capital expenditures	(340)
Operating free cash flow	242
Cash from nonoperating assets	40
FCF	$282

Alternatively, *FCF* can be calculated as:

$$FCF = \text{After-tax operating tax cash flow} - \text{Interest } (1 - t) - PD - RP - RD - EX$$

where

PD = preferred stock dividends
RP = expected redemption of preferred stock
RD = expected redemption of debt
EX = expenditures required to sustain cash flows

Calculation of Free Cash Flow

These projections are expected for 2011:
- Operating cash flow after taxes is estimated as $560,000.
- Interest payments on debt are expected to be $ 20,000.
- Redemption payments on debt are expected to be $75,000.
- New investments are expected to be $50,000.
- The marginal tax rate is expected to be 30 percent.

After-tax operating cash flow	$ 560,000
Less after-tax interest payments ($ 20,000 × (1 − .30))	(14,000)
Debt redemption payment	(75,000)
New investments	(50,000)
FCF	$ 421,000

 ## VALUATION AND BUSINESS CONCENTRATIONS

Business concentration is an important factor that should be considered during the valuation process. It typically is determined in terms of the institution's dependence on: (1) a single customer or a small group of customers for all or a major portion of offered financial products and services; (2) customers within a narrow industry segment for all or a major portion of financial products and services provided; (3) operations within a narrowly defined geographic territory; or (4) domination by a small group of management with no adequate oversight board or audit committee. Concentrations adversely affect the institution's value in two ways: (1) increased risk of potential decline in earning-generating power resulting from the possible inability to provide financial services or substantial decrease in demand for financial services; and (2) perception of a possible limit on future earnings growth due to lack of ability to satisfy customers' financial services needs. Appraisers should identify all relevant business concentrations and examine their impact on valuation by adjusting the discount rate, capitalization factor, and future earnings growth.

SPECIAL TOPICS—CLOSELY HELD STOCK

Companies that are closely held generally have a number of recognizable characteristics:

- They are privately held by a few stockholders, sometimes all members of the same family.
- There is a close relationship between ownership and management.
- There is little, if any, trading and that is usually among existing stockholders.
- The entity is publicly held, but with very narrow ownership, and it is thinly traded.

Closely held corporations (CHCs)—also known as close corporations, family corporations, or incorporated partnerships)—while enjoying many advantages of corporations, such as limited liability and tax benefits, maintain the internal attributes of a nonincorporated business. Stock of a CHC is held by a relatively small group of people, a family, or a single individual and is not available to the public. Thus, there is normally no established market for the CHC's stock. The valuation of a CHC's stock is a challenge when it is sold, exchanged, liquidated, or involved in mergers, buy-sell agreements, or stock options, and especially when the stock is held for estate and gift tax purposes. Since stock of a CHC is not publicly traded and has no readily available trading value, often there is conflict between the IRS and taxpayers in determining its FMV.

The Congress and the Treasury Department have addressed the issue of determining FMV for stock of CHCs by issuing Revenue Ruling 59-60, 1959-1 CB 237, code Section 2031. Revenue Ruling 59-60 states that the valuation process is distinctly different for sales/service companies than for holding/investment companies. The valuation standard often used in appraising stock in CHCs for estate and gift tax purposes is fair market value.

Reg. Sec. 20.2031-1 states:

The fair market value is the price at which the property would change hands between a willing buyer and a willing seller, neither being under any compulsion to buy or sell and both having reasonable knowledge of relevant facts.

The application of this definition in valuing stock of CHCs involves at least two problems: (1) Stock of CHCs is not easily traded in liquid markets, and any change that

EXHIBIT 8.21 Estate and Gift Tax Regulations

Regulations	Description
Estate Tax	
Reg. § 20.3031-1(b)	Defines fair market value as the value a willing buyer and willing seller would agree on given both parties have a reasonable knowledge of the relevant facts.
Reg. § 20.2031-2(a)	States that the fair market value is determined on the applicable valuation date.
Reg. § 20.2031-2(c)	Explains how to value securities when selling prices or bid and ask prices do not reflect fair market value.
Reg. § 20.2031-2(f)	Describes salient factors for determining stock value for unlisted securities where selling prices or bid and asked prices are unavailable.
Reg. § 20.2031-2(h)	States that restrictive agreements (e.g., option or contract to purchase stock at a stated price) may not be given any tax effect.
Reg. § 20.2031-3	Emphasizes the importance of valuing all assets, both tangible and intangible, and other relevant factors (e.g., earning capacity) to determine fair market value.

Regulations	Description
Gift Tax	
Reg. § 25.2512-1	Specifies that the value of a gift is determined on the date of the gift as the fair market value that a willing buyer and a willing seller would agree upon, both having a reasonable knowledge of the relevant facts.
Reg. § 25.2512-2(c)	Provides information for valuing securities when the selling prices or bid and asked prices do not represent a true fair market value (e.g., sale between family members).
Reg. § 25.2512-2(f)	Describes important factors for determining value of the gift.

may have occurred was probably within a family relationship; and (2) the criterion of objective and independent willing buyer, willing seller does not exist in estate and gift tax situations. Exhibit 8.21 shows relevant estate and gift tax regulations.

It is important to understand special aspects of closely held stock when undertaking a valuation. Several of these aspects are described next.

Revenue Ruling 59-60

The IRS originally issued Revenue Ruling 59-60 to be the guideline in the valuation of closely held capital stock for estate and gift tax purposes. The considerations in that ruling subsequently have been extended to cover all types of business interests for all income and other tax purposes. Revenue Ruling 59-60 defines FMV and suggests that all relevant factors and available financial information should be considered in determining FMV. More specifically, the ruling describes eight general factors that should be used in calculating the value of stock for which market quotations are either unavailable or are so scarce that they would not be useful in determining value. The eight specified factors outlined in Revenue Ruling 59-60 as listed below are applicable to all valuation assignments requiring determination of FMV. These eight factors have been considered in official opinions of the tax court whereas some factors (e.g., earnings, book value, dividend-paying capacity) are emphasized more than others.

The eight factors listed in Revenue Ruling 59-60 that should be taken into account when valuing closely held business interests are:

1. The nature of the business and the history of the enterprise from its inception
2. The economic outlook in general, and the condition and outlook of the specific industry in particular
3. The book value and the financial condition of the business
4. The earning capacity of the company
5. The dividend-paying capacity
6. Whether the enterprise has goodwill or other intangible value
7. Sales of the stock and the size of the block of stock to be valued
8. The market price of stocks of corporations engaged in the same or a similar line of business having their stocks actively traded in a free and open market

Discounts for Minority Position/Premium for Control

Currently, business owners have created a new class of nonvoting recapitalizations in Subchapter S corporations for use in succession and estate planning by giving away this class of nonvoting shares and taking valuation discounts for minority interest status, lack of voting rights, and lack of marketability. Nonvoting recapitalizations enable the founder (owner) of the company to remain in control until successors (e.g., next generation) are ready, willing, and able to effectively operate the business. These three discounting opportunities may be available for these types of nonvoting shares:

1. *Minority discount.* Minority interest typically is discounted for lack of control.
2. *Nonvoting discount.* Nonvoting shares generally are worth significantly less than the equivalent voting shares.
3. *Lack of marketability discount.* Shares that are not readily tradable and marketable are often discounted for lack of marketability and liquidity.

Minority and marketability discount is often available for a small, limited partner interest in the family limited partnership (FLP). The person buying the limited partner interest in FLP does not have the assurance or expectation to obtain the underlying value of the assets in FLP. When family members hold minority interests, the value of such shares may be discounted for lack of control.

A fundamental principle of valuation is that a single share of stock is not worth its pro rata value of the total company. In other words, if a company in total is valued at $1,000,000, and it has 100,000 shares of common stock, the value of a single share is less than $10.00. Conversely, the total value of a company is worth more than the price of a single share of stock multiplied by the shares outstanding. The reason for this anomaly is that control positions command a premium (and conversely minority positions require a discount). Control commands premiums because controlling interest involves such prerogatives as the power to: acquire or liquidate, select management, guide policy, declare and pay dividends, and set compensation.

Normally when a business is valued, it is on a 100 percent ownership basis—that is, the value of the company if 100 percent interest is purchased. Once the total value is known, the discount for a minority position is applied to arrive at the aggregate minority value. This figure then is divided by the shares outstanding to derive per-share value on a minority basis. Mathematically, the calculation is:

$$\text{Minority value per share} = [\text{Total value of business} \times (1 - \text{Minority discount \%})]/\text{Shares outstanding}$$

For example, if the total value of the business on a control basis is \$1,000,000, there are 100,000 shares outstanding, and a minority discount of 40 percent is appropriate, the value per share on a minority basis is:

$$\text{Minority value per share} = [\$1,000,000 \times (1 - .40)]/100,000 = \$6.00$$

This calculation also determines the premium for control, which is the percent increase from per-share minority value to per-share control value; in this example, 66.7 percent. In general, the premium for control and minority discount are related as:

$$\text{Control premium \%} = [1/(1 - \text{Minority discount \%})] - \text{Minority discount \%}$$
$$= 1 - [1/(1 + \text{Control premium \%})]$$

The minority value of the stock also can be estimated directly if data on minority position sales are available. Also, quoted stock prices for comparable companies can be used since by definition they reflect minority positions.

Discount for Lack of Marketability

Closely held stocks are not as readily marketable as shares of widely held, actively traded stocks. This lack of marketability and resulting lower liquidity has an adverse effect on the value of the stock, especially if it is a minority position. Consequently, a minority position in a closely held company would be valued with both minority and marketability discounts. Marketability discounts as high as 30 percent to 40 percent are not uncommon for minority positions in small corporations.

 SPECIAL TOPICS—VALUING WIDELY TRADED COMPANIES

An entire field of study has developed around the valuation of widely traded stock and other equity instruments. This area of finance often involves the use of complex mathematical and economic models to simulate the behavior of public equity markets.

When a widely traded bank holding company is an acquisition target, its quoted stock price represents the per-share value of the institution on a minority basis. The premium offered for controlling interest will depend on the buyer's assessment of the investment value of the target. Therefore, when a widely traded bank is being targeted for acquisition, the value measure relevant to the buyer is the value of a 100 percent interest. The market price of a share of stock is of secondary importance. Consequently, the types of analyses and valuation approaches described in this chapter are essentially the same, irrespective of whether the target is closely or widely held.

 ## CONCLUSION

This chapter presented basic business valuation models of cost, market, and income approaches. These valuation models are built based on valuation standards of generally accepted accounting principles that are used as standards to guide the preparation of financial statements as well as Uniform Standards of Professional Appraisal Practice that are issued by the Appraisals Standards Board. Valuations often are calculated to determine value of the equity of the target company. This chapter presents drivers of banks' intrinsic value, such as profitability, growth prospects, and cost of equity capital, as well as financial and nonfinancial key performance indicators that reflect on the reliability of the measured drivers. This chapter also discusses major valuation models that translate value drivers into value estimates.

 ## NOTES

1. This is essentially the same as the principle of substitution described in Chapter 5.
2. The deficiencies inherent in using book value are discussed in Chapter 5.
3. In discussing the income approach, the term "income" can apply to any measure of monetary receipts: earnings, cash flow, dividend capacity, and so on. The specific type of income used in a given situation does not affect the conceptual basis. From a practical standpoint, however, proper application of the income approach requires careful consideration of the type of income to be used. The different types are discussed later in this chapter.
4. Financial Accounting Standards Board, Statement of Financial Accounting Concepts No. 7: *Using Cash Flow Information and Present Value in Accounting Measurement* (Norwalk, CT: Author, 2000).
5. Financial Accounting Standards Board, Statement of Financial Accounting Standards (SFAS) No.159: *The Fair Value Option for the Financial Assets and Financial Liabilties* (Norwalk, CT: Author, February 15, 2007).
6. As mentioned at the beginning of this chapter, it was assumed for the sake of discussion of valuation principles that appropriate information on the subject asset and other data as necessary have been gathered.
7. Chapter 9 contains a more thorough discussion of the legal, tax, and accounting aspects of intangible assets.
8. The rate of return on net tangible assets must reflect a return on capital as well as a return of capital. The return on capital would be analogous to the discount rate. The return of capital would be analogous to a sinking fund contribution to return the capital (less any salvage value). If the net tangible assets are those that tend to increase in value, then return of capital is not a factor. Depreciating and wasting assets, however, need to be reflected as a higher rate of return.

CHAPTER NINE

Valuations for Tax and Accounting Purposes

VARIOUS TAX AND ACCOUNTING requirements drive the need for valuations. Valuations can provide both a basis for depreciation or amortization and a means to revalue the balance sheet for purchase accounting transactions. This chapter addresses the pertinent tax and accounting aspects of mergers and acquisitions (M&A) and the role valuation can play.

 TAX ASPECTS OF MERGERS AND ACQUISITIONS

This section discusses the income tax effects of the business combinations. In a business combination, the structure and accounting for M&A are affected by income tax considerations. The structure and types of business combinations determine the accounting method and income taxes that should be used. A merger or acquisition will be either a taxable or a nontaxable transaction. In a nontaxable transaction, the seller receives payment in a form that will not result in taxes paid on any gain realized. In a taxable transaction, the seller is liable for tax on the gain. Valuations can be an important part of either transaction type. Before addressing the valuation issues, it is useful to describe some of the basic characteristics of nontaxable and taxable transactions. This discussion is not intended to provide a comprehensive examination of the tax attributes of various transactions. It is an overview of the basic tax nature of bank M&A transactions.

Nontaxable Transactions

A common type of nontaxable transaction is the *Type A* reorganization (called a statutory merger). In this type of transaction, the seller receives stock, cash, and/or securities of the buyer equal to the purchase price. The seller's shareholders can receive different types of consideration (e.g., one may receive stock, another cash) and still qualify as nontaxable,[1] provided the continuity of interest test is met. This test requires that the seller's shareholders must have an equity position in the surviving company equal to at least 50 percent of the value of their formerly outstanding stock. Any boot received is taxable to the seller's shareholders only to the extent of the value of the boot.[2] In the case of a Type A reorganization, a boot is usually cash received by those shareholders who do not want stock or debt.

The *Type B* transaction (stock for stock) is one in which the seller's shareholders receive *voting* stock of the buyer in exchange for their shares. The buyer must acquire at least 80 percent of the voting and other classes of stock of the seller. No other consideration can be paid to the seller's shareholders (except cash for fractional shares) and still qualify as a Type B nontaxable transaction.

A *Type C* transaction (stock for assets) is similar to a Type B except that the buyer is exchanging voting stock for the assets of the seller. Under a Type C reorganization, the buyer may give the seller a limited amount of property in addition to voting stock—up to 20 percent of the fair market value of the net assets received.

The *Type D* reorganization involves the transfer of the assets of one company to another, and immediately thereafter the transferor and/or its shareholders are in control of the transferee. The Type D reorganization is most commonly used for spin-offs, split-offs, and split-ups. The requirements are extremely complex, but it can be a useful tool when a bank desires to transfer certain of its assets to a new, separate company.

A *Type E* reorganization is a recapitalization and involves only one corporation. A recapitalization occurs when a corporation issues a new type of debt or equity in exchange for its current debt or equity.

The last type of reorganization is a *Type F* and involves a change in identity, form, or place of a corporation. This type of reorganization is used when banks desire to change their legal status. It is not generally applicable to a merger transaction.

Taxable Transactions

Taxable transactions are relatively straightforward in their process: The stock or assets of a corporation are acquired for cash or its equivalent. The seller of the stock or assets is subject to tax at the time of the sale on the excess of the purchase price received over their tax basis in the stock or assets sold.

In a sale of assets, there are two layers of tax. The selling corporation recognizes any gain on the sale and pays tax on that gain. Then, when the net proceeds of the sale are paid to shareholders, they will be taxed on the gain of the receipts over their basis in the stock. Prior to the Tax Reform Act of 1986, the first layer of tax (at the corporate level of the seller) could be avoided by adopting a complete plan of liquidation under Section 337. The result of such a liquidation was that no tax at the corporate level was paid, except for certain tax recapture items. However, under the rules established by the 1986 tax law, the so-called General Utilities doctrine, which allowed the avoidance of double taxation, was repealed. Now double taxation is the rule rather than the exception. Additionally, if the buyer steps up the tax basis, it is subject to recapture of depreciation on real and personal property and investment tax credits. Although these recaptures were required under the old law, along with repeal of General Utilities, they have made a Section 337 asset acquisition even less desirable.

In a taxable sale of assets, their tax attributes generally do not survive the transaction. The buyer's new tax basis in the assets will equal the purchase price. In a taxable sale of stock, however, the tax attributes of the purchased company's assets will survive. In other words, the tax basis of the seller's assets would not change after the transaction and would carry over to the buyer.

Section 338 of the Internal Revenue Code allows a stock acquisition to be treated, for tax purposes, as an asset acquisition if a corporation acquires 80 percent or more of the stock of another corporation. The buyer elects to take this approach to step up the tax basis of the acquired assets, thus generating higher depreciation to reduce future tax liabilities. Unfortunately, under the 1986 tax law, the gain on the assets (i.e., the purchase price over tax basis) becomes a cost to the buyer because of the mechanics of a 338 election and repeal of General Utilities described previously. To understand why the buyer of the assets becomes liable for taxes on the gain in a sale, it is necessary to clarify the process of a 338 election.

1. On the day of the stock sale, the selling corporation is treated (for tax purposes) as having sold all its assets at the close of business in a single transaction to a hypothetical new corporation.
2. On the day after the stock sale, the selling corporation is treated (again, for tax purposes) as the hypothetical new corporation that purchases the same assets. The gain on the sale is now the responsibility of this new corporation.
3. This hypothetical new corporation is then liquidated into the buying corporation with the tax attributes and liabilities of the new corporation becoming those of the buyer. Consequently, the buyer now has responsibility for tax on the gain of the assets' values.

The 338 election allows the buyer to achieve the tax objective of allocating the price paid for stock to the underlying assets (i.e., to step up the tax basis) without actual transfer of assets or liquidation.

Prior to the 1986 tax law, Section 338 elections were very common in taxable bank acquisitions. The buyer could acquire stock, step up the tax basis of depreciable assets, and reduce future tax liabilities. Under General Utilities, the buyer could establish a new tax basis without incurring a tax liability on the gain. The 1986 law, however, makes this a much less desirable alternative. In order for a 338 election to be economically sound, the net present value of future tax savings from higher depreciation and amortization must be greater than the immediate tax liability payable on the gain. For all practical purposes, the benefits of a 338 election evaporated with the repeal of General Utilities.

TYPICAL TAX-ORIENTED VALUATIONS

Virtually all tax-related valuation requirements are driven by the need to establish a new tax basis of an asset: for computing taxable gain, for determining depreciation, for allocating purchase price among various assets, or for new property taxes. Even in nontaxable transactions, however, there are often tax-oriented valuation requirements. For example, in a Type A reorganization (statutory merger), it may be necessary to value the seller's (mergee's) stock to confirm that the 50 percent continuity of interest test is met. Additionally, if the buyer (merger) is issuing new securities or a new class of stock, it may be necessary to value them to determine the taxable gain of the seller.

Valuations can also be critical in the success of a Type C reorganization (stock for assets). If the parties of the transaction seek to exchange boot, the parties must be very certain of their valuations. Items that must be valued include:

- Stock of the buyer
- Boot if it is property other than cash
- Property acquired
- Seller's property that is not acquired

The last item can be a problem if the seller has widely scattered assets of which the buyer has little knowledge. This can be a problem because the 80 percent voting stock requirement means 80 percent of the *total value of all property* of the seller, not just 80 percent of the value of property acquired. If retained property is found to be such that less than 80 percent of total value was exchanged, the transaction would be denied nontaxable treatment.

Valuation requirements are far more common and visible with taxable transactions, particularly cash for assets and cash for stock with a Section 338 election. In either of these types of transactions, a new basis in the assets must be established, thus requiring an estimate of fair market value of the assets for determining future depreciation or amortization.

The most common reason for valuation in a taxable transaction is for *purchase price allocation.* This is the process of allocating—distributing—the total purchase price paid among the acquired net assets. Exhibit 9.1 illustrates how a purchase price allocation would proceed in a bank acquisition.

In this example, the total fair market value of acquired assets is $210 million. Subtracting the market value liabilities of $190 million, the net asset value is $20 million. Since the buyer is paying $28 million for the stock, $20 million is allocated to the identified net assets, with the balance of $8 million allocated to goodwill. The identified assets and liabilities are put on the buyer's books at their respective market values. The $8 million difference is put on the buyer's books as goodwill. This allocation to goodwill has significant tax ramifications for the buyer because goodwill is a nonamortizable asset, thus no tax benefit is realized, whereas other assets can be expensed against taxable income (through depreciation or amortization) over their

EXHIBIT 9.1 Tax-Oriented Purchase Price Allocation ($000,000)

	Tax Basis	Fair Market Value Basis	Difference
Assets of Selling Bank			
Cash	$ 10	$ 10	$ 0
Investments	50	52	2
Loans (net)	100	98	(2)
Premises	30	34	4
Other	10	11	1
Core deposit intangible	—	5	5
Total	$200	$210	$10
Deposits	$175	$180	$ 5
Other	10	10	0
Total	$185	$190	$ 5
Net Asset Value	$ 15	$ 20	$ 5
Total Liabilities and Net Asset Value	$200	$210	$10

Transaction:
  Buyer agreed to pay $28 million for 100 percent of seller's stock. The assets and liabilities are revalued to market value. Identified assets less liabilities equals $20 million, leaving $8 million ($28 million purchase price less $20 million net identifiable assets) to be "allocated" to goodwill. After the transaction, the buyer will have an $8 million intangible asset called goodwill on its balance sheet.

useful life. Consequently, it is important that accurate and supportable valuations be made of all assets of the seller.

Income Tax Implications of a Business Combination

In a business combination, assets acquired and liabilities assumed may give rise to deferred taxes that should be recognized and measured. The acquirer should account for the potential tax effects of temporary differences, carryforwards, and income tax uncertainties of an acquiree. To analyze the income tax implications of a business combination, six steps generally are performed:

1. Determine the tax structure of the transaction and tax status of the entities involved in the business combination.
2. Determine financial statement and tax bases of the net assets acquired.
3. Identify and measure temporary differences.
4. Identify acquired tax benefits.
5. Consider the treatment of tax uncertainties.
6. Consider deferred taxes related to goodwill.

Determine the Tax Structure and Status

The legal structure and the tax status of entities acquired (e.g., corporate entities, partnerships, limited liability corporations) are the most important determinants of the accounting and tax considerations of business combinations. How to record the deferred tax assets and liabilities will depend on the acquired enterprise's tax status. Furthermore, it is important to consider the tax structure of the transaction in order to determine whether the business combination transaction is taxable or nontaxable. If taxable, based on the rules of the specific tax jurisdiction, the tax bases of the assets acquired and liabilities assumed should be adjusted to fair value. If nontaxable, the historical tax bases of the assets and liabilities, net operating losses, and other tax attributes of the target company should be carryover to the acquirer company.

Determine Financial Statement and Tax Bases of the Net Assets Acquired

As a general rule, the tax bases of the identifiable assets acquired and liabilities assumed are determined based on other certain conditions and specific tax jurisdiction and related tax laws and regulations. For instance, it is different when determining the tax bases in a taxable transaction and a nontaxable transaction. In a taxable transaction, the tax bases are described at fair value. If there is excess, it will be treated as goodwill for tax purposes and may be tax-deductible. Other differences should also be considered between financial reporting and tax purposes. In a nontaxable transaction, historical tax bases of acquired assets and assumed liabilities, net operating losses, and other tax attributes of the acquiree carryover from the acquired company.

Identify and Measure Temporary Differences

Any temporary differences related to book bases and tax bases of the acquired identifiable assets and assumed liabilities should be determined in light of whether they are deductible or taxable, and the pertinent deferred tax assets or deferred tax liabilities should be recorded. Generally, deferred taxes may be caused by outside basis differences, contingencies, research and development activities, and acquisition-related costs, among others. The expected manner of recovery or settlement can also influence the deferred tax accounting. Moreover, the applicable tax rate may also affect the valuation of deferred tax assets and liabilities, so it should be considered based on certain facts and circumstances.

Identify Acquired Tax Benefits

In a business combination, the acquirer should recognize if there are any acquired net operating losses, credit carryforwards, or other relevant tax attributes that should be recorded as part of acquisition accounting. The extent of recognized tax benefits depends on the accounting standards being complied with. For example, based on the International Financial Reporting Standards (IFRS), whether the deferred tax assets could be recognized and recorded in the financial statements depends on whether the future taxable profits are sufficient to be available against which the deductible temporary difference can be utilized. However, based on U.S. generally accepted accounting principles (GAAP), typically a deferred tax asset is recorded in full. A valuation allowance will be required to reduce deferred tax assets if they are not considered to be realizable.

Consider the Treatment of Tax Uncertainties

An acquirer should identify and determine the accounting requirements for uncertain tax positions. When a business combination is taxable, acquisition price and subsequent tax returns often are challenged by the taxing authority and perhaps litigated. Thus, the tax positions may be uncertain. If a business combination is nontaxable, the tax basis of individual assets may be uncertain. The preacquisition tax returns of the acquired business may be uncertain as well.

Consider Deferred Taxes Related to Goodwill

An acquirer company should determine whether a deferred tax asset should be recorded when there are temporary differences associated with tax-deductible good-will. For financial reporting purposes, goodwill is a residual amount, and acquired goodwill is not amortized but capitalized as an asset. The amount assigned to goodwill for book and tax purposes will be different, if it is considered in different valuation and allocation rules.

 ## ACCOUNTING ASPECTS OF MERGERS AND ACQUISITIONS

Traditionally, when two banks have been combined, the transaction could be reflected, from an accounting perspective, as either a pooling of interests (pooling for short) or a purchase in compliance with Accounting Principles Board (APB) Opinion No. 16.[3] In an attempt to improve the financial reporting for business combinations, the Financial Accounting Standards Board (FASB) issued Statements of Financial Accounting Standards (SFAS) No. 141, *Business Combinations*,[4] which became effective in June 2001 along with SFAS No. 142, *Goodwill and Other Intangible Assets*.[5] SFAS No. 141 prohibited pooling-of-interest accounting for business combinations, introduced certain changes in purchase method, and imposed the additional disclosure requirements for business combinations. Prior to the adoption of SFAS No. 141, the accounting for business combinations lacked the adequate disclosures and provided too much flexibility to management to justify the preferred method (pooling versus purchase) for a particular case. Thus, business transactions of a similar economic nature could result in different accounting treatments. The FASB issued SFAS No. 141 to mitigate the difficulties associated with the dual treatment of business combinations and for the failure of the pooling method to reflect the value of purchased intangibles.

Effective implementation of provisions of SFAS No. 141 is intended to improve the transparency of business combination reporting by:

- Providing more accurate assessment of the investment made in the acquired entity through the "fair value" focus of purchase method.

- Enhancing comparability of financial statements through uniform business combinations treatment.
- Presenting a more complete information through extended disclosure requirements.

Provisions of SFAS No. 141 are based on these nine understandings of the underlying economics of business combinations:

1. Generally, all business combinations are acquisitions.
2. All business combinations are associated with a clearly identifiable price.
3. The purchase price is the best evidence of the values exchanged.
4. When the purchase price exceeds the fair values of the net assets acquired, goodwill must be recognized as a permanent asset of the combined company.
5. Recognized goodwill should not be amortized; instead, it should be tested periodically for impairment.
6. Goodwill is recognized regardless of the extent of ownership acquired.
7. A change of ownership control is a precondition to the recognition of a business combination.
8. Goodwill is measured by subtracting the fair values of the net assets of the acquired company from the purchase price.
9. For accounting measurement purposes, it is assumed that the operations of the acquired company are discontinued.

By adopting SFAS Nos. 141 and 142, the FASB reached the conclusion that "virtually all business combinations are acquisitions" where ownership control of one of the combining entities changes hands. However, in a real world, when two banks combine, sometimes it is difficult to determine whether a change of ownership control actually has taken place primarily for three reasons. First, ownership control is a matter of degree and factual control may be obtained with less than the majority of legal voting rights.Thus, the rationale for eliminating the pooling-of-interests method appears to be questionable. Second, the assumption that "virtually all business combinations are acquisitions" ignores the existence of mergers, even though at least one-third of business combinations in leading economies actually are mergers. Third, business combinations are complex and significant events in the current economic organization and dynamics of business firms. This complexity is expected to continue and demands a search for the distinctive features of business combinations that distinguish between different types of transactions (pooling versus purchase).

The elimination of pooling was based on the assumption that the underlying combination was an exchange of ownership interests between the owners of the combining entities. This assumption is valid when the combination is effected exclusively through an exchange of shares, and it is understood to be a mere change in legal form. However, when a significant change in ownership interests is involved, the pooling method can distinguish entity equity from shareholder equity. The acquired company's shareholders typically receive a form of consideration directly from the entity for ratifying the merger, particularly when the business combination takes place among entities not under common control. By making a distinction between shareholders' equity and entity equity, the pooling approach can charge or credit the acquisition differential to entity equity. The accounting treatment of a business combination as a purchase transaction requires the identification of an acquired entity and the measurement of an acquisition price. Assumption of being able to meet these requirements in a real-world business combination underestimates the complexities associated with the synergistic transformation. The measurement of the acquisition price requires an excessive reliance on the consideration paid and the estimation of fair value. It appears that the elimination of the pooling method was based on a particular understanding of the underlying economics of business combinations. The existence and persistence of complexities in business combination demands a new comprehensive framework for accounting for business combinations that allows the use of both pooling and purchase accounting method for business combinations. Thus, the remainder of this chapter addresses both pooling and purchase accounting methods for business combinations that are applicable to both M&A.

Pooling versus Purchase Accounting

An acquisition that qualifies for pooling allows the balance sheets of the two banks to be combined without adjustments to the values of assets or liabilities. In this type of transaction, it is assumed that two shareholder groups mutually accept the risks and rewards of combining their banks and agree to an exchange of their ownership interests. Exhibit 9.2 illustrates how the pooling of interest results in a new balance sheet and income statement.

The other method of M&A acquisition accounting, the purchase method, is more complex. Under purchase accounting rules, a new balance sheet is created that reflects the current value of assets and liabilities of the seller rather than their historical book values. The effect of this method on the resulting balance sheet, especially capital, can be significant. Exhibit 9.3 illustrates the results of purchase method accounting on the balance sheet, using the same facts as in Exhibit 9.2. In the purchase accounting example (an all-cash sale), the equity-to-asset ratio falls significantly, from 7.41 percent to 5.48 percent. If the transaction had been less than all cash (some stocks and notes), the effect on equity ratios would not be quite as dramatic but relative capital levels would still decline.

The only time purchase accounting does not cause a lower equity-to-asset ratio is when the seller receives only equity instruments of the buyer as payment. In general, the greater the percentage of purchase price that is in cash and the higher the premium over book, the greater the decline in the capital ratio.

Requirements for Use of Pooling Accounting

The determination of whether to use pooling or purchase accounting is not an option of the bank. There are 12 very clear requirements that must all be met in order for the buying bank to use pooling to account for an acquisition.

EXHIBIT 9.2 Example of Pooling of Interest Accounting Where Bank A Is Acquirer, Bank B Is Target ($000, Except Book Value per Share)

	Bank A	Bank B	Adjustments	Combined
Assets				
Cash and due forms	$ 15,000	$ 6,000	—	$ 21,000
Investments	75,000	45,000	—	120,000
Net loans	160,000	42,000	—	202,000
Premises and equipment	9,000	5,000	—	14,000
Other assets	11,000	2,000	—	13,000
Total Assets	$270,000	$100,000	—	$370,000
Liabilities				
Deposits	$200,000	$ 80,000	—	$280,000
Short-term debt	30,000	10,000	—	40,000
Other liabilities	17,000	5,000	—	22,000
Long-term debt	3,000	0	—	3,000
Total Liabilities	$250,000	$ 95,000		$345,000
Shareholders' Equity				
Common stock	$ 5,000	$ 1,000	($2,440)*	$ 3,560
Surplus	6,000	1,000	2,440*	9,440
Retained earnings	9,000	3,000	—	12,000
Total Equity	$ 20,000	$ 5,000	—	$ 25,000
Total Liabilities and Equity	$270,000	$100,000	—	$370,000
Common shares outstanding	150,000	40,000	—	206,000*
Book value/share	$ 133	$ 125	—	$ 121.36
Equity/assets	7.41%	5.00%	—	6.76%

*Assumes an exchange ratio of 1.4:1 (about 1.5 times B's book value); therefore, Bank A must issue 56,000 shares at $133 to issue to Bank B shareholders to redeem their 40,000 shares. Because Bank A is "buying" shares worth $125 for 1.4 of its shares that are worth $186, there must be offsetting adjustments to common stock and surplus equal to the difference in book value ($61) times shares redeemed (40,000). These entries do not affect the total equity, only the relative composition of the equity account.

These 12 requirements are spelled out in paragraphs 46-48 of APB Opinion No. 16. The essence of these 12 requirements is summarized next.

1. Each of the entities must be autonomous and may not have been a subsidiary or division of another company within two years before the plan of consolidation is initiated.
2. Each of the combining companies must be independent of each other from initiation to consummation of the transaction. Independence means that the companies can hold no more than 10 percent of each other's stock.
3. The combination must be effected in a single transaction or in accordance with a specific plan within one year after the acquisition is initiated.

EXHIBIT 9.3 Example of Purchase Accounting—100% Cash Acquisition Where Bank A Is Acquirer, Bank B Is Target ($000, except book value per share)

	Bank A	Bank B	Adjustments	Combined
Assets				
Cash and due forms	$ 15,000	$ 6,000		$ 21,000
Investments	75,000	45,000	($1,000)[a]	119,000
Net loans	160,000	42,000	(2,000)[b]	200,000
Premises and equipment	9,000	5,000	440[c]	14,440
Other assets	11,000	2,000		13,000
Core deposit intangible	—	—	4,000[d]	4,000
Goodwill	—	—	1,000[e]	1,000
Total Assets	$270,000	$100,000	($ 5,000)	$372,400
Liabilities				
Deposits	$200,000	$ 80,000	—	$280,000
Short-term debt	30,000	10,000	—	40,000
Other liabilities	17,000	5,000	—	22,000
Long-term debt	3,000	0	$ 7,440[f]	10,440
Total Liabilities	$250,000	$ 95,000	$ 7,440	$352,440
Shareholders' Equity				
Common stock	$ 5,000	$ 1,000	($1,000)[g]	$ 5,000
Surplus	6,000	1,000	(1,000)[g]	6,000
Retained earnings	9,000	3,000	($3,000)[g]	$ 9,000
Total Equity	$ 20,000	$ 5,000	($5,000)[g]	$ 20,000
Total Liabilities and Equity	$270,000	$100,000	($5,000)	$365,000
Common shares outstanding	150,000	40,000	(40,000)[h]	150,000
Book value/share	$ 133	$ 125	—	$ 133
Equity/assets	7.41%	5.00%	—	5.48%

[a] Assumed market value of investments $1,million less than book value.

[b] Assumed market value of loans $2 million less than book value.

[c] Assumed market value of premises $440,000 more than book value.

[d] Value of core deposit base (described in Chapter 16).

[e] Excess of purchase price ($7,440,000) over market value of Bank B's assets ($6 million cash, $44 million in investments, $40 million in loans, $5,440,000 in premises, $2 million in other assets, and $4 million core deposit value) less liabilities ($95 million).

[f] Debt incurred of $7,440,000 (equal to $186 per share as in pooling example in preceding exhibit).

[g] Since Bank B ceases to exist, the equity account is completely distributed and also ceases to exist.

[h] All of Bank B's stock acquired for cash.

4. One of the corporations offers and issues only common stock with rights identical to those of the majority of its outstanding voting common stock in exchange for substantially all (90 percent or more) of the voting common stock interest of the other company.
5. None of the combining entities may have changed the equity interest of the voting common stock in contemplation of effecting the combination either within two years before the plan of combination is initiated or between the dates the combination is initiated and consummated.
6. Each of the combining companies reacquires shares of voting common stock only for purposes other than business combinations, and no company reacquires more than a normal number of shares between the date the plan of combination is initiated and the date it is consummated. Acquisitions of voting common stock of the issuing corporation by any of the combining corporations or their subsidiaries are treated as reacquisitions by the issuing company.
7. The ratio of the interest of an individual common stockholder to those of other common stockholders in a combining company must remain the same as a result of the exchange of common stock to effect the combination.
8. The voting rights to which the common stock ownership interests in the resulting combined corporation are entitled must be exercisable by the stockholders; the stockholders may neither be deprived of nor restricted in exercising those rights for a specified period.
9. The combination must be resolved at the date the plan is consummated, and no provisions relating to the issue of securities or other terms of consideration may be pending.
10. The combined corporation may not agree directly or indirectly to retire or reacquire all or part of the common stock issued to effect the combination.
11. The combined corporation may not enter into other financial arrangements for the benefit of the former stockholders of a combining company, such as guaranty of loans secured by stock issued in the combination, which, in effect, negates the exchange of equity.
12. The combined corporation may not intend or plan to dispose of a significant part of the assets of the combining companies within two years after the combination, other than disposals in the ordinary course of business of the formerly separated companies to eliminate duplicate facilities or excess capacity.

The requirements for pooling are complex and strictly enforced. If the transaction does not pass all the tests, it will be accounted for as a purchase. If a bank is contemplating a transaction that is to be accounted for as a pooling, competent accounting and legal advice should be sought.

Advantages and Disadvantages of Purchase and Pooling Accounting

The two methods of accounting for M&A each have their advantages and disadvantages, some of which are summarized in Exhibit 9.4.

EXHIBIT 9.4   Pooling and Purchasing Accounting: Advantages and Disadvantages

	Pooling Accounting	Purchasing Accounting
Advantages	Straightforward from accounting perspective	Negotiations usually more flexible
	No borrowing or debt issuance	Ownership dilution can be avoided
		Opportunity to revalue assets
	Avoids potential regulatory concerns relating to debt issuance or goodwill	Opportunity to sell off major assets
	Capital of both entities survives transaction	
Disadvantages	Hard to qualify for (the 12 strict rules)	Accounting more complex
	Less flexibility in negotiations	Can adversely impact capital ratios and future earnings
	Stock issuance can dilute earnings	Goodwill and intangible asset considerations
	Historical asset values retained	Reduces capital ratios in most cases
	Merger costs expensed in year of transaction	

TYPICAL ACCOUNTING-ORIENTED VALUATIONS

If a transaction qualifies for pooling accounting, there are no accounting requirements for valuation of assets. The balance sheets and income statements of the banks are combined at their book values without adjustment.

Valuations for accounting purposes usually are required when a transaction is treated as a purchase. When purchase accounting is used, the seller's assets are restated to current fair market values. Liabilities assumed are recorded at their present value under current interest rates. The value of the payment made (whether in cash, stock, or debt) becomes the basis of the transaction.

The purpose of the purchase accounting valuation is to allocate the price paid to the net assets purchased (i.e, to the net value of the acquired tangible and intangible assets less liabilities assumed). The concept is similar to the tax-oriented valuations for a Section 338 election described earlier in this chapter.

The concept of allocating acquisition cost (including fees and expenses) to acquired net assets is fairly straightforward: The fair market value of all assets acquired (both tangible and intangible) less liabilities assumed must equal the acquisition cost. The basic steps in this process are described next.

First, the tangible assets must be valued. Then the intangible assets are valued. This topic is addressed in general in Chapter 10 and specifically for core deposits in Chapter 17. Then liabilities are valued. The bulk of a bank's liabilities are in customer deposits. Short-term, variable rate, or non-interest-bearing deposits are usually valued at their current levels. Deposits that are long term (over one year) and at fixed rates should be revalued to reflect a premium, if current market rates exceed the deposit instrument's rate, or to reflect a discount, if current rates are below the deposit instrument's rates.

If the acquisition cost exceeds the value of tangible and identified intangible assets net of liabilities, the difference is accounted for on the buyer's balance sheet as goodwill. APB Nos. 16 and 17, and SFAS No. 72 deal with the accounting treatment of goodwill.

Exhibit 9.5 illustrates conceptually how various values interrelate to form the basis of a purchase price allocation for accounting purposes. In this example, the composition of the book assets and liabilities is shown on the left. On a book basis, the net asset book value (the book value of equity) is $8 million. After the valuation, asset values total $108 million. Liabilities are revalued from $92 million book to $93 million market. Therefore, the net asset value is $15 million. This example has a $20 million acquisition cost. Consequently, there will be $5 million of goodwill (the $20 million purchase price less $15 million of market value of net assets).

The valuation of acquired assets and assumed liabilities has a substantial impact on the economics of the transaction. First, goodwill will be amortized in accordance with APB No. 17, thus reducing future reported income. Second, goodwill cannot be used to reduce taxable income (as discussed previously). Third, goodwill is excluded from calculation of Tier 1 capital. In general, a buyer usually wants to minimize the amount of the purchase price allocated to goodwill. Consequently, a thorough identification and valuation of all assets, both tangible and intangible, becomes critically important.

ACQUISITION METHOD

In a business combination, there are explicit standards and provisions for the acquisition method, which contains the steps of application, the accounting for assets acquired and liabilities assumed, and the recognition of gains and losses. Some divergences still exists, even though the new guide is trying to combine the differences in accounting for business combination between U.S. GAAP and IFRS in their prior standards.[6]

According to the IFRS, four steps are required in applying acquisition method:[7]

1. Identifying the acquirer.
2. Determining the acquisition date.
3. Recognizing and measuring the identifiable assets acquired, the liabilities assumed, and any noncontrolling interest in the acquiree.
4. Recognizing and measuring goodwill or a gain from a bargain purchase.

Identifying the Acquirer

The first step in a business combination is to determine which one of the parties should be the acquirer in a business combination. Generally, the party that obtains control is identified as acquirer, and the party that holds directly or indirectly greater than 50 percent of the voting shares has control. However, some parties under certain

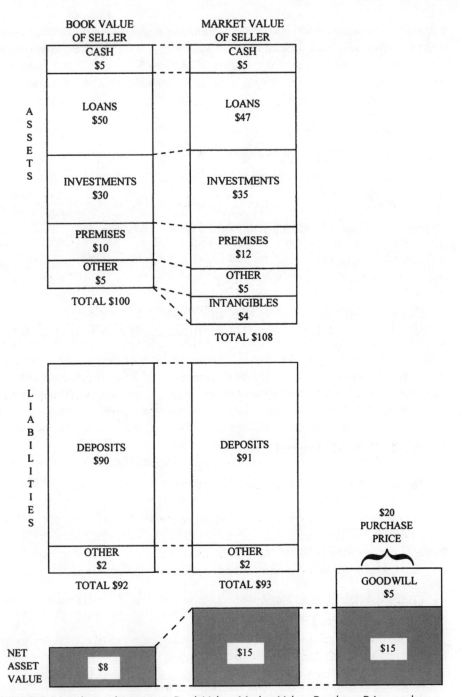

EXHIBIT 9.5 Relationship among Book Value, Market Value, Purchase Price, and Goodwill ($Millions)

uncommon conditions could also be identified as the acquirers. For instance, a variable interest entity that is consolidated could be an acquirer under the U.S. GAAP. Another example is, under IFRS, some entities may hold less than 50 percent of voting power but could identified as acquirers because these entities may have control under certain circumstances.

Determining the Acquisition Date

The second step is to determine the acquisition date. According to IFRS, generally the date on which the acquirer obtains control of acquiree is the acquisition date (i.e., usually the closing date). However, there are exceptions. For instance, the acquisition date may be the date control is obtained through the other transaction or event, such as a business combination achieved without the transfer of consideration. Consequently, it could be earlier or later than the closing date under the circumstance that control transfers by writing agreement. Thus, all relevant facts and situations surrounding should be taken into account in determining acquisition date in a business combination.

Recognizing and Measuring the Identifiable Assets Acquired, Liabilities Assumed, and Any Noncontrolling Interest in the Acquiree

On the acquisition date, identifiable assets acquired and liabilities assumed should be recognized by the acquirer based on the standards of U.S. GAAP and IFRS. In a business combination, certain assets acquired and liabilities assumed that are not considered as the part of assets and liabilities exchanged will be identified as separate transactions.

Subsequently, the acquirer will measure the identifiable assets acquired and liabilities assumed. Generally, the measurement is applied at fair value that has different definitions in U.S. GAAP and IFRS. Based on U.S. GAAP, fair value is the price that would be received from the sale of an asset or paid to transfer a liability in an orderly transaction between market participants. Based on IFRS, fair value is the amount that an asset could be exchanged or a liability settled between knowledgeable, willing parties in an arm's-length transaction.

In this process, all these factors should be recognized and measured, if any:

1. Assets that the acquirer does not intend to use, such as defensive intangible assets
2. Asset valuation allowances
3. Inventory
4. Contracts like loss contracts
5. Intangible assets
6. Reacquired rights, such as determining the value and useful life of reacquired rights
7. Property, plant, and equipment including government grants, consideration of decommissioning, and site restoration costs
8. Income taxes
9. Recognition of assets held for sale
10. Employee benefit plans
11. Payables and debt

12. Guarantees
13. Contingencies, such as initial recognition and measurement, subsequent measurement, and contingent liabilities
14. Indemnification assets
15. Recognition of liabilities related to restructurings or exit activities
16. Deferred or unearned revenue
17. Deferred charges arising from leases
18. Classifying or designating identifiable assets and liabilities
19. Long-term construction contracts

Recognizing and Measuring Goodwill or a Gain from a Bargain Purchase

Goodwill is an asset that represents the future economic benefits caused by other assets acquired in a business combination. Some measurement differences are caused by certain assets and liabilities not being recorded at fair value. The measurement differences will affect the amount of recognized goodwill. In a business combination, goodwill is considered as an asset and not amortized. However, annual impairment tests will influence goodwill if an indication of impairment exists.

According to IFRS, bargain purchases will happen when the acquisition-date amounts of the identifiable net assets acquired, excluding goodwill, exceed the sum of (1) the value of consideration transferred, (2) the value of any noncontrolling interest in the acquiree, and (3) the fair value of any previously held equity interest in the acquire.

It is necessary to identify a gain for a bargain purchase. In addition, a bargain purchase should be recognized immediately by the acquirer in earnings, because it represents an economic gain. After all assets acquired and liabilities assumed have been identified and recognized, the acquirer should review the procedures used to measure these items: (1) identifiable assets acquired and liabilities assumed; (2) noncontrolling interest in the acquiree, if any; (3) acquirer's previously held equity interest in the acquiree, if any; and (4) consideration transferred.

If there is still an indication of a bargain purchase after this review, it should be recognized in earnings and attributed to the acquirer. In this process, consideration transferred should be measured and recognized. Consideration transferred includes acquisition date fair values of the assets transferred, the liabilities caused by the acquirer to the former owners of the acquiree, and the equity interests issued by the acquirer to the former owners of the acquiree. Generally, consideration transferred is measured at fair value. An acquirer should also consider contingent consideration and relevant issues. It is the acquirer's obligation to transfer additional assets or equity interests to the selling shareholders in case of future events occur or conditions are met. Contingent consideration is usually utilized to enable the buyer and seller to agree on the terms of a business combination, even if the ultimate value of the business has not been determined.

Assessing What Is Part of a Business Combination Transaction

According to the IFRS, the acquirer will identify whether any part belongs to a business combination transaction under the circumstance that the acquirer and acquiree may have a preexisting relationship. A transaction could be recognized and accounted for separately from a business combination if it is unrelated to the business combination. It is primarily done for the benefit of the acquirer or the combined entity.

Measurement Period Adjustments

Generally the measurement period is less than a year from the acquisition date. During the measurement period, certain adjustments are needed if there are some changes or new transactions. First, if some new changes may influence the measurement of the amounts, the provisional amounts recognized at the acquisition date should be adjusted according to the new facts and circumstances. Second, if additional assets or liabilities happened as of the acquisition date may influence the recognition of those assets and liabilities as of that date, the adjustments should represent these changes. Finally, if the initial accounting for a business combination is incomplete by the end of the reporting period in which the combination occurs, the acquirer should report in its financial statements provisional amounts for the items for which the accounting is incomplete.

Reverse Acquisitions

Reverse acquisitions that are also business combinations should use the acquisition method as well. A reverse acquisition would happen only if the accounting acquiree meets the definition of a business under the standards. For instance, a reverse acquisition would occur if the entity that issues securities is identified as the acquiree for accounting purposes, and the entity whose equity interests are acquired is the acquirer for accounting purposes.

PRESENTATION, DISCLOSURE, AND TRANSITION REQUIREMENTS OF BUSINESS COMBINATIONS

In many instances, these Federal Deposit Insurance Corporation (FDIC)–assisted transactions can result in significant day one gains. Day one gain is related to the fair value concept. Day one gain is an initial exit price less transaction price. Transaction price is a price that is initially paid to acquire an asset, and exit price is what has been paid for an asset during the acquisition. The computation of the day one gain requires the application of Accounting Standard Codification (ASC) No. 820, *Fair Value Measurements and Disclosures* (formerly SFAS No. 157, *Fair Value Measurements*).[8] The revised standards are intended to move U.S. M&A accounting toward the international standards concept of "fair value" reporting. They are likely to result in greater postclosing volatility in reported earnings for some deal structures. The major point of the standard is the establishment of the fair value hierarchy, which is a three-level hierarchy. Fair value measurements will be classified based on the level of inputs used.

> Level 1. Observable input, which consists of quoted prices in active markets.
> Level 2. Observable input but allows the use of quoted prices for similar assets in active markets.

Level 3. The least preferable but acceptable level on inputs that are based on the entity's own assumptions about what the market participants assumptions would be.

The standard explicitly states that the use of observable inputs should be maximized. Although the rule change of FASB has greatest impact on publicly traded companies, it also will impact companies subject to SFAS No. 141R, which that requires acquirers to:

- Use fair value when recording a target's assets and liabilities.
- Determine the fair value of the consideration paid (such as the acquirer's stock) as of the acquisition date rather than as of the signing date.
- Record earn-outs and other forms of contingent consideration at their fair value as of the acquisition date.
- True up the recorded amounts to actual payments and changes in potential payments through postclosing adjustments to earnings.
- Expense acquisition-related costs as they are incurred.
- Expense most restructuring and exit activity costs at the time of the acquisition.
- Recognize acquired in-process recearch and development as an indefinite-lived intangible asset.
- Accrue lawsuits and other preacquisition contingencies at their fair value if, at the time of the acquisition, they are "more likely than not" to occur (although the FASB is considering cutting back on this change).

SFAS No. 160, *Accounting for Non-Controlling Interests*, deals with the accounting and reporting of M&A transactions.[9] One of the most significant changes is the requirement that transaction costs related to an acquisition, including fees for attorneys, investment bankers, and accountants, be expensed as incurred rather than capitalized over time. Another significant change relates to the way companies account for earn-out arrangements. Under the current accounting rules, earn-outs are recorded when the contingency is resolved, and the earn-outs are considered part of the cost of the acquisition. Under the new accounting rules, earn-outs and other forms of contingent consideration will be recorded at fair value on the acquisition date regardless of the likelihood of payment. U.S. GAAP and IFRS have the same requirements in a majority of the disclosures. The standards of disclosure requirements for business combinations are more extensive and comprehensive than previous guidance under APB Opinion No. 16. The next sections discuss the minimum disclosure requirements, effective dates, and related transition provisions.

Disclosures for Business Combinations

Users of financial statements need to evaluate the relevant nature and financial effects according to the disclosures. When an acquirer completes several business combinations in the same accounting period, each material business combination should report all disclosures. Some disclosures could be aggregated for immaterial business combinations that are collectively material. All disclosures should be made in the period in which the business combination occurs. Based on U.S. GAAP, if an acquisition occurred in a prior reporting period and that period is presented in the financial statements, the disclosures should be included in subsequent financial statements. It is also required that companies disclose information about acquisitions made after the balance sheet date and before the financial statements are issued. If the initial accounting for the business combination is incomplete, the company should describe which disclosures could not be made and why they could not be made.

When the market is declining and banks have a high level of unrealized losses, providing a fair value measurement becomes challenging. To address those issues, FASB issued SFAS No. 157-4 in 2009 to determine fair value when the volume and level of activity for the asset or liability has decreased significantly. The unrealized losses of debt securities for banks when markets are inactive have to be treated as other-than-temporary impairments (OTTI) and be recorded on the bank's financial statement. SFAS No. 157-4 require disclosure of the inputs and valuation techniques used to measure fair value during interim and annual periods. Securities should be segmented into major categories, such as equity securities, debt securities issued by foreign governments, and corporate debt securities, and be disclosed in the financial statements. The new rules give strict guidelines on how to write off losses related to bad debt securities or other financial instruments affecting the structure, timing, and other considerations. Impairment related to credit loss should be recognized in earnings while impairment related to other factors should be recognized in other comprehensive income, net of applicable taxes. The OTTI related to the security's credit loss should be measured as the difference between the present value of the expected cash flows and the amortized cost basis. Pro forma information should also be prepared for the business combination. However, no additional guidance is provided about how entities should calculate pro forma revenue and earnings amounts. One approach would be to add the results from the financial statements of the acquiree to the historical financial results of the acquirer after making some or all of these adjustments: (1) alignment of accounting policies, (2) effect of fair value adjustments, (3) taxation, and (4) financial structure.

Income Statement

Under U.S. GAAP, many items should be identified in income, including transaction costs, restructuring charges, revaluations of contingent consideration, adjustments to acquired contingencies, gain or loss on previously held equity interests, and gain on bargain purchases. Companies should exercise judgment in determining the appropriate income statement classification for these items based on their nature. Generally, the income statement recognition of items should mirror their recognition outside of a business combination, and most items recognized in income should be classified as part of operations. The implementation of SFAS No. 144, *Accounting for the Impairment or Disposal of Long-Lived Assets*, may also affect income statement.[10]

Statement of Cash Flows

Under U.S. GAAP, in most conditions, cash paid to purchase a business, net of any cash acquired, should be presented as a separate line in the investing activities section of the statement of cash flows. Under IFRS, the cash flows arising from obtaining and losing control of subsidiaries or other businesses are required to be reported separately under investing activities in the cash flow statement. The amount of cash paid or received as consideration by obtaining or losing control of subsidiaries or other businesses is reported in the statement of cash flows net of any cash and cash equivalents acquired or disposed of as part of such transaction, events, or changes in conditions. SFAS No.115, *Accounting for Certain Investments in Debt and Equity Securities*, also should be considered as its implications can have some cash flow implications.[11]

CONVERGENCE IN ACCOUNTING STANDARDS ON MERGERS AND ACQUISITIONS

M&A are occurring at a fast pace as companies worldwide look for new ways to improve their efficiency and effectiveness. During the past decade, the volume of mergers and acquisitions has grown. Furthermore, the Gramm-Leach-Bliley Financial Modernization Act of 1999, by allowing combinations between banks and other financial services companies including insurance companies, mutual funds, and stock brokerages, encourages more M&A in the financial services industry. The pace of M&A escalated rapidly during the 1990s and is expected to continue in the twenty-first century. Together, the combined companies should achieve a greater rate of return on investment regardless of the accounting method used to account for business combinations. The International Accounting Standards Board (IASB) in 2008 issued a revised version of its standards for accounting for business combinations such as mergers and acquisitions, in coordination with the FASB.

There have been significant changes in the accounting treatment of M&A transactions; the use of the pooling method has been practically eliminated and it is required that all business combinations be accounted for utilizing the purchase method. The use of the purchase method, which results in goodwill recognition, coupled with the requirement of periodic testing for the goodwill impairments, can cause dilution in the reported earnings and the related earnings per share for M&A deals. Despite the accounting method used in M&A deals, cash flows of the combined companies remain the same, and, accordingly, the cosmetic dilution of earnings and earnings per share under the purchase method reflects artificial accounting differences rather than real economic consequences. Business combinations occur in a situation when an entity acquires either the net assets that constitutes a business or equity interests of one or more other entities and obtains control over that entity or entities. The FASB issued SFAS No. 141 (Revised 2007), *Business Combinations*. The object of this statement is to improve the relevance, representational faithfulness, and comparability of reported information about a business combination and its effects. This statement replaces FASB No. 141 but retains the fundamental requirements that the acquisition method of accounting (previously called the purchase method) be used for all business combinations. The accounting for business combinations has changed substantially with the issuance of FASB ASC No. 805, *Business Combinations* [previously SFAS No. 141(R)]. IFRS business combination standards were also revised in 2008. Both U.S. GAAP and IFRS business combination standards significantly change accounting treatment of M&A activities, how business combinations are accounted for, and effects of financial statements on the acquisition date and in subsequent periods.

Changes are more significant for those banks that prepare their financial statements in accordance with U.S. GAAP than for companies that prepare their statements under IFRS. It is expected that implementation of provisions of both FASB and IASB standards on business combination accounting in ASC No. 805, *Business Combinations,* and in IFRS No. 3 (revised 2008), *Business Combinations,* relevant to M&A activities will continue to have significant impacts on measurement, recognition and disclosure of M&A transactions.[12]

Compliance with U.S. GAAP ASC No. 805 has been effective for all business combinations for which the acquisition date was on or after the beginning of the first annual reporting period beginning on or after December 15, 2008. IFRS accounting standards on business combinations have been applicable for all business combinations for which the acquisition was on or after the beginning of the first annual period beginning on or after July 1, 2009. Prior to the implementation of these standards, there was divergence between the definitions of a business combination between U.S. GAAP and IFRS. The two definitions are basically now converged with some minor differences. For example, both sets of standards require that for a business combination to occur, an acquirer must obtain control over a business; "control," however, is defined differently under U.S. GAAP and IFRS. These differences may cause divergent accounting results.

Both U.S. GAAP and IFRS accounting standards on business combinations are applicable to acquisition transactions. M&A transactions of formation of joint ventures where no one party obtains control in the creation of a joint venture and acquisitions of an asset or a group of assets that does not constitute a business are not within the scope of these standards. An alternative to these standards, which require elimination of the pooling-of-interest method, is to permit the pooling method when an acquirer cannot be identified in situations when: (1) the significant majority of voting common shares of the combining entities are exchanged or pooled; (2) the fair value of one entity is not materially different from that of the entity to be combined with; and (3) the shareholders of each entity maintain substantially the same voting rights and interest in the combined entity. Under the pooling-of-interest method: (1) carrying amounts on the books of the combining entities should be carried forward; (2) no goodwill should be recognized; and (3) prior financial statements should be restated as if the combining entity always had been combined.

 ## CONCLUSION

This chapter presented tax and accounting aspects of M&A. The accounting and tax treatment of M&A transactions has fundamentally changed during the past decade; use of the pooling method has been eliminated and now it is required that all business combinations be accounted utilizing the purchase method. The use of the purchase method results in goodwill recognition and periodic testing for goodwill impairments that affect both reported income and taxes of combined companies. In a business combination, assets acquired and liabilities assumed may give rise to deferred taxes that should be recognized and measured. The acquirer should account for the potential tax effects of temporary differences, carryforwards, and income tax uncertainties of an acquiree. Disclosure requirements under current U.S GAAP and IFRS for business combinations are extensive and comprehensive, as discussed in this chapter.

 NOTES

1. The overall transaction would be considered nontaxable, although shareholders receiving cash would be taxed on their gain.
2. "Boot" is the designation for property that, transferred in an otherwise nontaxable transaction, gives rise to taxable income.
3. Accounting Principles Board Opinion No. 16, *Business Combinations.*
4. Financial Accounting Standards Board, Statement of Accounting Standards Board No. 141, *Business Combinations*, and FASB Statement No. 141 (Revised 2007), *Business Combinations*, and now Accounting Standards Codification No. 805 (Norwalk, CT: Author 2009).
5. Financial Accounting Standards Board, Statement of Accounting Standards Board No. 142, *Goodwill and Other Intangible Assets*, and now Accounting Standards Codification (ASC) 350, (Norwalk, CT: Author 2009).
6. PricewaterhouseCoopers, *A Global Guide to Accounting for Business Combinations and Noncontrolling Interests*, 2010. Available at: www.pwc.com.
7. Ibid.
8. Financial Accounting Standards Board. Statement of Financial Accounting Standards No. 157, *Fair Value Measurements* (Norwalk, CT: Author, 2006).
9. Financial Accounting Standards Board, Statement of Financial Accounting Standards No. 160, *Accounting for Non-controlling Interests* (Norwalk, CT: Author, 2006).
10. Financial Accounting Standards Board, Statement of Accounting Standards Board No. 144, *Accounting for the Impairment or Disposal of Long-Lived Assets*, and now Accounting Standards Codification 360-10 (Norwalk, CT: Author, 2009).
11. Financial Accounting Standards Board, Statement of Accounting Standards Board No. 115, *Accounting for Certain Investments in Debt and Equity Securities*, and now Accounting Standards Codification No. 320 (Norwalk, CT: Author, 2009).
12. International Accounting Standards Board, International Financial Reporting Standard No. 3 (revised 2008), *Business Combinations.*

CHAPTER TEN

Intangible Asset Valuation

O FTEN IT IS NECESSARY for tax and accounting purposes, as described in Chapter 9, to value the intangible assets of an acquired company. This chapter addresses the unique characteristics of intangible assets and their role in the acquisition process. Specific examples of bank intangible assets are used where appropriate.

 ## NATURE AND TYPES OF INTANGIBLE ASSETS

Intangible assets do not have physical substance but are nonetheless integral components of the overall value of a business. The value of an intangible asset is usually a result of economic benefits that accrue to the owner. The fact that the purchase price of a business exceeds the net value of tangible assets confirms that intangible assets have benefits and the buyer perceives them to have value.

Criteria for Defining Intangible Assets

By standards of common law, assets such as stocks, bonds, and loans are considered intangible. For tax and accounting purposes in acquisitions, however, these types of assets are not considered intangible. For tax and accounting purposes, an asset is intangible if it possesses two key characteristics:

1. *Immateriality*[1]. This criterion distinguishes an intangible asset from a nontangible asset. Intangible assets are considered immaterial noncurrent assets, which means they have a relatively permanent nature and are not intended for sale. Nontangible

assets, however, are claims against other parties, such as notes and receivables, and could be sold individually. It is for this reason that the loans of a bank are not considered intangible assets even though they are incorporeal property. In Chapter 9, these were referred to as tangible financial assets.

2. *Inseparability.* Assets are considered intangible if they are inseparable from the active business. In other words, the intangible asset, separated from the business, is usually worthless or meaningless.

Under most circumstances, it is necessary to identify and value intangible assets only for tax and accounting reasons. Substantial tax benefits can be derived from valuing the intangible assets, and there are financial reporting requirements that need to be met. The common types of intangible assets likely to be found in an acquired bank are described next. Not all of these will or can be amortizable for tax purposes. Nonetheless, it is useful to consider their value when analyzing an acquisition.

Core Deposit Base

The core deposit base of a bank is composed of the funds associated with stable customer deposit relationships. An intangible asset is created because the bank has a source of funding that is usually less costly than the market rate of alternative funds on the open market.

Deposits are a liability of a bank, and for many this has negative implications: How can a liability be an asset? To understand this seemingly contradictory statement, it is necessary to view deposits as the raw materials of banks. With them, banks invest in earning assets at a spread to generate a profit. Deposits are so beneficial that banks are willing to pay to attract them through branches, advertising, and premiums in addition to interest paid. Consequently, when a bank and its deposits are acquired, there is a definite economic benefit to the buyer. Chapter 17 addresses the core deposit base as an intangible asset in detail because it is such a crucial part of bank acquisition valuation.

Claim for Future Income

The point that earnings give the value of intangible assets is implicitly acknowledged in statements of those who claim the existence of intangible assets, that is, a legal claim to some future benefit, typically a claim to future cash such as goodwill, intellectual property, patents, copyrights, and trademarks, and so on. In terms of stocks, a stock's worth is equal to the present value of all its estimated future cash flows. Analysts analyze the projected revenues, costs, and capital requirements associated with commercializing the intangible, estimated time to commercialize the asset, estimated cost of noninfringing alternatives, time value of money (cost of capital) associated with the intangible, and impact of the commercialization on working capital (accounts receivables and account payables) in order to construct a clear financial projection for future cash flows.

Loan Servicing Contracts

Often a bank will sell a loan it has made but retain the right to service it—take payments, keep records, and so on—for a fee. The buyer of the loan receives the interest and principal payments without the responsibilities and costs of operations. The fee the bank receives for servicing the loan in excess of the operations costs incurred is the economic benefit, and an intangible asset.

Safe Deposit Box Contracts

Banks that have safe deposit boxes rent these boxes to customers for specified monthly fees. Often the book value of the boxes is minimal or nonexistent—the boxes have long since been depreciated. Because they still have economic utility, they continue to generate income. The value of this future income stream in excess of the expenses associated with the safe deposit boxes is an intangible asset.

Proprietary Computer Software

When a bank develops computer software for its own use, it does so at considerable expense and consequently creates an asset that has value. The extent of that value usually is based on the cost necessary to acquire similar software or on the time that was required to develop it originally. With the proliferation of packaged banking software, proprietary programs are becoming less common, especially in smaller community banks.

Trust Accounts

Banks that maintain trust departments manage assets for customers for a fee. Like loan servicing contracts, the fees received for managing trust accounts, in excess of costs, create an intangible asset.

Leasehold Interests

Often banks operate branches in leased quarters or on leased ground. These leases are often long term in nature and sometimes at rental rates below the market for similar properties. The difference between the lease rate paid by the bank and the current market rate over the life of the lease, discounted to present value, is an intangible asset.

Assembled Workforce

When a bank is acquired, the in-place staff represents an intangible asset. The costs to attract, recruit, and train an equivalent staff—their replacement cost—would be substantial. Consequently, there is value in the staff of the acquired bank.

Goodwill

Goodwill is a catchall intangible asset. It reflects the difference between the price paid for a bank (or any business) and the bank's value of the tangible and identified intangible assets, less the liabilities assumed. From a strategic valuation standpoint, separating goodwill from other intangibles is not that critical. From a tactical standpoint, however, the separation can be very important for tax and accounting reasons, as discussed in Chapter 9. Goodwill represents the future economic benefits caused by other assets acquired in a business combination. In a business combination, goodwill is considered as an asset and not amortized.

Intangible Asset Impairments

Intangible asset impairment is a rather complex issue. To better reflect the underlying market value of the intangible assets, the Financial Accounting Standards Board (FASB) issued Statement of Financial Accounting Standard (SFAS) No. 142, which provides a clear path to measure intangible asset impairments. Intangible assets have to be tested annually according to the guidelines using a two-step process that begins with an estimation of the fair value of a reporting unit. The first step is a screen for potential impairment, and the second step measures the amount of impairment, if any. However, if certain criteria are met, the requirement to test intangibles for impairment annually can be satisfied without a remeasurement of the fair value of a reporting unit.[2]

Asset Management

The asset management (investment management or fund management) provision includes many different aspects and relative fields. Among them are asset and stock selection, monitoring of investments, elements of financial statement analysis, and plan implementation. Asset management with a global aspect can mean managing local and physical (tangible) assets of a company; or it can be detailed management of intangible assets. As intangible assets are a major component of market capitalization and price stability, the application of the uniform valuation metrics and active risk management are the new challenges according to the Intangible Asset Finance Society.

 ## AMORTIZABLE VERSUS NONAMORTIZABLE INTANGIBLE ASSETS

As discussed in Chapter 8, the total value of a business is the sum of the tangible and intangible asset values less liabilities assumed. The intangible assets can be identified intangibles (such as core deposit base and loan service contracts) or unidentified intangibles (goodwill). Moreover, the identified intangibles can be either amortizable (enabling a depreciationlike deduction against taxable income to be taken) or non-amortizable (not eligible for the deduction). Consequently, the total value of a business could be described as:

$$\text{Total value of a business} = \text{Tangible asset value}$$
$$+ \text{Amortizable intangible asset value}$$
$$+ \text{Nonamortizable intangible asset value}$$
$$+ \text{Goodwill}$$
$$- \text{Liabilities assumed}$$

The ability to first identify an intangible asset and then prove it amortizable can yield significant tax savings and result in increased postacquisition cash flow.

Benefits of Amortization

"Amortization" refers to the depreciation of an intangible asset. It is based on the concept of the wasting or exhaustible asset, although an intangible asset does not waste away as a physical asset does. The wasting away of an intangible asset is legal fiction but is necessary to consider in order to spread the recovery of a payment for that intangible asset over its fixed or useful life.

If an intangible asset can be amortized, significant tax savings often can be realized. The potential tax savings is equal to the amortization amount multiplied by the marginal tax rate. For example, if intangible assets valued at $10 million are amortizable over, say, ten years, and the marginal tax rate is 35 percent, annual tax savings to the acquiror of $350,000 are possible.

Requirements for Amortization

The Internal Revenue Service (IRS) has issued several rulings that relate to the issue of intangible assets amortization. The two most significant are Revenue Ruling 68-483 and Revenue Ruling 74-456. In general, these rulings hold that in order for an intangible asset to be amortizable for federal income tax purposes, it must meet three tests:

1. It must be separated and isolated from goodwill; that is, it must be separately identifiable.
2. It must have a limited useful life.
3. That limited life must be measurable with reasonable accuracy.

Separating intangible assets from nonamortizable goodwill is never considered easy. In general, the IRS has been very aggressive in its interpretation of goodwill and tends to allocate as many intangible assets as possible to that category. However, separate identification of intangible assets historically has not been the main cause for denial of the amortization deduction. The more common reason for disallowance is the inability to establish and measure a limited useful life. Consequently, it may be possible to identify an intangible asset but not be able to life it (i.e., to establish and measure its useful life). Then it is classified as a nonamortizable identified intangible asset and treated no differently from goodwill for tax purposes.

The ability to life an intangible asset depends on (1) proving the asset has a limited life and (2) measuring that life. In determining whether an intangible has a limited life, it is useful to ask these two questions:

1. Does the asset's value to the business diminish progressively over time?
2. Is the availability of the asset to the business limited, irrespective of that asset's current or future value?

The first question applies to intangible assets that do not regenerate naturally. Core deposit accounts tend to be viewed as nonregenerative intangibles. In other words, over time, core deposit relationships will naturally dwindle as customers move and businesses close.

An example of the second question is the intangible asset created by a below-market lease rate on a branch. The value actually may increase if market lease rates escalate, but if the lease is in effect for only five years, its availability to the bank is limited and so it has a limited useful life.

The second key aspect in lifing an intangible asset is measuring the length of that useful life. Unless the intangible asset has a clear duration (as in the branch lease example), estimating the life is usually the most difficult aspect of proving it to be amortizable. The courts have indicated in numerous cases that the life need only be determined with *reasonable*, not *perfect*, accuracy. In practice, the most supportable lives are based on in-depth, comprehensive analyses of the experiences of the business owning the asset.

 ## MEASURING THE USEFUL LIFE OF AN INTANGIBLE ASSET

Measuring the life of an intangible asset is relatively straightforward if there is a contractual life without renewal possibilities. Unfortunately, few intangible assets as part of a bank acquisition are this clear-cut. Most have lives that can be determined only by experience, such as being based on the historical pattern of the availability and usefulness of the intangible asset to the bank. For example, the core deposit base of a bank is composed of individual customer relationships and theoretically could stay active in perpetuity. In reality, however, the deposit base acquired at a given time has a finite life and eventually will diminish through the natural process of customers moving and businesses closing. This same concept can be applied to many other bank-related intangibles, such as safe deposit box contracts and trust accounts.

Intangibles without a stated contractual life are those most vulnerable to IRS attack and potential disallowance of amortization deduction. Consequently, it is essential that the life of intangible assets to be amortized be established from thorough, objective analysis. Two factors appear to improve the supportability of a useful life calculation:

1. Using the unique experience of the business being acquired relative to the intangible asset being lifed—in other words, not using industry averages or other businesses' experiences as the basis for the life
2. Where possible, lifing each component of the intangible asset base or as small a component as possible—for example, with loan servicing contracts, estimating the average life of each contract based on its characteristics rather than an overall average

Both of these factors are discussed next in more detail.

Unique Experience

The *unique experience* aspect necessitates a detailed analysis of the historical data of the bank being acquired. This requirement often results in tedious data collection, especially in smaller banks where historical records are not always in machine-readable form. Often the investment in such data gathering, however, is justified by the potential tax savings.

The types of historical data to be gathered to measure useful life will vary depending on the nature of the particular intangible asset. In most cases, however, it is desirable to determine a start date (when the account was opened or the contract started) and an end date (when the account was closed or the contract terminated) for the various components of the intangible asset. If these two dates can be identified for each component for a significant historical time period (say, five years), the historical attrition rates can be gauged and an overall average useful life measured.

Very few banks maintain the meticulous records necessary to determine the start and end dates for each component of an intangible asset over a five-year historical period. This information is especially difficult for components that are not active at the time of analysis but are needed to establish the statistical base. For example, if the life of a core deposit base is being measured, it is necessary to retrieve data on accounts opened and already closed as well as accounts opened and still active. It is the closed accounts that can be difficult to analyze, since most banks purge them from their automated systems.

One technique used to compensate for this lack of data involves first identifying the active accounts at the end of each year for, say, the past five years and at the date of the acquisition. Then, starting with the first year, the account numbers (or contract numbers) are tracked through each successive year to determine if they were still active at the end of the second year, at the end of the third year, and so on to the time of acquisition. At some point, the accounts or contracts may disappear from the list, showing that their closing date was during that year. This technique is not perfectly accurate because the exact end date is not known, but if applied properly, this method usually achieves the reasonable accuracy criterion for the courts. A detailed discussion of the use of a bank's unique experience to establish core deposit life is included in Chapter 17.

Individual Component Analysis

Tax law surrounding intangible assets involves a concept known as the *mass asset rule.* The courts have defined a mass asset to be a group of intangible assets grouped together for the convenience of the owner of the business. If one mass asset is acquired and not a group of individual intangible assets, the amortization deduction will not be allowed. The courts have reasoned that a mass asset does not have a determinable or measurable useful life, even though some of the individual components do. Consequently, to support an amortization deduction, it is necessary to prevent intangible assets from being classified as mass assets.

The mass asset rule was first applied in a 1925 court case when a buyer of a newspaper subscription list was denied amortization of the list's value.[3] This case and a number of others through the mid-1960s took a hard line on mass assets being in the nature of goodwill and therefore nonamortizable. This rule typically was invoked when the intangible asset in question was some type of customer or subscription list.

The first break in the hard-line application of the mass asset rule came in the *Seaboard* case.[4] The taxpayer was allowed an amortization of the premium paid for loan servicing contracts. The aggregate premium was valued based on an analysis of each loan and its unique characteristics. In this case, the methodology led the court to conclude that each loan contract had a separately identified value to the taxpayer, and, therefore, the taxpayer acquired separate loan contracts and not a mass asset.

After the *Seaboard* case, it appeared that amortization required each component to be lifed and valued individually. This made the practical application difficult and expensive. In 1969, however, in the *Western Mortgage* case, the taxpayer was allowed an amortization deduction on mortgage loan servicing rights even though each loan was not lifed and valued individually.[5] The court held that the taxpayer properly measured an *average* service life of the acquired mortgage portfolio. This important case expanded the practical applicability of supporting intangible asset lives. The IRS was, however, still arguing that intangible assets were inseparable from goodwill.

The most crucial case in the erosion of the mass asset rule was the *First Pennsylvania* case.[6] This 1971 case also involved loan servicing contracts and the estimate of the useful life of these contracts, which varied due to prepayment and refinancings by borrowers. The arguments in the case centered on the useful life estimate, not on whether the loan servicing contracts represented an intangible asset separable from goodwill. The potential amortization of the asset was conceded by the IRS by virtue of the fact that the IRS introduced witnesses to dispute the taxpayer's estimate of useful life. If the intangible asset had been no different from goodwill, there would have been no need to dispute the life estimate. Revenue Ruling 68-483 (issued in 1968) stated "whether or not an intangible asset, or a tangible asset, is depreciable for Federal income tax purposes depends on the determination that the asset is actually exhausting, and that such exhaustion is susceptible to measurement." Here the IRS explicitly states that if the intangible asset can be proven to be wasting (i.e., having a measurable and finite useful life), it can be amortized.

Revenue Ruling 74-456 (issued in 1974) stated that certain intangible assets, such as customer and subscription lists, generally have indeterminable useful lives and are not amortizable, except in unusual cases where the asset's life can be measured and its value determined. The IRS, therefore, is on record as stating that unusual circumstances may exist to justify intangible asset amortization even where the useful life is not known with certainty.

In general, given the history of the mass asset rule and the IRS position of requiring unusual circumstances, it is best to have a detailed analysis of the individual intangible assets. The useful life estimation will be on more solid foundation with a detailed analysis.

 ## ESTABLISHING VALUE OF INTANGIBLE ASSETS

Once the intangible asset has been identified (thus being separable from goodwill) and lifed (avoiding the mass asset problem), it needs to be valued. Identifying and lifing an intangible asset establishes it as amortizable. The value is needed to arrive at the dollar amount of that amortization deduction.

The general techniques used to value intangible assets are the same as those used to value any asset: the *cost*, *market*, and *income* approaches. The particular situation and nature of the asset will determine the best approach.

Cost Approach

The cost approach values an intangible asset based on the cost necessary to replace it with one of comparable utility. This approach can be used, for example, to value proprietary software based on the cost to purchase or develop similar software. The cost approach could also be applied to such intangible assets as the core deposit base, based on the cost to create an equal level of deposits. This particular technique, however, is rarely applied to core deposits because other techniques are available that are more supportable.

This approach uses the concept of replacement as an indicator of fair value and is based on the principle of substitution. In general, in order to use the cost approach to value an intangible asset it is necessary to estimate with reasonable accuracy the cost to purchase, develop, or create a similar asset. It is this requirement that causes the cost approach to be difficult to apply to many intangible assets. If some intangible assets are readily replicated or replaced, such as routine software, the cost approach that commonly is used to value machinery and equipment will be used to estimate the fair value.

Market Approach

The market approach to valuation requires comparable transaction data. This approach estimates fair value by analyzing observed trading prices and other relevant information in market transactions. Due to the nature of intangible assets, especially their in- separability from the total business, they are rarely sold individually. Consequently, direct market comparables are virtually nonexistent. Even indirect comparables are usually not available. Publicly reported data might show total premium paid for an acquisition, but the allocation of that premium among various intangible assets is not reported. Only in unusual circumstances can the market approach be used to value an intangible asset.

When market data is reasonably available, this approach will be used to measure the fair value of an intangible asset. For example, when some types of intangible assets may trade as separate portfolios, such as brands, cable television, or wireless telephone service subscriptions, they could be valued in this approach.

Income Approach

The income approach typically uses the discounted cash flow method to convert future amounts to a single present value. The income approach is the most common technique used to value intangible assets is. This technique is directly applicable because most intangible assets result from an economic benefit (some level of income) that accrues to the asset's owner. In simplest terms, the value of an intangible asset is the income stream (less related expenses) over the useful life of the asset, discounted to present value. The income approach is the most common method for valuing intangible. Some other variations of the income approach are the (1) multiperiod excess earnings method, (2) relief-from-royalty method, (3) Greenfield method, and (4) with and without method.

A simple example using safe deposit box contracts can illustrate the calculation. (For this illustration, tax benefits are assumed to be zero. As described in Chapter 9, however, when amortization of an intangible results in tax savings, those future tax savings should be reflected in the value.) Assume that the average life of a safe deposit box contract is five years, the total safe deposit income to a bank is $100,000 a year, and annual costs associated with the safe deposit boxes (depreciation, maintenance, salary for clerk, etc.) total $60,000. The value of these safe deposit contracts is calculated as

EXHIBIT 10.1 Valuation of Safe Deposit Box Contracts

Year	Safe Deposit Boxes Net Income	Discount Factor @ 8.5%	Present Value
1	$40,000	9217	$ 36,868
2	40,000	8495	33,980
3	40,000	7829	33,316
4	40,000	6650	26,600
5	40,000	6129	24,516
	Net Present Value		$155,280

shown in Exhibit 10.1. The value of the safe deposit box contracts in force on the date of acquisition is about $155,000.

A variation of the income approach is the cost savings method. This method is used when the intangible asset does not produce income but allows the owner to avoid costs that otherwise might be incurred. The value is equal to the cost savings over the life of the asset, discounted to present value. A favorable lease can be valued using the cost savings method. For example, suppose that a bank has a 2,500-square-foot branch in the lobby of an office building leased at a rate of $15 per square foot per year, but market rates for comparable space are $20 per square foot each year. Also, suppose the lease has seven years remaining before the bank must renew at market rates. The value of the intangible asset created by a below-market rate leasehold interest is calculated as shown in Exhibit 10.2. The value of the intangible asset created by the lease, because of cost savings, is about $64,000.

EXHIBIT 10.2 Valuation of a Below-Market Rate Lease

Year	Market Rent[*]	Lease Rate Rent[†]	Cost Savings	Discount Factor @ 13%	Present Value
1	$50,000	$37,500	$12,500	.885	$11,025
2	50,000	37,500	12,500	.783	9,728
3	50,000	37,500	12,500	.693	8,663
4	50,000	37,500	12,500	.613	7,663
5	50,000	37,500	12,500	.543	6,788
6	50,000	37,500	12,500	.480	6,000
7	50,000	37,500	12,500	.425	5,313
			Net Present Value		$55,340

[*]2,500 square feet multiplied by $20, for simplicity, assumes market rate does not increase over lease period.

[†]2,500 square feet multiplied by $15.

AMORTIZATION METHODS

Once the intangible asset has been valued, the annual deduction for taxes must be calculated to determine the annual amortization. The most common way to ascertain the annual amortization deduction of an intangible asset is the *time method.* This method computes the deduction in this way:

Annual amortization deduction = Value of intangible/Useful life in years

This method is analogous to straight-line depreciation used for tangible assets.

Another approach is the *income forecast method,* which measures the amortization in a given year based on the percent of total income or cost savings from the asset likely to be generated in that year. This approach is used when the total benefit of an intangible asset is not evenly distributed over its useful life. A good example, outside of banking, is film rights. Typically the income from a film is higher in the first few years because it is most likely to be popular when it is new. Consequently, the owner of the film rights would amortize more of the value in early years than in later years of the useful life. Tax court rulings, especially the *Citizens & Southern Bancorporation* case described in Chapter 17, support the possibility of using the income forecast method for core deposit base amortization.[7]

The *cost recovery method* is a third technique of determining amortization deduction. This approach uses the actual experience during a taxable year to determine the decline in value of an asset. This method has been used to amortize magazine subscription lists based on the actual number of lost subscribers during a year.

 ## SUPPORTING INTANGIBLE ASSET VALUATION AND AMORTIZATION

Intangible asset valuation should not be an afterthought but an integral part of the negotiations and acquisition agreement. To improve the supportability of intangible asset amortization, it is beneficial to follow these seven key guidelines:

1. *Be familiar with the latest IRS rulings.* The acquiring bank and its counsel should become familiar with cases involving intangible assets, especially cases related to financial institution related. Understanding the reasoning of the courts and the IRS positions is helpful in designing a more supportable acquisition tax plan.
2. *Include intangible asset value in acquisition agreement.* The binding acquisition agreement should state the classes of tangible and intangible assets being acquired and the allocation of the purchase price among them. This will help support the separability of amortizable intangible assets from goodwill and nonamortizable intangible assets.
3. *Avoid the temptation to eliminate goodwill completely.* Very seldom is there a bank acquisition that does not involve some element of goodwill. Consequently, a portion of the purchase price should be allocated to goodwill and included in the contract.

4. *Be meticulous when establishing useful lives.* The establishment of a useful life is the area the IRS is likely to find fault. Consequently, the best techniques, using the bank's own unique data and experiences when possible, should be employed. Perfect accuracy is not required, only reasonable accuracy. In general, however, the closer to perfect, the better the argument can be supported.

5. *Establish intangible asset values professionally.* The supportability of value is strengthened when independent, qualified valuation professionals are used. Their experience and objectivity strengthen the taxpayer's evidence if valuation professionals called on to defend the amortization deduction. Moreover, professionals will be aware of the best techniques to use in a given situation.

6. *Maintain good records.* From the first step in the acquisition process, the buyer should maintain complete records, especially related to the assets purchased and their value. Consequently, it is often beneficial to have preliminary valuations of major intangible assets early in the process.

7. *Be reasonable and logical.* Once all the research and analysis is completed, it should be checked for reasonableness and logic. Consider how the IRS might attack assumptions and techniques used.

By following these seven guidelines, the likelihood increases that intangible asset amortization will be supportable.

 ## GOODWILL IMPAIRMENT

As discussed in Chapter 9, in a business combination, goodwill is considered as an asset and should not be amortized. Instead, annual impairment tests should be conducted to determine whether an indication of goodwill impairment exists.

Impairment Test

SFAS No.142 requires goodwill be assigned to reporting units and test for impairment periodically. There are two steps of goodwill impairment test. Step 1 is comparing a reporting unit's fair value to its carrying amount. It is used as a screening process to identify potential goodwill impairment. Step 2 is to measure the amount of the reporting unit's goodwill impairment loss, if the carrying amount of a reporting unit is more than the reporting unit's fair value. To perform step 1 of the goodwill impairment test, an entity must:

1. *Identify its reporting units.* The unit of accounting for goodwill is at a level of the entity referred to as a reporting unit. For the annual or event-driven impairment assessment, it is important to identify the reporting units.

2. *Assign assets and liabilities to its reporting units.* An entity should be assigned the appropriate assets and liabilities to the respective reporting units in a goodwill impairment test, if both of these criteria are met:
   a. The asset will be employed in or the liability related to the operations of a reporting unit.

b. The asset or liability will be considered in determining the fair value of the reporting unit.

3. *Assign all goodwill to one or more of its reporting units.* Goodwill must be assigned to one or more reporting units as of the acquisition date, no matter whether other assets or liabilities of the acquired entity also are assigned to those reporting units. An entity might follow one of two approaches when assigning goodwill to reporting units: an acquisition method approach and a with-and-without approach.

4. *Determine the fair value of those reporting units to which goodwill has been assigned.*

Impairment Model

Goodwill is deemed impaired if its carrying amount exceeds its implied fair value. To identify a potential impairment and measure an impairment loss, a two-step impairment test is performed:

Step 1. Compare the fair value of the reporting unit with the reporting unit's carrying amount, including goodwill, to identify any potential impairment.

1. If the reporting unit's fair value is more than its carrying amount, the reporting unit's goodwill is considered not impaired, and step 2 is not needed.

2. If the reporting unit's fair value is less than its carrying amount, the reporting unit's goodwill may be impaired, and step 2 must be applied to detect the amount of the goodwill impairment loss.

Step 2. Compare the implied fair value of the reporting unit's goodwill with the carrying amount of the reporting unit's goodwill.

1. If the carrying amount of the reporting unit's goodwill is more than the implied fair value of the reporting unit's goodwill, an impairment loss should be recognized for the excess.

2. After a goodwill impairment loss for a reporting unit is measured and recognized, the adjusted carrying amount of the reporting unit's goodwill becomes the new accounting basis for that goodwill. A subsequent reversal of previously recognized goodwill impairment losses is prohibited if the measurement of that impairment loss is recognized.

Disposal Considerations

When a reporting unit is to be disposed of in its entirety, the entity must include in the reporting unit's carrying amount the goodwill of that reporting unit in determining the gain or loss on disposal. When some, but not all, of a reporting unit is to be disposed of, the accounting for that reporting unit's goodwill will depend on whether the net assets that are to be disposed of constitute a business.

 CONCLUSION

This chapter examined the unique characteristics of intangible assets and their role in the acquisition process. All identifiable intangible assets acquired should be recognized in a business combination. Whether an intangible asset is identifiable depends on whether it meets the contractual-legal criterion or the separability criterion as discussed in this chapter. Intangible assets that cannot be disposed of individually should be combined if they have similar useful lives that can be determined by relevant economic and legal considerations. Generally, if intangible assets have a determinable useful life, they will be amortized over the useful life using an appropriate method presented in this chapter. The method of amortization for all intangible assets with a finite life should reflect the pattern in which the economic benefits are expected to be consumed by the entity.

 NOTES

1. "Immateriality" as used here is a legal term meaning the assets do not have material—physical—substance. It does not mean immaterial in the economic or accounting sense.
2. Financial Accounting Standards Board, Statement of Accounting Standards Board No. 142, *Goodwill and Other Intangible Assets*, and now Accounting Standards Codification No. 350 (Norwalk, CT: Author 2001).
3. *Danville Press Inc. v. Comr.*, 1 B.T.A. 1171 (1925).
4. *Comr. v. Seaboard Finance Co.*, 367 F.2d 646 (9th cir. 1966), cert. denied, 372 U.S. 935 (1963).
5. *Western Mortgage Corporation v. Comr.*, 308 F.Supp. 333 (C.D. Cal. 1969).
6. *First Pennsylvania Banking & Trust Co. v. Comr.*, 56 T.C. 677 (1971), acq. 1972-1 C.B. 2.
7. See the discussion of the *Citizens & Southern Bancorporation* case in Chapter 17 for an example of core deposit amortization.

PART FOUR

IV

Assessment of Financial Institutions

CHAPTER ELEVEN

Financial Analysis of Banks and Bank Holding Companies

THE ANALYSIS OF THE financial performance of a bank to be valued is one of the most essential parts of the valuation research process. The financial performance, however, is only the quantified reflection of the management of the institution. In other words, the financial statistics are not the bank, but they represent a scorecard of how well the bank is organized and operated. Consequently, a thorough analysis of the financials provides an objective assessment of performance. The financial data presented in this chapter are taken from the Uniform Bank Performance Report (UBPR) prepared by the Federal Financial Institutions Examination Council, the National Information Center (NIC) and the Bank Holding Company Performance Report (BHCPR).[1]

 ## TYPES AND SOURCES OF FINANCIAL DATA

Banks, because of their regulated nature, are required to submit substantial amounts of financial data to regulators. Much of the financial information is made available to the public. The format of reporting is identical, which allows for apples-to-apples comparisons across banks of different sizes and in different locations with the knowledge that the information is probably 99 percent consistent.

Financial information on banks and bank holding companies (BHCs) is available on an individual basis or in total for various peer groups. In a typical valuation, information at both levels is beneficial; then it is possible to analyze the bank directly and to compare it with its peer group.

Uniform Bank Performance Report

One of the more useful reports available is the Uniform Bank Performance Report (UBPR) prepared by the Federal Financial Institutions Examination Council primarily for bank management as an analytical tool to help supervise and examine financial institutions. It emphasizes trends in profitability, asset quality, liquidity, and asset-liability management. This report presents a comprehensive profile of a bank for a five-year period, along with comparisons to peer groups. It serves as an analysis of the impact that management and economic conditions can have on a bank's balance sheet. Data in this report are collected by a survey of commercial banks and shared with participating banks, although, unlike call report data, they are not publicly disclosed. The statistics presented in a UBPR for a given bank are divided into four broad sections. The first section of the UBPR presents summary ratios that provide an overview of the bank. Key ratios are shown in the areas of income and expenses as percents of average assets, nonperforming loans, liquidity and rate sensitivity, capitalization, and overall growth rates. Ratios for banks in the peer group are also shown. This allows for easy comparison between Example Bank and its peers.

The second section of the UBPR presents a wide variety of statistics relative to income performance. A summary five-year income statement is shown, along with ratios of expenses to assets, margins, yields on earning assets, cost of funds, noninterest income, and overhead expenses as a percent of both assets and total income.

The UBPR's third section is a dissection of the bank's balance sheet. A detailed breakdown of loans and investments is shown, along with nonearning assets. The liabilities are also shown, with core and noncore deposits listed separately. The capital levels and composition are analyzed in great detail. This section also presents in-depth statistics on loans and loan losses, asset/liability management, and liquidity.

The fourth and final section of the UBPR presents a variety of ratios for banks in the same state as the Example Bank and those in the same peer group. Also presented are statistics on any foreign offices of the subject bank.

Bank Holding Company Performance Report

A report similar to the UBPR is the Bank Holding Company Performance Report (BHCPR). This is an essential report if the banking organization being analyzed is a holding company. The Federal Reserve System provides this report to the public.

The BHCPR contains four major sections. The first section contains various ratios of profitability, loan losses, liquidity, and debt and equity on a consolidated basis (i.e., for the parent company and all subsidiaries). The ratios for the peer group are also shown.

The second section is a summary of various income and expense levels and ratios. Income and expenses are shown as a percent of assets, with margins and yields also computed. These statistics are presented on a consolidated basis.

The third section is a detailed balance sheet analysis, including a five-year summary of assets, liabilities, and capital, along with a multitude of balance sheet ratios. Special tables are produced for loan losses, liquidity, and capital. As in the preceding two sections, the statistics are presented on a consolidated basis.

The last section presents the balance sheet and income statement of the parent company only and selected ratios with peer group comparisons. Unless the holding company has significant nonbanking activities, the parent company statistics should be relatively minor in relation to the consolidated total.

Other Public Sources

The UBPR and BHCPR are invaluable sources of financial data on a bank or BHC. If specific call reports—the financial statements banks submit to regulators—are desired, these can be obtained from the National Information Center (NIC) Web site (www.ffiec .gov/nicpubweb/nicweb/nichome.aspx). The NIC provides comprehensive information on banks and other financial institutions, including both domestic and foreign institutions operating in the United States in which the Federal Reserve has a supervisory, regulatory, or research interest.

In recent years, various regulatory agencies have used the same format for every bank and BHC irrespective of whether it is state, national, Federal Reserve System member, or non-Fed member. There are, however, degrees of detail in the call reports depending on the size of the bank and whether it has non-U.S. offices. For banks, there are four call reports:

1. *FFIEC 031.* For banks with domestic and foreign offices
2. *FFIEC 032.* For banks with assets over $300 million and domestic offices only
3. *FFIEC 033.* For banks with assets between $100 million and $300 million, and domestic offices only
4. *FFIEC 034.* For banks with assets below $100 million and domestic offices only

These reports are all in the same basic format, with slightly less detailed reporting requirements for smaller banks.

BHCs, which report consolidated and parent company financial data to the Federal Reserve, have three different forms:

1. *FR Y-9C.* Consolidated financial statements for BHCs with more than $150 million in assets and all BHCs with two or more subsidiary banks
2. *FR Y-9LP.* Parent-only financial statements for BHCs with more than $150 million in assets and all BHCs with two or more subsidiary banks
3. *FR Y-9SP.* Financial statements for one-BHCs with assets less than $150 million

If stock of the bank or BHC is widely traded, a copy of its annual report can provide a wealth of financial data as well as other information on operations. If the institution is registered with the Securities and Exchange Commission (SEC), a copy of its 10-K report provides extremely beneficial information.

Private Sources

A number of private companies have been preparing and marketing specialized reports, using the public data as input. Most of these private sources are quite good and prepare a product that is often more readable than data from public sources. Two such sources of data are Sheshunoff Information Services, Inc. of Austin, TX, and the investment banking firm of Keefe, Bruyette & Woods. These companies also offer bank data on computer disk that allows for easy manipulation and analysis.

Finding financial information on private companies is difficult and, at times, impossible. These are some steps for finding what financial information does exist on private companies. Merger Online provides some private company financials, although the amount of information is limited compared to what is available for public companies. Not all private companies are included in Merger Online. Some private companies do publish annual reports for internal or promotional use and that can be obtained by contacting the company. Company Profiles sources usually provide annual sales and employee figures. A search for articles about the company can be conducted to get the financial conditions. Someone may have written about the company and included some financial details. Also, you can develop some impressions about a company's financial condition by reading about its activities.

Internal Data Sources

If access to the subject bank's internal records is possible, there is a wealth of potential data. However, reports produced by banks differ widely. Some banks are very sophisticated and generate excellent management reports in a wide variety of areas. Others produce very minimal data. Consequently, each situation must be assessed individually. Nonetheless, some basic reports are likely to exist in every bank.

The most common is the daily statement of condition, which is a detailed balance sheet and income statement created after the close of every business day. This report is useful because of its detailed nature, but it rarely follows the same format as the regulatory reports. Therefore, some rearranging of the daily statement is usually necessary if comparison with historical call reports is desired.

The delinquent (past due) loan report should also be reviewed. This report usually shows loans that have not received payment within seven days of the due date. The report segregates the loans by length of delinquency (for example, 7–30 days, 31–60 days, 61–90 days, and so on).

The bank should also have records regarding the loans charged off and those that have had reserves established but not yet completely charged off. This information provides detail regarding problem loans and any possible future losses likely to surface.

Another excellent source of information, financial and otherwise, is the bank's examination report. The report issued by the bank's regulatory agency will contain detailed analyses of nonperforming loans, foreclosed property, investment risks, and a wide variety of insights into the operations and organization. This report is highly confidential and is not available through public sources. If, however, the bank is cooperating in the valuation, it may be possible to view this report.

The annual budgets of the bank can also be beneficial. Depending on the sophistication of the institution, the budget can be a detailed forecast of financial performance based on strategic plans, or it can be a simplistic extrapolation of the preceding year's performance. The particular situation will determine the usefulness of budgets in the valuation research process.

Asset/liability (A/L) management reports are also beneficial if the bank has a formal A/L system. Such a system monitors the repricing opportunities for all interest-earning assets and interest-bearing liabilities. From these reports it is possible to assess the interest rate risk the bank faces. For example, a bank may have $500 million in commercial loans, with some adjustable at 30 days, some at 60 days, and some at 90 days. Consequently, the $500 million would be allocated into time groups depending on their "rollover" date. This is called a repricing opportunity because the bank can adjust the interest rate (i.e., reprice it) during that time period. The same process is undertaken on the liability side, except that repricing is based on the deposits or other funding sources' maturity dates.

The internal information sources described here are just a few of those likely to be available in any given bank or BHC. Each situation must be assessed individually to determine the applicability and availability of financial data beyond the basic reports.

OVERVIEW OF FINANCIAL STATEMENTS

Financial statements are prepared as part of the accounting cycle that documents the activities of the business. Users of financial statement information do not necessarily need to know everything about accounting to use the information in basic statements. Banks and BHCs are required to maintain financial records and reports for regulators, in addition to the normal financial information kept by any prudent business. The format and level of detail of various financial reports will differ from bank to bank. The conceptual framework, however, will be similar. This framework is described next. Financial data used in this section pertain to the Example Bank as presented in related Exhibits throughout the chapter.

Income Generation and Income Statement

The income statement, also known as the profit and loss (P&L) statement, shows revenues earned and expenses incurred for a period of time by reflecting the various sources of income and expenditures. Depending on the financial requirements, businesses will prepare either a single-step or multistep income statement. Banks' and savings institutions' keen focus is often on the interest margin of the difference between interest earned and the cost of funds which requies the use of a specialized income statement format. Supplemental income statement information can also be provided to reflect the impact of investing in certain tax-exempt securities.

Exhibit 11.1 illustrates how income is created by a bank. The major source of income is interest, which is generated mainly by loans and investments. Subtracted from that figure is the interest expense (mostly interest paid on deposits). The resulting difference is called net interest income. The noninterest income (mostly from service charges and fees) is added, which results in total income. Overhead expenses include such costs as personnel, office occupancy, data processing supplies, utilities, and insurance. The provision for loan losses is a charge against income to reflect bad loans. The resulting figure, after subtracting operating expenses and loan loss provision, is pretax income. With taxes subtracted, the final figure is net income.

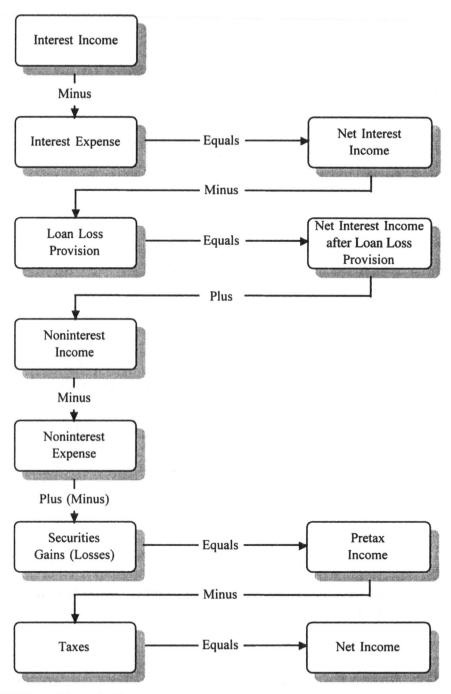

EXHIBIT 11.1 Schematic of Bank Income Generation

The internal financial reports and/or annual reports of a bank or BHC may not be in the same format as the regulatory reports. Occasionally, the income statement will be in this general format.

> Interest income
> − Interest expense
> = Net interest income
> − Loan loss provision
> = Net interest income after loan loss provision
> + Noninterest income
> − Noninterest expense
> + Securities gains (or minus losses)
> = Pretax income
> − Taxes
> = Net income

Consequently, it is sometimes necessary to rearrange either the internal or regulatory reports to allow comparison between the two types.

Balance Sheet

The balance sheet is a statement reflecting the financial position of an entity by showing economic resources owned (assets) and claims against the assets (liabilities and owners' equity) on a particular date. The balance sheets of banks and savings institutions typically are not classified into short-term and long-term categories for assets and liabilities; instead, they are generally presented in descending order of maturity. Supplemental information often is prepared by banks showing average balances of assets and liabilities and the related income or expense and average rates paid or earned.

The major items shown on a bank or BHC balance sheet include:

- Cash, cash balances at other depositary institutions, and due from accounts
- Securities (investments) held by the bank
- Federal Reserve funds sold (short-term loans to other banks) and securities purchased under agreement to resell (also called reverse repos)
- Total loans and lease financing receivables (net of unearned income)
- Loan loss reserves
- Net loans (total loans less loan loss reserves)
- Assets held in bank's own trading account
- Bank premises and fixed assets
- Other real estate owned (property temporarily owned by the bank, usually as a result of loan foreclosure)
- Investment in subsidiaries or other companies not consolidated in financial statements
- Customer liabilities on acceptances outstanding
- Intangible assets (as a result of acquisitions)
- Other assets

Assets can be either earning or nonearning. Earning assets are principally the loans and investments held by the bank, with Federal Reserve funds sold and interest-bearing balances at other banks usually being a smaller part. Earning assets are about 91 percent of the total assets of all banks. Of the earning assets, loans comprise about 57 percent; investments about 34 percent, Fed funds sold about 6 percent, and interest-bearing balances at other banks about 3 percent. Of the nonearning assets, most are in noninterest balances at other banks and due from accounts. About one-fifth of non-earning assets are in premises and equipment.

The liability side of the balance sheet is arranged in order of priority claim on the bank's assets (from highest to lowest). The categories typically listed include:

- Customer deposits
- Fed funds purchased (short-term borrowings from other banks) and securities sold under agreement to repurchase (repos)
- Demand notes issued to the U.S. Treasury
- Miscellaneous borrowed funds
- Mortgages and capitalized leases
- Bank's liability on customer acceptances outstanding
- Notes and debentures subordinated to depositors
- Other liabilities

Deposits account for about 97 percent of banks' liabilities.

Another entry on the liability side of the balance sheet is limited-life preferred stock. This type of preferred stock has a stated maturity (or it is redeemed at the option of the holder, not the bank) and is *not* convertible to perpetual preferred or common stock. Limited-life preferred stock is technically not debt, and therefore it is not a liability, but it is not counted fully as equity. Limited-life preferred stock is addressed in greater detail later in this chapter as part of the discussion of bank capital.

The equity portion of the balance sheet represents the owners' interest in the bank. Equity consists of: perpetual preferred stock; common stock; surplus; undivided profits and capital reserves; and cumulative foreign currency translation adjustment. Equity is about 8 to 9 percent of assets at all U.S. banks.

Cash Flow Statement

The statement of cash flow shows sources and uses of cash generated and spent through operating investing and financing activities. The statement of cash flow is presented in accordance with Statement of Financial Accounting Standards (SFAS) No. 95, *Statement of Cash Flows*, amended by SFAS No. 102, *Statement of Cash Flows—Exemption of Certain Enterprises and Classification of Cash Flows from Certain Securities Acquired for Resale (an Amendment of FASB Statement No. 95)*, and SFAS No. 104, *Statement of Cash Flows—Net Reporting of Certain Cash Receipts and Cash Payments and Classification of Cash Flows for Hedging Transactions (an amendment of FASB Statement No. 95)*.[2] The amendments permit certain financial institutions, such as banks and savings institutions, to net the cash flows for selected activities, such as trading, deposit taking, and loan activities.

COMPOSITION OF BANK ASSETS

The assets of a bank represent the uses of funds. Each major category of assets is discussed is this section. Unless otherwise noted, the asset items are equivalent for a bank or BHC.

Cash

The cash and due forms category accounts for about 8 percent of all assets. There are five major types of assets in this category: (1) actual vault cash; (2) cash items (usually checks) in process of collection; (3) deposits at banks in the United States; (4) deposits at foreign banks; and (5) deposits at the Federal Reserve Bank.

If the bank simply sticks its cash in a vault, it will have a hard time making a profit. Thus, a bank keeps most of its money tied up in loans and investments, which are called earning assets because they earn interest. Cash items in process of collection are usually the largest component of the cash and due from total. This represents the value of checks that have been deposited by customers but not yet collected from the bank on which those funds are drawn.

Investment Securities

Investment securities comprise about 29 percent of all bank assets. Banks do not like putting their assets into fixed-income securities, because the yield is not great. However, investment-grade securities are liquid, and they have higher yields than cash, so it is always prudent for a bank to keep securities on hand in case it needs to free up some liquidity. Banks hold a variety of investment securities, the most common of which are: Treasury securities such as T-bills, Treasury notes, and Treasury bonds; obligations of U.S. government agencies and corporations; and securities issued by states and municipalities.

Historically, banks were able to record the value of investments at the purchase price, adjusted for amortization of premiums and accretion of discounts. Two new accounting rules, SFAS No. 107 and SFAS No. 115, impact how banks report the value of investments on their balance sheets.

SFAS No. 107 requires business entities, including financial institutions, to disclose the fair value of investments where it is practicable to estimate such fair value. The definition of fair value for SFAS No.107 is "the amount at which the instrument could be exchanged in a current transaction between willing parties other than in a forced or liquidation sale." From a practical standpoint, most investments held by banks have quoted market prices. Therefore, the estimation of fair value is reliable and consistent.

SFAS No. 115 requires banks to classify each investment security into one of three types: trading account, held to maturity, and available for sale. Most banks will have a very small portion of their portfolios, if any, in the trading account category. This new reporting gives greater insights into the nature of the bank's balance sheet.

Fed Funds Sold and Reverse Repos

Fed funds sold are excess reserves of the bank that are loaned to other banks on a short-term basis, usually overnight. Reverse repurchase agreements (or reverse repos) provide another use for excess funds. To create a reverse repo, the bank purchases an investment security from another bank for a short period of time under an agreement to resell. At the end of that time period, it sells the investment back to the bank from which it was purchased. This action allows the bank to earn a market rate of interest, or close to it, on excess funds that may be available only for a day or two. About 5 percent of total bank assets are in Fed funds and reverse repos.

Loans and Lease Financing Receivables

Loans represent the majority of a bank's assets. A bank typically can earn a higher interest rate on loans than on securities, roughly 6 to 8 percent. The financial statements provide detailed information about the rates earned on loans and investments. Loans and lease financing receivables are extensions of credit made directly to bank customers or the purchase of such assets from other financial institutions. Loans, net of reserves, constitute approximately 52 percent of total assets of all banks.

Total loans, as reported by banks, are not the aggregate face value of those loans. The difference between the amount reported as total loans and the face value of all loans is the unearned income of those loans. A simple example illustrates the difference.

If an individual borrows $10,000 for three years at 11 percent annual interest with monthly payments, the total payback will be $11,786. The actual note amount (the total loan) is $11,786, but that figure includes unearned income of $1,786 at the beginning of the loan. Consequently the amount recorded at the inception of the loan is $10,000, not the $11,786 note amount. As the borrower makes payments, the principal owed is reduced, as is the amount reported on the balance sheet. Not all loan types are structured like a consumer loan. Some loans, most commonly real estate, do not include future income in the note amount. For example, a $10,000 real estate loan has a face value of $10,000 and is reported as such. As the principal is repaid, the face value and reported amount decreases.

Loans and leases are generally reported in these categories:

- Secured by real estate
- To depository institutions
- Agricultural
- Commercial and industrial
- Acceptances from other banks
- To individuals
- To foreign governments
- To state and local governments
- Other loans

The allowance for loan and lease losses is subtracted from total loans and lease financing receivables. This is a reserve account to cover anticipated losses on loans and leases.

Loans, however, come with risk. If the bank makes bad loans to consumers or businesses, the bank will take a hit when those loans are not repaid. Another subtraction from loans is the *allocated transfer risk reserve*. This is a special reserve account used by banks that have loans to specific countries which have not been able to make payments on external debt and where no definite prospects exist for orderly restoration of debt service. This is a minor amount in virtually all nonmoney center banks.

Loans and lease financing receivables less the reserves (both loss and allocated transfer risk) results in *net loans and lease financing receivables.* For simplicity, throughout this book the term "loans" is used for this asset group unless otherwise stated. Also, the term "loan loss reserves" is used for all types of loan, lease, and allocated transfer risk reserves.

Assets Held in Trading Accounts

Securities and other investments held by banks for their own trading account are recorded on the balance sheet at market value. Trading account assets include most of the same types of investments banks hold for the securities portion of their balance sheet. This asset type is found almost exclusively in larger banks with full-time trading departments that regularly deal in securities. Trading assets are segregated from the investment portfolio.They are recorded separately when acquired until they are disposed or sold, and are recorded at the price in effect when these securities are purchased or sold. Trading assets held for other banks are marked to market (adjusted to current market value) while held by a bank. Banks with over $10 billion in assets have about 1.5 percent of their assets in trading account securities. The figure was 0.26 percent for banks with $3 to $10 billion of assets, 0.2 percent for banks with $1 to $3 billion, and virtually none for banks under $1 billion. Held-for-trading financial assets are recognized at fair value with transaction costs being recognized in profit or loss.

Premises and Fixed Assets

The term "fixed assets" refers to premises, and this asset category includes the cost, less accumulated depreciation, of land, buildings, furniture, fixtures, and equipment used by the bank, its branches, or consolidated subsidiaries in its normal business. This includes vaults, fixed machinery, parking lots, and real estate acquired for future expansion. Overall, less than 2 percent of the total assets of all banks is made up of premises and fixed assets. Included in this category are any loans to, or investments in, groups that will purchase premises and lease them back to the bank. Other leased premises and/or equipment are carried at their capitalized value net of depreciation. The requirements for a capitalized lease are complex; they are specified in FASB No. 13. Essentially, most arm's-length long-term leases are capitalized. The bank's assets appear as if the bank purchased the premises with the corresponding liability being obligations for capitalized leases. Fixed assets can further be classified in the company's balance sheet as intangible, tangible, or investments. The benefits that a business obtains from a fixed asset extend over several years.

Specifically excluded from the premises and fixed assets accounts are valuable art objects (recorded as other assets) and favorable leases (recorded as intangible assets).

Other Real Estate Owned

Real estate owned by the bank, but not used in its normal business, is part of the other real estate (ORE) portfolio (also called OREO, or REO). It is usually property the bank has acquired through foreclosure, although there are other reasons for ORE (e.g., there may be closed but unsold branches or land originally purchased for expansion but no longer needed). Overall, about 0.5 percent of banking assets are in ORE.

ORE is reported at book value (not to exceed fair market value) less accumulated depreciation and any loss reserves established for the properties. If a bank owns only a portion of a property (perhaps as a result of participation loan foreclosure), its pro rata share of the property's value is recorded as ORE.

Investments in Unconsolidated Subsidiaries and Associated Companies

This asset category is a minor entry on most banks' balance sheets. It includes the amount of a bank's investment in the stock of all subsidiaries that have not been consolidated into the financial statements. The amount owed by unconsolidated companies that arises mainly from dividend receivables and administrative charges receivable is interest free and has no fixed terms of payment.

Investments in associated companies (generally investments of between 20 and 50 percent in a company's equity) where a significant influence is exercised by the group are accounted for by using the equity method. An assessment of investments in associates is performed when there is an indication that the asset has been impaired or the impairment losses recognized in prior years no longer exist.

Customer Liabilities to Bank on Acceptances Outstanding

The term "acceptances outstanding" represents unmatured drafts and bills of exchange accepted by a bank (i.e., full amount of customers' liabilities to the bank for the bank's guarantee of certain drafts and bills of exchange, usually for financing of imports and exports). There is an offsetting liability entry for the bank's obligation to honor the acceptance, usually for the same amount as the asset. The liability, called a bankers' acceptance, is a marketable investment for the holder, much like a large certificate of deposit (CD) issued by a bank would be marketable. It is a component of liabilities including acceptances and guarantees, own acceptances, and promissory notes outstanding.

Intangible Assets

Intangible assets are recorded on a buying bank's balance sheet as a result of a business combination under the purchase method of accounting. The typical types of *identified* intangible assets in a bank are core deposit base, computer software, mortgage servicing rights, and favorable leases.

The primary *unidentified* intangible is goodwill.

When intangible assets, especially goodwill, are high, it usually means that the bank or BHC has acquired another institution at a significant premium over book value. Since most acquisitions are by BHCs, intangibles usually are found on their books rather than on the books of individual banks.

Other Assets

Other assets is a catchall category for assets that do not fit the other categories and are not large enough to warrant a separate line item.

COMPOSITION OF BANK LIABILITIES

The liabilities of the bank represent the sources of funds used to invest in assets. There are many different types of liabilities. Some offer transaction capabilities with relatively low or no interest. Others offer limited check-writing capabilities but pay higher interest rates. Liabilities with long-term fixed maturities generally pay the highest rates. Customers who hold each instrument respond differently to interest rate changes. The major liability groups of a bank are described in this section. These liabilities are virtually the same for both banks and BHCs.

Deposits

The most prevalent liabilities of a bank are customer deposits. They are stable deposits that customers are less likely to move when interest rates on competing investments rise. Overall, deposits represent about 97 percent of all bank liabilities. They are influenced more by location, availability, and price of services. Not only do most checking, demand, and savings deposits yield low or no interest rates, which means the bank is paying almost nothing for the use of this money, but they are often a stable and growing financing base.

The types of deposits reported are shown in Exhibit 11.2. Deposit levels are also segregated by IPC (Individuals, Partnerships and Corporations) and public funds.

One other deposit segregation reported in the UBPR is a core versus noncore deposit. The core deposits of a bank are generally considered to be those that are the result of a stable customer relationship and are not likely to be volatile. About 75 to 80 percent of banking deposits are usually in the core deposits category. Noncore deposits are usually considered to be CDs of $100,000 or more (called jumbo CDs), public funds, and brokered deposits.

Fed Funds Purchased and Repos

Banks purchase Fed funds for an extended period when they see their borrowing needs lasting several days or they believe short-term rates may rise and they want to lock in the current rate. Fed funds purchased for an extended term, like overnight federal funds, are not subject to reserve requirements and sometimes are preferred to other purchased liabilities of comparable maturity. Fed funds purchased are the opposite of Fed

EXHIBIT 11.2 Deposits by Type in U.S. Banks—2010

Deposit Type	Approximate % of All Deposits
Demand	9%
Savings, NOWs	16%
CDs under $100,000	41%
CDs over $100,000	11%
Super NOW/MMDAs	16%
Foreign Office Deposits	7%

funds sold. The bank that "purchases" Fed funds—borrows excess reserves from another bank—is satisfying a temporary deficiency in its reserve position. By using Fed funds, the bank is able to satisfy its reserve needs without liquidating part of its security holdings. (If the Fed funds transaction involves funds that are immediately available but mature in more than one business day, they are called term Fed funds and are recorded as other borrowings.)

Repos serve the same basic purpose as Fed funds purchased; the bank sells a security to a third party with the agreement to repurchase it within a short period of time, sometimes overnight. The selling bank receives needed short-term funds without actually liquidating securities.

Demand Notes Issued to U.S. Treasury

Demand notes are designed to provide investors with a convenient means of investing funds directly with banks. Demand notes pay a floating rate and are in book-entry form with no stated maturity. An investment in demand notes involves risks. Prospective investors in demand notes should consider carefully the risk factors as well as the other information contained or incorporated.

From time to time, banks involved with the Treasury Tax and Loan note program receive funds that are to be credited to the U.S. government. The day after such funds are received, they are recorded as demand notes of the U.S. Treasury and constitute a liability of the bank. This liability is essentially a special type of deposit.

Other Borrowed Money

Banks tend to shun the use of other sources of borrowings, such as borrowings from other banks through federal funds purchases and repo agreements, bank notes, long-term debt, and commercial paper. Unlike core depositors, who for the most part are happy to receive any interest at all, these lenders demand and receive higher yield, so banks try not to use too much in the way of other borrowings. Banks and BHCs have a variety of techniques for borrowing money for short-term or long-term needs. A bank can borrow funds:

- On its promissory notes (if it is a holding company)
- On notes and bills rediscounted (including commodity drafts rediscounted)
- Through loans sold with agreement to repurchase
- By creation of due bills (an obligation that results when a bank sells a security or asset and receives payment but does not deliver the security or asset)
- From the Federal Reserve Bank
- By overdrawing correspondent accounts
- On purchase of term federal funds
- By selling assets short (in other words, selling an asset it does not actually own)
- Issuing notes and debentures

The liability category "all other borrowed money" comprises only one-tenth of 1 percent of total liabilities. Liabilities are either customer deposits or money that banks borrow from other sources to use to fund assets that earn revenue. The bank's liability items or obligations such as capital stock and cashier's check outstanding are due to its stockholders and creditors.

Mortgage Indebtedness/Capitalized Leases

Capitalized lease is an accounting approach that identifies a bank's lease obligation as an asset on its balance sheet. Under this method, the expenses are higher in the earlier years and gradually decline over the term of the lease. This liability encompasses the debt a bank has incurred for purposes of building or acquiring premises and fixed assets. This category also includes any obligations for long-term capitalized leases. The rate of indebtedness represents a significant source of financial distress, especially for households, and the estimated effects are particularly strong in countries with less expanded mortgage markets.

Bank's Liability on Acceptances Executed and Outstanding

This balance sheet category reflects the bank's liability from customers' drafts and bills of exchange that the bank has agreed to pay. This liability is an offset of the customers' liability to the bank on acceptances outstanding asset described in the preceding section. The bank reports the amount of liability represented by drafts and bills of exchange that have been accepted by domestic offices of the reporting bank, or by others for the account of such offices, and are outstanding.

Subordinated Notes and Debentures

A subordinated note or debenture is a type of debt issued by a bank or BHC or its subsidiaries that is subordinate to depositors' claims on the bank's assets. When issued by a bank directly, a subordinated note or debenture is not insured and matures in seven or more years. When issued by a BHC, it is considered unsecured long-term debt. Such debt shall be issued by a bank with the approval of, or under the rules and regulations of, the appropriate federal bank supervisory agency. Banks report mandatory convertible securities with subordinated notes and debentures while holding companies record them separately.

Other Liabilities

The last liability group includes all miscellaneous liabilities of the bank, including accrued but unpaid expenses, deferred income taxes, dividends payable, accounts payable, and deferred gains.

OFF–BALANCE SHEET ITEMS

In addition to items that are recorded on the balance sheet of a bank, there are *off–balance sheet* items, which are obligations that are contingent liabilities of a bank, such as letters of credit and interest rate swaps, and thus do not appear on its balance sheet. In large money center banks, off–balance sheet commitments can be substantial, sometimes more than the value of recorded assets. Most of these commitments are related to futures and options contracts and foreign exchange dealings. In general, off–balance sheet items include:

- Direct credit substitutes in which a bank substitutes its own credit for a third party, including standby letters of credit
- Irrevocable letters of credit that guarantee repayment of commercial paper or tax-exempt securities
- Risk participations in bankers' acceptances
- Sale and repurchase agreements
- Asset sales with recourse against the seller
- Interest rate swaps
- Interest rate options and currency options

The area of off–balance sheet commitments, and the risk associated with such commitments, is very complex. Risk-based capital guidelines discussed later in this chapter attempt to factor in that risk in determining capital adequacy. Where off–balance sheet commitments are substantial, in-depth research by a knowledgeable professional is necessary. Hence the risks that are involved include:

- Standby letters of credit
- Risk participations
- Asset sales with recourse
- Risk participations in bankers' acceptances
- Unused portions of loan or lease commitments with original maturities of more than one year
- Revolving underwriting agreements
- Note issuance facilities

 ## COMPOSITION OF BANK CAPITAL

The capital of a bank or any other business serves three basic purposes:

1. To absorb unanticipated losses
2. To provide operating funds
3. To measure ownership

Banks are unique in that they have *equity capital* and *regulatory capital*. The equity capital of a bank is measured the same way as the equity of any business—assets less liabilities. The principal components of equity capital are: par value of stock (common, limited life preferred, and/or perpetual preferred); surplus; undivided profits; and capital reserves.

Regulatory capital is a measure used by regulatory agencies to assess the financial condition of a bank under their supervision. The components of equity capital are described in this section, and regulatory capital definitions and guidelines are given in the next section.

Par Value of Stock

Banks in many states require that the stocks have a par value, or nominal value, to provide a minimum amount of legal capital to pay creditors. The aggregate par value of common, limited life preferred, and/or perpetual preferred stock is simply the par (or stated) value of the stock multiplied by the number of shares outstanding. Par value bears no relation to the market value of the stock. The par value is printed on each stock certificate. The par value of each stock is also changed accordingly by stock splits. A two-for-one split, for instance, would halve the par value. The par value of preferred stock is much higher than common stock because preferred stock pays a fixed dividend that is a designated percentage of par value.

Surplus

Surplus is the net amount of funds that have been formally transferred to this account as a result of capital contributions and any amount received for common stock and perpetual preferred stock in excess of par value. It is the excess of assets over liabilities accumulated throughout the existence of a business, excepting assets against which stock certificates have been issued; excess of net worth over capital stock value, that is, an amount of assets in excess of obligations to outsiders (creditors). The allocation to the surplus account is a bookkeeping entry and does not affect financial performance. This capital account is more pertinent for various legal and accounting requirements than for understanding the capital base of the bank. For example, the surplus account is considered part of permanent or legal capital in virtually all states and is not returned to owners through cash dividends or purchase of their shares unless creditor claims are adequately protected. In order to provide some measure of protection to creditors, most states designate a minimum level of permanent capital. From an accounting standpoint, the surplus account is used to keep track of this permanent capital and to meet various state incorporation laws. From a valuation and financial analysis standpoint, the delineation between aggregate par value and surplus is not important.

Undivided Profits

The undivided profits of a bank are the accumulated net income, gains, and losses less dividend distributions to shareholders and amounts transferred to the surplus account. It is the account shown on a bank's balance sheet representing profits that have neither been paid out as dividends nor transferred to the bank's surplus account. Current earnings are credited to the undivided profits account and are then either paid out in dividends or retained to build up total equity for expected future growth. As the account grows, round amounts may be transferred periodically to the surplus account. The undivided profits account increases through net income, including any extraordinary gains. This account can decrease through net losses, including extraordinary losses, and dividends paid to shareholders. The issuance or retirement of stock does not affect the undivided profits accounts. These transactions affect the surplus account, as described.

Capital Reserves

The last component of equity capital is capital reserves or accounts established to prepare for future uses, such as: reserves for undeclared dividends, either stock or cash (although each would have a separate reserve account); retirement of limited life preferred stock or notes and debentures subordinated to deposits, if the issues called for such a reserve; and reserves for contingencies such as lawsuits or other claims against the bank.

Capital reserves are in reality segregations of the retained earnings account and normally do not show on publicly available financial data as separate items. Therefore, without access to a bank's internal records, it may be hard to determine the existence of special capital reserves. From a valuation standpoint, separating out capital reserves is not of critical importance. It is the resource created by the accumulated capital surplus (not revenue surplus) of a bank, including an upward revaluation of its assets to reflect their current market value after appreciation.

Stress Test

The stress test essentially looks at a bank's loans and further evaluates the worthiness of its borrowers in an attempt to determine when and which loans could go bad. The stress test also would include whether banks have money in buffer when loans go unpaid. In a stress test, a lot depends on the assumptions made. The bank can look rosy and at the same time be highly distressed.

A leverage ratio can be used to measure the stress. It is defined as total equity divided by assets. For banks, the majority of assets are essentially loans. The lower the ratio, the more stressed the bank is. Regulators prefer to see at least a 5 percent leverage ratio. Lower than 5 percent could mean that the bank could be completely distressed.

Basel rules require that bank stress tests consist of four elements:

1. The stressed value at risk (SVaR), which is computed on a ten-day, 99 percent confidence level; three times the ten-day, 99 percent SVaR should be maintained.
2. Model inputs are calibrated to historical data from a continuous 12-month period of significant financial stress.
3. The capital requirement is determined based on the higher of its latest SVaR number and an average of SVaR numbers calculated over the preceding 60 business days multiplied by the multiplication factor.
4. Risk factors considered in pricing models should also be included in VaR calculations.

 REGULATORY CAPITAL COMPONENTS

Banking regulators take a much more complex view of capital than the simple accounting definition described earlier. The details of regulatory capital and definitions of components vary from time to time, but the major elements are consistent. Regulators categorize bank and BHC capital as core capital elements (Tier 1), supplement capital elements (Tier 2), and total capital (Tier 1 plus Tier 2). The components of each tier differ slightly between banks and BHCs. Each is discussed separately in this section.

Capital Components—Banks

The foundation components for banks to use for Tier 1 capital are:

- Permanent shareholders' equity
- Disclosed reserves
- Common stock
- Surplus
- Undivided profits (also called retained earnings)
- Capital reserves
- Cumulative foreign currency translation adjustments
- Minority interest in consolidated subsidiaries
- Perpetual preferred stock that is noncumulative (means that if dividends are not paid, they do not accumulate to the next period)
- Mortgage servicing rights up to 50 percent of Tier 1 capital
- Purchased credit card relationships up to 25 percent of Tier 1 capital
- Intangible assets that have been grandfathered for regulatory capital purposes

Items that must be subtracted from these components to calculate Tier 1 capital are:

- Intangible assets
- Unrealized holding losses in the available-for-sale equity portfolio
- Deferred tax assets disallowed for regulatory capital purposes
- Goodwill
- Perpetual preferred stock

Tier 1 capital represents the highest form of capital and generally is defined as the sum of core capital elements less intangible assets including goodwill, unrealized holding losses in the available-for-sale equity portfolio, and any investment in subsidiaries that the Federal Reserve determines should be deducted from Tier 1 capital.

Tier 2 capital includes these components:

- General provisions/general loan loss reserves
- Reevaluation reserves
- Hybrid capital instruments
- Subordinated term debt
- Undisclosed reserves
- Allowance for loan and lease losses, up to 1.25 percent of gross risk-weighted assets
- Perpetual preferred stock not qualifying as Tier 1 capital
- Mandatory convertible debt, net of common or preferred stock, set aside to redeem such debt
- Subordinated debt, intermediate-term preferred stock, and other limited-life capital instruments with value qualifying as Tier 2 capital based on remaining maturity:
  Over five years: 100% qualifies
  Four to five years: 80% qualifies
  Three to four years: 60% qualifies

Two to three years: 40% qualifies
One to two years: 20% qualifies
Under one year: 0% qualifies
■ Intermediate-term preferred stock
■ Unrealized holding gains on qualifying equity securities

Total regulatory capital in a bank is simply Tier 1 plus Tier 2 capital, with the restriction that Tier 2 may account for no more than 50 percent of total capital. The sum of Tier 1 and Tier 2 capital less any deductions makes up total capital, which is the numerator of the risk-based capital ratio discussed in Chapter 6. A bank's risk-based capital ratio is the ratio of qualifying capital to assets and off–balance sheet items that have been risk weighted based on perceived credit risk.

Capital Components—Bank Holding Companies

For a BHC, the foundation components of Tier 1 capital are: total equity capital; minority interests in consolidated subsidiaries; and intangible assets recorded before February 19, 1992, except goodwill, purchased mortgage servicing rights, and purchased credit card relationships.

From these amounts, the next items must be subtracted to calculate Tier 1 capital for a BHC:

■ Auction rate preferred stock and any other perpetual preferred stock deemed by the Federal Reserve to be eligible for Tier 2 capital only
■ Cumulative preferred stock in excess of 25 percent of Tier 1 capital
■ Goodwill
■ Identified intangible assets recorded February 19, 1992, or later
■ Purchased credit card relationships in excess of 25 percent of Tier 1 capital
■ Mortgage servicing rights plus purchased credit card relationships in excess of 50 percent of Tier 1 capital

Components eligible for Tier 2 regulatory capital in a BHC include:

■ Intermediate preferred stock with a weighted average maturity of five years or more, subordinated debt with a weighted average maturity of five years or more, and subordinated debt with an original maturity of five years or more based on the remaining term of the instrument:
Over five years: 100% qualifies
Four to five years: 80% qualifies
Three to four years: 60% qualifies
Two to three years: 40% qualifies
One to two years: 20% qualifies
Under one year: 0% qualifies
■ Unsecured long-term debt issued by the BHC prior to March 12, 1988, with the remaining time to maturity impacting the percent that qualifies as Tier 2 capital:

Over five years to maturity: 100% qualifies
Four to five years to maturity: 80% qualifies
Three to four years to maturity: 60% qualifies
Two to three years to maturity: 40% qualifies
One to two years to maturity: 20% qualifies
Under one year to maturity: 0% qualifies

- Auction rate preferred stock and any other perpetual preferred stock deemed by the Federal Reserve to be eligible for Tier 2 capital only
- Cumulative perpetual preferred stock in excess of 25 percent of core capital
- Total perpetual debt
- Mandatory convertible securities, both equity contract notes and equity commitment notes
- Long-term preferred stock based on remaining term to maturity:
Over five years: 100% qualifies
Four to five years: 80% qualifies
Three to four years: 60% qualifies
Two to three years: 40% qualifies
One to two years: 20% qualifies
Under one year: 0% qualifies
- Allowance for loan and lease losses, up to 1.25 percent of gross risk-weighted assets, limited to 100% of Tier 1 capital amount

From these Tier 2 qualifying amounts for BHCs, these must be subtracted:

- Common or perpetual preferred stock set aside to retire or redeem outstanding equity contract notes or equity commitment notes
- Capital investments in unconsolidated companies controlled by the BHC
- Reciprocal holdings of the banking organization's capital instruments

RISK-BASED CAPITAL

The risk-based capital is a stated requirement of liquid reserves placed on banks and institutions that deal in risky ventures. One dollar in cash is much less risky than an unsecured promissory note for one dollar from a con artist. Everything in between is a matter of degree. That is the premise that forms the basis of risk-based capital requirements. The Board of Governors of the Federal Reserve System sets the requirements for financial institutions. The risk-based capital requirements impact the sizes and types of real estate loans financial institutions are willing to make. In evaluating the financial strength of a bank or BHC, regulators evaluate the capital level (Tier 1 and Tier 2) relative to risk-weighted assets. The calculation of risk-weighted assets is done to reflect the fact that not all assets are of the same risk of loss and, therefore, do not need the same capital cushion.

In calculating risk-weighted assets, the "true" assets on the balance sheet and off–balance sheet items are assigned a risk weight of 100, 50, 20, or zero percent. Total risk-weighted assets is the sum of all assets and off–balance sheet asset equivalents times their respective risk weight.

The major balance sheet items that have a zero percent risk weighting (that is, riskless and not requiring capital) are:

- Cash
- Federal Reserve Bank balances
- U.S. government guaranteed debt
- U.S. government securities
- Book value of paid-in-stock at the Federal Reserve Bank

Significant items that have a 20 percent risk weight are:

- Cash items in process of collection
- Claims on domestic and Organisation for Economic Co-operation and Development (OECD) banks
- Claims on any other bank maturing in less than one year
- Claims guaranteed by U.S. financial institutions
- Securities issued or guaranteed by U.S. government agencies and state and local governments
- Portions of loans or other assets collateralized by securities issued by U.S. government agencies, U.S. Treasury, OECD countries, or cash
- Local currency claims on foreign central governments up to value of local liabilities in that country
- Privately issued mortgage-backed securities representing indirect ownership or mortgage-related U.S. government agency or U.S. government sponsored agency
- Portion of securities and loans conditionally guaranteed by the U.S. government

The 50 percent risk-weight assets are:

- U.S. state or local government revenue bonds or similar securities
- Residential real estate mortgage loans representing first liens on one- to four-family dwellings
- Credit equivalent amounts on interest rate and foreign exchange rate contracts, unless assigned to a lower risk-weighting category

The 100 percent risk-weight assets are:

- Loans and other claims on private obligors except residential real estate first liens
- Claims on non-OECD banks with over one year maturity
- Claims on foreign central governments not included elsewhere
- Obligations of state and local governments repayable solely by a private party or enterprise
- Fixed assets
- Investments in unconsolidated subsidiaries, joint ventures, or associated companies (if not deducted from capital)
- Instruments used by other banking organizations that qualify as capital
- All other tangible or intangible assets not deducted from capital

Off–balance sheet items are also taken into account in calculating regulatory capital requirements. These off–balance sheet items also carry a 100, 50, 20, or zero percent weighting.

The off–balance sheet items with a zero percent risk weight are unused commitments with original maturity under one year or that can be unconditionally canceled at any time.

The only 20 percent weighted items are short-term, self-liquidating, trade-related contingencies that arise from the movement of goods.

The 50 percent weighted items are:

- Transaction-related contingencies
- Unused commitments with original maturity over one year
- Revolving underwriting facilities and not issuance facilities where the borrower can issue short-term paper in its own name on a revolving basis and the underwriting banks have a legally binding commitment either to purchase notes not sold by the borrower or to advance funds to the borrower

The 100 percent weighted items are:

- Direct credit substitutes
- Sales and repurchase agreements and asset sales with recourse not already on the balance sheet
- Principal amount of assets to be purchased as part of forward agreements
- Securities lent where bank is at risk

An example of calculating risk-weighted assets is shown in Exhibit 11.3.

In determining the capital adequacy of a bank or BHC, the risk-adjusted capital ratio is calculated. In general, regulators look for at least an 8 percent total risk-adjusted capital ratio. The ratio is calculated as:

- Bank total risk-adjusted capital ratio:

Total capital (Tier 1 and Tier 2)

_____

Gross risk-weighted assets—loan and lease loss allowance over 1.25% of risk-weighted assets—allocated transfer risk reserve BHC total risk-adjusted capital ratio:

Total capital (Tier 1 and Tier 2)

_____

Gross risk-weighted assets—mortgage servicing rights over 50% of Tier 1 capital—purchased credit card relationships over 25% of Tier 1 capital— all other identified intangible assets—goodwill—loan and lease loss allowance over 1.25% of risk-weighted assets—allocated transfer risk reserve

EXHIBIT 11.3 Illustration of Calculation of Risk-Weighted Assets

Balance Sheet	Book Value	Weight	Risk-Weighted Amount
Cash and Equivalents	$ 100	0%	$ 0
Cash Items	200	20%	40
Securities	700	20%	140
Revenue Bonds	50	50%	25
Residential Mortgage Loans	500	50%	250
Other Loans	2,000	100%	2,000
Revenues and Fixed Assets	60	100%	60
Other Real Estate Owned	12	100%	12
Other Assets	78	100%	78
	$ 3,700		$ 2,605
Off–Balance Sheet	Notional Value	Conversion Factor	Balance Sheet Equivalent
Loan Commitments (under 1 year)	$ 100	100%	$ 100
Standby Commitments	160	100%	160
Loan Commitments			
(over 1 year)	80	50%	40
	$ 340		$ 300
		Total Risk-Weighted Assets	$ 2,905

The valuation implications of these capital requirements is that the required annual contribution of capital from earnings must be sufficient enough to maintain at least the regulatory minimums.

 VALUE-AT-RISK MODELS

Banks' regulatory capital changes and requirements for the market risk exposure in the United States are in conformity with an amendment to the 1988 Basel Capital Accord. Currently, the three methods employed in determining regulatory capital changes for market risk exposure are: standardized approach, precommitment approach, and internal models.[3] The standardized approach is based on standard risk management procedures consistent with regulatory rules that assign capital charges to specific assets in estimating the selected portfolio effect on banks' risk exposure. The precommitment approach suggested by the Federal Reserve Board of Governors is another method that can be used. The third method is based on banks' internal models utilizing the standardized regulatory parameters of a ten-day holding period and 99 percent coverage.

Recently commercial banks have used time-series VaR models to determine their regulatory capital requirements for market exposure.[4] VaR estimates, generated by banks' internal VaR models, are forecasts of the maximum portfolio value that could be lost over the specified time horizon with a specified precision and confidence level. VaR estimates are crucial and relevant to banks and their regulators in assessing regulatory capital requirements. Thus, the reliability of these forecasts and the accuracy of their underlying VaR models are essential.

Bank regulators have utilized four statistical methods, suggested in the literature,[5] for assessing the accuracy and reliability of VaR models. Banks often report their specified VaR internal estimates to the regulators who assess whether the trading losses are less than or greater than these estimates. This regulatory assessment is conducted by evaluating VaR estimates based on (1) the binomial distribution; (2) internal forecasts; (3) distribution forecasts; and/or (4) probability forecasts. These statistical assessment methods are intended to verify the accuracy and reliability of the forecasted VaR as well as reasonableness of assumptions and estimates used in forecasting VaR using a hypothesis-testing concept. The binomial distribution assessment method is based on the assumption that the VaR estimates are independent across time and determined from independent binomial random variables. The VaR interval forecasts valuation method considers VaR estimates as interval forecasts of the lower left-hand interval at a specified probability level. The VaR distribution forecasts assessment method determines whether the observed quantities derived under the interval model's distribution forecasts exhibit the properties of observed quantities from accurate distribution forecasts. The VaR probability forecasts evaluation method is based on standard forecast evaluation tools that measure the accuracy of VaR interval models in terms of how well their generated probability forecasts of specified regulatory actions minimize a loss function relevant to regulators. The loss functions relevant to regulators are determined based on proper scoring rules of probability forecasts.

 ## COMPOSITION OF BANK INCOME

The income of a bank is derived primarily from interest and fees. Interest income is earned from various earning assets (e.g., loans and investments) while fee income can be a result of many different activities (e.g., service charges, safe deposit box rental, foreign exchange transactions, and trust fees). Larger banks can also generate significant income through trading gains.

Interest Income

Interest income represents about 90 percent of gross income of all banks in the United States and about 85 percent of BHC income. Nearly two-thirds of that amount is derived from loans. Bank call reports identify interest income from these sources:

- Loans to businesses, individuals, and governments
- Lease financing receivables
- Deposit accounts at other financial institutions
- Treasury and U.S. agencies securities
- Other municipal securities

- Other domestic securities (debt and equity)
- Foreign securities
- Assets held in trading accounts
- Fed funds sold and securities purchased under agreements to resell

Every earning asset on the balance sheet generates some level of income. In general, the income associated with an earning asset is equal to interest income from the earning asset which is typically 5% of the average balance of the earning asset.

If an earning asset has an average balance during the year of $1,000 at a rate of 9 percent, about $90 in income for the year would result. It is "about" $90 because there are different techniques of accruing interest income, especially on loans. For example, the rule of 78s is a technique for recognizing interest income that gives slightly greater interest in the early periods. Therefore, if the example just used is a $1,000 loan at 9 percent that is being accrued by the rule of 78s, the income earned may be slightly over $90 in the early years and slightly less than $90 later on. On average, however, the formula just used is a good approximation of interest income based on the level of earning assets.

Noninterest Income

The noninterest income of a bank is reported in these categories:

- Income from fiduciary (trust) activities
- Service charges on deposit accounts
- Securities gains and losses
- Trading gains and fees from foreign exchange transactions
- Other foreign transaction gains (or losses)
- Gains (or losses) and fees from assets held in trading accounts
- Other noninterest income

The last category, other noninterest income, covers a wide variety of income-generating activities, including:

- Fees for services provided to others (such as data and correspondent services)
- Safe deposit box rentals
- Gains on sale of assets
- All service charges, commissions, and fees not related to deposit accounts and foreign exchange transactions
- Rental income
- Credit card fees
- Teller overages

The relationship is indirect between the magnitude of noninterest income and the size of the balance sheet. Some banks are more fee-oriented than others. On average, noninterest income represents about 8 percent of gross income (interest income plus all other income) of all U.S. banks. In the largest banks (with over $10 billion in assets), noninterest income represents over 15 percent of gross income. In general, smaller banks have greater reliance on interest income than on fees and service charges.

The area of securities gains (or losses) is one that should be examined carefully in a bank, especially in times of volatile investment markets. Because banks hold securities in their investment portfolio, buying and selling of such securities is a normal part of the financial management of the institution. When securities are bought, there is always the possibility that a gain (or loss) over the carrying value will be realized if the security is ultimately sold. This can be a relatively unpredictable part of the bank's income, especially if it holds long-term investments in its portfolio. In general, however, securities gains represent a very small portion of a bank's gross income.

Extraordinary Gains (Losses)

Like any business, banks can realize nonrecurring gains or losses on transactions that are unusual and infrequent. Both the unusual and infrequent criteria must be met for a transaction to be classified as extraordinary. To be unusual, an event or transaction must be highly abnormal or obviously unrelated to the normal operations of the bank. To be infrequent, the event or transaction should not be reasonably expected to recur in the foreseeable future.

The rules are very strict for reporting a gain or loss as extraordinary. If a bank sells an asset—for example a branch office—and realizes a gain (i.e., if sales proceeds exceed book value), the amount would not be considered an extraordinary gain even if the bank had never before sold a branch. Such a transaction would not pass the "unusual" test because banks buy and sell branches routinely, even though that particular bank had not done so in the past. If, however, a natural disaster destroyed a branch, thus causing a net loss, this amount would be an extraordinary loss and would be reported as such. Such an occurrence would be defined as both unusual and infrequent.

As would be expected, extraordinary items are an insignificant portion of all bank incomes, less than 0.1 percent of total income. However, for a given bank during a given year, the impact can be significant.

 ## COMPOSITION OF BANK EXPENSES

The expenses incurred by a bank or BHC usually fall into four main categories:

1. Interest expense—paid on deposits and other sources of funds
2. Noninterest expense—normal expenditures for personnel, facilities and other overhead, amortization expense, and all other functional expenses that are not related to interest, loan losses or taxes
3. Provision for loan and lease losses and allocated transfer risk—set aside in anticipation of losses from loans
4. Taxes—on income at federal, state, and local level as applicable

Interest expense constitutes about 54 percent of total expenses; noninterest expenses, 38 percent; provisions for loan and lease losses and allocated transfer risk, 4 percent; and taxes, 4 percent.

Interest Expense

The interest expenses of a bank reflect the price paid to attract and keep funds. The annual interest expense associated with a liability is equal to the average balance of that liability during a year multiplied by the annual interest rate. The most significant funding source is customer deposits, which represent about 97 percent of all bank liabilities. The expenses associated with these deposits are segregated into two groups: (1) interest on certificates of deposit of $100,000 or more (jumbo CDs) and public funds; and (2) interest on other deposits.

This separation is made because jumbo CDs and public funds usually are not considered to be core deposits, and it is beneficial to separate the cost of attracting these more volatile funds.

The next major interest expense category is expenses of Fed funds purchased and securities sold under agreements to repurchase. Expenses in this category reflect the cost of borrowing short-term funds from other banks to meet reserve requirements.

Interest on demand notes issued to U.S. Treasury and other borrowed money is the third category of interest expense. The costs in this area are a result of normal borrowings of a bank that do not fall into other categories as well as the cost of demand notes (part of the Treasury Tax and Loan program described earlier in this chapter).

Any interest paid by the bank on mortgage indebtedness and capitalized leases also is shown separately on the income statement. The interest portion of a mortgage payment (e.g., on funds borrowed to build a branch) would be determined by the amortization schedule of the debt. On a capitalized lease, the interest payment is imputed from the total lease payment. In other words, the capitalized lease is viewed as financing and is reported as such, with a portion of the lease payment imputed to interest and a portion to equivalent principal reduction.

The last category of interest expense is interest on notes and debentures subordinated to deposits. These costs reflect the issuance of such debt instruments by the bank. Included with these costs are the fees incurred to issue the notes, amortized over the life of the note.

Noninterest Expense

The noninterest expenses of a bank include operating and overhead expenses. The major classifications of expenses are salary and employee benefits, premises and fixed asset expense, and other noninterest expenses.

The expense category of salary and employee benefits includes virtually all costs associated with the staff: salaries, overtime pay, bonuses, Social Security, unemployment tax, insurance, pension plans, and other direct employee benefits. The only employee-related expenses not included are training and professional organization dues, which are both included in other noninterest expense.

Premises and fixed asset expenses include the costs associated with the operation and maintenance of facilities, equipment, vehicles, furniture, and fixtures used by the bank in the normal course of business. Both direct out-of-pocket costs and depreciation expenses are included in this category. Expenses associated with property owned by the bank but not used in the normal course of business, such as foreclosed real estate, are included in other noninterest expenses.

Other noninterest expense is a catchall category for expenses not applicable elsewhere. Examples of expenses in this category include:

- Director fees
- Fidelity insurance premiums
- Regulatory assessment fees
- Legal and other professional fees
- Net losses on sale of assets
- Expenses associated with ORE
- Management fees paid to parent BHC
- Intangible asset amortization
- Advertising and public relations fees
- Office supplies and telephone
- Data processing

Provision for Loan and Lease Losses and Allocated Transfer Risk

The provision for loan and lease losses and allocated transfer risk is an expense item in that it is a charge against current income. The allocated transfer risk is a reserve for bad loans made to certain countries that appear unable to resume debt repayment. This is a minor expense item even for large international banks.

The amount of the provision for normal loans and leases is based on anticipated losses on loans, including any accrued but unpaid interest. When a provision for a loan loss is made, the destination of the expense is the loan loss reserve described earlier in this chapter in the asset discussion. Any subsequent actual loan charge-off is applied against the loan loss reserve, never directly against retained earnings. Conversely, recoveries of loans previously charged off are credited to the loan loss reserve.

The provision for loan loss expense is an item that is reported differently for accounting and income tax purposes (where it is called reserve for bad debts). The difference is referred to as a *timing difference.* The tax effect of such a timing difference is accounted for and reported as a deferred income tax credit or debit on the income statement and in the balance sheet as an other liability (if a credit balance) or an other asset (if a debit balance). Any difference between the bank's loan loss reserve and its reserve for bad debts for tax purposes can be eliminated only through subsequent differences between the bad debt deduction for taxes and the provision for loan losses.

Income Taxes

The last category of expenses is income tax at federal, state, and local levels. The income tax expense shown in a bank's call report is the applicable income tax of the bank based on the reported income. The calculation of the actual income tax liability to be paid is based on rules prescribed in the regulations of the various taxing authorities. These rules are usually different from those used to prepare call reports. Therefore, the tax liability arising from the pretax income on a call report probably will be different from the actual taxes paid. The differences arise from two primary sources:

1. *Timing differences.* Caused when a bank reports an item of income or expense in one period for call report purposes but in another period for income tax purposes. An example is a bank that uses straight-line depreciation for book purposes and accelerated depreciation for tax purposes. The total depreciation is the same, but the reported amount in any one period will be different because of timing.
2. *Permanent differences.* Caused when a bank reports an item of income or expense for call report purposes that will never be reported for tax purposes. An example is goodwill amortization, which is an expense for book purposes but not for tax purposes.

The income tax figures reported in a bank's call report are generally determined by these four steps:

1. Determine income before taxes and extraordinary items and other adjustments (equal to total bank income less interest expense less noninterest expenses less provision for loan loss).
2. Adjust for any permanent differences in book versus tax income by adding back expense items not eligible for tax deductions (e.g., amortization of goodwill and premiums paid on officer life insurance where the bank is the beneficiary) and subtracting income not taxable (e.g., qualifying municipal bond interest and 85 percent of cash dividends received on the stock of U.S. corporations).
3. Apply the combined federal, state, and local income tax rates to the results of steps 1 and 2.
4. Reduce the amount from step 3 by any tax credits expected to be taken on the bank's tax return.

The resulting figure in step 4 is the applicable income tax line on a bank's call report. If this figure is different from the actual taxes to be paid by the bank during the year, the difference is shown as deferred portion of applicable income taxes. If applicable taxes are less than actual taxes, the deferred portion is a debit balance and is carried in other assets, subject to certain limitations. If the applicable taxes are greater, it is a credit balance and carried as an other liability.

 BALANCE SHEET ANALYSIS ILLUSTRATION

A key component in the understanding of a bank for valuation purposes is the analysis of historical balance sheet trends. This is an important part of the financial analysis and is essential to establishing value accurately. The primary sources of balance sheet data are the call reports, the UBPR, and other internal reports as available.

Exhibit 11.4 shows the balance sheet items and selected ratios for Example Bank. The analysis described in the balance of this chapter is based on these statistics. These statistics are used in the example of valuation by the income approach described in Chapter 15.

EXHIBIT 11.4 Example Bank Balance Sheet Summary ($000)

	2010	2009	2008	2007	2006	2005
Assets						
Cash and Due Forms						
Non-Interest Bearing	$ 26,992	$ 20,991	$ 24,096	$ 22,122	$ 19,577	$ 18,306
Interest Bearing	8,972	6,390	2,509	10,120	2,450	1,309
Subtotal Cash and Due Forms	35,964	27,381	26,605	32,242	22,027	21,615
Securities	70,309	58,345	52,700	38,264	36,658	32,129
Fed Funds Sold and Securities Purchased	2,786	2,596	7,189	18,609	14,709	12,064
Total Loans	266,235	243,665	214,201	171,553	143,707	121,350
(Loan Loss Reserve)	2,879	2,559	2,180	1,554	1,398	998
Net Loans	263,356	241,106	212,021	169,999	142,309	120,352
Trading Account Assets	0	0	0	0	0	0
Premises and Fixed Assets	5,885	6,214	5,816	5,131	4,718	5,237
Other Real Estate Owned	854	332	529	450	717	834
Intangible Assets	2,423	2,524	2,971	3,321	3,488	2,888
Other Assets	6,629	4,587	6,805	3,794	3,409	4,117
Total Assets	$388,206	$343,085	$314,636	$271,810	$228,035	$197,236
Liabilities						
Deposit of Customers						
Demand Deposits	$ 67,947	$ 67,264	$ 78,121	$ 62,271	$ 59,974	$ 45,677
Other Transaction Deposits	21,330	18,475	17,606	11,780	12,030	21,223
MMDA Savings	60,699	47,827	54,573	47,541	27,623	15,083
Other Savings	14,617	12,659	10,565	8,413	8,669	7,328
CDs under $100,000	53,302	44,937	34,679	34,863	32,258	29,853
Subtotal Core Deposits	217,895	191,162	195,544	164,868	140,554	119,164
Other Deposits	54,538	45,149	35,018	33,364	30,586	27,851
Total Deposits	272,433	236,311	230,562	198,232	171,140	147,015
Fed Funds Purchased and Securities Sold	85,491	78,047	50,240	39,478	33,845	28,650
Other Borrowed Money	132	141	3,403	4,569	160	113
Mortgages and Capitalized Leases	1,249	1,269	1,299	1,304	1,271	1,195
Subordinated Notes and Debentures	798	827	935	960	1,010	1,123
Other Liabilities	6,530	7,001	10,662	10,878	7,186	6,903
Total Liabilities	$366,633	$323,596	$297,061	$255,691	$214,612	$184,999
Limited Life Preferred Stock	0	0	0	0	0	0

(Continued)

EXHIBIT 11.4 (*Continued*)

	2010	2009	2008	2007	2006	2005
Equity Capital	21,573	19,489	17,575	16,119	13,423	12,237
Total Liabilities and Equity Capital	$388,206	$343,085	$314,636	$271,810	$228,035	$197,236
As Percent of Assets						
Net Loans						
Bank	67.8%	70.3%	67.4%	62.5%	62.4%	61.0%
Peer	55.0%	54.2%	56.2%	54.6%	52.1%	52.7%
Investments						
Bank	21.1%	19.6%	19.8%	24.7%	23.6%	25.1%
Peer	21.9%	22.2%	23.0%	24.3%	26.4%	26.0%
Premises and Fixed Assets						
Bank	1.5%	1.8%	1.9%	1.9%	2.0%	2.2%
Peer	1.8%	1.8%	1.8%	1.8%	1.9%	2.0%
Other Real Estate Owned						
Bank	0.22%	0.10%	0.17%	0.17%	0.31%	0.42%
Peer	0.55%	0.51%	0.39%	0.28%	0.25%	0.18%
Earning Assets						
Bank	89.9%	87.2%	87.2%	86.0%	86.1%	84.1%
Peer	89.5%	89.4%	89.5%	89.5%	89.0%	88.6%
Loan Loss Reserve						
Bank	0.74%	0.75%	0.69%	0.57%	0.61%	0.51%
Peer	0.71%	0.70%	0.70%	0.61%	0.61%	0.60%
Core Deposits						
Bank	56.3%	55.7%	62.2%	60.6%	61.6%	60.4%
Peer	69.8%	70.9%	70.5%	69.1%	69.8%	65.1%
Demand and Transaction Deposits						
Bank	23.0%	25.0%	30.4%	27.2%	31.6%	33.9%
Peer	23.2%	24.4%	26.0%	26.5%	26.2%	26.4%
MMDA and Other Savings						
Bank	19.4%	17.0%	20.7%	20.6%	15.9%	11.4%
Peer	24.9%	23.0%	21.3%	19.6%	19.7%	11.8%
CDs, $100,000						
Bank	13.7%	13.1%	11.0%	12.8%	14.2%	15.1%
Peer	21.0%	21.8%	23.2%	23.5%	23.7%	26.3%
Capital Composition						
Common Equity	$ 21,573	$ 19,489	$ 17,575	$ 16,119	$ 13,423	$ 12,237
Loan Loss Reserve	2,879	2,559	2,180	1,554	1,398	998
Permanent and Convertible Preferred	0	0	0	0	0	0

(*Continued*)

EXHIBIT 11.4 (Continued)

Total Primary Capital	$ 24,452	$ 22,048	$ 19,755	$ 17,673	$ 14,821	$ 13,235
Changes in Common Equity						
Balance—Beginning of Year	$ 19,489	$ 17,575	$ 16,119	$ 13,423	$ 12,237	$ 10,953
Net Income	3,007	2,729	2,394	1,605	1,142	1,724
(Cash Dividends)	(923)	(815)	(938)	(409)	(456)	(440)
Other Changes (New Capital)	0	0	0	1,500	500	0
Balance—End of Year	$ 21,573	$ 19,489	$ 17,575	$ 16,119	$ 13,423	$ 12,237
Capital Ratios						
Primary Capital/Assets						
Bank	6.3%	6.4%	6.3%	6.5%	6.5%	6.7%
Peer	8.0%	8.0%	8.1%	7.9%	7.9%	8.1%
Equity/Assets						
Bank	5.6%	5.7%	5.6%	5.9%	5.9%	6.2%
Peer	7.0%	7.1%	7.5%	7.5%	7.5%	7.7%
Net Income/Average Equity						
Bank	14.7%	14.7%	14.2%	10.9%	8.9%	15.6%
Peer	10.1%	9.9%	13.9%	14.6%	14.5%	14.7%
Dividends/Average Equity						
Bank	4.5%	4.4%	5.6%	2.8%	3.6%	3.8%
Peer	6.1%	6.5%	7.2%	6.4%	6.4%	6.2%
Dividends/Net Income						
Bank	30.7%	29.9%	39.2%	25.5%	39.9%	25.5%
Peer	55.2%	65.6%	51.8%	43.8%	44.1%	42.1%

Asset Growth Rates

Example Bank's total assets have grown rapidly from $197 million at year-end 2005 to over $388 million at year-end 2010. The year-to-year increases are shown in Exhibit 11.5. This rate of growth has been generally consistent with the bank's aggressive philosophy, especially in the lending areas. While asset growth averaged 14.5 percent compounded annually, loans grew at over 17 percent each year. When valuing Example Bank, it probably would be overly optimistic to assume such growth can continue. This is especially true given the fact that much of the asset growth was supported by funding other than core deposits (as discussed later).

Asset Composition

From 2005 to 2010, loans consistently increased as a percent of total assets: from 61.0 percent to 70.3 percent. In 2010, however, that ratio declined to 67.8 percent,

EXHIBIT 11.5 Example Bank Asset Growth Rates

	Change in Total Assets
2005–2006	15.6%
2006–2007	19.2%
2007–2008	15.7%
2008–2009	9.0%
2009–2010	13.1%
Compounded 2005–2010	14.5%

reflecting a more conservative balance sheet management policy. Also, Example Bank has improved on its non-interest-bearing cash and due forms, reducing to 6.9 percent of assets in 2010 from 8.3 percent in 2005. In general, Example Bank has significantly reduced its level of nonearning assets relative to total assets between 2005 and 2010, from 13.9 percent of assets to 11.0 percent.

Asset Composition—Peer Group Comparison

Also shown in Exhibit 11.4 are various ratios for Example Bank and a peer comparison. From these statistics, it is clear that the bank is an aggressive lender; 68 percent of its assets are in loans versus 55 percent for peers. Most of the other asset categories are generally consistent with the peer group, except Example Bank appears to have less of an REO problem.

The one area where Example Bank compares unfavorably is in its funding base; core deposits are significantly lower than its peers on a percentage of deposits basis, as are smaller CDs. The danger sign is that the bank may be susceptible to volatile funding costs. The rapid growth in assets was funded by a variety of liabilities that are not necessarily stable.

This potential weakness in the balance sheet must be considered in the valuation process.

Liability Growth Rates

Between 2005 and 2010, liabilities at Example Bank grew at a 14.7 percent compounded annual rate. Core deposits grew at a 12.8 percent rate while other deposits increased at 14.4 percent per year on average. Other interest-bearing liabilities grew at a 23 percent rate, further indicating the bank's reliance on volatile funding sources.

Liability Composition

Example Bank's liabilities are clearly oriented toward customer deposits, although that orientation has decreased in recent years. At year-end 2010, 74.3 percent of all the bank's liabilities were in customer deposits and 59.4 percent were in core deposits. The other major category of liabilities is Fed Funds Purchased and Securities Sold with Repurchase Agreements, accounting for 23.3 percent of liabilities in 2010 versus 15.5 percent in 2005.

Liability Composition—Peer Group Comparison

Example Bank has relied more on volatile funding sources during the past few years than has its peers. This is evidenced by the fact that core deposits are lower as a percent of assets at the bank than for the peer group. Within the core deposit base, Example Bank tends to have a much lower small CD base than its peers.

Capital Levels and Trends

Despite fairly good levels of net income, Example Bank's equity and primary capital position declined slightly between 2005 and 2010. This has been a direct result of the rapid growth in the asset base, which has made it more difficult to grow capital at the same rate.

In general, Example Bank has been adequately capitalized since 2005 but below peer group averages on a capital ratio basis. However, good income growth has enabled the bank to grow the absolute level of capital at an impressive rate: 12 percent per year between 2005 and 2010. Net income to average equity has been above peer group averages, except for down years in 2006 and 2007. The price for internal generation of capital has been a low level of dividends. Dividends paid have been below peer averages, measured by both dividends to average equity and dividends as a percent of net income. From 2005 to 2010, Example Bank paid dividends equal to 31.7 percent of net income, whereas peer groups averaged 50.4 percent of net income—60 percent more.

INCOME STATEMENT AND PROFITABILITY ANALYSIS ILLUSTRATION

Once the trends and composition of the balance sheet have been analyzed, the next analysis focuses on the income statement and related measures of profitability. The purpose of this analysis is to understand fully the sources and nature of all income and expenses. Each major type of analysis needed for valuation is described in this section. Exhibit 11.6 presents income statement components and summaries.

Overall Income and Expenses

Along with assets, income and expenses at Example Bank have grown rapidly. Total interest income on a tax equivalent basis grew at an annual rate of 9.17 percent between 2005 and 2010. Over the same period, interest expense grew at an 8.8 percent rate. Tax equivalent net interest income increased at a 9.5 percent annual rate. Noninterest income increased at a 16.1 percent annual rate and increased from 24.6 percent of total tax equivalent income in 2005 to 30.4 percent in 2010. Total income increased at an annual rate of 11.2 percent.

Overhead expenses grew at a 9.6 percent annual rate, slower than asset increases and total income. It appears that Example Bank is improving its cost effectiveness.

The expenses associated with loan losses were extremely high in 2009, reflecting a cleaning up of the loan portfolio. Before that time and in 2010, loan loss provision expense generally has been a relatively constant percent of loans.

EXHIBIT 11.6 Example Bank Income and Expense Summary ($000s)

	2010	2009	2008	2007	2006	2005
Interest and Fees—Loans and Leases						
Real Estate Loans	$11,207	$ 8,883	$ 6,627	$ 4,690	$ 3,654	$ 3,590
Loans to Individuals	5,088	5,119	5,868	5,658	5,532	5,426
Commercial Loans	14,027	11,989	10,411	9,913	9,114	8,920
All Other Loans	0	0	0	0	0	0
Leases	393	368	217	278	237	331
Subtotal Loans and Leases	$30,714	$26,358	$23,124	$20,539	$18,537	$18,267
Interest and Fees—Investments						
Balances at Other Institutions	$ 483	$ 207	$ 233	$ 376	$ 345	$ 233
Securities	4,636	4,247	3,240	2,790	2,767	2,234
Fed Funds Sold	69	206	597	895	693	503
Other Investments	92	77	75	73	160	94
Subtotal Investments	$ 5,280	$ 4,737	$ 4,145	$ 4,134	$ 3,965	$ 3,054
Interest Income—Other	$ 0	$ 0	$ 0	$ 0	$ 0	$ 0
Total Interest Income:						
Actual as Reported	$35,994	$31,095	$27,269	$24,673	$22,502	$21,321
Memo: Tax Equivalent (TE)	$36,401	$31,561	$27,990	$25,618	$23,589	$22,119
Interest Expense—Deposits						
Transaction Accounts	$ 1,445	$ 1,385	$ 1,304	$ 1,248	$ 1,148	$ 1,031
MMDAs	5,109	4,205	3,960	3,792	3,485	3,232
Other Savings	1,109	957	902	863	794	713
CDs under $100,000	5,843	4,443	4,986	4,763	4,077	3,492
CDs over $100,000	3,724	3,160	2,521	2,420	2,395	2,307
Other Deposits	0	0	0	0	0	0
Subtotal Deposits	$17,229	$14,149	$13,672	$13,085	$11,897	$10,774
Interest Expense—Other						
Fed Funds Purchased	$ 5,672	$ 4,432	$ 2,678	$ 2,541	$ 3,077	$ 2,911
Other Borrowed Money	42	44	137	32	18	23
Mortgages and Capitalized Leases	109	114	108	101	71	55
Subordinated Notes/ Debentures	59	66	71	74	75	69
Subtotal Others	$ 5,882	$ 4,656	$ 2,994	$ 2,748	$ 3,241	$ 3,058
Total Interest Expense	$23,111	$18,805	$16,666	$15,833	$15,138	$13,832
Net Interest Income:						
Actual as Reported	$12,883	$12,290	$10,603	$ 8,840	$ 7,364	$ 7,489
Memo: Tax Equivalent (TE)	$13,290	$12,756	$11,324	$ 9,785	$ 8,451	$ 8,287

(Continued)

EXHIBIT 11.6 (*Continued*)

Loan Loss Provision	$ 1,377	$ 1,980	$ 1,251	$ 809	$ 400	$ 539
Net Interest Income after Loan Loss Provision						
Actual as Reported	$11,506	$10,310	$ 9,352	$ 8,031	$ 6,964	$ 6,950
Memo: Tax Equivalent (TE)	11,913	10,776	10,073	8,976	8,051	7,748
Noninterest Income						
Fiduciary Activities	$ 599	$ 514	$ 441	$ 356	$ 293	$ 204
Service Charges	2,427	2,031	1,796	1,595	1,367	1,123
Trading Gains (Losses)	0	0	0	0	0	0
Other Noninterest Income	$ 2,781	2,648	2,349	1,995	1,098	683
Total Noninterest Income	$ 5,807	$ 5,193	$ 4,586	$ 3,946	$ 2,758	$ 2,010
Total Income before Loan Loss Provision						
Actual as Reported	$18,690	$17,483	$15,189	$12,786	$10,122	$ 9,499
Memo: Tax Equivalent (TE)	19,097	17,949	15,910	13,731	11,209	10,099
Total Income after Loan Loss Provision						
Actual as Reported	$17,313	$15,503	$13,938	$11,977	$ 9,722	$ 8,960
Memo: Tax Equivalent (TE)	17,720	15,969	14,659	12,922	10,809	9,758
Noninterest (Operating) Expenses						
Salaries and Benefits	$ 5,734	$ 5,495	$ 5,026	$ 4,539	$ 3,747	$ 2,994
Premises and Fixed Assets	2,777	2,522	2,320	1,987	1,514	1,007
Other Noninterest Expenses	4,973	4,785	4,353	3,821	3,280	2,886
Total Noninterest Expenses	$13,484	$12,802	$11,699	$10,347	$ 8,541	$ 6,887
Securities Gains (Losses)	$ 28	$ 80	$ 373	$ 365	$ 10	($ 65)
Pretax Income						
Actual as Reported	$ 3,857	$ 2,781	$ 2,612	$ 1,995	$ 1,191	$ 2,008
Memo: Tax Equivalent (TE)	$ 4,208	$ 3,087	$ 2,587	$ 2,210	$ 2,258	$ 2,738
Income Tax Liability (Credit)	$ 850	$ 52	$ 218	$ 390	$ 49	$ 284
Net Income	$ 3,007	$ 2,729	$ 2,394	$ 1,605	$ 1,142	$ 1,724
(Memo: Dividends Paid)	$ 923	$ 815	$ 938	$ 409	$ 456	$ 440
Net Interest Margin on Average Earnings Assets*						
Bank	4.03%	4.34%	4.40%	4.49%	4.59%	
Peers	4.77%	4.89%	5.01%	5.01%	5.02%	
Noninterest Income to Total Income						
Bank	30.4%	28.9%	28.8%	28.7%	24.6%	
Peers	18.1%	17.3%	15.1%	14.2%	13.7%	

(*Continued*)

EXHIBIT 11.6 *(Continued)*

	2010	2009	2008	2007	2006	2005
Operating Expenses to Total Income						
Bank	70.6%	71.0%	73.5%	75.3%	76.2%	
Peers	65.1%	63.5%	63.0%	61.1%	62.9%	
Loan Loss Provision to Average Total Loans						
Bank	0.54%	0.86%	0.65%	0.51%	0.30%	
Peers	0.78%	1.15%	0.78%	0.61%	0.53%	
Net Income to Average Total Assets						
Bank	0.82%	0.83%	0.82%	0.64%	0.54%	
Peers	0.97%	0.71%	1.00%	1.05%	1.04%	

*Tax equivalent.

Net income has been strong except for a decline in 2006. Since then, however, Example Bank has achieved returns on equity above its peers. As discussed below, the higher return on equity is due more to higher leverage than to stronger earnings.

Sources of Profitability

The best way to examine the sources of profitability is to calculate the performance of the bank in the key areas that drive income. There are four key measures examined for Example Bank:

1. *Net interest margin.* Usually expressed as a percent of average earning assets, sometimes shown after loan loss provision to arrive at a "loss-adjusted" margin.
2. *Noninterest income to total income.* The proportion of total income accounted for by noninterest sources.
3. *Operating expenses per dollar of total income.* The outlays made by the bank to generate a dollar of income.
4. *Loan loss provision to average loans.* Measures the credit quality and risks.

Clearly, there are other measures that can be used to assess performance. A focus on these four, however, provides an excellent overview of a bank's performance.

Example Bank's net interest margin has been declining since 2005 (as has those of its peers), reflecting the overall squeeze on margins felt by all depositary institutions. Of more concern, however, is the fact that Example Bank's margins are much smaller than those of its peers, and the gap appears to be widening. Much of this is due to the fact that Example Bank is using higher-cost noncore deposits as a significant source of funding.

Example Bank is, however, doing an excellent job of generating noninterest income. Over 30 percent of total income in 2010 was from noninterest sources versus 18.1 percent for its peers. Moreover, the proportion of income from noninterest sources has increased from 2005.

A major weakness of Example Bank is operating expense control, although it has improved in that area. In 2010, the bank required nearly 71 cents to generate one dollar of income versus 65 cents for peers. Example Bank has improved dramatically since 2006 when it required 76 cents, but improvement is still needed, particularly because margins are low and declining.

The last area, loan loss provision to average loans, is something that Example Bank does very well. Despite aggressive loan growth, its rate of losses (measured by the provision made to loan loss reserves) has been consistently below that of its peers.

The end result is that Example Bank has had a return on assets below its peer group every year except 2009. The major cause of this low level of profit is the small margins on earning assets. High operating expenses have compounded the problem.

 ## LOAN RISK ANALYSIS ILLUSTRATION

The analysis of the loan position of a bank being valued is of critical importance. Loans are usually the major source of income and potentially the major source of losses. The danger to a buyer who is valuing a bank for acquisition purposes is that the loan portfolio may not be as strong as historical financial statements would indicate. In other words, substantial and abnormal losses may be looming on loans already on the books. A bank with expected future loan losses of, say, $500,000 is clearly valued higher than if those loan losses were $1 million.

Like many other aspects of valuation, estimating future loan losses requires judgment. Determining the percent of a loan that ultimately will be collected is difficult, especially with turbulent domestic and international economic conditions.

Before discussing strategies to assess a loan portfolio, it is beneficial to demonstrate why an accurate estimate of loan quality is essential. The next analysis illustrates how loan losses dramatically affect future income and consequently value.

Magnified Impact of Loan Losses

Using Example Bank as an illustration, consider its 2010 income under two scenarios: actual conditions and with an additional and unexpected one-half of 1 percent of loans going bad. This would result in a loan loss provision of $830,000 more than the actual level as shown in Exhibit 11.7. With just an additional 0.5 percent of the loan portfolio going bad, income declined by nearly 35 percent.

Another way to view the impact of loan losses is to calculate the new good loans Example Bank must make to offset the impact of the unexpected additional one-half of 1 percent of the portfolio going bad—in other words, the dollars in new loans needed to replace the $1,038,000 decrease in pretax income. Example Bank would need to make just over $12 million in new good loans to equal $1,038,000 pretax income. Stated alternatively, about $19 in new loans are needed to generate sufficient income to offset $1 of loans that go bad.

Clearly, the future level of loan losses has a substantial impact on financial performance. It is imperative that these losses be quantified as accurately as possible before a valuation of the bank is made. One systematic technique to quantify future loan losses is described next.

EXHIBIT 11.7 Illustration of Impact of Loan Losses on Net Income: Example Bank—2010 Income ($000)

	Actual	With Additional 1/2 of 1% Loans Going Bad
Total interest income	$35,994	$35,994
Total interest expense	23,111	23,111
Net interest income	12,883	12,883
Provision for loan losses	1,377	2,708
Noninterest income	5,807	5,807
Total operating expenses	13,484	13,484
Securities gains (losses)	28	28
Pretax income	3,857	2,526
Taxes	850	557
Net income	3,007	1,969

Delinquent and Classified Loan Analysis

When a loan portfolio is being analyzed as part of an overall bank valuation, the loans of particular interest are those that are delinquent and those that are classified. Delinquent loans are late in payment (anywhere from a few days to a few months); classified loans are those that are beyond delinquent and are no longer accruing income. Depending on the bank's and the regulatory examiner's judgment, reserves may be established to cover losses for a given classified loan, at a rate of 10 to as much as 90 percent. When a loan is charged off, this is, in effect, reserving 100 percent of the outstanding balance.

There are two alternatives to projecting the loss level on delinquent and classified loans. The easiest way is to use the historical experience of the bank to estimate future losses on a group of loans. For example, the bank's experience may indicate that 75 percent of the principal balance of delinquent loans and 25 percent of the principal balance of classified loans eventually are recovered. These rates could be applied to loans in those categories as of the date of valuation. This approach works reasonably well when there are large numbers of fairly small loans, such as auto loans and credit card receivables.

The more difficult approach is to assess each delinquent and classified loan individually. This can be a tedious process, but often it is appropriate where the loans are large and complex. For most banks, larger commercial and real estate loans would fit these criteria.

Exhibit 11.8 presents a tabular format that can be used to analyze individual delinquent loans. This tabular format lists the loan (by name, number, or other relevant description), the amount outstanding, the days past due, reserves established to date (if any), any comments on the loan's outlook, the future loss percentage on book value, and the dollar amount of loss. The total dollar amount of loss for all delinquent loans is the figure of interest in the valuation process.

Exhibit 11.9 illustrates a format that can be used to analyze classified loans. This form is slightly different from that used for delinquent loans. The reason is that classified loans usually have some reserves already established—that is, some loss has been

EXHIBIT 11.8   Format for Delinquent Loan Analysis

Loan Name/Number	Amount Outstanding on Date of Valuation*	Days Past Due	Loss Provisions to Date	Outlook for Loan	Estimated Loss%	Estimated Loss Amount

*Includes principal balance and any accrued but unpaid interest.

EXHIBIT 11.9 Format for Classified Loan Analysis

Loan Name/Number	Amount Outstanding on Date of Valuation*	Loss Provisions to Date	Accrued but Unpaid Interest	Status as of Date of Valuation	Additional Future Losses

*Includes principal balance and any accrued but unpaid interest.

EXHIBIT 11.10 Example Bank Loan Risk Analysis

	2010	2009	2008	2007	2006
Loan loss provision/average loans					
Bank	.54%	.86%	.65%	.51%	.30%
Peer	.43%	1.15%	.78%	.61%	.53%
Net loan losses/average loans					
Bank	.41%	.70%	.32%	.42%	.27%
Peer	.58%	.81%	.61%	.65%	.58%
Loan loss reserves/nonaccruals					
Bank	95%	158%	277%	181%	140%
Peer	173%	182%	198%	173%	197%
Past due loans/assets					
Bank	0.33%	0.31%	0.21%	0.28%	0.47%
Peer	1.18%	1.22%	1.22%	1.29%	1.32%

recognized and reflected in past net income. For example, a $100,000 original balance loan may have already had a 25 percent reserve established. Therefore, on date of valuation, $75,000 is the potential loss amount. A $25,000 expense item to loan loss reserves is already reflected in past net income figures.

Another difference in the form is in accrued but unpaid interest. This situation occurs when a borrower stops payments but the bank continues to accrue the interest income and reverse income accrued but not received. After 90 days, most banks will discontinue the accrual of interest income. If the loan eventually becomes a total loss, the principal must be charged off as well as whatever interest income was accrued but never actually received.

Historical Loan Risk Analysis

Exhibit 11.10 contains several loan risk analysis measures for Example Bank. Except for 2010, Example Bank has had a very good loan portfolio performance. Its losses as a percent of loans have been below those of its peers since 2006. The reasons appear to be diligent collection efforts and superior assessment of credit risk. This conclusion is based on the fact that Example Bank's net loan losses and past due loans are below peer levels. Reserves for future losses may be somewhat low for 2010, as it dipped below 100 percent of nonaccruals for the first time since 2006.

 ## LIQUIDITY AND INVESTMENT PORTFOLIO ANALYSIS ILLUSTRATION

Any banking organization must ensure that adequate liquidity is maintained in order to meet customer withdrawal requirements, satisfy contractual liabilities, fund operations, and provide funds for loans. Sources of liquidity include those assets

EXHIBIT 11.11 Example Bank Liquidity and Investment Portfolio Summary

	2010	2009	2008	2007	2006	2005
Loans/Core deposits						
Bank	122.1%	124.7%	118.4%	107.3%	103.2%	102.6%
Peer	84.9%	85.2%	85.8%	81.4%	76.1%	80.1%
% of securities, 1 year						
Bank	88.2%	86.4%	86.6%	100.0%	69.3%	46.0%
Peer	32.7%	30.1%	33.6%	33.0%	30.2%	26.5%
% of securities 1 to 5 years						
Bank	6.0%	7.2%	6.5%	0%	5.3%	30.2%
Peer	40.4%	42.7%	41.1%	41.3%	42.2%	30.2%
% of securities, 5 years						
Bank	5.8%	6.4%	6.9%	0%	25.4%	23.8%
Peer	26.9%	27.2%	25.3%	25.7%	27.6%	43.3%

readily convertible to cash. These usually include investments and other securities maturing in one year or less, interest-bearing balances at other banks, and short-term debt that is money market related.

Exhibit 11.11 shows that Example Bank seems to be relatively illiquid in that it has a high loan volume relative to its stable funding base. (Loans exceeded core deposits every year since 2005.) However, this high level of loans has been balanced somewhat by the fact that the investment portfolio is overwhelmingly short term. In the last four years, Example Bank has had about 90 percent of its investment portfolio in short-term instruments.

In general, Example Bank does not seem to face a major problem in liquidity. The high level of loans is offset by a short-term investment portfolio. However, if the bank could replace some of its higher-cost liabilities with core deposits, its margins would likely increase.

 PORTFOLIO EQUITIES ANALYSIS (REALM MODEL)

REALM is a duration-analysis model designed to predict changes in market value of portfolio equities by determining how different interest-rate scenarios would affect the market value of an institution's portfolio equity. REALM currently is being used by some banks such as Eastern Bank in Boston and originally was developed by Chase Financial Technologies.[6] REALM can assist financial institutions in taking a proactive approach to their asset/liability management process by determining the impact of different interest-rate scenarios on the market value of equity portfolio. REALM enables banks to download all their loan and deposit portfolios, item by item, into the model rather than using aggregated information and then analyze the effect of fluctuations in interest rates on each asset/liability item.

SPECIAL BANK HOLDING COMPANY CONSIDERATIONS

Many banks are owned by BHCs. The financial statements of a holding company can differ from those of a bank in several respects. First, the holding company reports its financials on a consolidated basis. This means that the financial statements of the individual banks, and any other owned businesses, are added together along with any assets, liabilities, income, and expenses at the parent company level. Second, because nonbank entities can be part of a holding company, some of the income and expenses will be attributable to activities other than traditional banking. Third, because the holding company is usually the vehicle for acquisitions, any associated debt and intangible assets normally are found at the holding company level.

In most cases, the difference between the format and content of holding company financials and bank financials will be minor. In terms of valuation, establishing value of a bank or a BHC will, in nearly all cases, involve the same types of analyses. It is useful, however, to understand the major differences.

The consolidated financial statements of a holding company reflect all the subsidiaries added together, plus any assets, liabilities, income, and expenses at the parent company level. The parent in a BHC structure is usually just a legal entity that is not directly engaged in income-generating businesses. The income of the parent is mainly the dividends paid by the subsidiaries. Miscellaneous parent company income might include interest income from miscellaneous investments owned by the holding company or interest-bearing deposits it has. In general, the income reported on a consolidated basis will be the aggregate of the subsidiaries' incomes.

Expenses of the holding company can vary widely. Some holding companies are shells and have no expenses outside of miscellaneous legal and accounting fees for filing regulatory statements and preparing annual reports. Other holding companies, conversely, are complete service centers for their subsidiaries, offering diverse services such as operations, audit, courier, data processing, check clearing, and investment management. In this case, expenses are incurred at the holding company level that otherwise would be incurred by the bank. The bank is charged a management fee for these services.

With assets, the main difference between a BHC and a bank is in the area of intangible assets. In nearly all instances, intangibles created by an acquisition are booked at the parent company. Also, the stock of the subsidiaries is an asset of the parent company. These two assets account for 90 to 95 percent of the assets of the parent company in a typical BHC structure.

For most parent companies, the only liability of any consequence is debt, usually incurred to acquire subsidiaries. The stockholders' equity account of the parent is essentially the same as a bank—that is, stock, surplus, and retained earnings.

In general, the existence of a holding company as owner of a bank does not complicate the financial analysis. There are a few differences, as described, that are useful to bear in mind during the analysis. The techniques of analysis and eventual valuation of a holding company are essentially the same as those for an individual bank. The exception would be a holding company that has many nonbank businesses. Such a situation would require different valuation research, analysis, and techniques.

LIABILITY MANAGEMENT

Liability management constitutes a vital part of a bank's bottom line. The SEC[7] has now proposed stricter rules on securities, which worsened the financial crises. The SEC has proposed that the risk of losses, when issuing asset-backed securities, must be shared with the banks.[8] The SEC has further proposed that more disclosure about the loans should be made; often their contents are not reviewed. The SEC proposals came when the securitization market is exploding back with more than $30 billion in repackaged loans in 2010. This amount is more than twice the amount in 2009. The SEC does not have the authority to decide what kind of loans are given to borrowers, but the measures are intended to make better loan decisions. For instance, more transparency in the system will make the issuers bring better-quality assets. The proposed rule addresses concerns that financial services firms may continue to generate fees, securitize subprime and risky morgages into investments, and sell them to investors without proper assessment of their risk and management of their liabilities.

One of the heated debates in the proposals has been the fact that banks would be obligated to own 5 percent of the securities they sell. This requirement would provide incentices for bank to align their interests with those of investors. Although banks traditionally have invested in the same types of risky securities that they sold to investors in the years before the crisis, the new proposal would make it mandatory. The SEC's new rule (33-9175), issued in January 2011, pursuant to Section 943 of the Dodd-Frank Act of 2010, require securitizers including banks to release more data on the loans in asset-backed securities so investors are able to make more informed and sound decisions.[9] Financial services firms are now required to disclose fulfilled and unfulfilled purchase requests and warranties in asset-backed securities.

 CONCLUSION

This chapter discusses financial analysis, performance evaluation, and capital requirement of banks. The capital requirement is determined based on applicable regulations, which provides guidance on how banks and depositary institutions must maintain their capital. The 2007–2009 financial crisis and regulatory responses (Dodd-Frank Act of 2010 and Basel III Accord) require banks and other depositary financial institution to maintain adequate levels of capital and be more transparent in disclosing their loans and asset-backed securities. Specifically, Basel III will require banks to: (1) maintain top-quality capital (tier1 capital, consisting or equity and retained earnings) up to 4.5percent of their assets; (2) hold a new separate "capital conservation buffer" of common equity worth at least 2.5 percent of their assets; and (3) build a separate "counter-cyclical buffer" of up to 2.5 percent when their credit markets are booming.

 NOTES

1. Sources: www.ffiec.gov/nicpubweb/nicweb/SearchForm.aspx and https://cdr .ffiec.gov/public/Default.aspx

2. Source: www.gasb.org/home
3. P. Kupiec and J. M. O'Brien, "A Pre-Commitment Approach to Capital Requirements of Market Risk," Manuscript, Division of Research and Statistics, Board of Governors of the Federal Reserve System, 1995.
4. D. Hendricks, "Evaluation of Value-at-Risk Models Using Historical Data," *Federal Reserve Bank of New York Economics Policy Review* 2 (1995): 39–69.
5. Jose A. Lopez, "Regulatory Evaluation of Value-at-Risk Models." Research Paper #9710. Federal Reserve Bank of New York, 1997. P. Kupiec,. "Techniques for Verifying the Accuracy of Risk Measurement Models," *Journal of Derivatives* 3 (1995): 73–84.
6. Wayne S. Fassett, "REALM Improves Interest-Rate Risk Reading," *Bank Management* (August 1991): 54–55.
7. Zachary A. Goldfarb, "SEC Proposes Tighter Rules on Securities that Helped Fuel Financial Crisis," *Washington Post*, April 8, 2010.
8. Securities and Exchange Commission, Asset-Backed Securities, Proposed Rule 33-9117, April 7, 2010. Available at: www.sec.gov.
9. Securities and Exchange Commission, Disclosure for Asset-Backed Securities Required by Section 943 of the Dodd-Frank Wall Street Reform and Consumer Protection Act, Rule 33-9175, January 20, 2011. Available at: www.sec.gov.

12

Internal Characteristics Assessment

THE FINANCIAL ANALYSIS DESCRIBED in Chapter 11 provides extensive insight into the characteristics of the banking company being valued. The numbers, however, do not tell the full story. To understand the bank completely, it is necessary to analyze the internal characteristics of the institution. It is these internal characteristics that create the financial performance. Consequently, an assessment of the business behind the numbers is essential to a thorough and accurate valuation.

The requirements for a proper internal characteristics assessment are fairly easy to identify but more difficult to achieve. They are:

- *A complete financial profile.* Based on publicly available data, a financial profile (as described in Chapter 11) should be developed prior to internal investigation.
- *Access to the bank being analyzed.* Proper analysis cannot be undertaken without access to staff and records. Consequently, it is unlikely that the assessment can be undertaken much before the due diligence review.
- *A work plan to follow.* Because acquisitions are time critical, it is necessary to have a definite plan of action, including areas to be analyzed, priorities, responsibilities, data required, and schedules.
- *Knowledge analysts.* Banks are unique types of businesses, and the people undertaking an internal characteristics assessment should be experienced in bank analysis and terminology. The pressured time of an acquisition is not the proper forum for training.

Assessing the internal characteristics is a more difficult task than analyzing the financial performance. With financial data, there are rules and definitions that allow an objective comparison of a bank over time and with its peers. Internal characteristics, however, are often less objective and require greater creativity and intuition. Some techniques can be used to organize the research and ensure that important internal characteristics are not overlooked.

OBJECTIVES AND BENEFITS OF AN INTERNAL CHARACTERISTICS ASSESSMENT

The primary reason for undertaking an assessment of internal characteristics of a bank is to provide a greater understanding of the institution, thus allowing better assumptions to be made in the valuation process. As discussed in Chapter 4, valuation is an inexact science at best and requires a variety of assumptions about future performance. The more background information considered, the more accurate the assumptions of future performance. Consequently, the main benefit of a thorough internal characteristics assessment is a better estimate of the bank's value.

Another reason for an internal characteristics assessment is a more complete due diligence review. Too often, due diligence reviews focus on the loan and investment portfolio, almost to the exclusion of other critical factors. Obviously, loans and investments are extremely important aspects of the bank, but other aspects also should be analyzed carefully. The internal characteristics assessment described in this chapter helps provide for a more complete due diligence review.

Identifying potential integration problems is a third reason for a thorough internal characteristics assessment. Knowledge gained during the analysis often uncovers weaknesses that must be addressed in order to integrate the two entities. Executives who have been involved with acquisitions say that 80 percent of the value is created *after* the transaction is closed during the integration period. The most creative, well-priced acquisition usually will not realize its full benefit potential without proper integration. The earlier problems are identified, the easier it will be to resolve them with minimum disruption.

The fourth reason for an internal characteristics assessment is profit improvement. In every bank, there are opportunities to increase income and/or decrease expenses. If undertaken properly, the assessment of internal characteristics can result in ideas for improving profits after the acquisition.

TEN P FACTOR FRAMEWORK

Because banks are complex business entities, it is useful to have a framework for assessing the internal characteristics. Such a framework allows better organization of the analysis and delegation of blocks of research to appropriate staff and outside consultants.

For a complete assessment, research should be undertaken in ten areas labeled the *ten P factors* for convenience. Each of these factors covers a relatively distinct portion of a complete internal characteristics analysis. The ten P factors are:

1. Profits
2. People

3. Personality
4. Physical distribution
5. Portfolio
6. Products
7. Processes
8. Property
9. Planning
10. Potential

The types of analyses appropriate in each of these ten areas are described next.

Profits

The financial analysis described in Chapter 11 addressed in great detail the *quantity* of the profits. The *profit factor* considers the *quality* of the profits. "Quality" refers to the likelihood of the profits continuing or growing from historic levels. To assess quality, it is necessary to go beyond the financial statements. The nature and sources of profit performance must be assessed. It is critically important to determine whether abnormal business conditions affected past profits. The publicly available financial statistics are seldom sufficient to make this assessment. Some key factors to consider when assessing profit quality include sources of net interest income, sources of noninterest income, importance of nontraditional activities, and expenses.

The basis of interest income should be investigated to determine whether the sources are stable over the long term. For example, interest income may be abnormally high due to high risk loans made by the bank. Also, the basis of interest expense should be identified, particularly any reliance on purchased funds, which may indicate a need to replace those funds at an even higher cost.

The noninterest income generated by fees, service charges, and trading gains can provide significant revenue to the bank without a corresponding increase in overhead. To a buyer, it is essential to determine whether those sources of noninterest income can continue. Service charges on deposit accounts are relatively stable and predictable, as are service charges and commissions on such routine items as money orders, credit life insurance, and safe deposit boxes. However, other gains are transitory, such as sale of assets, trading account activities, and foreign currency transactions. If the bank generates income from nontraditional activities, it is important to assess the stability of that income and of the outlook for the future.

Expense trends should also be scrutinized. The most likely area of potential window dressing by a seller is expenses. It is important to analyze the type of expenses to identify any category of expenses that has grown much faster or slower than others. For example, lower equipment expenses may be a sign of deferred maintenance. Decreasing personnel expenses may be the result of wholesale, short-term layoffs rather than structural improvements in operational efficiency. Many expense reductions are, in reality, expense deferrals for which payment eventually will be incurred by the buyer. These types of reductions do not truly increase a bank's performance or long-term value.

People

The *people factor* considers the impact of the staff on the bank's future success. To effect a successful integration, it is crucial to understand the unique nature of the acquired bank's staff.

The first area of analysis is the organizational structure. This can be a complex topic requiring a creative analysis in order to judge the organization's strengths and weaknesses. There are, however, six common organizational characteristics that a buyer should investigate for potential problems:

1. *Lack of a reasonably accurate organization chart.* Having one does not imply there is a good organization, but lack of one suggests there is a poor organizational structure.
2. *Unclear lines of authority.* When the authority (and derivatively, the responsibility) is unclear, there are likely to be organizational problems.
3. *Multiple reporting relationships.* If some staff report to more than one superior, this is a sign of potential weakness in the organization.
4. *Excessive spans of control.* The number of subordinates to which a manager can effectively provide functional and technical direction is limited. A very common situation, indicative of potential organizational weaknesses, is the assignment of too many direct reports to one manager and too few to others. This type of imbalance indicates poor use of managerial talent. The right number of subordinates depends on the variety and complexity of tasks being performed. Typically, however, more than six or seven direct reports per manager is excessive.
5. *Inappropriate reporting relationships.* In weak organizations, there are likely to be numerous instances of staff reporting to a superior unrelated to their functions. This is a symptom of an organization that just happened rather than one that has been planned.
6. *Mismatched positions and responsibilities.* Another sign of an unplanned organization is the lack of relationship between a person's position and his or her responsibility. Some vice presidents may be glorified clerks while key staff are in lower positions.

Evaluating organizational structure is a very subjective exercise. If, however, the organization is analyzed in relation to the six factors just described, major potential problems and weaknesses are likely to be observed.

The next aspect of the people factor is management depth. Successful integration requires competent, motivated staff on both the buyer's and seller's side. It is important to evaluate the depth and breadth of management talent at the bank. Frequently, especially in smaller banks, a small number of key people run the bank. If these people leave after the acquisition, which can happen after a change of ownership, there will be few replacements, and a disproportionate share of the acquirer's management resources would be necessary to fill the void.

The actual level of staffing is another important people factor concern. Overstaffing is a problem for many banks and can reduce the potential value of an acquisition target. Unfortunately, it is not possible to make a judgment about overstaffing using simple rules of thumb, such as "one employee for every 2 million in assets." The proper staffing

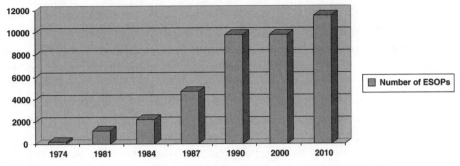

EXHIBIT 12.1 Growth of Employee Stock Ownership Plans in United States

Source: Author's calculation based on data from the Employee Stock Ownership Plans Association.

level is dependent on a multitude of factors unrelated to size, such as number of branches, types of operational systems, location, loan mix, liability mix, and lines of business. Determining whether a bank is staffed properly requires an analysis of the workload and operations of each department.

Another aspect of the people factor is the existence of employee stock ownership plans (ESOPs). An ESOP is defined by the Employee Retirement Income Security Act of 1974 (ERISA) as a qualified retirement plan designed to invest primarily in the employer's securities. An ESOP provides a means for employees to have an ownership interest in the employee corporation. There are a number of organizational, financial, and taxation benefits to ESOPs, including: (1) providing a means for employees to invest in the employer's securities; (2) generating liquidity for closely held corporation shareholders by purchasing stock directly from shareholders and creating a partial market for corporate stock; (3) providing income tax benefits for employers; and (4) creating motivations for employees, improved employee rations, and employee productivity. Exhibit 12.1 shows the growth of ESOPs during the past three decades, resulting from the perceived benefits of such plans.

Many companies created leveraged employee stock ownership plans by borrowing funds to purchase company stocks in the late 1980s. ESOPs originally were created in 1974 when Congress permitted the establishment of ESOPs by the enactment of ERISA. In 1984, Congress added an exclusion from gross income for 50 percent of the interest a qualified lender receives on a securities acquisition loan. Furthermore, in 1986, Congress made dividends paid on ESOP shares deductible when they were used to repay exempt loans. The use of ESOPs grew substantially during the 1990s primarily because of: (1) a rising stock market, (2) increased tax advantages, (3) hostile takeover activities, and (4) the availability of high yield debt to purchase companies.

Current ESOPs are created to finance leveraged buyouts, known as ESOPLBO, for the purpose of purchasing part of a company being taken private. The ESOP issues debt to third parties to generate funds necessary to buy a substantial portion of the shares. The company is allowed to deduct dividends on ESOP shares used to repay the exempt loan, and a qualified lender is permitted to exclude from gross income 50 percent of the interest earned on certain loans. As the loan is being paid, the purchase shares are allocated to participating employees under the ESOPs. This ownership granted to employees under the ESOPs can create better incentives for employees to be more effective and efficient and lead to loyalty and increased productivity.

Family-owned businesses can use ESOPs as devices to sell the business through tax-advantaged Section 1042 sales. Small businesses can utilize ESOPs to reduce taxes through the use of ESOP-owned S corporations. The American Institute of Certified Public Accountants issued Statement of Position (SOP) No. 93-9, *Employers' Accounting for Employee Stock Ownership Plans,* in 1993. The SOP requires that when a company allocates shares to participants' ESOP accounts, a compensation expense measured by the fair market value of the stock on the allocation date should be recognized. Any dividends on stock held in an ESOP should be treated the same as dividends on non-ESOP shares, which should reduce retained earnings.

The Section 133 interest exclusion for qualified ESOP lenders was restricted by the Revenue Reconciliation Act of 1989 (RRA). The RRA limited loans to 15 years and also required that, for loans made after July 10, 1989, the ESOP owns more than 50 percent of each class and of the total value of all of the corporation's outstanding stock. This exclusion was repealed by Section 1602(a) of the Small Business Job Protection Act of 1996, which allowed loans in existence on or before August 10, 1996, to be grandfathered.

The last aspect of the people factor is personnel administration. It is essential that a buyer review the system in place for the personnel-related functions, such as salary administration, benefits, performance reviews, grade structure, payroll system, recruitment, pension, and general employment practices. It is beneficial to know of any discrepancies between the buyer's and seller's personnel administration policies as early as possible.

Personality

Every organization has a personality, or culture, that has evolved over the years. The *personality factor* considers this aspect of the organization. An organization's personality has a powerful influence on the actions of individuals within that organization. Some personalities are clear and obvious while others nearly defy description. Some different types of organizational personalities that might be found in an acquisition target could include profit oriented, growth oriented, participatory, autocratic, informal, process oriented, results driven, or conservative. However, when assessing an organization's personality, it is far more important to examine actions than words.

The personality factor is related to the people factor, but the personality of an organization outlives staff and is carried on through successive generations of personnel. Consequently, it can be extremely difficult to change an organization's personality or to merge two different ones. The more divergent the buyer's and seller's organizational personalities, the greater the risk that integration after acquisition will be difficult.

Physical Distribution

The *physical distribution factor* considers all means by which services are delivered to customers, such as branches, automated teller machines (ATMs), automated clearinghouse (ACH), audio response, point of sale (POS), and home banking. These physical distribution components usually represent a significant financial investment and can create a basis for future growth. There are four key factors to analyze with respect to the physical distribution system: location, costs, technology, and synergy opportunities.

The location is a critical factor for branches and ATMs. If they are well located, they can provide a significant competitive advantage, but if they are poorly located, they can be a drain on income. Factors to consider include the desirability of the market served, growth prospects, nearby competition, site characteristics, traffic flows, visibility, accessibility, and exposure.

Costs are another key concern. The cost effectiveness of the physical distribution system components must be addressed on the basis of expenses incurred relative to benefits derived. If the bank has a reasonably accurate cost allocation system, it is useful to develop a comparison table for branches, such as the one shown in Exhibit 12.2. In this example, Branches C and D are far more cost effective than the other three, even though Branch C has the second lowest transaction volume and branch D has the highest costs. This type of analysis also can be applied to gauge the effectiveness of other components of the physical distribution system.

The third element is technology. The sophistication of the physical distribution system is an important concern, because if it is used properly, technology can lead to lower transaction costs. The situation to be aware of is one of overtechnology, where the investment has been made in hardware and software but is not being utilized fully because of lack of training, customer resistance, or poor vendor support.

The fourth point of analysis is synergy opportunities in the physical distribution system. Often a principal objective in an acquisition is the expansion of the market in geographic and/or market segment terms. A physical distribution system that complements the buyer's own system has greater potential value than one that results in overlapping markets and duplicate coverage.

EXHIBIT 12.2   Example of Branch Cost-Effectiveness Comparison

Branch	Fully Allocated Monthly Expenses*	Transactions[†]	Cost-Effectiveness Ratio[‡]
A	$150,000	70,000	.92
B	200,000	75,000	.74
C	75,000	62,000	1.63
D	300,000	175,000	1.15
E	100,000	38,000	.75

*Includes direct operating expenses and pro rata share of indirect expenses based on consistent allocation formula.

[†]Teller transactions, used as a surrogate measure of benefits derived by the branch. Other measures could be used, such as accounts opened, deposits, or loans made.

[‡]Ratio is computed as the percent of total transactions at the branch divided by percent of expenses incurred by the branch (i.e., the five-branch average would equal 1.0).

Portfolio

The *portfolio factor* addresses the mix of earning assets and interest liabilities in the bank's portfolio. Much of the financial analysis of the portfolio was described in Chapter 9. This assessment expands on that analysis and provides qualitative input.

The loan part of a bank's portfolio typically receives the most attention during an acquisition, which is appropriate because unanticipated loan losses have a potentially devastating impact on value. In addition to the financial-oriented analysis of loans detailed in Chapter 11, it is beneficial to evaluate the quality of the credit systems, including credit approvals, documentation, audits, collateral appraisal, funds disbursement procedures, and undue concentrations in certain industries. It may be necessary to investigate the underlying physical collateral on large loans to ensure that realistic values are assigned and that potential problems will not surface after the acquisition.

The investment part of the portfolio is usually fairly easy to analyze from safekeeping records. These records normally list the type of security, rate, yield, maturity, book value, and market value. It is prudent, however, to verify the actual existence of the securities.

On the liability side, the portfolio factor considers the deposit base funding the assets, especially the mix of stable core deposits versus other more volatile sources of funds. Within the core deposit base it is useful to assess (1) concentration of deposits from a limited number of customers; (2) cost of the deposits; (3) maturity dates of the accounts; and (4) trend in deposit mix over the last five years.

This analysis complements and enhances the financial analysis described in Chapter 9.

Products

Another key aspect is the *product factor*, which addresses what products the bank offers and how they fit in the competitive environment. For example, the range of products may be too limited to meet market needs, thus necessitating significant investment by the buyer for development and promotion of new products. Conversely, the target bank's range of products may be adequate but incompatible with the buyer's, for strategic and/or operational reasons.

When analyzing the products of a bank, these five criteria are relevant:

1. *Features.* The characteristics of the product that make it successful or unsuccessful.
2. *Support.* The backroom systems in place to support the products, including hardware, software, and staff.
3. *Pricing.* The fee structure, including both implicit and explicit charges.
4. *Promotion.* Programs and approaches used to promote the product in the marketplace.
5. *Competitive comparison.* How the quality, range, and price of services compares with competition.

These five criteria allow for a thorough analysis of the products of the bank.

Processes

The *processes factor* addresses the procedural aspects of the bank, which can include all functions but normally focuses on high-volume, labor-intensive activities due to the limited time available during an acquisition analysis.

The purpose of the analysis is to understand the operational strengths and weaknesses of the bank to the greatest extent possible. The high-priority functional areas to be analyzed should, at a minimum, include: loan processing, proof and transit, bookkeeping and tellers, and data processing.

The types of analyses useful to undertake in each area include: (1) staff scheduling relative to volume requirements; (2) equipment utilization; (3) inter- and intradepartmental work flow; (4) methods and procedures; and (5) automation opportunities.

A thorough analysis can identify weakness in the current processes, potential integration problems, and profit improvement opportunities in addition to providing a better base of information for valuation.

Property

Banking is a labor-intensive business, but significant amounts of capital are invested in property. The *property factor* addresses the fixed assets owned and leased by the bank being valued and the potential contribution of these properties to the future success of the institution.

The bank's facilities should be analyzed from four principal perspectives: (1) physical, (2) functional, (3) locational, and (4) financial.

A review of the physical aspects of the facilities will uncover deferred maintenance and the need to invest in repairs in order to bring the structures to standard. When a bank is to be sold, maintenance and repair expenditures can be delayed to improve earnings. A relatively quick analysis, performed by a knowledgeable architect or engineer, can uncover potentially significant future expenditure requirements.

The functional characteristics of the facilities relate to the suitability of size, layout, and configuration. For example, large, opulent branches may constitute the bulk of a bank's branch system, but they may be functionally inefficient and/or obsolete.[1] In such a case, the appraised value of the branches may overstate the true value of the branch network to the buyer. Conversely, a system of efficient, functional branches may have value to the buyer far in excess of the appraised real estate value (due to enhanced market position and locational advantage).

The locational aspects of the facilities should also be analyzed carefully. If buildings (especially branches) are well located, they can be invaluable in maintaining and expanding the bank's market reach. Conversely, if the facilities are poorly located in declining areas, there may be negative value in the buildings—that is, they may detract from the overall value of the bank. The locational analysis requires input from professionals who have experience analyzing both the market and the placement of bank facilities based on market potential.

The last aspect of the property analysis is the financial aspect. In this analysis, the costs of operating the facilities are evaluated, including utilities, maintenance, insurance, and taxes. The purpose is to understand the facilities costs as well as to identify any abnormal expenditures.

Depending on the stage of the acquisition process, a full appraisal of the premises may or may not be necessary. During the early acquisition stages, an overall review is normally sufficient. Later, when specific points are being negotiated or tax allocations are being made, a full appraisal of all property may be necessary. This appraisal may also point out significant gains possible from sale of facilities. If any such facilities could be sold after acquisition, this could enhance the investment value of the bank.

The fixtures of the bank should also be examined. Furniture, teller counters, and other routine equipment are not likely to have a substantial impact on value. There are, however, instances of valuable objects in the fixtures category—for example, art or coin collections. In such a case, sale of those items may result in gain unanticipated from a review of the financial statements.

The equipment used by the bank is important to analyze. Banks have a substantial amount of equipment, such as computers, terminals, and item processors. The important aspect from a buyer's perspective is the compatibility of equipment. For example, if the seller's computer equipment does not interface with the buyer's, it may be necessary to acquire a completely new system that can accommodate the new, larger bank. This situation can affect how a target bank's value is viewed by the buyer.

Planning

The quality of the preparation and implementation of the strategic plan is indicative of the bank's overall approach to its business. The *planning factor* assesses whether the bank has established a defensible market position or is wandering aimlessly with no particular direction. The results of the bank's planning efforts are major influences on the strength of the bank's franchise value. This banking franchise concept reflects the correct observation that a buyer is purchasing a current and future market position, as well as physical and financial assets, when it buys another bank.[2] How well the bank has planned (and subsequently executed the plan) often is the crucial element in determining its position in the market, and derivatively its franchise value.

From a practical standpoint, very few banks have done a particularly good job at strategic planning. If they go through the exercise at all, many view it as a waste of time that detracts from real work. In many cases, the unique franchise a bank has developed (if any) is a result of location or luck. When valuing such a bank, it is essential to consider the uniqueness of the franchise, how it developed, and the likelihood of sustaining and improving it.

Potential

The *potential factor* considers the future opportunity available to the bank and the level of resources necessary to capitalize on those opportunities. To a great extent, the true value of a bank is determined by the potential. As described in Chapter 4, value is the net present value of the future benefits of ownership. Because the future is so critical to value, it is essential that the potential of the bank's market be analyzed carefully.

Potential can be measured a number of ways. For a retail-oriented community or regional bank, the key measures may be future population and income growth, which measure future deposit and loan potential. For a global money center bank, the measures of potential become far more complex as they are based on worldwide economic conditions, conditions within targeted market segments, and a host of other macro factors. Nonetheless, some measure of potential should be quantified.

The direct impact of potential can be illustrated by a simple example. Assume two banks of identical size and profitability, equal in all respects except that one is located in a growing, dynamic metropolitan area and the other in a stable rural community. Using the stabilized income approach as described in Chapter 8 for simplicity and illustration, the value of each of the two banks would be calculated as:

$$\text{Value} = \text{Stabilized income}/\text{Capitalization rate}$$

Suppose "stabilized income" at each bank is $5 million; then value is:

$$\text{Value} = (\$5,000,000)/\text{Capitalization rate}$$

As discussed in Chapter 8, the capitalization rate is the discount rate *minus* the expected growth rate of income. Assume the risk structures of both banks would require a 15 percent discount rate. Therefore, the value of either bank would be:

$$\text{Value} = \$5,000,000/(.15 - \text{Growth rate})$$

Only the growth rate differentiates the two banks. If the metropolitan bank can expect growth of 7 percent, its value would be:

$$\begin{aligned}\text{Value of metropolitan bank} &= \$5,000,000/(.15 - .07) \\ &= \$62.5 \text{ million}\end{aligned}$$

If the rural bank can expect growth of only 4 percent, its value would be:

$$\begin{aligned}\text{Value of rural bank} &= \$5,000,000/(.15 - .05) \\ &= \$50.0 \text{ million}\end{aligned}$$

The lower growth potential resulted in a 20 percent decrease in value. Clearly, the future income growth potential of the bank has a substantial bearing on its value.

SHAREHOLDER VALUE CREATION

Shareholder value creation should be one of the most important goals of financial institutions. Indeed, any consolidation and convergence in the financial services industry is executed in an attempt to improve shareholders' value creation of the combined organization. Several internal performance measurement techniques can be used by financial institutions in assessing shareholder value creation. These techniques are risk assessment, economic value added, and balanced scorecard.

Risk Assessment

The risk assessment method focuses on the risk assessment and risk management units to measure shareholder value creation. This method entails identification of all types of risk, including credit, market, strategy, operation, and political risks. Financial institutions should incorporate all types of potential risks into their internal value-at-risk (VaR) model, which determines an estimate of the maximum loss amount of a particular portfolio over a given holding period. The VaR estimates are determined based on the behavior and movements of underlying risk factors (e.g., credit risk, market risk, liquidity risk). Financial institutions should measure and manage the interrelated nature of all of their risks and minimize them to a prudent acceptable business risk in order to enhance their shareholder value creation.

Economic Value Added

Economic value added (EVA) can be used to assess shareholder value creation through a set of matrices that determines whether the actual reported net income exceeds the predetermined expected earnings. The EVA equals the difference between the reported net income and the dollar cost of capital charged to earnings [EVA = net income – (cost of capital) (investment)]. When the EVA is positive, it indicates value creation, and when the EVA is negative, it measures that shareholder value is destroyed.

The concept of EVA implies that an investment must generate returns equivalent to at least cost of capital to be considered profitable and economically justified. Cost of capital is the weighted average cost of debt and equity and is the return that both shareholders and bondholders could have earned by investing in equally risky investments. EVA measures the combined banks' performance based on its return on capital, both equity and debt. It measures how well shareholders of the merged banks are rewarded for investing in the combined banks rather than another. Traditional income measurement only considers one type of capital cost, namely the "interest" on debt, while ignoring the cost of equity finance. The external financial reporting process does not measure the cost of finance provided by the entity's shareholders because these costs, like all opportunity costs, cannot be observed easily and directly. However, this cost should be estimated and considered in performance measurement to assess properly how successful a bank has been, after the merger, in creating value for its shareholders.

Mergers and acquisitions deals can be considered successful in improving shareholder value creation when they increase the combined banks' market value added (MVA). MVA is the difference between the market value of the merged bank and its invested capital (including both equity and debt).

$$
\begin{aligned}
\text{MVA} &= \text{Market value of the merged bank} - \text{Invested capital} \\
\text{PVA} &= \text{Present value of expected future EVAs} \\
\text{EVA} &= \text{Reported accounting income} - \text{Capital charges} \\
\text{Capital charges} &= \text{Weighted average cost of capital} \\
&\quad \times \text{Invested capital, including both equity and debt}
\end{aligned}
$$

To ensure the success of the combined bank in creating shareholder value, management should measure EVA for all of the provided services and products. The use of EVA as a performance benchmark encourages managers and even employees to think and act more like shareholders in an attempt to create shareholder value.

Balanced Scorecard

The balanced scorecard (BSC) method is the most commonly used technique of assessing shareholder value creation. The BSC is a relatively new measurement tool developed originally by Kaplan and Norton in 1992.[3] The BSC approach suggests a balance between financial measures (e.g., net income, profitability, return on investment) and nonfinancial measures (e.g., service quality, customer satisfaction and retention, innovativeness, employee satisfaction), in assessing shareholder value creation. The key distinction of the BSC is that it measures both financial and nonfinancial factors, including financial indicators, customer satisfaction, internal operations, and employee growth and learning. Financial measures including net income, operating margin, earnings per share, and new product revenue are ultimately used to assess shareholder value creation. Operational measures consist of productivity, operational efficiency and effectiveness, product innovations, technological advances, and safety. The customer perspective measures used to assess customer satisfaction indices with information such as repeat business or results from customer surveys. These measures enable financial institutions to assess the quality of their products and services by improving customer satisfaction and meeting the needs of customers. The learning and growth measures determine how well a work force is prepared for and motivated to be creative and innovative. These measures include in-house and on-the-job training, continuing professional education, certifications, designations, and other credentials of employees.

An effective BSC should balance between performance drivers (leading indicators) and outcome measures (lagging indicators). Examples of banks that are currently using the BSC are Citicorp, and JPMorgan Chase . Financial institutions should use the BSC to ensure that their goals are being achieved by providing answers to these questions:

- How do their customers see them?
- How do they look to their shareholders?
- How can they improve quality and be more efficient and effective?
- Can they continue to improve and create value?

Answers to these questions should provide adequate input to the BSC method to customize an appropriate mix of outcomes (lagging indicators) and performance drivers (leading indicators) into the institution's strategy. This strategy should include the next steps to ensure the institution's success in using the balanced scorecard:

- Top management's establishment of vision for the institution and define mission, goals, and strategies to achieve them

- Communication of the BSC to all affected personnel and the requirement of feedback from them
- Alignment of the BSC with the institution's business units
- Utilization of a rewards system that links performance measures to key success factors
- Implementation of the BSC into the institution's planning and budgeting systems
- Utilization of the BSC as an everyday management tool in creating an appropriate balance between performance and outcome indicators
- Continuous improvement of the BSC approach by finding better performance drivers (leading indicators) and outcomes (lagging indicators)

The BSC is becoming a very popular performance measure system in assessing shareholder value creation. Financial institutions should be aware of and utilize the BSC approach in order to compete effectively in today's global market.

Cost of Capital

Cost of capital can be defined as the cost of company's funds, including debt and equity. It is also considered the expected rate of return on a portfolio for investors. It is a pivotal criterion used to evaluate the feasibility of businesses and projects in the industry, which actually sets a threshold that the business has to achieve because it is the minimum expected rate of return for investors. Weighted average cost of capital (WACC) is the combined cost of debt and equity.

Managing Risk

Risk management is a process of assessing and managing the entity-wide risk. It is not a static activity but rather a continuous process. The 2007–2009 financial crisis has drawn a significant amount of attention to model risk management. Effective risk management requires proper assessment of all types of risks and allocation of capital to all assessed risks. For example, an international bank may desire to allocate 50 percent of its economic capital to credit risk, 30 percent to operational risk and other risks (liquidity), and 20 percent to market and asset-liability rate risks. These risks are defined in next.

Interest Rate Risk

Interest rate risk is the risk of adverse movements in interest rates on a bank's asset and liability positions. This risk may cause loss of profits since banks routinely earn on assets at one rate and pay on liabilities at another rate. Techniques used to minimize interest rate risk are a part of asset/liability management. Interest risk is the risk which has the potential to change the value of an investment caused by the change in the spread of two interest rates. These risks can be minimized by diversifying and hedging. These changes also affect the securities adversely.

Market Risk

Market risk is defined as the day-to-day risk borne by the investor. It also is known as systemic risk, and it cannot be diversified away. Market risk results from trading activities and is the risk associated with earnings volatility caused by adverse price movements in the bank's principal trading positions. Market risk modeling has developed in response to the 2007–2009 financial crisis and now is measured in terms of VaR.

Credit Risk

Credit risk is the risk of potential loss arising from the failure of borrowers to repay a loan or any financial obligation. The higher the credit risk, the higher the borrower has to pay interest. Credit risk is computed based on the borrower's ability to pay the loan amount or the financial contract obligation. This computation takes into consideration the borrower's financial strength, including collateral assets, revenue-generating ability, and taxing authority (such as for government and municipal bonds). Credit risks are considered pivotal for fixed-income investing. This is one reason why credit risk agencies evaluate credit risks of thousands of corporate issuers and municipalities on a continuous basis. Credit risk also is directly correlated with the yield on bonds for investments.

Basel I lays down the international standards of bank capital. These standards were further altered by the Basel II norms for interpretation regarding capital requirement for credit risk. Credit risk basically includes the 5 Cs: character, cash flow, collateral, conditions, and capital. Credit risk modeling has been developed by utilizing credit VaR techniques to address bank capital requirements of the Basel Committee.

Regulatory Risk

The risk involving any change in laws, regulations, or legislation impacting securities, businesses, market, and industry sectors is called regulatory risk. It can result in increases associated with the costs of operating businesses and change in investments.

Foreign Exchange Risk

Risk that has the potential to change the investment value caused by the change in currency exchange rates is called foreign exchange risk, or currency risk.

Sovereign Risk

Sovereign risk is the risk that a foreign bank will change its foreign exchange regulations, impacting the value of foreign exchange contracts.

Liquidity Risk

Liquidity risk is the risk that a bank is not able to meet its obligations as they become due. A bank may acquire funds short term and lend funds long term to obtain favorable interest rate spreads; this process may cause liquidity risk if depositors or creditors demand repayment. The main operating activities of banks in transforming short-term deposits into long-term loans makes them vulnerable to liquidity risk. Effective liquidity risk management is essential to banks to ensure their ability to meet cash flow and earnings targets. The Basel Committee has established guidance on managing liquidity risk that provides details on eight functions. The Basel Committee provides this guidance on managing liquidity risk:

- The importance of establishing a liquidity risk tolerance
- The maintenance of an adequate level of liquidity, including through a cushion of liquid assets
- The necessity of allocating liquidity costs, benefits and risks to all significant business activities
- The identification and measurement of the full range of liquidity risks, including contingent liquidity risks
- The design and use of severe stress test scenarios
- The need for a robust and operational contingency funding plan
- The management of intraday liquidity risk and collateral
- Public disclosure in promoting market discipline.[4]

Operational Risk

Operational risk is the risk that losses can occur from internal failures and external events aside from financial, market, and credit risks. It is the risk of loss resulting from inadequate or failed internal processes, people, and systems, or from adverse effects of external events according to Basel III rules. Operational risk modeling, such as cash flow at risk (CaR) and earnings at risk (EaR), has been developed to deal with possible disruptions in the bank's operations and to meet requirements of the Basel Committee by allocating capital to operational risk.

Asset Management

Asset management can be defined as investing in the best available assets by evaluating risks embodied in them. Defining financial goals, timelines, and continuous monitoring of assets is critical to a good asset management practice.

Liability and Liquidity Management

Liquidity management is essentially managing cash flows to run operations and is measured in terms of CaR.

Capital Adequacy

Capital adequacy is calculated as a bank's risk weighted credit exposure. It is calculated as the sum of Tier 1 and Tier 2 capital and divided by the risk-weighted assets. This ratio essentially is used to have a stable and efficient financial systems and protect the interests of depositors.

Diversification

Diversification is minimizing risks by investing in different class of assets. It is also considered a risk management technique in finance involving a variety of investments within a portfolio.

Overall Risk Management

Financial services firms should assess the level of risk for their entire activities and positions, which is better known as aggregated firm-wide risk, and then decide whether this level of risk is optimal or whether it should be decreased or could be increased without impairing operations or capital adequacy. Exhibit 12.3 presents overall risk metrics for banks. Effective risk management requires adequate assessment of all types of risks shown in the exhibit and proper allocation of capital to these risks. A survey conducted in 2010 reveals that the majority of financial executives are not adequately prepared to meet ever-increasing complexities associated with risk management and continued growth in business analytics. Nonetheless, after the 2007–2009 financial crisis, financial services firms are doing more analysis and assessment of liquidity risk and operational risk.[5]

Risk management modelings of VaR, CaR, and EaR often are used to optimize risk level and minimize potential losses. For example, VaR as a measure of downward risk determines the maximum loss at a certain confidence level. A bank daily VaR of $50 million at the 90 percent confidence level means that in 10 days out of 100, the bank expects to incur a loss that exceeds $50 million. CaR and EaR are measures of

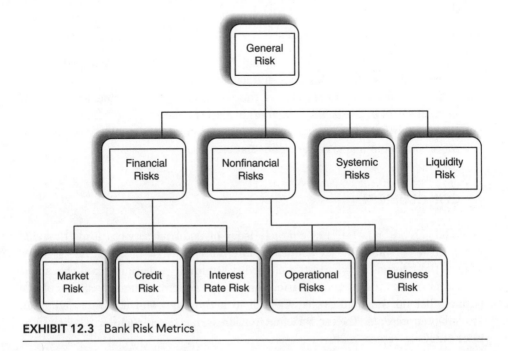

EXHIBIT 12.3 Bank Risk Metrics

downward risk for cash flows and earnings accordingly and determine whether the bank is able to meet its cash flows and earnings targets.

An effective risk management should:

- Consider firm-wide risk, which consists of all types of risks and the relationships among them.
- Understand the nature, dynamics, and drivers of risks and ways to assess them effectively.
- Develop appropriate risk management models (VaR, CaR, EaR) to mitigate potential negative impacts of risks.
- Understand accounting, legal, regulatory, and financial requirements to deal with all kinds of risks.
- Determine whether the assessed firm-wide risk level is optimal in meeting capital adequacy and financial targets or whether it should be decreased or could be increased.
- Recognize that general risk is the firm-wide risk associated with volatility in earnings and cash flows.
- Understand that financial risk is the risk associated with financial activities.
- Recognize that nonfinancial risk is the risk involved with operations.
- Understand that systemic risk is the risk associated with the likelihood of financial distress that may cause multiple simultaneous defaults of large international service firms.
- Recognize that liquidity risk is the risk associated with inadequate bank's liquidity positions.
- Understand that market risk is the risk associated with adverse market price fluctuations in bank's trading activities.
- Recognize that credit risk is the risk of losses due to the failure to pay or credit counterparties.
- Understand that structural asset/liability risk is the risk involves with volatility in interest rates on the bank's asset and liability positions.
- Recognize that operational risk is the risk associated with inefficiencies and ineffectiveness in the bank's operation processes.
- Understand that business risk is the risk due to the losses resulted from residual sources of nonfinancial earnings fluctuations.

 CONCLUSION

This chapter presents internal characteristics of financial services firms that add value. To understand these value-added internal characteristics, it is necessary to analyze the internal characteristics of the institution. It is these internal characteristics that create the financial performance. Consequently, an assessment of the business behind the numbers is essential to a thorough and accurate valuation. This chapter presented the ten P factors in addressing a complete internal characteristics analysis.

NOTES

1. This problem of superadequacy of branches was discussed in Chapter 8 as a form of functional obsolescence.
2. The concepts of franchise and franchise value are discussed in Chapter 15.
3. Robert S. Kaplan and David P. Norton, "The Balanced Scorecard—Measures that Drive Performance," *Harvard Business Review* (January/February 1992): 71.
4. Basel Committee on Bank Supervision, "Principles for Sound Liquidity Risk Management and Supervision," June 2008. Available at: www.bis.org/publ/bcbs138.htm.
5. Peggy Bresnick Kendler, "Firms Not Prepared for Increased Risk Analytics Demands," *Wall Street & Technology*, October 29th 2010. Available at: http://ba.wallstreetandtech.com/articles/227600161.

CHAPTER THIRTEEN

External Environment Assessment

T HE ANALYSES DESCRIBED IN Chapters 11 and 12 provide important insight into the bank being valued. They are, however, inwardly focused analyses. To complete the analysis, it is essential that an assessment be made of the external environment in which the bank operates.

This chapter reviews techniques that can be used to determine the viability and future prospects of the market served by the bank. Each situation will be different, but there are certain basic measures that are indicative of market potential and banking opportunity. Here the classic PEST analysis, which contains *p*olitical analysis, *e*conomic analysis, *s*ocial analysis, and *t*echnological analysis, is used to discuss the external environment (see Exhibit 13.1).

 IMPACT OF EXTERNAL ENVIRONMENT ON VALUE

The condition and viability of the external environment has an important bearing on a bank's value. All other things being equal, the better the market, the higher the value of a bank operating in that market. In an active, growing market, there tends to be greater opportunity, less price competition, and more customers. Growing, vibrant markets create opportunity and, if capitalized on, create value.

In Chapter 12, the tenth P factor, potential, addressed the issue of opportunity and how well the bank seizes on this opportunity as a contributor to value. The degree of success is a result of internal factors, such as marketing, pricing, and strategic planning. No matter how well the bank seizes opportunity, however, that opportunity first must exist. A bank in a stagnant economy may not be able to maintain growth at the rate of inflation, no matter how well it is managed. Consequently, it is

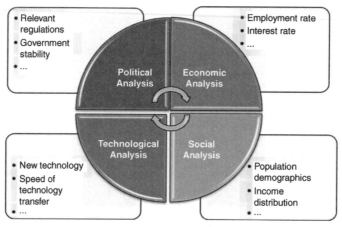

EXHIBIT 13.1   PEST Analysis

---

imperative that the future potential of the market be assessed and wherever possible quantified.

 POLITICAL ANALYSIS

Political factors may have significant influences in the economy, and this may affect the valuation of business organizations to some extent. Specifically, political factors maintain tax policy, labor law, environmental law, trade restrictions, tariffs, and political stability. For financial institutions, there are some relevant laws, regulations, and acts which could affect the assessment to some extent. For instance, the effective implementation provision of the Dodd-Frank Act requires many rules and regulations to be established within the next several years (2010–2015). For example, the newly established Consumer Financial Products Commission will make rules for most retail products offered by banks, such as certificates of deposit and consumer loans.

 ECONOMIC ANALYSIS

The next broad type of analysis of the external environment is economic, which considers the business and employment activity in a market and assesses its future potential. Examining the economic characteristics of a market is an essential adjunct to the demographic analysis. Jobs and business opportunity are the principal factors that retain existing residents and attract new ones.

The most basic measure of economic activity is employment. It is important to examine the trend in employment over the last five to ten years and to analyze the levels of employment by industry. These statistics normally are gathered by the state employment service. The breakdown by industry can highlight potential weaknesses in the local or regional economy. This analysis can also indicate whether the market is overly dependent on one industry or employer.

Another good indicator of economic health is the level and trend in retail sales. In a growing market, the trend in retail sales is usually upward and at a rate exceeding inflation—usually there is real growth in retail sales. The level of retail sales can be assessed by comparing the sales per person in the market versus the sales per person in the state overall. If the market average is higher than the state average, it means that residents are better off on average and/or that the market is an economic and service center for a larger region, one that draws people from outside the immediate area. Either situation is indicative of above-normal banking market potential.

A third important gauge of economic health is the number and type of business firms in a market. The *County Business Patterns* report of U.S. Department of Commerce provides a detailed listing of the number of businesses by Standard Industrial Classification (SIC) code in every U.S. county. In addition, financial health, systemic risk and likelihood of fraudulent activities (e.g., phenomenon of mortgage fraud) must also be considered. Mortgage fraud may involve a large number of participants, which may include borrowers, loan officers, real estate agents, appraiser, attorneys, and so on. Thus, the phenomenon of mortgage fraud may significantly affect the financial institutions.

Depending on the size, type, and sophistication of the market being analyzed, there may be a wide variety of other economic statistics available that provide greater insight into the economy. Such measures might include building permits, office vacancy rates, industrial productions, tonnages shipped, and tourists.

Each market should be approached as a unique entity, with different types of data indicative of economic health analyzed as appropriate.

 ## SOCIAL ANALYSIS

Social factors include cultural aspects and health consciousness, population growth rate, age distribution, career attitudes and emphasis on staff job satisfaction, corporate social responsibility, and environmental matters. These factors may affect how organizations operate, how competitive organizations are, and how much organizations are worth.

Sources of Data

There are a variety of sources for data useful to the external environment assessment. The most widely used is the U.S. Department of Commerce, which gathers and publishes an enormous amount of economic and demographic data. The Census of Population and Housing, an important data source, contains detailed data on virtually every aspect of demographics at a small-area level—data by township, census tract, and even block. The disadvantage of the census is that the bureau conducts a variety of censuses and surveys, including the once-a-decade census (as required by the U.S Constitution with updates only in selected areas such as people/household, business/industry, and geography).

The population of the United States was counted as 308,745,538 in 2010 with an increase of 9.7 percent from the 2000 census. The 2010 census can be obtained by visiting the U.S. Census Bureau's home page (http://www.census.gov/). None-theless, the census is the most complete and authoritative demographic database available.[1] The results of the 2010 census determined the number of seats each state receives in the United States House of Representatives starting with the 2012 elections. Consequently, the census affected the number of votes in each state. Because of population changes, 18 states had changes in their number of seats. Changes in the number of seats can affect banks' lobbying efforts regarding regulatory, accounting, auditing, and tax reforms.

Local data sources include planning agencies and Chambers of Commerce. Planning agencies usually are excellent sources of information on a variety of demographic and economic trends. Many agencies are well staffed and maintain sophisticated, up-to-date databases. A directory of planning agencies is available from the National Association of Regional Councils in Washington, DC. Chambers of Commerce provide a variety of information, especially regarding local business activity. Like planning agencies, how-ever, the range of sophistication is wide. In general, larger urban areas tend to have more complete and timely data available from their Chambers of Commerce.

A number of private sources offer demographic and economic data on hardcopy or computer disk or via online computer connections. Most of these sources offer updates to census data and provide customized reports at a county, city, census tract, or zip code level.

Data on financial institution competitors can be gathered from a variety of public and private sources. If detailed financial statistics on competing banks are desired, the Uniform Bank Performance Reports provide a complete database.[2] Deposit statistics at bank and savings and loan branches are available from the Federal Deposit Insurance Corporation (FDIC) and Office of Thrift Supervision (OTS) respectively as well as from a number of private companies.[3]

Demographic Analysis

In most cases, the success of local businesses is related to the local population. Therefore, demographic characteristics of the population in the market served by the bank should be analyzed first. To determine the future viability of the market, it is essential that the nature of the people living and working there be analyzed. Even if the bank being valued does not primarily serve consumers but serves businesses, it is essential to examine demographics.

The most basic assessment is a look at the number of people in the market, how that number has changed over time, and projected changes if available. A summary popula-tion table might be constructed as shown in Exhibit 13.2(a) along with the graphical display of the population change since 1910 until 2010 in Exhibit 13.2(b) based on the census results, which was drawn up for a bank with a market area of three counties. From these statistics, a wide variety of percentage increases and growth rates can be computed.

The same type of analysis can be undertaken for the number of households, which will not necessarily show the same pattern as the population analysis. Because of declining average household sizes (due in part to more divorces and fewer children), population often increases at rates less than household growth.

EXHIBIT 13.2(a) Population Trends by County, 1990–2011 (Projected)

	Actual		Estimated		Projected
	1990	**2000**	**2009**	**2010**	**2011**
County A	42,540	44,950	45,500	46,000	45,000
County B	59,380	60,125	63,520	65,000	70,000
County C	18,760	20,175	24,350	29,000	35,000
Total	120,680	125,250	133,100	140,000	150,000

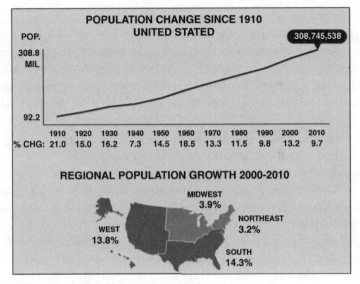

EXHIBIT 13.2(b) Population Change since 1910

Source: U.S. Census Bureau, 2010. Available at http://2010.census.gov/.

Income is the next major area of analysis. There is a strong correlation between the income of households in a market and the banking potential (as measured by deposits and loans). Of the variety of ways to measure income, the two most common are:

1. *Per-capita income.* The average income of all people in an area
2. *Median household or family income.* The income level where half the households or families make less and half make more.

Normally, median income is a more useful figure and should be used where possible.

To analyze income trends, a table like the one shown in Exhibit 13.3 might be constructed. The annual increases in income then can be compared to the rate of inflation to determine whether real income growth has occurred. The real median household income in 2009 was $49,777, not statistically different from the 2008 median. Real median income declined by 1.8 percent for family households and

EXHIBIT 13.3 Median Household Income by County, 1990–2011 (Projected)

	Actual		Estimated		Projected
	1990	**2000**	**2009**	**2010**	**2011**
County A	$ 8,500	$17,500	$22,000	$29,000	$33,000
County B	10,000	21,000	26,500	30,500	35,000
County C	9,500	10,000	12,000	14,000	27,000
Weighted Average	$ 9,393	$17,972	$22,308	$26,590	$32,533

increased 1.6 percent for nonfamily households between 2008 and 2009. Unlike medians, per capita and means are affected by extremely high and low incomes.

Another demographic measure of interest is the age distribution of the population. The pattern of age can have an impact on whether the market is deposit-oriented, loan-oriented, or a mix of the two. In general, markets with a greater proportion of middle-age and older residents tend to be deposit-intensive. Conversely, younger residents tend to generate greater loan demand. Change in real median household income by age of the householder between 2008 and 2009 was not uniform across the age groups. The median income of households with householders under 65 declined (1.3 percent) while the income of households with householders 65 and older increased (5.8 percent). More precisely, declines in median income were experienced by households with house-holders aged 15 to 24 (4.4 percent decline), 25 to 34 (2.0 percent decline), and 35 to 44 (2.6 percent decline).

The median age figure is not a good measure of the age distribution. A better measure is the percent of residents within various age groups. By comparing the percent of residents age 18 to 34 or 45 to 64 in the market and in the state, a hypothesis can be made about whether the market will be more loan- or deposit-oriented, or whether it will be both.

Education level is another indicator of market viability. Higher levels of education normally are associated with greater earning power and more banking potential. The percent of residents with four or more years of college should be compared with regional or state figures.

The combination of population, households, income, age, and education provides a sound basis for understanding the nature of the residents in a market and the future viability of the area. Wherever possible, it is beneficial to examine historical trends and projections as well as comparisons to a larger region or the state.

 TECHNOLOGICAL ANALYSIS

Technological factors include technological aspects such as research and development activity, automation, technology incentives and the rate of technological change. They can determine barriers to entry and minimum efficient production level and can influence outsourcing decisions. Furthermore, technological shifts can affect costs and quality and lead to innovation. Specifically for financial institutions, technology such as Internet banking, visual and audio communications systems, and e-commerce are very common nowadays. New technologies are coming out continually. It is crucial to determine whether a financial institution can do well in catching up with the technology speed and taking advantage of technology.

 ## OTHER ANALYSIS

Market-Wide versus Small-Area Analysis

There are two potential levels of external environment analysis. The market-wide level analysis considers the broad trend of demographic and economic characteristics at, for example, a regional or county level. A small-area analysis examines these character-istics at a census tract, zip code, or city level.

The nature of the market and bank being valued determines whether a market-wide analysis or small-area analysis is needed. For example, if a bank being valued operates county-wide, an analysis with county level data is probably sufficient. Conversely, if a bank is located in only one section of a city or county, it may be necessary to analyze that small area, in addition to the market-wide characteristics. Unless small-area data are clearly required, it is usually necessary to undertake only a market-wide analysis. Demographic and economic statistics at a county or regional level are easier to gather, usually more accurate, and updated more often. Small-area information, such as at a census tract level, is more difficult to gather and, unless it is taken from the census, has a greater potential for error. The discussions in this chapter focus on external environ-ment assessment at a market-wide level.

Competitive Analysis

Reviewing the performance of competitors provides excellent information on the general economy and how the bank being valued fits into the competitive landscape. All the information needed for this analysis is available from the FDIC, the Uniform Bank Performance Reports, OTS (for savings and loans), or National Credit Union Adminis-tration (for credit unions).

The first type of competitive analysis is to review the deposit trends for all banks, savings and loans, and credit unions in the market. It is usually best to examine deposits of individuals, partnerships, and corporations (IPC deposits). The difference between total deposits and IPC deposits is public funds. Distortions in deposit trends can result from public funds since these are usually attracted by a bidding process and do not necessarily reflect market forces. Exhibit 13.4 shows a useful way to organize basic deposit data.

This same type of table also could be constructed for each type of deposit (demand, savings, and time) as well as for loans.

It is also beneficial to evaluate the strengths of the different types of institutions. In the example shown in Exhibit 13.4, banks dominate the market with 67 percent of 2010 deposits, but that is down from 71 percent in 2006. Credit unions are almost inconsequential in this particular market. The savings and loans are a little stronger with nearly 32 percent of deposits in 2010, up from 28 percent in 2006.

EXHIBIT 13.4 Example: Regional IPC Deposit Trends ($000,000)

	2010	2009	2008	2007	2006
Banks	$1,025	$1,007	$ 989	$ 975	$ 949
S&Ls	482	465	440	409	382
Credit unions	18	15	14	12	10
Total	$1,525	$1,487	$1,443	$1,396	$1,341
Subject bank	$ 372	$ 350	$ 307	$ 281	$ 259
Share	24.4%	23.5%	21.3%	20.1%	19.3%

When evaluating deposits, it is important that deposit figures be gathered only for branches located in the market being analyzed. For example, suppose the market being analyzed is one county, and one branch of a statewide bank is located in that county. It would be erroneous to include all that bank's deposits in the analysis, since only one branch is represented in the market. Consequently, only the deposits for that one branch should be included. The FDIC reports branch deposit data for banks, as does the OTS for savings and loans. Credit unions do not report branch data, but they usually have few branches or are so small that their effect is negligible.

No information, except for deposits, is publicly reported by branch offices. Assets, income, and expenses are reported by the entire institution only and not branches. Therefore, the local area competitive market share analysis is limited to deposits for banks' branches. Wherever possible, however, the relative standing of the subject bank in terms of loans, income, and expenses should be analyzed.

The intensity of financial institution activity is another useful analysis. The intensity can be measured by the ratio of households per financial institution office. When this ratio is compared to other markets, it provides an assessment as to the overbanked or underbanked nature of the market. This information can give some clue as to the opportunity to expand market share, which is likely to be easier in an underbanked market. Exhibit 13.5 can be used to organize the analysis. The statistics

EXHIBIT 13.5 Gauge of Competitive Intensity

	Market	State
Number of offices		
Banks	43	901
S&Ls	16	194
Credit unions	2	30
Number of Households per office	56,300	880,300
Banks	1,309	977
S&Ls	3,519	4,538
Credit unions	28,152	29,343
All	923	782

indicate that the market being analyzed is slightly underbanked relative to the state average (because the market tends to have more people per financial institution office).

There are many other ways in which a bank can be compared with its competitors, including locations of facilities and automated teller machines, services offered, interest rates and fees, profitability measures, and markets served.

By analyzing the competition thoroughly, a clear picture of the bank's standing relative to the competition evolves. This can be important input to the assessment of the future opportunity of the bank being valued.

 ## CONCLUSION

This chapter presented environmental factors, such as national market, global competition, technological advances, economic, regulatory and political developments that affect banks' operation, sustainable performance, and value. The condition and viability of the external environment factors must be assessed, and their impacts on banks' performance, value, and sustainability should be determined.

 ## NOTES

1. Other U.S. Department of Commerce publications can be secured at most public and university libraries. This source should be investigated to determine the availability of special reports for the market area being analyzed.
2. www.ffiec.gov/nicpubweb/nicweb/SearchForm.aspx
3. www.fdic.gov/bank/statistical/

PART FIVE

Valuation of Mergers and Acquisitions

CHAPTER FOURTEEN

Bank Merger and Acquisition Process

T HE PROCESS OF MERGING or acquiring two banking organizations is extremely complex; it requires a great deal of time and effort from both buyer and seller. The business, legal, operational, organizational, accounting, and tax issues all must be addressed if the merger or acquisition is to be successful. Throughout the process, valuation can be an important input to the decision-making process, from initial target analysis through integration of the entities.

Merger and acquisition (M&A) strategies are extremely important in order to derive the maximum benefit out of a merger or acquisition deal. It is quite difficult to decide on the strategies of M&A, especially for those companies that are going to make a merger or acquisition deal for the first time. In this case, they take lessons from the past M&A that took place in the market between other companies and proved to be successful.

The M&A process, shown graphically in Exhibit 14.1, can be viewed as having three broad phases: strategy phase, negotiation and investigation phase, and finalization and integration phase.

This chapter reviews the three broad phases of a merger or acquisition and describes the steps normally undertaken. These are not necessarily the steps that would be taken in every situation. They represent, however, the general process that could be undertaken to ensure a successful M&A program.

STRATEGY PHASE

The first phase of any merger or acquisition is the development of a *strategy*, which defines the direction of the bank and establishes the long-range goals to be pursued. There are typically seven parts to the first phase:[1]

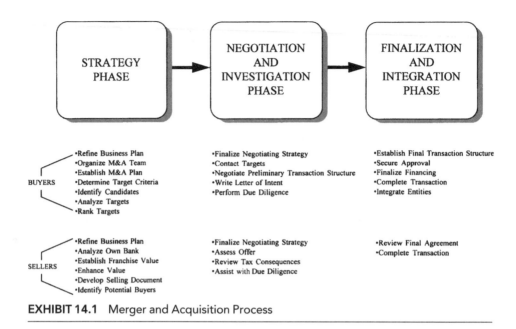

EXHIBIT 14.1 Merger and Acquisition Process

1. Overall strategic plan
2. M&A team
3. M&A plan
4. Candidate criteria
5. Candidate identification
6. Candidate analysis
7. Preliminary valuation and financial feasibility

This process tends to be oriented to buyers, but sellers should plan just as thoroughly as buyers. Sellers should be prepared for unexpected offers and possibly even unwanted suitors. A seller should have an overall business strategy defined and know the value of the bank, based on the way a buyer would view it. A selling bank should extend as much effort in the strategy phase as will the buyer.

Overall Strategic Plan

It is essential that a bank establish an overall strategic plan as it identifies the its competitive position and sets objectives to exploit its relative strengths while minimizing the effects of its weaknesses. The bank's M&A strategy should complement this process by targeting those industries and companies that can improve the acquirer's strengths or alleviate its weaknesses. With the acquisition plan focused on this goal, management can reduce the cost and time involved in analyzing and screening investment opportunities that arise. Opportunities that fail to meet these criteria can be rejected quickly for being inconsistent with the overall strategic plan. Thus acquitison should be viewed as one of several alternative strategies to achieve a basic business objective. This overall plan outlines the focus, direction, and objectives of the bank, usually over a three- to five-year time horizon. Such a plan specifies how and where the bank will compete and identifies markets to be served, resources required, products, pricing, delivery systems, financial structure, growth objectives, and a host of other management variables. Any decision on M&A, whether as a buyer or seller, should be made only after broader business direction and goals have been established.

The overall strategic planning process must begin with an honest assessment of the bank's strengths and weaknesses in the areas of finance, management, operations, organization, productivity, market position, delivery systems, and the like. An objective and occasionally overcritical analysis of the bank is absolutely essential for the development of a realistic business plan.

It is then necessary to analyze the market and competitive environment facing the bank thoroughly. Such factors as economic activity, population growth, demographic characteristics, commercial activity, market shares, and legal restrictions are all factors that are external to the bank but have an impact on its strategic alternatives.

Once the bank understands itself and the external environment it faces, major strategic objectives can be identified. Strategic objectives are long term in nature and define the major thrust and direction of the organization, as opposed to specific quantified targets (which come later in the process). Examples of possible strategic objectives include:

- Expanding geographic trade area into an adjacent market
- Improving operational capabilities in loan processing
- Enhancing product lines to include more sophisticated credit products
- Broadening management capabilities in middle-market commercial lending

In the normal strategic planning process, there may be hundreds of objectives. The next task is to identify which objectives are most critical and therefore deserve priority attention.

Strategic objectives do not define the means by which they will be accomplished. There can be several alternative approaches to meet a given objective. For example, a merger or acquisition could be one way to accomplish any one of the strategic objectives just listed. There are, however, other ways that could be used to achieve these objectives. In other words, M&A *is not an objective but a way to achieve other business objectives.* This is a critical distinction because it places M&A in proper perspective: a means to an end, not an end in itself.

Once the strategic objectives of the bank have been identified and ranked, the next task is to establish approaches to achieve the objectives. For any given objective, there can be a variety of alternative approaches. For example, consider the objective of *expanding a geographic trade area into an adjacent market.* There are a number of approaches that could achieve that objective, such as an acquisition, branches, or a new charter bank. Each alternative approach must be evaluated on its own risks and merits, and the one selected should best meet the needs of the bank. It is usually in this stage of the strategic planning process that the buy/sell/stay independent decisions are made.

After the preferred approach to achieve an objective is selected, the tactical operating plans that will be used to implement the approach can be developed. These tactical plans detail the actions, time frames, responsibilities, resource requirements, and output of the multitude of tasks required to implement a broad program.

The tactical plans can be in a variety of areas, such as finance, organization, operations, human resources, marketing, delivery systems, products, and M&A. All the individual plans are related in the sense that they help in achieving the overall objectives of the bank. The M&A plan, whether the bank will be a buyer or seller, should be developed only within the context of the bank's overall objectives.

A company's strategic plan provides the major stakeholders with a shared vision of where they are today, where they are going, and how they intend to get there. When considering a merger or acquisition, the strategic plan should clearly articulate why it is being considered and how it will be achieved successfully. The acquisition plan should tie very closely to the company's overall strategic plan. An acquisition plan that starts to drift from the strategic plan, or when its connection to the strategic plan blurs or becomes less well defined, is a clear warning to return to the company's basic strategy and goals and investigate whether this acquisition fits. The strategic plan strategies should respond to three key questions:

1. Is this strategy breaking the mold to compete and grow the business (or enhance your area) in a nontraditional way?
2. What does your customer require from you that will enable you to earn higher performance results?
3. What marketplace rationales or internal limitations and commitments can support each of your strategies and convince stakeholders that you are doing the right thing?

Sale Side of Merger and Acquisition

No matter how good the business is, banks should have an alternative exit strategy in case things go south in business or a potential buyer offers an extremely lucrative multiplier. A seller's main goal is to achieve the highest possible price. To prepare the business for sale, it is important to understand what exactly attracts buyers and how would they potentially value the business, what financial targets are they planning to achieve (earnings before interest, taxes, depreciation, and amortization; valuation; market capitalization; or enterprise value). Typically sellers need to understand the fundamental motives for buying their business and what potentially can give the combined business the ability to generate excess returns to the shareholders over a period of time (excluding the lock-up period). To understand why sellers would fit business into the buyer's development strategy, sellers need to understand the primary rationale behind the business combination.

Hence the sale side of M&A includes these 12 steps:

1. Assessment and analysis of the business plan or compiling a business plan including financial modeling
2. Company valuation

3. Detailed analysis of the transaction targets of clients
4. Structuring of the transaction
5. Preparation of a professional, convincing information memorandum
6. Rigorous analysis of potential buyers
7. Definition of the long list of potential strategic and, if applicable, financial buyers
8. Coordination, preparation, and moderation of management meetings
9. Preparation and support in the due diligence
10. Coordination of all other parties involved in the process
11. Conduct of negotiations
12. Process management up to the closing of the transaction

Buy Side of Merger and Acquisition

Buyers can be in the market for banks for different reasons. But the successfully devised and implemented strategy can be a differencing factor in a competitive banking business. To be successful, strategy must be flexible and proactive. The most common strategies are the assimilation strategy, convergence and risk/portfolio management, and the takeover strategy.

The assimilation strategy can be defined as the strategy where buyers purchase smaller banks in a close geographic proximity and keep the leadership in place. The main purpose of the acquirer is to grow the customer base within the familiar business settings. The assimilation strategy is convenient for both the acquirer and the target because it mitigates the negative consequences of M&A, such as layoffs, or skyrocketing integration expenses. That strategy is also appropriate when banks intend to conduct a number of acquisitions in the future, not just one.

The convergence strategy is used when banks are looking to expand into other product or services within the industry. Companies are looking to capitalize on the goodwill and established reputation. For example, First Tennessee, a traditional lending institution, expanded to provide wealth management services to its clients. The danger of the convergence strategy is that the focus of the company's tradional strength that used to bring the bank competitive advantage and helped to retain clients can be blurred.

Consolidation for risk management purposes has become more and more popular and are expected to be even more in demand for the next five years. The 2007–2009 financial crisis can be attributed to many factors including an inadequate risk assessment of business transactions. Risk management has become and will continue to be an integral component of managerial functions affecting every transaction and economic event. The importance of the systemic risk assessment through risk management is underscored in the Dodd-Frank Financial Reform Act of 2010 which requires financial services firms including banks to place a keen focus on compliance risk that should be integrated into the risk management process and its integration into corporate governance best practices. The banking business is in need of the products that can mitigate risk. To reduce the risk levels that banks are exposed to, financial institutions are looking into buying a different line of business: for example, commercial banks purchasing investment banks or vice versa. The purpose is to achieve uncorrelated streams of income and diversify business as much as possible to ensure financial stability. The risk management strategy takes a long time to integrate. The key to this strategy is risk management experts who bring the most value to the business.

And last, but not least, the takeover strategy is currently the most widely used strategy. It takes place when a stronger company acquires a weaker competitor. Takeovers can be opportunistic in nature, when companies hope that the combined business will deliver a better result. They can also be strategic in nature, when the acquirer wants to access a competitor's customer base in a new geographic area. That strategy is hard to implement. Obviously, the target company has some efficiency problems; otherwise, it would not be for sale. Resources and capital needed to navigate a combined business sometimes exceed the discount the company received by purchasing a weaker rival.

Hence the buyer side of M&A includes:

- Engagement structure
- Steps and techniques used by buyers
- Following the buyer-side rules
- Predeal strategic planning and platform philosophy
- Acquisition process
- Discount and capitalization rate determination
- Buyer types and motivations
- Synergies valuation
- Sources and uses of deal financing techniques
- Buyer-side due diligence (light)
- Structuring M&A deals

Merger and Acquisition Team

If a merger or acquisition is part of the overall plan, the next step in the strategy phase is to organize the M&A team, as all M&A face security issues and concerns. To handle them properly, security managers need to be involved. The M&A team should consist of key bank staff in areas such as lending, administration, finance, operations, marketing, and human resources. The team leaders should be sufficiently senior executives to ensure that extremely critical decisions receive the attention they deserve. The M&A team has a mission to identify potential targets for acquisition, assess those target companies, and execute the merger or acquisition.

Outside assistance can be valuable throughout the M&A process. Specialists involved with the M&A team usually include lawyers, accountants, strategy consultants, appraisers, investment bankers, operational consultants, public relations experts, and special examiners. The input from specialists throughout the process can be crucial to a successful merger or acquisition.

The formation of an M&A team usually is thought of as the buyer's responsibility. A seller, however, should also have a team. The decision to sell and the planning for it is one of the most important decisions in the life of a bank, and it should not be taken lightly. The team organized by the seller would have these types of functions:

- Improve the operational and financial condition of the bank as much as possible.
- Quantify the value of the bank's franchise as well as from the perspective of potential buyers.
- Prepare a profile of the bank for potential buyers.
- Determine optimal transaction structure from a tax standpoint.
- Identify potential buyers, and determine the potential value of the bank to each of these buyers.

As with the buyer, the seller's team should consist of key staff and outside experts. Sellers must plan as carefully and prepare just as thoroughly as buyers.

Merger and Acquisition Plan

With the overall business strategy developed and the team identified, the next task is to develop an M&A plan. The elements of this plan should include: (1) timing of activities; (2) preparing for sale (if seller); (3) desired structure of transaction; (4) financial and tax ramifications; and (5) negotiating strategy.

An effective M&A plan consists of several interrelated steps. These steps include: (1) initial criteria development; (2) candidate generation and screening; (3) candidate assessment; and (4) detailed target evaluation. The plan developed at this point in the M&A sequence provides a framework for the remainder of the process which is discussed in the following sections.

Candidate Criteria

The bank that intends to buy must establish the criteria to select potential acquisition candidates. These criteria define what kind of institution will be considered by the buyer. The range of possible criteria is almost endless; however, they usually include:

- Size, usually measured by level of assets or deposits
- Location
- Quality of loan portfolio
- Asset mix
- Liability structure
- Type of customer or market served
- Market position
- Capital levels
- Extent of delivery system

Any given buyer will have its own list of specifications for acquisition candidates. Whatever those criteria are, they should be established early, so that subsequent work is focused in areas where the objectives of the bank will best be met.

Candidate Identification

Candidate identification and screening builds on a clearly defined M&A strategy and sound criteria for relative measurement. Determining which companies possess strong patented technology in a specific area can help to identify acquisition candidates. The acquisition criteria provide the framework from which a list of potential candidates can be developed. At this point, the analysis is usually undertaken using data available from public and private sources. Unless inside information is available, it will be difficult to assess many of the selected candidates on the nonfinancial criteria. Nonetheless, publicly available financial data and information can reveal much about a target institution. Review of the financial data often can reveal strategies, such as retail versus commercial orientation (from loan mix) and degree of aggressiveness (loan-to-deposit ratios and market shares). Field research can help in the evaluation of the target's service delivery system, pricing philosophies, product mix, and marketing programs. Direct consumer research can yield insights about the candidate's image in the marketplace.

After thorough review of the financial data and sound field research, the list of potential candidates can be reduced to a few high-priority targets. Frequently, a priority ranking of the candidates will also emerge. While this first cut will not yield all required information, it does reduce the possibilities and thereby facilitates a more detailed analysis of the remaining banks. The buyer's management and staff time is, therefore, used more effectively in the subsequent stages of the acquisition process.

Candidate Analysis

The initial candidate list should be assembled from multiple sources, such as SIC codes, industry databases, trade associations, mailing lists, and industry journals. When multiple or conflicting opinions exist, a comprehensive list will facilitate consensus building and result in more objective decisions. With the list of potential targets reduced to a select few, a more thorough analysis can be undertaken. Inclusion and exclusion criteria can now be applied to the comprehensive list. Data may come from secondary sources and primary research. Some clients use a numerical rating system, which give scores to each criterion. Some may allocate weightings while others may perform the assessment on a qualitative basis. The first analysis is a detailed review of the banks' financial conditions. An examination of five-year trends can be beneficial in identifying strengths and weaknesses of the banks. (Chapter 11 addresses the financial analysis in detail.)

The market and competitive environments should also be analyzed. The economic activity and demographic patterns in the target's market area should be investigated to determine the future growth and expansion opportunities for each target. Part of this review should also be an assessment of competitive activity, especially relative market shares of financial institutions. (Chapter 13 discusses market and competitive analyses.)

Once the final list of potential targets has been refined, it is critical to develop a profile. Typical profiles may include:

- Key company information such as history, ownership structure, size, location(s) and organizational structure
- Background and contact information on key company decision makers

- Management team background
- Product and patent information
- Segment trends, customer and market data
- Current business alliances and competitive situation

Preliminary Valuation and Financial Feasibility

With information from the preceding steps (candidate criteria, identification, and analysis), it is possible to place a preliminary value on each candidate. This value estimate is based on information available from public sources and the buyer's market research, and provides a general guideline to the value of each candidate bank. These preliminary valuations are undertaken using the same basic approaches as any other valuation, but the input assumptions are not as complete at this stage as they may be later in the process. Preliminary valuation models provide the key metrics to help understand the costs and return potential of a specific acquisition. At this point in the process, these models are high level and preliminary in nature. They are intended to provide an indication of potential costs and value. Definite analysis of acquisition opportunities occurs after the initial strategy has been developed and approved.

One of the biggest mistakes firms make is setting up ownership transition plans that simply will not work in the real world. Hence, financial models analyze the impact of stock repurchases and sales under various valuation formulas as well as repurchase and sale schedules. Therefore, it is also useful to simulate the financial impact on the buying bank assuming various prices and transaction structures. Computer models allow a variety of acquisition assumptions to be assessed in terms of impact on earnings, dilution, and capital levels. From the range of alternatives, it is possible to identify the preferable transaction structures. This does not mean that the seller will necessarily agree to the proposed structure, but the buyer should know the impact of other options.

 ## NEGOTIATION AND INVESTIGATION PHASE

The second broad phase in the M&A process is *negotiation and investigation.* This phase covers the activities from initial contact between buyer and seller to the point where the final M&A agreement can be prepared. After selecting a target company, it is the time to start the process of negotiating an M&A and so, a negotiation plan is developed based on several key factors, such as the benefits of the target company, the bidding strategy and how much to offer in the first round of bidding, and so on.

The most common approach to acquiring another company is for both companies to reach agreement concerning the M&A; that is, a negotiated merger will take place. This negotiated arrangement is sometimes called a bear hug. The negotiated merger is the preferred approach to an M&A since having both sides agree to the deal will go a long way to making the M&A work. In cases where resistance is expected from the target, the acquiring firm will acquire a partial interest in the target; this sometimes is referred to as a toehold position. This toehold position puts pressure on the target to negotiate without sending the target into panic mode.

In cases where the target is expected to strongly fight a takeover attempt, the acquiring company will make a tender offer directly to the shareholders of the target, bypassing the target's management. Tender offers are characterized by these points:

- The price offered is above the target's prevailing market price.
- The offer applies to a substantial number, if not all of, outstanding shares of stock.
- The offer is open for a limited period of time.
- The offer is made to the public shareholders of the target.

There are five major aspects of this phase of the M&A process: (1) the use of proper and applicable negotiation principles and techniques; (2) negotiation strategy; (3) candidate contact and preliminary negotiations; (4) letter of intent; and (5) due diligence.

Negotiation Principles and Techniques

The main principles of the M&A process negotiations are to achieve a compromise that would minimize the complications and allow both parties to think that they are in a fair agreement with one another. The main principle of the victorious negations is the information availability. Both buyers and sellers need to gather as much financial, legal, operational, and regulatory information as possible before entering into the discussion. As a rule, an acquirer makes the first move by sending a letter of intent (LOI); then the phase of due diligence and negotiation starts. Both parties should be flexible and accommodate the other party's informational needs in a timely manner. If a conflict of interests arises, both parties should do their best to seek a compromise that would benefit shareholders of both financial institutions. Both the seller and buyer must understand the underlying motive behind the combination and have a bottom-line negotiations position. To sum up, the keys to successful negotiations is to achieve a win-win situation where both parties feel that they benefit from the deal and to be thoroughly prepared. A high degree of preparation may cost the company a significant amount, but it became a necessity after the passage of the Sarbanes-Oxley in 2002. Noncompliance may cost way more down the road.

Sometimes a compromise is not that easily achieved; then negotiation techniques and tools come into play. Earn-outs are one of the few possible negotiation tools that can be used in M&A negotiation process. Enrique C. Brito of the McLean Group suggests that earn-outs typically are used in negotiations to arrive to the compromise between buyer and seller. An earn-out is a contingent form of payment that is dependent on the acquired company's achievement of certain performance targets after the transaction closes. The buyer pays in installments, and the amount depends on the completion of the agreed-on milestones. Both parties have to agree on the key performance indicators (KPIs) that need to be achieved. Gross profit and gross margin often are used as KPIs in earn-out agreements. In short, the main purpose of earn-outs is to find a common ground for both the buyer and seller.

In M&A transactions, the objective is to arrive at a convergence of points of view in which each party walks away with a feeling that they have a fair agreement. This requires the deal maker to fine-tune the person's negotiation skills to guide the parties toward such convergence. An effective convergence can be achieved in actual M&A transactions when the applied fundamental negotiation principles and strategies are comparable and consistence for both the sales side and the buyer side of the M&A deal.

Negotiation Strategy

Integrating market position into negotiation process plays as one of the key roles for a successful M&A. The first step is to decide how the initial contact with the target will be made, who will be contacted at the target, who from the buyer will do the contacting, and the general approach to the negotiations. This part of the M&A process does not lend itself to generalizations. There is an infinite variety of potential strategies. The best approach depends on the unique nature and personality of the buyer and seller.

Candidate Contact and Preliminary Negotiations

The first contact with a target usually is made with the chair or president. There are situations, however, where a large shareholder may be the appropriate initial contact. Identifying that shareholder may be difficult; consequently, in any first meeting, one should attempt to identify key shareholders.

During the preliminary negotiations, the buyer and seller typically discuss their respective goals and objectives in general terms. The basic structure of the proposed transaction is discussed, but price usually is not addressed until the preliminary negotiations are under way. The objective of the preliminary negotiations is for both parties to come to a meeting of the minds.

Obviously, price must be addressed at some time in the preliminary negotiations. At this point, however, the buyer does not have sufficient information to establish a firm price. Consequently, the price usually is discussed as a *range*, either in dollars or as the stock exchange ratio in a stock-for-stock transaction.

Letter of Intent

If the preliminary negotiations yield positive results, a *letter of intent* should be sent by the buyer to the seller. Such an LOI is an agreement in principle to acquire or be acquired, but it is usually not a legally binding commitment. The letter of intent provides the approval for a close inspection by the buyer, and should protect both parties. The LOI should cover these six points:

1. The purchase price range and consideration to be paid
2. Approval to provide access to necessary information and staff
3. Commitment to maintain confidentiality
4. A date by which the transaction is either completed or canceled
5. Conditions under which either the buyer or seller can escape (usually unforeseen events that could impact the value of the seller significantly or events that cause a decline in the buyer's stock below a specified level)
6. Prohibition of the seller from soliciting other offers (to avoid price shopping)

The LOI can address as many issues as necessary based on the buyers and sellers circumstances and needs. At a minimum, however, the six areas just described should be covered.

Due Diligence

Possibly the most critical step in the M&A process is the *due diligence review.* This is the in-depth analysis of the selling bank by the buyer to ensure that initial assumptions of performance and value are valid. Identification of an attractive target or deal of interest is an essential first step in M&A strategy; however, tactical deal diligence is the point in the process where clients really can focus on risk mitigation and reward maximization. This review is essential to ensure that the underlying business is sound. A thorough due diligence review also can be valuable in identifying weaknesses that will have to be addressed if the acquisition is consummated. The bank works closely with strategic clients and financial investors to understand the targets business and operational fundamentals. Taking an outside-in perspective, the bank helps potential buyers understand the target's core market dynamics, its relative positioning with customers and competitors, the health of its current and future revenue streams, and the potential risks associated with the acquisition. Areas normally covered during the due diligence period include:

- Asset quality, especially loan portfolio
- Investments
- Organization, personnel, and staffing
- Delivery systems and facility locations
- Future loan losses and adequacy of existing reserves
- Data processing
- Operations
- Management depth
- Physical plant and property
- Asset/liability management
- Customer base
- Market position
- Interest rate risk exposure
- Concentration of risk
- Contingent liabilities
- Other real estate–owned portfolios
- Tax liabilities
- Cash management

Also, an extremely detailed analysis of the financial statements of the bank is appropriate to ensure that all reported financial data are compiled in accordance with generally accepted accounting principles, regulatory requirements, and sound business practices.

A team approach usually is taken in the due diligence review. In addition to the buyer's staff, outside auditors, consultants, lawyers, valuation experts, and investment bankers can play an important role in ensuring that all relevant facts are uncovered. Once the due diligence review is completed, there should be no surprises after the transaction is consummated.

The five elements of negotiation and investigation described above (proper principles and techniques, negotiation strategy, candidate contact, letter of intent, and due diligence) take a buyer's perspective, but the seller also must play an active role. To negotiate effectively, the seller must have a negotiation strategy. Once the LOI is received, the preliminary price and deal structure must be analyzed, especially the tax consequences.

One important element that often is not given adequate attention by sellers is the value of the *currency* to be used as payment in a stock-for-stock transaction. In this context, the currency is the stock of the buyer's bank or bank holding company. If the stock received in the transaction is not worth the value the buyer established in the LOI, the price actually received by the seller is reduced. This can be a particularly important concern when the buyer's stock is not widely traded. In this case, a prudent seller values the buyer's stock to ensure that a fair exchange ratio is established. Even if the buyer is widely traded, a seller still should have an independent valuation of the buyer's stock.

The seller should also assist in the due diligence review by providing reasonable access to information and staff. The more helpful the seller, the less time the buyer's due diligence team will spend, thereby reducing disruptions to normal activities.

 ## FINALIZATION AND INTEGRATION PHASE

The last broad phase in the M&A process is *finalization and integration.* In this phase, the transaction terms are finalized, the transaction is consummated, and the task of integrating the entities begins.

Postmerger integration is a difficult process, with potential long-term implications for the acquiring company. Cost and performance improvement opportunities often are not fully realized during initial postmerger integration efforts.

The five major aspects of this phase are: (1) final agreement; (2) regulator and shareholder approval; (3) final review; (4) transaction finalization; and (5) integration.

Final Agreement

The *final agreement* is the formal, detailed document that specifies the exact conditions of the transaction. The agreement is a complex legal document that should be prepared and reviewed by legal counsel of both buyer and seller. For the final agreement, banks try to negotiate access to leaders and a set of communication principles, such as sign-off procedures and a promise to coordinate internal communication. The communication plan should include minute details to avoid any critical communication issues that need attention in this phase.

An M&A agreement usually includes these significant items:

- Description of transaction and closing
- Determination of price, means, and conditions for adjustment from the initially agreed-on price
- Representations and warranties of the seller—for example, existence of authority to sell, capitalization, approvals/consents, undisclosed liabilities, taxes, litigation, contracts/commitments, and title
- Covenants of the seller—for example, access provision, conduct of business, cooperation, shareholder approval, and avoidance of inconsistent activities
- Covenants of the buyer—for example, filing of regulatory forms, shareholder approval and confidentiality
- Special agreements—for example, management contracts, purchase/sale of assets, and tax sharing
- Employee benefits
- Allocation of the purchase price to net assets acquired including intangible assets such as core deposits
- Conditions of closing
- Termination of contract
- Any other special agreements as necessary

No two final agreements are the same, as each transaction has different requirements. The areas listed, however, typically are found in most agreements.

Regulator and Shareholder Approval

All changes in bank control, whether a merger or acquisition, require some type of regulatory approval. The regulatory authorities for various types of banking organizations are:

- *Federal Reserve Bank.* Regulates holding companies.
- *Comptroller of the Currency.* Regulates national banks.
- *Federal Reserve Banks and State Banking Department.* Regulate state banks that are Federal Reserve System members.
- *Federal Deposit Insurance Corporation and State Banking Department.* Regulate state banks that are not Federal Reserve System members.

Usually, the criteria used to evaluate a merger or acquisition is similar for all regulators. The most important criterion is the *safety and soundness* of the combined banks. This criterion considers the resulting financial condition of the combined banks, specifically the so-called *CAMEL* factors—*c*apital, *a*sset quality, *m*anagement, *e*arnings, and *l*iquidity. Regulators search for evidence that indicates whether the transaction would weaken the financial condition of the buyer, especially postmerger capital levels.

The second regulatory criterion is *antitrust*, which considers the effect on competition and concentration of economic power. Until 1980, this was the most common reason for denial of a bank merger or acquisition. Since that time, however, the application of antitrust guidelines has been less stringent. One major difference has been in the definition of competition. Before, only commercial banks were counted in the calculation of antitrust concentration ratios. (The Herfindahl-Hirshmann Index measure of market concentration was the most widely used of these ratios.) Regulators now include competition from other financial institutions in their calculations. Consequently, many M&A that would have been denied before 1980 are routinely approved.

The third area of regulatory consideration is *community impact*, especially compliance with the Community Reinvestment Act. Regulators do not look favorably on mergers or acquisitions that would reduce service and convenience to the community. Community activists have been successful in holding up mergers and gaining certain commitments from the parties for low-income housing loans.

Shareholder approval also must be received. The seller's shareholders must always approve the transaction. Moreover, in certain financing arrangements, the buyer's shareholders also must approve the transaction. The proxy statements sent to shareholders, which must be approved by regulators, normally include information on the transaction in these areas:

- Reason for the transaction
- Structure of the transaction, including complete description of consideration to be received
- Historical financial data of seller
- Historical financial data of buyer and pro forma presentation of combined historical results if the buyer is issuing securities as part of the transaction
- Pertinent information about directors and senior management of the buyer and seller
- Explanation of dissenting shareholder rights
- Copy of the merger agreement

The process of securing regulatory and shareholder approval is extremely complex. The advice of legal, financial, and accounting counsel is required to avoid problems that can delay the transaction. A shareholder rights plan is a defensive tactic used by a corporation's board of directors against a takeover. In the field of M&A, shareholder rights plans were devised as a way for directors to prevent a takeover bidder negotiating a price for sale of shares with shareholders and instead forcing the bidder to negotiate with the board. In many jurisdictions, shareholder rights plans are unlawful without shareholder approval.

Final Review

Because bank acquisitions are complicated transactions, the length of time between the due diligence review and all approvals may be six months or more. Often it is beneficial to conduct another brief review of the seller during the six months of waiting to get the final approval for the negotiated M&A deal to ensure that there have not been any material changes during that period.

Transaction Finalization

Once all necessary approvals have been received, the transaction can be closed. The financing is completed and the change of ownership is made. It is at this point that many believe that the process is over. The final task, however, is the most crucial and probably the most difficult.

Integration

To realize the potential benefits of a merger or acquisition, successful integration of the two entities usually is required. Integration management has become a critical component in the overall M&A process. Integration is not glamorous, but without it all the preceding effort may be wasted.

Early in the process, usually during the due diligence period, a fundamental decision should be made by the buyer. This decision involves the degree of integration to apply after the deal is closed. In other words, how far and how fast will the buyer move in combining the entities? The answer depends on the unique situation and objectives of the buyer, but the options normally fall into one of four categories:

1. *Hands-off.* The seller retains its operations and organization as before the transaction, with the only integration being financial statement consolidation.
2. *Coordinate activities.* This option combines the straightforward and easy elements (e.g., property insurance, employee benefits, and auditing) but retains separate major operational and organizational systems.
3. *Back-room consolidation.* This option combines virtually all the activities not involved with customer contact (e.g., data processing, proof, and investments) in addition to the straightforward functions.
4. *Intervention.* This option involves the total integration of the seller into the buyer's organization. Under this approach, the seller essentially becomes a branch of the buyer.

Each type of integration approach has been used with varying degrees of success. The buyer should decide early in the process which level is appropriate for a given transaction.

Irrespective of which approach is to be used, the first important task is to appoint an integration project manager. This function should be considered full time, at least for the duration of the integration. The person should be a high-level executive (but not the chief executive officer, as a full-time commitment is unlikely) who has a good understanding of the various aspects of a bank. This position should be given high status and direct access to executive management.

The integration manager should select the team that will work full time to formulate the integration strategy and identify the priority projects needed to integrate the entities successfully. These staff members should be quality people drawn from both the buyer and the seller. Also, it is often beneficial to utilize outside resources as necessary to facilitate the integration and provide objective viewpoints. Consultants in a variety of disciplines can be of assistance on an as-needed basis.

With the required projects identified, the integration team forms task forces of staff to assist on a given project. The members of the task force will not be full-time integration team members, but they will be drawn from the appropriate operational and functional areas.

The integration manager and team have the responsibility of reporting results and ensuring that progress is made according to plan. They also have responsibility to communicate to the task forces the feedback from other areas and senior management. Timely and open communications are essential in successful integration.

 ## OTHER CONSIDERATIONS

Financial Aspects

Added value is what most of the M&A deals determine as a success. Deloitte Consulting LLP indicates that the deal is not successful until the value of the transaction is delivered.[2]

Possibility to generate future earnings to bring in substantial return on investment to the shareholders is usually what differentiates the acquisition targets. Return on investment, also referred to as return on equity, is a performance measure that usually is expressed as a percentage and is calculated as a return on investment (gain minus cost) divided by the cost of investment. Return on equity measures the payback potential of the initial investment. The advantage of that method is that it calculates the future cash flows of the combined entity and computes the rate of return. In fact, due to uncertainty, future earnings can be manipulated, so it is essential to understand the underlying drivers behind the earnings numbers. Acquiring companies want the combined entity's return on capital to be higher than the weighted average cost of capital. Depending on how established the acquiring company is and how risky the project is, the appropriate discount rate is assigned when the discount rate is applied to the future cash flow.

In addition to increased value of the combined entity value, M&A also affect the stock prices of the companies. Research evidence suggests that the target's stockholders typically benefit from the M&A announcement because of the stock price increase. Hawawini and Swary suggest that stock value of the target company increase on average 11% during the week of the combination announcement.[3] The effect on the bidder may not be that dramatic (usually the acquirer's stock value declines a few percentage points), but in the long run, banks involved in acquisitions demonstrate an ability to generate higher-than-average cash flows and greater asset growth.

Tax and Legal Aspects

Tax and legal aspects of M&A can be quite complicated. Tax considerations are critical for an M&A transaction. Tax is the major issue that either the buyer or seller has to deal with when combining two separate entities. During the sensitivity analysis, the buyer should consider several deal structures to determine how tax ramifications will affect the deal outcome. The seller must also understand the tax implications of the proposed deal structure in order to realize the intended gain.

Typical buyer-seller conflicts arise due to the following issues: stock sale versus asset sale (assets sale requires the payment of the sales tax of furniture, fixtures, and equipment [assets] while stock sale mandates no such tax); and taxable sales versus tax-free reorganizations (in taxable sales, assets of the target can be written off, so the depreciation deductions will increase, but the shareholders who would want to sell their shares will have to a pay capital gains tax, and vice-versa with tax-free reorganization). Assumptions of liabilities and double taxation are also complicated issues in an M&A transaction. For example, depending on the type of M&A, an acquirer may assume up to 100 percent of the target liabilities, including those that were not revealed or uncovered during the due diligence process.

An M&A does provide tax-saving opportunities if structured properly, so various tax implications should be accounted for long before the deal is officially announced. Changing regulations is a major legal concern in the M&A process. It is costly to employ a legal advisor in house who can keep up to date in a dynamic environment.

Special Topics

M&A is a complex and creative process, and there is more to it than standard accounting/finance, legal, and environmental considerations. Take the earn-out agreements, for example, that we mentioned earlier. Earn-out agreements have increased in popularity due to limited access to the capital markets. Earn-outs are designed to align buyer and seller incentives posttransaction and also present an attractive option for dealing with current market conditions and valuation disagreements.

Considering the complex nature of earn-out agreements, it is recommended that both the buyer and seller to attract the best available outside expertise to be included in the M&A team.

Another special tool to assist the M&A process that currently has been underutilized are so-called M&A collars. M&A collars are contractual agreements that modify the traditional fixed-price stock agreements based on the risk exposure of the deal and preferences of both parties. The most common type of M&A collars are fixed-price collars. The target receives a guarantee that the price paid by a bidder will be within the specified range. If the bidder price falls below the lower bound, then the stock is priced based on the exchange ratio. If the bidder price rises, then the stock is priced again based on the exchange ratio.

To illustrate, an exchange ratio of 0.5 means that each share of target stock will be exchanged for half of the bidder stock if the bidder price does not fall within the boundary.

Depending on the complexity of the situation, the deal can be tailored in a more sophisticated manner. M&A collars facilitate the negotiation process greatly. Collars have a number of other benefits, including reducing the ability of either party to arbitrage, reducing the uncertainty of the deal value, and lowering the volatility (beta), hence decreasing the risk exposure. There are also disadvantages to collar agreements. For example, for both the bidder and target, a prearranged collar may result in over- or underpayment, respectively, due to the limited flexibility in the later stages of M&A. Renegotiation is possible, but it can result in a substantial increase of legal and financial costs.

The Johnson & Johnson (J&J) 2006 merger with Guidant provides an interesting example of the need to stay flexible in M&A practice. J&J was in the process of purchasing Guidant, a leading heart pacemaker manufacturer, and had a collar agreement in place. However, in the midst of the deal, the Food and Drug Administration announced the recall of the Guidant implantable heart devices, and Guidant was under scrutiny. The collar agreement contained a "materially adverse effects clause," which gave J&J leverage to renegotiate the purchase price and lower the offer. If J&J had walked away from the deal, it would have had to pay $700 million fee for terminating the deal prematurely.

Merger and Acquisition in Action

This section presents several actual M&A deals with the intention of providing guiding best practives for M&A transactions. In May 2010, United Airlines and Continental Airlines confirmed a $3 billion merger that would create the world's biggest airline, with ten major hubs, dominating in New York, Chicago, and Los Angeles. The deal is a subject to antitrust approval from the Department of Justice, but if the merger goes through, it will create the largest carrier in the United States.

The Bank of America deal to buy Merrill Lynch was a merger that united the nation's largest consumer bank with one of its most celebrated investment banking firms. Merrill Lynch was one of the largest producers and sellers of complex securities at the heart of the economic crisis. The Wells Fargo deal to merge with Wachovia including the troubled Charlotte bank's banking operations, Wells Fargo is set to gain the large retail banking network it has long sought. Management at Bank of America and Merrill Lynch failed to exercise fiduciary prudence in their mergers; management at Wells Fargo and Wachovia did exercise fiduciary duty in their merger. Comparing the performance of the two banks, Bank of America and Wells Fargo, in terms of how corporate governance had an impact on their stock performance after their respective acquisitions. Wells Fargo's effort in adhering to proper corporate governance, such as no irregularities in executive compensation during and after the merger, conservative credit practices, transparency of information, and proper due diligence in the merger, are relatively quite ethical and transparent. Hence, Wells Fargo's effective governance led to its better stock performance compared to Bank of America, and can set a benchmark and best practices that can be used for future business combinations in the banking industry.

Post–Merger and Acquisition Accounting Issues

This section presents some of the accounting issues of post-M&A, including accounting for intangible assets, goodwill, and contingent consideration. Fair value must be used to measure investment properties; biological assets; property, plant, and equipment; and a limited category of intangible assets. All identifiable intangible assets acquired should be recognized in a business combination. Whether an intangible asset is identifiable depends on whether it meets the contractual-legal criterion or the separability criterion. The contractual-legal criterion arises from contractual or other legal rights. The separability criterion is capable of being separated from the entity and sold, transferred, licensed, rented, or exchanged. Some postacquisition accounting issues that are caused by the recognition of intangible assets include the grouping of intangible assets that have similar attributes and lives; selection of useful lives that maintain the assessment of an indefinite useful life; amortization methods; and specific issues relating to impairment testing. Generally, if intangible assets have a determinable useful life, they will be amortized over their useful life using an appropriate method. Economic and legal factors affect their useful lives. The method of amortization for all intangible assets with a finite life should reflect the pattern in which the economic benefits are expected to be consumed by the entity. If amortization charges are not included in the carrying amount of another asset as permitted or required, they should be recognized as an expense.

Goodwill must be tested annually for impairment, because it does not generate independent cash flows and must be allocated to one or more cash-generating units for the purpose of impairment testing. Thus, goodwill should be recognized in a business combination after all the identifiable assets, liabilities, and contingent liabilities of the acquiree have been recognized. Generally, goodwill may include: (1) The fair value of expected synergies from the combination; (2) assets that are not capable of recognition (such as skilled workforce, noncontractual customer relationships); and (3) assets and liabilities that are not measured at fair value, such as deferred tax and employee benefits.

To identify the constituent parts of goodwill, the acquirer may assist in allocating the goodwill to the cash-generating units or groups of cash-generating units.

 CONCLUSION

This chapter presented an M&A process composed of several phases of strategy, negotiation, investigation, finalization, and integration to ensure the success of a business combination. The business, legal, operational, organizational, accounting, and tax issues should be considered during an M&A process.

 NOTES

1. Federal Reserve Board. Remarks by Governor Roger W. Ferguson, Jr. At the College of Management, University of Massachusetts, Boston, Massachusetts October 27, 1998. Available at: www.federalreserve.gov/boarddocs/speeches/1998/19981027.htm.
2. Deloitte 2011. Available at: www.deloitte.com/view/en_US/us/Services/additional-services/Merger-Acquisition-Services/Merger-Acquisition-Library/Merger-Acquisition-Strategy/index.htm?id=maflash.
3. Hawawini and Swary, "Mergers and Acquisitions in the U.S. Banking Industry: Evidence from the Capital Markets" North-Holland (Amsterdam and New York) February 27, 2002.

CHAPTER FIFTEEN

Valuing a Bank as a Business Enterprise

ALUING A BANK OR bank holding company is one of the more crucial and highly visible aspects of valuation as part of a merger or acquisition. A mistake at this point can be very costly. Overestimate value, and a buyer is left with a difficult premium to earn back; underestimate value, and the seller does not realize the best price or maximize shareholder value. This chapter presents techniques that can be used to establish the value of a bank as an ongoing business entity. To examine the process, Example Bank is used to illustrate specific application of the valuation principles. The Example Bank referred to in this chapter is not a particular bank. It is a composite of several real banks with characteristics that allow illustration of a straightforward valuation. Conditions that can make a valuation more complex and difficult are addressed in Chapter 19.

 BUSINESS ENTERPRISE VERSUS A COLLECTION OF ASSETS

When establishing the value of a bank as a business enterprise, the assets owned by the bank need not be valued individually except in unusual circumstances. The relevant value estimate is based on the future income-generating capabilities of the bank as a whole operating unit, not on the specific assets it happens to own. At this level of analysis, the individual assets are important only to the extent that they help explain the basis for future income. For example, understanding the overall mix and quality of loans and investments is essential to forecasting future income levels. It is usually not necessary, however, to know the value of each individual loan and investment, except in cases where large losses are possible or unrealized on the balance sheet.

There are instances where individual assets may need to be examined, even within the context of the valuation of the total business enterprise. Situations where non-performing loans or other real estate are a substantial part of the asset base may require a special analysis. Individual assets are also more important when recent earnings have been poor and the outlook is not good. In such a case, a more accurate indicator of the bank's overall value may be its net asset value (NAV) rather than future earnings potential.

In this chapter, it is assumed that the Example Bank is a profitable institution with favorable prospects for continued profitability. Chapter 19 discusses approaches to situations different from this one.

CONCEPT OF THE BANKING FRANCHISE

The valuation of a bank as a business enterprise is essentially the valuation of its *franchise*. This term is used frequently in merger and acquisitions (M&A), but there seems to be a range of opinion as to exactly what "franchise" means.

When people speak of a banking franchise, they usually are referring to the composite nature of all the bank's individual characteristics that make it an economically viable entity. These individual characteristics can include:

- Customer base
- Deposit insurance as part of charter
- Management and staff
- Office locations
- Operational systems
- Technological capabilities
- Financial acumen
- Delivery systems
- Image
- Market share

These and many other individual characteristics combine and work together to form the franchise. The stronger these characteristics are and the more effectively they work together, the more valuable the franchise.

Theoretically, a buyer should pay no more for a bank than its current franchise value. In other words, the buyer should not pay the seller for value the buyer may create in the future through better management and planning. This was the difference between fair market value and investment value discussed in Chapter 7. In reality, however, the market for banks, especially sound and healthy ones, is competitive, with multiple buyers usually bidding for one seller. Consequently, the price paid will almost always reflect a sharing of the value creation opportunities the buyer expects to bring. For example, suppose a selling bank's as-is franchise is valued at $100 million.[1] Two buyers are bidding, with one projecting a value creation potential of $20 million over current franchise value and the other projecting an additional $10 million. Each of these buyers believes it can bring skills that will lead to enhanced value of the selling bank. If each buyer has a great desire to own the seller, the eventual price is likely to be over $110 million. The first buyer was willing to share value creation potential with the seller up to the point of outbidding the second buyer. The problem arises if the buyer overestimates its ability to add value. If the buyer does not add $10 to $20 million of value, its shareholders suffer the consequences.

The entire subject of franchise value, both current and potential, is critical to the proper valuation of an acquisition target. An astute buyer usually will value a target bank given its current franchise, analogous to the value if purchased and left alone. This provides a starting point for further valuation based on various value creation assumptions: that is, a buy-and-improve value. The smart buyer knows to walk away when the price to be paid requires too much sharing of value creation potential with the seller.

DIFFERENCE BETWEEN STRATEGIC AND TACTICAL VALUATIONS

The types of valuation thought of most often during an M&A are those at a *strategic* level. These types of valuations are critical to the overall decision-making process, especially in assessing franchise value, quantifying value creation potential, pricing a target, or evaluating an offer.

The stated objective in virtually all M&A is enhancement of shareholder value. Given this objective, the postcombination earnings, return on equity, and/or stock price should be higher than before the combination. For these conditions to be met, the transaction price must reflect a realistic value of the selling bank to that buyer. Consequently, the most critical valuation task at a strategic level is establishing a value of the target bank's franchise, both as is and potential, as discussed earlier. This is especially important to the buyer (so as not to overpay), but it is also important to the seller (to ensure a fair price is received).

In the early stages of the M&A process, it is possible to value an institution from the outside as a free-standing entity. For this type of valuation, the needed information is publicly available. This value is not as accurate as it would be after full access to the subject bank, but it provides a general starting point. The buyer's financial analysts and tax advisors can then simulate the impact on the buyer of various combinations of payment, price, and transaction structures. Also, the effect on value creation of different assumptions about the target's growth rates, future loan losses, spreads, and expenses can be quantified. It is essential that a range of values be established for a target early in the process and that the effect on the buyer's financial structure and performance be quantified. This knowledge allows the buyer to negotiate with a better understanding of the impact of different assumptions on key financial variables.

The seller should also have a valuation of its own franchise to provide a basis for assessing an offer price. The value of the franchise can be assessed on an as-is basis and from the perspective of specific potential buyers. Early on, the seller should have a review of tangible asset value as well as potential intangible assets.

Once buyer and seller agree to proceed, strategic valuation requirements still exist. From the buyer's perspective, a more detailed valuation is required based on full access to the seller's internal records. The additional information will allow for better assumptions on which to estimate value. The internal information will also allow for identification of intangible assets that may exist. (The early identification of intangibles, and their inclusion in the final acquisition agreement, can be useful in supporting certain tax allocations and deductions.)

The seller should also value the buyer's stock if such stock is part of the consideration received. Doing this ensures that the stock exchange ratio is appropriate relative to the values of the two banks. The valuation of the buyer's stock is especially important if it is a closely held bank with a limited market for the stock.

Although strategic-level valuations are the well-known type, *tactical-level* valuations usually require the most effort and are necessary to meet a variety of regulatory, legal, tax, and/or accounting purposes. From the buyer's perspective, detailed valuations of premises and other tangible assets are required for accounting and tax reasons, especially if purchase accounting is used. Moreover, the valuation of intangible assets can have tax advantages under certain transaction structures. The buyer should also value the major components of the seller's loan portfolio and underlying collateral of substantial book value. This type of valuation can provide valuable input for making decisions on the structure of the transaction as well as strategic moves after the acquisition.

WHY THE COST APPROACH IS NOT USED FOR STRATEGIC BANK VALUATIONS

The cost approach values a property based on the expenses incurred to replace it, less any physical, functional, and economic obsolescence. From a practical standpoint, this approach is very difficult to use when valuing a bank (or any type of business) as an operating entity, especially where significant intangible assets are involved.

The cost approach is better suited for valuation of the individual tangible assets of a bank, such as its building and equipment. The value of the bank's franchise, as mentioned, is more than the collective value of the assets. Consequently, the cost approach generally is not used to value a bank at a strategic level.

APPLICATION OF THE MARKET APPROACH TO VALUING A BANK

The market approach values a bank based on the prices paid to acquire similar banks, with adjustments as necessary to compensate for the lack of direct comparability. This valuation approach must be used very carefully, as every acquisition situation is different and the prices paid in other transactions must be assessed thoroughly. Since each situation is unique, the exact same circumstances of buyer and seller will not be replicated. Consequently, great care must be taken when selecting comparable transactions and using the data as a basis for determining the value of a bank.

The previous discussion of value creation potential and its impact on price is the reason that the market approach must be used carefully. Because the market for financially solid banks is relatively competitive, buyers often bid up prices based on value creation possibilities (either real or perceived). Consequently, the prices reported often reflect as-is value and a value creation factor. This is the investment value described in Chapter 7. When these prices are used to value another bank, something above as-is or stand-alone value is being measured. Notwithstanding these problems, the market approach is used widely in pricing bank acquisitions.

Identification of Comparable Transactions

The first task in applying the market approach is to gather data on similar bank acquisition transactions. There are public and private data sources on banking acquisitions. The Federal Reserve Bank or State Banking Department with jurisdiction over the proposed acquisition should be able to assist in identifying comparable transactions.

The result of this research should yield a chart similar to that shown in Exhibit 15.1. These ten bank sales fit the general characteristics of Example Bank—they are all roughly the same asset size and historically profitable. Information that is not shown on

EXHIBIT 15.1   Bank Sales Comparable to Example Bank ($000)

Name	Sales Date	Asset Size	5-Yr. Annual Asset Growth	5-Yr. Avg. Return on Assets	Form of Payment	Price to Book Equity	Price to Recent Year's Earnings
Bank 1	4/12/98	$316,129	12.7%	0.95%	Cash/Stock	1.25	18.1
Bank 2	6/19/98	369,178	18.2%	1.22%	Cash	1.47	9.2
Bank 3	8/1/98	558,496	9.7%	0.94%	Cash	1.03	11.7
Bank 4	8/10/98	423,048	13.1%	1.15%	Stock	1.35	12.3
Bank 5	9/27/98	341,911	6.8%	1.32%	Stock	1.78	13.8
Bank 6	1/17/99	534,715	15.2%	0.78%	Cash	0.95	9.2
Bank 7	3/15/99	478,776	12.9%	1.17%	Cash	1.17	13.1
Bank 8	5/19/99	310,160	16.1%	0.80%	Cash/Stock	1.51	14.4
Bank 9	6/12/99	322,399	7.9%	1.20%	Cash	1.33	12.7
Bank 10	8/28/99	412,315	13.7%	1.04%	Cash	1.14	10.5
Average $ (unweighted)	—	$406,713	12.6%	1.06%	—	1.30	12.5
Example Bank	12/31/99	$388,206	14.5%	0.73%	Cash	—	—

the exhibit but should be analyzed nonetheless includes other characteristics, such as asset/liability mix, capital levels, market area, and general lines of business.

Basis of Comparability

No two transactions will be comparable in every way. Consequently, the identified transactions may have to be adjusted to be more comparable to the bank being valued. Although an infinite number of variables can affect the purchase price, these six key factors are the most significant:

1. *Type of market.* Comparable transactions should be in similar types of businesses and sizes of markets. This factor should also reflect the various market risks associated with the comparable bank sales.
2. *Sales dates.* Sales within the last two years are preferred, because changing economic and competitive conditions can alter the acquisition environment.
3. *Asset size.* Comparables should be of approximately the same size, preferably no smaller than half the size and no larger than twice the size.
4. *Five-year asset growth.* Because asset growth is positively correlated with value in many cases, it is best to compare banks that have grown at about the same rate.
5. *Five-year return on assets.* Because profitability has a direct influence on value, the nearer the return on assets, the more comparable the transaction. Also, the degree of volatility of income should be considered.
6. *Form of payment.* Because form of payment affects tax and liquidity issues, it can affect price paid. Consequently, it is better to have transactions that involve the same payment medium.

No transaction will be identical to another, but if the six factors described previously are used as a basis, transactions that are sufficiently similar to allow valid comparison or that can be adjusted to reflect the conditions of the proposed transaction can be selected.

Publicly Traded Companies as Comparables

If the bank or bank holding company being valued is publicly traded, then other such banks can be used as comparables. Market price per share plus a control premium provides a basis for a value estimate.

Great care must be taken, however, when using data on publicly traded banks as a basis for establishing value of a closely held bank. The dynamics and economics of their respective markets are quite different. Also, the types of institutions are usually dissimilar—with different lines of businesses, leverage, debt structure, markets, and so on. It can be useful to investigate the price-to-earnings (P/E) ratios for publicly traded bank stocks to gauge, in general, what other investors are paying for an income stream. Reliance on that information alone for value estimation of a closely held bank is risky. In general, it is advisable to avoid exclusive or predominant use of data on publicly traded banks when valuing a closely held one. Other techniques and data sources that involve greater certainty usually are available.

Value Estimation by Market Approach—An Example

The data in Exhibit 15.1 show the price paid for the ten comparable transactions as a multiple of book equity and earnings. The average for the comparables is also shown. The application of these statistics to the proposed transaction requires careful judgment, as the publicly available data may mask underlying factors and conditions that affected the purchase price, including adverse market conditions, unusual loan losses, or any number of other unique circumstances.

The ten comparable banks are slightly larger in asset size, slower growing, and more profitable than Example Bank. How these factors interrelate to form value is a subjective measure. In the Example Bank case, faster asset growth is a positive factor only if profitability can support the higher capital requirements, but the somewhat lower profitability is negative. Based on an in-depth analysis of Example Bank and its market, it is known that such asset growth is unlikely to continue, given changes in its market served, and that future asset growth will be nearer or less than the ten-bank average.

The profitability of Example Bank has been increasing slightly but is still well below the ten-bank sample for a five-year average. A thorough analysis of Example Bank indicates that a 0.9 to 1.0 percent return on average assets is a reasonable long-term expectation.

Two measures are used to compute the value of Example Bank by the market approach: price to book equity and P/E.[2] Because Example Bank is expected to be less profitable than the ten comparables, a P/E ratio of 10 is reasonable, resulting in a value estimate of $30.7 million. Because of expected future performance, a P/E multiple of 1.1 was used, resulting in a value estimate of $23.7 million. Averaging the results yields an estimate of value of Example Bank using the market approach of $27.0 million.

Advantages and Disadvantages of Market Approach

The market approach has one overriding advantage: It considers real transactions. In other words, it reflects actual conditions in the marketplace. The disadvantages, however, are significant, especially if the bank being valued and the comparables are closely held.

Price paid reflects much more than book value of equity or last year's earnings. As described in Chapter 7, book value has little or no relevance to market value. Consequently, relating a market price to a nonmarket measure is comparing apples to oranges. Moreover, value is a reflection of future benefits whereas last year's earnings are historical.

The most significant disadvantage, however, is that comparable prices often reflect more than the current franchise value of the selling bank. As discussed earlier in this chapter, the eventual price will, in all probability, reflect current franchise value plus the level of value creation potential the buyer is willing to share with the seller. The relation between price and value depends on the unique circumstances and perceptions of buyer and seller. The value of a bank established by comparing it to other transactions is likely to be higher than its current franchise value. Therefore, the market approach must be used very carefully with full awareness of what is, and what is not, included in comparable sales data.

Notwithstanding the disadvantages of the market approach, this technique can be a good check on values derived by other approaches if used properly. Also, because the information on bank transactions is reported widely, the data needed to utilize this approach are fairly easy to gather.

 APPLICATION OF THE INCOME APPROACH TO VALUING A BANK

The income approach values a bank based on the net present value (NPV) of future income (best measured by available cash flow) generated by the bank. This future income has two components:

1. Actual cash available to owners each year after meeting all expenses, reserves, and capital requirements necessary to sustain and grow the bank
2. The residual value of the bank at the end of a specified projection period (ten years is typical)

The first component, cash available to the owners, can be thought of as the dividend-paying capacity of the business. The second component, residual value, is analogous to the value of the bank's franchise if it were sold at the end of the projection period. The bank need not be sold, but a residual value must be computed as part of the valuation mathematics. These two sources of income are comparable to the potential benefits of any investment: current income and future income from appreciation of the asset.

Measuring Available Cash Flow

Available cash flow in the context of a bank acquisition is the amount of cash available to the owners at the end of an accounting period. This is true cash flow because it quantifies the monetary amounts that can be paid to owners. This is not the same as cash flow in an accounting sense as reported by banks in their annual reports.

Available cash flow is driven by the net income of the bank after it adds to capital the amounts necessary to meet regulatory requirements. As a formula:

Available cash flow = Net income − Required additions to equity capital

This is also the formula for potential dividends. Therefore, the available cash flow from a bank to owners can be thought of as the potential dividends the bank could pay.

This formula is consistent in every bank because all regulated banks come under specific rules with respect to dividends and capital:

▪ Banks have very specific minimum capital requirements that cannot be violated (at least beyond short periods of time).

- Dividends can be paid only to the extent that capital is not reduced (except with special permission).
- Net income is the basis for determining allowable/potential dividends.

Overview of Income Approach Model

The general form of the income approach model that can be used to value a bank is shown in the next equation.

$$\text{Value of bank by income approach} = \frac{\text{Present value (PV) of available cash flow for}}{\text{10 years} + \text{PV of residual value after tenth year}}$$

The most crucial aspect of the valuation is the forecast of available cash flows. To arrive at that figure, it is necessary to project the balance sheet and income statement of the bank being valued. Techniques to project these variables are discussed in the next two sections of this chapter.

Projection of Key Balance Sheet Items

The first step in projecting available cash flows is to project the key balance sheet items of the bank. The balance sheet contains the "drivers" of income and expenses, such as loans, investments, deposits, and so on. Estimating future income based on drivers is a more complex approach than simply extrapolating historical income and expenses. Use of this approach is justified, however, because it is a more accurate reflection of the way income actually is generated at a bank.

Exhibit 15.2 illustrates some key balance sheet items and techniques that can be used to forecast each item. As with any projection, judgment and analysis must interact to form a reasonable, informed estimate.

A number of techniques can be used to project a bank's balance sheet. The one used in this book requires these seven steps:

1. Project the year-end asset levels for the next ten years and the residual period, based on a percentage increase over the preceding year.
2. Project earning and nonearning assets as a percentage of year-end total assets.
3. Project total loans as a percentage of earning assets and net loans based on a target loan loss reserve to total loans ratio.
4. Project investments and other earning assets as the difference between total earning assets and net loans.
5. Project total liabilities as the difference between total assets and equity.
6. Project core deposits, noncore deposits, and other interest-bearing liabilities as a percentage of total liabilities.
7. Project capital requirements under new risk-weighted rules, given the projected asset mix.

The assumptions used to project the balance sheet of Example Bank are summarized in Exhibit 15.3. The resulting projected balance sheet is shown in Exhibit 15.4.

EXHIBIT 15.2 Possible Approaches to Projecting Key Balance Sheet Items

Item	Alternative Projection Techniques
Loans	• Market share
	• Percentage change from preceding year
	• Percent of total assets
	• Absolute value
Loan loss reserves	• Target percent of total loans
	• Absolute levels
Investments	• Percentage change from preceding year
	• Percent of total assets
	• Absolute value
	• Difference between total earning assets and net loans
Other earning assets	• Percentage change from preceding year
	• Percent of total assets
Nonearning assets	• Difference between total assets and earning assets
	• Percent of total assets
	• Percentage change from preceding year
	• Absolute value
Total assets	• Percentage change from preceding year
	• Summation of individual asset values
	• Absolute value
Core deposits	• Market share
	• Percentage change from preceding year
	• Percent of total liabilities
	• Absolute value
Other deposits	• Percentage change from preceding year
	• Percent of total liabilities
	• Absolute value
Other liabilities	• Percentage change from preceding year
	• Percent of total liabilities
	• Absolute value
	• Difference between total liabilities and deposits
Total liabilities	• Difference between total assets and equity
	• Summation of individual liability values

Projection of Income, Expenses, and Available Cash Flow

Simultaneously with the projection of the key balance sheet items, the future income, expenses, and cash flows can be estimated based on a variety of assumptions. The derivations of the income assumptions are summarized next.

EXHIBIT 15.3 Assumptions to Project Balance Sheet of Example Bank

Variable	Assumptions
Asset growth per year	8% in year 1, 7% in year 2, 5% thereafter
Nonearning assets	11% of total assets in year 1, 10% in year 2, 9% thereafter
Total loans	69% of total assets in year 1, 70% in year 2, 71% in year 3, 72% thereafter
Loan loss reserves	1.0% of total loans in year 1, 0.9% in year 2, 0.8% in year 3, 0.7% thereafter
Investments and other earning assets	Balance of total assets minus total loans minus loan loss reserves minus nonearning assets
Total deposits	80% of liabilities in year 1, 85% in year 2, 90% in year 3, 95% in year 4
Non-Interest-bearing core deposits	23% of total deposits in year 1, dropping by 2% per year and stabilizing at 11% in year 7
Interest-bearing core deposits	75% of total deposits in year 1, increasing by 2% per year to 80% in year 6
Noncore deposits	2% of total deposits all years

- *Net interest income.* This is total interest income minus total interest expense. Rather than attempt to project each individually (which requires a forecast of interest rates), it is more reasonable to project the interest spread that is achievable over a base cost of funds. The base cost of funds used in the valuation of Example Bank is the cost of interest-bearing core deposits during the last year. The yield on loans, investments, and other earning assets is expressed as a *spread* over the base cost of funds. Similarly, the cost of noncore deposits is expressed as a premium over the cost of core deposits. This approach does not require a projection of absolute interest rates, just the difference—the spread—between them.
- *Noninterest income.* The income from sources other than interest (including trust fees, service charges, and so on) is forecast as a percent of total income.

These two sources of income are added to derive total income.

Forecasting operating expenses can be as detailed as appropriate for a given situation. Normally, the next categories are sufficient.

- *Personnel expenses.* This expense category includes all salaries, benefits, payroll taxes, and other costs related to staff. The most straightforward way is to express personnel expenses as a percentage of total income.
- *Premises and fixed asset expenses.* This expense category includes all occupancy and related fixed asset costs. These expenses can also be projected as a percentage of total income.
- *Other operating expenses.* This category includes all other costs and can be expressed as a percentage of total income.

EXHIBIT 15.4 Projected Balance Sheet of Example Bank ($000)

	Year 1	Year 2	Year 3	Year 4	Year 5	Year 6	Year 7	Year 8	Year 9	Year 10	Residual
Assets											
Net Loans	$286,398	$310,887	$331,095	$352,546	$370,174	$388,682	$408,116	$428,552	$449,948	$472,446	$496,068
Investments and Other Earnings Assets	86,745	92,862	97,533	97,534	102,411	107,531	112,908	118,553	124,481	130,705	137,240
Total Earning Assets	373,144	403,750	428,648	450,080	472,584	496,213	521,024	547,075	574,429	603,150	633,308
Nonearning Assets	46,119	44,861	42,394	44,513	46,739	49,076	51,530	54,106	56,812	59,652	62,635
Total Assets	$419,262	$448,611	$471,041	$494,593	$519,323	$545,289	$572,554	$601,181	$631,241	$662,803	$695,943
Liabilities											
Non-Interest-Bearing Core Deposits	$73,175	$76,007	$76,449	$75,458	$69,992	$63,734	$56,607	$59,420	$62,373	$65,474	$68,730
Interest-Bearing Core Deposits	238,614	278,692	317,868	359,535	387,287	416,722	447,713	469,958	493,315	517,842	543,595
Noncore Deposits	6,363	7,239	8,047	8,877	9,332	9,805	10,292	10,804	11,341	11,904	12,496
Total Deposits	318,152	361,938	402,364	443,871	466,611	490,261	514,612	540,181	567,029	595,220	624,822
Other Liabilities	79,538	63,871	44,707	23,362	24,558	25,803	27,085	28,431	29,844	31,327	32,885
Total Liabilities	$397,689	$425,809	$447,071	$467,232	$491,169	$516,065	$541,697	$568,612	$596,873	$626,548	$657,707
Total Equity	$21,573	$22,801	$23,970	$27,361	$28,154	$29,225	$30,857	$32,570	$34,368	$36,225	$38,235
Total Liabilities and Equity	$419,262	$448,611	$471,041	$494,593	$519,323	$545,289	$572,554	$601,181	$631,241	$662,803	$695,943

Note: Historical financial data for Example Bank presented and analyzed in Chapter 11.

EXHIBIT 15.5 Assumptions Used to Project Income Statement of Example Bank

Variable	Assumptions
Spread over cost of interest-bearing core deposits	For loans: 550 basis points, all years
	For investments: 75 basis points, all years
	For other earning assets: 75 basis points, all years
Premium paid over core deposits	For noncore deposits: 100 basis points, all years.
	For other interest-bearing liabilities: 125 basis points, all years.
Noninterest income	31% of total income in year 1, increasing by 1% per year to 40%.
Operating expenses	Salaries and benefits: 28% of total income, all years
	Occupancy and fixed assets: 13% of total income, all years
	Other operating expenses: 25% of total income, all years
Loan loss provision	Provision is set so as to maintain a 1.0% reserve to total loan ratio, and assuming net charge-offs equal 0.3% of total loans
Securities gain/losses	None
Taxes	30% on fully tax-equivalent income

The tax rate must also be projected. Because the model projects tax-equivalent income, the maximum marginal rate for that tax bracket should be used as a starting point. The actual effective rate may be lower due to loss carryforwards, accelerated depreciation, and so on. This is a judgment call and must be made on a case-by-case basis.

The last projection assumption is the minimum capital-to-asset ratio required under risk-based capital rules. This is a critical assumption as it has an impact on the levels of available cash flow used in the valuation process. Capital rules spell out clearly the minimum level of capital that must be maintained. As is often the case, however, the bank being valued has excess capital. The projection model should not, however, assume that capital in excess of regulatory minimum can be used as dividends. In fact, banking regulators normally do not allow dividends to be paid if those dividends reduce the absolute level of capital. Consequently, if there is excess capital in the bank being valued for acquisition, it means that the new owner may have greater flexibility in paying dividends as long as the capital ratios are adequate.

The assumptions used in projecting the income and available cash flow of Example Bank are summarized in Exhibit 15.5. The resulting projected income and cash flow statement is shown in Exhibit 15.6.

Value Estimation by Income Approach—An Example

With the total and available cash flows projected, the valuation process can be completed. The future available cash flows are discounted to PV, the residual value is determined, and they are added together. The key elements are the discount rates used to convert future cash flows into PV and the residual value of the bank after the end of the tenth year.

EXHIBIT 15.6 Projected Income Statement and Available Cash Flow of Example Bank ($000)

	Year 1	Year 2	Year 3	Year 4	Year 5	Year 6	Year 7	Year 8	Year 9	Year 10	Residual
Net Interest Income (Tax Equivalent)	$14,590	$15,026	$16,171	$15,759	$15,911	$16,039	$16,140	$16,947	$17,794	$18,684	$19,618
Noninterest Income	6,555	7,071	7,965	8,118	8,567	9,022	9,479	10,387	11,377	12,465	13,079
Total Income (Tax Equivalent)	$21,145	$22,098	$24,136	$23,877	$24,478	$25,061	$25,619	$27,334	$29,171	$31,140	$32,697
Operating Expenses											
Salaries and Benefits	$ 5,920	$ 6,187	$ 6,758	$ 6,686	$ 6,854	$ 7,017	$ 7,173	$ 7,654	$ 8,168	$ 8,719	$ 9,155
Premises and Fixed Assets	2,749	2,873	3,138	3,104	3,182	3,258	3,331	3,553	3,792	4,048	4,251
Other Operating Expenses	5,286	5,524	6,034	5,969	6,120	6,265	6,405	6,834	7,293	7,785	8,174
Total Operating Expenses	$13,956	$14,584	$15,930	$15,759	$16,156	$16,540	$16,909	$18,040	$19,253	$20,553	$21,580
Provision for Loan Losses	882	1,189	1,207	1,285	1,300	1,365	1,433	1,505	1,580	1,659	1,742
Securities Gains (Losses)	0	0	0	0	0	0	0	0	0	0	0
Pretax Income	6,308	6,324	6,999	6,833	7,023	7,156	7,278	7,789	8,338	8,929	9,375
Taxes	1,892	1,897	2,100	2,050	2,107	2,147	2,183	2,337	2,501	2,679	2,813
Net Income	$ 4,415	$ 4,427	$ 4,899	$ 4,783	$ 4,916	$ 5,009	$ 5,094	$ 5,452	$ 5,837	$ 6,250	$ 6,563
ROA	1.09%	1.02%	1.07%	.99%	.97%	.94%	.91%	.93%	.95%	.97%	.97%
Required Additions to Capital	$ 1,713	$ 1,653	$ 3,876	$ 1,278	$ 1,555	$ 1,632	$ 1,713	$ 1,798	$ 1,887	$ 1,981	$ 2,079
Available Cash Flow	$ 2,702	$ 2,773	$ 1,024	$ 3,506	$ 3,361	$ 3,377	$ 3,381	$ 3,654	$ 3,950	$ 4,270	$ 4,484

Note: Historical financial data for Example Bank presented and analyzed in Chapter 11.

The discount rates used in the valuation of Example Bank are shown in Exhibit 15.7. These rates were derived using the techniques described in Chapter 8. The discount rate of 14 percent reflects the risk-free rate plus an appropriate risk premium.

The residual value of Example Bank was calculated based on the capitalization of its residual available cash flow.[3] It was assumed that a 3 percent long-term growth of income was reasonable. Therefore, a capitalization rate of 11 percent was used (discount rate of 14 percent minus growth rate of 3 percent).

Given all the assumptions of balance sheet growth and composition, income expenses, capital needs, and discount rates, the value of Example Bank using the income approach is $25.2 million, about 1.17 times 2010 book value.

SENSITIVITY OF VALUE ESTIMATE TO ASSUMPTION CHANGES

The discounted cash flow (DCF) should be used in valuing M&A deals with great caution, given the dynamic and uncertain nature of the market. More sophisticated methods, such as the capital asset pricing model (CAPM) and option pricing model, are superior to DCF primarily because they capture the full value of financial engineering—such as lowering the cost of capital, gaining tax and accounting advantages, reducing unnecessary regulatory costs, and restructuring particular assets through securitization; and measure unique synergies in distribution and product lines. The acquirer can create value in these ways:

- *Universal synergies,* which often are fully reflected in the M&A price, can be created by improving the yield on investments, eliminating excess cost, or improving productivity and pricing.
- *Endemic synergies,* which are less reflected in M&A deal pricing, can be achieved by selling the products of a new company.
- Unique synergies are distinctive and the deciding factor in most M&A deals, achieved through earning revenue from special skills or assets, leveraging an entity's base to create new business opportunities, and restructuring to gain a distinct competitive advantage.

In general, the final estimates of value are very sensitive to changes in assumptions. It is for this reason that two prospective buyers could value a selling bank completely differently, yet both still could be justified. Consequently, it is essential that valuation assumptions be selected very carefully and only after thorough analysis of the target bank.

Many different assumptions that can affect value, but some cause more changes in the final value estimate than others. The more critical assumption areas are:

- Net interest margin
- Operating expenses
- Loan loss provision

EXHIBIT 15.7 Valuation of Example Bank Using Income Approach ($000)

	Year 1	Year 2	Year 3	Year 4	Year 5	Year 6	Year 7	Year 8	Year 9	Year 10	Residual
Available Cash Flow	$2,702	$2,773	$1,024	$3,506	$3,361	$3,377	$3,381	$3,654	$3,950	$4,270	$4,484
Discount Rate	14%	14%	14%	14%	14%	14%	14%	14%	14%	14%	14%
Present Value of Available Cash Flow	$2,370	$2,134	$691	$2,076	$1,746	$1,539	$1,351	$1,281	$1,215	$1,152	—
Growth Rate of Available Cash Flow in Perpetuity	—	—	—	—	—	—	—	—	—	—	3.0%
Capitalization Rate on Residual Available Cash Flow	—	—	—	—	—	—	—	—	—	—	11%
Capitalized Value of Cash Flows	—	—	—	—	—	—	—	—	—	—	$42,828
Net Present Value of Available Cash Flows (Years 1–10)						$15,555					
Present Value of Capitalized Cash Flows						$9,645					
Value of Example Bank (rounded)						$25,200,000					

EXHIBIT 15.8   Sensitivity of Value Estimates to Changes in Key Assumptions ($000,000)

Assumption Area	Base Assumptions	Revised Assumptions[1]	Original Value	Revised Value	Percentage Change in Value
Net Interest Margin on Average Earning Assets	3.91% in year 1, 3.87% in year 2, 3.89% in year 3, 3.59% in year 4, 3.45% in year 5, 3.31% in year 6, 3.17% thereafter	4.30% in year 1, 4.26% in year 2, 4.28% in year 3, 3.95% in year 4, 3.80% in year 5, 3.64% in year 6, 3.49% thereafter	$25.2	$29.9	+18.5%
Operating Expenses	66% of total income all years	59.4% of income all years	$25.2	$34.2	+35.8%
Loan Loss Provision	Target loan loss reserve to total loans of 1%, with charge-offs equaling 0.3% of loans	Charge-offs equal 0.27% of loans, same reserve balance	$25.2	$25.8	+2.4%
Discount Rate on Cash Flow	14% all years	12.6% all years	$25.2	$29.4	+16.5%
Growth Rate of Available Cash Flow in Perpetuity	3.0% annually	3.3% annually	$25.2	$25.5	+1.2%

[1]Revised assumptions equal base assumptions changed by 10 percent in direction that would tend to increase value.

- Discount rate on available cash flows
- Capitalization rate on residual available cash flow

Exhibit 15.8 summarizes the impact on Example Bank's value of a 10 percent change in the six key assumptions. Each assumption was altered 10 percent in the direction that normally would increase value. From the data, it is clear that net interest margin and operating expenses have the largest magnifying impact on value. Therefore, the assumptions in these two areas need to be considered very carefully when establishing value.

VALUE-CREATION OPPORTUNITIES AND THE ACQUISITION PRICE

The value just estimated by the income approach is the franchise value of Example Bank as a stand-alone entity on an as-is basis to a hypothetical buyer. Consequently, it is a starting point in establishing a purchase price. As a passive investment, Example Bank is worth about $25.2 million, given the assumptions used. To a particular buyer, however,

Example Bank may be worth more for a variety of reasons. For example, a particular buyer may be able to reduce operating expenses by combining facilities and staff. Another buyer may be able to increase the net interest margin due to sophisticated financial management and loan-pricing capabilities. There are any number of reasons why the price a particular buyer is willing to offer for Example Bank may be higher than its value as a stand-alone entity.

The next list illustrates how three different types of buyers might offer different yet equally justifiable prices for Example Bank. Different buyer situations and assumptions significantly influence their perceptions of value and the price each believes would be justified.

- *Cost-cutter buyer.* Able to reduce operating expenses to total income by 20 percent over four years; resulting value would be $40.8 million (+ 62 percent).
- *Money-manager buyer.* Able to sustain 3.91 percent margin on earning assets; resulting value would be $32.5 million (+ 29 percent).
- *Expansion buyer.* Able to grow assets at rate two percentage points higher; resulting value would be $23.6 million (– 6.3 percent).[4]

From these scenarios, it is clear that different assumptions and situations of buyers can have a significant impact on the perceived value of a target.

The figures just shown quantify the impact of different value creation scenarios. Actually achieving enhanced shareholder value through an M&A depends on the distinctive benefits the buyer can bring.[5] To justify the premiums paid for many banks, the buyer must be able to improve the performance of the seller and/or the combined entities. If not, shareholder value will be diminished, not enhanced.

The first area of potential improvement is through enhancement of the operations of buyer and seller so that each is better than before the merger. Enhancements can be in the areas of processing (lowering per-unit costs through economies of scale), personnel (bringing needed skills to the seller), and asset utilization (putting assets to more profitable use). Describing these enhancement areas is easy; implementing plans to achieve them is very difficult. There seems to be mounting evidence that many buyers of banks do not realize sufficient benefits to justify the premiums paid.

The second area is market benefits. Through merger, the combined entities may have a stronger position in a market, reach the critical mass needed to enter certain businesses and be able to develop and deliver services more efficiently. Like operational enhancements, however, market benefits can be extremely difficult to realize.

A third area of potential improvement is financial. Typically, the types of benefits include diversification of the types of businesses in which the bank is engaged to reduce cyclical risk, lower borrowing costs, and increase debt capacity. These benefits are mentioned infrequently in bank acquisitions. The market has tended not to reward these potential benefits with higher stock prices. Investors do not pay a premium for diversified firms and in fact seem to discount them. ("Diversification" as used here means the variety of types of businesses, not diversification of customer types within a certain line of business. In fact, there does seem to be some advantage to, for example, a diversified commercial loan portfolio.) Moreover, lower borrowing costs and increased debt capacity are difficult to associate with enhanced shareholder value.

The fourth area of benefit potential is tax. Many acquisitions have been motivated by the opportunity to use net operating loss carryforwards and to step up the tax basis of assets to get higher depreciation. Since the Tax Reform Act of 1986, virtually all the benefits that used to motivate certain acquisitions have been eliminated. There are, however, potential benefits to reduce future tax liability through amortization of some acquired intangible assets.

A fifth area is the buyer's ability to collect loans that have been charged off. Some buyers have the staff skills and support systems to do a better job in collecting bad assets. If loans already charged off are included in the acquisition, any collections on them fall to the bottom line and increase available cash flow, thus value.

In the final analysis, the most straightforward way to enhance shareholder value is to improve the earnings. Under normal circumstances, a bank earning 1.2 percent on assets after an acquisition, compared with 1.1 percent before, will have enhanced its shareholders' value.

 ## VALUATION METHODS FOR MERGERS AND ACQUISITIONS

Valuation can be one of the most tedious but crucial steps in the entire M&A process. A wide variety of valuation methods for M&A can be used, ranging from simplistic rules of thumb to highly sophisticated mathematical models. The primary purpose of any valuation process is to determine the price or a range of reasonable prices for an M&A deal. In an acquisition deal, the acquirer tries to estimate the target's intrinsic value and the synergistic value that the combined entity will create.

The intrinsic value is determined based on the earning power and earnings quality. Earning power is measured in terms of the entity's capability to constantly increase profitability and rate of return in light of plausible assumptions based on both internal sources and external economic and benchmark data. Earnings quality is assessed by factors such as customer base, profitability, customer satisfaction, employee satisfaction, and relative risk. Synergistic value is determined based on the perceived synergy in the form of economies of scale, risk reduction, increased power, lower funding or capital costs, increased sales, improved management efficiency, or improved productivity. The acquirer should assess these values in determining and negotiating a price for the M&A deal. Although the price actually is determined in the negotiation process, considerations are given to the valuation assumptions and estimates.

To maximize shareholders' value under the arm's-length dealing concept, the acquiring company attempts to negotiate the lowest possible price below the sum of the target's intrinsic value and the acquisition's synergistic value. The target, however, tries to obtain the highest price possible. Within this framework, there is typically a range of acceptable prices to both the acquirer and the target. PV of an entity can be measured as the total current wealth enjoyed by the owners of the entity. The current wealth consists of (1) the current market value of the shares purchased and (2) the total cash dividends received.

A business combination can be considered successful if it results in increases in the total current wealth of the owners of the combined entity. A number of valuation approaches and methods can be used in recognizing and measuring the fair value of identifiable assets acquired and liabilities assumed in a business combination. The assets acquired usually include working capital, tangible assets, and intangible assets. The liabilities assumed include contingent consideration, the previously held equity interest, noncontrolling interest. Fair value is described differently in U.S. generally accepted accounting principles (GAAP) and International Financial Reporting Standards (IFRS). According to U.S. GAAP, fair value is the price that would be received to sell the asset or paid to transfer the liability at the measurement date of a business combination. Under the IFRS, fair value is the amount for which an asset could be exchanged, or a liability settled, between knowledgeable, willing parties in an arm's-length transaction.

The three most commonly used valuation approaches in determining a bank's intrinsic value are the: (1) income approach (earnings/cash flow); (2) asset approach (balance sheet); and (3) market approach (market valuations).

Income Approach

The income approach estimates the target bank's value based on its historical and projected earnings and cash flows. Under the income approach, the acquirer bank must: (1) determine the target's core accrual earnings; (2) estimate the synergies and costs arising from the combination; (3) make adjustment for noncash earnings to estimate cash earnings; and (4) discount the estimated cash earnings at a rate appropriate to reflect risk. The core earnings are income from continuing and normal operations (e.g., services and products) not affected by nonrecurring events, such as the sales of assets, extraordinary loan loss provisions, or any income from real estate activities or other abnormal/nonrecurring events. The acquirer should estimate both the synergistic gains and transaction costs resulting from the combination. Estimating synergistic gains and transaction costs resulting from economies of scale, revenue enhancement opportunities, and regulatory and legal needs is perhaps the most difficult task in determining the value of the target bank.

Synergies can be achieved through economies of scale and scope, risk reductions, lowering funding or capital costs, and increased sales. Thus, examples of synergistic gains resulting from revenue enhancements and economies of scale are:

- Increased net interest margin from improving loan yield and/or reducing deposit costs
- Increased fee income provided from opportunities to offer new financial products and services previously unavailable
- Cost savings resulting from consolidating overlapping branches; administrative, marketing, accounting, and operating activities; and personnel expenses
- Other related revenue enhancements or cost reductions

Transaction or incremental costs are estimated according to the M&A strategies. Examples of incremental costs are:

- Increased loan loss provisions
- Possible increases in deposit insurance premiums
- Early retirement and severance costs resulting from consolidating management and personnel
- Other incremental costs resulting from the combination

Two calculations often are used to determine normalized earnings and cash flows: (1) capitalization of historical earnings/cash flow, and (2) discounted projected earnings/cash flow. Under the capitalization of historical cash earnings approach, normalized historical cash earnings are viewed as an indication of an institution's future capacity to provide returns to both debt and equity holders. The capitalization approach requires the determination of normalized historical cash earnings and the calculation of a capitalization rate that is appropriate for the particular cash earnings base. The normalized cash earnings are determined using an appropriate rate of return that reflects the risk associated with the cash earnings stream and the market's required rate of return for an investment in the bank. The capitalization rate is the weighted average cost of capital (WACC) calculated based on both cost of debt and cost of equity capital. The normalized cash earnings for each year are calculated in this way:

Item	Amount
Core earnings from normal operations	$1,000,000
+ Synergistic benefits	200,000
− Incremental costs	100,000
Accrual-adjusted earnings	1,100,000
+ Noncash charges (e.g., depreciation, goodwill)	150,000
Cash earnings (CE)	$1,250,000

The most commonly used formula for the capitalization of historical cash earnings is:

$$PV_t = \frac{CE(1 + g)}{r - g}$$

where:

PV_t = present value of the target bank (long-term debt and equity)
CE = normalized cash earnings ($1,250,000 as calculated above)
g = long-term annual growth rate (assumed 5 percent)
r = weighted average cost of capital (WACC) representing the required rate of return on cash earnings (assumed 15 percent)

Thus,

$$PV_t = \frac{\$1,250,000(1 + .05)}{.15 - .05} = \$13,125,000$$

PV_t ($13,125,000) is the estimate of fair market value (FMV) of the target's capital (long-term debt and equity). If the FMV long-term debt is estimated to be $3,000,000, then the target's FMV of equity will be $10,125,000 ($13,125,000 − 3,000,000).

The discounted net cash flow methodology determines the value of the target bank based on the PV of the future economic benefits to both debt and equity holders. The future economic income is measured by the projected net cash flows, which are then discounted using the WACC as a discount rate. The sum of the discounted projected cash flows represents the FMV of the target bank based on this formula:

$$PV_v = CF_0 + \frac{CF_1}{(1+r)^1} + \frac{CF_2}{(1+r)^2} + \cdots + \frac{CF_n}{(1+r)^n}$$

where:

PV_v = present value of cash flows representing the FMV
CF = net cash flow for a given period
r = discount rate using weighted average cost of capital (WACC)

The precision of the PV analysis depends on the accuracy of forecasted cash flows, selected discount rates, time periods, and terminal value. To accurately forecast reasonable cash flows expected from an M&A deal, the appraiser must develop a projected balance sheet and income statement for the target on the relevant time horizon (e.g., five years). Using the previous formula in calculating PV of future cash flows indefinitely is a meaningless exercise, primarily because the PV effect of distant cash flows is immaterial. To shorten the time horizon, the appraiser must incorporate a terminal cash flow for the final year, which could be thought of as a sale or liquidation of the investment, determined based on a market value multiple such as P/E or price/book.

Using the PV method, the value of the target bank under the following assumptions is determined.

1. Total assets are $5,000 million and are expected to grow at 8 percent per year.
2. Equity is $375 million and desired equity/assets ratio is 7 percent.
3. Return on assets (ROA) is 1 percent each year.
4. Terminal value in year 6 is projected at 10 percent year five averages assets.
5. The discount rate is 12 percent.

The results presented in Exhibit 15.9 show that under these assumptions, the bank has an intrinsic value of $610.1 million. This acquisition value is determined based on the given assumption. The appraiser can use sensitivity analysis and simulation analysis to determine the effect of changes of these assumptions on the PV. Although PV analysis requires a number of projections and assumptions, it can produce relevant valuation estimates for acquisition analysis.

Balance Sheet Approach

The underlying premise of the asset approach is that the value of the target bank equals the current value of its net assets (Assets – Liabilities) plus a premium to account for its intangible value, such as goodwill. Using this approach, the value of the target bank

EXHIBIT 15.9 Present Value Analysis ($ in Millions)

Year	Average Assets	Earnings	Required Equity	Actual Equity	Cash Flow	Discount Factor	Present Value
0 (Acquisition date)	$5,100	$50	$350	$375	$ 25	1.0	$ 25
1	5,200	52	362	405	43	.8929	38.4
2	5,400	54	378	437.4	59.4	.7972	47.4
3	5,624.3	56.2	393.7	472.4	78.7	.7118	56.1
4	5,849.3	58.5	409.5	510.2	100.7	.6355	64.0
5	6,083.3	60.8	425.8	551.0	125.2	.5674	71.1
6	608.1					.5066	
Terminal value							308.1
Total present value							610.1

is determined by estimating the FMV of its assets and liabilities. The asset approach assesses the FMV of all types of assets and liabilities including: current assets (cash, deposits, loans, securities, receivables); property, plants, and equipment; intangible assets (e.g., core deposits, customer lists, goodwill); current liabilities; and long-term liabilities.

One of the most commonly used methods to estimate the NAV is to assess deposit valuation. The deposit valuation method is appropriate when estimating the value of a branch or a failed bank acquisition. Deposit valuation requires information regarding the amount and types of deposits, estimated lives, interest and operating costs, discount rate, fee income, and marginal earnings rate for the deposits. The balance sheet approach to valuation of the target bank is determined by this simple formula:

1.	Recorded historical value of net assets (assets – liabilities)	xxxx
2.	Add:	
	• Premiums for undervalued assets and/or overstated liabilities	xx
	• FMV of off–balance sheet assets	xx
	• FMV of intangibles (e.g., goodwill)	xx
3.	Total:	xxxx
4.	Subtract	
	• Discounts for overvalued assets and/or undervalued liabilities	(xx)
	• Value of off–balance sheet liabilities	(xx)
5.	Value of the target bank	xxx

Market Approach

The market approach is based on two concepts. The first premise is that the value of the target bank should be determined according to how its stock is being valued in the market where it is traded. The second concept is to compare prices of similar acquisitions with the target bank to estimate the acquisition market value for the target. The market valuation approach based on the comparable bank market multiple, and comparable bank transactions rely on analyzing financial data, ratios, and price multiples obtained from publicly traded banks. The next measurements or price multiples from comparable bank data can be used to estimate FMV of the target bank:

1. Premium to market $= \dfrac{\text{Merger price per share}}{\text{Market price per share before announcement}}$

2. Price/Earnings $= \dfrac{\text{Merger price per share}}{\text{Earnings per share}}$

3. Price/Book $= \dfrac{\text{Merger price per share}}{\text{Book value per share}}$

4. Premium to deposits $= \dfrac{\text{Merger price per share}}{\text{Total deposits}}$

5. Invested capital/Assets $= \dfrac{\substack{\text{Market value of invested capital} \\ \text{(Market value of long-term debt and equity)}}}{\text{Total assets}}$

Using a bank stock's trading value to estimate acquisition valuation has several limitations. First, the majority of bank shares traded are not within the organized stock exchanges (e.g., the New York Stock Exchange or the American Stock Exchange) or even regional over-the-counter markets. Thus, the trading price may not represent an objective and relevant valuation. Second, if the acquiring bank attempts to gain control through "open market" purchases, the price would rise to reflect an acquisition premium or to induce others to sell. Finally, capital markets fluctuate based on economic and capital market forces rather than just the intrinsic value of individual stocks.

Compiling relevant data on previously comparable M&A deals and comparing them to the target is not without problems. Each M&A deal has its own attributes and characteristics distinguishable from other deals. However, the usefulness of comparable merger market analysis depends on how the sample M&A transactions are selected (e.g., size, location, market position, performance in market, and market extension). These limitations of the market approach should be considered when using it to estimate the intrinsic value of the target bank. If the intrinsic value is below the suggested merger price for other similar banks, the acquirer should not attempt to negotiate the price. Conversely, if the intrinsic value is above previous merger prices for comparable banks, then the acquirer has more room to negotiate the price.

SOPHISTICATED VALUATION TECHNIQUES FOR MERGERS AND ACQUISITIONS

Appraisers most often use the valuation approaches discussed in the previous section (e.g., income approach, balance sheet approach, and market approach) when valuing the acquisition under consideration. Although these approaches can be useful in estimating the intrinsic value of the target bank, the more sophisticated valuation methods presented in this section can improve the precision and accuracy of valuation. The sophisticated valuation techniques can be empirically estimated with a high degree of reliability.

The valuation of M&A has received much attention in finance and accounting literature during the past five decades. A number of valuation techniques have been employed to assess the value and results of M&A transactions. Early empirical studies of M&A[6] utilized a portfolio or paired sample technique of calculating the differences in return to the sample of acquiring firms and the return on a portfolio of like firms or a paired sample of comparable firms. Thus, differences in the returns of the paired samples indicate the impact of M&A deals. These studies used different versions of this return equation:

$$\Delta R_n = \frac{P_n \sum_{t=0}^{N} D_t}{P_0} - \frac{P'_n \sum_{t=0}^{N} D'_t}{P_0}$$

where

ΔR_n = differences in return to shareholders

P_n = price of share at time period n

P_0 = price of share at time 0 (merger announcement or completion)

D_t = dividend at time t

$$P_n = \frac{\sum_{t=0}^{N} D_t}{P_0} \left[\begin{array}{l} \text{= return to investor who purchased a share of the merging firm} \\ \text{at time 0 and held this share until time } n \end{array} \right.$$

$$P'_n = \frac{\sum_{t=0}^{N} D'_t}{P_0} \left[\begin{array}{l} \text{= return to investor of no merging firms or investor based on an} \\ \text{estimation of the price and dividend stream had no merger} \\ \text{occurred} \end{array} \right.$$

Results of early studies of M&A transactions are inconsistent and inconclusive. Some mergers showed positive benefits, and other mergers were not deemed successful or there were no significant differences between the merged firms and the nonmerged firms in risk, growth rate, or financial structure.

Recent studies of M&A transactions have used the capital market event methodology to measure market returns to M&A deals. Dodd[7] investigated both completed and canceled mergers by employing the market model to assess market reactions to merger announcements and found that shareholders of target firms earn large positive abnormal returns. Merger-related event methodology is based on three underlying M&A theories. The first theory refers to non-value-maximizing behavior by management of acquiring firms and implies that acquisitions are attempts by acquiring management to maximize growth in sales or assets or to control a large firm. Acquisitions of this type would have no real economic impact on the combined business, indicating that any positive gains made by the target shareholders would be offset by a loss to the acquiring firms' stockholders.

Empirical studies in support of this theory of M&A are Trito and Scanlon[8] and Hannan and Rhoades,[9] which found that target banks gain positive returns while acquiring banks accrue a negative return surrounding the merger announcement day.

The second theory of M&A refers to value maximization motivations of increasing the value of acquiring firms' shareholders. Current merger studies found evidence in support of the value maximization theory. Desai and Stover[10] employed an event study methodology for measuring returns and found a positive average abnormal return for shareholders of acquiring banks during the two days surrounding the merger announcement and on the date the Federal Reserve Board approved the acquisition.

Capital Asset Pricing Model

The CAPM is based on capital market theory, which describes how investors must behave when selecting a particular security (e.g., common stocks) for their portfolios under a given set of assumptions. The CAPM has been used in the literature to evaluate capital market reactions to M&A announcements and changes in market participants' (e.g., investors') behavior resulting from the M&A deal. The CAPM is calculated based on this following formula:

$$R_{it} = \alpha_i + \beta_i R_{mt} + e_{it}$$

$$e_{it} = R_{it} - (\alpha_i + \beta_i R_{mt})$$

where:

R_{it} = return on security i for period t
α_i = constant for security i
β_i = systemic risk of security i
R_{mt} = return on market portfolio for period t
e_{it} = residual of abnormal return for security

The CAPM typically is utilized to calculate average abnormal return and cumulative abnormal return.

$$\text{Average residual} = \bar{e}_i t_t = \frac{\sum\limits_{i=1}^{N} e_{it}}{N}$$

$$\text{Cumulative average residual} = CART = \sum\limits_{T-t}^{T-t} e_t$$

where

$\bar{e}_i$ = Average of all residuals for period t_i
e_{it} = Firm i residual at time t
N = Number of firms within group
T = Number of periods aggregated

The abnormal residuals can be used in measuring the synergistic benefits of M&A deals. CAPM is used to estimate the fair rate of return on capital market investment securities of M&A transactions. Another use of CAPM in the valuation process is to estimate the cost of equity capital component of an overall income capitalization value. CAPM explains rational investment decision making, which is relevant to any business valuation, especially valuation of M&A deals.

Accounting-Based Valuation Approach (Ohlson Model)

The Ohlson model utilizes the noncontroversial dividend discount model to measure stock price in terms of current book value and future residual income. The model is based on the assumption that the accounting system is an effective means of recognizing and accumulating wealth by business entities. More specifically, recorded book value serves as a static measure of firm value at a given point in time while earnings measures the increment to shareholder wealth over a specified period of time. The theoretical framework of the model is that book value and earnings are relevant valuation attributes. Book value represents a stock measure of value while earnings measure increments to book value and are indicators of future dividend-paying ability of an entity.

The Ohlson model is based on the noncontroversial assumption that the market value of an entity's equity P_t is equal to the PV of current and future dividend payments, d_{t+j}

$$P_t = \sum_{j=1}^{\infty} (1 + r)^{-j} E_t \left[dt + j \right]$$

where

P_t = market value of equity
r = discount rate or cost of equity capital
E_t = expected future earnings
d_{t+j} = future dividend payments at time j

This model also assumes that the accounting data follow the clean surplus relation:

$$b_{vt} = b_{vt-1} + x_t - d_t$$

where:

b_{vt} = net book value
x_t = earnings for period t

This clean surplus relation implies that the current book value is a function of previous book value, future earnings, and dividends. The payment of dividends at time t reduces future-period earnings due to the reduction in the firm's asset base rather than reducing current earnings. The clean surplus assumption allows the rewriting of the dividend discount model in terms of accounting data:

$$PV_t = b_{vt} = \sum_{j=1}^{\infty} (1 + r)^{-j} E_t [x_{t+j}^a]$$

where

$$x_t^a = \text{residual income or abnormal earnings}$$

This formula indicates that the estimated value of a firm's equity is determined by discounting its future abnormal earnings or residual income and adding it to the firm's current book value. The practical implementation of the Ohlson model requires the: (1) prediction of future earnings; (2) determination of the appropriate forecast horizon; and (3) selection of the appropriate discount rate. The implication of this discounted residual income model for assessing an M&A deal is that the book value provides an important beginning reference point in the valuation process.

Fama-French Three-Factor Market

The Fama-French three-factor model describes market behavior. Fama and French based their conclusion on the observation that two classes of stocks tend to do better than the market as a whole:[11]

- Small caps
- Stocks with a high book to market ratio (also called value stocks)

They then incorporated these two factors in the CAPM model to indicate a portfolio's exposure to these two classes:

$$r = R_f + \beta_3(K_m - R_f) + bs \times SMB + bv \times HML + \alpha$$

where

$$r = \text{portfolio's rate of return}$$
$$R_f = \text{risk-free return rate}$$
$$K_m = \text{return of the whole stock market}$$
$$SMB = \text{small minus big}$$
$$HML_t = \text{high minus low}$$

Arbitrage Pricing Theory

Arbitrage is the practice of taking advantage of the inefficiencies of two or more markets and making a risk-free profit. Arbitrage pricing theory (APT) states that the expected return on a financial asset is the linear function of different macroeconomic factors. The sensitivity to each factor is indicated by a factor-specific beta coefficient. The rate of return derived by the model will further be used to price the asset. The asset price should be equal to the expected end-of-period price discounted at the rate implied by model.

The APT model:

$$r_j = E(r_j) + b_{j1}F_1 + b_{j2}F_2 + \cdots + b_{jn}F_n + \epsilon_j$$

where

$E(r_j) = j$th asset's expected return

$b_{jk} = $ sensitivity of the jth asset to factor k, also called factor loading

$F_k = $ systematic factor (assumed to have mean zero)

$\varepsilon_j = $ risky asset's idiosyncratic random shock with mean zero

In relation to the CAPM model, the APT has less restrictions in its assumptions. While the CAPM model assumes that the market portfolio is identical, the APT assumes that each investor will hold a unique portfolio with its own particular array of betas. The APT can be considered a supply-side model essentially because of its beta coefficients reflecting the sensitivity of the underlying asset to economic factors. Hence, any change in the factors will make a difference in expected return on asset. CAPM, however, is seen as a demand side model. Its results are based on maximizing the investor's utility function and from the resulting market equilibrium.

Multiples in Valuation

Multiples in valuations are commonly used for cross-checking or double-checking other calculations. They are also used to compute multiples for DCF valuation to compare to industry multiples. However, they are highly influenced by one-time events and difficulties of accounting for future events and diffirences in risks.[12]

Some common principles that should be kept in mind while doing multiple valuations are:

- *Use peers with similar prospects for return on invested capital and growth.* The firms to be valued should be comparable. They should be similar in sizes and in the same industry. Abnormal firms and exceptions should not be included.
- *Use forward-looking multiples.* Both principles of valuation and empirical evidence lead us to recommend that multiples be based on forecast rather than historical profits.
- *Use enterprise-value multiples.* The traditional basis for comparison—the P/E ratio— is not enough for comparison. Other ratios such as the market-to-book ratio should also be used as a proxy for growth and conservative reporting. The higher the market-to-book ratio ratio, the less likelihood of financial manipulation.
- Adjust the enterprise-value-to-EBITDA (earnings before interest, taxes, depreciation and amortization) multiple for nonoperating items. Although the one-time non-operating items in net income make EBITDA superior to earnings for calculating multiples, even enterprise-value-to-EBITDA multiples must be adjusted for non-operating items hidden within enterprise value and EBITDA, both of which must be adjusted for these nonoperating items, such as excess cash and operating leases.[13]

RELATION BETWEEN PRICE AND VALUE AND EFFECT ON STOCKHOLDERS

This chapter has focused on the determination of a banking company's value. As described in Chapter 7, however, there is a difference between price and value. The price that one bank pays to acquire another usually reflects the value the particular buyer places on an acquisition (the investment value concept), not necessarily the as-is or consensus value (the FMV concept). Consequently, any given acquisition price reflects individual negotiations between buyer and seller. Depending on the competitive situation, the buyer's willingness to share future value creation potential with the seller could vary substantially. High multiples for interstate acquisitions reflect, in part, the desire for banks to expand their franchise and their willingness to pay the price while the window of opportunity is open. In other words, to ensure entry into the market, buyers are willing to share with the seller a substantial portion of the value creation potential.

The price paid reflects the buyer's perception of the value of the target, based on future expectations of the performance of that target and the added value the buyer can bring. More frequently, buyers examine the price-to-value value relationship in terms of the effect on stockholders and what levels of earnings and growth are needed to justify the price paid relative to value received by stockholders. Buyers are also looking much more carefully at the strategic actions necessary to achieve the added value.

The most common measure of impact on shareholders is *earnings dilution,* which is the reduction in earnings per share (EPS) after an acquisition. Dilution occurs because the earnings of the combined entities are not sufficient to offset the increased stock issued (if a stock-for-stock transaction) or the interest on acquisition debt (if a cash-for-stock transaction with debt). Exhibit 15.10 illustrates the dilution resulting from a stock-for-stock acquisition. In this example, dilution of over 10 percent will be experienced by shareholders of the buying bank. This particular bank may believe a 10 percent dilution is acceptable and be willing to pay $4.5 million for the selling bank. Another bank, however, may face different circumstances. For example, if the buyer's stock sold for 60 percent of book (instead of the 80 percent shown in the exhibit), the dilution would be over 18 percent. A potential buyer in this situation may find this level of dilution unacceptable.

EXHIBIT 15.10 Illustration of Earnings per Share Dilution Resulting from Stock-for-Stock Acquisition (Assumes Pooling of Interest Accounting)

	Buyer	Seller	Combined
Earnings (latest year)	$ 2,000,000	$ 500,000	$ 2,500,000
Shares outstanding	1,500,000	—	—
Equity (book value)	$14,000,000	$3,000,000	$17,000,000
Purchase price	$ 4,500,000	—	—
Market price of stock/book value	80%	—	—
Market price/share	$7.47	—	—
Number of new shares issued to seller's shareholders	602,410	—	—
Total shares outstanding	—	—	2,102,410
Earnings/share	$1.33	—	$1.19
Dilution percentage	—	—	10.5%

EXHIBIT 15.11 Illustration of Earnings per Share Dilution Resulting from Cash-for-Stock Acquisition (Assumes Purchase Accounting)

	Buyer	Seller	Combined
Earnings	$ 2,000,00	$ 500,000	$2,500,000
Share outstanding	1,500,000	—	1,500,000
Equity (book value)	$14,000,000	$3,000,000	—
Purchase price	$ 5,500,000	—	—
Interest rate on acquisition debt	12%	—	—
Goodwill	—	$2,000,000	—
Goodwill amortization	—	25 years	—
Tax rate	35%	—	—
Acquisition debt interest expense (after tax)	—	—	$ 439,000
Goodwill amortization	—	—	$ 80,000
Earnings	—	—	$1,981,000
Earnings/share	$1.33	—	$1.32
Dilution percentage	—	—	0.8%

In general, dilution of the buyer's EPS will occur during a stock-for-stock acquisition when the purchase price, as a multiple of the selling bank's earnings, is greater than the market price of the buyer's stock as a multiple of its earnings. In the example described, the purchase price is nine times the seller's earnings while the buyer's stock price is less than six times earnings. For there to be no dilution, the buying bank's stock would have to be priced at a 28 percent premium over book ($11.95) rather than at a 20 percent discount ($7.47).

The same type of dilution analysis can be undertaken in a cash-for-stock acquisition, except the price is evaluated based on debt costs (or the opportunity cost of an earning asset liquidated to fund the acquisition) instead of stock. Exhibit 15.11 illustrates the dilution in a cash-for-stock acquisition. In this case, the buyer experienced an EPS dilution of about 1 percent. In a cash acquisition, dilution will occur if the interest expense on acquisition debt and goodwill amortization exceed the selling bank's earnings.

The key point is that the price paid for one particular acquired bank reflects value to that buyer, not necessarily to other banks. The final price of an acquisition is the combination of the value of the bank as a stand-alone investment *plus* its value to the particular buyer as a result of synergies and franchise expansion opportunities. The ultimate test of the appropriateness of price paid is the extent to which shareholder value is enhanced, and this may not be evident until several years after the transaction. Consequently, some of the high premiums are justified by the unique circumstances and strategies of a particular buyer. However, if the perceived opportunities of value creation do not materialize, then the high premiums will not be justified.

CONCLUSION

Valuing a financial services firm is one of the most significant aspects of valuation as part of a merger or acquisition. This chapter presents techniques that can be used to establish the value of a bank as an ongoing business entity and differenciates between strategic valuation techniques intended for the overall decision-making process and tactical valuation methods designed to meet specific requirements, such as legal regulatory, taxes, and accounting. Valuation methods are developed based on value drivers of profitability, growth prospects, cash flows, market performance, and cost of equity capital. This chapter also describes relative and fundamental valuation models that convert those value drivers into value estimates.

 ## NOTES

1. The term "as-is" means the bank with its current strategies, markets, financial structures, and so on.
2. Deficiencies in these measures were described in Chapter 8, but application of the market approach is very difficult without using these two widely reported figures.
3. There are alternative ways of computing residual value, such as multiple of earnings and book value. Use of these measures to determine residual value suffers from the same deficiencies as using these measures to determine total value.
4. Faster asset growth results in lower value because a greater proportion of income must be allocated to capital to meet regulatory requirements. Consequently, this buyer would destroy value if it did nothing else but increase the bank's assets at a faster rate.
5. For an excellent discussion, see Alfred Rappaport, "Converting Merger Benefits to Shareholder Value," *Mergers & Acquisitions* (March/April 1987): 49–55.
6. Thomas Hogarty, "Profits from Mergers: The Evidence of Fifty Years," *St. John's Law Review*, Special edition, 44 (1970): 378–391. B. Lev and G. Mandelker, "The Microeconomic Consequences of Corporate Mergers." *Journal of Business* 45 (1972): 85–104.
7. P. Dodd, "Merger Proposals, Management Discretion and Stockholder Wealth," *Journal of Financial Economics* 8 (December 1980): 105–137.
8. J. W. Thrifts and K. P. Scanlon. "Interstate Bank Mergers: The Early Evidence," *Journal of Financial Research* 10, No. 4 (1987): 67–74.
9. T. H. Hannan and S. A. Rhoades, "Acquisition Targets and Motives: The Case of the Banking Industry," *Review of Economics and Statistics* (February 1987): 67–74.
10. Anand Desai and R. D. Stover. "Bank Holding Company Acquisitions, Stockholder Returns, and Regulatory Uncertainty," *Journal of Financial Research* 8, No. 2 (1995): 145–156.
11. E. Fama and K. R. French, 1993. "Common Risk Factors in the Returns on Stocks and Bonds,"*Journal of Financial Economics* 33, 3–56.
12. Source: http://finance.wharton.upenn.edu/~benninga/fnce728/chap10.pdf.
13. Marc Goedhart, "The Right Role for Multiples in Valuation," Spring 2005. Available at: www.nd.edu/~scorwin/fin70610/McKinsey%20on%20Multiples%202005.pdf

CHAPTER SIXTEEN

Valuation of Tangible Bank Assets

V ALUING A BANK AS a business enterprise (as discussed in Chapter 15) does not necessarily require the valuation of each individual tangible asset owned by the bank. Nonetheless, it is appropriate in some situations to value some or all of the tangible assets. Three primary reasons to value specific tangible assets are to:

1. Determine a new taxable basis in a merger that uses purchase accounting rules (discussed in Chapter 9).
2. Compute the portion of the purchase price that is attributable to goodwill (also discussed in Chapter 9).
3. Gauge the extent of unrealized gains or losses on the balance sheet that could impact future earnings potential of the bank, particularly in loans and investments (a real-world complication discussed in Chapter 19).

Tangible assets to be valued fall into two categories: physical and financial. Physical tangible assets are those with true physical substance, such as furniture, fixtures, equipment, and premises. Financial tangible assets are those that involve a clear legal claim on future income or underlying assets, such as loans and investments.

The context in which tangible bank assets are valued is usually the fair market value in the current productive use of the asset—value in use. This is an important distinction because it assumes continuation of the current use of the property or asset. Value in use is not necessarily the theoretically highest value of the asset. For example, a bank that maintains a branch at a major intersection may have a locational advantage for new and existing customers. This particular site, however, might be worth far more to the developer of a fast food restaurant. At some point in the future, the bank may decide that the sale of the branch would yield a profit substantial enough to warrant such action, but current valuation cannot presume such future actions.

This chapter addresses the valuation of both physical and financial tangible assets in the context of their value in use. The extent to which a theoretically higher value exists in some other use is outside the scope of this discussion.

TANGIBLE PHYSICAL ASSETS

The physical assets of a bank include primarily the premises, furniture, fixtures, and equipment—the assets the bank uses in its daily operations. Depending on the size and complexity of the bank, identifying all the physical assets may be difficult or impossible. Some banks maintain excellent fixed asset management systems; others do not. Nonetheless, unless the internal records are grossly inadequate, it usually is possible to identify the major assets that will account for 90 to 95 percent of the total physical asset value. Listed next are many of the physical assets likely to be found at a typical bank:

- Buildings
- Vacant land for expansion
- Leasehold improvements
- Vaults
- Parking lots
- Furniture and fixtures
- Computers and peripherals
- Automated teller machines
- Automobiles
- Computer software
- Art objects and decorations
- Item processing equipment

Even with an accurate inventory of physical assets, it is worthwhile to conduct an investigation to identify and verify the major physical assets in the bank.

Placing a value on a bank's physical assets nearly always requires the cost rather than the market or income approaches. The cost approach is applicable because it values a physical asset based on the cost to replace it with one of equal utility, less any physical, functional, and/or economic obsolescence. Because the bank's property is used in the course of business and does not generate income directly, the income approach is not applicable. Also, because bank property is often very specialized (it includes vaults, teller counters, and proof machines), it is difficult to apply the market approach, which requires comparison with recent sales of similar properties. There is not a sufficiently large market for used bank physical assets to generate comparable sales data. The discussion of approaches to value in Chapter 8 describes the cost approach in detail.

The overall value of a bank's balance sheet is unlikely to be significantly impacted by the difference between market value and book value of tangible physical assets because they account for such a small percentage of total assets. Tangible financial assets are the real drivers of asset value, as discussed next.

TANGIBLE FINANCIAL ASSETS

Normally, one thinks of tangible assets as those with physical substance, such as buildings, machinery, or inventory. The majority of assets of many businesses fit this description. In a bank, however, the bulk of the assets are financial, such as loans and investments. These assets are not truly physical but are tangible in that they are usually marketable and involve a legal claim to property and/or future income.

Valuing the tangible financial assets of a bank typically requires the discounted future income approach. Since the loans and investments of a bank represent rights to future income, the values of these instruments are equal to that future income, discounted to present value (PV) at a rate commensurate with the risks.

Two major categories of tangible financial assets are important to value for merger or acquisition: investment securities and the loan portfolio. These two categories account for over 90 percent of a typical bank's total assets.

Investment Securities Valuation

Valuing the investments of a bank can be very simple if the types of investments are plain vanilla such as U.S. Treasury securities or municipal bonds. Because of the depth of the market for these types of investments, daily price quotes provide the best, most reliable guide to market value.

If the bank has a significant exposure to more exotic investments such as derivatives or collateralized mortgage obligations, the valuation can be extraordinarily complex. Many of these types of investment activities are off–balance sheet items, which affect the earnings of the bank but do not show up on the balance sheet.

The majority of banks do not have substantial exposure to exotic investment vehicles and off–balance sheet activities. Consequently, the discussion in this chapter focuses on more traditional investments made by banks: U.S. Treasury securities, government agency securities, and municipal bonds. As mentioned, price quotes are easily obtained, but it is useful to understand how the market determines values for these types of investments.

All valuation models for investment securities are based on the income approach— that is, the current market value of the particular investment is equal to the net present value (NPV) of the cash flows to be received by the owner of that investment. The primary parameters needed to value an investment security are the cash flows to be received, time to maturity, and the discount rate. Exhibit 16.1 illustrates a simple valuation of a bond with known cash flows for a defined time period.

The current market value of the investment generating this cash flow stream, with an annual discount rate of 8.5 percent, is $2,386.29.

From a practical standpoint, a bank is able to track the value of its investment portfolio better than it can track most other assets on the balance sheet. Most banks, or

EXHIBIT 16.1 Valuation of a Bond Paying $100 Semiannually for Three Years, $2,500 Face Value

Payment #	Payment	Maturity Value	Discount Factor @ 8.5%/yr	Present Value
1	$100	—	.9593	$ 95.93
2	100	—	.9203	92.03
3	100	—	.8826	88.26
4	100	—	.8467	84.67
5	100	2,500	.7790	2,025.40
				2,386.29

their safekeeping agents, revalue the investment portfolio frequently; often it is done daily. A report is generated showing, among other things, the type of security, its par value, maturity date, coupon rate, yield to maturity, book value, and market value. In most cases, this is the best source of investment portfolio market value amounts. Very seldom is there a need to establish value independently of the normal types of investments most banks hold.

Loan Portfolio Valuation

Loans can present a much more difficult valuation problem, even though the mathematical approach is similar to that used for investments. The difference is that most types of bank loans do not have an active, organized market with a free exchange of information. Therefore, a bank is not able to value its loan portfolio each day based on the input of the market. This situation is changing somewhat with active secondary mortgage markets and loan securitization. For the most part, however, the loan portfolio of a bank must be valued on a case-by-case basis. Much of the valuation process is subjective and open to disagreement. Numerous assumptions must be made about timing of payments, prepayments, default risk, and future interest rates. Nonetheless, it is important that the value of the loan portfolio be carefully considered.

A good starting point for the loan valuation is the book value of the portfolio. The book value of a loan is the original balance of the loan less the reduction in principal from payments made until the day of valuation plus loan charge-offs, if any. The book value is usually easy to determine from the information carried in the bank's loan systems. Most computerized loan systems carry previous-day book values.

The market value of a loan is the NPV of the future income stream generated by that loan discounted at a rate that reflects current interest rates and the timing and risk of the future income. Banks are not generally in favor of measuring their loans based on market prices that may cause earnings volatility. Banks typically prefer their current practices of valuing their loans based on the original cost less a reserve to account for probable losses. The position of the Financial Accounting Standards Board (FASB) on bank loan valuation, as of February 2011, has been controversial and inconsistent as the FASB has yet to decide to require banks to value loans using market prices or allow banks to continue using the prevailing cost method for loan valuation. There are two primary reasons why book value and market value are unlikely to be the same for a given loan:

1. The current interest rate that would be charged on a similar loan made today is different from the rate actually charged on the loan. For example, if the interest rate charged on a loan is 8 percent but the current rate on a similar loan is 10 percent, the market value of the loan would be less than its book value, all other things being equal.
2. The loan is nonperforming—interest payments are not being made—and the collateral value does not cover the outstanding principal balance and unpaid interest due. In this case, the market value would be less than book value.

For performing loans, the valuation is virtually identical in approach to the valuation of an investment security—the NPV of the future income stream discounted by an appropriate rate of interest.

When valuing performing loans, the rate used to discount future income to PV is the rate that would be charged for an equivalent loan at the time of the valuation, not the interest rate stated on the loan. As with investments, current rates determine the value of an income-generating asset, not the rate stated on that asset.

Nonperforming loans cannot be valued by calculating the NPV of future income, because there is no income, and there may never be. The valuation of a nonperforming loan is a more subjective process that must consider the likelihood of payments beginning again and/or the value of any underlying collateral. If a loan is non-performing, it does not mean that its market value is necessarily less than its book value. If a loan is well collateralized with marketable property, the liquidation value of the collateral may cover the debt sufficiently.

When valuing the loan portfolio of a bank, it is useful to assign each loan being valued to one of five categories:

1. Commercial loans
2. Consumer loans
3. Mortgage loans
4. Lease financing
5. Nonperforming loans

Commercial Loans

Commercial loans are larger and more complex, and can have a disproportionate impact on the overall value of a bank's assets. Consequently, these types of loans must be examined very carefully. The value of these loans depends on the timing of repayments, assumptions about prepayment, and prevailing interest rates. The approach is similar to that used for investment securities, except that cash flow (payments) for commercial loans can be irregular. Consequently, often it is necessary to project the future cash flow of the loan until its maturity date, then apply the discount rate to calculate NPV.

EXHIBIT 16.2   Valuation of a Commercial Loan

Month	Cash Flow	Discount Factor @ 8.5%	Present Value of Cash Flow
1	$ 4,167	.993	$ 4,138
2	4,167	.986	4,109
3	4,167	.979	4,079
4	4,167	.972	4,050
5	4,167	.965	4,022
6	170,834	.959	163,398
7	4,167	.952	3,967
8	4,167	.945	3,938
9	170,834	.938	159,820
10	4,167	.932	3,884
11	4,167	.925	3,954
12	170,834	.919	156,583
			$515,842

For example, a commercial loan with book value of $500,000 at 10 percent, one year remaining life, and interest-only payments for six months with bullet payments in months 6, 9, and 12 has cash flow and valuation as shown in Exhibit 16.2. Because the loan is paying a 10 percent rate in an environment where an 8.5 percent discount rate is appropriate, market value is somewhat higher than current book value.

This type of valuation analysis, while time consuming, may be justified for the larger commercial loans. It is not unusual to find 4 or 5 percent of loans constituting a third to a half of dollar volume. Clearly, an in-depth valuation of these larger loans is worthwhile.

Consumer Loans

Consumer loans are relatively easy to value, because they usually have fixed payments for a specified period of time. There is some prepayment risk with consumer loans, but it is typically less of a problem than with other types of loans, particularly mortgage loans.

A straightforward formula can be used to calculate the value of a portfolio of fixed-payment consumer loans that share the same number of remaining payments and contractual interest rate:

$$\frac{\left(\dfrac{1}{DR}\right) \times \left(1 - \dfrac{1}{(1+DR)^n}\right)}{\left(\dfrac{1}{IR}\right) \times \left(1 - \dfrac{1}{(1+IR)^n}\right)} \times \text{Loan amount}$$

where

DR = discount rate per payment period

n = number of payment periods remaining

IR = contractual interest rate per payment period on the loans

An example illustrates the use of this formula. Suppose a portfolio of auto loans with a book value of $20 million is to be valued. These loans are all four-year auto loans at 13 percent (1.083 percent per month) with 27 months remaining on their original 48-month life. An annual discount rate of 12 percent is being used, resulting in a 1 percent rate per payment period.

$$\frac{\left(\frac{1}{.01}\right) \times \left(1 - \frac{1}{(1+.01)^{27}}\right)}{\left(\frac{1}{.01083}\right) \times \left(1 - \frac{1}{(1+.01083)^{27}}\right)} \times \$20,000,000$$

$$= \frac{23.56}{23.30} \times \$20,000,000$$

$$= \$20,223,176$$

This portfolio of loans has a value of about $20.22 million.

To account for potential prepayment risk, this same formula could be used with a different assumption of remaining periods n. For example, if the remaining life is assumed to be 20 periods instead of 27 (i.e., if early payoffs bring down average life), the value of the portfolio declines slightly to $20.17 million.

Mortgage Loans

Mortgage loans present a particularly difficult valuation challenge because of the variety of payment streams and the general availability of no-penalty prepayment options. Because mortgage borrowers are very rate sensitive, the slightest decrease in rates causes massive prepayments and refinancing, as was experienced in 1992 and 1993. Also, the widespread success of adjustable and graduated payment mortgages with caps, collars, and floors gives even more uncertainty to the value of a mortgage.

In its simplest form, a mortgage loan with fixed payments over a known remaining time period can be valued exactly like a consumer loan or a bond. In the case where mortgage rates are expected to fall, thus creating prepayments, the calculated value of a mortgage portfolio can change dramatically. For example, a $150 million portfolio of 30-year monthly pay, fixed-rate loans at 7 percent with 26 years remaining (312 months) discounted at 8 percent has a value of $137 million. If the assumption of remaining life changes to, for example, 13 years (156 months), the value of the portfolio is $142 million. In this particular, example the value is higher with a shorter life because the prevailing interest rate environment (the discount rate of 8 percent) is higher than the interest rate of 7 percent on the portfolio.

Lease Financing

Lease financing loans are similar to normal loans with regular payments, except that a residual value of the collateral exists at the end of the lease term. During the term of the lease, the payment stream can be valued exactly as a consumer loan. The driver of the valuation of the lease portfolio, however, is the residual value of the assets being financed. Therefore, careful attention must be paid to the collateral underlying the lease and the assumptions of residual value.

Nonperforming Loans

Nonperforming loans need to be evaluated on a case-by-case basis because there is no cash flow to value. An examination of the underlying collateral can gauge the liquidation value of the loan. Liquidation value provides a worst-case scenario of the value. Individual analysis may lead to assumptions of resumed payments that can be valued through discounting.

TANGIBLE ASSETS IN BANK MERGERS AND ACQUISITIONS

When banks are acquired, the acquisition is seldom a case of a purchase of individual assets. The buyer is interested in the future income-generating capabilities of the bank as a business entity (the franchise). The quality of the individual assets, however, can be a primary determinant of that future income. A clean loan portfolio, a well-balanced investment mix, and efficient fixed assets are all signs of a profitable bank. Consequently, from a business decision-making perspective, the value and corresponding quality of the tangible assets are important factors.

From a tax and accounting perspective, the individual assets and their values are also important. Purchase price allocations and establishing new depreciable basis of assets are both critical factors affecting tangible assets in a bank merger or acquisition. Business enterprise value (BEV) analysis and related internal rate of return (IRR) analysis are used to measure the fair value of assets acquired and liabilities assumed. BEV analysis is a critical valuation tool in measuring the fair value of the identified assets and liabilities of the entity. BEV that supports many of the valuation assumptions, such as discount rate, projected cash flows, and synergies, typically is performed without considering a third-party valuation specialist or the acquirer. IRR analysis uses market participant assumptions and the consideration transferred to measure the fair value of assets acquired and liabilities.

The BEV is performed using either the income approach, such as discounted cash flow method; or the public company market multiple or the market transaction multiple methods of the market approach

INTANGIBLE ASSETS IN BANK MERGERS AND ACQUISITIONS

The identifiable intangible assets acquired should be recognized separately from goodwill in a business combination. Income, market, and cost techniques may be considered when measuring the fair value of acquired intangible assets.:

- *Income approach for intangible assets.* This method is based on the income-producing capacity of bank's intangible assets. Based on the unique nature of the intangible assets, this is the most common approach to value such assets. Some of the most common variations of the income approach include:

- Multiperiod excess earnings method
- Relief-from-royalty method
- Greenfield method
- With and without method

- *Market approach for intangible assets.* When a market date is reasonably available, this approach is used to measure the fair value of an intangible asset. For example, when some types of intangible assets may trade as separate portfolios, such as brands, cable television, or wireless telephone service subscriptions; they could be valued in this approach.
- *Cost approach for intangible assets.* This approach uses the concept of replacement as an indicator of fair value and is based on the principle of substitution. If some intangible assets are readily replicated or replaced, such as routine software, the cost approach, which commonly is used to value machinery and equipment, will be used to estimate the fair value.

 ## CONCLUSION

This chapter addresses the valuation of both physical and financial tangible assets as well as intangible assets. Financial service firms often value their assets, both tangible and intangible, by focusing on book values. This chapter also discusses some common valuation approaches and methods of recognizing and measuring the fair value of both tangible and intangible assets. As a general rule, tangible assets will be measured by using market approach or the income approach because the data typically are available and can be easily verified. Some tangible assets, such as specialized properties or plant and equipment, and often intangible assets are measured by using the replacement cost method of the cost approach.

CHAPTER SEVENTEEN

Core Deposits as a Special Type of Intangible Asset Valuation

T HE CORE DEPOSIT BASE is an intangible asset unique to banks. It is usually the single largest potentially amortizable intangible asset associated with a bank acquisition. Recent tax court and Supreme Court rulings have made the amortization deduction opportunities clearer, but the whole issue still must be approached carefully. This chapter presents a variety of issues related to core deposits as an intangible asset and some different points of view on definition and measurement of their value.

CONCEPT OF CORE DEPOSIT BASE AS AN INTANGIBLE ASSET

Deposits are a liability of a bank, but their existence may create an intangible asset. On the surface this can appear to be a contradiction, but it is not. Deposits are the lifeblood of a bank, without which there would be no funds for loans and investments. When a bank is acquired, the buyer receives a built-in base of usually stable customer relationships. This customer base has demonstrable economic benefits to the buyer.

Clearly, bankers place value on deposits and depositors. In order to attract depositors, branches are built and staffed, premiums are offered, and advertising is undertaken. These activities are all evidence that deposits have value, and banks are willing to pay more than just the interest cost to attract them. Core deposits can be valued a number of ways. Generally a cost savings method, an income approach, is utilized when valuing an acquired core deposit base. The premise underlying this approach is that a rational buyer would be willing to pay a premium to obtain a group of core deposit accounts only if the accounts are a source of funding that is less expensive than the buyer's marginal cost of funds. In the early 1990s, tax incentives existed for allocating value to core deposit intangible assets. Such incentives disappeared when the tax code was changed to permit the deductibility of goodwill amortization. However, with the issuance of Statement of Financial Accounting Standard No. 141 (SFAS No. 141), the need for core deposit intangible asset valuations has been revived.[1]

The critical issues associated with core deposits are not related to whether they have economic benefit, which they clearly do, but to the measurement of that economic benefit and determination of whether the customer relationship is a wasting asset—that is, whether it has a measurable, finite life.

INTERNAL REVENUE SERVICE POSITION ON CORE DEPOSITS

The Internal Revenue Service (IRS) historically has challenged the concept that core deposits represent an intangible asset separate and distinct from goodwill. The IRS concedes that stable customer relationships have economic value, but it historically has put forth the theory that they are part of the overall goodwill of the bank. In the past, all amortization deductions of core deposits for federal income tax purposes have been challenged. The IRS has spent a great deal of effort attempting to invalidate the deduction of core deposit value amortization for federal income tax purposes. Typically, the IRS has focused on these areas to deny the deduction of core deposit value: inappropriate deposit types included in core deposit base; incorrect alternative funds rates used in cost-savings approaches; and faulty statistical data.

The implications of the IRS's strategy is that buyers who plan to amortize and deduct the core deposit base premium for federal income tax purposes must have a thorough, well-documented core deposit valuation methodology and statistical basis. The IRS now recognizes the existence of intangible assets and allows for their amortization over their economic useful life. To be an amortizable intangible asset, it must be separately identifiable and have a reasonably determinable economic life. Prior to the enactment of Internal Revenue Code (IRC) Section 197, the Code did not specify whether customer-based intangibles, such as core deposits, were intangible assets subject to amortization.

IMPORTANT CORE DEPOSIT TAX COURT CASES

For many years, the idea has been put forth that the core deposit base of an acquired bank is an intangible asset that could be amortized for federal income tax purposes. The IRS has challenged such efforts, with the result being a number of cases that give insight into the thought process and direction of the courts. Five cases in particular are important. Each of these cases is discussed in this section.

Midlantic Case

The first case, *Midlantic*,[2] involved a purchase and assumption of a failed bank. The taxpayer argued that the premium paid to acquire a failed bank should not be considered goodwill or going-concern value, because the bank was failing. Only the right to solicit depositors of the former bank should be considered an intangible asset. The tax court held that this right to solicit was an intangible asset with a limited useful life and was, therefore, amortizable. *Midlantic* was not definitive because it involved a failed bank and was not considered applicable to voluntary combinations of healthy banks.

Banc One Case

The second important case, *Banc One*,[3] was a 1985 case involving several issues that affected the purchase price allocation, some of which were related to core deposit value. Other issues involved the valuing of goodwill and other unrecorded intangible assets. Although the ruling went against the taxpayer, the tax court's reasoning offered positive indications that it believed that core deposits could exist as an amortizable intangible asset.

In 1973 and 1974, through cash transactions, Banc One Corporation acquired the assets and assumed the liabilities of two banks. In both cases, the purchase price was allocated to the acquired net assets using a second-tier approach (a technique that is no longer available for tax valuations). Initially, Banc One did not value the deposit base but did allocate a portion of the purchase price to a loan premium. During litigation in 1984, Banc One amended its petition in order to claim that it acquired an amortizable deposit premium. The IRS agreed that core deposits possessed a value but argued that the value was inseparable from nonamortizable goodwill and that the deposit base is self-regenerative—that it is not a wasting asset—and thus its useful life could not be determined.

The important aspect of this case, with respect to core deposits, is the reason for the court's ruling against Banc One. Amortization for tax purposes was denied not because the tax court believed core deposits were, across the board, inseparable from goodwill but because the court believed the methodology used by Banc One's appraiser to establish useful life was improper. Facts after the date of acquisition were used to establish the life of the deposits acquired in 1973 and 1974. The tax court stated that because the life of the deposit base was established based on data after the close of the tax year in which the acquisition occurred (and therefore improperly established), there was no need to rule whether the value of deposits were or were not separable from goodwill. The court's reasoning was such that the issue of whether a definite life existed or not was not decided. Some observers felt that had the court believed core deposit value was not separable from goodwill, it would have based its ruling on that determination.

AmSouth Case

The third important case, *AmSouth*,[4] was decided in favor of the IRS on February 25, 1988. The court held that AmSouth had not demonstrated that the value of the acquired core deposit was separate and distinct from goodwill. Therefore, the value of the core deposit relationship was not amortizable and thus not deductible for federal income tax purposes.

In February 1979, AmSouth Bancorporation acquired the assets and assumed the liabilities of the Bank of East Alabama (BEA), with a premium paid of $4.8 million. At the time of the acquisition, BEA was having financial difficulties and capital adequacy problems. Nonetheless, BEA was not in immediate danger of failing nor had it experienced a deposit outflow. In fact, deposits were still growing at a modest rate.

In 1977, the board of directors of BEA decided to sell the bank, and on December 30, 1977, it was announced that AmSouth agreed to purchase the assets and assume the liabilities of BEA. The acquisition was finalized in February 1979.

On June 12, 1978, BEA signed the merger agreement with AmSouth. This agreement contained the purchase price but did not allocate that price to specific assets or liabilities. An agreement of purchase was signed on August 25, 1978, which allocated to goodwill $1.7 million of the $4.8 million purchase price. On February 25, 1979, the final purchase agreement was signed, which assigned $1,679,045 of the purchase price to the customer deposit base with no allocation to goodwill.

The $1,679,045 customer deposit base figure was arrived at by the residual method. AmSouth first allocated the purchase price to the fixed assets, the loan portfolio, the investment portfolio, cash, and other assets. The amount of liabilities assumed was then deducted from the value of the assets to arrive at a net tangible asset figure of $3,120,955. The entire excess of $1,679,045 (the residual) of the purchase price ($4,800,000) over the value of net tangible assets ($3,120,955) was assigned to core deposit value. To arrive at net tangible asset value, the book values of loans were used; no fair market value (FMV) calculations were made. Moreover, it is not clear whether any assets were revalued to market or if only the book values were used. AmSouth did not perform, or have performed, a valuation of the core deposit base prior to or at the time of the acquisition. After the amortization deduction was challenged, AmSouth retained two appraisal firms to value the customer deposit base independently. The results of these valuations were used in the *AmSouth* case.

One appraisal firm valued the deposit base at $3.1 million as of December 31, 1987 (rather than the February 28, 1979, acquisition date) with a remaining life of 40 years for the business customers and 25 years for individual customers. All deposits were valued, including jumbo certificates of deposit (CDs; those over $100,000). The appraisal firm determined the value of the deposits by calculating the difference in the marginal cost of deposits for AmSouth and the actual cost of deposits for BEA. This difference was multiplied by the projected average balances of the customer deposit base over its estimated remaining useful life.

The second appraisal firm estimated the deposit base value at $3.0 million (also as of December 31, 1987) with a useful life of 40 years. This value was derived by calculating the PV of the projected net income to be obtained from that part of the acquired deposit base that remained in each successive year over its useful life. This net income was determined to be the difference between the cost of the deposits and the income derived from investing those deposits in typical bank assets.

Both appraisal firms estimated the remaining useful life by analyzing closed account history. Also, both used a snapshot approach that assumed that all deposits remain at their current balances until closed and that deposit relationships do not provide value in the form of cross-selling opportunities.

AmSouth presented several arguments to support its amortization claim. The major one, however, was the assertion that BEA had no goodwill because it was in financial difficulty at the time of the acquisition and there had been negative publicity about certain activities of its past president. AmSouth cited the *Midlantic* case as support. The court disagreed because BEA did not fail (as was the situation in the *Midlantic* case) and, in fact, had continued to experience deposit growth. Although the court decided the *AmSouth* case on fairly narrow grounds, a number of aspects of the case, summarized next, probably diminished AmSouth's position.

- In the final purchase agreement, AmSouth allocated nothing to goodwill even though BEA was solvent and had continual deposit growth.
- The purchase agreement included a value for core deposits, but this value was not supported by any valuation procedure undertaken before the acquisition. The core deposit value was not part of the determination of purchase price but was the leftover between price and net tangible asset value (the residual method).
- AmSouth used two appraisal firms that employed substantially different approaches yet arrived at approximately the same values after several revisions. The credibility of these valuations was suspect.
- All deposits, not just core deposits, were included in the valuation.
- AmSouth failed to revise the values of all assets as required by Accounting Principles Board (APB) Opinion No. 16 and 17; instead, the bank used book values for all acquired assets.
- The values of the two appraisal firms were much higher than AmSouth's original core deposits value estimate. AmSouth should have proportionately reduced the value of other assets to ensure no negative goodwill.

In the end, the court did not explicitly state that core deposits in general do not have value separate from goodwill. It held only that AmSouth had not demonstrated that the deposits of BEA it acquired had value separate and distinct from goodwill. The conclusion from a number of observers was that the unsupported valuation and less-than-comprehensive documentation were the main reasons for the unfavorable ruling.

Citizens & Southern Case

The fourth major case related to core deposits is *Citizens & Southern* (C&S).[5] In this case, the court ruled on September 6, 1988 that C&S had demonstrated that the value of acquired core deposits was separate and distinct from goodwill, thereby permitting C&S to amortize the cost of the core deposits.

Beginning in the late 1950s, C&S developed close relationships with a number of banks located throughout Georgia. These correspondent associates, as they were known, utilized certain operational and banking services of C&S, and in some cases they used the C&S name. During 1981 and 1982, C&S acquired nine of these correspondent associates and, after the acquisition, conducted business in substantially the same manner as before. C&S paid a premium of $52 million (for all nine banks) of which $42 million was allocated to the core deposit base and $10 million to goodwill.

To establish the purchase price, C&S used a computer acquisition model developed by its finance staff. This model projected future dividend potential, then discounted those dividends to present value to arrive at acquisition value. An integral part of the projections was the funding provided by core deposits, which was shown separately in the model. While the model did not explicitly value the core deposits, when assumptions of greater core deposit funding were made, the model did produce higher value estimates, all other assumptions being the same.

C&S acquired the nine banks in taxable mergers or stock purchases that constituted taxable asset purchases for federal income tax purposes. C&S allocated the purchase price of the acquired banks in a manner consistent with generally accepted accounting principles (GAAP). The FMVs of the loan and investment portfolios were determined, the intangible assets other than core deposits were valued at cost, and the deposit base was valued and classified as a separately identifiable intangible asset. Goodwill was calculated as the excess of the purchase price over the value of net tangible and identifiable intangible assets.

The valuation of the core deposit base was thoroughly prepared and became crucial to the favorable ruling C&S received. C&S included only transaction accounts (demand deposit account [DDA] and negotiable order of withdrawal [NOW]), regular savings, and time deposit open accounts. All of these accounts represented deposits that were relatively low-cost funds, reasonably stable over time, and more or less insensitive to interest rate changes.

The C&S valuation considered only those accounts that existed at the time of valuation and reflected market information and conditions at the time. These valuations were completed prior to the acquisition date.

An income approach was used by C&S to value the core deposits (described in detail later in this chapter). The four steps C&S used were:

1. Determine account survival probabilities by examining the past rate of closure of deposit accounts. (C&S used actual account closure data, for each type of account, for each acquired bank.)
2. Project net investable balances (net of reserves and float) of each type of account open at each year into the future.
3. Calculate expected income on deposits by multiplying the spread (interest earnings and service charge income less interest and operating cost on the deposits) by the net investable balances. The interest earnings assumed the funds would be invested in loans. Service charge income was estimated based on the acquired banks' records and Federal Reserve Functional Cost Analysis data. The cost of deposits included both the interest expense, if any, and the overhead costs required to service accounts.
4. Discount projected income to present value. (C&S used the yield on the acquired banks' loan portfolios as the discount rate, a relatively conservative approach.)

The appraiser retained by C&S also used the cost savings approach to core deposit value estimation. This approach measured the value of an asset as the PV of the difference between the ongoing cost of the asset and its market rate alternative. The appraiser used the rate on insured CDs as the market alternative, another conservative approach. The value of the core deposit base using the cost savings approach was $34 million (versus the $42 million using the income approach).

To derive the annual depreciation deduction, C&S computed the PV at the acquisition date of the projected income for the taxable year. Since deposit accounts tend to run off faster in early years, the net effect is that C&S was able to take greater deductions in early years than would be possible with straight-line amortization.

C&S presented a number of circumstances and facts that led to the ruling in its favor and that made the case substantially different from *AmSouth* or *Banc One*:

- C&S made it clear through documentation that its primary motivation for the acquisition was to garner deposits.
- C&S contended that under GAAP, deposit base is recognized as being separate from goodwill (APB Opinion No. 17 and Financial Accounting Standards Board Statement of Financial Accounting Standards No. 72).
- C&S claimed that there were reliable techniques to value core deposits and estimate their useful life.
- Allocations to core deposits were made prior to the acquisitions and became an integral part of the pricing process (and there was ample evidence to prove this).
- C&S used only true core deposits in its valuation.
- All core deposit accounts were examined in the valuation, not just a sample of accounts.
- The life of the core deposit base at each acquired bank was estimated based on the actual history of that bank. Moreover, C&S used an independent competent statistician to establish the deposit lines and conducted follow-up studies that corroborated the projections.

In general, the process used by C&S was thoroughly documented and well thought out, and these facts were essential in the favorable ruling it received.

One important issue that was decided by the court in the *C&S* case was that of valuation methodology. Both an income and cost savings approach were used to value the acquired core deposits. The IRS claimed that by using the income approach to value the core deposit intangible asset, C&S allocated the purchase price to the earning assets twice. The IRS's reasoning was:

- C&S valued the loans and investments (the earning assets) of the nine acquired banks based on the PV of the income stream they were expected to generate— interest income from the earning assets less cost of funding.
- C&S calculated the value of the deposit base as the PV of the income stream the deposits could generate by being invested in earning assets.
- C&S assumed that all core deposits were immediately available for investment, but in reality C&S could invest the core deposits already funding earning assets only when those earning assets matured or rolled off.
- Therefore, C&S should have adjusted the core deposit base by that portion that was invested in earning assets it had previously valued.

The court agreed with this logic and held that the income approach was not proper and that the cost savings approach was the correct valuation method to be used.

Another key issue decided in the *C&S* case was the basis of the amortization deduction. IRC Section 167(c) indicates that straight-line depreciation is the only method available for intangible assets. In the *C&S* case, however, the court held that the evidence supported an accelerated method because it was shown that the deposit base does decline more rapidly in the early years after an acquisition. The court agreed that the amount of depreciation is equal to the PV, on the acquisition date, of the projected cost savings for each taxable year.

Newark Morning Ledger Case

Another recent case applicable to core deposit valuation is the *Newark Morning Ledger.*[6] On April 20, 1993, the Supreme Court overturned an appeals court ruling that assets such as customer lists should be classified as goodwill and not be deductible for tax purposes. In a 5–4 ruling the Court reaffirmed that an intangible asset can be depreciated for federal income tax purposes if it can be valued and has a limited useful life that can be measured with reasonable accuracy.

In 1976, The Herald Company (later acquired by the Newark Morning Ledger Company) purchased the outstanding shares of Booth Newspapers, Inc. As a taxable transaction, The Herald Company allocated its adjusted income tax basis in the Booth shares among the assets that were acquired. Among the assets identified and valued was the "paid subscriber" list, valued at $67.8 million based on the estimate of future value derived from the identified subscribers of Booth's eight newspapers. The IRS denied the claimed depreciation deduction on the ground that the concept of a paid subscriber was indistinguishable from goodwill and therefore was not depreciable.

The IRS did not contest the estimate of useful life nor the assumptions underlying The Herald Company's estimate of value using the income approach (the PV of subscription revenue stream less the cost of collecting those subscriptions). The IRS claimed that the value of an acquired paid subscriber list is only the cost of replacing them with an equal number of new subscribers (estimated by the IRS at $3 million) and that asset is still indistinguishable from goodwill.

The Supreme Court held for the Newark Morning Ledger (as successor to The Herald Company) by stating that the company proved that a paid subscriber list is an intangible asset with an ascertainable value and a limited useful life that can be measured with reasonable accuracy. The court also stated that The Herald Company proved that the asset is not self-regenerating; rather, it wastes as a finite number of subscriptions are canceled.

The importance of this case cannot be overstated as a foundation to deduct core deposit value for tax purposes. Nonetheless, the case did not relieve the taxpayer of the responsibility to properly value the intangible asset and estimate its useful life with reasonable accuracy. In fact, it reemphasized the need for solid, well-documented valuation work.

Another aspect of *Newark Morning Ledger* that is relevant to bank core deposit valuations is the Court's implied support of the income approach. While it did not explicitly rule for this particular method, it did state that the value was more than the cost of generating new customer names. Had the method of valuation been in question, the Court could have allowed a deduction on just the $3 million value the government placed on the "paid subscriber" list.

 ## DEPOSITS TO BE INCLUDED IN VALUATION

There appears to be less than complete agreement among regulators as to which deposit accounts should be considered core besides the fact that acquirers of banks, thrifts, or branches need deposit valuations in order to record identifiable intangible assets separately from goodwill related to the transaction. Another reason is that core deposits have no default risk and hence the standard method of valuing core deposits is the same as maturity to price deposits. The Office of the Comptroller of the Currency defines "core deposits" as the base of demand and savings accounts that—while usually not legally restricted—the bank can expect to maintain for an extended period of years because of generally stable relationships. Although CDs are not explicitly listed, the *Citizens & Southern* case seems to support the exclusion of CDs in the core deposit base. The specific types of deposit accounts to be considered core at a given bank should be evaluated on an individual basis. The safest approach appears to be to include only noninterest-bearing DDA, NOWs, and savings in the core deposit base value calculations.

 ## ALTERNATIVE APPROACHES TO VALUING A CORE DEPOSIT BASE

Alternative approaches to core deposit gathering create deposit bases with very different contributions to profitability and value. The highest-performing core deposit-gathering model combines all dimensions of the funding attracted growth, interest expense, fee income, noninterest expense and deployable term-related behaviors to maximum advantage. As with other types of assets, there are several ways to approach the valuation of a core deposit base. A superior core deposit-gathering approach will attract funding that has maximum direct and echo effect earnings contributions. Because each core deposit category presents a different mix of finance and ambiguous influences on depositor behaviors, the best core deposit-gathering approach will in fact be the one that creates funding in certain categories. Each approach has advantages and disadvantages as well as practical limitations. Moreover, the *Citizens & Southern* and *Newark Morning Ledger* cases demonstrated that the court favored the cost savings approach over others. Nonetheless, three possible approaches to core deposit valuation are described next. Applications of the techniques are described later in this chapter.

Historical Development Cost Approach

One possible way to establish the value of a core deposit base is to determine the costs actually incurred to attract those deposits—the amount spent, for example, on branches, advertising, and so on. This approach is analogous to the cost approach to valuing assets described in Chapter 8.

The historical development cost approach presents some very serious practical difficulties. Assigning historical costs incurred to attract core deposits, as opposed to the attraction of other types of business, is virtually impossible. Even for banks that have excellent cost accounting and management information systems, identifying the relationship between certain costs and resulting depositor relationships would be suspect at best. Consequently, basing the core deposit value on historical development costs is rarely, if ever, used.

Another problem with the historical development cost approach is that a bank has already deducted, for tax purposes, the cost of acquiring deposits as part of normal operating expenses. Therefore, to reflect those acquisition costs in determining core deposit value for tax purposes may imply double counting of those expenses. In general, the valuation of a core deposit base using historical costs should be avoided.

Cost Savings Approach

Conceptually, the cost savings approach to core deposit valuation is based on the premise that the deposits being acquired have value because the cost of alternative funding is higher. The most supportable alternative funding to use to make this comparison is usually retail CDs (as was used in the successful *Citizens & Southern* case). The alternative funding rate would include the interest cost and maintenance expenses of CDs.

The cost savings approach to valuing the core deposit base is approached in much the same way that an investment is valued, except that when an investment is valued, cash *inflows* are discounted to PV, whereas when a deposit base is valued, cash *outflows* are discounted. These cash outflows associated with the deposits include the interest costs on the deposits, the maintenance costs (net of any fees), and the runoff of the deposits themselves. These future outflows are discounted at a market rate of interest that reflects the yield curve for the alternative source of funds (e.g., CDs) at the time of the valuation. The difference between the actual level of the deposits acquired and the net present value (NPV) of discounted future cash outflows is the value benefit of the deposit base.

A practical problem arises in that a yield curve on retail CDs is normally not available. A reasonable assumption to make is that the shape of the CD yield curve is the same as the shape of the yield curve of zero-coupon Treasury instruments. Another reasonable assumption is that the difference in the rates between zero-coupon Treasury instruments and CDs at any point on the yield curve is equal to the maintenance cost of those CDs.[7] Therefore, the total of CD interest and maintenance costs would equal the rate on zero-coupon Treasury instruments. Consequently, using this yield curve to discount future cash outflows from the acquired deposit base is a reasonable and supportable assumption.

Future Income Approach

A third technique of core deposit valuation is the future income approach. This technique establishes value based on the difference between the cost of deposits (both interest and maintenance) and the income generated by using those deposits to make loans and investments as well as fees from deposit accounts. The weakness in this approach, as shown in the *Citizens & Southern* case, is the potential for double counting of value.

Core deposit intangibles relate to the future earnings potential of the membership that is acquired. Generally, this must be amortized over a period, typically seven to ten years. The income approach uses estimates of future cash flows and PV techniques to derive current value and hence is based on the premise that the value of a business is equal to the PV of the entity's future stream of cash flows. There are two primary methods within this approach: capitalization of earnings that derives the current present fair value of an entity and discounted future earnings that converts the earnings to value. The future income approach starts with the interest income generated by earning assets (mostly loans and investments), minus the interest costs associated with the deposits funding those earning assets. The result is *net interest income.* Any fee and service charge income associated with the deposits is added, and then the maintenance expenses associated with the deposits are subtracted. Finally, taxes are subtracted. The net income for each year is then discounted to PV. The resulting figure is the value of the core deposit base to the owner.

The discount rate used to convert future income flows to PV must reflect the riskiness of the business of taking deposits and making loans. Consequently, there are risks with the deposits and the loans. The selection of a discount rate would follow the procedures described in Chapter 8 and would be analogous to discounting the future income of a business as described in Chapter 16.

Establishing value based on future income is often the most complex and difficult approach, because various operations and maintenance expenses must be assigned to earning assets and deposits. Without a good cost accounting or product profitability system, this cost assignment can be difficult.

It should be noted that the future income approach may not be the most supportable technique for establishing a tax basis, but it can be a good way to establish acquisition value. When a bank is considering the acquisition of a branch, the better way to establish the economic value of the deposits to be assumed (as opposed to the tax value) is probably the income approach.

 ## CORE DEPOSIT BASE LIFE ESTIMATION

Core deposits bring multiple economic advantages to financial institutions. The most obvious is their often low rate paid, which reduces interest expense. In addition, core deposits are often a platform for generating fee income and added revenue by cross-selling other services to depositors. Irrespective of which approach to valuation is used, establishing a life of the core deposit base is the most essential element of the valuation process if this asset is to be considered as an amortizable intangible asset by the IRS. Without an accurate estimate of useful life, the value of the core deposit base may be treated no differently, for tax purposes, than goodwill. Consequently, it is very important that the life of the deposit base be established with reasonable accuracy.

In general, to establish the life of the acquired deposit base, it is best to use the actual experience of the bank being acquired. Use of industry or peer group averages may be reasonable, but it is less supportable if challenged by the IRS. The completeness and accuracy of records maintained by the bank will, to a great extent, determine how much reliance must be placed on industry data. For the discussion that follows, it is assumed that the necessary information is available from automated and/or manual sources at the bank.

Historical Retention

The initial step in lifing a core deposit base is to quantify the historical retention rate for each type of core deposit account (DDA, savings, etc.). This retention rate, sometimes called a survival rate, can be defined as the percent of accounts for each deposit type open at the beginning of a year that still will be open at the end of that year.

One method to quantify historical retention rates is to construct a table similar to that shown in Exhibit 17.1. The first step in constructing such a table is to start with a base year (2006 in this example) and find the number of accounts active at year end (1,000 in this example). These are the *base year* accounts. The next step is to determine the number of base year accounts that were still open one year later, two years later, three years later, and so on. In the example, of the 1,000 base year accounts, 690 were still active one year later, 518 two years later, 400 three years later, and 350 four years later. In 2007, 360 accounts were opened during the year and remained open at

EXHIBIT 17.1   Illustration of Historical Retention Rate Calculation

| Age of Account (yrs.) | Number of Accounts Open at Date | | | | | Retention Rate | |
	12/31/ 2006	12/31/ 2007	12/31/ 2008	12/31/ 2009	12/31/ 2010	Age of Account (yrs.)	Probability of Account Remaining Open in Next Year
0–1	1,000	360	548	429	419	0–1	67.9%[a]
1–2	—	690	234	370	300	1–2	76.8%[b]
2–3	—	—	518	176	296	2–3	77.0%[c]
3–4	—	—	—	400	135	3–4	87.5%[d]
4–5	—	—	—	—	350		
Total	1,000	1,050	1,300	1,375	1,500		

Notes:

[a] $\left(\dfrac{690}{1,000} + \dfrac{234}{360} + \dfrac{370}{548} + \dfrac{300}{429}\right) \div 4 = 67.9\%$

[b] $\left(\dfrac{518}{690} + \dfrac{176}{234} + \dfrac{296}{370}\right) \div 3 = 76.8\%$

[c] $\left(\dfrac{400}{518} + \dfrac{135}{176}\right) \div 2 = 77.0\%$

[d] $\dfrac{350}{400} = 87.5\%$

year-end. Of those 360, 234 were still open one year later, 176 two years later, and 135 three years later. A similar pattern can be developed for the 548 accounts opened in 2008, the 429 opened in 2009, and the 419 opened in 2010.

Using the table in Exhibit 17.1, the retention rate for first-year accounts can be computed. (It is 67.9 percent in this example with the calculations shown at the bottom of the exhibit.) This figure means that if an account is open less than one year, there is a 67.9 percent chance it will stay open another year. If an account has been open between one and two years, there is a 76.8 percent chance it will stay open another year. If an account has been open between two and three years, the chance that it will stay open an additional year increases to 77.0 percent. Over three years, the retention rate is 87.5 percent. A higher retention rate as an account ages is common. Bankers have long recognized that the longer a customer has been with the bank, the less likely it is that he or she will leave during a given year.

If historical records are available in automated form, it is easier to apply this technique. Special computer programs may be necessary to extract the data from historical records, but basic data should be available. The problem arises when records are in manual form or nonexistent. Such situations must be assessed on a case-by-case basis to determine if a sampling of accounts is possible or if less historical information provides a sufficient basis for estimating retention rates.

There are several typical deficiencies in data availability likely to be found. The most common among smaller banks is the lack of historical account data in machine-readable form. Normally, the information on active accounts is available. The problem arises in tracking accounts that have been opened and already closed during the four- or five-year-long historical period being studied.

One technique to determine the active or closed status of accounts is to examine the year-end trial balances for each account type. If accounts are opened and numbered sequentially (i.e., if the latest account has the highest account number), it is relatively easy to determine the number of accounts opened during a year:

$$\text{New accounts during year} = \text{Last account no. this year}$$
$$- \text{First account no. this year}$$

This figure is then subtracted from the number of active accounts at the end of the year. The difference is the number of accounts retained. For example, suppose there were 1,000 accounts active at the beginning of a year. Through examination of account number sequence, it is found that 400 new accounts were opened, and from the trial balance report, it is known that there were 1,090 accounts active at the end of the year. The number of the original 1,000 accounts retained would be 690 (1,090 − 400).

The second and subsequent years become somewhat more complex because multiple years and multiple groups of account numbers are tracked. The basic approach, however, is the same.

Another common data deficiency occurs when a bank has changed data processing systems. Occasionally, the data can be reconstructed using various conversion programs. If not, it may be necessary to take a sample of accounts and track manually, or use less historical data.

There are a number of ways to establish the life of a core deposit base. The method described is one of those ways. If the historical information is available, construction of a table showing the accounts open by age group is an excellent technique to establish the retention rates for the bank being analyzed. This analysis provides a basis for estimating the likely retention of the acquired deposit accounts.

Projected Lifing of Acquired Core Deposit Accounts

Intangible assets must be amortized uniformly, depending on the type of asset and circumstances in which it was acquired. Based on the retention rates computed from historical data, it is possible to project the run-off of the acquired deposit accounts. The age distribution of those acquired accounts is determined based on account opening dates. The number of accounts in each age group (0 to 1 years, 1 to 2, etc.) form the beginning of the account retention projection.

As shown in Exhibit 17.2, the 1,500 accounts acquired in 2010 are distributed in five age groups; 419 were under 1 year old, 300 were 1 to 2 years old, 296 were 2 to 3 years old, 135 were 3 to 4 years old, and 350 were over 5 years old. At the end of 2011, the projected number of accounts that will be retained is computed based on the historical retention rates. For example, of the 419 acquired accounts that were less than one year old, at year-end 2010, 67.9 percent (285) will be retained to year-end 2011. During 2012, those 285 accounts that will then be one to two years old will be retained at a rate of 76.8 percent (ending with 219). During 2013, those 219 accounts which are now two to three years old will be retained at a rate of 77 percent (ending with 169). During 2014, the 169 accounts will be retained at a rate of 87.5 percent (ending 2009 with 148 accounts). The retention rate then stabilizes at 87.5 percent.

The same process is undertaken for each account age group, except that acquired deposit accounts that are one to two years old begin with the 76.8 percent retention rate, accounts two to three years old begin at 77.0 percent, and accounts over three years old begin at 87.5 percent.

The net result of these calculations is a projection of the number of acquired accounts remaining active at the end of each year (the column titled "Total Acquired Accounts" in Exhibit 17.2). When the number of accounts still open reaches about 5 percent of the original group (in this example, 75 accounts), it is assumed that the next year the remaining accounts run off.

The final step is to compute the average number of accounts open during each future year. This average is calculated as the midpoint between two year-end figures. This method of calculating the average implicitly assumes accounts are closed at a fairly constant rate during a year. Under most conditions, this is a reasonable assumption.

 ## APPLICATION OF THE COST SAVINGS APPROACH

As described previously, the most supportable way to measure the value of a core deposit base is to gauge the differential between the costs associated with the core deposits and

EXHIBIT 17.2 Calculations of Projected Balances of Acquired Deposit Accounts (Acquisition Date: 12/31/2010)

	Age of Acquired Deposit Accounts					Total Acquired Accounts	Average Number of Accounts	Average Balance*
	0–1	1–2	2–3	3–4	5+			
12/31/2010 (actual/ acquired)	419	300	296	135	350	1,500	—	$2,000
12/31/2011	285	230	228	118	306	1,167	1,334	2,040
12/31/2012	219	177	199	103	268	966	1,067	2,080
12/31/2013	169	155	175	90	235	824	895	2,125
12/31/2014	148	136	153	79	205	721	773	2,175
12/31/2015	130	119	133	69	180	631	676	2,200
12/31/2016	113	104	117	60	158	552	592	2,250
12/31/2017	99	91	102	53	138	483	518	2,300
12/31/2018	87	80	90	46	120	423	453	2,350
12/31/2019	76	70	78	41	105	370	397	2,400
12/31/2020	66	61	69	35	92	323	347	2,440
12/31/2021	58	53	60	31	81	283	303	2,490
12/31/2022	51	47	52	27	71	248	266	2,535
12/31/2023	44	41	46	24	61	216	232	2,590
12/31/2024	39	36	40	21	54	190	203	2,640
12/31/2025	34	31	35	18	48	166	178	2,690
12/31/2026	30	27	31	16	41	145	156	2,750
12/31/2027	26	24	27	14	36	127	136	2,800
12/31/2028	23	21	24	12	31	111	119	2,860
12/31/2029	20	18	21	10	28	97	104	2,920
12/31/2030	17	16	18	9	25	85	91	2,970
12/31/2031	15	14	16	8	21	74	80	3,030
12/31/2032	13	12	14	7	16	0[†]	37	3,100

*5% annual increase.

[†]It is assumed that when the remaining accounts reach 5 percent of the original number acquired (75 in this example), all accounts run off the next year.

the costs of alternative funding at market rates. The next discussion uses the data from the preceding example to illustrate how the cost savings approach can be applied.

The cost savings approach is similar in concept to the valuation of a bond, except that in the case of deposits, the amount of the deposit base originally acquired is compared with the future cash outflows (principal, interest, and maintenance costs net of fees) associated with that deposit base. Exhibit 17.3 shows an illustration of the calculations.

EXHIBIT 17.3 Illustration of Cost Savings Approach to Valuation of Core Deposit Base (Rounded to $000, Using Data from Exhibit 17.2)

Year	Average Deposits during Year from Acquired Accounts[a]	Cash Outflows Associated Deposits				Discount Rate[d]	Discounted Value of Cash Outflow
		Interest[b]	Mainte-nance[c]	Runoff	Total		
2011	$2,721	$177	$54	$279	$510	7.85%	$ 472
2012	2,219	144	44	502	690	8.05%	591
2013	1,902	124	38	317	479	8.16%	379
2014	1,681	109	34	221	368	8.17%	269
2015	1,487	97	30	194	321	8.17%	217
2016	1,332	87	27	155	269	8.23%	167
2017	1,191	77	24	141	242	8.26%	139
2018	1,065	69	21	126	216	8.30%	114
2019	953	62	19	112	193	8.34%	94
2020	847	55	17	106	178	8.35%	80
2021	754	49	15	93	157	8.37%	65
2022	674	44	13	80	137	8.39%	52
2023	601	39	12	73	124	8.40%	43
2024	536	35	11	65	111	8.41%	36
2025	479	31	10	57	98	8.41%	29
2026	429	28	9	50	87	8.40%	24
2027	381	25	8	48	81	8.41%	21
2028	340	22	7	41	70	8.41%	16
2029	304	20	6	36	69	8.39%	15
2030	271	18	5	33	56	8.35%	11
2031	242	16	5	29	50	8.35%	9
2032	115	7	2	127	136	8.33%	23
						TOTAL	$2,866

Core Deposit Value = Deposits Acquired ($3,000) − Discounted Value of Outflow ($2,866) = $134 (4.5% premium).

[a]Average number of accounts that were open during year times average balance (from Exhibit 17.2).
[b]At 6.5 percent.
[c]At 2 percent of balances, per Fed Functional Cost Analysis, for regular savings.
[d]Using a yield curve on zero-coupon 30-year U.S. government instruments.

The first step is to determine the volume of the originally acquired deposits retained at the end of each year through the life of that deposit base. This is based on the average number of accounts open during the year multiplied by the average balances. (Results of that calculation are shown in column 1 of Exhibit 17.3, using the data from Exhibit 17.2.)

The next step is to determine the cash outflows associated with the deposits. The interest costs in this example are assumed to be 6.5 percent of deposits during the year (results shown in column 2). Maintenance costs are based on Federal Reserves Functional Cost Analysis figures at 200 basis points (2 percent) of deposits (results shown in column 3). Runoff is simply the reduction in deposit balances during the year (balances during preceding year less balances during current year, results in column 4). The total outflows (column 5) are discounted at the rate on zero-coupon Treasury instruments (usually the average of the four quarterly rates for the year being discounted). The sum of these discounted values ($2,866,000) is subtracted from the deposits acquired ($3,000,000) to arrive at the deposit base value ($134,000).

The cost savings approach to core deposit base valuation can be difficult to understand. To address this difficulty, it is useful to think of two streams of cash that a bank will have to pay out over some period of time. The first stream of cash outflow is that which the bank will pay to the depositors who own the deposits being acquired (column 5 in Exhibit 17.3). The bank has acquired a liability with a book value of $3,000,000, but because the payout occurs over time, the value of the liability is less than $3,000,000 even considering interest and maintenance costs.

The second stream of cash outflow to think of is one associated with the payout on a portfolio of CDs paying market rates and having the exact same runoff characteristics as the deposit base that was acquired. Since it is assumed that the cost of alternative funding at market rates is equal to the cost of CDs, the NPV of that portfolio of CDs (including interest and maintenance) will be enough to replace the acquired deposits ($3,000,000).

Returning to the first stream of cash, those future outflows are discounted to PV at a rate that reflects only the risk of the future cash outflows. The yields on zero-coupon Treasury instruments are an excellent proxy for the market's assessment of future investment income risk at a specific point in time. Using these rates, the NPV of the future cash outflows can be computed (in the example, $2,866,000).

The PV of the future liability of the bank for the deposits it acquired is $2,866,000. The PV of an alternative source of funding liabilities at market rates is $3,000,000. The difference between these two represents the advantage to the bank of being able to use core deposits instead of market rate alternatives. Consequently, the value of those core deposits is equal to that advantage, or $134,000.

APPLICATION OF THE FUTURE INCOME APPROACH

The future income is influenced by both external factors, such as general economic conditions, yields available on alternative investments, industry conditions and outlook, and internal factors, such as financial risk (leverage, liquidity, etc.), operating risk (management, markets, competition, etc.), and risk associated with estimating annual earnings capacity. The future income approach to valuing a core deposit base requires three steps:

1. Determine the earnings per acquired account based on the interest expense and operating costs associated with each account.

2. Project the total earnings from all acquired accounts as they run off over the average life of the account base.
3. Compute the value of the deposit base by discounting the future earnings to PV.

Each of these three steps is described next.

Earnings per Account Calculation

The fundamental basis of the future income approach is that deposits are invested in interest-bearing assets. Consequently, the first step is to calculate how much is earned from each dollar of deposit that is invested. The procedure here explains the after-tax earnings generated by $100 of deposits (assuming same type of savings deposit base as in the cost savings example).

1. Gross deposit received of $100.00
2. Minus reserves and float of $5.00
3. Equals net investable deposits of $95.00
4. Multiplied by yield on earning assets of 8.16 percent equals $7.75
5. Minus interest expense on gross deposit of 4.0 percent equals $3.95
6. Minus operations costs of $2.00 equals $1.95
7. Minus taxes of $.68
8. Equals after-tax earnings on deposit of $1.27 (1.27 percent)

The foundation of the future income approach becomes the 1.27 percent after-tax earnings rate on deposits.

Projection of Earnings from Acquired Deposit Base

Once the percent return from each deposit account type is calculated, the future earnings of the acquired deposit base can be computed. Exhibit 17.4 illustrates the earnings calculation. The average number of accounts is multiplied by the average balance (which results in total deposit balances). The after-tax income percent (1.27 percent) is applied, resulting in the earnings attributable to the acquired deposits each year over the life of the deposit base.

Computation of Deposit Base Value

The value of the deposit base under the future income approach is the NPV of the after-tax income attributable to the acquired deposits. Applying a 12 percent discount rate, the NPV of all after-tax income shown in Exhibit 17.4 is about $136,000—a 4.5 percent premium. This is the value of the acquired deposit accounts (for that one type of account) to the buyer.

Notice that in the income approach, a discount rate of 12 percent was used, but for the cost savings the discount rate used was based on the yield curve for zero-coupon Treasury securities. The main difference is that the 12 percent reflects what a bank would apply to a comparable business taking deposits. Consequently, there is a risk

EXHIBIT 17.4 Calculation of Core Deposit Base Value Using Income Approach (Rounded to $000, Using Data from Exhibit 17.2)

Year	Average Deposits during Year from Acquired Accounts[a]	After-Tax Income[b]	Discount Rate[c]	Discounted Value of Income
2011	$2,721	$34	12%	$ 30
2012	2,219	28	12%	22
2013	1,902	24	12%	17
2014	1,681	21	12%	13
2015	1,487	19	12%	11
2016	1,332	17	12%	9
2017	1,191	15	12%	7
2018	1,065	14	12%	6
2019	953	12	12%	4
2020	847	11	12%	4
2021	754	10	12%	3
2022	674	9	12%	2
2023	601	8	12%	2
2024	536	7	12%	1
2025	479	6	12%	1
2026	429	5	12%	1
2027	381	4	12%	1
2028	340	4	12%	1
2029	304	4	12%	.5
2030	271	3	12%	.3
2031	242	3	12%	.3
2032	115	1	12%	.1
				$136

[a] Average number of accounts open during year times average balance (from Exhibit 17.2).

[b] At 1.27 percent, as described in text.

[c] The 12 percent discount rate reflects what a bank would expect to apply to a comparable business that takes deposits and makes loans. This is fundamentally different from the discount rate used in the cost savings approach to valuation, and will never be the same.

factor associated with the business activity in addition to the normal time value of money reflected in the yield curve of zero-coupon Treasury securities.

The core deposit value by the cost savings approach was $134,000. By the future income approach, the value was estimated at $136,000. As with the valuation of any asset, different approaches will yield different results. In general, it is unlikely that two different approaches to core deposit value will result in estimates that are this close to one another.

SYSTEMICALLY IMPORTANT FINANCIAL INSTITUTIONS

The wave of consolidations in the financial services industry during the 1990s and the first half of the 2000s has resulted in fewer but bigger financial institutions, and they are often perceived as too big to fail (TBTF). Moral hazards can be raised if these TBTF firms assume the government's reluctance to hold them accountable for their business failures as signaling aversion to tough regulatory reforms and actions. Recent debates suggest that different sizes of financial services firms may receive different regulatory scrutiny and treatment. The elite public companies and banks may receive protection and benefits from the perception by policy makers, regulators, and the capital market that they are TBTF. The common definition of the TBTF firms is that their failure will threaten the overall financial stability of the nation and thus government bailout is the only way to rescue them.

The financial services industry traditionally has been regarded to be vital to the nation's economic growth, development, and prosperity. Nonetheless, recent financial difficulties in the industry and related financial crisis have been treated as TBTF, which has resulted in large government bailouts. Anecdotal evidence suggests that government bailouts through the Troubled Asset Relief Program have aided those troubled financial institutions to recover; others believe that the bailout provides only a short-term cure and just postponed their inevitable demise. Thus, these institutions should be unwound or effective regulatory reforms are needed to discipline the institutions. These financial services are considered TBTF primarily because: (1) they play a vital role in our economy and thus their demise could be devastating to the nation's economic growth and sustainability; and (2) financial markets hold a significant portion of bank securities and investments.

The Dodd-Frank Wall Street Reform and Consumer Protection Act of 2010 creates a new council of regulators, named the Financial Stability Oversight Council (FSOC) to examine U.S. financial stability. The FSOC is charged with identifying "systemically important" (SI) financial institutions, including banks and nonbank financial firms, and addressing their financial risks. In this section, we examine the financial health of SI financial services firms. The common definition of the SI and/or TBTF firms is that these firms play an important role in U.S. financial stability and are basically so large that their failure would threaten the overall financial stability of the nation. Investors are concerned about their failures. Thus, the market tends not to adequately discipline them and regulators hesitate to severely scrutinize them. The Dodd-Frank Act empowers the FSOC to identify large bank holding companies (BHCs) and other financial institutions such as nonbank financial companies, technology services providers, and financial market utilities that are systemically important to the financial system. The next paragraphs provide backgound information regarding some of the financial services firms that might be perceived as SI/TBTF. Indeed, a few have already bankrupted.

Lehman Brothers

Lehman Brothers Holdings Inc. was a global financial services firm with worldwide headquarters in New York City and regional headquarters in London and Tokyo as well as offices located throughout the world. It operated business in investment banking, equity and fixed-income sales, research and trading, investment management, private equity, and private banking. Lehman Brothers, which was named in early 2007 one of the largest investment banks, was also a primary dealer in the U.S. Treasury securities market. However, this superfirm declared bankruptcy on September 15, 2008 with $613 billion in debt. The share price dramatically fell in the first two weeks of September 2008 until it bottomed at $0.10 on September 17, 2008. Lehman Brothers also was downsized by cutting more than 6,000 employees throughout the process. After being in operation for 158 years, it is a tragedy that Lehman Brothers became history. However, society can learn an important lesson from its failure, which was due to not focusing on sustainability and pursuing high profit without considering the underlying risk.

Goldman Sachs

Goldman Sachs Group Inc. is a global investment banking and securities firm with headquarters in New York City and with additional offices throughout 23 countries in major international financial centers, such as Tokyo, London, and Hong Kong. It engages in investment banking, securities, investment management, and other financial services primarily with institutional clients. It also engages in proprietary trading and private equity deals and is a primary dealer in the U.S. Treasury security market. In 2008 and 2009, Goldman Sachs received billions of dollars in taxpayer money to help it stay afloat. Goldman Sachs and Morgan Stanley became traditional BHCs on September 21, 2008, which meant an end of the era of investment banking on Wall Street. Both of them will be under stricter supervision from more federal supervision organizations including the Securities and Exchange Commission to minimize their potential conflicts of interest in providing financial services and to oversee their operational and reporting activities.

Morgan Stanley

Morgan Stanley is a global financial services firm headquartered in New York City serving a diversified group of corporations, governments, financial institutions, and individuals. It also operates in 36 countries around the world with over 600 offices and a workforce of over 60,000. It was separated from J.P. Morgan & Co. in 1935. The other part of Morgan is J.P. Morgan. Because of the subprime crisis, it, like Goldman Sachs, was finally confirmed as a BHC on September 21, 2008. Although big changes have occurred, Morgan Stanley seems to be performing well since that time.

JPMorgan Chase

JPMorgan Chase & Co. is a global securities, investment banking, and retail banking firm. It was formed in 2000, when Chase Manhattan Corporation merged with J.P. Morgan & Co. It is the second largest market capitalization bank in the United States institution, just behind Bank of America. The hedge fund unit of JPMorgan Chase is the largest hedge fund in the United States with $53.5 billion in assets as of the end of 2009.[8]

JPMorgan Chase, in its current structure, is the result of the combination of several large U.S. banking companies over the last decade.

Bank of America

Bank of America Corporation is a financial services company serving clients in more than 150 countries and having a relationship with 99 percent of the U.S. Fortune 500 companies and 83 percent of the Fortune Global 500. As of 2010, Bank of America was the fifth largest company in the United States by total revenue[9] as well as the second largest non-oil company in the United States, only after Wal-Mart. In 2010, *Forbes* listed Bank of America as the third "best large company in the world."[10] The bank's 2008 acquisition of Merrill Lynch made Bank of America the world's largest wealth manager and a major player in the investment banking industry.

Bank of America performed very well, even in the subprime crisis. However, sometimes it still is criticized. For example, in January 2008, Bank of America began notifying some customers without payment problems that their interest rates were being more than doubled, up to 28 percent. This attracted national attention from television and Internet commentators and definitely hurt its goodwill to some extent.

Citigroup

Citigroup Inc. is a global financial services company with the world's largest financial services network, spanning 140 countries with approximately 16,000 offices worldwide. The company employs approximately 260,000 staff around the world and holds over 200 million customer accounts in more than 140 countries. Even such a huge company suffered huge losses during the global financial crisis of 2007–2009 and was rescued in November 2008 in a massive bailout by the U.S. government.[11] It is one of the Big Four banks in the United States, along with Bank of America, JPMorgan Chase, and Wells Fargo.

Wells Fargo

Wells Fargo & Company is a diversified financial services company with operations around the world. It is the fourth largest bank in the United States by assets, the largest bank by market capitalization,[12] and the second largest bank in deposits, home mortgage servicing, and debit cards. In 2007, it was the only bank in the United States to be rated AAA by Standard & Poor's, although its rating has since been lowered to AA in the light of the financial crisis of 2007 to 2009.[13] Wells Fargo delineates all its financial services into three different business segments when reporting results: community banking; wholesale banking; and wealth, brokerage, and retirement. In October 2008 Wells Fargo issued an offer to buy Wachovia superseding Citigroups offer, which was in conjunction with the FDIC. Citigroup protested the takeover and ultimately lost the battle paving the way for Wells Fargo to buy Wachovia. Citigroup ultimately stepped aside but is seeking damages for a breach of an exclusivity agreement to buy Wachovia.

 **CONCLUSION**

This chapter presents several emerging issues relevant to financial services firms including those related to core deposits as an intangible asset, valuation methods, and estimation of credit losses using an incurred loss model, which requires evidence of a loss before financial assets can be written down. It is the author's hope that the emerging regulatory requirements and accounting standards move toward a more forward-looking expected loss model of accounting for credit losses that better reflects the economics of lending decisions. There will be more global efforts to address the overriding issue of systemically important financial institutions that many believe contributed to the 2007–2009 global financial crisis.

 NOTES

1. Financial Accounting Standards Board, "Financial Accounting Series NO 299-A," DECEMBER 2007. Available at: www.gasb.org/cs/BlobServer?blobcol=urldata&blobtable=MungoBlobs&blobkey=id&blobwhere=1175820919432&blobheader=application%2Fpdf

2. *Midlantic National Bank* v. *Comr.*, T.C. Memo 1983–58.

3. *Banc One Corp.* v. *Comr.*, T.C. Memo 1983–35.

4. *AmSouth Bancorporation* v. *United States*, 88–1, U.S.T.C.

5. *Citizens & Southern Bancorporation & Subs* v. *Commissioner*, 91 T.C. No. 35 (1988).

6. *Newark Morning Ledger Co., as successor to the Herald Company, petitioner* v. *United States.* Supreme Court of the United States; 91–1135, 4/20/93, 113 set 1670.

7. The economic argument underlying this assumption is based on the principle of substitution. If CDs plus maintenance cost yielded a rate higher than zero-coupon Treasury instruments, the bank would substitute open market funding for CDs. Admittedly, this ignores potential relationships with the customer for other product sales, but it is a supportable and reasonable assumption.

8. www.marketfolly.com/2010/03/worlds-largest-hedge-funds.html.

9. CNN, "Fortune 500 2010: Fortune 1000 Companies 1-100." Available at: http://money.cnn.com/magazines/fortune/fortune500/2010/full_list/.

10. Forbes.com, "The Global 2000," March 1, 2010. Available at: www.forbes.com/lists/2010/18/global-2000-10_The-Global-2000_Rank.html.

11. Eric Dash, "U.S. Approves Plan to Help Citigroup Weather Losses," *New York Times*, November 23, 2008. Available at: www.nytimes.com/2008/11/24/business/24citibank.html?hp.

12. Google.com, "Wells Fargo & Company: NYSE:WFC quotes & news—Google Finance." Available at: www.google.com/finance?q=NYSE:WFC.

13. "S&P Downgrades Wells Fargo, U.S. Bancorp, Other Banks," *BusinessWeek*. June 17, 2009. Available at: www.businessweek.com/investor/content/jun2009/pi20090617_892748_page_2.htm.

CHAPTER EIGHTEEN

Derivative Financial Instruments

D ERIVATIVES ARE FINANCIAL PRODUCTS, such as futures contracts, options, and mortgage-backed securities. Most of the value of derivatives is comprised on the value of an underlying security, commodity, or other financial instrument that has a value, based on the expected future price movements of the asset to which it is linked called the underlying asset. Derivative financial instruments have grown rapidly because of the dynamics of the global financial markets, the ever-lasting fluctuation in interest and currency exchange rates, the complexity of financial engineering, and their potential profitability. Commercial banks in the United States reported outstanding derivatives contracts with a national value of $33 trillion in 1999 comparing to $ 231.2 trillion in 2010. The trend in derivatives transactions shows a steady growth of about 20 percent compound annual rate increase since 1990. Of the $33 trillion reported outstanding derivatives national value, only $4 trillion were exchange-traded derivatives. The remainder were off-exchange or over-the-counter (OTC) derivatives.[1] Derivatives are defined as any financial instruments or other contracts (e.g, futures, forwards, options, swaptions, caps, collars, and floors) with one or more underlyings (e.g., interest rate, index security price, commodity price, foreign exchange rate, or some other variables) with one or more notional amounts or payment provisions or both (e.g., face amount expressed in currency units, number of shares, bushels, pounds, or other units specified in the contract). Key elements of this definition are "underlying," "notional amount," and "payment provision." An under-lying is a specified interest rate, security price, commodity price, foreign exchange rate, or some other variable or index whose market movements cause the fair market value or cash flows of a derivative to fluctuate. A notional amount is a number of currency units, shares, bushels, pounds, or other units specified in the contract that determines the size of the change caused by the movement of the underlying. The underlying and notional amount typically determine the amount of settlement and whether a settlement is required in most cases. A payment provision determines a fixed or determinable settlement that is to be made if the underlying behaves in a certain manner. A net settlement indicates that a derivative can be settled in cash rather than the delivery of the underlying item.

Derivatives typically derive their value from underlying traditional financial instruments. Participants in derivative markets (e.g., dealers, financial institutions, business firms, mutual and pension funds, state and local governments) use derivatives for a number of reasons, including risk management purposes and speculation activities. The widespread use of derivatives, coupled with the concerns raised by the financial community regarding complexities, risks, failures, and insufficient measurement, recognition, and disclosures of derivative transactions, has caused regulators and the accounting profession to issue authoritative guidelines on derivatives.

Derivatives have been used for: (1) managing financial risks, (2) speculating on the price of financial instruments, (3) reducing the cost of raising capital, (4) earning higher investment returns, (5) adjusting investment portfolios to take advantage of mispricing between stock baskets and stock index futures, and (6) combining derivatives with other financial instruments to create new and more powerful financial products. Most commonly, active end users of derivatives are financial institutions, mutual funds, pension funds, and commercial firms. Derivatives are being traded through both organized exchanges and OTC, and their "notional value" exceeds the estimated total value of the world's bonds and stocks. Exchange-traded derivatives typically are more standardized and offer greater liquidity than OTC derivatives, which are individually arranged contracts. Most of the risk associated with exchange-traded derivatives is market risk rather than credit risk. OTC derivatives are privately traded instruments that are customized to meet specific needs and for which the counterparty is not an organized exchange.

Derivative transactions have grown significantly in volume and complexity from the traditional interest rate and currency swaps to more sophisticated, computer-driven risk management derivatives. This ever-increasing use of derivatives and recent losses by some derivatives end users have raised numerous issues of concern among regulators, the financial community, and the accounting profession as to the appropriate use, proper risk assessment, and adequate disclosures of derivative transactions by both issuers and end users of these financial products. Improved oversight by regulators and new accounting standards by the accounting profession have been suggested as a means of addressing these issues.

The global financial community is concerned with the frequency and magnitude of derivatives losses suffered by public companies (e.g., Gibson Greetings, Procter & Gamble, Air Products & Chemicals, and American International Group), mutual funds and municipal governments (e.g., Orange County, California), and British merchant banks (e.g., Barings PLC). These well-publicized derivative losses focused on renewed attention on OTC derivatives sold by banks and brokers. As a result, several congressional and private initiatives have been taken to address derivatives issues.

AUTHORITATIVE GUIDELINES ON DERIVATIVES

A number of reports[2] studied derivatives and made recommendations to Congress, financial regulators, the Securities and Exchange Commission (SEC), and the Financial Accounting Standards Board (FASB) to take proper actions to: (1) close the perceived regulatory gaps related to dealers of derivatives; (2) establish new regulations for derivatives brokers, dealers, and end users to ensure investors' protection; (3) issue new accounting standards and guidelines for proper disclosures of derivatives; and (4) require reasonable capital requirements for derivatives dealers and brokers to mitigate unexpected derivatives losses or failures. The Government Accountability Office (GAO) report places the responsibility for managing derivatives on a strong system of corporate governance consisting of responsible boards of directors, independent audit committees, and effective internal and external auditors.

In April 1998, the Federal Financial Institutions Examination Council (FFIEC) published a rule that affects investment activities of financial institutions: "The Supervisory Policy Statement on Investment Securities and End-User Derivatives Activities."[3] The FFIEC consists of the main five regulatory agencies that oversee financial institutions: the Federal Reserve System, the Federal Deposit Insurance Corporation, the National Credit Union Administration, the Office of Thrift Supervision, and the Office of the Comptroller of the Currency. This policy statement states that management should establish and maintain appropriate risk management practices to continuously assess the risks of investment securities and derivatives activities for the entire institution in the context of the portfolio as a whole. The statement describes five types of risk associated with investment securities and derivatives transactions: (1) market or interest risk, (2) credit risk, (3) liquidity risk, (4) operational or transaction risk, and (5) legal risk. These risks and their related control activities are discussed in the section entitled "Derivatives Risk Management Policy" later in this chapter and Exhibit 18.2.

The FASB issued Statement of Financial Accounting Standards (SFAS) No. 133, *Accounting for Derivative Instruments and Hedging Activities*, in June 1998 and its successor Accounting Standards Codification (ASC) No. 815 provides a comprehensive and consistent standard for the recognition and measurement of derivatives and hedging activities. ASC No. 815 resolves the inconsistencies that existed with respect to accounting for derivatives and changes considerably the way many derivatives transactions and hedged items are reported. Over the past decade, the FASB has issued several other guidelines on accounting and disclosure requirements of derivatives to address the ever evolving nature and types of derivative transactions. These guidelines are further discussed in the section entitled "Accounting for Derivatives" later in this chapter.

Prior to 2000, almost all derivatives were traded on regulated central exchanges overseen by the Commodity Futures Trading Commission; after 2002, the derivative market became unregulated and exempt from all regulations, including state gambling laws. With no regulatory scrutiny of derivative trades, the determination of the true value of those exotic instruments became subjective, manipulative, and complex. The recent financial crisis has underscored the lack of regulations for nonsecurities-based derivatives contracts such as credit default swaps (CDS). Unlike other derivative contracts (insurance, securities, commodities, and futures), CDS are not regulated. Thus they are perceived as a form of legalized gambling that are traded primarily in the OTC markets. Proper regulations require transparent information on OTC transactions to restore investors' confidence on speculative derivatives transactions (credit derivatives). Global regulators, particularly in the United States and Europe, have considered regulating CDS and other OTC derivatives by establishing a clearinghouse to serve as a central counterparty (CCP) for those derivatives. Proper regulation of derivatives trades requires full transparency, true competition in determining trading prices and volumes, adequate capital reserves, effective internal controls, and sound financial reporting. Effective regulation and vigilant oversight of derivative trades would eliminate secret pricing and differences in what commercial banks charge their consumers and what they pay to hedge their trades. The Dodd-Frank Act of 2010 addresses derivative transactions; it is discussed in the section titled "Derivatives under the Dodd-Frank Act of 2010," later in this chapter.

 ## DERIVATIVE MARKETS

Derivative markets are investment markets for contractual financial instruments whose value is determined based on the value of underlying assets or instruments. Their performance is measured by how underlying assets or instruments perform. Like any other contracts, derivatives are agreements between two parties (buyer and seller) dealing on an arm's-length basis. The price of these contracts is determined based on bargaining power of the two involved parties, when the buyer tries to purchase as cheaply as possible and the seller attempts to sell as dearly as possible. Like any other investment market, the derivatives market determines the prices of the derivatives trading therein, which theoretically should reflect their fair values or true economic values to investors. In efficient derivatives markets, prices are determined by using investment models (e.g., the capital asset pricing model, the arbitrage pricing theory, or the Black-Scholes option pricing model) in such a way that prices fluctuate randomly as investors cannot consistently earn abnormal returns (returns above those that would compensate them for the level of risk they assume). Return measures investment performance, which represents the percentage increase in the investor's wealth resulting from making the investment (for stock, this is the percentage change in price plus the dividend yield). Risk is the uncertainty of future returns.

To increase their wealth, investors attempt to maximize their return subject to minimum level of risk. However, in an investment market, there is a positive correlation between risk and return, known as the risk-return trade-off. Derivative prices (e.g., options, forwards) are based on the prices of the underlying traditional financial instruments (e.g., stocks, and bonds) traded in capital markets. Derivatives often are used for hedging purposes to manage the risk of investing in the underlying instruments. Derivatives also can be utilized for speculation purposes of trading derivative contracts rather than the underlying securities. Nevertheless, derivative markets typically offer three advantages over security markets: (1) Commissions and other trading costs of derivative markets are much lower than transaction costs of spot markets; (2) derivative markets (e.g., options and futures) typically have greater liquidity than the underlying securities market; and (3) short selling is readily available and possible in derivative markets but not in securities markets. Derivative markets allow speculators willing to assume risk to accommodate hedgers wishing to reduce it and, thus, help financial markets become more efficient, which provides better opportunities to managing risk.

There are actually two distinct forms of the derivative market: over-the- counter and exchange-traded derivatives. It is possible to purchase and sell derivatives in the form of futures or as OTC offerings. In this scenario, the derivatives focus on larger clients, such as government entities, investment banks, and hedge funds. It is not unusual for investors who are interested in derivatives to actively participate in both of these financial markets. OTC derivatives often are traded on computer networks and by phone and are traded directly between two parties. Some firms use online systems through which traders can assess the availability of credit lines for the counterparty and within overall trading limits. Automation of trading traditionally has been limited in the OTC derivatives market, which makes it difficult to determine the online fair value of OTC derivative transactions. Brokers are being utilized to locate counterparties who are willing to transact at the quoted price. After counterparties have been identified, they determine for themselves whether each other's credit quality is acceptable and whether the exposure can be accommodated within credit limits. Foreign exchange dealers, especially bank dealers, have developed electronic trading facilities, such as Web sites, that allow their customers to trade electronically. Therefore, the online fair value quotations are easily available for foreign exchange derivatives. Exchange-traded derivative contracts are those derivatives instruments that are traded via specialized derivatives exchanges or other exchanges where individuals trade standardized contracts that have been defined by the exchange.

Forward foreign exchange and forward foreign agreements are two derivative products that have attracted significant volumes. Development of electronic trading systems for swaps has facilitated execution of online swap tradings between dealers. Participants in this system electronically express their desire to enter into specific swap transactions while other participants (e.g., dealers) accept the transaction as offered or suggest possible changes in terms. The credit limits of all participants (dealers) are also loaded into the system prior to trading. These electronic systems allow online, accurate capture of data, especially fair value for swap transactions. The rapid growth and widespread acceptance of electronic online brokering of derivatives has made the pricing process of determining fair value more accurate and timely.

The rapid growth and increasing use of derivatives by many large banks has concerned banking authorities and regulators and has provided sufficient incentives for market participants and policymakers to reevaluate derivatives risk management procedures, especially the risk assessment and management of counterparty credit risk and the probability that a counterparty will not settle an obligation for full value, either when the obligation is due or at any time thereafter.

DERIVATIVES RISK MANAGEMENT

The collapse of Long-Term Capital Management prompted several professional groups to study derivatives and their related risks. The President's Working Group on Financial Markets, Counterparty Risk Management Policy Group, and the International Swaps and Derivatives Association (ISDA) are the most active groups that have suggested ways to strengthen risk management for derivatives.[4] The Working Group's report evaluates the regulatory framework for OTC derivatives and suggests policies, procedures, and techniques by which individual firms measure and manage counterparty risk associated with derivatives. The Counterparty group and the ISDA called for important cooperative efforts related to collateral programs to strengthen market infrastructure to reduce derivative risk. The ISDA has developed templates for confirmations that market participants use for many derivative products. The confirmation lists both the economic features and legal terms of derivative transactions.

Banks involved in derivative transactions should establish and maintain an adequate and effective risk management system that promotes risk management policies and procedures, develops effective risk assessment and monitoring systems, and requires both internal and external audits and sound accounting systems in properly measuring, recognizing, and disclosing fair value of derivatives. Banks should establish an adequate and effective derivatives risk management system consisting of: (1) appropriate board of directors, audit committee, and management oversight; (2) sufficient risk management policies and procedures; (3) adequate and effective risk measurement and monitoring systems; (4) adequate and effective internal controls; and (5) independent external audit.

Derivatives can be utilized to manage (e.g., increase or decrease) the risk of investing in the spot items (underlying instruments) primarily because the value of derivatives is related to the prices of the underlying spot market goods. Derivative markets enable investors to manage their risk to their tolerant and preferable levels by transferring risk from those wishing to reduce it to those willing to increase it. Thus, risk management is essential to the valuation and long-term performance of derivatives. Financial institutions are facing significant risks of changes in interest rates, foreign currency value, equity, and commodity prices as well as loan defaults and changes in market conditions. Therefore, financial institutions often use derivatives to manage, transfer, or hedge such risks. Indeed, one study reveals that financial institutions consider derivatives as critical or imperative risk management strategies.[5]

The Committee of Sponsoring Organizations of the Treadway Commission (COSO) in 1996, issued a report titled "Internal Control Issues in Derivatives Usage—An Information Tool for Considering the COSO Internal Control-Integrates Framework in Derivatives Applications." The COSO report suggests the application of the COSO framework control principles to derivatives in their overall risk management processes. These risk management processes, depending on the nature and extent of derivatives used, should consist of:

1. Understanding operations and entity-wide objectives.
2. Identifying, measuring, assessing, and modifying business risk.

3. Evaluating the use of derivatives to control market risk and link use to entity-wide and activity-level objectives.
4. Defining risk management activities and terms relating to derivatives to provide a clear understanding of their intended use.
5. Assessing the appropriateness of specified activities and strategies relating to the use of derivatives.
6. Establishing procedures for obtaining and communicating information and analyzing and monitoring risk management activities and their results.[6]

The COSO report also suggests that entities, including financial institutions and their boards of directors, senior management, and others involved with derivatives, consider a number of actions to manage the use of their derivatives. These suggested actions are:

1. Initiating a self-assessment of entity-wide control systems, directing attention specifically to areas of derivative operations that are of primary importance.
2. Fully integrating management of derivative activities into the enterprises' overall risk management system by developing and implementing a comprehensive risk management policy.
3. Ensuring that policy objectives specifying the use of derivatives are clearly articulated and documented.
4. Requiring that any use of derivatives be clearly linked with entity-wide and activity-level objectives.[7]

The complexity of derivative instruments is largely the result of the pricing mechanisms, flexibility and options features, and value calculation formulas and associated risks. Derivatives are important tools used by management for mitigating risks. The ever-increasing growth of derivatives suggests that market participants including management find those useful tools for risk management. Credit derivatives can be useful to commercial banks to manage loan portfolio risks and to investment banks to manage risks of underwriting securities and to asset managers or hedge funds to achieve the desired credit risk portfolio. Nonetheless, credit derivatives can create conflict of interest when a bank performs all three commercial, investment, and insurance activities. Credit derivatives enable banks to take additional risks or transfer risks of loans to another party.

 ## DERIVATIVES RISK MANAGEMENT POLICY

An appropriate risk management policy for derivatives should address all aspects and issues pertaining to derivatives including their purposes, risks, and accounting methods to measure their fair value. Such a risk management policy should become part of the risk management process which addresses all aspects and key considerations of the use of derivatives. This process is described in the following sections.

The Extent of Derivatives' Use

Recently, derivatives have grown rapidly because of the dynamic state of financial markets, the volatility in interest and currency exchange rates, the complexity of financial engineering, and the impact of derivatives on profitability and risk management. As of December 2007, exchange-traded derivatives amounted to $289 trillion and OTC contracts exceeded $549 trillion; together these represent about 11 times the global gross domestic product.[8] The extent of the use of derivatives should be considered when constructing investment portfolio and risk management because it determines the degree to which the institution is affected by fair value measurement and recognition requirements of accounting standards (e.g., SFAS No. 133).[9]

Identification and Analysis of All Types of Derivatives

Derivatives are generally classified into three categories: (1) stand-alone (freestanding) derivatives, (2) compound derivatives (derivatives combined with other derivatives), and (3) embedded derivatives (derivatives that are bifurcated from the instrument in which they are embedded). The proper classification of derivatives is important because SFAS No. 133 requires that accounting for and reporting of gains and losses resulting from changes in fair value depend on the purpose and reasons for holding derivatives as well as their intended use and the resulting designation. For financial reporting purposes, derivatives should be designated as: (1) a fair value hedge of an existing asset, liability, or firm commitment; (2) a cash flow hedge of a forecasted transaction; (3) a hedge of a foreign operation; or (4) not intended as a hedge.

The description, examples, and accounting for each of these four categories are summarized in Exhibit 18.1. The basic premise of the three types of hedges—cash flow, fair value, foreign currency—is that a derivative must be expected to be "highly effective" in offsetting exposure due to changes in fair value attributable to the risk of being hedged. Derivatives, in terms of their contract, can be described as either forward based, option based, or hybrid. A forward-based derivative (e.g., futures, forwards, and swaps) is a two-sided contract in which each party can incur a favorable or unfavorable outcome resulting from changes in the value of the underlying instrument or the amount of the underlying reference factor. An option-based derivative (e.g., options, interest rate caps, and interest rate floors) is a one-sided contract in which the holder of such a derivative has an option to exercise the right, which would result in a favorable outcome for the holder and an unfavorable outcome for the buyer. However, if market conditions would result in an unfavorable outcome for the holder, the holder can leave the right to expire unexercised.

Identification and Assessment of Derivative Risk

Derivatives typically expose issuers, holders, and investors to various types of risk. Financial institutions should establish adequate and effective internal control structure and procedures to manage derivative risks by (1) identifying and classifying derivative risks, (2) measuring the effects of these risks on the institutions' value and reputation, (3) determining the likelihood of risk occurrence and magnitude of their expected losses

EXHIBIT 18.1 Derivatives Categories, Description, Examples, and Their Accounting Treatment under SFAS No. 133

Type	Description	Example	Accounting
Fair value hedge	Hedge of an exposure to changes in fair value of an asset, liability, or an unrecognized firm commitment attributable to a particular risk.	a. Use of an interest rate swap to change fixed-rate debt into floating-rate debt. b. Use of futures contracts to hedge fair value of copper or other types of inventory. c. Use of a derivative to hedge fair value of a firm commitment (e.g., to sell crude oil at a fixed price).	a. Derivatives should be measured at their fair value and reported as assets or liabilities. b. Any changes in fair value (gains or losses) of hedged items attributable to risk being hedged should be recognized in earnings in period of change and as adjustment to carrying amount of item. c. Any changes in fair value (gains or losses) of derivative designated as fair value hedge must be recognized in income.
Cash flow hedge	Hedge of an exposure to variability in cash flows of recognized assets, liabilities, or forecasted transactions attributable to a particular risk.	a. Hedge of a forecasted sale or purchase of natural gas (or another commodity) with futures contracts. b. Hedge of variable interest payments using an interest rate swap to convert the variable payments into fixed payments.	a. These derivatives should be measured at fair value and reported as assets or liabilities. b. Effective portion of derivatives' gains or losses (changes in fair value) should be reported initially as a component of other comprehensive income (outside earnings) and subsequently reclassified into earnings when forecasted transaction affects earnings. c. Ineffective portion of gains or losses (unrealized) should be reported in earnings immediately when derivative transactions are expected to occur.

(Continued)

EXHIBIT 18.1 (*Continued*)

Type	Description	Example	Accounting
Foreign currency hedge	Hedge of foreign-currency exposures of net investment in foreign operations attributable to a particular risk.	Hedge of foreign-currency exposure of: a. An unrecognized firm commitment (a fair value hedge). b. An available-for-sale security (a fair value hedge). c. A forecasted transaction (a cash flow hedge). d. A net investment in a foreign operation.	a. These derivatives should be measured at fair value and recognized as assets or liabilities. b. Any changes in fair value (gains or losses) should be reported in other comprehensive income (outside earnings) as part of cumulative translation adjustment to the extent of offsetting translation gain or loss recorded in other comprehensive income. c. Any ineffective portion of derivative gain or loss may not be included in cumulative translation adjustment account in other comprehensive income. d. Translation gains or losses should be reported in other comprehensive income (outside earnings).
Derivatives not intended to hedge			a. These derivatives should be reported at fair value. b. Any changes in fair value should be recognized in earnings in period of change.

and unfavorable outcomes, and (4) managing derivative risks to an acceptable prudent risk. Derivative risks are:

- Market risk
- Credit risk
- Liquidity risk
- Operational risk
- Legal risk
- Control risk
- Basis or correlation risk
- Systemic risk
- Settlement risk
- Valuation or model risk

Many of these risks and their related control activities described in this section were derived from the sources identified in the chapter and listed in this chapter's Notes.[10]

Exhibit 18.2 presents these types of derivative risks and their related attributes and control activities.

Market Risk

Market risk is defined as the exposure to an institution's financial condition causing economic losses resulted from adverse changes in the fair value of the derivative. Any significant and unexpected movements in interest rates, foreign exchange rates, equity prices, commodity prices, and other factors related to market volatilities of the rate, index, or price underlying the derivative can increase the derivative market risk.

Credit Risk

With credit risk, an end user would incur economic losses if the counterparty fails to meet its financial obligations under the contract. The derivative credit risk is positively correlated with the derivative's market value, which is the economic benefit that can be lost if the counterparty fails to fulfill its obligation.

Liquidity Risk

Liquidity risk is related to the institution's failure to achieve its cash flow projections and liquidity characteristics of derivatives used in accomplishing institutional objectives. The institution should identify the types and sources of funding liquidity risk of all derivatives and consider the effects that market risk can have on liquidity for different types of instruments.

Operational Risk

Operational risk is defined as the failure of the institution to:

1. Establish appropriate risk management policy consistent with derivative objectives set for the board of directors authorization.

EXHIBIT 18.2 Derivatives Risks, Attributes, and Control Activities

Risk	Attributes	Control Activities
Market	1. Market risk measurement system addressing capital at risk and value at risk	1. Board-approved limits (e.g., trade, counterparty position, levels of unhedged market exposure, stop-loss, open position by product type)
	2. Ongoing mark-to-market valuation of derivative positions	2. Mark-to-market derivatives
	3. Sensitivity and simulation analysis of derivative portfolios in determining their performance under stress conditions (e.g., abnormal volatility of market, market shocks)	3. Incorporation of stress testing, sensitivity analysis, and scenario analysis into derivative model estimates
	4. Determination of overall market risk limits (e.g., net and/or gross position, stop loss, rate change, options, value at risk)	4. Continuous assessment of board-approved limits
	5. Selection of appropriate model estimations of market values	5. Review model estimations of market values especially when market values are not readily available
Credit	Appropriate credit risk management that:	1. Assessing creditworthiness of issuer or counterparty
	1. Addresses complexity of derivative transactions	2. Third-party verification of counterparty credit.
	2. Identification of various types and sources of credit risk	3. Continuous monitoring of counterparty credit
	3. Policy provisions for counterparty default, settlement, and presettlement credit risk	4. Ongoing monitoring of credit risk limits
	4. Proper credit risk limits on individual and counterparty exposure	5. Procedures for monitoring of credit exposure on institution-wide basis
	5. Mechanism for monitoring credit risk on ongoing basis	6. Review and reapproval of credit risk policies, procedures, and limits
	6. Establishment and documentation of credit risk policies and procedures	
Liquidity	1. Identification of types and sources of market liquidity risk	1. Reviewing types and sources of market liquidity risk
	2. Participation in OTC markets	2. Close monitoring of OTC market in which institution participates
	3. Preapproval of liquidity characteristics of derivatives	3. Continuously monitoring liquidity limits and characteristics of derivatives
	4. Board-approved liquidity limits	

(Continued)

EXHIBIT 18.2 (Continued)

Operational	1. Proper authorization of derivative transactions	1. Approving every derivative transaction according to established authorization policies and procedures
	2. Effective execution of derivative transactions	2. Evaluating and monitoring derivative's internal control structure on ongoing basis
	3. Establishment of adequate and effective internal control structure for derivatives	3. Continuous monitoring of valuation and pricing models
	4. Operational policies and procedures to ensure proper pricing and valuation of derivatives	4. Ensuring that derivative's information system conforms to applicable accounting and reporting standards
	5. Sound accounting information systems that gather, classify, measure, recognize, and report derivative transactions	
Legal	1. Identification of different types and sources of legal risk	1. Continuous assessment of nature of derivatives and authority of counterparties
	2. Involvement of legal counsel for derivative activities	2. Use of standard contract or master agreement
	3. Enforceable procedures for derivative transactions	3. Continuous monitoring by legal counsel
	4. Adequate legal documents of derivative contracts	
	5. Due diligence contract enforcement activities	
Control	1. Risk management policy consistent with derivative objectives set forth by board of directors	1. Ensuring that only authorized derivative transactions take place and that unauthorized transactions are detected and corrected
	2. Existence of adequate and effective internal control system for derivatives	2. Ensuring that magnitude, complexity, and risks of derivatives are commensurate with purpose established for derivative activities
	3. Achievement of internal operational goals	3. Maintaining appropriate source documents to support management intent for issuing, holding, and classifying derivatives
	4. External financial reporting requirements	4. Keeping accurate subsidiary ledgers for all derivatives and periodically reconciling all derivatives on general ledger to supporting subsidiary ledgers
	5. Compliance with all applicable laws and regulations	

(Continued)

EXHIBIT 18.2 (Continued)

Risk	Attributes	Control Activities
Basis or Correlation	1. Identification of types and sources of derivative basis or correlation risk 2. Board-approved correlation limits 3. Methodology of correlation measurements	1. Assessing the correlation between derivative instruments priced off of different yield curves 2. Measuring and evaluating correlation coefficient 3. Ensuring that correlation limits are within approved level
Systemic	1. Identification of different types and sources of systemic risk 2. Effective risk management system 3. Existence of contingency plans to minimize losses when market disruptions occur	1. Continuous monitoring of systemic risk. 2. Taking appropriate action based on approved contingency plans when market disruptions occur
Settlement	1. Identification of different types and sources of settlement risk 2. Board-approved maximum settlement risk limits	1. Monitoring payments on appropriately timely basis 2. Closely monitoring unsettled items
Valuation or Model	1. Identification of all appropriate valuation models of pricing all types of derivatives. 2. Use of value-at-risk methodology to measure market risk	1. Assessing different valuation models 2. Continuously monitoring variable of valuation models 3. Using value-at-risk methodology in measuring market risk

2. Develop adequate and effective control activities to ensure that only authorized derivative transactions take place and that unauthorized derivative transactions are detected and corrected.
3. Ensure that the magnitude, complexity, and risks of derivatives are commensurate with the purposes established for derivatives activities.
4. Maintain appropriate source documents to support management intent as well as justification regarding issuing, holding, and classifying derivatives.
5. Keep accurate subsidiary ledgers for all derivatives.
6. Periodically reconcile all derivatives on the general ledger to the supporting subsidiary ledgers.

Legal Risk

Legal risk is the failure of the institution to comply with applicable rules, laws, and regulations pertaining to derivatives that may cause losses due to legal or regulatory actions taken against the institution. Legal risk can arise from: (1) misunderstanding of terms of derivative contracts; (2) insufficient documentation of the contract; (3) adverse changes in applicable laws and regulations, including tax laws and regulatory requirements that prohibit the institution from investing in or even holding certain types of derivatives; and (4) inability to enforce a netting arrangement in bankruptcy.

Control Risk

Control risk is the failure of the institution's internal control structure pertaining to derivatives to prevent, detect, and correct errors, irregularities, and fraud that negatively affect the institution's ability to achieve operational, financial, and compliance objectives of its derivatives. Control risk could arise from: (1) absence of an adequate and effective internal control structure for derivatives; (2) lack of appropriate managerial policies and procedures to continuously monitor derivative transactions; (3) noncompliance with applicable laws, regulations, and contract requirements; and (4) noncompliance with financial reporting requirements for derivatives.

Basis or Correlation Risk

Basis or correlation risk mostly relates to hedging contracts and measures the differing effects market forces have on the performance or value of two or more distinct instruments used in a combination. Basis risk is determined by calculating the difference between the cash market price of the derivative being hedged and the price of the related hedging contract. This risk indicates the lack of proper correlation between hedging contract prices and the price movement in the cash market when the basis changes while the hedging contract is open.

Systemic or Interconnection Risk

Systemic or interconnection risk risk relates to the institution's particular risk resulting from operating in a particular market segment, across specific markets or borders, and/or to a settlement system.

Settlement Risk

Settlement risk is the institution's inability to settle derivative contracts in cash or other assets that are readily convertible into cash, such as Treasury securities or marketable equity securities, rather than the delivery of the underlying items on an appropriately timely basis.

Valuation and Model Risk

Valuation and model risk relates to the imperfection and subjectivity of models and the associated assumptions used to value derivatives. Valuation model is the failure of the utilized derivative models to determine the true fair value of derivatives. This risk is further discussed in the section titled "Derivatives Valuation Models" later in this chapter.

 ## ACCOUNTING FOR DERIVATIVES

Financial derivatives have grown rapidly during the past decade, primarily because of fundamental changes in global financial markets, advancements in computer technology, and fluctuations in interest and currency exchange rates. Derivatives have become increasingly important and widely used in global business. They have been utilized for a variety of purposes, including risks management, financing schemes, tax planning, earnings management, and speculation activities. However, the nature and risks associated with derivatives and how entities use them are not well understood by many users of published financial statements (e.g., investors, creditors, customers). The financial community and standard-setting bodies are concerned with complexities, risks, lack of uniform accounting practices for derivatives, and insufficient disclosures of their fair values.

SFAS No. 133 establishes accounting and reporting standards for derivative instruments and hedging activities by requiring that affected entities recognize all derivatives as either assets or liabilities in financial statements and measure them at fair value. The adoption of SFAS No. 133 provides for the first mandated source of public information about fair value of derivatives. The fair value measurement and recognition requirements of the statement provide some detailed information about previously unreported derivatives extensively used by all entities, including not-for-profit organizations.

Derivatives are commonly defined as financial products such as swaps, options, futures, forwards, and unstructured receivables, which derive their value from underlying financial instruments such as stocks, bonds, and foreign currencies. SFAS No. 133 (paragraph 6) defines a derivative instrument as:

> a financial instrument or other contract with all three of the following characteristics: (a) It has (1) one or more underlyings and (2) one or more notional amounts of payment provisions or both . . . ; (b) it requires no initial net investment or an initial net investment that is smaller than would be required for other types of contracts . . . ; (c) Its terms require or permit net settlement.

These derivatives have been used for:

1. Managing financial risks
2. Speculating on the price of financial instruments
3. Reducing the cost of raising capital
4. Earning higher investment returns
5. Adjusting investment portfolios to take advantage of mispricing between stock baskets and stock index futures
6. Combining derivatives with other financial instruments to create new and more powerful financial products

The most common active end users of derivatives are financial institutions, mutual funds, pension funds, and commercial firms. Derivatives are being traded through both organized exchanges and OTC, and their "notional value" exceeds the estimated total value of the world's bonds and stocks.[11] Exchanged traded derivatives typically are more standardized and offer greater liquidity than OTC derivatives, which are individually arranged contracts.

Derivative transactions have grown significantly in volume and complexity from the traditional interest rate and currency swaps to more sophisticated computer-driven risk management derivatives. This ever-increasing use of derivatives and recent losses by some derivatives end users have raised numerous issues of concern among regulators, the financial community, and the accounting profession as to the appropriate use, proper risk assessment, and adequate disclosures of derivative transactions by both their issuers and end users. Improved oversight by regulators and new accounting standards by the accounting profession have been suggested as a means of addressing these issues. SFAS No. 119 provides more guidance for proper disclosures of derivatives than SFAS Nos. 105 and 107. However, SFAS No. 119 deals only with disclosures of derivatives, not their measurement and recognition, and is considered just a step in the right direction for providing better and more adequate guidance for companies to present quantified disclosure of the risks they face from on- and off-book financial instruments. SFAS No. 119 is intended to improve the quality of disclosures about derivatives instruments while SFAS No. 133 addresses accounting for recognition and measurement of derivative transactions.

SFAS No. 133 requires all derivative instruments to be measured at fair market value and be reported on the balance sheet as assets or liabilities. The accounting method and reporting of the change in fair values depend on the reason for holding derivatives, their intended use, and the resulting designation. The FASB rationales in issuing SFAS No. 133 (paragraph 3) were that: (1) derivatives represent rights or obligations that meet the definitions of assets or liabilities and, accordingly, should be reported in financial statements; (2) fair value is the only relevant measure for derivatives and hedging activities, and, therefore, they should be measured at fair value; (3) only derivatives and hedged items that are considered either assets or liabilities should be reported as such in financial statements; and (4) special accounting for hedging activities should be provided only for qualified hedged items that are attributable to the risk being hedged.

Other initiatives by the SEC and Congress have been introduced that eventually would require more quantitative disclosures about derivative risks and risk management activities of companies under the SEC's jurisdiction. In response to derivatives concerns, six of Wall Street's biggest securities firms have voluntarily agreed to impose more controls over their derivatives activities.[12] The firms have agreed to provide adequate disclosures to the SEC and Commodity Futures Trading Commission (CFTC) about how they manage their internal derivative risks and their capital standards and reporting requirements. These standards are intended to avoid direct legislative action on derivatives by Congress. These standards address four derivatives issues: (1) adequate and effective internal controls for monitoring derivatives risks; (2) proper disclosure and reporting of derivatives activities to regulators; (3) sufficiency of the firm's capital standards in terms of the risks involved; and (4) counterparty relationships in dealing with the firm's customers. The SEC has amended and expanded the disclosure requirement for derivatives under SFAS No. 119 in Release No. 33-7386.[13] The amendments require enhanced disclosure of accounting policies for derivatives as well as quantitative and qualitative information about market risk inherent in market risk–sensitive instruments.

The current guidance in the ASC No. 815, titled *Derivatives and Hedging*, as originally established by SFAS Statement No. 133, *Accounting for Derivative Instruments and Hedging Activities*, as of July 1, 2009, when the FASB codification became the single source of authoritative nongovernmental U.S. generally accepted accounting principles (GAAP). The FASB has amended the accounting guidance in ASC No. 815 for certain derivatives by issuing SFAS No. 138, *Accounting for Certain Derivative Instruments and Certain Hedging Activities, an Amendment of SFAS No. 133* in June 2000 and again in April 2003 with the issuance of SFAS Statement No. 149. In May 2008, significant amendments were made to the disclosure requirements in ASC No. 815-10-50 with the issuance of SFAS No. 161, *Disclosures about Derivative Instruments and Hedging Activities, an amendment of FASB Statement No. 133.* In March 2010, the FASB issued Accounting Standards Update (ASU) No. 2010-11, *Scope Exception Related to Embedded Credit Derivatives*, which amends and clarifies the accounting for credit derivatives embedded in interests in securitized assets. The International Financial Standards Board issued International Accounting Statement No. 39, *Financial Instruments: Recognition and Measurement*, in proving IFRS guidance on derivative transactions. Although there are some differences between U.S. GAAP and IFRS regarding derivatives and hedge accounting, the remainder of this chapter refers to accounting guidance on derivative transactions as provided in ASC No. 815. ASC No. 815 affects all entities that use derivative instruments to hedge business risks.

Financial and Managerial Impacts of ASC No. 815

Adoption of ASC No. 815 provides the first mandated source of public information about fair value of derivatives. The fair value recognition requirements of ASC No. 815 provide some details of these previously unreported derivatives used extensively by financial companies to service customers and generate income and by other entities to manage risk, including interest rate and foreign currency exposures. Thus, issuers and end users of derivatives are affected by the fair value recognition of the statement. The FASB has addressed several problems associated with current accounting practices for derivatives. These problems include inconsistent, incomplete, and complex accounting guidance for derivatives and the fact that the effect of derivatives is not transparent in the financial statements. As a result, under current accounting practices, derivative transactions are not properly recognized in the financial statements, making it difficult for users to determine the nature, extent, and effects of derivatives on a firm's financial positions and results of operations.

ASC No. 815 is intended to address and resolve the perceived problems of lack of visibility, completeness, and consistency of accounting practices for derivative transactions. All derivatives should be reported in the statement of financial position at fair value, and their related changes in fair value should be recognized in income when they occur. There is one exception: for derivatives that qualify as hedges. Depending on the nature of the exposure, changes in the fair value can be reported in other comprehensive income (via shareholders' equity). The requirement of recognition of changes in fair value would, depending on the accounting method used (hedge or nonhedge accounting), create volatility in either income or equity. Thus, under the current accounting standards, all derivatives would be reported on the balance sheet at fair value. The accounting for gains or losses that result from changes in fair value depends on the reasons for holding the instrument, its intended use, and whether it qualifies for designation as a hedge of a fair value exposure, a cash flow exposure, or a net investment in a foreign entity.

The FASB rationales for issuing ASC No. 815 were: (1) derivatives represent rights or obligations that meet the definition of asset or liabilities and, therefore, should be reported as such in financial statements; (2) like other financial instruments, derivatives should be measured at fair value because fair value is the only relevant measure for derivatives; (3) any adjustments to the carrying amount of hedged items should reflect changes in their fair value (gains or losses) associated with the risk being hedged; (4) only hedged items that are qualified as assets or liabilities should be reported in financial statements; and (5) special accounting for items designated as being hedged should be provided only for qualifying items. ASC No. 815 requires matching the timing of gain or loss recognition on the hedging instrument with the recognition of the changes in the fair value of the exposure-hedged asset or liability and the earnings effect of the hedged-forecasted transaction.

Adoption of ASC No. 815 may increase volatility in earnings and equity through comprehensive income. The degree of volatility, however, depends on the entity's intended use of derivatives and their nature and the type and extent of derivatives and hedging activities. The increased volatility results primarily from the requirement for recognition of any changes in fair value (gains or losses) in either earnings or components of other comprehensive income, depending on the reason for holding derivatives or hedging activities. Traditionally, any gains or losses resulting from changes in fair value of derivatives and hedging activities were either ignored or disclosed in footnotes to financial statements. Under ASC No. 815, all derivatives are recorded at their fair value on the balance sheet as assets or liabilities, and changes in their fair value are reported on the income statement or balance sheet, depending on their intended use and their designation as a fair value hedge, cash flow hedge, or foreign currency exposure hedge.

The balance sheet effect of adopting ASC No. 815 is an increase in the size of the balance sheet because of the fair value recognition of derivatives as assets or liabilities. The income statement effects of changes in fair value of derivatives depend on the intended use of derivatives and whether they are qualified and designated as hedging instruments. If the derivative does not qualify as a hedging instrument or is not designated as such, any changes in its fair value and the resulting gain or loss should be recognized currently in earnings. If the derivative qualifies for special hedge accounting, the resulting gain or loss should be either recognized in income or deferred in other comprehensive income (e.g., equity). To qualify for special hedge accounting, the derivative must be designated as a fair value hedge, cash flow hedge, or foreign currency hedge.

Adoption of ASC No. 815 can affect risk management strategies in several ways. Traditionally, management has used synthetic-instrument accounting techniques to convert variable-rate debt into fixed-rate debt by using an interest rate swap. Prior to ASC No. 815, synthetic-instrument accounting techniques had affected the income statement as if the entity had actually issued fixed-value debt. Under ASC No. 815, these techniques should qualify as a cash flow hedge with essentially the same income statement effect as before; however, the balance sheet effect of these techniques should reflect the swaps' fair value and their changes in fair value that are deferred in other comprehensive income.

How Does ASC No. 815 Work?

ASC No. 815 is very complicated, its implementation is complex, and it requires substantial changes in accounting information systems of financial institutions that use derivatives. However, ASC No. 815 provides an excellent opportunity for financial institutions to further examine their risk management practices and policies on derivatives. It requires that all derivatives be measured at their fair value and be recognized as assets or liabilities in the statement of financial position. The accounting for changes in the fair value of a derivative (gains or losses) depends on the intended use of the derivative, the reason for hedging the instruments, and the resulting designation as a hedge of a fair value exposure, a cash flow exposure, or a net investment in a foreign currency.

The fact that derivative activities are to be made publicly available increases the responsibility of management to ensure that measurement, recognition, reporting, and disclosures are reliable, relevant, and adequately supported. The magnitude of derivatives being used by entities, coupled with their associated risk and the first-mandated source of public information about their fair value, necessitates that the affected entities organize an implementation team to adopt ASC No. 815 effectively and efficiently. The implementation team should include auditors and individuals knowledgeable in global financial markets, risk management, accounting, law, tax, information systems, operations, treasury, and asset and liability management. The implementation team should analyze and understand the nature, terms, and extent of derivatives and consult with the entity's independent auditors, advising them of key decisions. ASC No. 815 does not delineate a specific methodology for assessing whether a hedge is expected to be highly effective or for measuring hedge ineffectiveness. The implementation team should clearly define the intended use of derivatives, because the only requirement under ASC No. 815 is that there be a "reasonable basis" for assessing hedge effectiveness.

Extensive information system modification may be necessary to ensure compliance with substantial fair value requirements of ASC No. 815. The implementation team should: (1) identify all derivatives that meet the definition of derivatives as stated in ASC No. 815; (2) determine whether existing hedging strategies qualify for hedging accounting under ASC No. 815; (3) consider the changes in the existing accounting system and disclosure policies that should be made to satisfy the fair value accounting requirements of ASC No. 815; (4) assess and document the entity's risk management strategies, including objectives and policies consistent with the requirements of ASC No. 815; and (5) communicate the financial and managerial impacts of adopting ASC No. 815 to all internal (e.g., executive management, audit committee) and external (auditors, shareholders) parties.

Financial Requirements

Financial institutions should establish accounting policies and procedures pertaining to the classification and reasons for holding derivatives. The proper classification of derivatives is important because ASC No. 815 requires that accounting for and reporting of gains and losses resulting from changes in fair value depend on the purpose and reason for holding derivatives. For financial reporting purposes, derivatives should be specifically designated as: (1) a fair value hedge of an existing asset, liability, or firm commitment; (2) a cash flow hedge of a forecasted transaction; (3) a hedge of a foreign operation; or (4) not intended as a hedge. The hedge accounting should consider: (1) the type of hedge relationship (e.g., fair value, cash flow, or foreign currency); (2) how effectively hedged items are measured; and (3) potential alternatives to existing hedging strategies.

Accounting systems of financial institutions should: (1) measure, recognize, and report fair value of derivatives and hedging activities, including related gains and losses in financial statements; and (2) provide adequate disclosure while not revealing critical data about characteristics of related assets to competitors. The complexity and extensive use of derivatives requires that the financial institution's accounting information system: (1) accurately assess valuation considerations in light of the related derivatives' risk; (2) provide income adjustments for fluctuations in fair value of derivatives and hedging activities; (3) keep track of other comprehensive income fair value adjustments and their subsequent recognition in earnings; and (4) consider the procedures for bifurcating and subsequent measurement of the component of hybrid instruments. Financial institutions, according to provisions of ASC No. 815, should also provide documentation of:

1. The reason for issuing or holding derivatives
2. Derivatives' intended use and resulting designation

3. The nature of the cash hedge strategy
4. The nature and assessment of the risk that is being hedged
5. How the hedging instrument's effectiveness is being assessed
6. The designation of derivatives and hedged items in hedging relationships

The FASB, in June 2000, issued an amendment to ASC No. 815 titled *Accounting for Certain Derivative Instruments and Certain Hedging Activities* to address major implementation problems of adopting ASC No. 815. The amendment was intended to resolve major implementation problems of ASC No. 815, including restrictions on cross-currency hedges, specific risks-that can be hedged, expansion of the normal purchase and normal sales expectations, hedges of interest rate risk, and hedges of foreign currency–denominated assets and liabilities. The amendment: (1) permits the use of a benchmark interest rate that excludes the sector spread; (2) relaxes restrictions on hedging recognized foreign currency–denominated assets and liabilities; and (3) reduces earnings volatility resulting when the changes in those foreign currency items are measured at fair value.

Disclosure Requirements

Financial institutions should disclose the objectives for issuing or holding derivatives, the context needed to understand the objectives, and strategies for achieving those objectives. ASC No. 815 requires disclosure of the classification of derivatives into those designated as fair value hedging instruments, as cash flow hedging instruments, and as hedging instruments for hedges of the foreign currency exposure of a net investment in a foreign operation and as all other derivatives. Financial institutions should indicate the risk management policy for each of these types of hedge, including a description of the items or transactions for which risks are hedged. Furthermore, the SEC requires disclosures based on the type of market risk that is being hedged (e.g., interest rate, foreign currency, commodity). If appropriate and feasible, qualitative disclosures about objectives and strategies for using derivative instruments should be provided.

The extensive disclosure requirements of ASC No. 815 are classified into qualitative information and quantitative information. Qualitative disclosures are: the entity's objectives and strategies for holding and issuing derivatives, and a description of the transactions or other events that will result in the recognition of gains and losses in earnings resulting from changes in fair value of cash flow hedges, deferred in accumulated other comprehensive income. Quantitative disclosures are: (1) the net gain or loss recognized in earnings for the period representing aggregate ineffectiveness for all hedges and the component of the derivatives' gain or loss excluded from the assessment of hedge effectiveness; (2) an estimate of the amount of gains and losses related to cash flow hedges, included in other comprehensive income that will be recognized in earnings within the next 12 months; (3) the amount of gains and losses reclassified into earnings as a result of the discontinuance of cash flow hedges because it is probable that the original forecasted transaction will not occur; (4) the maximum period of time over which the entity is hedging cash flows related to forecasted transactions; and

(5) the net amount of the foreign currency transaction gain or loss on the hedging instrument included in the cumulative translation adjustment during the period.

 ## TAX CONSIDERATIONS OF DERIVATIVES

Financial institutions should identify and examine the applicable tax rules on derivatives to determine: (1) how derivatives should be classified for tax purposes (debt or equity); (2) how their related trading revenues (gains or losses) should be measured and classified (capital or ordinary); and (3) what is the timing of derivative gains or losses for tax purposes. Determination of the tax treatment of derivative transactions depends on the: (1) type of derivatives; (2) status of the taxpayer holding derivatives (e.g., corporations, individuals, dealers, and investors); (3) purpose of holding derivatives (e.g., capital asset, inventory, and holding instrument); and (4) manner of acquisition, holding, or disposition of derivatives.

The tax effects of the transition adjustments should also be considered. Transition adjustment is the difference between a derivative's previous carrying amount and its fair value at the time of the adoption of ASC No. 815. This transition adjustment should be reported in net income or other comprehensive income, as appropriate, as the effect of a change in accounting principles and presented in a manner similar to the cumulative effect of a change in accounting principles as described in Accounting Principles Board (APB) Opinion No. 20. Many of the transition adjustments required under ASC No. 815 create temporary differences. Depending on the nature of the hedge relationship (e.g., fair value or cash flow hedge), the deferred tax impacts of the temporary differences should be netted in the cumulative effect of adoption on net income or on other comprehensive income as set forth in the statement. Consult with tax experts (e.g., public accounting firms) and seek advice from the Internal Revenue Service for reasonable assurance of compliance with tax laws regarding classification, measurement, and recognition of derivative transactions for tax purposes.

 ## AUDIT OF DERIVATIVE TRANSACTIONS

Financial institutions should communicate the financial and managerial impacts of issuing and/or holding derivatives to all interested parties, including executive management, the audit committee, shareholders, creditors, regulators, and independent auditors. Risk management strategies will be more visible under ASC No. 815 primarily because of the required extensive justification and documentation regarding how derivatives and hedging activities are initially designed, measured, and recognized, and subsequently tracked and disclosed. ASC No. 815 eliminates managerial practices of "synthetic or accrual accounting" with the intention of keeping derivatives off the balance sheet with net periodic settlements being recorded through earnings.

Adoption of ASC No. 815 may increase volatility in earnings and equity through comprehensive income. The degree of volatility resulting from the requirement for recognition of any changes in fair value (gains or losses) in either earnings or components of other comprehensive income depends on the reason for holding derivatives or hedging activities. The balance sheet effect of adopting ASC No. 815 is an increase in the size of the balance sheet because of the fair value recognition of derivatives as assets or liabilities. The income statement effects of changes in fair value of derivatives depend on the intended use of derivatives and whether they are qualified and designated as hedging instruments. If the hedged item fails to meet general criteria applicable in all circumstances as well as criteria specific to the type of hedge (fair value, cash flow, or net investment in a foreign operation), it cannot be treated as a hedge and would be marked to market with no offset. If the derivative does not qualify as a hedging instrument or is not designated as such, any changes in its fair value and the resulting gain or loss should be recognized currently in earnings. If the derivative qualifies for special hedge accounting, the resulting gain or loss should be either recognized in income or deferred in other comprehensive income (equity). Auditors' involvement in assessing and classifying derivatives is important in preparing financial statements in conformity with accounting standards (ASC No. 815) as well as in complying with applicable laws and regulations on derivatives. External auditors should be provided with appropriate answers to the set of questions suggested by the AICPA[14] and other authoritative bodies (e.g., FASB). The questions are:

- Has the board established a clear and internally consistent risk management policy, including risk limits (as appropriate)?
- Are management's strategies and implementation policies consistent with the board's authorization?
- Do key controls exist to ensure that only authorized transactions take place and that unauthorized transactions are quickly detected and appropriate action is taken?
- Are the magnitude, complexity, and risks of the entity's derivatives commensurate with the entity's objectives?
- Are personnel authorized to engage in and monitor derivative transactions well qualified and appropriately trained?
- Do the right people have the right information to make decisions?
- How are the fair value of derivatives and hedged assets and liabilities determined?
- Do derivatives previously designated as hedges continue to qualify under the requirements of ASC No. 815?
- How is management responding to the possible volatility in earnings and equity resulting from the changes in fair value of derivatives and hedging items?
- Are there any derivatives that qualify as hedges under ASC No. 815 that previously were not considered as hedged items (e.g., foreign currency futures in certain hedging relationships)?

The AICPA suggests that objectives of audit procedures for derivative transactions might include those designed to test that:

- Derivatives contracts have been executed and processed according to management's authorizations.

- Income on derivatives, including premiums and discounts, are properly measured and recorded.
- Derivatives accounted for as hedges meet the applicable criteria for hedge accounting.
- Changes in the market value of derivatives have been appropriately accounted for in the circumstances (whether or not hedge accounting is used).
- Information about derivatives in the financial statements is accurate and complete and has been properly classified, described, and disclosed.[15]

SOURCES OF INFORMATION ON DERIVATIVES

Derivative markets have become so visible in today's financial system that virtually any publication that covers the stock and bond markets contains some coverage of derivatives. A variety of specialized trade publications, academic and professional journals, and Internet sites are provided by a number of companies and governmental agencies. Many of the derivative failures have been caused by allowing individual employees to trade or invest in derivatives without proper knowledge and with lack of supervision and authorization of top-level management. Senior management should establish proper policies and procedures for issuing and/or holding derivatives and should monitor effective implementation of these policies and procedures.

Financial institutions should provide in-house training and education for employees directly involved with derivative transactions and ASC No. 815 on a continuous basis. Financial institutions should obtain and study existing publications on derivatives and provide education for employees dealing with derivative transactions and hedging activities. Employees should be provided with the most recent publications, regulations, and accounting standards on derivatives. Some of the current initiatives on derivatives are:

Group of Thirty, *Derivatives: Practices and Principles*, 1993

Comptroller of the Currency, *Risk Management of Financial Derivatives*, Banking Issuance Circular 277, October 27, 1993

U.S. General Accounting Office, *Financial Derivatives: Actions Needed to Protect the Financial Systems*, May 1994

Bank Administration Institute and McKinsey and Company, *Banking Off the Balance Sheet: Using Derivatives for Risk Management and Performance Improvement at Commercial Banks*, 1994

American Institute of Certified Public Accountants, *Six Common-Sense Questions About the Use and Risks of Derivatives*, 1994

American Institute of Certified Public Accountants, *Derivatives—Current Accounting and Auditing Literature*, 1994

Basel Committee on Banking Supervision, *Risk Management Guidelines on Derivatives*, July 1994

Office of the Comptroller of the Currency, Bulletin 94-31, *Risk Management of Financial Derivatives: Questions and Answers*, May 10, 1994

Federal Deposit Insurance Corporation, *Examination Guidance for Financial Derivatives,* May 18, 1994

Financial Accounting Standards Board, Statement of Financial Accounting Standards No. 119, *Disclosure about Derivative Financial Instruments and Fair Value of Financial Instruments,* October 1994

Financial Accounting Standards Board, Financial Accounting Series, Special Report, *Illustrations of Financial Instruments Disclosures,* December 1994

Committee of Sponsoring Organizations of the Treadway Commission, *Internal Control Issues in Derivatives Usage: An Information Tool for Considering the COSO Internal Control—Integrated Framework in Derivatives Applications,* 1996

U.S. Securities and Exchange Commission, *Disclosure of Accounting Policies for Derivative Financial Instruments and Derivatives Commodity Instruments and Disclosure of Quantitative and Qualitative Information about Market Risk Inherent in Derivative Financial Instruments, Other Financial Instruments, and Derivative Commodity Instruments,* Release No. 33-7386, 1997, Washington DC

Financial Accounting Standards Board, SFAS No. 113, *Accounting for Derivative Instruments and Hedging Activities,* 1998

Financial Accounting Standards Board Implementation Task Force on Derivatives

Federal Financial Institutions Examination Council, Supervisory Policy Statement on Investment Securities and End-User Derivatives Activities, issued April 23, 1998

ASC No. 815 has been issued with many unanswered implementation questions and, accordingly, implementation guidelines will evolve as the statement is adopted by affected entities. To facilitate the proper adoption of ASC No. 815 and to provide adequate answers to implementation questions, the FASB has appointed the Derivatives Implementation Group, which is a task force to assist the FASB in identifying implementation issues and in answering the related questions. The task force is in the process of compiling an implementation guide to highlight and resolve significant implementation problems in advance of the adoption of the statement. The status of the guidance will remain tentative until it is formally cleared by the FASB and finally is incorporated in a FASB staff implementation guide.

DERIVATIVES VALUATION MODELS

The increasing use of derivative contracts available OTC, on exchanges, and through private placements has raised serious concerns regarding their proper valuations. A number of valuation models for different types of derivatives (e.g., option, call, swap) have been developed based on the premise that if the suggested model accurately determines the value of a derivative, its market price should equal its theoretical fair value. Many of these models go far beyond the intended level of this book. The models range from the relatively simple models (e.g., binomial option pricing model) to more complex and sophisticated models (e.g., Black-Scholes model, digital contracts).

Binomial Model

To simplify the derivatives valuation models, the binomial model presented here is the one-period binomial option pricing formula.[16] This model determines the option price as a weighted average of the two possible option prices at expiration, discounted at the risk-free rate. Mathematically the option price is calculated as:

$$C = \frac{PCu + (1 - P)Cd}{1 + r}$$

where

C = theoretical fair value of call option

$P = \dfrac{r - d}{u - d}$ where r is the risk-free rate

Cu = price of call when it goes up = Max $[0, S(1 + u) - E]$ where S is stock price

u = the percentage increase in value of stock,

E = the exercise price of call

Cd = price of call and is equal to Max $[0, S(1 + d) - E]$

d = the percentage decrease in value of stock

Binomial Model—An Illustrative Example

Assume that a stock is currently priced at $150 and can go up to $177, an increase of 18 percent, or down to $120, a decrease of 20 percent, in just one period. Furthermore, the exercise price of a call option is $125, and the risk-free rate is 12 percent. The theoretical fair value of the call is calculated as:

$$C_u = \text{Max}\,[0, S(1 + U) - E] = \text{Max}[0, 150(1 + .18) - 125] = \$52$$

$$C_d = \text{Max}\,[0, S(1 + d) - E] = \text{Max}[0, 150(1 - 20) - 125] = \$\phi$$

$$P = \frac{r - d}{u - d} = \frac{.12 - (-.20)}{18 - (-.20)} = \frac{.32}{.38} = .842$$

$$1 - P = 1 - .842 = .158$$

$$C = \frac{PCu + (1 - P)Cd}{1 + r} = \frac{(.842)(52) + (.158)0}{1 + .12} = \frac{43.78}{1.12} = \$39$$

Black-Scholes Call Option Valuation Model

In a world of no taxes and no transaction costs, one could adjust hedge positions almost constantly within the short time period. Black and Scholesdeveloped a call option pricing formula known as the Black-Scholes option pricing model, which has been modified and used by valuation professionals to determine the theoretical fair value of call options.[17] The Black-Scholes call option valuation formula, as described next, determines the call value based on the stock price, exercise price, risk-free rate, time to expiration, and variance of the stock return. The formula is:

$$Pc = P_s N(d_1) - \frac{E}{e^{rt}} N(d_2)$$

$$d_1 = \frac{\ln\left(\frac{P_s}{E}\right) + \left(r + \frac{1\delta^2}{2}\right)t}{\delta\sqrt{t}}$$

$$d_2 = \frac{\ln\left(\frac{P_s}{E}\right) + \left(r + \frac{1\delta^2}{2}\right)t}{\delta\sqrt{t}}$$

where:

Pc = current price of the call option

P_s = current value of the stock

E = exercise price of the call option

e = 2.71828

t = time remaining before expiration (in years)

r = continuously compounded risk-free rate of return

δ = standard deviation of the continuously compounded annual rate of return on the stock

$\ln\left(\frac{P_s}{E}\right)$ = natural logarithm of $\frac{P_s}{E}$

$N(d_1)_i N(d_2)$ = cumulative normal probabilities, which is the probability that a derivative less than d will occur in a normal distribution with a mean of zero and a standard derivation of 1

The Black-Scholes option valuation formula can be applied to a variety of financial derivatives in light of these assumptions:

■ There are no taxes or transaction costs.
■ The stock pays no dividends prior to expiration.
■ The risk-free rate is constant throughout the life of the option.
■ The standard deviation of the return on the stock is constant throughout the life of the option.
■ The rate of return on the stock follows a lognormal distribution of a normal curve.
■ The calls are European style with a single payoff received on a maturity date known at the contract's inception.

Illustrative Example of the Black-Scholes Valuation Formula

Consider a stock is currently priced at $75. Assume a call option with an exercise price of $86. The risk-free rate is 10 percent, and the standard deviation of the continuously compounded annual return is 50 percent. The time remaining before the expiration is three months.

$$d_1 = \frac{\ln\left(\frac{75}{86}\right) + \left[.10 + \frac{1}{2}(.5)^2\right].25}{.50\sqrt{.25}} \approx -.319$$

$$d_2 = \frac{\ln\left(\frac{75}{86}\right) + \left[.10 + \frac{1}{2}(.5)^2\right].25}{.50\sqrt{.25}} \approx -.545$$

In the following equation

$$P_s = P_s N(d_1) - \frac{E}{e^{rt}} N(d_2) = (75 \times .3725) - \left[\frac{86}{e^{10 \times .25}} \times .2912\right] \approx \$10.29$$

$$N(d_1) = N(-.319) = .3725 \text{ (from a normal curve distribution)}$$

$$N(d_2) = N(-.545) = .2912 \text{ (from a normal curve distribution)}$$

Digital Contracts for Valuation of Derivatives

Digital contracts are simple building blocks that provide a unified approach for determining formulas for a wide variety of financial instruments. Unlike the specialized formulas (e.g., Black-Scholes) that can be applied only to the specific asset for which they were derived, digital contracts are applicable to a wide variety of financial assets. Digital contracts are simple because their payoffs are either "on" or "off," indicating that a digital option pays at maturity either one dollar (on) or nothing (off), depending on its payoff event.

Ingersoll suggested a three-step valuation process with digital contracts.[18] The first step is the determination of the (risk-neutral) probability of a particular payoff event. The second step involves development of the formulas for the digital contracts. The third step is to use these instruments (formulas) to value financial derivative contracts. To simplify mathematically, a pure European-style call option can be valued as follows:

$$P_c - \sum_i a_i k(S_i t_i T_i M_i) + \sum_j b_j L(S_j t_j T_j M_j)$$

where

$k(S_i t_i T_i M_i) =$ value at time t of receiving \$1 at time T, the maturity date, if and only if the event M occurs

$L(S_j t_j T_j M_j) =$ value at time t of receiving one share of stock at time T (no dividends), if and only if the event M occurs

The probability of event M happening depends on the current stock price (S), so the values of k and L are determined based on stock price (S). Thus, the value of the call option is determined based on the value of stock.[19]

Financial institutions should establish managerial policies and procedures regarding issuing and/or holding derivatives. Management initially should brainstorm various methods that can be used in issuing and holding derivatives in order to maximize the expected return and minimize the potential risk. Derivatives should be used in a manner consistent with the entity's overall financial and investment activities as well as risk management. The managerial policies on derivatives should be clearly defined, including the purposes for which derivatives are being issued or held, because the classification and the accounting for changes in the fair value of derivatives, under ASC No. 815, depend on their intended use. These policies should be reviewed and revised as business and market circumstances change to properly determine the value of derivatives. The institution's risk management philosophy should be properly documented and assessed in achieving the overall risk management objectives.

DERIVATIVES UNDER THE DODD-FRANK ACT OF 2010

The 2007–2009 financial crisis has underscored the lack of regulations for non-securities-based derivatives contracts such as CDS. Unlike other derivative contracts (insurance, securities, commodities, and futures), derivatives are primarily traded in the OTC markets. Proper regulations require transparent information on OTC transactions to restore investors' confidence regarding speculative derivatives transactions (credit derivatives). Global regulators, particularly in the United States and Europe, have considered regulatory CDS and other OTC derivatives by establishing clearinghouse to serve as a central counterparty for those derivatives. Prior to 2000, almost all derivatives were traded on regulated central exchanges overseen by the Commodity Futures Trading Commission; whereas after 2002, the derivatives market became unregulated and exempt from all regulations, including state gambling laws. With no regulatory scrutiny of derivative trades, the determination of the true value of those exotic instruments became subjunctive, manipulative, and complex.

The passage of the Dodd-Frank Wall Street Reform and Consumer Protection Act of 2010 has significantly changed the oversight and structure of OTC derivatives markets by promoting greater transparency and moderating of systemic risks of OTC derivative transactions. The effective impelementation of provisions of Dodd-Frank is expected to strengthen the structure, scope, executive mechanisms, supervision, margin/collateral requirements, and pricing of derivatives markets. Four specific expected requirements/ improvements are listed next.

1. Financial services firms will be required to trade on exchanges standardized OTC derivatives that are cleared by the CFTC and/or the SEC and accepted by a required clearing agency.
2. Many OTC derivatives participants are subject to CFTC and SEC registration, regulation, and oversight.

3. Many OTC derivatives participants are subject to the application of enhanced prudential standards and transparency requirements, such as margin and capital.
4. The CFTC and SEC are directed to issue business conduct rules for derivatives participants.

 ## CONCLUSION

Derivatives have grown significantly in volume and complexity from the traditional interest rate and currency swap to more sophisticated computer-driven risk management derivatives. The magnitude, complexity, risks, and incomplete as well as inconsistent accounting and reporting practices for derivatives have raised some concerns. Improved oversight requirements, regulatory initiatives, and new accounting standards have been suggested as a means of addressing these concerns. ASC No. 815 standardizes the accounting for derivatives by requiring that derivative instruments be measured at fair value and recognized in financial statements. Financial institutions should gain thorough knowledge and understanding of the provisions of regulatory requirements and accounting standards about derivatives.

The widespread use of derivative transactions presents new challenges and opportunities for financial regulators, the accounting profession, and the business community. Derivatives provide a means to: (1) access low-cost funds; (2) earn higher investment returns; (3) adjust investment portfolios to take advantage of mispricing between stock baskets and stock index futures; and (4) combine derivatives with other financial instruments to create new and more powerful financial products. The adoption of ASC No. 815 would cause financial institutions to report a fuller picture of their financial exposures by requiring measurement, recognition, and reporting of fair value of derivatives in their financial statements. The balance sheet effect of adopting ASC No. 815 is an increase in the size of the balance sheet because of the fair value recognition of derivatives as assets or liabilities. The income statement effects of changes in fair value of derivatives depend on the intended use of derivatives, whether they are qualified and designated as hedging instruments. Adoption of ASC No. 815 may increase volatility in earnings and equity through comprehensive income. Implementation of provisions of ASC No. 815 is very complex and requires substantial changes in financial information systems, internal control structure, and risk management strategies of affected entities. Currently, many financial institutions use derivatives for a variety of purposes, including accessing low-cost funds, earning higher investment returns, and creating more powerful financial products. Financial institutions must continually assess their risk management practices to ensure that their derivatives are properly valued and in compliance with board-authorized policies and procedures approved to facilitate the implementation of leveraged trading strategies.

 ## NOTES

1. Federal Reserve Board, remarks by Chairman Alan Greenspan on financial derivatives before the Futures Industry Association, Boca Raton, FL, March 19, 1999.

2. U.S. General Accounting Office, *Financial Derivatives: Actions Needed to Protect the Financial Systems*, GAO/GGD-94-133 (May 1994). Group of Thirty, "Derivatives: Practices and Principles," 1993.

3. Federal Financial Institutions Examination Council, *Supervisory Policy Statement on Investment Securities and End-User Derivatives Activities*, April 23, 1998.

4. Federal Reserve Board, remarks by Governor Laurence H. Mayer before the Derivatives Risk Management Symposium Institute on Law and Financial Services. Fordham University of Law, New York, New York, February 25, 2000.

5. Michael S.Gibson, *Credit Derivatives and Risk Management*, Financeand Economics Discussion Series Divisions of Research & Statistics and Monetary Affairs Federal Reserve Board, Washington, D.C. 2007-47. Available at www.federalreserve.gov/pubs/feds/2007/200747/200747pap.pdf

6. Deloitte and Touche LLP, Committee of Sponsoring Organizations of the Treadway Commission, *Internal Control Issues in Derivatives Usage: An Information Tool for Considering the COSO Internal Control-Integrated Framework in Derivatives Applications*, 1996, p. 4.

7. Ibid., p. 6.

8. Bank of Institutional Settlements, Semiannual OTC Derivatives Statistics at End December 2007, available at www.bis.org.

9. Financial Accounting Standards Board, Statement of Financial Accounting Standards No. 133, *Accounting for Derivative Instruments and Hedging Activities* (Norwalk, CT: Author, 1998).

10. American Institute of Certified Public Accountants (AICPA), *Derivatives—Current Accounting and Auditing Literature*, Financial Instruments Task Force of the Accounting Standards Executive Committee, 1994. Deloitte & Touche LLP, "Internal Control Issues in Derivatives Usage." Committee of Sponsoring Organizations of the Treadway Commission, 1996. Federal Financial Institutions Examination Council, *The Supervisory Policy Statement on Investment Securities and End-User Derivatives Activities*, April 1998. PricewaterhouseCoopers, *Guide to Accounting for Derivative Instruments and Hedging Activities*, March 31, 2010

11. www.bis.org/statistics/otcder/dt1920a.pdf BIS quarterly review states in June of 2010 the "notional value" of outstanding global derivatives contracts was $582 trillion, which exceeds the estimated total value of the world's bond and stocks of $143 trillion. While this notional value of outstanding derivatives contracts may not present the exact size of the financial derivatives market, it provides some indications of potential payments and growth associated with derivatives.

12. The six Wall Street firms that established the new standards for derivatives are CS First Boston, Inc.; Goldman, Sachs & Co.; Salomon Brothers, Inc.; Merrill Lynch & Co.; Lehman Brothers Holdings, Inc.; and Morgan, Stanley & Co.

13. U.S. Securities and Exchange Commission, *Disclosure of Accounting Policies for Derivative Financial Instruments and Derivative Commodity Instruments and Disclosure of Quantitative and Qualitative Information About Market Risk Inherent in Derivative Financial Instruments, Other Financial Instruments, and Derivative Commodity Instruments*, Release No. 33-7386 (Washington, DC: Author, 1997).

14. American Institute of Certified Public Accountants, *Derivatives—Current Accounting and Auditing Literature*, Accounting Standards Executive Committee. Financial Instruments Task Force, 1994.

15. Ibid.

16. Ibid.

17. Fischer Black and Myron Scholes, "The Pricing of Options and Corporate Liabilities." *Journal of Political Economy* 81, No. 3 (May/June 1973): 637–654.

18. Jonathan E. Ingersoll, Jr., "Digital Contracts: Simple Tools for Pricing Complex Derivatives," *Journal of Business* 73, No. 1 (2000): 67–89.

19. See ibid. for a more sophisticated mathematical illustration and examples of using digital contracts in determining the value of derivatives.

CHAPTER NINETEEN

Real-World Bank Valuation Complications

NOT ALL BANK VALUATIONS will involve normal conditions and clean banks that have healthy prospects for reasonable returns in the future. There are numerous instances where special circumstances require adjustments to the standard valuation approaches. This chapter addresses emerging issues facing financial services firms and describes the application of the various valuation approaches under nine real-world complicating circumstances:

1. A bank that has experienced losses in recent years because of low spreads, high overhead expenses, or excessive loan losses
2. A bank with inadequate capital levels
3. A bank that faces very uncertain loan loss exposure on a significant portion of its portfolio
4. A bank whose equity base consists of both preferred and common stock, but only the value of the common stock is needed
5. A bank that is highly leveraged
6. A branch of a bank that is to be purchased
7. Bank assurance
8. Initial public offering (IPO)
9. Islamic banking systems

Each of these situations requires slight modifications to the valuation approaches used in Chapter 16.

BANKS EXPERIENCING RECENT LOSSES

Banks and banking organizations in the United States traditionally have reported many consecutive years of record earnings, showing financial health and strength in rebounding from the financial difficulties of the late 1980s and early 1990s. In 1991, the Federal Deposit Insurance Corporation Improvement Act introduced mandatory procedures called prompt corrective action, which require regulators to promptly close depositary institutions when their capital falls below predetermined quantitative standards. During the 1990s and the first half of 2000s, the banking industry was profitable and financially healthy with the average annual return on assets (ROA) of above 1 percent and the average annual return on equity above 15 percent. However, the chairman of the Federal Deposit Insurance Corporation (FDIC) in her February 8, 2000 testimony before the U.S. House of Representatives raised some concerns regarding several recent failures of insured institutions.[1] In addition to her concerns, the loss rates, stated as the loss to the deposit insurance fund as a percentage of the total assets of the failed banks, were not significant and considered to be within the acceptable 12 percent range of the FDIC.[2]

The financial crisis of 2007–2009 is considered by many economists to be the worst financial crisis since the Great Depression. It was triggered by a liquidity shortfall in the U.S. banking system and has resulted in the collapse of large financial institutions, the bailout of banks by national governments, and downturns in stock markets around the world. The financial crisis of the late 2000s led to the failure of a number of banks in the United States. Twenty-five banks failed and were taken over by the FDIC in 2008, while 140 failed in 2009. In early 2010, the FDIC announced that despite the closure of banks in 2008 and 2009, over 700 banks remained at risk of failure in 2010. The receivership of Washington Mutual Bank by federal regulators on September 26, 2008, was the largest bank failure in U.S. history. In the last quarter of 2008, expenses incurred resulting from rising loan losses and declining asset values caused a net loss of $32.1 billion, the financial services industry's first quarterly loss since 1990. ROA for the last quarter of 2008 was –0.94 percent, which was the worst since the second quarter of 1987. The net income of the financial services industry for the entire year 2008 was $10.2 billion, down 89.8 percent from 2007 with ROA of 0.08 percent, the lowest since 1987. In addition, 23.6 percent of the industry experienced negative profit in 2008, and 62.8 percent reported lower full-year earnings than in 2007. A total of 25 banks failed in all of 2008 versus 3 in 2007. In August 2009, the FDIC reported that the list of troubled banks had climbed to over 400 banks, the highest level in 15 years. Since the beginning of the recent financial crisis in 2007, the number of problem financial institutions increased tenfold; a total of 775 institutions were on the FDIC's list of official problem institutions at the end of the first quarter of 2010.[3]

Exhibit 19.1 shows the number of troubled institutions increased tenfold in the three years from 2007 to 2010, from an average of 1 percent (during 1996 to 2007) up to 9.8 percent (2007 to 2010). These are the financial institutions that are most likely to fail in the future. The U.S. government has taken some measures to prevent those troubled financial institutions from failing. One measure was the Troubled Asset Relief Program (TARP), which was signed into law by U.S. President George W. Bush on

Number of Institutions

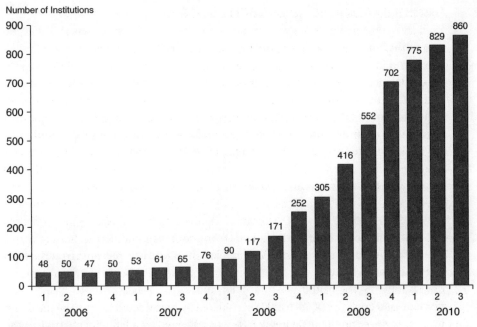

EXHIBIT 19.1 Number of FDIC-Insured Problem Institutions

Source: Author's calculation based on the data from FDIC Quarterly Banking Profile.

October 3, 2008. TARP is a program to purchase or insure assets and equity from financial institutions to strengthen the financial sector. Two categories of assets could be purchased or insured. The first category is residential or commercial mortgages and any securities, obligations, or other instruments based on or related to such mortgages that were originated or issued on or before March 14, 2008. The second category is any other financial instrument deemed necessary to promote financial market stability. TARP was intended to improve the liquidity of these assets by purchasing them using secondary market mechanisms, thus allowing participating institutions to stabilize their balance sheets and avoid further losses.

The ten primary reasons for recent bank failures are:

1. Extensive activity in subprime lending without prudential standards with regard to borrowers with blemished or limited credit histories and inadequate safeguards (e.g., capital) to meet anticipated losses
2. Valuation and liquidity risk resulting from "retained interests" generated from the securitization of high-risk assets for institutions with excessive concentrations of these assets in relation to capital
3. Fraudulent financial activities by failed bank managers and directors
4. Conflicts of interest created by mixing commercial and investment banking activities
5. Irrational business combinations in the financial services industry that created too-big-to-fail (TBTF) financial institutions that are not sustainable

6. Lack of proper focus on risk assessment and risk management
7. Excessive compensation of executives of perceived TBTF institutions that had no link to their performance and encouraged them to take excessive risks
8. Greed and incompetency of directors and officers of troubled financial institutions
9. Too much focus on achieving short-term results at the expense of sustainable performance
10. Too much focus on results (return on investment) primarily for shareholders with no consideration of outcomes for other stakeholders and contributors of both physical and human capital (customers, employees, society)

Financial services firms can minimize the risk of failure by engaging in these activities:

- Use of a more sophisticated risk management system
- Use of a risk-focused approach of emphasizing the adequacy and effectiveness of the internal control system
- Continuous testing of the loan portfolio and other transactions to ensure that prudent risk taking is occurring
- Continuous assessment of an institution's risk management system and overall risk profile
- Ongoing monitoring of control activities to ensure that the designed control activities are functioning effectively as intended
- In-depth review of the loan portfolio
- Identification of problems at an early stage
- Fraud prevention policy of reducing incidents of fraud
- Discouraging excessive risk taking by executives through redesigning executive compensation
- Refocusing executive efforts on achieving sustainable performance for all stakeholders and away from short-term results only for shareholders
- Aligning interests of management with those of stakeholders by linking executive compensation to sustainable performance
- Avoiding conflicts of interest by implementing the Volcker rule of prohibiting banks from engaging in proprietary trading unrelated to customer-driven business and banking activities of sponsoring or investing in hedge funds or private equity funds
- Maintaining capital adequacy that commensurate for all types of risks (market, systemic, liquidity, interest rates, operational, and credit)
- Implementing all applicable rules, regulations, and standards (Sarbanes-Oxley Act of 2002, Dodd-Frank Act of 2010, Basel Committee rules)
- Addressing the misperception of TBTF
- Complying with corporate governance reforms, measures, and best practices
- Cleaning tacit (problem) assets from the bank's balance sheet

An increasingly common situation in bank mergers and acquisitions is when the selling bank has experienced losses in recent years. Use of the market approach may not accurately reflect true value, and the income approach may be distorted by the recent losses. There are two options in such a situation. If the losses are expected to continue for at least the next few years—that is, if a turnaround is unlikely for whatever reason—it may be appropriate to estimate the bank's net asset value (NAV)—the market value of the bank's assets less the market value of its liabilities. In extreme situations, the liquidation value of the bank may be the most appropriate value measure. Liquidation value is the lowest price a business commands—a business is worth no less than what remains after assets are liquidated and liabilities satisfied.

The more likely situation is a bank that has experienced recent losses being evaluated by a buyer who will be able to improve its performance. In this case, it is first necessary to construct a detailed balance sheet as it would exist on the date of acquisition. This balance sheet should reflect adjustments to clean up the bank so that its performance can be forecast as a healthy entity. This clean balance sheet would be the starting point for the new income statement. It is essential that the new income statement immediately reflect the expenses associated with cleaning up existing problems, recognizing loan losses, undertaking needed deferred maintenance, and so on. The income approach as described in Chapter 16 could then be used. The difference is that cleanup costs are reflected as immediate outflows of cash when calculating available cash flow.

Exhibit 19.2 provides a simple example. In this case, the available cash flows have been forecast based on an acquired balance sheet free of problem assets. Without cleanup costs, the value of the bank is $94 million, but because of problems requiring $25 million, the value of the bank is only about $69 million. This simple example illustrates how estimated cleanup costs would be reflected in value calculations.

 ## BANKS WITH LOW EQUITY CAPITAL

A situation closely related to low earnings is a bank with low equity, often below regulatory minimums. In such a situation, it is difficult to apply the market approach unless banks with similarly low equity levels have been sold recently and can be used as comparables. A better approach is similar to the one just described: Project value by the income approach after a capital injection, and then adjust the value to reflect that capital injection.

The difference between the low-equity situation and the recent losses situation has to do with where the money goes. The cost of cleaning up the bank described earlier presumably went to outside parties. In a low-equity situation, a capital injection stays with the bank and helps with earnings but essentially is unavailable to the owners until the bank is sold or is sufficiently profitable that internal capital creation is adequate. For example, if a buyer is required to inject one dollar of new capital on acquisition, the assets will increase by one dollar, as will equity. All or virtually the entire additional dollar can be invested in earning assets, thus improving the income of the bank. And when the bank is sold, the one dollar is still part of the equity base. Contrast this scenario with one in which one dollar is a direct loss (say from the sale of investments). The dollar is removed from the bank, with no current or future benefit.

Despite the differences in effect, the valuation of a bank with low equity can be undertaken essentially in the same manner as for a bank with recent losses. The key is to

EXHIBIT 19.2 Illustration of the Impact on Value as a Result of Balance Sheet Cleanup Costs ($000,000)

	Year 1	Year 2	Year 3	Year 4	Year 5	Year 6	Year 7	Year 8	Year 9	Year 10
Available cash flow*	$10.0	$10.5	$11.0	$11.5	$12.2	$13.0	$13.8	$14.8	$16.0	$17.2
Discount rate	14%	14%	14%	14%	14%	14%	14%	14%	14%	14%
Capitalization rate on year 10 cash flow	—	—	—	—	—	—	—	—	—	11%
Sum of present values of cash flow	$57.8									
Present value of capitalized value of year 10 cash flow	$42.2									
Clean value†	$94.0									
Cleanup costs	($25.0)									
Value considering cost to clean up	$69.0									

*Based on a clean balance sheet that reflects the results of cleanup, such as realizing losses on an investment portfolio, taking loan losses, and so on.

†The value had the buyer acquired the clean balance sheet.

EXHIBIT 19.3 Reflecting Capital Injections in Starting Balance Sheet ($000,000)

	Acquired Balance Sheet	Capital Injection	Starting Balance Sheet
Assets			
Cash and Due Forms	$ 10		$ 10
Securities and Fed Funds	20	+5	25
Total Loans	130		130
(Loan Loss Reserves)	(10)		(10)
Net Loans	120		120
Premises and Fixed Assets	5	+1	6
Other Real Estate Owned	3		3
Other Assets	2		2
Total Assets	$160	+6	$166
Liabilities and Equity			
Non-Interest-bearing Deposits	$ 25		$ 25
Interest-bearing Deposits	115		115
Total Deposits	140		140
Other Liabilities	17		17
Equity	3	+6	9
Total Liabilities and Equity	$160	+6	$166

establish a starting balance sheet reflecting the capital injection. Exhibit 19.3 illustrates how a buyer would adjust a balance sheet of a $160 million bank to reflect a $6 million addition to equity. An income statement would then be projected based on this starting balance sheet. Available cash flow would be adjusted downward to reflect the required equity injection, with value estimated based on the income approach.

Another possibility is that the balance sheet is so weak that it cannot be cleaned up within realistic financial or time limits. In such an extreme case, the liquidation value, as described earlier, may be the most appropriate measure of value.

In some instances, the NAV may be negative; that is, the value of the bank's assets may be less than its liabilities. This is the typical situation with an FDIC-assisted sale. In this case, the buyer requires the FDIC to inject sufficient capital (and hold back certain nonperforming assets) to ensure that the acquired balance sheet is reasonably clean.

The Dodd-Frank Wall Street Reform and Consumer Protection Act of 2010 creates a new council of regulators, the Financial Stability Oversight Council (FSOC), to identify and address to U.S. financial stability. The FSOC is charged with identifying "systemically important" (SI) financial institutions including banks and nonbank financial firms and addressing their financial risks. The FSDC with the assistance of the newly established Official Financial Research in the department of Treasury will establish risk measurement and reporting methodologies. The FSOC considers many factors a in determining (SI) financial institutions. Among them are:

- The extent of leverage
- The nature and extent of off–balance sheet exposures providing liquidity and credit to households, businesses, governmental entities, low-income, minority or under-served communities
- Ownership structure (managed, owned)
- Nature and amount of financial assets
- Types and amount of liability including short-term funding
- Oother risk-related factors

The Federal Reserve is directed by Dodd-Frank to establish enhanced risk-based capital, liquidity requirements, leverage, overall risk management requirements, concentration limits, and resolution plans for the designated SI firms.

 BANKS WITH UNCERTAIN FUTURE LOAN LOSS EXPOSURE

Traditionally loans have comprised a significant proportion of bank assets, and therefore banks' financial reporting for loans, particularly loan loss provision, is essential. The most complicating situation is when the bank being valued faces uncertain future loan loss exposure. In other words, the loss facing the bank in its loan portfolio is difficult if not impossible to assess with any reasonable degree of accuracy, and existing reserves may or may not be adequate. This can be a particular problem in smaller banks where a few large problem loans have a disproportionate impact on the banks' financial condition and subsequent value to a buyer.

One way to reflect such uncertain exposure is to identify separately those problem loans on the projected income statement of the bank. Instead of one line item called loan loss provision, there would be two: loan loss provision for identified problem loans and loan loss provision for all other loans. The total of these two would be the loan loss provision for the bank. The normal income approach could then be used to value the bank.

The advantage of this separation technique is that a normal annual loan loss provision could be applied to all other loans while the specific impact of the problem loans on the value estimate can be assessed. Different assumptions of degree and timing of collectability can be simulated to determine how franchise value might be affected.

Loans and loan losses are somewhat unique aspects of banks (and other financial institutions) for two reasons: (1) Loans (which are, in effect, accounts receivable) constitute a large part of the asset base; and (2) losses on loans can be difficult to predict. It is this second aspect that is of most concern in the valuation process.

In the valuation of Example Bank in Chapter 15, the loan loss provision was based on a target loan loss reserve of 1 percent of total loans with a charge-off rate of 0.3 percent of total loans. Had these projections been different, the resulting value

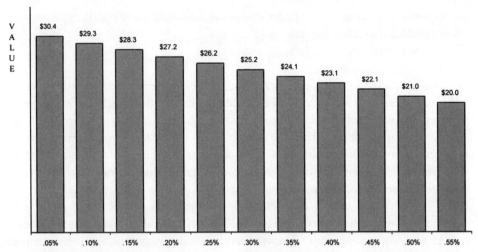

EXHIBIT 19.4 Impact on Estimated Value of Example Bank with Varying Assumptions of Loan Losses* ($ Millions)

Net charge-offs each year, as a percent of total loans (with constant 1 percent reserve for loan losses)
*From data in Chapter 16.

would also be different. Exhibit 19.4 illustrates how the value impact can be affected by relatively minor changes in assumptions. For every 0.05 percent increase in net charge-offs to average assets, the value of Example Bank declines by about $1.0 million to $1.1 million.

It should be noted that increasing or decreasing any expense item (salaries, occupancy, etc.) would have the same impact on value. The difference is that most operating expenses of a bank are either fairly predictable or controllable, or both. Loan losses are unique because they can be unpredictable. Banks in a given peer group tend to have much more consistent operating expense ratios than loan loss ratios. Loan losses are related to many factors outside the bank's control. Consequently, when a bank is being valued, it is critically important that the loan loss assumptions be as accurate as possible and based on a full knowledge of pertinent facts.

Securities and Exchange Commission (SEC) Staff Accounting Bulletin No. 102 requires that bank methodology in determining allowance for loan losses (ALL) should:[4]

1. Provide a detailed analysis of the loan portfolio performed on a regular basis.
2. Consider all loans (whether on an individual or group basis).
3. Identify loans to be assessed for impairment on an individual basis under Statement of Financial Accounting Standards (SFAS) No. 114, and segment the remainder of the portfolio into groups of loans with similar risk characteristics for evaluation and analysis under SFAS No. 5.
4. Consider all known relevant internal and external factors that may affect loan collectability.
5. Be applied consistently but, when appropriate, be modified for new factors affecting ALL.

6. Incorporate management's judgments about the credit quality of the loan portfolio through a systematic process.
7. Be overseen by the bank's audit committee.

Banks traditionally have been in compliance with accounting standards to determine their loan loss provision based on an incurred loss approach. Under an incurred loss approach, banks typically do not recognize a provision for a loan loss until there is an indication that the loan has been impaired. Consequently, a bank would not recognize losses based on external indicators of economic loss in the value of its loans, even though the economic and market indicators suggest that a significant number of borrowers will default on their loans (as occurred in the 2007–2009 financial crisis). The incurred loss approach is not as procyclical because it delays loss recognition until incurred. This delayed and asymmetric recognition of loan losses does not appropriately reflect the true value of bank assets. To determine the bank value effectively and to overcome the effects of delayed and asymmetric recognition of loan losses calculated under the incurred loss approach, the bank should implement an expected loss approach for loans. Under this approach, a bank determines its loan loss provision by considering all changes in expected future cash collections from its loans.

Banks are not typically in favor of measuring their assets (loans) based on the expected future cash flow or market prices that may cause earnings volatility. Banks prefer continuing their current practices of valuing their loans based on the original cost less a reserve to cover probable losses. During the recent financial crisis, which left many banks with inadequate capital and their investors vulnerable, the use of cost method proved problematic. In its meeting of December 21, 2010, the Financial Accounting Standards Board (FASB) decided to address this concern by considering three categories for bank assets:[5]

1. Fair value of net income (FV/NI). Fair value measurement with all changes in fair value recognized in net income
2. Fair value of other comprehensive income (FV/OCI). Fair value measurement with qualifying changes in fair value recognized in other comprehensive income
3. Amortized cost

As of January 27, 2011, the FASB's position is unclear. It may not require banks to value their loans using market prices, as previously planned, and it may allow the business strategy criterion to determine which bank assets would be measured at amortized cost.

 ## PREFERRED AND COMMON STOCK

In cases where a bank has both common and preferred stock, there are instances where a buyer is interested in the value of only one or the other. The technique is relatively straightforward. Preferred stock can be valued by either the market approach (comparing one issue with similar issues of preferred stock) or the income approach (the net present value of interest and return of principal).

Valuing just the common stock of a bank that has both preferred stock and common stock requires that the bank first be valued as a total economic entity. The market and income approaches used to value Example Bank in Chapter 16 provide this total economic entity value. The preferred stock value is then subtracted from the total economic entity value, with the result being the aggregate value of the common stock. This is the value on a 100 percent common stock ownership basis. Any minority position valuation would require that an appropriate minority and/or marketability discount be applied.

 ## HIGHLY LEVERAGED BANKS

Banks, or more likely bank holding companies, that have high debt-to-equity ratios may have historical earnings that belie their underlying earning potential. If a bank has a large debt burden, its fixed interest charges can have a significant impact on net income and available cash flow. Leverage ratios can vary widely among different-size holding companies.

Valuing a highly leveraged bank is best accomplished by examining it on a debt-free basis, both historical and projected. Historical income statements can be adjusted to reflect what income would have been without the debt or with a normal level of debt. Projected income then is estimated on a debt-free basis. Normal market and income approaches to value can then be used. The amount of debt is subtracted from the debt-free value to arrive at a with-debt value. This is essentially the approach described in the discussion of total enterprise value versus value of equity in Chapter 8.

Bank regulators do not typically disclose their assessment of the stability, financial health, and sustainability financial institutions; however, one simple method of such evaluation is the Texas ratio (TR). The TR is determined as the ratio of a bank's nonperforming assets and loans that are 90 days past due to the bank's tangible capital.[6] The TR of above 100 percent typically is considered as an indication of bank tendency to fail.[7] Ford and Phillips, 2010 The other key performance indicators of bank failures are capital adequacy, return on assets, return on equity, and loan loss reserve provisions. As of the second quarter of 2010, more than 120 banks had a TR of above 200, 387 banks showed a TR of 100 or above, and 661 banks had a TR between 50 and 99.[8]

 ## BRANCH ACQUISITIONS

As consolidation continues in the banking industry, more and more banks are finding that redundant branch coverage is causing excessive costs. Moreover, with a greater focus on optimal asset utilization, some banks are withdrawing entirely from selected markets. The net result is that branch acquisitions have become commonplace. Buyers of branches confront an unusual set of circumstances, including the problem of defining exactly what is being acquired. Some branches are almost self-contained banks with their own loyal customer base while others are simply service centers for routine deposit and loan services.

EXHIBIT 19.5 Example of Net Asset Valuation of Branch to Be Acquired ($000,000)

	Book Value of Assets and Liabilities	Market Value of Assets and Liabilities	Buyer's Opening Balance Sheet
Assets			
Vault cash	$ 10	$ 10	$ 10
Investments	20	18	$ 70*
Total loans	105	100	100
(Loss reserve)	(5)	(5)	(5)
Net loans	100	95	95
Fixed assets	15	20	20
Miscellaneous	5	5	5
Core deposit value	—	—	10
Total assets	$150	$148	$210
Liabilities			
Deposits	$200	$200	$200
Total liabilities	$200	$200	$200
Net asset value	($ 50)	($ 52)	$ 10

*Reflects $5.2 million injection by seller to balance market value of assets and liabilities.

In most instances, the value of a branch is more than the physical premises, furniture, fixtures, and equipment. If only these parts of a branch are being acquired, typical real estate and equipment valuation methods are sufficient. The more likely, and more complex, situation is when a bank is selling a branch as a business unit, including earning and nonearning assets and customer relationships.

The most straightforward technique to valuation of a bank branch as a business unit is to compute its NAV. Exhibit 19.5 illustrates this approach. The first column shows the book value of the assets and liabilities to be computed as part of the branch sale. (As is the case with many branch acquisitions, there are more assigned liabilities than assigned assets.) The second column shows the adjustments of assets and liabilities to market values. The third column shows the balance sheet the buyer would have. It reflects a $5.2 million injection by the seller and includes core deposit intangible value.

In essence, when a branch is acquired with equal assets and liabilities, the price paid reflects the value of the core deposit intangible—the customer base. Consequently, the buyer must be confident that a significant number of depositors will not move their accounts when the branch is sold. If this were to occur, the deposit base on which to value the intangible would be smaller, thus lowering the premium.

Another approach is to forecast the income and cash flows from the assets acquired and liabilities assumed. The normal income approach could then be used to value the branch. When using this approach, the required additions to capital must be factored into the available cash flow calculation. For example, if a branch with $20 million in assets and $20 million in liabilities is being acquired, the incremental equity capital needed for the buyer to inject, assuming a 5 percent equity-to-assets ratio, would be $1 million. Such a requirement should be considered in the valuation.

In some cases, the purchaser of a branch is taking over only the deposits and fixed assets of the branch. No assets except for the physical structures are being acquired. This is the typical scenario for an FDIC branch sale. In determining the value of this type of branch acquisition, the purchaser will pay a premium for the customer base, which represents the value of the core deposit intangible.

The premiums paid for a deposit purchase vary considerably, but most fall into the 2.5 to 5 percent range. This means that for every $100 of deposit the bank takes over, it will pay the seller $2.50 to $5.00 in addition to taking over the liability. The premium will depend on the types of deposits being acquired and the contractual interest rates the purchaser will have to pay depositors. Lower-cost stable deposits (such as checking and passbook savings) tend to command higher premiums.

 EUROPEAN BANKING MODEL

Consolidation, convergence, and global competition in recent years have encouraged banks to engage in insurance and investment activities. Especially, the passage of the Gramm-Leach-Bliley Financial Modernization Act (GLB) of 1999 allows banks to establish financial holding companies that could engage in a wide variety of financial services activities, including insurance and investment activities. The banking model under the GLB Act in which banks can fully integrate insurance and investment businesses into their core product and service offerings would resemble the European banking model of "bancassurance" (the selling of insurance through the banks' distribution channels, allowing banks to offer many products and services to customers). The bancassurance model has been used successfully by European banks and would be possible for U.S. banks under the GLB Act to increase their market share and profitability in nontraditional markets.

Traditionally, the investment marketplace was driven primarily by institutional investors and wealthy individuals. Recently, especially during the 1990s, individuals across all income and demographic segments have become active investors by investing in the rewarding stock market, 401(k) plans, and mutual funds. Exhibit 19.6 shows that in recent years (2006–2010) the amount of assets in mutual funds exceeded bank deposits and grew at a rapid pace. Banks will be able to meet all of their customers' basic financial needs by integrating insurance and investment products with their core banking operations.

This wave of convergence will create a number of challenges for banks in shifting away from offering traditional banking services (e.g., deposits, loans, and transaction activities) and moving toward engaging in nontraditional markets, including insurance and mutual funds. By enacting the GLB Act, the United States was almost the last developed economy to eliminate convergence restrictions in the financial services industry and to allow the financial systems to respond to changes in the global marketplace. With this convergence now being possible in the financial services industry, three issues arise about the future structure and directions of financial service providers. These issues are: (1) the possible impacts of the passage of the GLB Act on

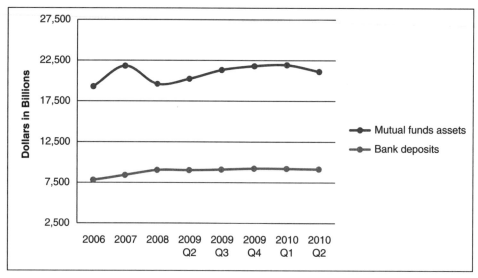

EXHIBIT 19.6 Trends in the Growth of Mutual Funds Assets and Bank Deposits

Source: Author's calculation based on bank deposit data from the Financial Deposit Insurance Corporation and mutual fund assets data from the Investment Company Institute.

future mergers and acquisitions in the financial services industry; (2) whether the convergence, specifically between banks and insurance companies, will limit consumer choice; and (3) whether banks and securities companies combine without imposing excess and unjustifiable levels of risk on the consumer and the economy in general. These and other related issues should be addressed in complying with the provisions of the GLB Act and in adopting the European bancassurance model in the United States. Effective and successful convergence requires banks to combine with insurance companies and mutual funds according to the provisions of the GLB Act. To achieve a successful level of convergence, banks should modify their financial reporting as well as their internal risk assessment policies and procedures. These changes require compliance with insurance and mutual funds laws and regulations and make bank valuations more complicated.

During the past decade, the mutual fund industry has grown substantially to the unprecedented level of over \$6 trillion and surpassed the total deposits at banks. The Investment Company Act of 1940 requires calculation and reporting of the NAV per share for a mutual fund. Mutual funds are not taxpaying entities; their earnings pass directly through to shareholders who report individual earnings information on their tax returns. Mutual funds calculate daily NAV per share by using the market value of funds' investments. The daily reporting of NAV in the financial press permits investors to determine the fair market value (FMV) of their investments. NAV is calculated as:

$$\text{NAV} = \frac{\text{Market value of shareholders' equity}}{\text{Outstanding shares of mutual funds}} = \frac{\text{Assets (at FMV)} - \text{Liabilities}}{\text{Outstanding shares of mutual funds}}$$

Exhibit 19.7 shows the calculation of the daily NAV for the hypothetical ABC mutual fund.

EXHIBIT 19.7 Calculating the Daily Net Asset Value for the ABC Mutual Fund

Assets	
Cash	$ 1500
Interest receivable	325,000
Dividend receivable	416,000
Investment at cost	395,000,000
Net appreciation of investments*	15,000,000
Total assets at FMV	$410,742,500
Liabilities	
Investment purchases payable	$ 2,100,000
Accrued expenses	216,000
Total liabilities	$ 2,316,000
Shareholders' equity	
Capital stock	$391,000,000
Net appreciation of investments	15,000,000
Retained earnings†	2,426,500
Total shareholders' equity (at FMV)	$408,426,500
Total liabilities and equity	$410,742,500
Shares outstanding	18,000,000

Net asset value (NAV) = 408,426,500 ÷ 18,000,000 = $22.69.

*"Net appreciation" and "net depreciation" of investments represent unrealized holding gains and unrealized holding losses.

†Retained earnings consist of capital gains, income, expenses, and distributions.

 ## INITIAL PUBLIC OFFERING

An Initial Public Offering (IPO) is another business area that requires determination of fair value of the company going public in order to assess the IPO pricing and fair value of the minority interests prior to the IPO. In the IPO process, the privately held company in the transition process of "going public" provides the public with the opportunity to buy shares in the public stock markets. The financial institution in the transition process of may be considered attractive to the public stock markets for these reasons: (1) generating new capital from the IPO; (2) increasing earnings capacity resulting from the new capital invested; (3) increasing growth prospects resulting from new capital and increased earnings capacity; and (4) accessibility to a public market for offering stock in an active market to a great number of potential shareholders.

In most of the aforementioned valuation services, the considerations in dispute are not bought and sold every day by able and willing involved parties. In other words, there is not a readily available FMV for them; accordingly, the proper valuation method should be employed to assess their value. Valuation experts utilize a number of valuation methods commonly derived from theories of finance (e.g., discounted cash earnings, and capital asset pricing model) to calculate a business's value.

EXHIBIT 19.8 Summary of Valuation Approaches in More Complex Situations

Situation	Valuation Approach
Bank has experienced losses in recent years	If losses are expected to continue, use market value of equity approach, which essentially measures liquidation value. If losses are not expected to continue, develop projected income statement based on detailed analysis of current balance sheet and yields, costs, etc. Factor in any costs necessary to divest of assets or liabilities that are draining earnings. Then use income approach.
Bank has very low equity	If current balance sheet is clean, prepare projected income statement based on yields, costs, etc. Then use income approach, taking into account any needed immediate capital injection. If current balance sheet is not clean and level of required equity is very high relative to likely asset quality, liquidation value approach may be warranted.
Bank faces uncertain loss exposure on a selected portion of its portfolio	Undertake detailed analysis of problem loans to reduce uncertainty as much as possible. Then include two line items for loan losses in projected income statement: one for problem loans, another for all others. This way, problem loans can be evaluated separately from the rest. Then use normal income approach.
Bank has preferred and common stock, and only value of common stock is desired	Total value of bank is equal to value of common stock plus value of preferred stock; conversely, value of common stock is equal to total value of bank less value of preferred stock. Therefore, the first step is to value bank in total, then value preferred stock using techniques described in Chapter 8. The difference is common stock value.
Bank is highly leveraged	Value bank on debt-free basis using income approach, then subtract debt to be assumed to arrive at value with debt.
Branch purchase	Compute net asset value taking into account value of core deposit intangible asset, or construct an opening-day balance sheet of branch, then project income statement based on yields, costs, etc. Value by income approach, taking into account any capital injections needed to support acquired assets.

The eight situations described in this chapter are not uncommon and are likely to be confronted in the course of most bank valuations. A summary of the approaches that should be considered is shown in Exhibit 19.8.

ISLAMIC BANKING SYSTEM

The Islamic banking system and practices are in some respects different from conventional banking systems in the sense that Sharia-compliant transactions are conducted by not charging interest. Nonetheless, the Islamic banking industry engages in global competition and is expected to improve its capital adequacy, risk management systems, and investor protection. Currently more than 600 Islamic financial institutions provide banking services in over 75 countries, and they are expected to grow internationally beyond boundaries of Islamic countries. Thus, the Islamic banking system is becoming an integral component of the international financial system.

The Islamic banking system primarily focuses on socioeconomic banking activities that comply with Sharia while achieving the socioeconomic objectives promoted by Islam. Sharia prohibits interest-based income to ensure banks do not harm others in the Islamic society while making money and to achieve a fair and equitable distribution of wealth. Conventional banks charge borrowers an interest rate through which they can reward their depositors and make some profit for being the broker. Islamic banks, however, enter a partnership with their depositors and invest their money in Sharia-compliant businesses. The profit from this investment is then shared between the depositor and the bank after a set time. In many cases, this "profit rate" is competitive with the conventional banking system's interest rate for savers. An Islamic bank can enter into a lease agreement for a car or a house with its customer where the bank buys a vehicle and then leases it back to the customer over a time period that would ensure that the capital was repaid and the bank made a profit.

The Islamic banking system can operate sufficiently in Sharia-compliant for basic bank lending and saving activities. For example, according to Sharia-compliant mortgage agreements, a bank can buy the property and then lease it out to its borrower at a price that combines a rental charge and a capital payment. At the end of the mortgage term, when the price of the property has been fully repaid, the bank transfers the house to the borrower. Alternatively, the bank can enter into a partnership with a potential homeowner by purchasing 60 percent of the house, the individual 40 percent. The bank then rents its share of the house back to the homeowner until the house is fully paid for by the homeowner. However, complex bank activities of structured financing, collateralized debt, convertible debt, derivative financial instruments, and hedging can present significant challenges for Islamic banks that strive to be Sharia compliant.

The 2010 survey of Islamic banking challenges addresses these aspects of the Islamic banking system:[9]

- Regulatory and Sharia compliance
- Risk management
- Corporate structuring and capital management strategy
- Investment and capital markets
- Human capital management

The survey suggests these improvements in the Islamic banking system:

- Establish effective enterprise-wide risk management systems that address the different types of risks faced by Islamic financial service offerings.
- Refine the Sharia governance structure.
- Improve the Sharia approval banking process and internal audit systems.
- Develop a wide range of Sharia-based investment instruments.
- Promote a culture of professional excellence in Islamic finance.
- Foster collaboration among Sharia scholars, Islamic bankers, and industry.
- Encourage practitioners to articulate thought leadership initiatives embracing innovative Sharia-based products and services.

EMERGING ISSUES IN THE FINANCIAL SERVICES INDUSTRY

Several issues have the potential to affect the financial services industry.

Final Report of the Financial Crisis Inquiry Commission

In May 2009, Congress formed the Financial Crisis Inquiry Commission (FCIC) to investigate causes of the 2007–2009 financial crisis in the United States.[10] The FCIC's report provides a summary of events and conclusions on the recent crisis, the majority of which have already been in public domain. The financial crisis created a worldwide economic meltdown, bankrupted several Wall Street investment banks (Countrywide and Wachovia), and contributed to significant global deficits and unemployment. The FCIC reviewed millions of documents, interviewed over 700 witnesses, and conducted 19 days of hearings for almost a year and issued its report on January 27, 2011. The overall conclusion of the FCIC report is that the 2007–2009 financial crisis could have been avoided and was caused by inadequate and ineffective regulations to ensure the safety and soundness of the financial system. Inadequacies ranged from lax oversight of derivatives to insufficient supervision by federal banking and securities regulators as well as greed, excessive risk taking, and mismanagement by executives of financial services firms.

The report concludes that 12 of the 13 largest U.S. financial institutions "were at risk of failure" in 2008. This overall conclusion is not endorsed by the commission's four Republican members, who wrote two dissents and criticized findings of the report by suggesting that the financial crisis was caused by the credit bubble. Six Democratic members of the FCIC focused on corporate governance and regulatory failures in their report whereas three Republican members emphasized economic factors and the U.S. moneitary policy that contributed to the crisis. Another Republican member wrote a dissent by concluding that government housing policy of promoting homeownership through unconventional subprime mortgage loans was the key cause of the crisis. Thus, all three reports, while differing about the role of regulation, are regarded as not relevant and useful because Congress enacted a major financial services reform (Dodd-Frank Act) in response to the financial crisis. These three reports failed to address corporate governance, business sustainability, motivational, accountability, and ethical and cultural failures of the major financial services firms.

Other Issues

Other issues affecting the financial services industry are the audit committee, internal control reporting, investment valuation, new accounting and auditing standards, derivatives and related risks, and business combinations. These issues are further discussed in the this section.

It is expected that a more effective audit committee will provide oversight of the bank's business and financial risks. The audit committee should understand and evaluate the effects of new financial reporting and regulatory requirements, work on the scope of changes of the proposed standards, and check if the bank is actively participating in the standard-setting process and providing comments to the FASB. The audit committee also needs to review the bank's risk management with respect to its economic condition, review and understand the changes in the key assumptions and business operations, determine the fair value (particularly for complex or illiquid securities), review the plans to reduce the expenditures, and understand the working of the management and company's disclosure.

Management is primarily responsible for a fair presentation of financial statements and the effectiveness of internal controls. Transaction risk can be substantial if the bank lacks adequate internal control. An effective internal control system requires that there are adequate and comprehensive internal financial, operational and compliance data as well as external market information about events and conditions that are relevant to decision making. Information should be reliable, timely, accessible, and provided in a consistent format along with the reliable information systems in place that cover all significant activities of the bank. Banks are now reporting on both fair presentation of their financial statements and the effectiveness of their internal control over financial reporting under the integrated financial and internal control reporting (IFICR). Thus, under the IFICR, management should establish a sound accounting system that conforms to applicable accounting and regulatory standards and maintain an effective internal control system.

The use of a proper investment valuation model is helpful in making informed decisions about what to buy or sell and determines whether a particular investment is a prudent intelligent, worthwhile investment. While estimating the potential market value of assets or liability, the fair values of certain assets, such as auction rate securities and mortgage-backed or other asset-backed securities, continue to present difficulties and complications in valuation under circumstances of the economic downfall. The 2007–2009 financial crisis and its impact on capital market volatility and performance have led to declines in the fair values of many investment securities. Hence investors should assess the debt and equity securities and determine whether an investment is considered impaired. Companies need to carefully evaluate portfolios, comparing the value of cash flows. Consideration to whether the fair value of the security is expected to recover investors' cost basis and having the management to possess the intent and ability to hold the security until the anticipated recovery of the security would help investors to evaluate the associated value of equity securities. The FASB's position on accounting for impairment of certain loans and specifying the fair value accounting treatment of all debt and equity securities is not clear and has changed several times in the past two years. In 2010, the FASB planned to require banks to measure, recognize, and disclose market prices of banks' assets. Banks are not typically in favor of measuring their assets based on market prices, which may cause earnings volatility; they prefer to continue their current practices of valuing loans based on the original cost less a reserve to account for probable losses. As of February 10, 2011, the FASB had yet to decide whether to allow banks to continue measuring their assets at amortized cost.

The implications of provisions of Dodd-Frank Act will substantially change the oversight and structure of OTC derivatives markets.[11] The Act is intended to strengthen transparency and risk assessment of OTC derivatives, which contributed to the recent financial crisis. It is expected that regulatory implication rules will significantly affect the scope, structure, oversight, pricing, margin/collateral requirements, and execution mechanisms of OTC derivatives. Dodd-Frank is intended to minimize the probability of future financial crisis and systemic distress by empowering regulators to require higher capital requirements and establish new regulatory regime for large financial firms, by developing regulatory and market structures for financial derivatives, and by creating systemic risk assessment and monitoring.

The Dodd-Frank Act regulates most derivatives transactions formerly deregulated by the Commodity Futures Modernization Act of 2000 by categorizing derivatives transactions into three groups: (1) "swaps" derivatives, which are subject to primary regulation by the Commodity Futures Trading Commission (CFTC); (2) "security-based swaps" derivatives, which are subject to primary regulation by the SEC; and (3) "mixed swaps" derivatives, which are subject to joint regulation by the CFTC and SEC. The most significant derivatives provisions of the Dodd-Frank Act are: (1) mandatory clearing through regulated central clearing organizations and mandatory trading through either regulated exchanges or swap execution facilities; (2) new categories of regulated market participants, including swap dealers and major swap participants; and (3) the push-out from banks into bank affiliates of many swap activities.

The relationship between risk and derivatives is especially important in banking since banks dominate most derivatives markets and, within banking, derivative holdings are concentrated at a few large banks. Hence the estimation of market value and interest rate sensitivity of bank derivative positions should be done along with the focus on the interest rate swaps to avoid severe problems. The excessive use of derivatives by banks may have external effects leading to the breakdown of the payments systems and collapse of credit markets for firms. There is also the need for the company with derivative assets to recognize a current loss in earnings for the decline in fair value and/ or impairment of its asset to avoid the hedge ineffectiveness and/or affecting the cash flow hedging relationships.

While bank failures are not the only driver of consolidation, growth-minded banks are looking for opportunities to expand similar to the ones that have taken place over the last two decades without any solutions in light of bank failures and crisis. The bulk of consolidation is likely to come at the expense of smaller banks, whose numbers have been dwindling for decades in the face of deregulation and technological advances that disproportionately aided bigger competitors. The current credit crisis and the transatlantic mortgage financial turmoil bring into question the effectiveness of bank consolidation program as a remedy for financial stability and monetary policy in correcting the defects in the financial sector for sustainable development. The consolidation of any financial services may not necessarily be a sufficient tool for financial stability and development if it is not market driven to allow for efficient processes. A study conducted by KPMG in 2007 reveals more interest in and demand for consolidation and acquisition strategies in the global private banking and wealth management industry.[12] The study also states that regulation has been the biggest obstacle to acquisition, when banks were seeking targets and have made acquisitions in the several years leading up to the 2007–2009 financial crisis.

Improper use of special-purpose entities (SPEs), also known as off–balance sheet arrangements, which is common when many banks are engaged in securitization, can be problematic for financial services firms. SPE transactions typically serve a legitimate business purpose of isolating financial risk and providing less expensive financing. These off–balance sheet arrangements may be called qualifying special-purpose entities

(QSPEs) if they meet the requirements set forth in SFAS No. 140, *Accounting for Transfers and Servicing of Financial Assets and Extinguishment of Liabilities.* This wave of mortgage modifications to address the financial crisis has raised a number of accounting, legal, and public policy/economic issues regarding the implications of QSPEs on various loan modification initiatives, including those sponsored by the government. The sponsors can therefore benefit from these off–balance-sheet entities through SPE to finance a capital project where neither the liability nor the assets of that project will be included in the sponsor's balance sheet.

As stated in previous chapters, the 2007–2009 financial crisis has increased the likelihood of bank failures, the inability of many banks to continue in existence as going concerns, and the pressure to manipulate their financial statements. The Public Company Accounting Oversight Board (PCAOB) in the postfinancial crisis period has identified instances where auditors apparently did not comply with PCAOB auditing standards in key areas, such as fair value measurements, impairment of goodwill, indefinite-lived intangible assets and other long-lived assets, allowance for loan losses, off–balance sheet structures, revenue recognition, inventory, and income taxes. Those deficiencies occurred in audits of financial institutions and other types of companies. In response to the increased risks stemming from the economic crisis, financial services firms need to continue to focus on making improvements to their quality control systems and the PCAOB should consider following up on whether the changes in firms' quality control systems have the desired effect. Goodwill and indefinite-lived intangible assets must be reviewed for impairment at least annually, with impairment losses charged to expense when they occur. Acquisition-related intangible assets other than goodwill and indefinite-lived intangible assets need to be amortized to be expensed over their estimated useful lives and should be reviewed periodically by management to assess recoverability. Impairment losses on other acquisition-related intangibles can be recognized as a charge to expense if carrying amounts exceed fair values. Goodwill is tested for impairment at the reporting unit level in a two-step test: (1) to identify the potential impairment and (2) calculate the fair value of goodwill for each reporting unit for which the impairment was indicated previously. Going concern that refers to a company's ability to continue functioning as a business entity raises questions about many banks' ability to continue as the result of experiencing declining operations and liquidity issues. Banks are required to disclose in notes to financial statements whether any factors may put their status as a going concern in doubt. Auditors must consider whether the use of the going concern assumption is appropriate.

Banks that file for protection should plan to reorganize the business and continue as a going concern, with careful considerations being given to accounting and financial reporting, consolidated subsidiaries, and distinguishing the liabilities.

Financial services industries are expected to be scrutinized by policy makers, regulators, standard setters, and the investing community regarding their compliance with the Dodd-Frank Act, capital requirements (Basel III), and their responses to the 2007–2009 financial crisis. Thus, full disclosures, transparency of reported financial statements, and disclosures set forth in the management's discussion and analysis, (MD&A) regarding future financial forecasts, new products and services, financial and nonfinancial key performance indicators (KPIs) are crucial in providing reasonable assurance of compliance with all applicable laws, rules, regulations, and standards. Bank financial reports should provide a more timely and clear reflection of the risks involved by the use of some sophisticated financial products (e.g., mortgage-backed obligations). Hence, management must look at its financial statement disclosures; evaluate the sufficiency of its MD&A and internal controls disclosures; and effectively assess the risk of all transactions, particularly those related to off–balance sheet arrangements and arrangements with variable interest entities.

 ## CONCLUSION

This chapter has presented emerging issues facing financial services firms and described the application of the various valuation approaches under nine real-world complicating circumstances from challenges caused by the 2007–2009 financial crisis and the global regulatory responses to the peculiarities of Islamic financial institutions. As discussed, the 2007–2009 financial crisis was caused by inadequate and ineffective regulations to ensure the safety and soundness of the financial system as well as greed, excessive risk taking, and mismanagement by executives of financial services firms and could have been avoided.

 ## NOTES

1. Donna Tanove, Testimony on Recent Bank Failures and Regulatory Initiatives before the Committee on Banking and Financial Services, U.S. House of Representatives, February 8, 2000.
2. Ibid.
3. Federal Deposit Insurance Corporation, Quarterly Banking Profile, 2010. Available at: www.fdic.gov.
4. Securities and Exchange Commission Staff Accounting Bulletin No. 102, *Selected Loan Loss Allowance Methodology and Documentation Issues*, 2001. Available at: www.sec.gov/interps/account/sab102.htm
5. Financial Accounting Standards Board Summary of Board Decision as of January 27, 2011. Available at: www.fasb.org.
6. W. F. Ford, and R. J. Phillips, "Will Your Bank Fail?" *American Institute for Economic Research* 77, No.13, July 19, 2010. Available at: www.aier.org.
7. Ibid.
8. Amateur-Investor.net. 2010. Texas Ratio. Available at: www.amateur-investor.net/TexasRatio.htm.
9. Deloitte, 2010. "First Deloitte Islamic Finance Leaders' Survey in the Middle East: Benchmarking Practices," 2010. Available at: www.islamicfinance.deloitte.com.
10. U.S. Financial Crisis Inquiry Commission, "Final Report of the National Commission on the Causes of the Financial and Economic Crisis in the United States," pursuant to Public Law 111-21, January 2011. Available at: www.fcic.gov/.
11. Dodd-Frank Wall Street Reform and Consumer Protection Act of 2010, Pub. L. 111-203 (2010).
12. KPMG, "Hungry for More: Global Update 2007." Available at: www.kpmg.com.

About the Author

Zabihollah Rezaee is the Thompson-Hill Chair of Excellence and Professor of Accountancy at the University of Memphis and served a two-year term on the Standing Advisory Group of the Public Company Accounting Oversight Board. He received his B.S. degree from the Iranian Institute of Advanced Accounting, his M.B.A. from Tarleton State University in Texas, and his Ph.D. from the University of Mississippi. Professor Rezaee holds a number of certifications, including Certified Public Accountant, Certified Fraud Examiner, Certified Management Accountant, Certified Internal Auditor, Certified Government Financial Manager, Certified Sarbanes-Oxley Professional, Certified Corporate Governance Professional, and Certified Governance Risk Compliance Professional.

Professor Rezaee has published six books: *Financial Institutions, Valuations, Mergers, and Acquisitions: The Fair Value Approach* (John Wiley and Sons); *Financial Statement Fraud: Prevention and Detection* (John Wiley and Sons); *U.S. Master Auditing Guide, Third Edition* (CCH Incorporated); *Audit Committee Oversight Effectiveness Post-Sarbanes-Oxley Act* (Bureau of National Affairs, Inc.); *Corporate Governance Post-Sarbanes-Oxley: Regulations, Requirements, and Integrated Processes* (John Wiley and Sons); and *Corporate Governance and Business Ethics* (John Wiley and Sons); His forthcoming book *Business Sustainability and Accountability: The Emerging Performance and Reporting Paradigm* (John Wiley and Sons) is scheduled to be published in 2011. He was a contributor author (Chapters 13 and 29) to the book edited by Bakers and Anderson *Corporate Governance 2010* (John Wiley & Sons) and contributed Chapter 31, titled "Financial Institutions (Revised)," to the *Accountants' Handbook, Eleventh Edition*, 2011 Supplement (John Wiley & Sons).

Professor Rezaee has published over 190 articles in a variety of accounting, finance, banking, and economic journals, including: *Journal of Accounting and Economics*; *Contemporary Accounting Research, Auditing: A journal of Practice and Theory Accounting Horizons*; *Journal of Business and Accounting, Journal of Accounting, Auditing and Finance*; *Advances in Public Interest Accounting*; *Journal of Accountancy*; *Internal Auditors*; *Internal Auditing*; *Management Accounting*; *Strategy Finance*; *Bankers' Economic and Investment Alert*; the *Research in Accounting Regulations*; *Advances in International Accounting*; *The Financial Review*; and *Journal of Business Ethics*. Professor Rezaee has made more than 200 presentations at national and international conferences and over 50 workshops worldwide on corporate governance, professional ethics, business sustainability, forensic accounting, and business valuation.

Professor Rezaee is very active within the accounting profession and the academic and financial communities. He teaches financial, management, and international accounting and auditing, corporate governance and ethics, and Ph.D. seminar courses in financial reporting and auditing, and has been involved in financial and management consulting with national and international organizations including the United Nations. Professor Rezaee has received numerous research grants from various sources. He received the 1998 distinguished research award at Middle Tennessee State University and the Lybrand Bronze Medal for the outstanding article selected by the Institute of Management Accountants. He was also a finalist for SOX Institute's SOX MVP 2007 and a 2010 Finalist SOX Institute, Corporate Governance and Risk Management Award, and a 2010 Excellence in International Award, School of Accountancy, at the University of Memphis.

Index